# MANAGING CULTURAL DIFFERENCES

## EIGHTH EDITION

Managing Cultural Differences:
Global Leadership Strategies for the 21st Century, Seventh Edition
Robert T. Moran, Ph.D., Philip R. Harris, Ph.D., Sarah V. Moran, M.A.

Managing Cultural Diversity in Technical Professions
Lionel Laroche, Ph.D.

Uniting North American Business—NAFTA Best Practices
Jeffrey D. Abbot and Robert T. Moran, Ph.D.

Eurodiversity: A Business Guide to Managing Differences
George Simons, D.M.

Global Strategic Planning: Cultural Perspectives for Profit and Non-Profit Organizations
Marios I. Katsioulodes, Ph.D.

Competing Globally: Mastering Cross-Cultural Management and Negotiations
Farid Elashmawi, Ph.D.

Succeeding in Business in Eastern and Central Europe—A Guide to Cultures,
Markets, and Practices
Woodrow H. Sears, Ed.D. and Audrone Tamulionyte-Lentz, M.S.

Intercultural Services: A Worldwide Buyer's Guide and Sourcebook
Gary M. Wederspahn, M.A.

EIGHTH EDITION

# MANAGING CULTURAL DIFFERENCES

## GLOBAL LEADERSHIP STRATEGIES FOR CROSS-CULTURAL BUSINESS SUCCESS

ROBERT T. MORAN
PHILIP R. HARRIS
SARAH V. MORAN

AMSTERDAM • BOSTON • HEIDELBERG • LONDON • NEW YORK • OXFORD
PARIS • SAN DIEGO • SAN FRANCISCO • SINGAPORE • SYDNEY • TOKYO

ELSEVIER

Butterworth-Heinemann is an imprint of Elsevier

Butterworth-Heinemann is an imprint of Elsevier
30 Corporate Drive, Suite 400, Burlington, MA 01803, USA
Linacre House, Jordan Hill, Oxford OX2 8DP, UK

**Library of Congress Cataloging-in-Publication Data**
A catalog record for this book is available from the Library of Congress

**British Library Cataloguing-in-Publication Data**
A catalogue record for this book is available from the British Library.

ISBN: 978-1-85617-923-2

For information on all Butterworth–Heinemann publications
visit our Web site at www.books.elsevier.com

Printed and bound in China
11  12  13  10  9  8  7  6  5  4  3  2  1

Working together to grow
libraries in developing countries

www.elsevier.com | www.bookaid.org | www.sabre.org

ELSEVIER    BOOK AID International    Sabre Foundation

*To my children Elizabeth, Sarah, Molly, Rebecca and Benedict. Learners and teachers, receivers and givers, all multilingual citizens in our global world.*

*Robert T. Moran*

*In honor of Dr. Dorothy Lipp Harris, my late wife and elegant professor who supported me in writing this text for a quarter century and taught with it in graduate school. And to her sister, Jeanne Lipp Conover, who first introduced me into the concept of culture when I was a Fulbright professor in Japan, 1962 . . . Plus in appreciation to two cosmopolitans who inspire me to continue writing in my 80s – my present wife, Janet Belport Harris and my stepson, Jason Winter Belport.*

*Philip R. Harris*

*To my parents, whose global humanitarian lives have influenced me profoundly, and to every person who has crossed my path whose diversity of backgrounds, ethnicities, cultures, and world views have opened my eyes and mind. You have all taught me that through respect and developing a deep understanding of what makes each of us unique, that humankind, in all our wonderful diversity, can find ways to harmoniously live and work together.*

*Sarah V. Moran*

# CONTENTS

UNIT 2

REGIONAL CULTURAL SPECIFICS*

# FOREWORD

That culture drives human success—or consigns it to failure—is among the preeminent elucidations of Western social science over the past century. From Max Weber to Ruth Benedict, and Margaret Mead to Edward Banfield, with an honorific nod toward Franz Boas, we have long since accepted that the character of a culture may shape and galvanize—or divert and even impede—everything from democratic governance to human productivity and social integrity. But do we understand what happens when *multiple* cultures intersect, when they are "flattened" by the polylinear tide of information and trade flows as well as human linkages? How do we manage that cross-cutting current of cultural differences as we continue to globalize at warp speed?

Two decades before the late Samuel P. Huntington and a group of his academic collaborators led by Laurence E. Harrison collectively declared in 1999 that Harvard's Academy of International and Area Studies was ready to reincorporate culture as a dominant paradigm in development, this volume, *Managing Cultural Differences*, was first published. The year was 1979. Eight editions later, co-authors Robert T. Moran, Philip R. Harris, and Sarah V. Moran are still mapping the shifting tide of culture in our globalized world and exposing the hidden shoals and open channels of power, space, context, and communication in values and attitudes. In the course of those 31 years, tens of thousands of multinational managers and executives as well as international business students in over 400 undergraduate and graduate programs have plumbed its pages for guidance and reflection. It is a remarkable achievement.

The message, then and now, has been the same:

Learning to manage cultural differences is a means for all persons to become more global in their outlook and behavior, as well as more effective personally and professionally. When cultural differences are understood and utilized as a *resource*, then all benefit. When they are not, the costs are significant.

This 8th edition of *Managing Cultural Differences: Global Leadership Strategies for the 21st Century* merits the classification as the Gold Standard of cross-cultural textbooks. Employing a wide range of cultural theories and multiple sets of skill development models and drawing on real-world vignettes as well as case profiles, with five specific geographic areas of managerial guidance, it seeks to form the "inter-culturally competent leader." It also calls for the development of "worldmindedness,"—"a trait that can be taught, just like language."

According to the authors, American business strategy cannot and should not be a one-size-fits-all model but rather the vanguard of world-minded learning about the complexity by which we remain human as we do business. At a time when the world is recovering from a culturally-blinkered, free market triumphalism, the return to cultural openness and sophistication (and the methods by which this volume helps you get there) seems especially timely and compelling.

The current global culture wars have at their source self-serving, ethnocentric caricatures—Huntingdon's "clashing civilizations" to name but one—that intellectually dignify a new century of conflict and bloodshed. Seeded throughout its 500-plus pages, *Managing Cultural Differences* stands for a diametrically different proposition and a powerful corrective to those overstated polarities: cultural peace and social pragmatism. It reminds me of John Dewey reflexive maxim for self- and societal-development: knowledge is experience and experience is knowledge.

Listen. Learn. Act.

Richard D. Mahoney
Elizabeth Evans Baker Professor and
Director of The Baker Institute for
Peace and Conflict Studies
Juniata College

# PROLOGUE

We are pleased to present to persons interested in working skillfully in a complex, changing and interdependent global world the 8th edition of Managing Cultural Differences. For those familiar with earlier editions you will see some new concepts and ideas such as the challenge to become global in mindset and still "be loyal to one's tribe" as Albert Einstein wrote and we quoted in chapter one. There are also many "evergreen ideas" such as the concept and examples of low or high context communication in chapter two.

The first edition was published in 1979. We presented the idea that "culture counts" in business. Culture influences most human activities. We compared culture to a jewel. Hold it to the light, turn it around and it reveals multiple dimensions.

We are grateful to the many readers of our book as well as university and college professors who have read and used the book in the classroom or in executive education programs.

The number of printed pages in this edition has been reduced but additional material is contained on the secure website http://booksite.bh.com/moran

Finding a balance between theory and practice has been our goal. And finding application and relevance has been in the forefront of all we write.

We invite you to begin reading.

Robert T. Moran, Ph.D.
Paradise Valley, Arizona, USA

Philip R. Harris, Ph.D.
La Jolla, California, USA

Sarah V. Moran, M.A.
Montreal, Quebec, Canada

# ACKNOWLEDGMENT

The eighth edition of Managing Cultural Differences: Global Leadership Strategies for the 21st Century would not have been possible without the help and commitment of many people. We thank you all.

We especially want to thank Richard D. Mahoney, a brilliant writer and teacher, for writing the Foreword. It is worth reading.

We also very much appreciate the assistance of William Youngdahl, Katrin Adler, John Riesenberger, Harry Owens and Thomas Stevens who made suggestions to the text and wrote reviews. All have full professional calendars. We thank you for taking the time to review and for making a number of excellent suggestions for improvements.

Matt Sutter and Christine Billy shared materials which we incorporated into several chapters. We also acknowledge the help of Heike Stroermer, Sophie Jaeger, Eileen Sheridan Wibbeke and Mike McManus.

Georgia Lessard is a very talented colleague from Thunderbird who worked her "magic" with various drafts of each chapter prior to sending them to the Kirubhagaran Palani and his colleagues at Elsevier.

We especially want to acknowledge Judith Soccorsy who played a significant editorial role in several previous editions. She was willing to work with us on the eighth edition but needed to spend most of her energy in fighting cancer.

We also thank the many professors and other users and readers of the previous edition who gave us feedback.

Every book is a work in progress. We look forward to learning from you how this book can become even better.

Robert T. Moran, Philip R. Harris, Sarah V. Moran

# Unit 1

## Cultural Impacts on Global Management

*"One can be an internationalist without being indifferent to members of one's tribe."*
Albert Einstein, as quoted in *Einstein, His Life and Universe*,
Walter Isaacson, Simon and Schuster Paperbacks, 2007


*"A global manager is set apart by more than a worn suitcase and a dog-eared passport."*
*Harvard Business Review*, August 2003


*"We don't look so much at what and where people have studied, but rather at their drive, initiative, cultural sensitivity…"*
Stephen Green, Group CEO, HSBC
*Harvard Business Review*, August 2003

# 1

# GLOBAL LEADERS AND CULTURE

The world has changed, and so must people living in this changed global world.

## DID YOU KNOW?[a]

- Twenty-five percent of the population in China with the highest IQs and 28% in India are greater than the total population of North America. Implication for parents, teachers, and politicians—China and India have more honor kids than most, if not all countries.
- China will soon be the number one English-speaking country in the world.
- Every 6 min, 60 babies will be born in the United States, 244 babies will be born in China, and 351 babies will be born in India.
- In the United States, 1 out of 2 people are working for a company for whom they have worked less than 5 years.
- The top 10 jobs that are in demand in 2010 didn't exist in 2004, according to a former U.S. Secretary of Education.
- One out of 8 couples married in the United States in 2006 met online.
- If MySpace were a country, it would be the 11th largest in the world.
- There are over 2.7 billion searches performed on Google each month.
- The amount of new technical information is doubling every 2 years.
- Predictions are that by 2013 a supercomputer will be built that exceeds the computation capability of the human brain.

---

[a]From *Did You Know?* By Karl Fisch and Scott McLeod. Adapted by Sony BMG. Full presentation can be viewed at http://www.youtube.com/watch?v=jpEnFwiqdx8.

Vérité en-deça des Pyrénées, erreur au delà. (There are truths on this side of the Pyrenees that are falsehoods on the other.)[1]

In 1492, Christopher Columbus set sail for India, going west...he called the people he met "Indians" and came home and reported to his king and queen, "The world is round." I set off for India 512 years later...I went east...I came home and reported only to my wife and only in a whisper, "The world is flat."[2]

The real voyage of discovery consists not in seeking new landscapes but in having new eyes—Marcel Proust, French novelist, 1871-1922

More people will graduate in the United States in 2006 with sports and exercise degrees than with electrical engineering degrees. So, if we want to be the massage capital of the world, we're well on our way.[3]

## LEARNING OBJECTIVES

In the twenty-first century, leaders in business, government, and the professions cope with the phenomenon of globalization. It prompts them to cross borders more frequently and to communicate with persons from other cultures, either in person or electionally.

This chapter provides a rationale and an imperative for all individuals working "globally" to understand and respect their counterparts, and to develop the skills required to work effectively in today's complex world. Ways to analyze and understand other cultures are presented, along with how to use the suggested strategies. Seeing global issues through "multiple lens" or "by hearing with new ears" is also important.

Why does the world appear flat to some, round to others, and what are the advantages or disadvantages of either? Thomas Friedman writes about his insights during an interview with Nandan Nilekani, CEO of Infosys Technologies Limited:

"Outsourcing is just one dimension of a much more fundamental thing happening today in the world," Nilekani explained. "What happened over the last (few) years is that there was a massive investment in technology, especially in the bubble era, when hundreds of millions of dollars were invested in putting broadband connectivity around the world, undersea cables, all those things." At the same time, he added, computers became cheaper and dispersed all over the world, and there was an explosion of software-e-mail, search engines like Google, and proprietary software that can chop up any piece of work and send one part to Boston, one part to Bangalore, and one part to Beijing, making it easy for anyone to do remote development. When all of these things suddenly came together around 2000, added Nilekani, they created a platform where intellectual work, intellectual capital, could be delivered from anywhere. It could be disaggregated, delivered, distributed, produced, and put back together again—and this gave a whole new degree of freedom to the way we do work, especially work of an intellectual nature...And what you are seeing in Bangalore today is really the culmination of all these things coming together.[4]

The point is, the playing field in the global marketplace is being leveled for some, and thus "flat." That is an advantage for many and a disadvantage for others. In either view, cultural competing is a requirement. Culture does count.

The coauthors of this book have worked for global organizations for many years. In the 1960s and early 1970s, we had to convince many business and government leaders that "culture counts." From the industrialized world, the perspective often voiced was, "We tell them what to do, and if they want to work with us, they do it." This is rarely or never the situation today.

We no longer have to convince anyone with any global experience that *culture counts*. And when organizations, nongovernmental organizations (NGOs), and political organizations ignore, dismiss, or minimize culture, the costs are often significant. This chapter will present proven frameworks, models, and paradigms relevant to working skillfully in today's global business and geopolitical world. We believe managing cultural differences skillfully for all individuals, organizations, NGOs, and governments from all countries is a human and business imperative. Understanding the environment is a fundamental requirement for maintaining a competitive advantage. To successfully adapt to changes in the environment is a requirement for survival. Culture impacts relationships and business operations. Schein states it profoundly:

> Consider any complex, potentially volatile issue—Arab relations, the problems between Serbs, Croats, and Bosnians, corporate decision-making, getting control of the U.S. deficit, or health-care costs, labor/management relations, and so on. At the root of the issue, we are likely to find communication failures and cultural misunderstandings that prevent the parties from framing the problem in a common way, and thus make it impossible to deal with the problem constructively.[5]

McNamara et al. cite a dialogue about the Vietnam War between Colonel Herbert Schandler and Colonel Quach Hai Luong that illustrates dramatically the importance of culture in perception.[6] The dialogue took place in Hanoi in 1998, when military historians from the United States and Vietnam came together to try to understand the lessons of the Vietnam War to be carried forward to the twenty-first century.

> Colonel Quach Hai Luong: I want to ask you: What do you think the American objectives were in Vietnam?
> Colonel Herbert Schandler: Our objectives in Vietnam, as stated by our various presidents, were the following. First, to establish an independent, noncommunist South Vietnam whose people had the ability to choose their own leaders and form of government. A second objective was to *convince* North Vietnam—not to defeat or crush or obliterate North Vietnam—but to *convince* North Vietnam not to impose its will on the South by means of military force. We had no burning desire even to harm

North Vietnam in any way. We just wanted to demonstrate to you that you could not win militarily in the South.

Colonel Quach Hai Luong: But Colonel Schandler, if I may say so, this was a critical difference between your understanding of the situation and our understanding of it. Let me put it this way: your fundamental assumption is that Vietnam was two distinct—two rightfully independent—countries. On that basis, your objectives and strategies follow. We did not make that distinction. We saw only one country. All our strategies were based on this basic premise: that Vietnam is one country, unfortunately and artificially divided in two. Our war was for the purpose of protecting our independence and maintaining our national unity.

Now imagine how different the outcomes of the Vietnam War might have been if, at the beginning of this conflict, the military leaders and negotiators of the respective countries had used sophisticated problem-solving skills and dug deeper to understand the cultural meanings and implications of their actions and behind their public statements about the war. The same might be said of present conflicts in Afghanistan and Iraq.

Also supporting the notion that "culture" is important is Alan Greenspan, former chairman of the U.S. Federal Reserve. Greenspan stated that he originally believed that capitalism was "human nature."[7] After the collapse of the Soviet economy, however, he concluded that "it was not human nature at all, but culture." Culture is finding its place of significance in the experience of global individuals.

Cultures have always been distinct, mostly separate and independent. Over the past 100 years, and especially during the last 25, cultures and nations have remained unique, but have become increasingly more interconnected in complex and nonobvious ways. This book covers many topics, but the threads of culture, differences, and leadership run throughout.

"In the early 1990s, I happened to come across early 1960s economic data on Ghana and South Korea, and I was astonished to see how similar their economies were at that time. These two countries had roughly comparable levels of per capita gross national product (GNP); similar divisions of their economy among primary products, manufacturing, and services; and overwhelmingly primary product exports, with South Korea producing a few manufactured goods. They were also receiving comparable levels of economic aid. Thirty years later, South Korea had become an industrial giant with the fourteenth largest economy in the world. No such changes had occurred in Ghana, whose per capita GNP was now about one-fifteenth that of South Korea's. How could this extraordinary difference in development be explained? Undoubtedly, many factors played a role, but it seemed to me that culture had to be a large part of the explanation. South Koreans value thrift, investment, hard work, education, organization, and discipline. Ghanaians had different values.[8] In short, culture counts."

Diamond's[9] statement that, "We all know that history has proceeded very differently for peoples from different parts of the globe," is one we can all agree with. The specific data that humans all came from Africa are not disputed. Diamond questions, why did different people develop in different ways? His answer, "History followed different courses for different peoples because of differences in peoples' environments, not because of biological differences among peoples themselves."[10]

Change is also a part of our daily lives, and impacts all. If culture counts, managing cultural differences or skillfully leading in a global world becomes of paramount importance. Most of the following events took place after the year 2000 and share aspects of culture, differences, conflict, consequences, and leadership.

"An internationalist without being indifferent to members of one's tribe."—Albert Einstein wrote the words in a letter to a friend in 1919. Einstein was a genius, but these words suggest he was also quite wise.

The following three examples are relevant and from the experiences of Robert Moran.[11] He was born in Canada, where he lived for 25 years, then moved to Japan and later settled in the United States. His stories, therefore, have a north american flavor.

## A Friendly Encounter

"In our neighborhood, trash is picked up every Monday and Thursday. I was born and spent my early years in Canada, and everyone then called the trash "garbage." One of my early chores as a young boy was to take out the garbage.

I still take out the garbage, usually on a Sunday night for an early Monday morning pickup. One Sunday, as I left a full bucket on our street, I met a neighbor who was taking her dog for a walk. We exchanged friendly pleasantries, and she asked about our adult children. She was genuinely interested.

"Elizabeth is still living and working in France," I said, "and we are about to have a second American/French grandchild." I told her that Sarah was working in Taiwan, Molly was in San Francisco working for the Gap, Rebecca was a volunteer bush pilot in Tanzania flying medical personnel to the Masaai, and Ben, our youngest, was in West Africa finishing his first year as a Peace Corps volunteer.

Our neighbor looked at me, and in a matter-of-fact way responded, "Well, at least you have one 'normal' one."

We believe our five adult children are all "normal," at least most of the time. Working and living in San Francisco—and working in Taiwan—are equally "normal" in today's world."

## You Can't Trust the French

"Many years before the above encounter, about 20 years ago, I took a sabbatical from the Thunderbird School of Global Management, where I have been a faculty member since 1976. With two stuffed duffel bags each, my spouse and I left for France with our five young children. I was going to teach at a grande école—a French Ivy League university—in the suburbs of Paris. We wanted our children to learn another language and have a genuine experience of another culture.

For several weeks, we had not yet met any other foreigners as we tried to find an affordable used car, a house to rent, and schools for our children. We had only met French people who, without exception, helped us figure out how things worked in their sometimes-bureaucratic country.

Our youngest child, Ben, however, who was seven at the time, had met an American whose name was Jack, and he asked if Jack could come over and have dinner with us. We immediately agreed. As it was my turn to cook, with the help of my eldest daughter, we decided that fish—4 trout from the local marché—would be the entree.

As Jack was our guest, I presented the fish on a platter to him first. As I did this, my daughter said, from across the table, "Be careful, everyone, there may be some small bones in the fish." Jack, also 7 years old, looked at me and responded, "Okay… (sigh)… You know, you just can't trust the French."

Surprised at his comment, I asked him where he had first heard it. "My mother says that all the time," he responded.

Later that night, when I was dropping him off at his home, I met Jack's mother. She told me that she hated living in Europe and wanted to go home to the United States. She was lonesome, missed her friends, and did not really like living in France.

Of course, there is nothing abnormal about being lonely and finding a new environment difficult to adapt to. But her feelings and attitudes clearly influenced Jack, who might have been less disparaging and closed to his new environment had she felt differently."

## The All-American Girl

"Last spring, as my work at the university slowed down, my spouse and I were able to spend a little more time together, and we were ready for a new adventure. So we rented a small house in the French countryside, thinking that we would spend our time studying French, the first language of two of our grandchildren.

When my spouse told one of her friends that we were leaving for several weeks, her friend responded, "That's not for me—I'm an all-American girl!"

Remaining an "all-American" would be a safe bet, I suppose, if the world in which we live had not changed drastically in the past 20 years from huge forces of globalization. In fact, leading economists comfortably predict that in a generation, the center of worldwide economic activity will shift out of the United States and into Asia, where countries are already preparing to take over this role.

Our world has been most influenced by the victors of a war that concluded over half a century ago—namely, the United States, Western

Europe, and Russia—but rising economic powers such as India, Brazil, and China are increasingly asserting themselves in the international arena. The United States will no longer be able to maintain its role as sole superpower.

But many people, including global businessfolks, to my great alarm, believe otherwise.

In order for all people to better prepare themselves for this tectonic shift, a new way of thinking is necessary. Those who learn new ways of living in a globalized world will have the tools necessary to step forward and participate, and even lead. Those who stick to being "all-American," however, will in all likelihood be left out of the process altogether.

Indeed, being a *global American* is, in many ways, just as important for all Americans as being a *global company* is for most, if not all, of American organizations, if they are to succeed in today's world. Companies that were late in adapting to the new global economy are struggling to catch up. The same must also be true for Germans, Japanese, Saudis, Indians, Nigerians, and people of all nations.

Such a shift in paradigm is not impossible. About 500 years ago, after the Earth was discovered to rotate around the Sun, humanity had to give up the then-held belief that the earth was at the center of the universe. It simply wasn't. Giving up old ideas or ideas that don't work, or ideas that are inaccurate, are difficult.

New skills and attitudes are required for businesspeople, students, and all individuals to find our way in a new and rapidly changing world. Being at ease in other cultures, and having the global awareness and curiosity that is necessary to follow the rapid transformations taking place outside our borders—*and even inside of them*—are important ingredients in a global psyche.

Global people are already active in the fields of politics, business, academics, health care and in other professions and walks of life. Indeed, millions—yes, millions—of individuals already live and work in countries other than their own. But today, it is increasingly important that every person develop a global attitude as well. We can no longer leave this to government or business leaders.

Importantly, the major issues that the world may be facing in the next century, that is, tectonic shifts in the global economy, terrorism, global warming and increased pollution, mass migration, and the threat of global epidemics (just to name a few), are not issues that any country, even if it wanted to, could deal with alone. An increased collaboration with other countries and organizations across a wide spectrum of cultures will be fundamental to overcoming these challenges."

## Not Only Global Americans, But Also Global French, Saudi, Chinese, and Others

"One final incident demonstrates an important motivation that I have held for the past 20 years.

During executive business seminars that I teach, I am often asked, "Is it only Americans who have to be global? What about the rest of the world?" I usually respond by relating the following incident.

Many years ago, in New York, I was in the office of a senior vice president of a very large U.S.-based company. A person who reported to the senior vice president, and who had just returned from Asia to conclude an important contract, was invited to meet me. During the meeting, he told me that the deal in Asia should be cancelled, as he explained, as "they don't understand us, or our business, and they are arrogant."

The senior vice president, in my presence, responded angrily, "If they are arrogant, don't understand us—or whatever—I expect you to be that much more skillful. If you tell me how bad anyone else is again, I'll fire you."

Talk about tension!"

## A Global Person

Warren buffet, the CEO of Berkshire Hathaway and one of the world's most successful, influential, and wealthy individuals, is quoted as saying, "Only when the tides goes out do you find out who is not wearing a bathing suit."

Globalization is exposing most countries to more interactions and relationships with people and products from other countries, yet many people from different countries are not prepared to work, live, and prosper in a global and highly competitive new world.

In an Apple white paper,[12] the authors cited a 2002 National Geographic Study showing as follows:

> Eighty-five percent of 18- to 24-year-old Americans were unable to locate Afghanistan and Iraq on a map, despite the fact that the U.S. Was at war or publicly preparing for war in both countries. Sixty-nine percent were unable to locate Great Britain, and 29 percent were unable to find the Pacific Ocean.

But what is a global person? A global person does not believe that his/her nation is the best at everything and that everyone else wants to be just like him/her—rather he/she is aware that other cultures of the world have lives and viewpoints different from his/her own. A global person may not speak more than one language or have lived in another country. He/she may not even own a passport. However, a global person is aware of and interested in the issues of people around the world. He/she is empathetic and sensitive, and has skills in interacting with people who may not look like, talk like, smell like, or act like him/her.

"Worldmindedness"—a global awareness of other cultures and people (in many ways, the opposite of hate and fear)—is a trait that can be taught, just like language. The growing importance of other countries in the global arena should not be a threat, but an opportunity for cultural education, growth, and creativity.

In the *Sage Handbook of Intercultural Competence*,[13] many models and paradigms are identified to describe an interculterally competent individual. In most models, there are a knowledge component (knowledge of self, knowledge of other cultures, etc.), a skill component (showing respect, listening, accurately interpreting meanings, etc.), and an attitudinal component (globally minded, not believing one's way is the best or only way, etc.). All can be learned. Knowledge is easier to acquire than a skill to act on. Learning a skill is easier than transforming an ethnocentric attitude. We will start with Culture and a short definition: "culture is the way we do things here."

It is important to remember the following, however:

1. All people are to some extent like all other people. This is the universal aspect which all humans share.

   All people are to some extent unique. This is the individual aspect, and no two human beings are exactly the same.

   All people are to some extent like some other people. This is the cultural aspect which we share, in part, with people from our own tribe (as Einstein said).

2. Culture is learned. This learning is on the basis of the following statements.

   An individual's early childhood experiences exert a lasting effect on his/her personality. Psychologists, sociologists, anthropologists, and others accept this. The issues being studied are the critical ages and the specific experiences.

   The early childhood experiences and parenting practices vary from culture to culture.

   As a result, if a child of a U.S. white woman would be adopted by a Chinese couple living in a village in China, that child would learn to speak, read, and write Chinese, and behave like most of the other children in the village, but look more like the U.S. mother than any others in the village. He or she would behave like a Chinese boy or girl and learn Chinese values.

   We begin with culture.

# CULTURE

Culture is a distinctly human means of adapting to circumstances and transmitting this coping skill and knowledge to subsequent generations. Culture gives people a sense of who they are, of belonging, of how they should behave, and of what they should be doing. Culture impacts behavior, morale, and productivity at work, and includes values and patterns that influence company attitudes and actions. Culture is dynamic. Cultures change...but slowly.

Culture is often considered the driving force behind human behavior everywhere. The concept has become the context to explain politics, economics, progress, and failures. In that regard, Huntington[14] has written:

It is my hypothesis that the fundamental source of human conflict in this new world will not be primarily ideological or primarily economic. The great divisions among humankind and the dominating source of conflict will be culture.

Culture and cultural identities…are shaping the patterns of cohesion, disintegration, and conflict in the postcold war world. Global politics is being reconfigured along cultural lines…peoples and countries with similar culture are coming together. Peoples and countries with different cultures are coming apart.

Prior to entering a new market, forming a partnership, or buying a company, organizations spend time and money on "due diligence." What is forgotten or minimized in both business and politics is "cultural due diligence." The following models or frameworks on cultural analysis might be important in any due diligence exercise that has a cultural component. Chomsky et al.,[15] for example, demonstrates his ability to master an incredible wealth of factual knowledge, and his skills exemplify political due diligence. Lewis[16] demonstrates the importance of cultural due diligence for business. Globally minded individuals did this routinely.

The following 10 categories are a means for understanding either a macroculture or a microculture, and can be useful for studying any group of people, whether they live in the rural south of the United States, India, the bustling city of Hong Kong, Bangalore, Arusha in Tanzanika, or Bagdad in Iraq.

*Sense of Self and Space.* The comfort one has with self can be expressed differently by culture. Self-identity and appreciation can be manifested by humble bearing in one culture and by macho behavior in another. Independence and creativity are countered in other cultures by group cooperation and conformity. Americans have a sense of space that requires more distance between individuals, while Latins and Arabs will stand closer together. Some cultures are very structured and formal, while others are more flexible and informal.

*Communication and Language.* The communication system, verbal and nonverbal, distinguishes one group from another. It is estimated that there are less than 7,000 human languages today and in 2008 it was estimated that between 20 and 30 languages were "lost."[17] Apart from the multitude of "foreign" languages, some nations have 15 or more major spoken languages (within one language group there are dialects, accents, slang, jargon, and other such variations). Furthermore, the meanings given to gestures, for example, often differ by culture. So, while body language may be universal, its manifestation differs by locality. Subcultures, such as the military, have terminology and signals that cut across national boundaries (such as a salute or the rank system).

*Dress and Appearance.* This includes the outward garments and adornments, or lack thereof, as well as body decorations that tend to be culturally distinctive. We are aware of the Japanese kimono, the African headdress, the Englishman's bowler and umbrella, the Polynesian sarong, and the Native American headband. Many subcultures wear distinctive clothing: the formal look of business, the jeans worn by youth throughout the world, and uniforms that segregate everyone, from students to police.

*Food and Feeding Habits.* The manner in which food is selected, prepared, presented, and eaten often differs by culture. One man's pet is another person's delicacy. Americans love beef, yet it is forbidden to Hindus, while the forbidden food in Muslim and Jewish culture is pork, eaten extensively by the Chinese and others. Many restaurants cater to diverse diets and offer "national" dishes to meet varying cultural tastes. Feeding habits also differ, ranging from hands and chopsticks to full sets of cutlery. Even when cultures use a utensil such as a fork, one can distinguish a European from an American by which hand holds the implement.

*Time and Time Consciousness.* Sense of time differs by culture—some are exact and others are relative. Generally, Germans are precise about the clock, while many Latins are more casual. In some cultures, promptness is determined by age or status. Thus, in some countries, subordinates are expected on time at staff meetings, but the boss is the last to arrive. Yet, there are people in some other cultures who do not bother with hours or minutes, but manage their days by sunrise and sunset.

Time, in the sense of seasons of the year, varies by culture. Some areas of the world think in terms of winter, spring, summer, and fall; but for others, the more meaningful designations may be rainy and dry seasons. In the United States, for example, the East and Midwest may be very conscious of the four seasons, while those in the West or Southwest tend to minimalize such designations.

Many industries operate on round-the-clock schedules. This is the concern of chronobiologists who specialize in research on the body's internal clock by analysis of body temperature, chemical composition of blood serum and urine, sleepiness, and peak periods of feeling good. Drastic changes in time, such as can be brought on by shift work, can undermine both performance and personal life, leading to serious accidents on the job.

*Relationships.* Cultures fix human and organizational relationships by age, gender, status, and degree of kindred, as well as by wealth, power, and wisdom. The family unit is the most common expression of this characteristic, and the arrangement may go from small to large—in a Hindu household, the joint family includes under one roof, mother, father, children, parents, uncles, aunts, and cousins. In fact, one's physical location in such houses may also be determined, with men on one side of the house, women on the other. There are some places where the accepted marriage relationship is monogamy, while in other cultures it may be polygamy or polyandry (one wife, several husbands).

In some cultures, the authoritarian figure in the family is the head man, and this fixed relationship is then extended from home to community, explaining why some societies prefer to have a dictator head up the national family. Relationships between and among people vary by category—in some cultures, the elderly are honored, whereas in others they are ignored; in some cultures, women must wear veils and appear deferential, while in others the woman is considered the equal, if not the superior, of the man.

*Values and Norms*. The need systems of cultures vary, as do the priorities they attach to certain behavior in the group. Those operating on a survival level value the gathering of food, adequate covering, and shelter, while those with high security need value material things, money, job titles, as well as law and order. Many countries are in the midst of a values revolution. In some Pacific Island cultures, the greater one's status becomes, the more one is expected to give away or share.

In any event, from its values system, a culture sets norms of behavior for that society. These acceptable standards for membership may range from work ethic or pleasure to absolute obedience or permissiveness for children; from rigid submission of the wife to her husband to a more equal relationship. Because conventions are learned, some cultures demand honesty with members of one's own group, but accept a more relaxed standard with strangers. Some of these conventions are expressed in gift giving; rituals for birth, death, and marriage; guidelines for privacy; a show of respect or deference; expression of good manners; and so on. The globalization process and telecommunications are leading to the development of some shared values that cross borders and express planetary concerns, such as protection of the environment.[7]

*Beliefs and Attitudes*. Possibly the most difficult classification is ascertaining the major belief themes of a people, and how this and other factors influence their attitudes toward themselves, others, and what happens in their world. People in all cultures seem to have a concern for the supernatural that is evident in their religions and religious practices. In the history of human development, there has been an evolution in our spiritual sense, so that today many individuals use terms like cosmic consciousness to indicate their belief in the transcendental powers. Between these two extremes in the spiritual continuum, religious traditions in various cultures consciously or unconsciously influence our attitudes toward life, death, and the hereafter. Western culture seems to be largely influenced by the Judeo-Christian-Islamic traditions, while Eastern or Asian cultures have been dominated by Buddhism, Confucianism, Taoism, and Hinduism. Religion, to a degree, expresses the philosophy of a people about important facets of life—it is influenced by culture, and vice versa.

*Mental Process and Learning*. Some cultures emphasize one aspect of brain development over another, so that one may observe striking differences in the way people think and learn. Anthropologist Edward Hall maintains that the mind is internalized culture, and the mental process involves how people organize and process information. Life in a particular locale defines the rewards and punishment for learning or not learning certain information or in a certain way, and this is confirmed and reinforced by the culture. For example, Germans stress logic, while logic for a Hopi Indian is on the basis of preserving the integrity of his/her social system and all the relationships connected with it. Some cultures favor abstract thinking and conceptualization, while others prefer rote memory and learning. What seems to be universal is that each culture has a reasoning process, but then each manifests the process in its own distinctive way.

*Work Habits and Practices.* Another dimension of a group's culture is its attitude toward work—the dominant types of work, the division of work, and the work habits or practices, such as promotions or incentives. Work has been defined as exertion or effort directed to produce or accomplish something. Some cultures espouse a work ethic in which all members are expected to engage in a desirable and worthwhile activity. In other societies, this is broadly defined to include cultural pursuits in music and the arts or sports. For some cultures, the worthiness of the activity is narrowly measured in terms of income produced, or the worth of the individual is assessed in terms of job status. In Japan, the cultural loyalty to family is transferred to the organization that employs the person and the quality of one's performance—it is expressed in work group participation, communication, and consensus.

Another way of observing a culture is to note the manner and method of offering praise for accomplishments, which can include testimonial dinners, pay increases, commendations, and medals.

These 10 general classifications are a basic model for assessing a particular culture. It does not include every aspect of culture, nor is it the only way to analyze culture. This approach enables one to examine a people systemically. The categories are a beginning means of cultural understanding as one travels and visits different cultures. Likewise, the model can be used to study the microcultures within a majority national culture. All aspects of culture are interrelated, and to change one part is to change the whole. There is a danger in trying to compartmentalize a complex concept like culture, while trying to retain a sense of its whole. Culture is a complex system of interrelated parts that must be understood holistically.

## SYSTEMS APPROACH TO CULTURE

There are many different anthropological approaches to cultural analysis, and many prefer to use a coordinated systems approach as an alternative to understanding other cultures. A system, in this sense, refers to an ordered assemblage or combination of correlated parts that form a unitary whole.[18]

*Kinship System.* The family relationships and the way a people reproduce, train, and socialize their children. The typical North American family is a nuclear and rather independent unit. In many countries, there may be an extended family that consists of several generations held together through the male line (patrilineal) or through the female line (matrilineal). Such families have a powerful influence on child rearing, and often on nation building. Family influences and loyalties can affect job performance or business negotiations.

*Educational System.* How young or new members of a society are provided with information, knowledge, skills, and values. Educational systems may be formal and informal within any culture. How people learn varies by culture.

*Economic System.* The manner in which the society produces and distributes its goods and services. The Japanese economic system is in some ways an extension of the family and is group-oriented. Until recently, the world was divided into capitalistic or socialistic economic blocks, and economies were labeled *First World* (advanced free enterprise systems); *Second World* (socialist or communistic societies based on centralized planning and control); and *Third World* (developing nations moving from the agricultural to industrial or postindustrial stages). These categories are now outdated. Today, economies are mixed—some supposed Third World economies have high technology sectors, as in India and China; and Second World, formerly in the European Eastern Bloc, are in transition to free market systems, such as in Poland or Lithuania. Another trend beyond national economies is toward regional economic cooperatives or association that cut across national and ideological boundaries, such as is happening with NAFTA and the European Union. Macroeconomics is the study of such systems.

*Political System.* The dominant means of governance for maintaining order and exercising power or authority. Some cultures are tribal where chiefs rule, others have a ruling royal family with an operating king, while some prefer democracy.

*Religious System.* The means for providing meaning and motivation beyond the material aspects of life, that is, the spiritual side of a culture or its approach to the supernatural. This transcending system may lift a people to great heights of accomplishment, as is witnessed in the pyramids of Egypt and the Renaissance of Europe. It is possible to project the history and future of India, for instance, in terms of the impact of its belief in reincarnation, which is enshrined in its major religion. Diverse national cultures can be somewhat unified under a shared religious belief in Islam or Christianity, for example. In some countries, Islam is becoming the basis for governance, legal, and political systems. In others, religion dominates legal and political systems, such as Judaism in Israel or Roman Catholicism in the Republic of Ireland. The influence of religion is culturally weakening in some states, as with Roman Catholicism in France and Lutheranism in Sweden. Religion can also be a source of divisiveness and conflict in society; for example, Northern Ireland, the former Yugoslavia (especially Bosnia and Kosovo), and Africa (including Algeria and Rwanda). Unfortunately, history demonstrates that in the name of religion, zealots and extremists may engage in culturally repressive behavior, such as religious persecutions, ethnic cleansing, terrorism of nonbelievers, and even "holy" wars.

*Association System.* The network of social groupings that people form, whether in person or electronically. These may range from fraternal and secret societies to professional/trade associations. Some cultures are very group-oriented and create formal and informal associations for every conceivable type of activity (e.g., the culture in the United States). In some countries, families organize into clans, finding it difficult to work together for the common national good, as in Afghanistan and Iraq. Other societies are individualistic and avoid such organizing, such as in France.

*Health System.* The way a culture prevents and cures disease or illness, or cares for victims of disasters or accidents. The concepts of health and wholeness, well-being, and medical problems differ by culture. Some countries have witch doctors, spiritual remedies, and herb medications. Others, like India, have fewer government-sponsored social services, while Britain has a system of socialized medicine. The United States is in the midst of a major transition in its health-care and delivery system, and there is increasing emphasis on universal coverage, prevention, and wellness health models, and alternative holistic medical treatments. Medical practitioners can be culturally biased. For example, Western medicine tended to ignore folk medicine, especially in Asia and Africa. Fortunately, in this century, modern health-care workers are more open and are even practicing cross-cultural medicine. If the method or cure relieves pain and suffering without causing harm, they are willing to try and even adopt it.

*Recreational System.* The ways in which a people socialize or use their leisure time. What may be considered play in one culture may be viewed as work in another, and vice versa. In some cultures, "sport" has considerable political implications; in others, it is solely for enjoyment; while in still others, it is big business. Some cultures cherish the creative and performing arts, providing financial support for artists and musicians. Certain types of entertainment, such as a form of folk dancing, seem to cut across cultures. Global communications are forcefully impacting the media and entertainment industries. Music, sports, films, and special cultural or athletic events can be quickly broadcast worldwide. As a result, the youth subculture has similar tastes that go beyond national differences. The mass media and Internet become forums for electronic commerce and exchange in terms of leisure and recreation.

## KEY CULTURAL TERMINOLOGY

The specialists who make a formal study of culture use terms that may be helpful to those trying to comprehend the significance of this phenomenon in business or international life.

### Patterns and Themes

Some cultural anthropologists search for a single integrated pattern to describe a particular culture. Thus, the Pueblo Indians may be designated as "Apollonian"—people who stick to the "middle of the road" and avoid excess or conflict in their valuing of existence. To pinpoint a consistent pattern of thought and action in a culture is difficult, so other scholars prefer to seek a summative theme. This is a position, declared or implied, that simulates activity and controls behavior; it is usually tacitly approved or openly promoted in the society. One can note that in most Asian cultures there is a "fatalism" theme, while in the American business subculture the theme is profits, or the "bottom line."

## Explicit and Implicit

Some aspects of culture are overt, while others are covert. Anthropologists remind us that each different way of life makes assumptions about the ends or purposes of human existence, about what to expect from each other, and about what constitutes fulfillment or frustration. Some of this is explicit in folklore, and may also be manifest in law, regulations, customs, or traditions. Other aspects are implicit in the culture, and one must infer such tacit premises by observing consistent trends in word and deed. The distinction between public and hidden culture points up how much of our daily activity is governed by patterns and themes, the origin or meaning of which we are only dimly aware, if not totally unaware. Such culturally governed behavior facilitates the routine of daily living so that one may perform in a society many actions without thinking about them. This cultural conditioning provides the freedom to devote conscious thinking to new and creative pursuits. It is startling to realize that some of our behavior is not entirely free or consciously willed by us. At times, this can be a national problem, such as when a society finally realizes that implicit in its culture is a form of racism, which requires both legislation and education to rectify. Most cultures tend to discriminate against certain groups and believers, and this too may be covert. Thus, there is a global movement to rectify such bias toward women, gays, and ethnic or racial minorities, as well as any outsider or foreigner.

## Micro- or Subcultures

Within a larger society, group, or nation sharing a common majority- or macroculture, there may be subgroupings of people possessing characteristic traits that distinguish them from the others. These subcultures may be described in group classification by age, class, gender, race, or some other entity that differentiates this micro- from the macroculture. Youth, or more specifically teenagers, share certain cultural traits, as do other ethnic groups. There are many microcultures, such as white- or blue-collar workers, police or the military, college students, or the drug culture. Within a particular religious culture, there may be many sects or subcultures. As with any profession or vocational field that also has unique cultures, there are differing specialties and focus that are subcultures of the main group. Academia has a general culture and many subdivisions by discipline of study or specialization. The application of this concept is endless.

## Universals and Diversity

The paradox of culture is the commonalties that exist in the midst of its diffusion or even confusion. There are generalizations that may be made about all cultures that are referred to as *universals*: age-grading, body adornments, calendar, courtship, divisions of labor, education, ethics, food taboos, incest and inheritance rules, language, marriage, mourning, mythology, numerals, penal sanctions, property rights, supernatural beliefs, status differentiation, toolmaking and trade, visiting, weaning, etc. Thus, certain activities occur across cultures, but their manifestation may be unique in a particular society. And that brings us to the opposite concept of cultural *diversity*. Some form of sports or humor or music may be common to all peoples, but the way in which it is accomplished is distinctive in various cultural groupings.

## Rational/Irrational/Nonrational Behavior

There are many definitions of culture. Consider it as historically created designs for living that may be rational, irrational, and nonrational. *Rational* behavior in a culture is on the basis of what that group considers reasonable for achieving its goals. *Irrational* behavior deviates from the accepted norms of a society and may result from an individual's deep frustration in trying to satisfy needs; it would appear to be done without reason and possibly largely as an emotional response. *Nonrational* behavior is neither on the basis of reason nor against reasonable expectations—it is dictated by one's own culture or subculture. A great deal of behavior is of this type, and we are unaware of why we do it, why we believe what we do, or that we may be biased or prejudiced from the perspective of those outside our cultural group. How often and when to take a bath frequently is a cultural dictate, just as what food constitutes breakfast. What is rational in one culture may be irrational in another, and vice versa.

## Tradition

This is a very important aspect of culture that may be expressed in unwritten customs, taboos, and sanctions. Tradition can program a people as to what are proper behavior and procedures relative to food, dress, and to certain types of people, and what to value, avoid, or de-emphasize. As the song on the subject of "tradition" from the musical *Fiddler on the Roof* extols:

> Because of our traditions, we keep our sanity... Tradition tells us how to sleep, how to work, how to wear clothes... How did it get started? I don't know—it's a tradition...Because of our traditions, everyone knows who he is and what God expects of him![19]

## EXHIBIT 1.1
## COUNTING ELEVATOR FLOORS

It is quite normal in the United States to see the 13th floor absent in the selection of floors on the elevator directory panel. This is due, of course, to our cultural bias regarding the number 13 being "unlucky." By omitting it in the numbering sequence of the hotel floors, one avoids the anxiety of a superstitious customer. After entering the Hai-Li Hotel elevator in China and punching in my floor selection, I quickly noticed that not only was number 13 absent, but 14 was as well. As one rose to the higher floors in the hotel, one passed from floor number 12 to floor number 15. I mentioned this to my friends, and they assured me that the Chinese culture had an aversion to an unlucky number as well, only it was number 14. So our culturally astute hotel had decided to delete both numbers, thus showing their sensitivity (and respect) to both cultures, while showing favor to neither. Similarly in some countries, the custom is to designate the entrance floor as the "ground" floor, while the next floor becomes labeled the "first" floor, as the numbering continues upward. This is confusing to foreigners from countries where the entrance area from the street is known as the "first floor"; the problem worsens when more floors are being built underground, and as you enter, the visitor may find him or herself on the second or even third floor. Even basements are being built downward in levels 1, 2, 3, etc., and may be given exotic names after fruit or flowers. All this shakes up the staid, but makes the world more interesting.

Traditions provide a people with a "mindset" and have a powerful influence on their moral system for evaluating what is right or wrong, good or bad, and desirable or not. Traditions express a particular culture, giving its members a sense of belonging and uniqueness. But whether one is talking of a tribal or national culture, or of a military or religious subculture, traditions should be reexamined regularly for their relevance and validity. Mass global communications stimulate acquisition of new values and behavior patterns that may more rapidly undermine ancient, local, or religious traditions, especially among women and young people worldwide.

The following struck the authors' imagination when a manager for a high tech company brought it to our attention, namely, tradition and superstition express themselves when numbering floors in a hotel. We added some observations of our own as well (see Exhibit 1.1).

Some of these cultural variables have been researched and a "cultural profile" developed by Schmitz[20] for many countries. There are 10 concepts in the model:

*cultural profile*
*10*

1. *Environment*. Social environments can be categorized according to whether they view and relate to people, objects, and issues from the orientation of *control* (change environment), *harmony* (build balance), or *constraint* (external forces set parameters).
2. *Time*. A *past* orientation is indicated by placing a high value on preestablished processes and procedures. A *present* orientation is indicated by placing a focus on short-term and quick results. A *future* orientation is indicated by placing a focus on long-term results.
3. *Action*. Social environments can be distinguished by their approach to actions and interactions. An emphasis on relationships, reflection, and analysis indicates a *being* orientation. A focus on task and action indicates a *doing* orientation.
4. *Communication*. An emphasis on implicit communication and reliance on nonverbal cues indicates *high-context* orientation. A *low-context* orientation is indicated by a strong value on explicit communication.
5. *Space*. Cultures can be categorized according to the distinctions they make between *public* and *private* spaces.
6. *Power*. Social environments can be categorized by the way they structure power relationships. A *hierarchy* orientation is indicated by a high degree of acceptability of differential power relationships and social stratification. An *equality* orientation is indicated by little tolerance for differential power relationships and the minimizing of social stratification.
7. *Individualism*. An emphasis on independence and a focus on the individual indicate an *individualistic* orientation. An emphasis on affiliation and subordination of individual interest to that of a group, company, or organization indicates a *collectivistic* orientation.
8. *Competitiveness*. An emphasis on personal achievements, individual assertiveness, and success indicates a *competitive* orientation. Valuing quality of life, interdependence, and relationships indicates a *cooperative* orientation.
9. *Structure*. Environments that value adherence to rules, regulations, and procedures are considered *order* oriented and prefer predictability and minimization of risk. Environments that value improvisation exhibit a *flexibility* orientation and tend to reward risk taking, tolerate ambiguity, and value innovation.
10. *Thinking*. Cultures can expect, reinforce, and reward either a *deductive* approach (an emphasis on theory, principles, concepts, and abstract logic) or an *inductive* approach (emphasis on data, experience, and experimentation). They may also either emphasize a *linear* approach (analysis and segmentation of issues) or a *systemic* approach (synthesis, holism, and the "big picture").

Of course, it is important to keep in mind that these constructs are not rigid and material diversity illustrates this. Though of the concepts along a continuum, where extremes are unlikely and placement is relative, it is this which leads us to Hofstede's research.

## Hofstede's Early Research

To create opportunities for collaboration, global leaders must learn not only the customs, courtesies, and business protocols of their counterparts from other countries, but they must also understand the national character, management philosophies, and mind-sets of the people. Dr. Geert Hofstede, a European research consultant, has helped identify important dimensions of national character. He firmly believes that "culture counts" and has identified four dimensions of national culture:

1. *Power distance*—indicates "the extent to which a society accepts that power in institutions and organizations is distributed unequally."
2. *Uncertainty avoidance*—indicates "the extent to which a society feels threatened by uncertain or ambiguous situations."
3. *Individualism*—refers to a "loosely knit social framework in a society in which people are supposed to take care of themselves and of their immediate families only." Collectivism, the opposite, occurs when there is a "tight social framework in which people distinguish between in-groups and out-groups; they expect their in-group (relatives, clan, organizations) to look after them, and in exchange for that owe absolute loyalty to it."
4. *Masculinity*—with its opposite pole, *femininity*, expresses "the extent to which the dominant values in society are assertiveness, money and material things, not caring for others, quality of life, and people."

A significant dimension related to leadership in Hofstede's original study of 40 countries is the power distance dimension. He assigned an index value to each country on the basis of mean ratings of employees on a number of key questions.

Exhibit 1.2 shows the positions of the 40 countries on the power distance and uncertainty avoidance scales, and Exhibit 1.3 shows the countries' positions on the power distance and individualism scales.

The United States ranked 15th on power distance, 9th on uncertainty avoidance (both of these are below the average), 40th on individualism (the most individualist country in the sample), and 28th on masculinity (above average).

In Hofstede's study, the United States ranked 14th out of 40 on the power distance dimension. If this had been higher, then the theories of

# EXHIBIT 1.2

## POSITIONS OF 40 COUNTRIES ON THE POWER DISTANCE AND UNCERTAINTY AVOIDANCE SCALES

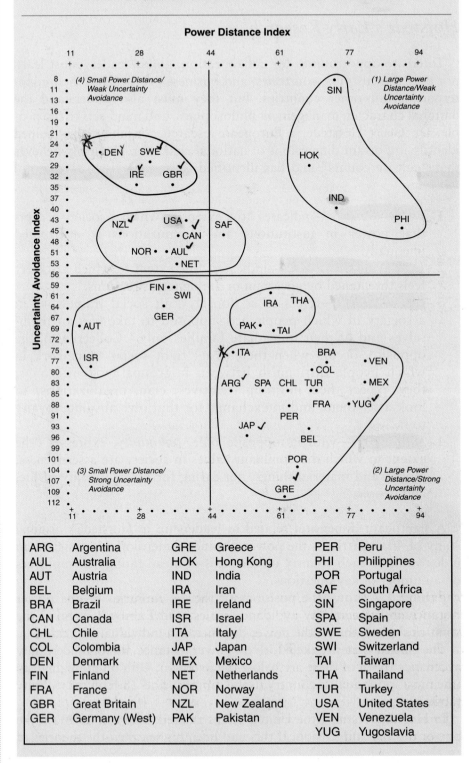

| ARG | Argentina | GRE | Greece | PER | Peru |
| AUL | Australia | HOK | Hong Kong | PHI | Philippines |
| AUT | Austria | IND | India | POR | Portugal |
| BEL | Belgium | IRA | Iran | SAF | South Africa |
| BRA | Brazil | IRE | Ireland | SIN | Singapore |
| CAN | Canada | ISR | Israel | SPA | Spain |
| CHL | Chile | ITA | Italy | SWE | Sweden |
| COL | Colombia | JAP | Japan | SWI | Switzerland |
| DEN | Denmark | MEX | Mexico | TAI | Taiwan |
| FIN | Finland | NET | Netherlands | THA | Thailand |
| FRA | France | NOR | Norway | TUR | Turkey |
| GBR | Great Britain | NZL | New Zealand | USA | United States |
| GER | Germany (West) | PAK | Pakistan | VEN | Venezuela |
|  |  |  |  | YUG | Yugoslavia |

EXHIBIT 1.3

## POSITIONS OF 40 COUNTRIES ON THE POWER DISTANCE AND INDIVIDUALISM SCALES

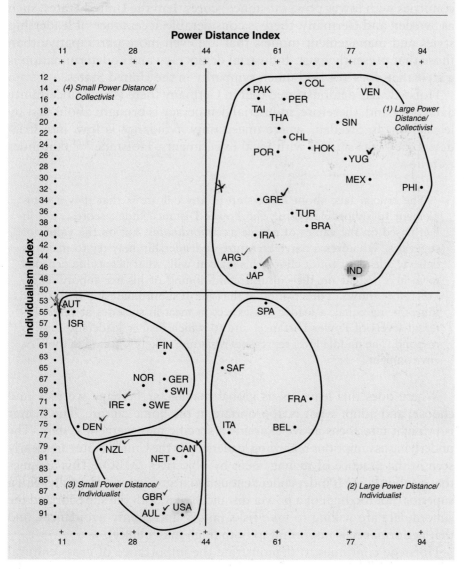

**Power Distance Index**

leadership taught in the United States might have been expected to be more Machiavellian. We might also ask how U.S. leaders are selected. Most are selected on the basis of competence, and it is the position of the person that provides his or her authority in the United States, which is, theoretically at least, an egalitarian society. In France, which has a higher power distance index score, there is little concern with participative management but great concern with who has the power.

Even today, French industry and the managers who run it are a mixture of the old and the new. France is still, in some ways, a country of family empires with many paternalistic traditions. There is also a remnant of a feudalistic heritage that is deeply rooted within the French spirit, which could account for the very conservative and autocratic nature of their business methodology. Hofstede has shown that in countries with lower power distance scores than the United States, such as Sweden and Germany, there is considerable acceptance of leadership styles and management models that are even more participative than those that presently exist. Industrial democracy and codetermination is a style that does not find much sympathy in the United States.

Hofstede has demonstrated that in Germany there is high uncertainty avoidance and, therefore, industrial democracy is brought about first by legislation. In Sweden, where uncertainty avoidance is low, industrial democracy was started with local experiments. Hofstede[21,22] continues as follows:

> The crucial fact about leadership in any culture is that it is a complement to subordinateship. The Power Distance Index scores...are in fact based on the values of people as *subordinates*, not on the values of superiors. Whatever a naive literature on leadership may try to make us believe, a leader cannot choose his style at will; what is feasible depends to a large extent on the cultural conditioning of his/her subordinates. I therefore show...a description of the type of subordinateship that, other things being equal, a leader can expect to meet in societies at three different levels of Power Distance, and to which his/her leadership has to respond. The middle level represents what most likely is found in the U.S. environment.

Where does this leave us as global managers? Perhaps we pick and choose, and adopt what is appropriate in the home culture. The matter is brought into focus as we examine a specific management system. The underlying assumptions regarding leadership in the United States are clearly seen in the practice of management by objectives (MBO). This assumes that a subordinate is independent enough to negotiate meaningfully with a superior (not too high of a power distance), that both the superior and the subordinate are willing to take risks (a low uncertainty avoidance), and that performance is important to both (high masculinity).

Hofstede continues to demonstrate the importance of cross-cultural research as MBO is applied to Germany.

> Let us now take the case of Germany. This is also a below-average Power Distance country, so the dialogue element in MBO should present no problem. However, Germany scores considerably higher on Uncertainty Avoidance; consequently, the tendency towards accepting risk and ambiguity will not be present to the same extent. The idea of replacing the arbitrary authority of the boss by the impersonal authority of mutually agreed-upon objectives, however, fits the low Power Distance, high Uncertainty Avoidance cultural cluster very well. The objectives become the subordinates' "superego."

The consequences of Hofstede's conclusions are significant. Leadership, decision making, teamwork, organization, motivation, and in fact everything managers do are learned. Management functions are learned, and they are on the basis of assumptions about one's place in the world. Managers from other business systems are not "underdeveloped" American managers.

## Bond's Confucian Cultural Patterns

Another researcher, Michael H. Bond, believes that the taxonomies developed by Western scholars have a Western bias.[23] In his research, he found four dimensions of cultural patterns: integration, human-heartedness, interpersonal harmony, and group solidarity. The *integration dimension* refers in a broad sense to the continuum of social stability. If a person scores high on this dimension, he or she will display and value the behaviors of tolerance, noncompetitiveness, interpersonal harmony, and group solidarity. *Human-heartedness* refers to the values of gentleness and compassion. People who score high on this dimension value patience, courtesy, and kindness toward others. *Moral discipline* refers to the essence of restraint and moderation in one's regular daily activities. If one scores high on this dimension, the behaviors valued are following the middle way, regarding personal desires as negative. The *Confucian work dynamic* refers to an individual's attitude and orientation toward work and life. According to Bond, the behaviors that are exhibited along this continuum are consistent with the teachings of Confucius.

Kong Fu Zen, renamed Confucius by Jesuit missionaries, was a Chinese civil servant who lived during the Warring States Period about 2500 years ago. He sought to determine ways in which Chinese society could move away from fighting among themselves so that through discipline, human relationships, ethics, politics, and business average themselves harmoniously. He was well known for his wisdom and wit and was regularly surrounded by followers who recorded his teachings. Confucianism is a set of practical principles and ethical rules for daily life.

Confucius taught that people should be educated, skilled, hard-working, thrifty, modest, patient, and unrelenting in all things. Human nature is assumed to be inherently good, and it is the responsibility of the individual to train his or her character in these standards of behavior.

Exhibit 1.4 represents a framework for understanding cultural differences along several dimensions and will be valuable for any person working in the global world.

Many other researchers, including Fons Trompenaars and Charles Hampden-Turner, have studied culture and written persuasively on culture's impact on global business in the twenty-first century.

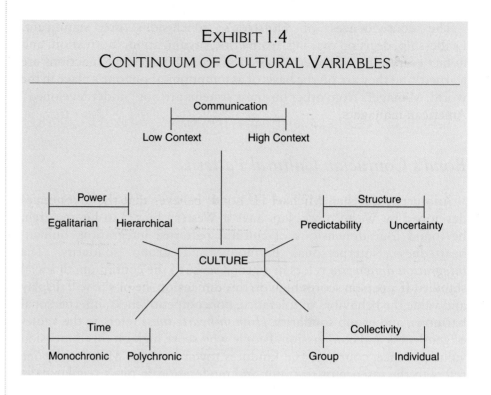

### EXHIBIT 1.4
### CONTINUUM OF CULTURAL VARIABLES

Communication
Low Context    High Context

Power
Egalitarian    Hierarchical

Structure
Predictability    Uncertainty

CULTURE

Time
Monochronic    Polychronic

Collectivity
Group    Individual

# GLOBAL LEADERS AS INFLUENCERS

A challenge global leaders experience today is how to influence across cultures and functions the individuals with whom they work and their global partners. Aware of the cultural influences on the personalities, motivations, and values of their counterparts, skillful leaders are able to influence others, whether it is by giving orders and directions to individuals under their authority or by "influencing with authority." Leaders know what they want to accomplish but how to achieve it and who are the key people they need to influence to succeed are routine unknowns.

According to Cohen and Bradford[24] the following points are key in successfully influencing others.

■ Assume any individual, even an adversary, can be an ally.
■ Be clear what you want.
■ Understand the "cultures" of all those to be influenced.
■ Identify your own and others currencies.
■ Build the relationships and develop partners.
■ Use formal and informal influencing skills.

Exhibit 1.5 shows a model of influence without authority.

All leaders have some power, which is the ability to influence others, inside or outside of an organization or enterprise whether it is a business, government agency, or a nation, to do what you want them to

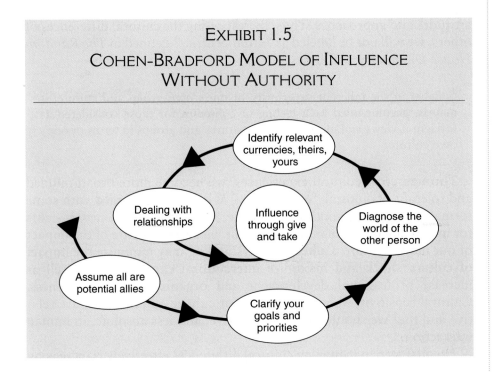

EXHIBIT 1.5
COHEN-BRADFORD MODEL OF INFLUENCE
WITHOUT AUTHORITY

do when you want them to do it. The total power of any individual is a combination of formal power or power associated with position plus informal power, which is personal and a function of one's skills, expertise, and credibility.

Verma[25] states that there are eight sources of power.

- Legitimate power—derives from position or status
- Persuasive—derives from personal skills and ability in winning others' cooperation
- Contact/network—derives from who we know and our connections
- Information—derives from the information we have and knowledge of how organizations work
- Expertise—derives from knowledge
- Referent—derives from our reputation in an organization
- Coercive—derives from our ability to punish
- Reward—derives from our ability to reward

# CULTURAL UNDERSTANDING AND SENSITIVITY

The global leader, sensitive to cultural differences, appreciates a people's distinctiveness and effectively communicates with individuals from different cultures. A global leader does not impose his/her own cultural attitudes and approaches. Thus, by respecting the cultural differences of others, we will not be labeled as "ethnocentric," defined in *The Random House Dictionary* as follows:

> Belief in the inherent superiority of one's own group and culture; it may be accompanied by a feeling of contempt for those considered as foreign; it views and measures alien cultures and groups in terms of one's own culture.

Through cross-cultural experiences, we become more broad-minded and tolerant of cultural "uniqueness." When this is coupled with some formal study of the concept of culture, we not only gain new insights for improving our human relations, but we become aware of the impact of our native culture. Cultural understanding may minimize the impact of culture shock and maximize intercultural experiences, as well as increase professional development and organizational effectiveness. Cultural sensitivity should teach us that culture and behavior are relative and that we should be more tentative, and less absolute, in human interaction.

The first step in managing cultural differences effectively is increasing one's general cultural awareness. We must understand the concept of culture and its characteristics before we can fully benefit from the study of cultural specifics and a foreign language.

Further, we should appreciate the impact of our specific cultural background on our own mind-set and behavior, as well as those of colleagues and customers with whom we interact in the workplace.[26] This takes on special significance within a more diverse business environment, often the result of increasing migration from less developed to more developed economies.

In the March 20, 2009, *Herald Tribune*, article by Nicholas D. Kristof, he wrote:

> That's because there's pretty good evidence that we generally don't truly want good information—but rather information that confirms our prejudices. We may believe intellectually in the clash of opinions, but in practice we like to embed ourselves in the reassuring womb of an echo chamber.

He ended his article:

> So perhaps the only way forward is for each of us to struggle on our own to work out intellectually with sparring partners whose views we deplore. Think of it as a daily mental workout analogous to a trip to the gym: if you don't work up a sweat, it doesn't count.

What follows are some ideas on how to learn and get good information.

# CROSS-CULTURAL LEARNING

To increase effectiveness across cultures, *training* must be the focus of the job, while *education* thought of with reference to the individual, and *development* reserved for organizational concerns. Whether one is concerned with intercultural training, education, or development, all employees should learn about the influence of culture and be effective cross-cultural communicators if they are to work with minorities within their own society or with foreigners encountered at home or abroad. For example, there has been a significant increase in foreign investments in the United States—millions of Americans now work within the borders of their own country for foreign employers. All along the U.S.-Mexican border, twin plants have emerged that provide for a flow of goods and services between the two countries.

A new reality of the global marketplace is the Information Highway and its impact on jobs and cross-cultural communications. Many skilled workers in advanced economies are watching their positions migrate overseas, where college educated nationals are doing high technology tasks for less pay. The Internet has changed how global business is and will be conducted for many decades.

Not considering computer language, most international exchanges take place with individuals using English as a second language. While a few corporate representatives will travel abroad, the main communication will occur by means of satellites on the Internet through modems connected to laptop or personal computers. Offshore operations done electronically in developing countries are stimulated by growing software applications that turn skilled tasks into routine work. Cross-cultural sensitivity is essential when participating in teleconferences or video conferences. Electronic media also require appropriate etiquette and protocols to create cultural synergy.

# GLOBAL TRANSFORMATIONS

To stay globally competitive, more and more corporations are increasing their investments and activities in foreign countries. U.S. engineers can work on a project during the day, and then send it electronically to Asia or elsewhere for additional work while they sleep. Such trends represent an enormous challenge for cross-cultural competence. C-Bay Systems in Annapolis, Maryland, for instance, transmits U.S. physicians' dictations about patients to their subsidiary operations in India where they are transcribed into English, sent back to headquarters by computer, and then the completed version is sent on to the medical office from which the communication originated.

Another example of "going global" is seen in personalized service firms such as law and accounting. These professions are increasingly engaging in cross-border activities, hiring local practitioners who comprehend their own unique culture, language, and legal or accounting systems. The need for international expertise and capital is one reason for this trend. Companies of professionals are forming alliances with their foreign counterparts such as the Alliance of European Lawyers. To be successful, the acquisition process then requires an integration of *national, organizational*, and *professional cultures*. Under these circumstances, culture becomes a critical factor ensuring business success, particularly with the twenty-first century trend toward economies of scale favoring large, multidisciplinary, and multinational professional service organizations.[27]

In only 10% of 191 nations are the people ethnically or racially homogenous. Never before in history have so many inhabitants traveled beyond their homelands, either to travel or work abroad, or to flee as refugees. In host countries, the social fabric is being reconfigured and strained by massive waves of immigrants, whether legal or illegal.[28]

Many corporate and government leaders, business students, and citizens still operate with dated mind-sets regarding the world, the people in various societies, the nature of work, the worker, and the management process itself. The Industrial Age has given way to the Information Age, and we can only speculate on its replacement in the next 100 years. Possibly the Space Age? Capra and Rast[29] state as follows:

> Now, in the old paradigm, it was also recognized that things are interrelated. But conceptually you first had the things with their properties, and then there were mechanisms and forces that interconnected them. In the new paradigm we say the things themselves do not have intrinsic properties. All the properties flow from their relationships. This is what I mean by understanding the properties of the parts from the dynamics of the whole, because these relationships are dynamic relationships. So the only way to understand the part is to understand its relationship to the whole. This insight occurred in physics in the 1920s and this is also a key insight of ecology. Ecologists think exactly in this way. They say an organism is defined by its relationship to the rest.

Thus, today's leaders are challenged to create new models of management systems. For that to happen, managers and other professionals must become more innovative and recognize the contribution of each individual or unit to the effective workings of the whole.

As the late Peter Drucker consistently observed, the art and science of management is in its own revolution, and many of the assumptions on which management practice was based are now becoming obsolete.

Foreign competition and the need to trade more effectively overseas have forced most corporations to become more culturally sensitive and globally minded. Managing people from different cultures is receiving the attention of business students as well as those in education and human resource development. Global management is a component in most executive education training programs worldwide.

According to Rhinesmith[30]:

Global managers must reframe the boundaries of their world...of space, time, scope, structure, geography and function; of functional, professional, and technical skills from a past age; of thinking and classification relative to rational to intuitive, national versus foreign, we versus they; of cultural assumptions, values and beliefs about your relations with others, and your understanding of yourself.

How do companies foster and create effective global managers? What is a global manager? Companies with worldwide operations are pondering these questions, plus many others. They find that the human resource component of the answer is, at times, more limiting than the capital investment in globalization. Bartlett and Ghoshal[31] state:

Clearly, there is no single model for the global manager. Neither the old-line international specialist nor the more recent global generalist can cope with the complexities of cross-border strategies. Indeed, the dynamism of today's marketplace calls for managers with diverse skills. Responsibility for worldwide operations belongs to senior business, country, and functional executives who focus on the intense interchanges and subtle negotiations required. In contrast, those in middle management and front-line jobs need well-defined responsibilities, a clear understanding of their organization's transnational mission, and a sense of accountability.

Percy Barnevik, former President and CEO of Asea Brown Boveri (ABB), responded when asked if there is such a thing as a global manager[32]:

Global managers are made, not born. This is not a natural process. We are herd animals. We like people who are like us. But there are many things you can do. Obviously, you rotate people around the world. There is no substitute for line experience in three or four countries to create a global perspective. You also encourage people to work in mixed nationality teams. You *force* them to create personal alliances across borders, which means that sometimes you interfere in hiring decisions.

You also have to acknowledge cultural differences without becoming paralyzed by them. We've done some surveys, as have lots of other companies, and we find interesting differences in perception. For example, a Swede may think a Swiss is not completely frank and open, that he doesn't know exactly where he stands. That is a cultural phenomenon. Swiss culture shuns disagreement. A Swiss might say, "Let's come back to that point later, let me review it with my colleagues." A Swede would prefer to confront the issue directly. How do we undo hundreds of years of upbringing and education? We don't, and we shouldn't try to. But we do need to broaden understanding.

Sheridan[33] found three clusters of leadership competencies and included intrapersonal competencies, interpersonal competencies, and social competencies. The following Seven C's apply not only to U.S. leaders but to any global leaders also. Her summary is shown in Exhibit 1.6.

# Exhibit 1.6
## Interculturally Competent Leader

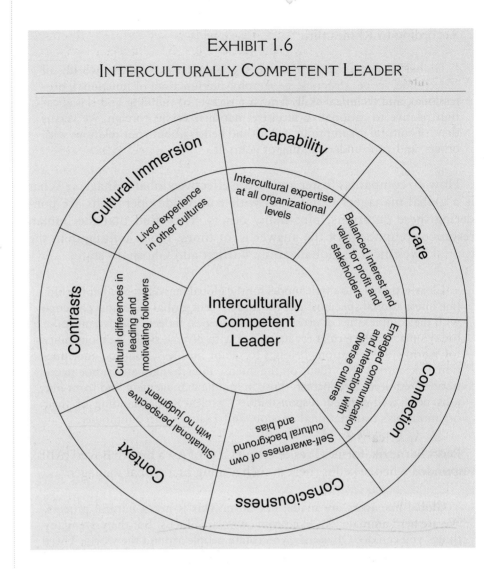

## *Self-Perception and Others' Perception of You*

Intentions are important but, like culture, perceptions count. And for the present and foreseeable future, what happens in our global world will be to a large extent influenced by the United States. China is increasingly becoming a world power. The United States is involved in many global economic, political, and religious disputes and conflicts. But in this complex, rapidly changing yet interconnected global world, the influence of even the most powerful is highly limited.

Now consider these comments, which provide a contrast.[34]

> Americans almost alone in the world, have a serious…even simplistic belief that their country is a force for enduring good. They acknowledge it does not always get it right, that at times its antics fall far short of its highest ideals, but all but the most hardened cynics really believe in America as a force for freedom and prosperity and in the universality of these goals.

This belief is born of the country's history, religion, and culture…. It is this self-faith as much as anything that defines and differentiates Americans from most of the rest of the world. There is not much doubt that outside the United States, American intentions, especially under the Bush administration, are regarded with a degree of suspicion and resentment…it is not hard to see why this self-belief evinces such cynicism around the world. The United States record—supporting tyrants, even in places such as Iraq—where it eventually topples them—is hardly unblemished. At times, America's commitment to liberty has looked a little selective.

## Denial

Most individuals, at some time in their lives, deny realities. In families, children deny that their parents are alcoholic, and women deny that their husbands are abusive. Similarly, in business organizations and academic institutions, "realities" are suppressed, "feelings" are stuffed, and intellectualization exercises force new realities into old paradigms.

The following humorous parody illustrates the denial of a country's competitiveness problem and a misdiagnosis. This example is American, but it can easily apply to most countries.

### THE AMERICAN WAY

The Americans and the Japanese decided to engage in a competitive boat race. Both teams practiced hard and long to reach their peak performance. On the big day they both felt ready.

The Japanese won by a *mile*.

Afterward, the American team was discouraged by the loss. Morale sagged. Corporate management decided that the reason for the crushing defeat had to be found, so a consulting firm was hired to investigate the problem and recommend corrective action.

The consultant's findings: The Japanese team had eight people rowing and one person steering; the American team had one person rowing and eight people steering.

After a year of study and millions spent analyzing the problem, the consulting firm concluded that too many people were steering and not enough were rowing on the American team.

So, as race day neared again the following year, the American team's management structure was completely reorganized. The new structure: four steering managers, three area steering managers, one staff steering manager, and a new performance review system for the person rowing the boat to provide work incentive.

That year the Japanese won by *two* miles.

Humiliated, the American corporation laid off the rower for poor performance and gave the managers a bonus for discovering the problem.

In this oversimplification, in the first race the Americans were overconfident and denied they had a competitiveness problem. In preparation for the second race, there was a serious misdiagnosis. Hamel states it well.

To fully understand our competitive advantage/disadvantage, we have to go deeper, and look at our "genetic Coding"—that is, our beliefs, our managerial frames. It is these beliefs that restrict our perceptions of reality and degrees of freedom. To be successful, a company needs "genetic variety." Our challenge must be to get outside our restrictive managerial frames.

If you want to enlarge your managerial frames, you must be curious about how the *rest of the world thinks*—and you must *have humility*. The real competitive problem is not that our institutional environment is hopelessly unhelpful, but that our managerial frames are hopelessly *inappropriate to the next round of global competition*.[35]

## THE COSTS OF GLOBAL INCOMPETENCE

Two additional skills are of fundamental importance today for global people. The first skill is *listening* to understand. Many global leaders, particularly of nation-states, do not seem to possess this skill to a high degree. Listening is a symbol of respecting the dignity of others.

The second is the skill of locating and using many very sophisticated *cultural interpreters*. It is impossible for any individual, given the complexity of culture, to have a free understanding of other systems. However, cultural interpreters, individuals from each culture, can teach leaders. Having listened and been a student with cultural interpreters as teachers, the global leader is equipped to face the many opportunities and challenges that will be continually presented.

Having a sense of culture and its related skills is a unique human attribute. Culture is fundamentally a group of problem-solving tools for coping in a particular environment. It enables people to create a distinctive world around themselves, to control their own destinies, and to grow. Sharing the legacy of diverse cultures advances our social, economic, technological, and human development. Culture can be analyzed in a macrocontext, such as in terms of national groups, or in a micro sense, such as within a system or organization. Increasingly, we examine culture in a global sense from the perspective of work, leadership, or markets.

Because management philosophies and practices are culturally conditioned, it stands to reason that there is much to be gained by including cultural studies in all management or professional development. This is particularly relevant during the global transformation under way. Culturally skilled leaders are essential for the effective management of emerging global corporations as well as for the furtherance of mutually beneficial world trade and exchange. In these undertakings, the promotion of cultural synergy by those who are truly global managers will help us to capitalize on the differences in people, while ensuring their collaborative action.

Learning to manage cultural differences is a means for all persons to become more global in their outlook and behavior, as well as more effective personally and professionally. When cultural differences are understood and utilized as a *resource*, then all benefit.[36] When they are not, the costs are significant.

---

## Mind Stretching

1. What was your reaction to the points in "Did You Know"?
2. Do you believe the world is really "flat," and what does this mean?
3. Is it possible to see events and issues through multiple lens?
4. When confronted with cultural differences, why do we often dig in and believe our way is right rather than listen?
5. What is your opinion regarding the Prophet Mohammed cartoon controversy?
6. In 5 years, with your "futurist hat" on, how would you describe our "global world"?
7. What is your opinion on the two words, "culture counts"?

## REFERENCES

1. Pascal, B. *Pensées*, Vol. 60, 1670, p. 294.
2. Freidman, T. "It's a Flat World, After All," *The New York Times Magazine*, April 3, 2005.
3. www.theglobalist@theglobalist.com. *Globalist Interview > Global Business, A CEO's Responsibilities in the Age of Globalization, Jeffrey Immelt*, March 17, 2006.
4. Freidman, T. *The World is Flat, a Brief History of the Twenty-First Century*. New York: Farrar, Strauss and Giroux, 2005, pp. 6–7.
5. Schein, E. H. "On Dialogue, Culture and Organizational Learning," *Organizational Dynamics*, Fall, 1993, Vol. 22, No. 2, pp. 40–51.
6. McNamara, R. S., Blight, J. G., and Brigham, R. K. *Argument Without End*. New York: Public Affairs, 1999, p. 191.
7. Brooks, D. "It's Culture That Counts," *International Herald Tribune*, February 21, 2006.
8. Harrison, L. and Huntington, S. P. (eds.). *Culture Matters*. New York: Basic Books, 2000, p. 111.
9. Diamond, J. *Guns, Germs, and Steel*. New York: Norton and Company, 1999, p. 13.
10. Ibid. p. 25.
11. Moran, R. Personal journal, 2010.
12. *Global Awareness and Education: American's Test for the 21st Century*. Apple Inc., February, 2007.
13. Deardorff, D. K. (ed.). *The Sage Handbook of Intercultural Competence*. Sage Publications, Inc., 2009.
14. Huntington, S. *The Clash of Civilizations and the Remaking of World Order*. New York: Simon & Schuster, 1996.

15. Chomsky, N., Mitchell, P. R., and Schoeffel, J. (eds.). *Understanding Power*. New York: Vintage, 2002.
16. Lewis, R. D. *The Cultural Imperative*. Yarmouth, ME: Intercultural Press, 2003.
17. *Science & Culture*, January/February 2008.
18. Miller, J. G. *Living Systems*. Niwot, CO: University Press of Colorado, 1994. See also *Systems Research and Behavioral Science*. Wiley Interscience, Baffins Lane, Chichester, West Sussex, UK PO19 1UD.
19. Stein, J. "Tradition," *Fiddler on the Roof*. Harnick, S., lyrics, Bock, J., music, 1964.
20. Schmitz, J. *Cultural Orientations Guide*. Princeton, NJ: Princeton Training Press, 2003, pp. 10–12.
21. Hofstede, G. *Cultures Consequences: International Differences in Work-Related Values*. Beverly Hills, CA: Sage Publications, 1984. See also Hofstede, G. *Cultures and Organizations: Software of the Mind*. London: McGraw-Hill, 1991
22. Hofstede, G. *Cultures and Organizations: Software of the Mind*. London: McGraw-Hill, 1991.
23. Lustig, M. W. and Koester, J. *Intercultural Competence: Interpersonal Communication Across Cultures*, Fifth edition. New York: Allyn and Bacon, 2005.
24. Cohen, A. R. and Bradford, D. L. *Influence without Authority*. Hoboken, NJ: John Wiley & Sons, Inc., 2005.
25. Verma, V. K. *Managing the Project Team*. Newton Square, PA: PMI Publications, 1997.
26. Thiederman, S. *Bridging Cultural Barriers to Success: How to Manage the Multicultural Workforce*. Lexington, MA: Lexington Books, 1990. *Profiting in America's Multicultural Workplace*. Lexington, MA: Lexington Books, 1991.
27. *The Economist*, August 29, 1998, p. 59.
28. Harris, P. R. *The Cultural Diversity Handbook*, Simons, G., Abramms, B., Hopkins, A., and Johnson, D. (eds.). Princeton, NJ: Pacesetter Books, 1996.
29. Capra, F. and Rast, D. S. *Belonging to the Universe*. San Francisco, CA: Harper, 1991.
30. Rhinesmith, S. H. *A Manager's Guide to Globalization*, Second edition. Chicago, IL: Irwin/ASTD, 1996, p. x.
31. Bartlett, C. A., and Ghoshal, S. "What is a Global Manager?" *Harvard Business Review*, September/October 1992, p. 131.
32. Taylor, W. "The Logic of Global Business: An Interview with ABB's Percy Barnevik," *Harvard Business Review*, March/April 1991, p. 95.
33. Sheridan, E. *The Global Business Leadership*. Burlington, MA: Elsevier, 2009.
34. Baker, G. "The Land of the Free Enjoys the Thrill of Being a Force for Good," *Financial Times*, April 12/13, 2003.
35. Hamel, G. "Pushing the Envelope of Global Strategy and Competitiveness," A summary of remarks by Gary Hamel for the Executive Focus International 1993 Executive Forum, February 12, 1993.
36. Gesteland, R. R. *Cross-Cultural Business Behavior—Marketing, Negotiating, and Managing Across Cultures*. Copenhagen, DK: The Copenhagen Business School Press (Handelshojskolens Forlag), 1999.

# GLOBAL
# LEADERS AND
# COMMUNICATIONS

There is more than a verbal tie between the words *common*, *community*, and *communication*. Try the experiment of communicating, with fullness and accuracy, some experience to another, especially if it be somewhat complicated, and you will find your own attitude toward your experience changing.

John Dewey

To effectively communicate, we must realize that we are all different in the way we perceive the world, and use this understanding as a guide to our communication with others.

Anthony Robbins

## LEARNING OBJECTIVES

We know that most leaders of organizations spend upwards of 70% of their time communicating. We also know that all business undertakings are comprised of communication.[1] We have learned from experience, and from extensive interaction with expatriates from all over the globe, that participating in these cross-cultural experiences while working internationally can be very challenging, especially when living or working in a foreign environment. It is for these reasons that this chapter provides an overview of interpersonal and intercultural communication.

Our world's population exceeds 6 billion. This is hard to imagine for most. However, if the global population was only 1000 people, it would include the following composition[2]:

Our world's population exceeds six billion.

584 Asians
124 Africans
150 Eastern and Western Europeans and former Soviets

84 Latin Americans
52 North Americans
6 Australians and New Zealanders

About 50% of the people speak the following languages:

165 Mandarin
86 English
83 Hindi/Urdu
64 Spanish
58 Russian
37 Arabic

The other half speaks Bengali, Portuguese, Indonesian, Japanese, German, French, and two hundred other languages. Communication, indeed, can be challenging in this global village.

Trade and business exchanges across cultural lines have played an important role in human history, and are perhaps the most important external incentive to increased human interaction across cultural and linguistic differences. When people who have different customs, values, behaviors, and communication styles interact together, the process can be quite difficult. Strangers, or those who are very dissimilar to ourselves, are often people who have a very different way of life, and their ways may *seem* unpredictable, unexplainable, or irrational. When strangers interact, this can cause anxiety for all parties involved, and communication can be difficult. Even after an appropriate median comes into existence, like having a second language in common, understanding can be hard to come by. Strangers, in general, are still not trusted in the same full sense that neighbors and kinfolk tend to be trusted.[3] With our globally interdependent economy, it is essential that we appreciate and understand the perspectives and goals of our world trade partners, especially when these trade partners are often working together for certain agreed-upon objectives.

We recognize that we are most comfortable communicating to those who are the most similar to us. This comfort level tends to decrease as dissimilarity increases. Research[4] has demonstrated that communication openness tends to be a precursor to different group members' response to conflict which can impact a diverse groups' performance. Reasons cited[5] are that members prefer to communicate and are more open with others who are most similar to themselves, and perceived dissimilarity tends to negatively impact communication. People are often unaware when misunderstandings occur or "errors" are committed while working with persons from different cultures. A cross-cultural *faux pas* results when we fail to recognize that persons of other cultural backgrounds have certain goals, customs, thought patterns, and/or values different from our own. This is particularly true in a diverse workforce with increasing numbers of expatriate workers not familiar with the home culture, its language, and communication systems.

Effective communication across cultural and linguistic boundaries is difficult, for it involves learning to use flexible approaches to listen, observe, and speak according to the specific situation at hand. Before a person is able to communicate effectively with people from different cultures, it is important to know about their culture, language, history, and where they live. The following is a list of questions that require a little more knowledge and sophistication. They are adapted from the booklet, "So You're Going Abroad: Are You Prepared?"[6] Can you answer the questions for any country in which you have done business?

1. There are many contemporary and historical people of whom a country is proud. Can you name a politician, a musician, a writer, a religious leader, a sports figure?
2. Are you familiar with that country's basic history? Date of independence? Relationship to other countries?
3. What are some routine courtesies that people are expected to observe in that country?
4. How do they greet each other? Foreigners?
5. What do you know about their major religions?
6. Are there role differences between men and women?
7. What kinds of foods are traditional?
8. What kind of humor is appreciated?
9. What is the relationship between that country and your country?

## CULTURAL FACTORS IN COMMUNICATION

Intercultural communication is a process whereby individuals from different cultural backgrounds attempt to share meanings. Lustig and Koester[7] provide definitions of communications. For example, *intercultural* communication is "the presence of at least two individuals who are culturally different from each other on such important attributes as their value orientations, preferred communication codes, role expectations, and perceived rules of social relationship." This is exemplified by a Japanese and an English negotiator discussing a joint venture. *Intracultural* communication occurs between culturally similar individuals. The study of child-rearing practices in different cultures would be referred to as *cross-cultural* or communication that pertains to the "study of a particular idea or concept within many cultures." *Interracial* communication refers to the "differences in communication between members of racial and ethnic groups," such as the Han Chinese, Zhuang Chinese, African-Americans, and Asian-Americans. In the classical anthropological sense, culture refers to the cumulative deposit of knowledge, beliefs, values, religion, customs, and mores acquired by a group of people and passed on from generation to generation.

Imagine yourself participating in the following cross-cultural situations that affect communication and understanding between two culturally different individuals. By the end of this chapter, we hope you will have a better sense of how to avoid or to effectively resolve these situations.

## Cross-Cultural Management

- You are involved in a technical training program in China, and one of your responsibilities is to rate persons under your supervision. You have socialized on several occasions, and spent time with one of the Chinese, who you are supervising. He is an extremely friendly and hardworking individual, but has difficulty exercising the leadership expected of him. On the rating form you indicated this, and his supervisor discussed it with him. Subsequently, he came to you and asked how you could have criticized his leadership skills. You indicated that you had an obligation to report deficiencies and areas of improvement. What cultural differences might cause misperceptions of this performance appraisal and evaluation?

- You are in Saudi Arabia attempting to finalize a contract with a group of Saudi businessmen. You are aware that these people are excellent negotiators; however, you find it difficult to maintain eye contact with your hosts during conversations. Furthermore, their increasing physical proximity to you is becoming more uncomfortable. You also have noticed that a strong handgrip while shaking hands is not returned. When invited to a banquet, because you are left-handed, you use your left hand while eating. Your negotiations are not successfully concluded. What may have been the reason for this? What cultural aspects are evidenced in this interaction; which, if known, could improve your communication with your Arab clients?

- You are the manager of a group of Puerto Rican workers in a New York factory, but you only speak English. You resent the use of Spanish among your subordinates. Why do your subordinates feel more comfortable in their native language? How could your company facilitate their instruction in the English language? Or should it?

- You are from a "developed country," and in your overseas travel to many poorer countries than your own, you can feel deep resentment that seems to be directed at you, your government, and your country. How do you respond to situations like this?

In the past, many businesspeople were not overly concerned with the way culture influenced individual or organizational behavior. However, serious and costly errors have made those working in a multicultural environment aware that insensitivity and lack of cultural knowledge can do much to injure, either permanently or temporarily, the relationship with their coworkers and colleagues. The following questions may prove helpful and expedient.

1. What must I know about the social and business customs of country X?
2. What skills do I need to be effective as a negotiator in country Y?
3. What prejudices and stereotypes do I have about the people in country Z?
4. How will these influence my interaction?

# VARIABLES IN THE COMMUNICATION PROCESS

Samovar and Porter[8] identify a number of variables in the communication process whose values are determined to some extent by culture. Each variable influences our perceptions, which in turn influence the meanings we attribute to behavior. In order to work effectively in a multicultural environment, one should recognize these and study the cultural specifics of the country or area to be visited.

*Attitudes* are psychological states that predispose us to behave in certain ways. An undesirable attitude for managers working in a multicultural environment is ethnocentrism, or self-reference criterion. This is the tendency to judge others by using one's own personal or cultural standards. For example, instead of attempting to understand Americans within their own cultural context, an ethnocentric person tries to understand them as similar to or different from himself or herself. It is vital to refrain from constantly making comparisons between our way of life and that of others. Rather, one must understand other people in the context of their unique historical, political, economic, social, and cultural backgrounds. In that way, it is possible to become more effective interactors.

*Stereotypes* are sets of attitudes that cause us to attribute qualities or characteristics to a person on the basis of the group to which that individual belongs. Stereotypes are outsiders' beliefs about groups. Stereotypes are certain generalizations that allow us to organize and understand our environment. For humans to survive, we need to be able to form instant judgments about a situation, object, or person, and to commit those judgments to memory. We draw on these stereotypes during similar situations so that we can quickly make judgments and act appropriately. Stereotypes aid us in predicting behavior by reducing our uncertainty. It was once said that "Stereotypes are in some ways a shorthand for us, but they have absolutely nothing to do with the person sitting across from you at the negotiating table."

*The Social organization* of cultures is another variable that influences one's perceptions. A *geographic society* is composed of members of a nation, tribe, or religious sect; a *role* society is composed of members of a profession or the elite of a group. Managers are members of the same role society, that is, the business environment, but they are often members of different geographic societies. At one level, communication between managers from two different cultures can be relatively smooth. On another level, significant differences in values, approach, pace, priorities, and other factors may cause difficulties.

*Thought patterns* or forms of reasoning may differ from culture to culture. The Aristotelian mode of reasoning prevalent in the West is not shared by people in the East. What is reasonable, logical, and self-evident to an Irish may be unreasonable, illogical, and not self-evident to a Japanese.

*Roles* in a society and expectations of a culture concerning behavior affect communication. Some roles have very prescriptive rules. For example, the *meishi* or name card of the Japanese businessperson identifies his or her position in a company and determines the degree of respect that is appropriately due for the individual.

*Language skill* in a host country is acknowledged as important by global leaders, but many believe that a competent interpreter can be helpful and, at times, necessary.

*Space* is also a factor in the communication process. Americans believe that a comfortable space around them is approximately two feet. The United States is a noncontact society. Latin Americans and Middle Easterners, for example, are contact societies and are comfortable with close physical proximity to others. Touching is common between men, and handshakes are frequent.

*Time sense* also impacts human interaction. North American cultures perceive time in lineal-spatial terms, in the sense that there is a past, a present, and a future. Being oriented toward the future, and in the process of preparing for it, one saves, wastes, makes up, or spends time. Zen treats time as a limitless pool in which certain things happen and then pass. A different time orientation can cause confusion when doing business in other cultures.

## COMMUNICATION AND INTERACTION

All business ultimately comes down to transactions or interactions between individuals. The success of an interaction depends almost entirely on how well managers understand each other and context of their interaction. To better understand the global leader's role as a communicator, we must comprehend what is involved in the complex process of communication. Communication occurs verbally and nonverbally and at different levels of formality, intellectuality, and emotionality, and is highly influenced by and influences context.

Most communication is manifested through symbols that differ in their meaning according to time, place, culture, or person. Human interaction is characterized by a continuous updating of the meaning of these symbols. In the past 25 years, we have expanded our capacities for symbolic communication beyond what was accomplished in the previous 2500 years. Despite the technological wonders of today's communications, international relations require us to deal with one another on a person-to-person basis. For this to be effective interaction, we have to overcome language and stereotype barriers. This may require the mental elimination of terms like "foreigner" or "alien," and more appropriately viewing the individual as having a background that is different.

## Communication and Context

The context of an interaction is found in the interactive relationship between those communicating and the environment. Fundamentally dynamic, communication is truly contextually bound, and is influenced by current realities, and by historical events that brought the communicating parties to the current state of interaction.[9] Context is seen as socially constructed phenomenon that is dynamic, being shaped by communication, relations, and the interactive nature of how people respond to and, in turn, shape context.[10]

Vital to the investigation of context[11] is learning to recognize how a person responds to and perceives the contextual events and situations that he/she is traversing through; what specific activities are in process; and the way in which a person utilizes his/her body, behavior, and language as a means to respond to and interact with this context; and fundamental to this is recognizing how background information and realities deeply influence the conversational exchange between different parties.

When considering how context shapes communication, and vice versa, we need to ask the following questions[12]: (1) Where is this conversation taking place? (2) Under what circumstances? and (3) What is the history behind this conversation? Add culture to this matter, and the first question becomes: Where, with whom, and how is this conversation taking place? The second becomes: Under what circumstances and what cultural contexts are involved?

And the third becomes: What is the history behind this interaction, and what is the history of interaction between the national and cultural groups represented in this discussion, and how might it influence this particular interactive communication? Language is often utilized as a mechanism to not only determine understanding, but also to influence action.[13] "Context and talk are now argued to stand in mutually reflexive relationship to each other, with talk, and the interpretive work it generates, shaping context as much as context shapes talk."[14]

## Axioms of Communication

*Every generation perceives life differently.* For example, the previous concepts of behavioral communication can be applied to a generation of people. The people of each generation project a unique image of "their" world at a certain point in time. This image reflects a generation's system of needs, values, standards, and ideals. The children who grew up during the early 1940s experienced life differently from today's children, and thus the problem of communication between the generations, and even cultures, becomes more understandable. The supervisor of a young worker, for example, may project his or her generation's view of the world (past-oriented) and find it difficult to facilitate communication by learning and accepting the reality of the younger employee (future- and global-oriented).

*Communication is at the heart of all organizational operations and international relations.* It is the most important tool we have for getting things done. It is the basis for understanding, cooperation, and action. In fact, the very vitality and creativity of an organization or a nation depends on the content and character of its communications. Yet communication is both hero and villain: it transfers information, meets people's needs, and gets things done, but far too often it also distorts messages, causes frustration, and renders people and organizations ineffective.

*Every person is a versatile communicator.* Language sets us apart from other creatures, and seemingly is characteristic of the more developed brain. But humans have a wide range of communication skills that go beyond words to include deliberate use of gestures, signs, shapes, colors, sounds, smells, pictures, and many other communication symbols. The diversity of human culture in this regard may be demonstrated by the "artist" who may communicate both thought and feeling in paintings, sculpture, music, and dance. Through such media, artists project themselves into people, things, and surroundings. We project our way of thinking, our temperament and personality, and our joys and sorrows into the world around us.

*Every person operates within his or her own private world or perceptual field.* This is what is referred to as life space, and it applies to individuals as well as to organizations and nations. Every individual communicates a unique perspective of the world and reality. Every culture reflects the group view of the world. From time to time, one must check whether one's view of the world, or that of an organization, synchronizes with the collective reality. This is particularly essential when "objective reality" is subject to the phenomenon of accelerating change. Even within-country cultural groups often have distinct views of world reality that may not coincide with other cultural groups' world views, as is exemplified by what occurred in China during the period of the Maoist Cultural Revolution.

*Every person projects himself or herself into human communication.* We communicate our image of self, including our system of needs, values, and standards as well as our expectations, ideals, and perceptions of peoples, things, and situations. We project this collective image through body, bearing, appearance, tone of voice, and choice of words.

*Every person is a medium or instrument of communication*, not just a sender and receiver of messages. If a person is comfortable with himself or herself and congruent in beliefs, actions and communications, people usually respond positively. If one is uncomfortable and incongruent, people will respond negatively. The more aware the individual is of the forces within him or her that affect behavior at work, the more that person is able to control his or her own life space.

## THE COMMUNICATION PROCESS

Communication is a process of circular interaction involving a sender, receiver, and message. In human interaction, the sender or receiver may be a person or a group of people. The message conveys meaning through the medium or symbol used to send it (the how), as well as in its content (the what). Both sender and receiver occupy a unique field of experience, different for each person. Essentially, it is a private world of perception through which all experience is filtered, organized, and translated; it is what psychologists call the individual's life space. This consists of the person's *psychological environment* as it exists for him or her. Each person experiences life in a unique way and psychologically structures his or her own distinctive perceptual field. Among the factors that compose one's field of experience are one's family and educational, cultural, religious, and social background. The individual's perceptual field affects the way he or she receives and dispenses all new information. It influences both the content and the media used in communicating.

An individual's self-image, needs, values, expectations, goals, standards, cultural norms, and perception affect the way input is received and interpreted. Essentially, people tend to *selectively perceive* all new data, and determine what aspects of the data are relevant to and consistent with their own perceptual needs. Two people can thus receive the same message and understand it as having two entirely different meanings. They actually perceive the same object or information differently. Communication, then, is a complex process of linking up or sharing perceptual fields between sender and receiver. The effective communicator builds a bridge to the world of the receiver. When the sender is from one cultural group and the receiver from another (and in the communication process, this is reciprocal), the human interaction is intercultural communication.

Once the sender conveys the message, the receiver analyzes the message in terms of his or her particular field of experience and pattern of ideas—usually, decoding the message, interpreting it for meaning, and encoding or sending back a response. Thus, communication is a circular process of interaction.

The communicator, whether as an individual from a cultural group or as a member of an organization, exhibits or transmits many kinds of behavior. First, the intended message is communicated on verbal and nonverbal levels. We also communicate unintended behavior, or subconscious behavior, on verbal and nonverbal levels. In other words, communication at any level involves a whole complex of projections.

There is also a "silent language" used in the process of human interaction, including tone of voice, gestures, and facial expressions. Some of these factors that affect the real meaning and content of messages are referred to as "body language"—the positioning of various parts of the sender's physique conveys meaning. The person is both a medium of communication and a message, and the way in which one communicates is vastly influenced by one's cultural conditioning.

## Select Models of Communication

Traditional Western models of communication are a reflection of Western cultural philosophical thought. The early models depict communication as a linear process, and were deemed process models which included the source, message, channel, and receiver.[15] In this case, Western communication models believe that the sender is in the principal position and that the main cause of understanding is derived from this principal position.[16] These traditional models of communication are being replaced by more current models of communication which tend to be more sociological and highlight culture. For example, one model includes the sender, message, channel, noise, receiver, feedback, and cultural context.[17] Where *noise* is perceptions of and the cultural backgrounds of each communicator, and *cultural filters* are the noise for both the sender and receiver.[18]

We have the same opinion with recent research[19] that asserts that language used in communication is not separable from its cultural context. Therefore, culture should no longer be viewed as noise, but rather as a key ingredient within the practice of communication. As such, culture influences how language is formed, culture influences how the linguistic communication is understood, and culture impacts how the language is constructed.[20] For example, "In Japanese and German prose, it appears that effectiveness has traditionally been the more valued dimension in developing texts, while English writing values efficiency."[21] Because we do not view culture as peripheral to communication, the values[22] that are espoused as part of one's culture become highly salient. Because values are aspects of actions that are determined to be "right or wrong," just as failing to concede that a person has a particular set of beliefs will lead to poor communication, failing to acknowledge or understand particular values will also lead to poor communication.[23]

The following view of communication is our preferred model of communication. This communication model places the focal point on the middle ground, where all parties involved in the communication cocreate meaning, and the position in between is the most important.[24] Clausen[25] researched global corporate communication challenges, and found that differences in cultural perception can impede communication, and that corporate headquarters practiced more western-style models of communication, which did not accommodate cultural differences and ultimately impeded communication. In fact, Clausen[26] found that the best communication outcomes were derived when communication and cultural outcomes were not determined beforehand, and a new culture was allowed to emerge on the basis of continuing to negotiate communication and to bridge learning between different cultures.

## COMMUNICATION GUIDELINES

Klopf[27] defines communication as "the process by which persons share information meanings and feelings through the exchange of verbal and nonverbal messages." The individual working and communicating in a multicultural environment must "remember that the message that ultimately counts is the one that the other person gets or creates in their mind, not the one we send."[28]

The following are practical guidelines to follow for more effective intercultural communication. These statements briefly outline several important characteristics of intercultural communication. Some are obvious, others are not, but all, if internalized and understood, will result in more effective communication.

- *No matter how hard one tries, one cannot avoid communicating.* Any behavior in human interaction has a message and communicates something. Body language communicates, as well as our activity or inactivity. Any behavior is communication because any behavior contains a message, whether intended or not.
- *Communication does not necessarily mean understanding.* Even when two individuals agree that they are communicating or talking to each other, it does not mean that they understand each other. Understanding occurs when the two individuals have the same interpretation of the symbols being used in the communication process, whether the symbols are words or gestures.
- *Communication is irreversible.* One cannot take back one's communication (although sometimes we wish one could). However, one's message can be explained, clarified, or restated. Once communicated, the message is part of the communicator's experience, and it influences present and future meanings. For example, disagreeing with a Saudi Arabian in the presence of others is an "impoliteness" in the Arab world, and may be difficult to remedy.
- *Communication occurs in a context.* One cannot ignore the context of communication that occurs at a certain time, in some place, using certain media. Such factors have message value and give meaning to the communicators. For example, a business conversation with a French manager in France during an evening meal may be inappropriate.
- *Communication is a dynamic process.* Communication is not static and passive, but rather it is a continuous and active process without beginning or end. A communicator is not simply a sender or a receiver of messages, but can be both at the same time.

Each of us has been socialized in a unique environment. Important aspects of the environment are shared, and these constitute a particular culture. Every person is part of many different identity groups simultaneously, thus learning and becoming part of all their cultures. Each of us is culturally unique because each adopts or adapts differently the attitudes, values, and beliefs of the groups to which we belong. Thus, communication becomes intercultural when all of the various group identities of those communicating interact. As the cultural variables and differences increase, the number of communication misunderstandings also increase. Our challenge is to examine the differences that make us unique and discover ways to be more effective in overcoming the barriers these differences create.[29]

# COMMUNICATION KEYS: LOW/HIGH CONTEXT AND LISTENING

## Low and High Context Communication

Anthropologist Edward Hall makes a vital distinction between high- and low-context cultures, and how this matter of *context* impacts communications. A high-context culture uses more vague forms of (or high-context) communications: information is either in the physical context or internalized in the person with little communicated in the explicit words or message. Japan, Saudi Arabia, Spain, and China are cultures engaged in high-context communications. On the other hand, a low-context culture employs more direct (or low-context) forms of communications: most information is contained in explicit codes, such as words. Canada and the United States, as well as many European countries, engage in low-context communications.

When individuals communicate, they attempt to find out how much the listener knows about whatever is being discussed. In a low-context communication, the listener knows very little and must be told practically everything. In high-context cultures, the listener is already "contexted" and therefore does not need to have much background information. When communicating with individuals of our own culture, we can more readily assess the communication cues so that we know when our conversation, our ideas, and words are being understood and internalized. However, communication between high- and low-context people is often fraught with impatience and irritation, because low-context communicators may give more information than is necessary, while high-context communicators may not provide enough information or background. Exhibit 2.1 is an excellent example of a low-context question responded to by a very high-context Middle Eastern communicator.

When communicating across cultures, communication misunderstandings can occur, but they are usually not serious and can be rectified. Exhibit 2.2 illustrates a communication misunderstanding that had grave results: excerpted (Exhibit 2.3) is the transcript of the conversation

## EXHIBIT 2.1

## RESEARCH IDENTIFIED BEHAVIORS MOST IMPORTANT FOR INTERCULTURAL EFFECTIVENESS

- Demonstrate respect (verbally and nonverbally)
- Respond to people in a nonjudgmental, nonevaluative manner
- Recognize that your exact knowledge, beliefs, and perceptions are unique and valid only for yourself
- Demonstrate empathy
- Have tolerance for ambiguity
- Turn off your behavioral auto-pilot and actively manage how you interact with others
- Demonstrate a willingness to adopt different roles and adapt your behaviors

## EXHIBIT 2.2

## MIDDLE EAST LOW/HIGH CONTEXT COMMUNICATION

"How many days did it take?"

"I will tell you. We watered at al Ghaba in the Amairi. There were four of us, myself, Salim, Janazil of the Awamir, and Alaiwi of the Afar; it was in the middle of summer. We had been to Ibri to settle the feud between the Rashid and the Mahamid started by the killing of Fahad's son."

Musallim interrupted, "That must have been before the Riqaishi was Governor of Ibri. I had been there myself the year before. Sahail was with me and we went there from…"

But al Auf went on, "I was riding the 3-year-old I had bought from bin Duailan."

"The one the Manahil raided from the Yam?" Bin Kabina asked.

"Yes. I exchanged it later for the yellow 6-year-old I got from bin Ham. Janazil rode a Batina camel. Do you remember her? She was the daughter of the famous grey which belonged to the Harahaish of the Wahiba."

Mabkhaut said, "Yes, I saw her last year when he was in Salala, a tall animal; she was old when I saw her, past her prime but even then a real beauty."

Al Auf went on, "We spent the night with Rai of the Afar."

Bin Kabina chimed in, "I met him last year when he came to Habarut; he carried a rifle, 'a father of 10 shots,' which he had taken from the Mahra he had killed in the Ghudun. Bin Mautlauq offered him the grey yearling, the daughter of Farha, and 50 *riyals* for this rifle, but he refused."

Al Auf continued, "Rai killed a goat for our dinner and told us…," but I interrupted: "Yes, but how many days did it take you to get to Bai?" He looked at me in surprise and said, "Am I not telling you?"

*Source*: Thesinger, W. *Arabian Sands*. London: Penguin Books, 1991.

EXHIBIT 2.3

AN EMERGENCY

*Captain to Copilot*:
"Tell them we are in emergency."

*Copilot to Controller*:
"We are running out of fuel."

*Controller*:
"Climb and maintain 3000."

*Copilot to Controller*:
"Uh, we're running out of fuel."

*Controller*:
"I'm going to bring you about 15 miles northeast and then turn you back...Is that fine with you and your fuel?"

*Copilot*:
"I guess so."

*The jet ran out of fuel and crashed.*

between the captain, copilot, and controller on the Avianca flight that crashed on Long Island in 1991.

The communication misunderstanding involves the high and low context of communication styles. It can be seen from this dialogue between the pilot, copilot, and controller that there was a critical misunderstanding between the copilot who was Colombian (native language Spanish—high context), and the American controller, who was a low-context communicator. "Emergency" is low context. "We are running out of fuel" is more high context (literally, all airplanes, once they take off, are running out of fuel). The controller's last question, "Is that fine with you and your fuel?" is more high context. The controller could have asked, "Are you declaring a fuel emergency?" If the controller had asked this question, perhaps the copilot would have responded "yes" because he or she had just heard the pilot say, "Tell them we are in emergency."

Unless global leaders are aware of the subtle differences, communication misunderstandings between low- and high-context communicators can result. Japanese communicate by not stating things directly, while Canadians usually do just the opposite—often declaring, "spell it all out, please." The former looks for meaning and understanding in what is not said—in the nonverbal communication or body language, in the silences and pauses, in relationships and empathy. The latter emphasizes sending and receiving accurate messages directly, usually by articulating words.

A third example in Exhibit 2.4 of low/high communication context involves a Chinese Human Resource (HR) director and a western HR director working for the same company, and Exhibit 2.5 illustrates the cultural variations in management style between Mexicans and Americans.

## EXHIBIT 2.4

## A QUESTION FROM A WESTERNER TO A CHINESE HR DIRECTOR CONCERNING ATTENDANCE AT A TRAINING PROGRAM

*Question*: "Do you think Mr. Sim will be able to come to the course next week, as I would like to make hotel reservations for him and the hotel is quite full?"

*Answer*: "It is possible he may have to attend a meeting in Shanghai."

*Follow-up question 2 days later and before the course begins*:

*Question sent by e-mail*: "I am following up my earlier conversation and am wondering if Mr. Sim will be attending the course."

*Answer by e-mail*: "As I told you previously, he will NOT attend."

*Result*: A significant misunderstanding between the Chinese HR director and the Westerner. The HR director ignored the Westerner at work for several days.


## EXHIBIT 2.5

## MANAGEMENT STYLES

| Aspect | Mexico | United States |
|--------|--------|---------------|
| Work/Leisure | Works to live | Lives to work |
| | Leisure considered essential for full life | Leisure seen as reward for hard work |
| | Money is for enjoying life | Money often ends in itself |
| Direction/ Delegation | Traditional managers autocratic | Managers delegate responsibility and authority |
| | Younger managers starting to delegate responsibility. Subordinates used to being assigned tasks, not authority | Executive seeks responsibility and accepts accountability |
| Theory vs. Practice | Basically theoretical mind | Basically pragmatic mind |
| | Practical implementation often difficult | Action-oriented problem-solving approach |
| Control | Still not fully accepted Sensitive to being "checked upon" | Universally accepted and practiced |

continued

## EXHIBIT 2.5
## MANAGEMENT STYLES (CONTINUED)

| Aspect | Mexico | United States |
| --- | --- | --- |
| Staffing | Family and friends favored because of trustworthiness | Relatives usually barred Favoritism is not acceptable |
| | Promotions based on loyalty to superior | Promotion based on performance |
| Loyalty | Mostly loyal to superior (person rather than organization) | Mainly self-loyalty |
| | Beginnings of self-loyalty | Performance motivated by ambition |
| Competition | Avoids personal competition; favors harmony at work | Enjoys proving her/himself in competitive situations |
| Training and Development | Training highly theoretical | Training concrete, specific |
| | Few structured programs | Structured programs general |
| Time | Relative concept | Categorical imperative |
| | Deadlines flexible | Deadlines and commitments are firm |
| Planning | Mostly short-term because of uncertain environment | Mostly long-term in stable environment |

*Source*: Abbot-Moran. *Uniting North American Business*. Butterworth-Heinemann, 2002, p. 71.

For low-context communicators to understand high-context messages, it is important to listen and observe the environment. Education seems to emphasize articulation over the acquisition of listening skills—which are essential to international negotiations. Lyman Steil pioneered scientific research on listening, and discovered that it is the communication competency that leads to true understanding; but, in some countries, like the United States, it is taught least. He summarized his findings in Exhibit 2.6. In high-context cultures, listening skills are highly valued and learned from an early age.

## *Listening*

We learn to listen and talk before we read and write. Should we have difficulties with reading, writing, and talking, we will receive special assistance while at school. Listening is a complex activity. The average person speaks approximately 12,000 sentences every day at about 150 words per minute, while the listener's brain can absorb around 400 words per minute. What do we do with this spare capacity? Many of us do nothing, and we can see that in the findings presented in Exhibit 2.6.

## EXHIBIT 2.6
## COMMUNICATION SKILLS

|         | Listening | Speaking  | Reading    | Writing |
|---------|-----------|-----------|------------|---------|
| Learned | 1st       | 2nd       | 3rd        | 4th     |
| Used    | Most      | Next most | Next least | Least   |
| (%–100) | (–45%)    | (–30%)    | (–16%)     | (–9%)   |
| Taught  | Least     | Next least| Next most  | Most    |

We become bored. A good listener is seldom bored. He or she uses this extra capacity to listen to the entire message and to more fully analyze the meanings behind the words.

Listening means different things to different people. It can mean different things to the same person in different situations. There are various types of listening behaviors:

1. *Hearing* is a physiological process by which sound waves are received by the ear and transmitted to the brain. This is not really listening in and by itself, though the two are often equated. Hearing is merely one step in the process of listening.

2. *Information gathering* is a form of listening. Its purpose is the absorption of stated facts. Information gathering does not pertain to the interpretation of the facts, and is indifferent as to the source.

3. *Cynical listening* is on the basis of the assumption that any communication is designed to take advantage of the listener. It is also referred to as defensive listening.

4. *Offensive listening* is the attempt to trap or trip up an opponent with his own words. A lawyer, when questioning a witness, listens for contradictions, irrelevancies, and weakness.

5. *Polite listening* is listening just enough to meet the minimum social requirements. Many people are not listening—they are just waiting for their turn to speak and are perhaps rehearsing their lines. They are not really talking to each other, but at each other.

6. *Active listening* involves a listener with very definite responsibilities. In active listening, the listener strives for complete and accurate understanding, for empathy, and assistance in working out problems.

Active listening, is what our normal listening mode should be, but rarely is.

Listening is, above all, a sharing of oneself. It is impossible for one to become an active listener without becoming involved with the speaker. Listening demonstrates the respect and concern that words alone cannot fully express. It has the unique power of diminishing the magnitude of problems. By speaking to someone who actively listens, a person has the sense of already accomplishing something. Listening fulfills another vital function as well. The listener provides feedback to the speaker concerning the speaker's success in transmitting his or her message clearly. In doing this, the listener exerts great control over future messages that might or might not be sent. Feedback will influence the speaker's confidence, delivery, content of the words, and nonverbal facets of communication.

Simons, Vázquez, and Harris state that when working within our own culture, we are very perceptive.[30] We know what ideas are being accepted or rejected and when others are following our conversation. However, when communicating across cultures, there is the real possibility of reading people incorrectly, and they us. Problems arise when one does not pay close enough attention or actively listen to what an individual is trying to communicate. Instead, when at work, in focusing on getting the job done, meeting business deadlines and agendas, one can easily pretend to listen or listen halfheartedly. Today, the workplace is a mix of individuals from different cultures, of different ages and genders, and with different work values. One must listen at three levels in cross-cultural exchanges.

1. *Pay attention* to the person, the message, and the nonverbal cues. One may subconsciously ignore a speaker whose thought process or thinking patterns are more convoluted or subtle than one's own. Also, the behavior of the speaker may be so emotional or subdued that one may selectively listen or not listen at all. To further complicate the listening process, an individual may speak with an accent, causing the listener to struggle to determine the words and put them in an understandable order.
2. *Empathize and create rapport.* Empathy, especially with people who have visible differences in language and culture, can build trust and loyalty. The verbal and nonverbal cues of the speaker reveal his or her thinking patterns. Attempting to emulate cues, after reading them properly and matching their style, increases the comfort and effectiveness of communication, especially a cross-cultural one.
3. *Share meaning.* Share your understanding of the speaker's message. Paraphrasing is an "active listening" skill that enables the listener to check the accuracy of his or her understanding of the message.

Through sharing meaning, active listening helps to ensure that correct attribution of the senders message is understood, by allowing for opportunity to correct mis-attributions.

## ATTRIBUTION

Triandis[31] cites the following interesting cross-cultural situation. In many cultures, domestic help does most of the tasks around a home, including the cleaning of shoes. In Canada, such employees usually do not clean shoes as part of their responsibilities. If Mr. Kato, a Japanese businessman, were a house guest of Mr. Smith, a Canadian businessman, and asked the "cleaning person" to shine his shoes, there could be a problem. It is, or at least could be, an inappropriate request. However, the crucial question is, what *attributions* do the cleaning person make concerning Mr. Kato's request? There are probably two possibilities. One is that he or she could say Mr. Kato is ignorant of Canadian customs, and, in this case, the person would not be too disturbed. The cleaning person could respond in a variety of ways, including telling the Japanese guest of the Canadian custom, ignoring the request, and speaking to his or her employer. However, if the cleaning person attributes Mr. Kato's request to a personal characteristic (he is arrogant), then there will be a serious problem in their interpersonal relationship. If a person from one culture is offended by a person from another culture and believes the offense is caused by culture ignorance, this is usually forgiven. If one "attributes" the offense or "error" to arrogance, there will be serious problems.

Attribution theory is concerned with how people explain things that happen. We interpret behavior in terms of what is appropriate for a role. Mr. Kato expected that it would be acceptable to ask the cleaning person to shine his shoes. From the perspective of the cleaning person, this is not acceptable. When each one's expectations were not realized, they attributed motives to the "offender" on the basis of their cultural construct. It helps answer such questions as given below:

1. Why did Mr. Kato ask the cleaning person to shine his shoes?
2. Why did Mrs. Lee ignore me when I tried to speak with her?
3. Why won't my supervisor tell me directly what she wants me to do?

There are many ways of perceiving the world. Given the almost limitless possibilities, we must subconsciously and habitually "screen" and organize the stimuli.

Attribution theory helps explain what happens and is applicable to cross-cultural management situations for the following reasons:

1. *Any Behavior is rational and logical from the perspective of the person behaving*. At a seminar involving Japanese and American businesspeople, an American asked a Japanese what was most difficult for him in the United States. The Japanese replied that "the most difficult part of my life here is to understand Americans. They are so irrational and illogical." The Americans listened with amusement and surprise.
2. *Persons from different cultures perceive and organize their environment in different ways so that it becomes meaningful to them.* To effectively work with people from different cultures requires that we make *isomorphic attributions* of the situation, that is, we put ourselves "in the other person's shoes." Isomorphic attributions result in a positive evaluation of the other person because they help us to better understand his or her verbal and nonverbal behavior.

Triandis[32] provides another attribution in Exhibit 2.7. As background, Greeks perceive supervisory roles as more authoritarian than

## EXHIBIT 2.7
## ATTRIBUTION IN GLOBAL MANAGEMENT

| Verbal Conversation | Attribution |
|---|---|
| *American:* How long will it take you to finish this report? | *American:* I asked him to participate. Greek: His behavior makes no sense. He is the boss. Why doesn't he tell me? |
| *Greek.:* I do not know. How long should it take? | *American:* He refuses to take responsibility. Greek: I asked him for an order. |
| *American:* You are in the best position to analyze time requirements. | *American:* I press him to take responsibility for his own actions. Greek: What nonsense! I better give him an answer. |
| *Greek:* 10 days. | *American:* He lacks the ability to estimate time; this time estimate is totally inadequate. |
| *American:* Take 15. Is it agreed you will do it in 15 days? | *American:* I offer a contract. Greek: These are my orders: 15 days. |

In fact, the report needed 30 days of regular work. So the Greek worked day and night, but at the end of the 15th day, he still needed one more day's work.

| Verbal Conversation | Attribution |
|---|---|
| *American:* Where is the report? | *American:* I am making sure he fulfills his contract. *Greek:* He is asking for the report. |
| *Greek:* It will be ready tomorrow. | Both attribute that it is not ready. |
| *American:* But we had agreed it would be ready today. | *American:* I must teach him to fulfill a contract. *Greek:* The stupid, incompetent boss! Not only did he give me wrong orders, but he does not even appreciate that I did a 30-day job in 16 days. |
| The Greek hands in his resignation. | The American is surprised. *Greek:* I can't work for such a man. |

Americans, who prefer participatory decision making. Read the verbal conversation first and then read the attributions being made by the American and the Greek.

These examples illustrate that each statement in cross-cultural communication leads to an intimation that does not match the attribution of the other. These are extreme examples of nonisomorphic attributions, and accordingly work to the detriment of the relationship.

The intercultural skill of making isomorphic attributions is vital to appropriate protocol and effective technology transfer.[33] Exhibit 2.8 provides an example of a discussion between an American and a Japanese.

EXHIBIT 2.8

DISCUSSION BETWEEN A JAPANESE AND AN
AMERICAN FIRM

A representative of a Japanese firm is discussing a business deal with a representative of an American firm. Americans value honesty and directness, while Japanese value harmony and group consensus. This was written during a seminar by a participant from an actual experience.

| Verbal Conversation | Attribution |
|---|---|
| *American:* Well, what do you think of this deal between our companies? | A: I wonder if they are as committed to the contract as we are. |
| | J: He knows our company's position in these dealings. Why does he ask me? |
| *Japanese:* Our firm is honored to do business with such a prestigious American company. | J: I will remind him of our group's agreement. |
| | A: That's nice, but doesn't he have any thoughts of his own on the matter. |
| *American:* Thank you, but how do you personally feel about the contract? | A: He must not understand that I want his opinion on the deal. I will rephrase the question. |
| | J: We have agreed on the matter. Perhaps the Americans are still unsure. |
| *Japanese:* The company is pleased that we have been chosen to represent your firm in Japan, and we wish to do the best job we can. | J: Our board is in agreement. |
| | A: I know his firm's position. I just wonder what he thinks. Maybe I better try again and be more direct about it. |
| *American:* I'm sure your firm will represent us well, but do *you* feel that the terms of the contract are equitable? | A: Is this guy stupid or something? Or maybe he's trying to hide something. |
| | J: Maybe he will feel better about the contract if I remind him that it was mutually agreed upon. |
| *Japanese:* This is what our two companies have agreed upon. Therefore, it must be the agreement. | A: He's really afraid to level with me. |

## Levels of Culture and Attribution

Using the analogy that culture is like an iceberg (part of it is seen, but most is not), the *technical* level of culture is the part of the iceberg that is visible. The technical aspects of a culture can be taught, and there is little emotion attached to this level. Few intercultural misunderstandings arise at this level, because the reason for any misunderstanding is usually quite easy to determine. Managers operate at the technical levels of culture when discussing the tolerance points of certain metals; however, when two managers are interacting over a period of time, it is difficult to remain exclusively at the technical level.

Continuing with the analogy of the cultural iceberg, the *formal* level of culture is partially above and partially below sea level. We learn aspects of our culture at the formal level usually by trial and error. We may be aware of the rules for a particular behavior, such as the rituals of marriage, but we do not know why. The emotion at the formal level of culture is high, and violations result in negative feelings about the violator, even though the violation is often unintentional. It is difficult to admit when the violated rule is local (i.e., an aspect of one culture and not another), and therefore does not apply to everyone. A business representative visiting France who uses a social occasion to discuss business with a French executive is violating a rule at the formal level of that culture.

The *informal* level of culture lies below "sea level," where actions and responses are automatic and almost unconscious. The rules of such behavior are usually not known, although we realize when something is wrong. Informal rules are learned through a process called modeling. One example of culture at the informal level is the male and female role behavior. In France, for instance, when is it appropriate for the American manager to begin calling her colleague "Denise," instead of "Mademoiselle Drancourt"? Emotion is usually intense at the informal level when a rule is broken, and the relationship between the persons involved is affected. Violations are interpreted personally; calling a person by his or her first name too soon could be interpreted as overly friendly and offensive.

## INTERNATIONAL BODY LANGUAGE

Words representing perhaps ten percent of the total (communication) emphasize the unidirectional aspects of communication—advocacy, law, and adversarial relationships—while behavior, the other ninety percent, stresses feedback on how people are feeling, ways of avoiding confrontation and the inherent logic that is the birthright of all people. Words are the medium of business, politicians, and our world leaders. All in the final analysis deal in power...The nonverbal, behavioral part of communication is the provenance of the common man and the core culture that guides life.

Edward T. Hall[34]

Do your actions really speak louder than your words? A study by Ting-Toomey[35] found that up to 65% (an estimate that goes up to 90%) of a message's meaning is sent through nonverbal cues. Nonverbal communication contributes to at least three reasons for cross-cultural conflict; one, the same signal has different meanings in different cultures; two, many nonverbal signals are sent in each interaction, which can make interpretation ambiguous; and three, the following factors influence nonverbal style in different cultural contexts—personality, gender, socioeconomic status, and the situation.[36] Exhibit 2.9 lists the many types of nonverbal communication.

Nonverbal signals or gestures are used in all cultures, and understanding the differences can help us become better cross-cultural communicators. An example of similar body language cues having different cultural reactions was reported by Furnham,[37] who states that, "Research in the United States has shown that tips tend to be larger if the waiter touches the diner…and if the waiter gives a big and 'authentic' initial smile." However, in the UK that same body language exhibited by a waiter may result in no tip at all. Body language is frequently culturally distinct. International body language can fall under three categories, two of which can create problems.

1. A gesture can mean something different to others than it does to you. For example, the A-OK gesture, as used in the United States, means that things are fine, great, or that something has been understood perfectly. But Brazilians interpret it as an obscene gesture, and to the Japanese it means money.
2. A gesture can mean nothing to the person observing it. Scratching one's head or drawing in breath and saying "saa" are common Japanese responses to embarrassment. One can miss these cues as these gestures may have no particular meaning in one's native culture.
3. A gesture can mean basically the same in both cultures and the meaning is accurately communicated with few possible misunderstandings.

## Hand and Arm Gestures

Most persons use their hands when speaking to punctuate the flow of conversation, refer to objects or persons, and mimic and illustrate words or ideas. Often, gestures are used in place of words. Generally,

Japanese speakers use fewer words and fewer gestures than Canadian speakers; French use more of both, and Italians much more.

In the Canada, patting a small child on the head usually conveys affection. But in Malaysia and other Islamic countries, the head, considered the source of one's intellectual and spiritual powers, is sacred and should not be touched.

Australians signal "time to drink up" by folding three fingers of the hand against the palm, leaving the thumb and little finger sticking straight up and out. In China, the same gesture means six.

To get someone's attention or to summon a waiter or waitress is often a problem. This task requires different gestures in different countries. For example, in restaurants in North American countries, one would call a waiter or waitress quietly, "sir," "miss," or "waiter," raise a finger to catch his or her attention, or tilt one's head to one side. Do not snap your fingers. In the Middle East, clapping one's hands is effective. In Japan, extend your arm slightly upward, palm down, and flutter your fingers. In Spain and Latin America, extend your hand, palm down, and rapidly open and close your fingers.

In a *Financial Times* advertisement, a major banking institution provided the following to illustrate the importance of local knowledge. One gesture in three countries has three different meanings.

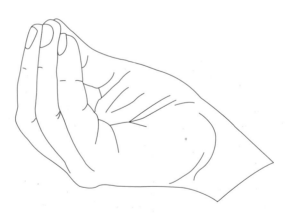

**EGYPT**

*Be patient*

**GREECE**

*That's just perfect*

**ITALY**

*What exactly do you mean?*

## Eye Contact

In many Western cultures, a person who does not maintain good eye contact is regarded as slightly suspect. Those who avoid eye contact are unconsciously considered unfriendly, insecure, untrustworthy, inattentive, and impersonal. In contrast, Japanese children are taught in school to direct their gaze at the region of their teacher's Adam's apple or tie knot, and, as adults, Japanese lower their eyes when speaking to a superior, a gesture of respect.

In Latin American cultures and some African cultures, such as Nigeria, prolonged eye contact from an individual of lower status is considered disrespectful. In the United States, it is considered rude to stare—regardless of who is looking at whom. In contrast, the polite English person is taught to pay strict attention to a speaker, to listen carefully, and to blink his or her eyes to let the speaker know he or she has been understood as well as heard. Americans signal interest and comprehension by bobbing their heads or grunting.

A widening of the eyes can also be interpreted differently. For example, take the case of an American and a Chinese discussing the terms of a proposed contract. Regardless of the language in which the transaction is carried out, the U.S. negotiator may interpret a Chinese person's widened eyes as an expression of astonishment instead of its true meaning of politely suppressed Asian anger.

# GUIDELINES FOR ENGLISH AND FOREIGN LANGUAGES

Much of the world's international business is conducted in English. When the mother languages in international business are different, generally the most commonly understood language is English. When Swedes negotiate with the Saudis in Saudi Arabia, the language most likely used is English. Following are 20 propositions for "internalizing" the use of English.[38]

1. Practice using the most common 3000 words in English; that is, those words typically learned in the first 2 years of language study. Be particularly careful to avoid uncommon or esoteric words; for example, use "witty" rather than "jocose," or "effective" rather than "efficacious."
2. Restrict your use of English words to their most common meaning. Many words have multiple meanings, and nonnative speakers are most likely to know the first or second most common meanings. For example, use "force" to mean "power" or "impetus" rather than "basic point." Other examples include using "to address" to mean "to send" (rather than "to consider") or using "impact" to mean "the force of a collision" (rather than "effect").

3. Whenever possible, select an action-specific verb (e.g., "ride the bus") rather than a general action verb (e.g., "take the bus"). Verbs to avoid include "do," "make," "get," "have," "be," and "go." For example, the verb "get" can have at least five meanings (buy, borrow, steal, rent, retrieve) in "I'll get a car and meet you in an hour."

4. In general, select a word with few alternate meanings (e.g., "accurate"—one meaning) rather than a word with many alternate meanings (e.g., "right"—27 meanings).

5. In choosing among alternative words, select a word with similar alternate meanings rather than a word with dissimilar alternate meanings. For example, "reprove" means to rebuke or to censure—both similar enough that a nonnative speaker can guess the meaning accurately. In contrast, "correct" can mean either to make conform to a standard, to scold, or to cure, leaving room for ambiguity in interpretation by a nonnative speaker.

6. Become aware of words whose primary meaning is restricted in some cultures. For example, outside of the United States, "check" most commonly means a financial instrument and is frequently spelled "cheque."

7. Become aware of alternate spellings of commonly used words and the regions in which those spellings are used: for example, colour/color, organisation/organization, centre/center.

8. Resist creating new words by changing a word's part of speech from its most common usage; for example, avoid saying "a warehouse operation" or "attachable assets."

9. Avoid all but the few most common two-word verbs, such as "to turn on/off (the lights)" or "to pick up" meaning "to grasp and lift."

10. Maximum punctuation should be used, for example, commas that help clarify the meaning, but could technically be omitted, should be retained.

11. Redundancy and unnecessary quantification should be avoided as they are confusing to the nonnative speaker trying to determine the meaning of the sentence. For example, factories cannot operate at greater than capacity—"peak capacity" is redundant.

12. Conform to basic grammar rules more strictly than is common in everyday conversation. Make sure that sentences express a complete thought, that pronouns and antecedents are used correctly, and that subordination is accurately expressed. For example, the sentence, "No security regulations shall be distributed to personnel that are out of date," needs to be rewritten as, "Do not distribute out-of-date security regulations to personnel."

13. Clarify the meaning of modal auxiliaries; for example, be sure that the reader will understand whether "should" means moral obligation, expectation, social obligation, or advice.

14. Avoid "word pictures," constructions that depend on invoking a particular mental image (e.g., "run that by me," "wade through these figures," "slice of the free world pie"). The use of absurd assumptions is a particular form of mental imagery likely to cause misunderstandings if taken literally; for example, "suppose you were me" or "suppose there were no sales."

15. Avoid terms borrowed from sports (e.g., "struck out," "field that question," "touchdown," "can't get to first base," "ballpark figure"), the military (e.g., "run it up the flag pole," "run a tight ship"), or literature (e.g., "catch-22").

16. When writing to someone you do not know well, use their last name and keep the tone formal while expressing personal interest or concern. Initial sentences can express appreciation (e.g., "We are extremely grateful to your branch…") or personal connection (e.g., "Mr. Ramos has suggested…"). Closing phrases can express personal best wishes (e.g., "With warmest regards, I remain sincerely yours…").

17. Whenever the cultural background of the reader is known, try to adapt the tone of the written material to the manner in which such information (i.e., apology, suggestion, refusal, thanks, request, directive) is usually conveyed in that culture. For example, apologies may need to be sweeping and unconditional (e.g., "My deepest apologies for any problems…"); refusals may need to be indirect (e.g., "Your proposal contains some interesting points that we need to study further…").

18. If possible, one should determine and reflect the cultural values of the reader on such dimensions as espousing controlling versus qualitative changes. When in doubt, a variety of value orientations should be included: "I want to thank you [individual] and your department [collective]…"

19. When the cultural background of the reader is known, try to capture the spoken flavor of the language in writing. For example, communications to Spanish speakers would be more descriptive, expressive, and lengthy than those to German speakers.

20. Whenever possible, either adopt the cultural reasoning style of your reader or present information in more than one format. For example, the following sentence contains both a general position statement and inductive reasoning: "Trust among business partners is essential; and our data show that our most successful joint ventures are those in which we invested initial time building a personal trusting relationship."

21. Oral presentations should be made plainly, clearly, and slowly, using visual aids whenever possible.

22. Paraphrase in intercultural conversations, encouraging your counterpart to do the same with your input.

23. Important international business communications by telephone should be confirmed by fax or written reports.

24. International meetings should be facilitated with a written summary, preferably in the language of the receiver or client.
25. Written brochures, proposals, and reports should be translated into the native language of the receiver or client.

## Foreign Language Competency

To survive and communicate, the average European speaks several languages. The typical Japanese studies English as well as other languages. This is not true of most U.S. citizens who, even when they study a foreign language, often lack fluency.

Although English is becoming a global language, bear in mind that many speak it as a second language. Also, American English is different from, though rooted in, British English, which is further modified when used in the British Commonwealth nations. Thus, in countries where "English" is the official language, human resource leaders should consider training programs for those workers whose native language is not English. Group sessions or self-learning modules can be presented by organizations under the title, "Improving Communications at Work." This instruction should also include improving pronunciation skills of nonnative employees.

The use of interpreters can further reduce misunderstanding in business and international relations. But translations are given in a cultural context, and linguistic specialists themselves require cross-cultural training. Because translation is the practice of generating one language on the basis of the information of another, the concept of equivalence, a term used to gauge the degree of reliability to the translated words, becomes highly salient.[39] As such, accurate translation is dependent upon knowledge of the intended group's culture and how their cultural values influence their perceptions. For example, Sang and Zhang[40] provide examples of translated corporate names into Mandarin Chinese that ensure sound is similar to the original, while highlighting positive Chinese values to create a basis for corporate trust:

■ Ford (福特 Fu Te, or Fortune and Uniqueness)
■ Nike (耐克 Nai Ke, or Endurance and Victory)
■ Desis (敌杀死 Di Sha Si, or Enemy, Kill, Dead- *a pesticide*)

The following announcements in English illustrate the problems in intercultural communication:[41]

Poorly translated materials can cause problems for corporations (Exhibit 2.10). For example, when Coca-Cola introduced its product into the Asian market, the Chinese characters sounded correct, but actually read, "Bite the wax tadpole." Pepsi-Cola had a comparable communication disaster when it moved into the Thai market using the American slogan, "Come alive, you're in the Pepsi generation." Only later did Pepsi discover that the Thai translation said, "Pepsi brings your ancestors back from the dead."

# THE INTERNET AND INTERCULTURAL COMMUNICATION

Both international education and business can be facilitated by competent simultaneous interpretation. New equipment for simultaneous interpreting, graphic presentations, and reporting have done much to foster international communication. The global use of the computer creates a universal language of another type. And through the wizardry of electronic technology, forthcoming inventions will translate for us. The following underscores the challenges and prospects in current communication technologies, particularly relative to the intercultural factors. Cross-cultural skills and sensitivity are just as much in demand when people meet electronically as when they meet in person.

## Some Conflicting Assumptions About Internet Communication

Hanna and De Nooy[42] researched the validity of four assumptions some have about how culture is present in cyberspace:

1. The Internet removes cultural differences.
2. The Internet is a direct access to cultural differences.
3. Communication over the Internet is similar to communication in other forms.
4. Computer-mediated communication influences cultural and genre-related communication.

Overall, they found that 1-3 were hard to validate as culture is discernible in online content and communication. "...It seems that since the ways in which a culture engages with a (new) genre depend on the way in which that genre is understood, the result is a function of an interaction between genre and culture that is not predetermined."[43] We feel that this research is worth noting because behavior is often influenced by the assumption a person subscribes to. If a person subscribes to the first three assumptions, then that person may be unaware of that those assumptions, in fact, can impede effective cross-cultural, cybercommunication.

## Communicating via Electronic Mail

Citizens of the global village increasingly use e-mail for business and personal reasons, with Internet subscriptions predicted to increase significantly every year. When e-mailing across cultures, avoid ambiguous messages, be specific, and provide background or context for the communication, so that there can be no misinterpretation. Summarize information in different words to clarify, remembering that body language and voice intonation are not present to nuance the message.

## Web Site Communications

The use of the Internet is an undeniable trend in global business with rising influence, and most corporations must learn effective strategies when using the Internet.[44] Pan and Xu's[45] study elaborated on the finding that culture shapes differences in how corporations communicate to their market. Their main finding was that culture in fact influenced corporate communications, for the U.S. corporations were more inclined to emphasize social responsibility, online marketing actions, and integrated public relations and marketing as an online communication strategy; while the Chinese corporations tended to focus on consumer-to-consumer interaction and corporation-focused information. Furthermore Kim et al.[46] determined that South Korean Web sites, as compared to U.S. Web sites, were more likely to favor high-context communication and contain polychronic time-management features. It is our opinion that if this study were replicated globally, we would find that cultures do impact Web site and cybercommunication and therefore influence cross-cultural cybercommunication.

New information technologies are like two-edged swords—they can facilitate or cause difficulties for transcultural communications.

## HANDLING TWO SWORDS AT THE SAME TIME: A GLOBAL SHIFT[47]

Is it possible to learn to shift one's style to fit different international situations? Is it possible to do what Miyamoto Musashi, a famous seventeenth century Japanese samurai, did? He developed the Nitoryu style of swordsmanship, or the act of handling two swords at the same time.

To be skillful, effective, and successful in one's own culture by being assertive, quick, and to the point is one mode of behavior. To be equally successful in another culture by being unassertive, patient, and somewhat indirect is another mode entirely—like intentionally handling two swords at the same time. Yo Miyoshi says he modifies his behavior to suit his audience: "When I discuss something with the head office in the United States, I try to be Western. But when I deal with my people in the company here, I am Oriental or Japanese."

Miyoshi is able to shift his style, or to handle two swords at the same time. He had to learn this behavior. In trying to teach "old dogs new tricks," we should focus on the teacher instead of the "dog." The following exercise is one way to focus on the teacher. The words listed below are some of the adjectives that could describe an international manager. Read the list and circle the ones that you believe apply to yourself.

Assertive, energetic, decisive, ambitious, confident, aggressive, quick, competitive, impatient, impulsive, quick-tempered, intelligent, excitable, informal, versatile, persuasive, imaginative, original, witty, colorful, calm, easy-going, good-natured, tactful, unemotional, good listener, inhibited, shy, absented-minded, cautious, methodical, timid, lazy, procrastinator, enjoy responsibility, resourceful, individualist, broad interests, limited interests, good team worker, enjoy working alone, sociable, cooperative, quiet, easily distracted, serious, idealistic, ethnocentric, cynical, conscientious, flexible, mature, dependable, honest, sincere, reliable, adaptable, curious.

Using these qualities skillfully is handling one sword—the sword that makes you successful in your business culture. The next step in the exercise is to think of the next international trip you will be taking, and consider the people you will be meeting. Now, go back to the same list of words and place a check beside those qualities that you believe these people will look for in you.

But we all carry basic personality characteristics—the sword that made us successful, our aggressiveness and competitiveness, for example. But in another culture, the second sword we are expected to carry might be characterized by qualities such as gentleness, cooperativeness, followership, indirectness, and commitment to relationships.

## CONCLUSIONS

The most basic skill that global leaders must cultivate is learning how to effectively communicate and listen cross-culturally. To facilitate our interactions with persons who do not share our values, assumptions, or learned ways of behaving requires new competencies and sensitivities so that the very cultural differences become resources. The complexities of the communication process have been reviewed here from the perspectives of cross-cultural behaviors and factors; listening, attribution, and foreign language skill levels, and variables when interacting; body language and gestures. This chapter has emphasized the possibilities and the pitfalls in intercultural communication, whether in personal or electronic encounters.

Global leaders should give a high priority to intercultural communication proficiency, as Hall and Hall observe:

> Each cultural world operates according to its own internal dynamic, its own principles, and its own laws—written and unwritten....Any culture is primarily a system for creating, sending, storing, and processing information. Communication underlies everything....Culture can be likened to an enormous, subtle, extraordinarily complex computer. It programs the actions and responses of every person, and these programs can be mastered by anyone wishing to make the system work.[48]

## MIND STRETCHING

Not only is the field of intercultural communication changing, but the relationship between culture and communication is—and probably always will be—complex and dynamic. We live in a rapidly changing world in which cross-cultural contracts will continue to increase, creating heightened potential for both conflict and communication.[49]

As you have read in this chapter, you of course understand yourself as formed in large part by your socialization in a particular culture. Therefore, we have a list of questions for you to consider. We ask that you take the time and look into the mirror to become better acquainted with your own style of communication and the societal and cultural influences that influence who you are, what you communicate about, and how you communicate your thoughts. In this manner, you will best understand how to improve yourself as a cross-cultural communicator within the global business context.

1. How does your culture tell you how to communicate and behave, and what are the messages that you feel are consistently reinforced?
2. How do you prefer to communicate? Directly? Indirectly?
3. How does your religion influence your values? Your beliefs? Your behavior? Who you associate with?
4. In your personal life, do you have many friends who are different from you? How are they different? Are they different in personality, ethnicity, culture, or are most of your friends of your own cultural background? Why?

5. How much time do you spend to understand another person's perspective? Or do you prefer to try to persuade others to change and adopt your own perspective?

*Everyone finds it easier to communicate and interact with people who have a similar personality, ethnicity, and culture.* We also prefer to be around people who share our religion, our beliefs, and our worldview. The challenge is to learn how to move beyond the inherent conflict that arises when two different people interact, and ultimately create an environment where all parties can find the common ground. The first step is to understand your own culture and communication style, and what barriers you may have toward positive cross-cultural communication interaction.

## REFERENCES

1. Adler, N. *International Dimensions of Organizational Behavior*. Fifth edition, Mason, OH: Thomson South-Western, 2008.
2. Meadows, D. H. "If the World Were a Village of 1,000 People," *Futures by Design: The Practice of Ecological Planning*, Aberley, D. (ed.). Philadelphia, PA: New Society Publishers, 1994.
3. Curtin, P. D. *Cross-Cultural Trade in World History*. United Kingdom: Cambridge University Press, 1984, p. 1.
4. Ayoko, O. B. "Communication Openness, Conflict Events and Reactions to Conflict in Culturally Diverse Workgroups," *Cross-Cultural Management*, Vol. 14, No. 2, pp. 105–124, 2007.
5. Ibid.
6. Moran, R. T. *So You're Going Abroad: Are You Prepared?* Self-published, Tenth Printing, 2003.
7. Lustig, M. W. and Koester, J. *Intercultural Competence*. New York: Addison Wesley, 1998.
8. Samovar, L. A. and Porter, R. E. *Intercultural Communication: A Reader*. Belmont, CA: Wadsworth Publishing Co., 1988.
9. Penman, R. *Reconstructing Communicating: Looking to a Future*. Mahwah, NJ: Lawrence Erlbawm Associates Publishers.
10. Duranti, A. and Goodwin, L. (eds.). *Rethinking Context: Language as an Interactive Phenomenon*. New York: Cambridge University Press, 1992.
11. Ibid.
12. Penman, R. *Reconstructing Communicating: Looking to a Future*, 2000. Mahwah, NJ: Lawrence Erlbawm Associates Publishers.
13. Duranti, A. and Goodwin, L. (eds.). *Rethinking Context: Language as an Interactive Phenomenon*. New York: Cambridge University Press, 1992.
14. Ibid., p. 31.
15. Clausen, L. "Corporate Communication Challenges: A 'Negotiated' Cultural Perspective," *International Journal of Cross-Cultural Management*, Vol. 7, No. 3, 2007, pp. 317–332.
16. Ibid.

17. Jandt, F. E. *Intercultural Communication. An Introduction*, Second edition, Thousand Oaks, CA: Sage, 1998.
18. Ibid.
19. Liddicoat, A. J. "Communication as Culturally Contexted Practice: A View from Intercultural Communication," *Australian Journal of Linguistics*, Vol. 29, No.1, 2009, pp. 115–133.
20. Ibid.
21. Ibid., p. 124.
22. Nordby, H. "Values, Cultural Identity and Communication: A Perspective From Philosophy of Language." *Journal of Intercultural Communication*, Vol. 17, No. 6–6, 2008, p. 1.
23. Ibid.
24. Clausen, L. "Corporate Communication Challenges; A 'Negotiated' Cultural Perspective," *International Journal of Cross-Cultural Management*, Vol. 7, No. 3, 2007, pp. 317–332.
25. Ibid.
26. Ibid.
27. Klopf, D. W. *Intercultural Encounters*. Englewood, CO: Morton Publishing Co., 1991.
28. Simons, G. F., Vázquez, C., and Harris, P. R. *Transcultural Leadership*. Houston, TX: Gulf Publishing Co., 1993.
29. Singer, M. R. *Perception & Identity in Intercultural Communication*. Yarmouth, ME: Intercultural Press, 1998.
30. Simons, G. F., Vázquez, C., and Harris, P. R. *Transcultural Leadership*. Houston, TX: Gulf Publishing Co., 1993. See also Elashmawi, F., and Harris, P. R. *Multicultural Management 2000*. Houston, TX: Gulf Publishing Co., 1998.
31. Triandis, H. C. (ed.). *Variations in Black and White—Perceptions of the Social Environment*. Urbana, IL: University of Illinois Press, 1976.
32. Ibid.
33. Nelson, C. A. *Protocol for Profit—A Manager's Guide to Competing Worldwide*. London: International Thomson Business Press, 1998.
34. Hall, E. T. *Dance of Life*. Garden City, NY: Anchor Press/Doubleday, 1983.
35. Ting-Toomey, S. *Communicating Across Cultures*. New York: Guildford Press, 1999.
36. Ibid.
37. Furnham, A. "Actions Speak Louder Than Words," *Financial Times*, April 4, 1999.
38. Riddle, D. I. and Lanham, Z. D. "Internationalizing Written Business English: 20 Propositions for Native English Speakers," *The Journal of Language for International Business*, 1985.
39. Sang, J. and Zhang, G. "Communication Across Languages and Cultures; A Perspective of Brand Name Translation from English to Chinese," *Journal of Asian Pacific Communication*, Vol. 18, No. 2, 2008, pp. 225–246.
40. Ibid.
41. Landers, A. "At Times Everything Gets Lost in the Translation," *Los Angeles Times*, January 28, 1996.
42. Hanna, B. and De Nooy, J. "Negotiating Cross-Cultural Difference in Electronic Discussion," *Multilingua: Journal of Cross-Cultural and Interlanguage Communication*, Vol. 23, No. 3, 2004, pp. 257–281.
43. Ibid., p. 277.

44. Pan, P. and Xu, J. "Online Strategic Communication: A Cross-Cultural Analysis of U.S. and Chinese Corporate Sites." *Public Relations Review*, Vol. 35, 2009, pp. 251–253.

45. Ibid.

46. Kim, H., Coyle, J., and Gould, S. "Collectivist and Individualist Influences on Web Site Design in South Korea and the U.S.: A Cross-Cultural Content Analysis." *Journal of Computer-Mediated Communication*, Vol. 14, 2009, pp. 581–601.

47. Moran, R. T. "Handling Two Swords at the Same Time," *Original and Modified*, 2003.

48. Hall, E. T. and Hall, M. R. *Hidden Differences—Doing Business with the Japanese*. Garden City, NY: Anchor/Doubleday, 1987.

49. Martin, J. N. and Nakayama, T. K. *Intercultural Communication in Contexts*. Boston: McGraw-Hill, 2004, p. xviii.

# NEGOTIATING LONG TERM FOR MUTUAL BENEFITS

In the game theory or economic theory, a zero-sum negotiation occurs when one participant s benefit (gain) or loss is balanced by the losses or benefits (gains) of the other participant. The result is zero. One gains 100, and the other loses 100, or vice-versa.

A non-zero sum negotiation occurs when the gains or losses of the participants in a negotiation are either less than or more than zero.

Globalization, because of the interdependence of nations and organizations, necessitates non-zero-sum activities, as the fortunes and welfare of two nations or two organizations depend to a certain extent on the fortunes and welfare of the other nations or organizations. In non-zero-sum approaches, the results for both parties are better.

"Skillful negotiators build trust and negotiate for mutual long-term benefit of all."[1]

## LEARNING OBJECTIVES

To understand the importance of "culture" when negotiating with individuals in today's global world: Dealing with conflicts, having a high degree of emotional intelligence, and being able to "profile" accurately one's negotiating counterparts are significant ingredients in negotiating success. It is also important for negotiators to develop a "partnership mindset" as each approaches a negotiation to achieve long-term mutual benefits.

The chapter is intended to be conceptual and immediately useful whether negotiating at home or abroad, and to persuade readers that skillful global negotiating is a necessary learned skill in today's business world.

There is a significant increase in business travel to and from the U.S., China, India, Russia, Brazil, and many other countries. Globalization has resulted in increased business travel to many countries in order to buy, sell, form mergers or acquisitions, build relationships, and for many other activities. Most of these business relationships will involve some form of negotiation.

Today's leaders seek business ventures in the global arena, crisscrossing the world to negotiate and bargain. Many claim the success rate of mergers and acquisitions to be less than 50% for successful integration, although little hard data is available, but state that "these mergers typically failed to achieve the targeted results."

Appreciating the complexities of labor negotiations in one's home country or negotiating a contract in a foreign country has made leaders understand the competency and skill needed to effectively work out these partnerships to mutual benefit.

In the twenty-first century, global leaders increasingly do their negotiating *electronically*, by telephone, fax, e-mail, and video conferencing. One of the most powerful communication tools for this purpose is the Internet. It offers quick and easy negotiation opportunities with manufacturers, suppliers, customers, and even government regulators. But it also requires more openness, transparency, and trust.

## TWO EXAMPLES OF "CULTURAL BAGGAGE"

### A United States Example

Graham and Herberger[2] describe a combination of characteristics typical of American negotiators. They are part of the cultural baggage such nationals bring to the negotiating table and, according to Graham and Herberger, typify the American "John Wayne" style of negotiating.

"I can go it alone." Many U.S. executives seem to believe they can handle any negotiating situation by themselves, and they are outnumbered in most negotiating situations.

"Just call me John." Americans value informality and equality in human relations. They try to make people feel comfortable by playing down status distinctions.

"Pardon my French." Americans aren't very talented at speaking foreign languages.

"Check with the home office." American negotiators get upset when, halfway through a negotiation, the other side says, "I'll have to check with the home office." The implication is that the decision-makers are not present.

"Get to the point." American negotiators prefer to come directly to the point, getting to the heart of the matter quickly.

"Lay your cards on the table." Americans expect honest information at the bargaining table.

"Don't just sit there, speak up." Americans don't deal well with silence during negotiations.

"Don't take no for an answer." Persistence is highly valued by Americans, and is part of the deeply ingrained competitive spirit that manifests itself in every aspect of American life.

"One thing at a time." Americans usually attack a complex negotiation task sequentially; that is, they separate the issues and settle them one at a time.

"A deal is a deal." When Americans make an agreement and give their word, they expect to honor the agreement no matter what the circumstances.

"I am what I am." Few Americans take pride in changing their minds, even in difficult circumstances.

These comments on American negotiators may appear to be harsh. They are not intended to isolate Americans as lacking in global negotiating skills. In today's marketplace, other nationalities can learn, as well as Americans, how to negotiate more effectively and skillfully.

## A European Example

A German Swiss buyer of goods is visiting a Chinese entrepreneur, trying to close a contract. The Chinese sits inscrutably while the Swiss expostulates his detailed proposal. The Swiss finishes his speech, a bit nervous at receiving so little feedback. Finally, the Chinese speaks: "This is not good for us." And then, "Let me take you for dinner."[3]

According to the German Swiss, the relationship may be in trouble, but the Chinese, in fact, "may be keenly interested and wants to strengthen the relationship" with a social event.

In Exhibit 3.1, Acuff[4] is not complimentary in his report card on American negotiators' skills.

### EXHIBIT 3.1
### THE U.S. NEGOTIATOR'S GLOBAL REPORT CARD

| Competency | Grade |
| --- | --- |
| Preparation | B– |
| Synergistic approach (win-win) | D |
| Cultural I.Q. | D |
| Adapting the negotiating process to the host country environment | D |
| Patience | D |
| Listening | D |
| Linguistic abilities | F |
| Using language that is simple and accessible | C |
| High aspirations | B+ |
| Personal integrity | A– |
| Building solid relationships | D |

We hope, as our horizons are widened by the global experience, that we are getting better at understanding the national character of our negotiating counterparts, confronting cultural stereotypes, and putting the negotiating process into a cultural context.

# NEGOTIATING ACROSS CULTURES

Negotiation is a process in which two or more entities come together to discuss common and conflicting interests in order to reach an agreement of mutual benefit. In international business negotiations, the negotiation process differs from culture to culture in language, cultural conditioning, negotiating styles, approaches to problem solving, and building trust, among many other factors.

## National Character

Studies of national character call attention to both the patterns of personality that negotiators tend to exhibit and the collective concerns that give a nation a distinctive outlook in international relationships. Foreign negotiators concerned with international image may be preoccupied with discussions of their national heritage, identity, and language. Cultural attitudes, such as ethnocentrism or xenophobia, may influence the tone of the argument.

Fisher maintains that foreign negotiators display many different styles of logic and reasoning. They frequently find that discussions are impeded because the two sides seem to be pursuing different paths of logic. Negotiation breakdown may result from the way issues are conceptualized, the way evidence and new information are used, or the way one point seems to lead to the next.

During the discussions, the foreign counterpart may pay more attention to some arguments than to others. Greater weight may be given to legal precedence, expert opinion, technical data, amity, or reciprocal advantage. A good international negotiator will discover what is persuasive to the foreign counterpart and use that method of persuasion.

Negotiators may place different values on agreements and hold different assumptions about the way contracts should be honored. The negotiator must find out what steps the counterpart intends to take in implementing the agreement. A signature on a piece of paper or a handshake may signify friendship rather than the closing of a contract.

## Cross-Cultural Noise

Noise consists of background distractions that have nothing to do with the substance of the foreign negotiator's message. Factors such as gestures, personal proximity, and office surroundings may unintentionally interfere with communication. The danger of misinterpretation of messages necessitates analysis of various contextual factors.

## Interpreters and Translators

Fisher points to limitations in translating certain ideas, concepts, meanings, and nuances. Subjective meaning may not come across through words alone. Gestures, tone of voice, cadence, and double entendres are all meant to transmit a message. Yet these are not included in a translation.

Sometimes a negotiator will try to communicate a concept or idea that does not exist in the counterpart's culture. For example, the American and English concept of "fair play" seems to have no exact equivalent in any other language. How, then, can an English national expect "fair play" from a foreign counterpart?

Interpreters and translators may have difficulty transmitting the logic of key arguments. This is especially true in discussions of abstract concepts such as planning and international strategy. The parties may think that they have come to an agreement when, in fact, they have entirely different intentions and understandings.

Fisher's five-part framework provides scholars and consultants with a launching pad for both theory building and practical applications. Two working papers, "Assess, Don't Assume, Part 1: Etiquette and Material Culture in Negotiation" and "Assess, Part II: Cross-Border Differences in Decision Making, Governance, and Political Economy" are also excellent in identifying the cultural variables in global negotiations.[5]

## ASSUMPTIONS AND NEGOTIATING

When people communicate, they make certain assumptions about the other's process of perceiving, judging, thinking, and reasoning patterns. These assumptions are made without realization. Correct assumptions facilitate communication, but incorrect assumptions lead to misunderstandings, and miscommunication often results.

The most common assumption is projective cognitive similarity; that is, one assumes that the other perceives, judges, thinks, and reasons the same way he or she does. Persons from the same culture, but with a different education, age, background, and experience, often have difficulty communicating. American managers experience greater difficulties communicating with managers from other cultures than with managers from their own culture. However, in some contexts, American managers share more interests with other members of the world managerial subculture than with their own workers or union leaders. The effects of our cultural conditioning are so pervasive that people whose experience has been limited to the rules of one culture can have difficulty understanding communication based on another set of rules.

To create cultural synergistic solutions to management problems and international negotiating, U.S. managers must identify and understand what is American about America, what common cultural traits are shared by Americans, and what values and assumptions form their foundation. Mark Twain stated, "The only distinguishing characteristic of the American character that I've been able to discover is a fondness for ice water." There are many more.

Awareness of cultural influences is essential for transferring concepts, technology, or ideas. Depending on the cultures, there may be an overlap of values in a specific area, and therefore the problems related to transferring ideas will be minimal. However, in some instances, the gap will be significant and cause serious problems. According to Graham,[6] there are four problems in international business negotiations: (1) language, (2) nonverbal behavior, (3) values, and (4) thinking and decision making.

The problems increase in importance and complexity because of their subtle nature. For instance, it is easy to ascertain the language differences between the French and the Brazilians. The solution is either state-of-the-art translating headsets or interpreting/translating teams to accommodate each side. The problem is obvious and relatively easy to address.

Cultural differences concerning nonverbal behavior are often not as obvious; we are not as aware of these behaviors. In face-to-face negotiations, we give and receive nonverbal behavioral cues. Some argue that these cues are the critical messages of a negotiation. The nonverbal signals from our counterparts can be so subtle that we may feel a sense of discomfort but may not know exactly why. For example, when a Japanese negotiator fails to make eye contact, it may produce a sense of unease in the foreigner, but it may simply be shyness on the part of the Japanese. Often, nonverbal intercultural friction affects business negotiations, but goes undefined and more often uncorrected.

Laver and Trudgill in Scheu-Lottgen and Hernandez-Campoy also point out that, during conversations, one must act almost as a detective, not only considering the words and speech but also attempting to establish, from an array of clues, the state of mind and the profile and perspective of the other's identity.[7]

The difference in values is even more obscure and harder to understand. For example, Americans value objectivity, competitiveness, equity, and punctuality, and often presume that other cultures hold the same values in high esteem. Regarding punctuality, Graham states, "Everyone else in the world knows no negotiation tactic is more useful with Americans. Nobody places more value on time. Nobody has less patience when things slow down."[8]

Generally, during a complex negotiation, Westerners divide the large tasks up into smaller ones. One can move through the smaller tasks, finishing one and moving on to the next, sensing accomplishment along the way. Issues are resolved at each step in the process, and the final agreement is the sum of the sequence. However, in Eastern thinking, all issues are discussed, often with no apparent order, and concessions, when made, occur at the conclusion of negotiations. The Western approach is sequential and the Eastern is holistic—the two are worlds apart. Therefore, American negotiators have difficulty measuring progress during negotiations with the Japanese, and the differences in the thinking and decision-making processes can result in blunders. For the Japanese, the long-term goal is a mutually beneficial ongoing business relationship.

## FRAMEWORK FOR INTERNATIONAL BUSINESS NEGOTIATIONS

A successful negotiation is a "win-win situation" in which both parties gain. Many factors affect a negotiation's outcome.

There are varied negotiation postures, bases from which to negotiate. One framework by Weiss and Stripp[19] maintains that there are 12 variables in every international negotiation that impact the negotiation, and can therefore significantly influence the outcome, either positively or negatively.

■ *Basic Conception of Negotiation Process.* There are two opposing approaches to the concept of negotiation: strategic and synergistic. In the strategic model, resources are perceived as limited. The sides are competitive and, as a result of bargaining, one side is perceived as getting a larger portion of the pie. In the synergistic model, resources are unlimited. Each party wants to cooperate so that all can have what they want. Counterparts look for alternative ways to obtain the desired results.

■ *Negotiator Selection Criteria.* These criteria include negotiating experience, seniority, political affiliation, gender, ethnic ties, kinship, technical knowledge, and personal attributes (e.g., affability, loyalty, and trustworthiness). Each culture has preferences and biases regarding selection.

■ *Significance of Type of Issue.* Defining the issues in negotiation is critical. Generally, substantive issues focus on control and use of resources (space, power, property). Relationship-based issues center on the ongoing nature of mutual or reciprocal interests. The negotiation should not hinder relationships and future negotiations.

■ *Concern with Protocol.* Protocol is the accepted practices of social behavior and interaction. Rules of protocol can be formal or informal. Americans are generally less formal than Germans, for example.

- *Complexity of Language*. Complexity refers to the degree of reliance on nonverbal cues to convey and interpret intentions and information in dialogue. These cues include distance (space), eye contact, gestures, and silence. There are high- and low-context communications. Cultures that are high context in communication (China) are fast and efficient communicators, and information is in the physical context or preprogrammed in the person. Low-context communication, in contrast, is information conveyed by the words, without shared meaning implied. The United States has a low-context culture.
- *Nature of Persuasive Arguments*. One way or another, negotiation involves attempts to influence the other party. Counterparts can use an emotional or logical approach.
- *Role of Individuals' Aspirations*. The emphasis negotiators place on their individual goals and need for recognition may also vary. In some cases, the position of a negotiator may reflect personal goals to a greater extent than corporate goals. In contrast, a negotiator may want to prove he or she is a hard bargainer and compromise the goals of the corporation.
- *Bases of Trust*. Every negotiator, at some point, must face the critical issue of trust. One must eventually trust one's counterparts; otherwise, resolution would be impossible. Trust can be based on the written laws of a particular country, or it can be based on friendship and mutual respect and esteem.
- *Risk-Taking Propensity*. Negotiators can be perceived as either "cautious" (low risk-takers), or "adventurous" (high risk-takers). If a negotiator selects a solution that has lower rewards but higher probability of success, he or she is not a risk-taker. If the negotiator chooses higher rewards, but a lower probability of success, then he or she is "adventurous" and a risk-taker.
- *Value of Time*. Each culture has a different way of perceiving and acting on time. Monochronic cultures emphasize making agendas and being on time for appointments, generally seeing time as a quantity to be scheduled. Polychronic cultures stress the involvement of people rather than preset schedules. The future cannot be firm, so planning takes on little consequence.
- *Decision-Making System*. Broadly understood, decision-making systems can be "authoritative" or "consensual." In authoritative decision making, an individual makes the decision without consulting with his or her superiors. However, senior executives may overturn the decision. In consensus decision making, negotiators do not have the authority to make decisions unless they consult their superiors.
- *Form of Satisfactory Agreement*. Generally, there are two broad forms of agreement. One is the written contract that covers possible contingencies. The other is the broad oral agreement that binds the negotiating parties through the quality of their relationship.

## Negotiation Insights for India, China, France, Brazil, South Korea, Germany, and Russia[9]

Can statements that are mostly accurate be made about a group of people or a "culture"? Is there a "national character" of a people, that is, a system of beliefs, attitudes, and values that are dominant in a country or nation as a result of common experiences?

In the definition of national character, there are three assumptions: (1) all people belonging to a certain culture are alike in some respects; (2) they are somewhat different from other cultures in the same respects; and (3) the characteristics ascribed to them are in some way related to the fact that they are citizens of a given country.

During negotiations, however, all anyone can observe is human behavior. We see what people do. What are the determinants of human behavior? We believe one has to consider three factors: culture (a national character); personality (no two people from the same culture are exactly alike); and context (where does the behavior take place—in New York? Sao Paulo? Tokyo? Jeddah?).

What follows is a summary of aspects of Indian, Chinese, French, and Nigerian "national character." Remember that "personality" and "context" are also determinants of behavior.

*Framework Applied to Indian Negotiators*

1. Basic Concept of the Negotiation Process
   - Building relationships and establishing rapport
   - Having conversations important
   - "Facilitation payments" often requested
   - Correct manners a requirement
2. Negotiator Selection Criteria
   - Technical experts always present
   - Status differences among team members a factor
   - Decisions made by senior management
3. Significance of Type of Issue
   - Price bargaining, reliability, credit, and local service important
   - Working rapport important
4. Concern with Protocol
   - Formality a norm
   - Friendly atmosphere
5. Complexity of Language
   - Concern with maintaining harmony
   - When Indians say "no problem," this is not to be taken literally
6. Nature of Persuasive Arguments
   - Maturity, wisdom, and self-control are valued behaviors
7. Role of Individual Aspirations
   - No attempt to "stand out"
   - Decision making at higher levels

8. Bases of Trust
   - Trust must be earned
9. Risk-Taking Propensity
   - Many are fatalists and are willing to take risks
10. Value of Time
    - Punctuality is important, but patience is often required
11. Decision-Making System
    - Highly centralized with only modest responsibility delegated to lower levels
12. Form of Satisfactory Agreement
    - Detailed agreements are the norm

*Framework Applied to Chinese Negotiators*

1. Basic Concept of the Negotiation Process
   - Intelligence gathering
   - Statements emphasizing "friendship"[20]
   - Hard bargaining
2. Negotiator Selection Criteria
   - Technical expertise
   - In times of turbulence/change political reliability
3. Significance of Type of Issue
   - Relationship-based issues receive attention
   - Connections (guanxi) important
4. Concern with Protocol
   - High concern with proper etiquette
   - Use "home court" as advantage
5. Complexity of Language
   - Very high context with implicit and unstated desires and approaches
6. Nature of Persuasive Arguments
   - "No compromising" to establish economic value
7. Role of Individual Aspirations
   - Individual aspirations are resurfacing but "standing out" is unusual
8. Bases of Trust
   - Past record is important
9. Risk-Taking Propensity
   - High avoidance of risk-taking resulting in meticulous and tough negotiating tactics and strategy
10. Value of Time
    - Long view of time, and masters at the art of stalling
11. Decision-Making System
    - Appearance of participative decision-making, but in reality is an authoritative system with higher levels always controlling
12. Form of Satisfactory Agreement
    - Carefully worded contracts, but legal infrastructure lacking

*Framework Applied to Brazilian Negotiators*

1. Basic Concept of the Negotiation Process
   - ■ Verbal facility, Harmony, and eloquence are valued
   - ■ Negotiating is often a long process
   - ■ Establishing trust is critical to success
2. Negotiator Selection Criteria
   - ■ Seniority is important
   - ■ Oratory skills, social and political connections, and academic training are significant
3. Significance of Type of Issue
   - ■ Early in the discussion, building relationships is important
4. Concern with Protocol
   - ■ Formal in social hierarchy and ceremony
   - ■ Dress is important
5. Complexity of Language
   - ■ Less direct and high context
6. Nature of Persuasive Arguments
   - ■ Inference, indirection, but with common sense
7. Role of Individual Aspirations
   - ■ Brazilians are individualistic, and outshining one's colleagues is acceptable
8. Bases of Trust
   - ■ Trust is built slowly
9. Risk-Taking Propensity
   - ■ Basically low on risk-taking
10. Value of Time
    - ■ Not hurried...a more polychromic approach to schedules
11. Decision-Making System
    - ■ Bureaucratic and hierarchical
12. Form of Satisfactory Agreement
    - ■ A handshake and words of honor are followed by details which are formalized by lawyers

*Framework Applied to South Korean Negotiators*

1. Basic Concept of the Negotiation Process
   - ■ Maintaining harmony and setting the stage for establishing the right kibun (feeling) of both sides is important
2. Negotiator Selection Criteria
   - ■ Status, knowledge, and expertise
3. Significance of Type of Issue
   - ■ Maintaining a positive business relationship is important but haggling over many aspects of the deal is typical
4. Concern with Protocol
   - ■ Basic rules of exchange must be followed

- Title, position, and formality are norms to be recognized
5. Complexity of Language
   - High context and indirect
6. Nature of Persuasive Arguments
   - Maintaining harmony
7. Role of Individual Aspirations
   - The group is more important than the individual
8. Bases of Trust
   - Established slowly on the basis of appropriate behavior
9. Risk-Taking Propensity
   - Avoid risk, and maintain face and harmony
10. Value of Time
    - Adhere to norms of punctuality
11. Decision-Making System
    - Decisions made at the highest levels
12. Form of Satisfactory Agreement
    - Written contracts with clauses to allow flexibility

*Framework Applied to German Negotiators*

1. Basic Concept of the Negotiation Process
   - Direct, explicit, analytical, and logical
2. Negotiator Selection Criteria
   - Excellent technical knowledge and strong educational background
3. Significance of Type of Issue
   - Get right down to business
   - Honest and straightforward
4. Concern with Protocol
   - Serious, controlled, and disciplined
5. Complexity of Language
   - Low context—frank and realistic
6. Nature of Persuasive Arguments
   - Careful research, orderly and persuasive presentation
7. Role of Individual Aspirations
   - Strong sense of duty and company loyalty
8. Bases of Trust
   - Convince with competence and performance, facts, and actions
9. Risk-Taking Propensity
   - Avoid risk by sticking to what is known
10. Value of Time
    - Being "on time" is always important
11. Decision-Making System
    - Top down
12. Form of Satisfactory Agreement
    - Written and binding documents

1. Basic Concept of the Negotiation Process
   - A competitive process where one side "wins"
2. Negotiator Selection Criteria
   - Professional, negotiators are selected on the basis of specialization
3. Significance of Type of Issue
   - Hard bargaining, personal relationships only play a small role
4. Concern with Protocol
   - Rules and protocol should be known and followed
5. Complexity of Language
   - Low context and direct
6. Nature of Persuasive Arguments
   - Delaying negotiations and wearing down their counterparts is often a style
7. Role of Individual Aspirations
   - Individualistic in contrast with the recent past
8. Bases of Trust
   - "Caution" is important
9. Risk-Taking Propensity
   - High risk-takers
   - Corruption endemic
10. Value of Time
    - Long and demanding
11. Decision-Making System
    - Very hierarchical
12. Form of Satisfactory Agreement
    - Contracts are cleverly written, and details are often omitted

# CONFLICT RESOLUTION AND NEGOTIATIONS[10]

By definition, all successful negotiations involve at least some resolution of conflicts. Unsuccessful negotiation involves at least one conflict, large or small, that has not been resolved.

Like leadership and power, conflict is a fascinating subject for research and discussion in organizations. Traditionally, the social scientists who have studied conflict have been keenly aware of its destructive element, which is observed in wars, strikes, family disruption, and disharmony. We will identify some themes reflecting the U.S. viewpoint with regard to conflict, and suggest ways that other cultures resolve disputes. As Rensis Likert stated many years ago, "The strategies and principles used by a society and all its institutions for dealing with disagreements reflect the basic values and philosophy in that society."[11]

What is conflict? Like the word culture, there is no single agreed-upon definition. Thomas[12] states, "Conflict is the process that begins when one party perceives that the other has frustrated, or is about to frustrate, some concern of his." This frustration may result from actions that range from intellectual disagreement to physical violence. Another definition of "conflict" holds that it results when two or more persons or things attempt to occupy the same space at the same time. The management of conflict is a major issue at the personal and organizational levels, and all negotiations involve a resolution of conflicting interests and needs.

Most U.S. negotiators view conflict as a healthy, natural, and inevitable part of relationships and negotiations. This constructive approach to conflict views the positive attributes in any conflict situation. The belief that conflict is constructive requires that problems be addressed directly, and that people can be motivated to search for solutions to these problems. Constructive disagreement may in fact be an integral part of American organizations. Stewart states, "When faced with a problem, Americans like to get to its source. This means facing the facts, meeting the problem head on, putting the cards on the table, and getting information straight from the horse's mouth. It is also desirable to face people directly, to confront them intentionally."[13]

However, conflict in organizations is perceived to have disadvantages when there are wide differences in viewpoints or perspectives and these are carried to the extreme. In this case, conflict is perceived as destructive, as the conflict creates a high level of stress for the individuals involved, which in turn affects their ability to perform. This undermines the cooperative dimension necessary in work groups, and results in time and energy being devoted to resolutions which could have been spent on organizational objectives. Such a situation also thwarts the decision-making process. Conflict resolution should be viewed as a win-win situation.

With the change in emphasis from the elimination of conflict to the management of conflict, Thomas[14] identified two models of conflict between social units. The process model appears as follows:

$$\text{Frustration} \rightarrow \text{Conceptualization} \rightarrow \text{Behavior} \rightarrow \text{Outcome} \rightarrow \text{Frustration}$$
$$\uparrow \qquad \uparrow$$
$$\text{Other's Reactions}$$

The frustration of one party leads to a conceptualization of the situation, to some behavior, to the reaction of the other party, and then to agreement or the lack of agreement. In the latter case, the conflict episode is continued with further frustration, a new conceptualization, etc. The process model is concerned with the influence of an event (e.g., the conceptualization of the problems, etc.). The structural model attempts to understand conflict by studying how underlying conditions shape events. "The structural model is concerned with identifying the pressures and constraints which bear upon the parties' behavior; for example, social pressures, personal predispositions, established negotiation procedures and rules, incentives and so on."[15] The structural model attempts to predict the effect of these conditions on the behavior of the individuals involved in conflict. Thomas maintains that the two models complement each other.

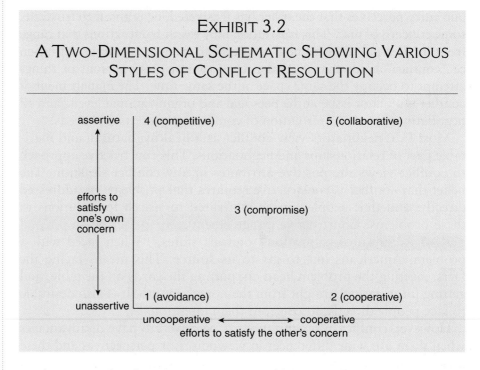

**EXHIBIT 3.2**

**A TWO-DIMENSIONAL SCHEMATIC SHOWING VARIOUS STYLES OF CONFLICT RESOLUTION**

assertive — 4 (competitive)     5 (collaborative)

efforts to satisfy one's own concern

3 (compromise)

unassertive — 1 (avoidance)     2 (cooperative)

uncooperative ⟷ cooperative

efforts to satisfy the other's concern

Thomas and Kilman suggest a two-dimensional scheme, with one dimension being the cooperative-uncooperative striving to satisfy the other's concern, and the second being the degree to which one assertively pursues one's own concerns.[16] In Exhibit 3.2, the assertive style (4) is competitive and represents a desire to satisfy one's concern at the expense of the other. The cooperative style (2) attempts to satisfy the other but not one's own concern. A compromising style (3) is a preference for moderate but incomplete satisfaction of both parties. Labor-management disputes in the United States characterize this style. A collaborative style (5) attempts to fully satisfy the concerns of both parties and is most synergistic. The avoidance style (1) is an indifference to the concerns of either party. The cooperative style as opposed to uncooperative is an Eastern mode of resolving conflict, and the assertive mode is more Western.

The effective global manager must achieve a synergistic solution, diagnosing conflict accurately and determining a strategy for managing the conflict.

## Conflict Management in the Arab World

In the Arab world, the role of the mediator is important in resolving conflict. Thus, "the greater the prestige of the mediator, and the deeper the respect he commands, the better the chances that his efforts at mediating a dispute will be successful."[17] Some highly regarded families and groups carry on ascribed status as mediators. The mediator must be impartial and beyond pressures, including monetary ones, from either side in the dispute. The mediator will often promote compromise by appealing to the wishes of other respected parties; for example, "Do it for the sake of...your father/brother." The ethical force of such an argument ("for the sake of") has three underlying assumptions, all of which remain unspoken but nonetheless understood by the disputants.

1. Each individual is obligated by ties of kinship to act in a manner that his kinsmen find gratifying.
2. The kinsmen, especially the older ones, are interested in the settlement of any conflict involving their kin group because every conflict represents a potential danger to the honor of the family.
3. By modifying one's position, the disputant can manifest generosity which, in turn, redounds to the honor of kin and bedouin values.

## Conflict Management in Japan

*To understand typical behavioral responses to conflict situations in Japan requires a basic understanding of the history and cultural environment of Japan.*[18] Accordingly, it is necessary to first ascertain the key psychological and cultural variables that affect Japanese conflict management phenomena, and then to determine how they interrelate with each other to create various deviations within a larger cultural norm. The Japanese conflict management system includes both institutionalized conflict management structures and behavioral conflict management techniques.

## Styles of Handling Conflict in Japan

Five styles of handling conflict are used in Japan: avoiding, compromising, obliging, integrating, and dominating; of these five styles, the Japanese prefer the avoiding style. In repeated examples of Japanese managers' response to the statement, "organizations would be better off if conflict could be eliminated," Japanese agree very strongly.

### Avoiding

On a behavioral level, the Japanese commonly employ a number of techniques to avoid conflict. Many of these techniques are not uncommon in cultures around the world, but they provide particular insight into Japanese conflict management.

One of their most effective techniques is sometimes referred to as triadic management. To avoid confrontation between two people, the Japanese often create a triad with another outside individual to manage the situation. Conflict between the two parties may be communicated through the third party in an indirect manner. The third party may take a more active role as an arbiter in situations where there is an apparent stalemate. In such a situation, the third party, who is respected by both of the other individuals, may provide a breakthrough by presenting her- or himself as the person on whose behalf the other two parties are to resolve the conflict. She or he urges the conflicting parties to relent so that she or he can "save face" *(kao)*, with an implicit threat that she or he will take offense if her or his intervention is not heeded. To prevent humiliation to the arbiter, both parties may comply, even though they might prefer to remain in conflict with each other. Although this triadic management technique is by no means unique to Japan, it is utilized extensively, and provides one of the greatest vehicles for conflict management within the culture. Those skilled in global negotiations often use this method in Japan.

### Compromising

A variant of triadic management, known as displacement, often can manifest itself in a variety of ways. Usually, the displacement will take place in the form of an offended individual attempting to convey his or her anger or resentment to a third party, who is in a far more favorable position to transfer the feelings of the injured party to the injuring party in a manner that is less conflicting.

### Obliging

Another technique often utilized to avoid direct confrontation is commonly referred to as conflict acceptance. Instead of rejecting or correcting an undesirable state of affairs, the individual persuades her- or himself or is advised by someone else to accept the situation. This somewhat fatalistic or deterministic approach is rooted in the strong Buddhist influence on the culture throughout the history of Japan.

### Integrating

Another, less-utilized technique employed to avoid direct confrontation may be referred to as self-aggression or self-confrontation. In this technique, one party expresses a grievance against another by exaggerated compliance.

### Dominating

This style of conflict resolution is contrary to the very nature of the Japanese character, and consequently is not used.

## *Interpreters and Translators During Negotiations*

The importance of an interpreter in business negotiations cannot be overemphasized. It is the interpreter who can assist with the accurate communication of ideas between the two teams. A linguistic interpreter can also be a cultural interpreter, letting the negotiators know of actual or potential cultural misunderstandings. It is advisable to remember the following points concerning the use of interpreters:

- Brief the interpreter in advance about the subject. Select an interpreter knowledgeable about the product or subject.
- Speak clearly and slowly.
- Avoid little-known words.
- Explain the major idea in two or three different ways, as the point may be lost if discussed only once.
- Avoid talking for more than a minute or two without giving the interpreter a chance to speak.
- While talking, allow the interpreter time to make notes about what is being said.
- Do not lose confidence if the interpreter uses a dictionary.
- Permit the interpreter to spend as much time as needed in clarifying points whose meanings are obscure.
- Do not interrupt the interpreter as he or she translates, to avoid misunderstandings.
- Avoid long sentences, double negatives, or the use of negative wordings when a positive form could be used.
- Avoid superfluous words. Your point may be lost if wrapped up in generalities.
- Try to be expressive, and use gestures to support your verbal messages.
- During meetings, write out the main points discussed. In this way, both parties can double-check their understanding.
- After meetings, confirm in writing what has been agreed.
- Do not expect an interpreter to work for over 2 h without a rest.
- Consider using two interpreters if negotiation is to last an entire day or into the evening, so that when one tires, the other can take over.
- Don't be concerned if a speaker talks for 5 min and the interpreter covers it in half a minute.
- Be understanding if the interpreter makes a mistake.
- Ask the interpreter for advice if there are problems.

## Successful Negotiation Procedures

Negotiations bring together two parties, each with an expectation of the outcome. On examination, the two parties evaluate their leverage, authority, and tactics. To close a negotiation that was the best possible deal for both sides means that, most likely, neither side feels cheated or duped and that a spirit of fairness pervaded the negotiation. When international negotiations take place, the cultural differences and implications can spin the negotiation in unanticipated directions. Weiss has established five steps for analyzing and developing a culturally responsive strategy for international negotiations.[19]

■ *Study your own culture's negotiation script.* When we are in our home culture, we behave almost automatically. Studying observations about our home culture by outsiders as well as our own self-examinations will enable a negotiator to construct an accurate national profile. What does your side bring to the party?

■ *Learn the negotiation script of your counterpart.* A first-time negotiator should build a profile of his or her counterparts from the ground up. An experienced negotiator should review and research his or her counterparts, adding new information. Beware of cultural biases. What does this party bring to the negotiations?

■ *Consider the relationship and circumstance.* Whether you are the buyer or the seller in a negotiation will affect the relationship, and an adjustment of strategy will have to occur. Any previous negotiating relationship with a counterpart, as well as his or her home culture and its familiarity with yours, will also affect the outcome. What is the context of the relationship?

■ *Predict the counterpart's approach.* If your counterpart's approach is similar to yours, or you perhaps can influence the selection of the approach, these deliberations will preview the possible interactions during preparation for the negotiation. Generally, approaches will be complementary or conflicting.

■ *Choose your strategy.* After completing the first four steps, the selection of the strategy must be feasible given the cross-cultural dimensions of the negotiations and the counterpart's approach, be appropriate to the relationship, and, with hope, be a win-win for both parties.

The following is a summary of a research project that analyzed actual negotiations.[20] The researchers' methods allowed them to differentiate between skilled negotiators and average negotiators by using behavior analysis techniques as they observed the negotiations and recorded the discussion. They identified "successful" negotiators as those who:

■ Were rated as effective by both sides.
■ Had a "track record" of significant success.
■ Had a low incidence of "implementation" failures.

A total of 48 negotiators who met all three success criteria were studied. They included union representatives (17), management representatives (12), contract negotiators (10), and others (9).

The 48 successful negotiators were studied over a total of 102 separate negotiating sessions. In the following description, the successful negotiators are called the "skilled" group. In comparison, the negotiators who either failed to meet the criteria or about whom no criterion data were available were called the "average" group.

## During the Planning Process

Negotiation training emphasizes the importance of planning.

- *Planning Time*—No significant difference was found between the total planning time of skilled and average negotiators prior to actual negotiation.
- *Exploration of Options*—The skilled negotiator considers a wider range of outcomes or options for action than does the average negotiator.
- *Common Ground*—The research showed that the skilled negotiators gave more than three times as much attention to common-ground areas as did average negotiators.
- *Long-Term or Short-Term?*—With the average negotiator, approximately one comment in 25 met the criterion of long-term consideration; namely, a comment that involved any factor extending beyond the immediate implementation of the issue under negotiation.
- *Setting Limits*—The researchers asked negotiators about their objectives, and recorded whether their replies referred to single-point objectives (e.g., "We aim to settle at 83") or to a defined range (e.g., "We hope to get 85, but we would settle for a minimum of 77"). Skilled negotiators were significantly more likely to set upper and lower limits—to plan in terms of range. Average negotiators, in contrast, were more likely to plan their objectives around a fixed point.
- *Sequence and Issue Planning*—The term "planning" frequently refers to a process of sequencing—putting a number of events, points, or potential occurrences into a time sequence. Critical path analysis and other forms of network planning are examples.

**Typical Sequence Plan Used by Average Negotiators**

A then B then C then D issues are linked.

**Typical Issue Plan Used by Skilled Negotiators**

A

D                                                                 B

C

Issues are independent and not linked by sequence.

The clear advantage of issue planning over sequence planning is flexibility.

## Face-to-Face Behavior

Skilled negotiators show marked differences in their face-to-face behavior, compared with average negotiators. They use certain types of behavior significantly more frequently, while they tend to avoid other types.

- *Irritators*—Certain words and phrases that are commonly used during negotiation have negligible value in persuading the other party, but do cause irritation. Probably the most frequent example of these is the term "generous offer" used by a negotiator to describe his or her proposal.
- *Counterproposals*—During negotiation, one party frequently puts forward a proposal, and the other party immediately responds with a counterproposal. Researchers found that skilled negotiators made immediate counterproposals much less frequently than average negotiators.
- *Argument Dilution*—This way of thinking predisposes us to believe that there is some special merit in quantity. Having five reasons for doing something is considered more persuasive than having only one reason. One may feel that the more he or she can put on his or her scale, the more likely it is to tip the balance of an argument in his or her favor. The researchers found that the opposite was true. The skilled negotiator used fewer reasons to back up each of his or her arguments.
- *Reviewing the Negotiation*—The researchers asked negotiators how likely they were to spend time reviewing the negotiation afterward. Over two-thirds of the skilled negotiators claimed that they always set aside some time after a negotiation to review it and consider what they had learned. Just under half of average negotiators, in contrast, made the same claim.

This research clearly indicates some of the behaviors of skilled negotiators. Negotiators need to practice these behaviors, and others, to increase their skills.

Wederspahn suggests that human resource development programs within global corporations should include an International Negotiations Workshop with a cultural overview of the counterpart party in negotiations.[21] The model is based on the high low-context approach to culture discussed elsewhere in our book. *Position-based negotiation* is based on the win-lose paradigm—the more one party receives, the more the other has to give up in the pursuit of self-interest and maximizing advantage. The main focus is on position—advancing, defending, and rationalizing it. Concessions made should be compensated by corresponding gains. Objective and impersonal data should be used to justify one's demands and trade-offs. Tactics include overstating demands, multiple fall-back positions, pressure and dramatic displays, hidden agendas, bluffing, and keeping one's opponents off balance. In contrast, *interest-based negotiation* assumes that a mutually advantageous agreement is possible and desirable; expectations are for collaboration that is win-win and that brings benefits to both parties. This approach looks to long-term payoff in the relationship, so that there is mutual openness and information sharing to better understand each other's needs, constraints, and aspirations. Trust building includes visits to each other's facilities, establishing explicit and objective standards of fairness, designing systems to share gain/risk, giving and receiving help from one another, as well as socializing and creating a common strategy and culture.

Surprises are avoided, pressure is not used, and agreements/contracts are flexible and adaptable to changing circumstances.

## THE PRICE OF FAILED NEGOTIATIONS

War is a conflict in the extreme, and often results when diplomacy and negotiations have failed. Recent research has suggested that serious conflict, such as war or occupation, can produce years of traumatic experiences, especially for many who have engaged in the extreme conflict. David Berceli, a trauma therapist and expert on Arab/American relations, has written on this (Exhibit 3.3).

### Emotional Intelligence and Negotiations

Everyone knows the meaning of IQ (Intelligence Quotient) and the importance of technical skills and intelligence to perform many job responsibilities. Some in an organization are referred to as "techies." Many also have personal experience with individuals who are very intelligent and have good technical skills but have failed in a leadership position.

Coleman[22] researched about 200 global companies, and found that the traditional attributes associated with leadership—intelligence,

---

EXHIBIT 3.3

WAR FORGES A NEW ERA IN CORPORATE
ARAB/AMERICAN RELATIONSHIPS

---

In the United States, "Roughly 3.6 days of work impairment per month associated with Post Traumatic Stress Disorder (PTSD)[a] translates into an annual productivity loss in excess of $3 billion."[b] These figures and subsequent loss in productivity increase dramatically in countries throughout the world that have been ravaged by war, political violence, or sectarian armed conflict. As a result of recent events in the Middle East, international corporations operating there need to seriously consider the staggering toll that emotional pain and suffering will have on the functional and productive capacity of their employees.

"There is no avoiding the traumatic aftermath of war; it reaches into every segment of society."[c] Work impairment due to secondary comorbid disorders of PTSD such as anxiety, depression, irritability, disturbed sleep, and elevated mood disorders all damage the cognitive and interpersonal skills of employees. This has a staggering impact on the social structure and eventually the economy of any corporation or society. As a result of this reality, whether they

continued

want to or not, corporations operating in war-torn countries of the Middle East will be forced to implement programs and procedures to deal with the systemic consequences of the trauma their employees have experienced....

As the average duration of each trauma episode is reported to be more than 7 years, "the typical person with PTSD has a duration of active symptoms for more than two decades. The process of healing, therefore, will have to be measured in terms of generations rather than years."[d] Beginning with the rebuilding of Iraq, corporate social responsibility and financial profitability should be seen as inseparable ideologies because of the severe and systemic trauma experienced by the Iraqi people. With some simple but strategic trauma behavior modifications, over time corporations will be able to break down antagonism and build alliances across opposing sides. They will be able to use the trauma of their employees as a common opportunity for gain. If they know what they are doing, they can use these opportunities to "reduce contentious behaviors and increase conciliation."[e]

[a]Post Traumatic Stress Disorder is the reexperiencing of disrupting emotions or behaviors following the initial trauma.
[b]This report is from the Department of Health Care Policy, Kessler. R. Harvard Medical School, Boston, MA. It can be found in the *Journal of Clinical Psychiatry*, 2000, Vol. 61 (Suppl. 5), pp. 4-12.
[c]Levine, P. We Are All Neighbors. Foundation for Human Enrichment, 2002, p. 3.
[d]This report is from the Department of Health Care Policy, R. Kessler. Harvard Medical School, Boston, MA. It can be found in the *Journal of Clinical Psychiatry*, 2000, Vol. 61 (suppl. 5), pp. 4-12.
[e]Baldwin, D. "Innovation, Controversy and Consensus in Traumatology," *The International Electronic Journal of Innovations in the Study of the Traumatization Process and Methods for Reducing or Eliminating Related Human Suffering*, Vol. 3, No. 1, Article 3.

vision, toughness, etc.—are insufficient. He states that effective leaders must have a higher degree of emotional intelligence as well. According to Coleman, there are five components of emotional intelligence:

1. Self-awareness or the ability to recognize and understand one's moods and emotions, as well as their effect on others. This is characterized by self-confidence and a realistic assessment.
2. Self-regulation or the ability to control or redirect disruptive impulses and moods and the propensity to suspend judgment. This is characterized by trustworthiness, integrity, and a comfort with ambiguity.
3. Motivation or the ability to work for reasons that go beyond money or status. This is characterized by a strong drive to achieve, and optimism even in the face of failure.

4. Empathy or the ability to understand the emotional makeup of other people. This is characterized by expertise in building and retaining talent.
5. Social skills or proficiency in managing relationships and building networks. This is characterized by skills in leading change and expertise in building and leading teams.

## CONCLUSIONS

Roger Fisher,[23] the negotiating guru, in an interview about emotions and negotiations, stated, "I don't have people criticizing me for talking about emotions...no one says it's a soft, fuzzy side." In short, keeping your feelings hidden, saying, "don't become emotional" during a heated argument, may become obsolete.

This perspective is supported by Fromm,[24] who wrote, "Emotions provide important information to us and to the other side. If we are able to express our emotions in a constructive way and at an appropriate time in the negotiation, rather than destroying or hurting the negotiation process, it can greatly enhance it."

Emotional intelligence contributes to a skillful negotiator's toolbox. The instruments and questionnaire to measure one's emotional intelligence or emotional competence are easily available and recommended to all global negotiators.

### MIND STRETCHING

1. As a negotiator, list your strengths and your weaknesses. Write an action plan to become a more skillful negotiator.
2. Become an astute observer of human behavior. As you observe the behavior of others in different situations, what are the determinants? Culture? Personality? Context?
3. How can you increase your styles of resolving conflicts when negotiating across cultures?
4. Apply the concepts in the chapter to any global dispute. Why are there as many unresolved issues?
5. Do our global business and political leaders have a high degree of observable emotional intelligence?

## REFERENCES

1. Moran, R. *Stated in a Session to Executives on Negotiation Across Cultures*, February 2010.
2. Graham, J. and Herberger, R. "Negotiating Abroad—Don't Shoot from the Hip," *Harvard Business Review*, July-August 1983.

3. Dierdorff, D. (eds.). *The Sage Handbook of Intercultural Competence*. PO 250. Sage Publications, 2009.

4. Acuff, F. L. *How to Negotiate with Anyone, Anywhere Around the World*. New York: Amacom, 1993.

5. "Assess, Don't Assume, Part 1: Etiquette and Material Culture in Negotiation" and "Assess, Part II: Cross-Border Differences in Decision Making, Governance, and Political Economy" are also excellent in identifying the cultural variables in global negotiating. HBR Working Paper 10–048 and Working Paper 10–050, 2009.

6. Graham, J. "*Vis-à-Vis*: International Business Negotiations," *International Business Negotiations*, Ghauri, P. and Usunier, J. C. (eds.). Oxford, UK: Pergamon, 1996.

7. Scheu-Lottgen, U. D. and Hernandez-Campoy, J. M. "An Analysis of Sociocultural Miscommunication: English, Spanish and German," *International Journal of Intercultural Relations*, Vol. 22, No. 4, November 1998.

8. Graham, J. "*Vis-à-Vis*: International Business Negotiations," *International Business Negotiations* Ghauri, P., and Usunier, J. C. (eds.). Oxford, UK: Pergamon, 1996.

9. Based on interviews conducted in 2010.

10. Moran, R. T. and Harris, P. R. *Managing Cultural Synergy*. Houston, TX: Gulf Publishing Company, 1982. Material updated in 2006.

11. Likert, R. and Likert, J. G. *New Ways of Managing Conflict*. New York: McGraw-Hill, 1976.

12. Thomas, K. W. *Conflict and Conflict Management*. Los Angeles: University of California. Working Paper, 74–3, 1974.

13. Stewart, E. C. *American Cultural Patterns: A Cross-Cultural Perspective*. LaGrange Park, IL: Intercultural Network, 1979.

14. Thomas, *Conflict and Conflict Management*.

15. Ibid.

16. Kilmann, R. H. and Thomas, K. W. *A Forced-Choice Measure of Conflict-Handling Behavior: The "Mode" Instrument*. Los Angeles Graduate School of Management, Working Paper, 1973, pp. 12–73.

17. Patai, R. *The Arab Mind*. New York: Charles Scribner & Sons, 1976.

18. Moran, R. T., Allen, J., Wichmann, R., Ando, T., and Sasano, M. "Japan," *Global Perspectives on Organizational Conflict*. Rahim, A. and Blum, A. (eds.). London: Praeger, 1994. Material updated in 2006.

19. Weiss, S. E. "Negotiating with 'Romans'—Part 2," *Sloan Management Review*, Massachusetts Institute of Technology, Spring 1994.

20. *Behavior of Successful Negotiators*. Huthwaite Research Group Report, 1976, 1982.

21. Wederspahn, G. M. "The Fine Art of International Negotiation," *HR News/ Society for Human Resource Management*, January 1993, pp. C6, 7.

22. Coleman, D. "Inside the Mind of the Leader," *Harvard Business Review*, January 2006.

23. www.news.harvard.edu/gazette/2005/10.13/03-reason.html.

24. Fromm, D. "Dealing with Your Emotions in Negotiations," *The Negotiation Magazine*, November 2005.

# GLOBAL LEADERS LEARNING FROM OTHERS AND CHANGE

> Global leaders must first and foremost be learners.
> —A fundamental theme in *Managing Cultural Differences*

Albert Einstein is recognized as genius. In Walter Isaacson's book, *Einstein: His Life and Universe*,[1] many aspects of Einstein's personal and professional life are documented with support from letters and Einstein's files and writing. One aspect of his professional life that is perhaps surprising to some readers is that throughout his life he displayed a "curiosity" for everything, and he asked colleagues and friends their opinions when he was "puzzled."

We believe that all persons and organizations can learn from others, and can adapt certain other systems to fit their own. The following example is based on Robert Moran's experiences in Japan a number of years ago.

I'd like to tell you how I first learned about an aspect of Japanese management techniques. Between 1965 and 1968, I was the playing coach of the Seibu Ice Hockey Team, the best team in Japan. The owner of the team and the president of the company, Yoshiaki Tsutsumi (at that time identified by *Fortune* magazine as one of the world's 10 wealthiest people), decided to devote some of his time to developing ice hockey in Japan in preparation for the 1972 Winter Olympics, which had just been awarded to the city of Sapporo in northern Japan.

In October 1968, shortly before leaving with a group of 25 Japanese hockey players for a 1-month, 17-game series against Canadian amateur and semiprofessional hockey teams throughout Canada, I was asked to attend a meeting with Mr. Tsutsumi. I was told the purpose of the meeting was to decide on the wardrobe for the players during their tour of Canada, which was to take place in January (Canada's coldest month).

There were six persons at the meeting, including the owner/president, his secretary, three other staff persons, and myself. After exchanging pleasantries, we began the serious business of selecting what would go into each player's luggage bag. Department managers from the Seibu Department Store were waiting in an adjoining room with samples of the various possibilities. The meeting lasted over 4 h. First, we decided on the outerwear—coats, hats, gloves, and overshoes—then the formal and informal suits and sweaters, and finally the *underwear*. Yes, we even decided on the kind and number of undershorts that each player would be allocated. The person making these decisions was the president himself, Mr. Tsutsumi. Of course, many hundreds of hours were spent planning other aspects of the tour.

Of the 17 games played in Canada, the Japanese team won 11, and, from both Canadian and Japanese perspectives, the tour was a total success. On several occasions, during the pregame discussion and between-period pep talks, the fact that the company president was concerned about them to the extent of assisting with the selection of their wardrobe was mentioned. He also telephoned before and after each game and spoke to several of the players a number of times. In my opinion, this was an example of Japanese management in its purest form.

What is the moral of this story? Is it that the owners of amateur and professional hockey teams (and perhaps baseball, football, and other teams as well) should select the underwear for their players? No, it isn't. But having worked and conducted communication and team-building workshops for a professional hockey team in the National Hockey League, I certainly believe that a little more care on the part of the owners in understanding the world of the players in getting to know them might have done wonders for their morale and have had a positive impact on their ability to win hockey games.

More recently in China, Robert Moran was in Shanghai and asked the U.S. National Managing Director of a very large organization headquartered in the United States this question: "You have been in China now almost 3 years working with Chinese at all levels in your organization. Could you tell me a few things you have learned from the Chinese that might make your organization a little better?" He paused and then said, "To be honest, I can't think of anything." Americans, British, and people from other countries have now been in Iraq and Afghanistan for a number of years. What has been learned that we might benefit from?

During this same trip to Asia, I met my daughter and two of her friends in Bangkok. All three had just completed 2 years as Peace Corps volunteers on the Gilbert Islands in the Pacific Ocean. One of my business school colleagues asked them, "Well, what did you learn from the locals when you were in Kirabah?" Without an instant hesitation, one person responded, "They taught me how to survive."

Over the years, the authors of this book have had the opportunity and privilege of working with or interviewing executives from many small and large global organizations. We also have interviewed a few politicians. Most did not appear to have a high degree of curiosity or inquisitiveness or interest in learning from executives in other countries.

# LEARNING OBJECTIVES

"Cultural imperialism" in the United States, in Europe, and in other developed countries is strong. History, however, has shown that it is never sustainable in the long term. This chapter presents the idea that global leaders—leaders of enterprises and governments, all leaders— can learn from others. "No one person has truth by the tail"—"nobody is right all the time"—"no nation is fully developed in all aspects." These are themes developed in this chapter.

## Nature and Nurture for Leaders

Does anyone believe that the mind is a "blank slate," which is a translation from two Latin words: "tabula rasa" which literally means "scraped table"? Most agree that all behavior is a result of the interaction between nature (the genes we receive from our parents) and nurture (the environment). However, everything is not genetic nor the environment.

Why do many leaders seem not to believe that they can also be learners? And learn from other cultures and management practices in our global world? The answer is not clear.

Many leaders, perhaps because they have become leaders, are not great learners, even though it is well known that curiosity and learning from others provide a sure way of increasing global savvy. "For curiosity to thrive, the first action is suspending assumptions and judgments, leaving our minds open to multiple perspectives," according to Janet M. Bennett.[2]

# LEARNING FROM OTHERS

Most studies in the management literature are comparative in nature. A book compares, for example, managerial processes and interdepartmental relations in the United States and Germany, or an article compares the career paths of Japanese and American managers. These kinds of cross-cultural studies are useful. However, because our world is becoming more pluralistic and interdependent, it is vital, though difficult, to study *interactions* between managers from more than one country.

Peter F. Drucker, perhaps the most significant management thinker of the twentieth century, died at the age of 95 in 2005. In 1954, he wrote *The Practice of Management*, which helped managers focus on the customer and what value means to organizations. Many of his ideas are universal and are timeless. The questions he asked and discussed in his books helped leaders shift their focus of reference and the categories they considered important. Dr. Drucker stated he wanted to learn from every student he met, and subsequently he became a great teacher.

Much of the management literature and textbooks (there are more MBA programs in the United States than in most, if not all, countries combined) are produced in the United States, along with much of the organizational and management behavior research. However, researchers in the United States should not assume that U.S. management techniques are necessarily the best, even for American managers or for managers of other countries. American management techniques are based on American values and assumptions (for example, that we can influence and control the future to a high degree). Managers from other countries do not necessarily have such values and assumptions—at least they may not place as much emphasis or importance on them.

It is generally accepted by managers that improved individual as well as organizational performance is the purpose of most organizational changes. In attempting to implement such change, one strategy that has not been sufficiently employed in the United States with any degree of consistency is that of studying other nations' management systems and asking what we can learn from them. Many managers feel that there's no need to do this. After all, they ask, "Hasn't the United States developed the most highly sophisticated system of management in the world? Don't the managers of the best foreign companies come to U.S. business schools for MBA degrees and executive management courses?" Yes, it may be true that many foreign managers come to the United States for training, but Americans can still learn from and borrow aspects of foreign management systems. Exhibit 4.1 identifies many U.S. values which are shared with people from a number of countries with possible alternatives which are shared by many other countries. Examples of how the cultural values might influence management practices are suggested in the third column.

The above exhibit is not only to compare cultural values affecting management practices in culture X with those in culture Y, but also to provide a basis whereby a manager might "synergistically" relate to managers trained in another cultural system and management practices developed in other cultures.

A word of caution from Hamel and Prahalad,[3] who suggest a pitfall in taking aspects of another culture, such as from Japan, and trying to integrate them into one's business philosophy. They cite a survey in which 80% of U.S. managers polled believed that "quality would be a fundamental source of competitive advantage." However, 82% of the Japanese believed "the ability to create fundamentally new products and businesses will be the primary source of competitive advantage."

Today, many countries, especially in Europe and Canada, have their own world-class programs in management education. Some of their MBA degree programs have unique features and adaptations worthy of emulation, particularly in cross-cultural management and organizational behavior.

EXHIBIT 4.1

## U.S. VALUES AND POSSIBLE ALTERNATIVES

| Aspects[a] of U.S. Culture | Alternative Aspect | Examples of Management Function Affected |
| --- | --- | --- |
| The individual can influence the future (where there is a will there is a way). | Life follows a preordained course, and human action is determined by the will of God. | Planning and scheduling |
| The individual can change and improve the environment. | People are intended to adjust to the physical environment rather than to alter it. | Organizational environment, morale, and productivity |
| An individual should be realistic in his aspirations. | Ideals are to be pursued regardless of what is "reasonable." | Goal setting and career development |
| We must work hard to accomplish our objectives (Puritan ethic). | Hard work is not the only prerequisite for success. Wisdom, luck, and time are also required. | Motivation and reward system |
| Commitments should be honored (people will do what they say they will do). | A commitment may be superseded by a conflicting request or an agreement may only signify intention and have little or no relationship to the capacity of performance. | Negotiating and bargaining |
| One should effectively use one's time (time is money, which can be saved or wasted). | Schedules are important but only in relation to other priorities. | Long- and short-range planning |
| A primary obligation of an employee is to the organization. | The individual employee has a primary obligation to family and friends. | Loyalty, commitment, and motivation |
| The employer or employee can terminate their relationship. | Employment is for a lifetime. | Motivation and commitment to the company |
| A person can only work for one company at a time (one cannot serve two masters). | Personal contributions to individuals who represent an enterprise are acceptable. | Ethical issues, conflicts of interest |

continued

EXHIBIT 4.1

# U.S. VALUES AND POSSIBLE ALTERNATIVES (CONTINUED)

| Aspects[a] of U.S. Culture | Alternative Aspect | Examples of Management Function Affected |
|---|---|---|
| The best qualified persons should be given the positions available. | Family considerations, friendship, and other considerations should determine employment practices. | Employment, promotions, recruiting, selection, and reward |
| A person can be removed if he or she does not perform well. | The removal of a person from a position involves a great loss of prestige and will rarely be done. | Promotion |
| All levels of management are open to qualified individuals (a clerk can rise to become company president). | Education or family ties are the primary vehicles for mobility. | Employment practices and promotion |
| Intuitive aspects of decision making should be reduced, and efforts should be devoted to gathering relevant information. | Decisions are expressions of wisdom by the person in authority, and any questioning would imply a lack of confidence in his or her judgment. | Decision-making process |
| Data should be accurate. | Accurate data are not as highly valued. | Record keeping |
| Company information should be available to anyone who needs it within the organization. | Withholding information to gain or maintain power is acceptable. | Organization, communication, managerial style |
| Each person is expected to have an opinion and to express it freely, even if his or her views do not agree with his or her colleagues. | Deference is to be given to persons in power or authority, and to offer judgment that is not in support of the ideas of one's superiors is unthinkable. | Communications, organizational relations |
| A decision maker is expected to consult persons who can contribute useful information to the area being considered. | Decisions may be made by those in authority, and others need not be consulted. | Decision making, leadership |

# EXHIBIT 4.1
## U.S. VALUES AND POSSIBLE ALTERNATIVES (CONTINUED)

| Aspects[a] of U.S. Culture | Alternative Aspect | Examples of Management Function Affected |
|---|---|---|
| Employees will work hard to improve their position in the company. | Personal ambition is frowned upon. | Selection and promotion |
| Competition stimulates high performance. | Competition leads to imbalances and to disharmony. | Career development and marketing |
| A person is expected to do whatever is necessary to get the job done (one must be willing to get one's hands dirty). | Various kinds of work are accorded low or high status, and some work may be below one's "dignity" or place in the organization. | Assignment of tasks, performance, and organizational effectiveness |
| Change is considered an improvement and a dynamic reality. | Tradition is revered, and the power of the ruling group is founded on the continuation of a stable structure. | Planning, morale, and organizational development |
| What works is important. | Symbols and the process are more important than the end point. | Communication, planning, quality control |
| Persons and systems are evaluated. | Persons are evaluated but in such a way that individuals will not be embarrassed or caused to "lose face." | Rewards and promotion, performance evaluation, and accountability |

[a]Aspect here refers to a belief, value, attitude, or assumption that is a part of culture in that it is shared by a large number of persons in any culture.

## Japanese and American Management

Studying managers solely through comparisons is not enough. One must also consider what happens when differences come together—namely, *interactions*. Aspects of North American or European managerial systems are not necessarily appropriate for managers of other geographic areas, and may not even be the best for their own managers. Furthermore, management is a dynamic process and is constantly changing. We can learn from the "way it was" by contrasting it with practices current at the end of the century. For example, the following research was conducted over

25 years ago, but shows how American and Japanese management styles have influenced each other and caused changes. Recent economic problems in Japan have forced many companies in that country to abandon some traditional customs, like "lifetime employment."

## The Type Z Hybrid

Ouchi and Jaeger[4] identify characteristics of typical American organizations (Type A):

1. Short-term employment
2. Individual decision making
3. Individual responsibility
4. Rapid evaluation and promotion
5. Explicit, formalized control
6. Specialized career path
7. Segmented concern

and characteristics of typical Japanese (Type J) organizations:

1. Lifetime employment
2. Consensual decision making
3. Collective responsibility
4. Slow evaluation and promotion
5. Implicit, formal control
6. Nonspecialized career path
7. Holistic concern

They then compare these organizations and relate them to their sociocultural roots. They conclude by presenting a hybrid organizational form (Type Z), which they suggest may be useful in the United States. Each of the two types of organizational structures (American and Japanese) represents a natural outflow and adaptation to the environments to which they belong.

Ouchi and Jaeger suggest the following characteristics for Type Z organization (modified American):

■ Long-term employment
■ Consensual decision making
■ Individual responsibility
■ Slow evaluation and promotion
■ Implicit, informal control with explicit formalized measures
■ Moderately specialized career path
■ Holistic concern for individuals

One of the most dramatic cases for East-West synergy lies in the interdependent relationship between Japan and the United States. This relationship has been tested many times, but overall it has been mutually beneficial.

Japan's previous success in production, distribution, and marketing has been due to the ability of the Japanese to learn from Western nations and then apply this knowledge to their own business situations. Nowhere is this more evident than in the field of management, where Japanese executives borrowed ideas from the United States and then refined them for increased productivity.

Many American companies have made significant changes in manufacturing techniques, including Kanban manufacturing, quality control circles, and just-in-time (JIT) purchasing, that are part of mainstream American/Japanese industrial production. Boosting the morale, knowledge, responsibility, and therefore productivity of a corporation's workforce by using these techniques can only be accomplished if employees realize that they have a growing role in the firm's processes, problems, and profits.

## Total Quality Management (TQM)

Who originated the quality initiatives that are a fundamental part of most, if not all, organizations? Japan? Germany? United States? A review of the history of quality initiatives shows that the beginnings were in the United States, but the quality concept was taken to Europe and Japan following World War II by Edward Deming and others. Subsequently, after Japan's great reconstruction success, it was reintroduced to the United States. "Total quality management" became a buzzword. Goldman outlines the history of quality initiatives and the present-day quality initiatives used worldwide.[5]

- ■ Customer involvement—customers' requirements are integrated into the product services.
- ■ Company cultural change—everyone's responsibility—labor and management to instill a quality orientation in any organization.
- ■ Continuous improvement and statistical measurement—measuring changes resulting from a quality process that can always be improved.
- ■ Employee empowerment—the mentality of the employee changes, and the quality becomes the most important objective.
- ■ Teamwork—working together on mutual goals.
- ■ Benchmarking—comparing your organization to the best of your competition.
- ■ Cycle time reduction—reducing the time to deliver a product from the beginning to customer satisfaction.

Six Sigma and "learn" adopt the above including ISO (International Standards Organization) which results as a business practice used in many organizations for financial improvement.

We invite our readers to analyze the following material[6] and complete the exercise with colleagues from other cultures in light of the chapter messages:

Trivial Pursuit™ is a board game that has sold millions of copies throughout the world. The game requires players to answer questions in a number of categories such as geography, entertainment, history, art and literature, science, and nature and sports. The category of the question is determined by a roll of the dice.

I would like to invite you, the reader, to play this game. You have rolled the dice and drawn the category "Global Management." This is your question: "Which countries produce the most skillful global leaders?"

If the question were in Trivial Pursuit M, it would be in the genius edition—a very difficult question. Two words in the question contribute to the difficulty—skillful and leader. A standard dictionary provides this definition of skillful: "well qualified, capable, fit." "Leader" is a little more murky. The dictionary definition is "someone who acts as a guide." One person I asked suggested Japan.

Japan indeed has a successful track record of best-selling products, including cars, electronic equipment, and steel, among others. This is largely accomplished through Japanese businessmen who work for the nine giant Japanese trading companies—the *sogo shosha*. But the Japanese cheat in trade, he said. They have been found guilty of commercial piracy, bribery, and falsifying documents. They also distort the international value of the yen, my friend said, so that some Japanese goods sell for less in other countries than in Tokyo. Moreover, they have exploited the open-door policy of some countries while vigorously pursuing a closed-door policy for themselves.

## A Vote for the United States

Another businessman who was listening to this conversation said he thought that the United States produced the most competent internationalists in business. The United States is the biggest economic entity in the history of the world, with dominant positions worldwide in computers, space, medicine, biology, and so on. Its competent internationalists in business make this possible.

This was overheard by a French manager, who said that Americans are naïve internationally. American businessmen, according to him, are the most ethnocentric of all businessmen (the dictionary definition is "one who judges others by using one's own personal or cultural standards").

Besides, he said, American businessmen have their priorities mixed up. They are too materialistic, too work oriented, too time motivated, and equate anything "new" with the best. Americans also have the highest attrition rate (dictionary definition: "return early from an international assignment") of any country, said the French manager.

The question is indeed a tough one. At a recent meeting of American managers attending a seminar on international joint ventures, I posed the same question. It evoked considerable discussion but no agreement. One person suggested they vote, and most hands were raised when Sweden was proposed. But Sweden, said one person who voted for another country, couldn't be the winning answer. Sweden is too small and the Swedish economy has declined sharply since the late 1970s because Swedish internationalists aren't aggressive enough. At this point, another participant suggested the right answer was the Soviet Union. Most people laughed at this suggestion. I assume that implied some disagreement.

Britain has had foreign operations for centuries. May be the British manager is the most competent internationalist. But when business travelers from several countries discussed this possibility while caught in Geneva International Airport recently during a snowstorm, no one thought Britain was the winning answer because Britain has lost so much in the international marketplace. Several businessmen from Britain were among those who participated in the discussion.

Since no agreement could be reached on the correct answer to my first question, I decided to rephrase it: What contribution to a multinational organization is made by managers of various nationalities?

## Different Contributions

Hari Bedi, an Indian expatriate working for a large multinational company in Hong Kong, believes that Asian internationals use the five C's of *continuity* (a sense of history and tradition), *commitment* (to the growth of the organization), *connections* (where social skills and social standing count), *compassion* (balancing science and political issues), and *cultural sensitivity* (a respect for other ways).

These qualities are among the contributions made by Asian managers to a multinational organization, he says. Western managers, according to Bedi, use the five E's: *expertise* (experience in managerial and technical theory), *ethos* (practical experience), *eagerness* (the enthusiasm of the entrepreneur), *esprit de corps* (a common identity), and *endorsement* (seeks unusual opportunities).

The answer is that managers of every country contribute something to a multinational organization. The usefulness of that contribution depends on the situation. Skilled global leaders are able to recognize the contribution made by managers of various nationalities. They are also able to develop solutions to problems faced by global organizations by using these contributions and cultural diversity as a resource, rather than a barrier to be overcome. They are first and foremost learners.

# STRATEGIC COLLABORATIONS AND MERGERS

"Companies are just beginning to learn what nations have always known: in a complex, uncertain world filled with dangerous opponents, it is best not to go it alone."[7] Mergers and acquisitions result. Some thrive, some survive, and some die. Some are perceived as an act of desperation, and others are more strategic. The following points are relevant:

- Internal growth possibilities are diminished for many organizations, and mergers or acquisitions are strategies to survive or grow.
- Increasing products, markets, and technology lowers risk.
- Organizational culture clash is a major problem in integrating different companies.
- Making the deal is easy; making it work is difficult.
- Ashkenas et al.[8] outline the following lessons learned by GE Capital.
- Acquisition integration begins with the due diligence studies of all aspects of the organization.
- Integrating management is a full-time business function like marketing.
- Decisions on structure, roles, and other important aspects of integration should be announced soon after the merger or acquisition is reported.
- Integration involves not only technologies and products, but cultures also.

These lessons are relevant when the integrated organizations are from the same national culture. When they are from different national cultures, the challenges are more significant, and the skills required to make them succeed are broader, deeper, and more sophisticated.

Global leaders are required to meet, socialize, and negotiate with foreign business persons and government officials. The manager must be able to communicate and work with persons who have been socialized in a different cultural environment. Customs, values, lifestyles, beliefs, management practices, and other aspects of their personal and professional life are therefore different. For the global leader to be effective, one must be aware of the many beliefs and values that underlie his or her country's business practices, management techniques, and strategies. Awareness of such values and assumptions is critical for managers who wish to transfer technology to another culture or who wish to collaborate with those who hold different values and assumptions.

The observations in this section take on added significance when computer networking and the Internet are used to form strategic alliances and partnerships. The *connectivity* of the Internet enables us to create *information partnerships* with personnel, customers, suppliers, contractors, and consultants. The key in such electronic endeavors is to treat them as *collaborators* rather than competitors.

## Performance Appraisals

This is a "hot topic" among many human resource professionals. The lingering question underlying most performance appraisal systems is, are these categories of performance measurement universal and of equal importance? Also, do they really measure this individual's contribution to the organization in any meaningful way?

Edwards et al.[9] ask whether employment practices in subsidiaries can be transferred to practices in the country of origin. The descriptions for Saudi Arabia and Japan might provide suggestions for United States and European organizations regarding performance appraisals.

Exhibit 4.2 illustrates the cultural variations in performance appraisals between Japanese, Americans, and Saudi Arabians.

### EXHIBIT 4.2
### CULTURAL VARIATIONS: PERFORMANCE APPRAISALS

| Dimensions— General | United States— Low Context | Saudi Arabia— High Context | Japan— High Context |
| --- | --- | --- | --- |
| Objective of P.A. | Fairness Employee development | Placement | Direction of company/ employee development |
| Who does appraisal | Supervisor | Manager—may be several layers up—appraiser has to know employee well | Mentor and supervisor Appraiser has to know employee well |
| Authority of appraiser | Presumed in supervisory role or position | Reputation important (Prestige is determined by nationality, age, gender, family, tribe, title, education) | Respect accorded by employee to supervisor to appraiser |
| | Supervisor takes slight lead | Authority of appraiser important—don't | Done equally |
| How often | Yearly or periodically | Yearly | Developmental appraisal monthly Evaluation appraisal—after first 12 years |
| Assumptions | Objective appraiser is fair | Subjective appraiser more important than objective Connections are important | Objective and subjective important Japanese can be trained in anything |

continued

*good to know*

EXHIBIT 4.2

| Dimensions— General | United States— Low Context | Saudi Arabia— High Context | Japan— High Context |
|---|---|---|---|
| Manner of communication and feedback | Criticism direct Criticisms may be in writing Objective/ authentic | Criticisms subtle Older more likely to be direct Criticisms not given in writing | Criticisms subtle Criticisms given verbally Observe formalities |
| Rebuttals | U.S. will rebut appraisal | Saudi Arabians will retreat | Japanese will rarely rebut |
| Praise/motivators | Given individually Money and position strong motivators Career development | Given individually Loyalty to supervisor strong motivator | Given to entire group Internal excellence strong motivator |

*Source*: Adapted from report of the Association of Cross-Cultural Trainers in Industry, now Pacific Area Communicators of International Affairs, 16331 Underhill Lane, Huntington Beach, CA 92647.

# LEADERSHIP IN A KNOWLEDGE CULTURE

Global leaders are engaged in a continuing change process, primarily through strategic planning and management. As the introduction of any change threatens both the existing culture and power structure, strategic response to change needs to be both decisive and planned.

Our cultural conditioning affects our attitudes toward the phenomenon of change, as well as our concept of leadership. The *Random House Dictionary* definition may provide a base for understanding—a *leader* is one who guides, directs, and conducts, while *leadership* is the position or function or ability to influence or lead others. Just as there is some cultural difference between American and European understanding of both leaders and leadership, so is there even greater diversity about these terms between Western and Eastern cultures. R. D. Lewis reminds us that whereas with the former, leadership is supposedly on the basis of "meritocratic" achievement, the latter accepts that leadership resides with strong persons at the top of a hierarchy. The Asian cultural view is influenced by Confucianism that seeks a stable society through hierarchy of five unequal relationships, extending from ruler and father to older brother, husband, and senior friend. Lewis underscores the cultural contrasts that affect the exercise of leadership in terms of values, communication styles, and organizational patterns. Exhibit 4.3 summarizes differences between the West and Asia.

# EXHIBIT 4.3

## VALUES, COMMUNICATION STYLES, AND ORGANIZATIONAL PATTERNS

| WESTERN CULTURAL VIEWS | ASIAN CULTURAL VIEWS |
|---|---|
| **Values** | |
| Democracy | Hierarchy |
| Equality | Inequality |
| Self-determination | Fatalism |
| Individualism | Collectivism |
| Human Rights | Acceptance of Status |
| Equality for Women | Male Dominance |
| Social Mobility | Established Social Class |
| Status through Achievement | Status through Birth or Wealth |
| Facts and Figures | Relationships |
| Social Justice | Power Structures |
| New Solutions | Good Precedents |
| Vigor | Wisdom |
| Linear Time | Cyclic Time |
| Results Orientation | Harmony Orientation |
| **Communication Styles** | |
| Direct | Indirect |
| Blunt | Diplomatic |
| Polite | Very Courteous |
| Talkative | Reserved |
| Extrovert | Introvert |
| Persuasive | Recommending |
| Medium-Strong Eye Contact | Weak Eye Contact |
| Linear-Active | Reactive |
| Unambiguous | Ambiguous |
| Decisive | Cautious |
| Problem Solving | Accepting of the Situation |
| Interrupts | Does Not Interrupt |
| Half Listens | Listens Carefully |
| Quick to Deal | Courtship Dance |
| Concentrates on Power | Concentrates on Agreed Agenda |
| **Organizational Patterns** | |
| Individual as a Unit | Company and Society as a Unit |
| Promotion by Achievement | Promotion by Age or Seniority |
| Horizontal or Matrix Structures | Vertical Structures |
| Profit Orientation | Market Share Priority |
| Contracts as Binding | Contracts as Renegotiable |
| Decisions by Competent Individuals | Decisions by Consensus |
| Specialization | Job Rotation |
| Professional Mobility | Fixed Loyalty |

*Source:* Lewis, R. D. Cultural Orientations Affecting Leadership Styles. *The Cultural Imperative.* Boston, MA: Nicholas Brealy/Intercultural Press, 2003.

This exhibit contains generalizations based on Lewis's research and experiences in more than a dozen countries. Obviously, within both Western and Eastern cultures, there will be many exceptions. Within Asia, there are national differences to be observed. Furthermore, the listings under Asian culture may be found somewhat applicable in the Near and Middle Eastern countries. However, these insights do underscore why there would be differences in leadership perception between the two cultural groupings. For example, in the more traditional Asian cultures, change might be more feared and resisted, while occurring more limitedly and slowly, unless revolutions determine otherwise. In the twenty-first century, China is rapidly changing. But these contrasts also provide clues for improving behavior and performance when living or working in the opposite cultural environment. By seeking to understand the other cultural position, a Westerner in Asia might focus on relationship and harmony building, as well as observing, when feasible, local precedents and customs. In this way, one learns to appreciate the other's life space and the limitations of one's own cultural conditioning.

> How do you turn transition into an advantage? By looking at every change, looking out every window. And asking: could this be an opportunity? Is this new thing a genuine change, or simply a fad? And the difference is very simple: a change is something people do, and a fad is something people talk about....
>
> Peter F. Drucker[10]

The twenty-first century is dominated by accelerating change, driven by continuing and rapid scientific and technological innovations. Those who would be global leaders need not only to plan and cope with change, but also to increase their management skills for this transition to a knowledge economy and industries. Perhaps the greatest challenge is for people to be more flexible in their mindsets, and willing to build continuing change into their lifestyles.

## AN OPPORTUNITY FOR CHANGE

### THE CATHOLIC CHURCH AND CHANGE IN THE TWENTY-FIRST CENTURY

The Catholic Church in many countries is facing outrage because of their leaders' responses to crimes of pedophilia. This sexual abuse scandal, some say, is the most complex that the church has experienced since the beginning.

However, the present Pope, Benedict XVI, seems to go from crisis to crisis, as a very old institution struggles with change and modernity.

## Human Factors in Change

We have a set of highly organized constructs around which we organize our "private" worlds. Literally, we construct a mental system for putting order, as we perceive it, into these life spaces. This intellectual synthesis relates to our images of self, family, role, organization, nation, and universe. Such constructs then become psychological anchors or reference points for our mental functioning and well-being. Our unique construct systems exert a pushing/pulling effect on all other ideas and experiences we encounter. We assign meaning almost automatically to the multiple sensations and perceptions that bombard us daily.

Not only do individuals have such unique filters for their experiencing, but groups, organizations, and even nations develop these mental frameworks through which information coming from the environment is interpreted. Intense interactions of various segments within our varied groupings form sets that enable us to achieve collective goals. In this way, a group, organizational, or national "style" or type of behavior emerges. Through their communication, people share themselves, so that individual perceptions converge into a type of "consensus" of what makes sense to them in a particular environment and circumstance. *Culture then transmits these commonly shared sets of perceptions and relationships.*

But because human interaction is dynamic, pressures for change in such constructs build up in both individuals and institutions. For example, when a manager from Grand Rapids, Michigan, is transferred for 3 years to Riyadh, Saudi Arabia, or Bangalore, India, that person is challenged to change many of his or her constructs about life and people. The same may be said for the corporate culture when a company attempts to transplant operations from Paris, France, to the Middle East or Asia. These forces for change can be avoided, resisted, or incorporated into the person's perceptual field. If the latter happens, then change becomes a catalyst for restructuring our constructs, giving us an opportunity for growth. In other words, individuals and institutions can adapt and develop.

When leaders do not prepare their people for necessary and inevitable change, the consequences can be disastrous. For example, many national, educational, political, and religious systems suffer from "culture lag." That is, as the human mainstream has moved ahead to a new stage of development, this particular community is locked into a past mindset. In the twenty-first century, many countries are burdened with obsolete and archaic religious, political, educational, and economic systems. In Asia, for instance, inadequate banking and lending practices hold back prosperity for their citizens. In the Middle East, ultratraditional religious views and practices diminish the role of women, deterring development of female potential and positive contributions. In Europe, centuries-old educational systems are badly in need of reform and updating. In Africa, the tribal ruling system has broken down, and the instability has led to a series of military coups and local despots, along with social chaos and ethnic killings. In North America, open door policies to foreigners and visitors are being undermined by fears of terrorism, forcing modernization of immigration and travel regulations, as well as security practices.

When a society or a system is imprisoned by its traditions, attitudes, and beliefs from the past, it may produce unsavory results. Terrorists or anarchists, for example, often come from countries where the needs of people, especially the young, are so frustrated that violence erupts. The sense of despair or righteousness may turn naïve youth into suicide bombers who destroy property and take human life. The subculture of global terrorism recruits young men and even women who are alienated and conditioned to an ideology of violence. At the same time, many perceive themselves as oppressed, and so they resort to rioting, fire bombings of property, and even the taking of innocent lives—witness the Black Power movement of the 1960s in the inner-city ghettos of America; the Irish Catholic minority and the IRA fighting of Northern Ireland; and the immigrant revolts that recently occurred in both Great Britain and France—which provides further insights into negative results when societies resist change and do not satisfy human needs.

In today's *changing culture*, people are also challenged to alter the way they perceive or think about their work and how it is to be performed. The shifting context of the work environment has been described as the new work culture.[12] The driving forces behind these social and technological changes are given below:

- Globalization of markets, consumerism, and workforces.
- Transformation of traditional organizational hierarchy into a more participative, multinational, or global network.
- Fragmentation of work and creation of a global job market.
- Ascendancy of knowledge and information services as primary global products.

One outcome of such trends is the reshaping of views of our various roles in the family, community, or workplace.

## Role Changes

For five decades, researchers have studied the changing roles of men and women, discovering that gender differences are mostly in our minds and cultures, rather than in biological realities.

Limitations in *gender roles* are largely created and kept in place by social, not biological, forces. As such, they are more readily subject to change. Scholars have demonstrated the resulting harm for persons and organizations when individuals are typecast and culture-bound in their career aspirations. Further, social progress is deterred when such attitudes prevail, as we have seen historically in the caste system of India and the class system of England. Fortunately, within modern societies changes in this regard are rapid, as workers move beyond traditional role concepts while assertively seeking equal opportunity and empowerment.

Similar representations may be made of *organization roles* and their place in society. Because human systems are collections of people, institutions may also suffer identity crises. Caught between a disappearing bureaucracy and an emerging "adhocracy," the institution may experience downturns in sales; poor morale and declining productivity; membership reductions; bankruptcy threats; obsolete product lines and services; and increasing frustration with unresponsive management. Organizations, then, are challenged to go through planned renewal to project new images of their positive roles among both personnel and the public. Simply hiring a public relations firm to redesign corporate image with the public is insufficient—organization members have to be involved in the process of institutional change!

So, too, with *national roles*. When a country's social fabric unravels or wavers, national identities may experience crises. Examples abound, such as the following:

- The United States' "loss of face" in Vietnam; the seizure of U.S. diplomats in Iran; the 9/11 double bombings of New York City's World Trade Center and the Pentagon; and the treatment of prisoners or insurgents in the "war on terrorism."
- Great Britain lost its empire and colonies, nearly bankrupting the nation, or the country's inappropriate policies and responses to the influx of immigrants from British Commonwealth nations.
- Japan's economic and technological progress threatens its traditional culture; and its youth reject "feudal" customs and practices.
- The Catholic Church and the pedophilia crisis.
- Continuing challenges in Iraq and Afghanistan.
- The global economic crisis.

People of various countries have sought to rediscover their collective selves in this postnation period. So geographers continuously redraw maps to reflect the changes in national borders. In some lands, the struggle for national identity is epitomized in a name change, as from Congo to Zaire or Rhodesia to Zimbabwe. Elsewhere, as in the former USSR, especially the Baltic Republics of Lithuania, Latvia, and Estonia, the countries became independent, with citizens seeking greater ethnic identity and autonomy. Whereas in the People's Republic of China, turmoil centers around information access, private enterprise, and democratization versus totalitarian control by the Communist Party. Often, the identity struggles within or among nations produce violence based on ancient rivalries or on tribal, clan, or even religious affiliation. Such regressive behavior not only transgresses the UN Declaration on Human Rights, but also acts to reverse changes toward a modern, multicultural society.

## Environmental Forces Influencing Change

Global leaders with foresight gather information about the real environment, local and worldwide, that may cause changes in strategies, polices, and technologies. They analyze and anticipate trends that influence their futures. Some positive forces of change drive us to increase or decrease workforce, to be more aware or responsive to community needs. In other words, global leaders create *adaptive systems*! This implies overcoming resistive and negative forces seeking to restrain necessary shifts in production and manufacturing, as well as making necessary alterations in roles, rules, regulations, and even markets.

As a case in point, many corporations, nongovernmental organizations (NGOs), and other institutions go global to survive. Over a decade ago, Moran and Riesenberger described 12 environmental forces impacting organizations and influencing change that are still evident today.[13] Some *proactive environmental* forces are as follows:

1. *Global sourcing*—organizations are seeking nondomestic sources of raw materials because of cost and quality.
2. *New and evolving markets are* providing unique growth opportunities.
3. *Economies of scale*—today's marketplace requires different approaches, resulting in competitive advantages in price and quality.
4. *Movement toward homogeneous demand*—globalization is resulting in similar products being required worldwide.
5. *Lowered transportation costs*—world transportation costs of many products have fallen significantly because of innovations.
6. *Government tariffs and taxes*—the protectionist tendencies of many governments are declining, as evidenced by the North American Free Trade Agreement (NAFTA) and the European Union (EU) policies and agreements.[14]
7. *Telecommunications*—falling prices as a result of privatization and new technologies are impacting globalization.

8. *Homogeneous technical standards*—the International Organization for Standardization (ISO) has been successful in developing global standards (known as ISO 9000).

Some *reactive forces* present in the global environment are as follows:

1. *Competition for nondomestic organizations*—new competitive threats are regularly experienced by organizations.
2. *Risk for volatile exchange rates*—the constant fluctuation of exchange rates in many countries impacts profits.
3. *Customers are becoming more global consumers*—globalization is impacting customers in ways that increase "local content" in subsidiary-produced goods.
4. *Global technological change*—technological improvements coming from many areas of the world require organizations to adjust their strategies to survive.

In a knowledge culture, smart global leaders do environmental scans. That is, they employ future research methods or consultants to help them to anticipate the future. They try to identify trends that will affect their businesses or organizations in the near- or long-term future. For example, they anticipate developing movements—such as the growth of environmental and ecological awareness and coalitions; the rise of activists organized to protect human or animal rights; and the development of space resources.

## Transforming Business Culture

Breakthroughs in paradigms, inventions, and technologies trigger rapid change in our professional lives and practices. Leading-edge thinkers maintain that the computer and the Internet are among the most transforming inventions in human history. Seemingly, they have the capacity to change everything—the way we work, the way we learn and play, and perhaps the way we sleep and cohabit. Andrew Grove, a founder and former chairman of Intel, predicted what has come to pass—that all corporations would become Internet companies. The global power of the Internet with its Web sites and chat rooms now dominates our lives, whether commercially or otherwise. Grove uses the term *Internet time* when referring to change, citing his own experience as a chipmaker when the Pentium processor was in full-scale production.[15] As CNN reported the story worldwide, a minor design error resulted in "a rounding error in division once every nine billion times." After this global report, the new Pentium users immediately requested replacement chips. Intel's response was to quickly set up a "war room" to instantly answer a flood of inquiries on the subject. Gradually, they replaced chips with this minor defect by the hundreds of thousands. This crisis not only shows the planetary power of satellite communications, but the kind of global leadership necessary to *manage such change*!

Writing about global electronic connecting, Symonds[16] observed, "The Internet is turning business upside down and inside out. It is fundamentally changing the way companies operate, whether in high tech or metal bashing. This goes far beyond buying and selling over the Internet, and deep into the processes and culture of an enterprise." Some of the sociotechnical changes that Symonds underscores are as follows:

■ Connecting through the Internet with buyers and sellers as well as trading partners.

■ Using the Internet to lower costs dramatically across integrated supply and demand chains.

■ Developing e-business (electronic) at hypergrowth rates by intercompany trade over the Internet.

■ Using Web sites to enrich the multimedia experience by integrating customer/suppliers, databases, monitoring sites visited, supporting online transactions, integrating personal/telephone call center operations, and supporting multiple payment operations.

■ Establishing organizational *intranets* to improve departmental and personnel exchanges, manage travel and expenses, and employee benefits, and share the latest information.

This whole process of instant, electronic communication is also transforming organizational cultures and business strategies. It fosters synergistic relations by the practice of connecting and collaborating. It encourages the formation of *information partnerships* between suppliers and customers, as well as between systems. It facilitates customized services, outsourcing for both personnel and manufacturing, and inventory control, as well as innovation with new products and services. The emerging e-speak technology connects us with electronic experts from mediators and brokers to physicians and consultants. Through networking, the software permit industry, service organizations, and nonprofit institutions become part of a worldwide, dynamic ecosystem.

## Utilizing Change Strategies

Global leaders should not only be sources of innovation, but also be skilled in using change strategies and methods. Agents of change may apply their efforts to alter personal, organizational, and national cultural goals. Operating globally in diverse cultures and circumstances necessitates appropriate adaptation of organizational objectives, management procedures, corporate processes, and technologies. Global leaders must learn to be as knowledgeable as possible wherever they are located, even if it means creative circumvention of local constraints. Innovators may respect the established system while working to bend or beat it to make it more responsive to satisfying human need.

The *New York Times* once ran this interesting advertisement:

WANTED—CHANGE AGENTS—Results-oriented individuals able to accurately and quickly resolve complex tangible and intangible problems. Energy and ambition necessary for success!

What, then, would be the responsibilities of such persons if employed? Obviously, to bring about planned change in an organization or culture. That would imply examining the prospects for alterations in the status quo within these basic categories: *structure* (the system of authority, communication, roles, and work flow)...*technology* (problem-solving mechanisms, tools, and computers)...*tasks* (activities accomplished, such as manufacturing, research, service)...*processes* (techniques, simulations, methods, scenario-building procedures, such as management information systems)...*environment* (internal or external atmosphere)...*people* (personnel or human resources involved).

Having decided on which category or combinations will be the focus of one's energy for change, the leader might follow these additional steps: (a) identify specific changes that appear desirable to improve effectiveness; (b) create a readiness in the system for such change; (c) facilitate the internalization of the innovation; and (d) reinforce the new equilibrium established through the change. This process is to be utilized in *force field analysis*—a systematic way to analyze the driving and resisting forces for change within individual or group life space as well as institutional or national space. The skilled change maker is also aware that any change introduced in one element of the previous chain affects the other factors. The parts of complex systems are interdependent, so the innovator attempts to forecast the ripple effect. Successful change agents take a multidimensional approach, considering legal, economic, and technological aspects of the change without ignoring its social, political, and personal implications. They also operate on certain assumptions:

■ People are capable of planning and controlling their own destinies within their own life space.
■ Behavioral change, knowledge, and technology should be incorporated into the planning process.
■ Human beings are continually in the midst of cultural change or evolution.

The implication of the latter statement is that the people involved in the change process may be suspicious of simplistic solutions as a result of the information/media blitz to which they have been exposed. They may already be suffering from information overload, experiencing a sense of powerlessness and loss of individuality. Essentially, the effective change maker may employ three change models to bring about a shift in the status quo:

- *Power*—political or legal, physical or psychological influence or coercion to bring about change, which may be legitimate or illegitimate. It depends on the purpose of change, its ingredients, and the method of application. For example, legislative power may be used to promote equal employment opportunity or to prevent a disease epidemic, while authority of role or competence may be called upon to overcome resistance to change.
- *Rationale*—the appeal to reason and the common good. This approach must recognize that people are not always altruistic and that self-interest may block acceptance of the proposed change, no matter how noble or worthwhile for the majority.
- *Reeducative*—conditioning by training, education, and positive rewards becomes the means to not only create readiness for the change, but to also provide the information and skills to implement it.

Each approach has its strengths and weaknesses, so a combination of the models may be most effective. Bellingham proposes examination of business drivers on strategy, structure, system, and personnel requirements in terms of new skills, styles, and the need for renewal.[17] To maximize commitment to change, 10 competencies are developed among personnel.

1. Mobilize people behind a shared vision, strategy, and structure—especially by involvement.
2. Empower people by defining job directions/boundaries, as well as by providing autonomy and support.
3. Recognize individual and team contributions by clarifying requirements, expectations, motivators, and rewards.
4. Build capacity by developing people, especially by attending to health needs (physical, emotional, intellectual, and spiritual).
5. Create a learning organization by using a systems approach that seeks input, knowledge, and partnerships.
6. Realign the culture through review of stated values and operating principles, as well as by translating norms and expected behaviors.
7. Create a cultural revolution by diagnosis, training, and targets.
8. Promote understanding by describing events and identifying feeling.
9. Facilitate acceptance by moving ahead on commitment and putting the past behind.
10. Enable the change to happen, moving to the new, demonstrating the benefits, and providing transitional steps for implementation.

There are a variety of methods and techniques to facilitate planned change. An approach can be as simple as "imagineering" at a staff meeting about changes likely to become realities in a decade, on the basis of present trend indicators. Or it may be using the more elaborate

Delphi technique, in which a questionnaire is developed with about a dozen situations likely to occur in the future of a company or a culture. Members or experts may then be asked to rate on a percentage basis the probability of the event's happening. Results are then tabulated and median percentages for each item determined. A report of results is circulated among participants, and they are asked to again rate the alternative possibilities after studying peer responses.

Today, the words "reengineering" or "reinventing" the organization are used to describe planned system-wide change. One consultant maintains that reengineering is not about downsizing, reorganizing, or restructuring. It is about thinking outside of the box, rethinking your work and company. It is a fundamental and radical redesigning of all the processes of business to obtain improvements in critical measures of performance (cost, quality, capital, service, and speed). It is throwing away what is and replacing it. For instance, if IBM, Merck, Boeing, etc., did not already exist today, how would they be created and structured?

## Organizational Culture Changes

Responding to change in today's organizations is difficult. At times, corporations that do not change or transform themselves effectively open the door to merger or acquisition by another company. In the worst scenario, such companies and associations go bankrupt. The annual *Fortune 500* list is filled with examples of firms that no longer exist because of inability to keep up with changing markets, technologies, or personnel needs.

According to Beatty and Ulrich,[18] four principles can serve as the framework if change and renewal are to be understood and implemented in mature organizations. Although stated over 20 years ago, their guidelines are still applicable to all human systems.

*Organizations renew by focusing on the customer's perspective and demands.* To sustain a competitive advantage, organizations must be devoted to customer or client needs in unique ways. When a mindset is embedded in employees that affects their work habits, they can be encouraged to focus more on the perspectives of those they seek to serve, despite political boundaries and internal company policies. For such a change, Hewlett Packard asked their teams to pretend they were the buyers of a particular product. As customers, they were to shop their four major competitors and evaluate why they chose one supplier over another, what the image of the supplier/competitor was, and the reasons for their choice. After going through this analysis from a purchaser's perspective, teams were better able to understand the perceived mindsets of their competitors, which gave them insight into their own customers' needs.

*Organizations renew by increasing their capacity for change.* Like humankind, systems have internal clocks that determine how swiftly change will move from definition to action. Today, organizations want to reduce the cycle time for how and when decisions are made and activities completed, so that they can move more quickly from idea conception to production, thereby increasing their capacity for adaptation and flexibility. "Alignment, symbiosis, and reflexiveness" can be helpful in this process. Alignment refers to the common goals of the company. When organizations have a sense of alignment, they can move toward shared goals in a shorter time frame because less time is spent building commitment and more time can be spent on work. Symbiosis is the speed with which organizations can remove barriers inside and outside the company to effect change. The Ford Taurus is a good example. To reduce boundaries and speed up internal clocks, Ford chose a cross-functional team removing boundaries between departments to design and deliver the car. Consequently, the Taurus moved from conception to production in 50% less time than established internal clocks. Reflexiveness is the time to reflect and learn from past activities, ensuring a sense of continuity.

*Organizations renew by adjusting both the hardware and software within their company.* These researchers refer to the hardware as issues of strategy, structure, and systems. These domains of activity are malleable and measurable and can be heralded with high visibility; for example, timely announcement of new alterations in any or all of these three issues. Unless the hardware is connected to the appropriate software, however, computers are useless. The same is true of the less-visible domains of the organization—the software, which includes employee behavior and mindset. Change begins by altering hardware, but often not enough resources are spent in making sure that employee behavior, mindset, and work activities match the change.

*Organizations need empowered employees to act as leaders at all levels.* Employees are to be trusted and empowered to act on issues that affect their work performance. Leaders have the obligation of articulating a vision and of ensuring that the vision will be implemented. Leaders must be credible, effective communicators, articulating changes so that they are readily understood and accepted.

For organization renewal to succeed, leaders at all levels must be both inspirational and able to express the new vision/strategy mindset, encouraging their followers to give the extra effort needed to make the vision a reality. Change agents are more apt to alter the status quo within organizations or institutions when they endeavor to take the following steps:[19]

■ include in the planning process everyone concerned about the change
■ avoid discrepancies between words and actions relative to the change
■ set realistic time frames for bringing about the change
■ integrate the activities involved in the change with available budget and resources

- avoid overdependence on external or internal specialists
- avoid data gaps between the top, middle, and lower levels of the system
- avoid forcing innovations into old structures incapable of handling them
- avoid simplistic, cookbook solutions to the problems connected with change
- realize that effective human relations are a condition for change, not an end
- apply change intervention strategies appropriately
- identify personnel capable of diagnosing the need for change
- capitalize on the pressures, both from within and without the system, for the change
- search the system at all levels for the leadership to effect the change
- promote collaborative efforts between line and staff in planning and implementing changes
- take strategic risks to inaugurate necessary change, while maintaining a realistic, long-term perspective relative to the change
- initiate systems to reward people who cooperate in carrying out the change and establishing more effective behaviors
- collect data to support and evaluate the change
- set measurable objectives and targets relative to the change that are both tangible and immediate.

Introducing change in multicultural organizations is more difficult than in domestic organizations. The change agent then needs to consider the cultural underpinnings resisting the change and make appropriate interventions. Technological, economic, market, and social forces, such as mass immigrations, drive changes in the workplace. Pritchett & Associates, a Dallas-based consultancy in organizational change, specializes in downsizing, turnarounds, and mergers during the "Age of Instability." In an employee handbook on the subject, Pritchett and Pound write that myths about change influence mindsets, and must be dispelled.[20] They advise workers that the reality is as follows: *change is dynamic and here to stay; controlling emotions helps workers to control the fluid situation; progress often masquerades as trouble; company changes require that workers also change; problems are a natural side effect of implementing change.*

Management usually tries to be as straightforward as the situation permits, while making tough decisions about the alterations. Workers can be part of the problem or the solution. Both managers and workers must act as a team to make the change plan succeed. In the shift toward an emerging global economy and work culture, Pritchett advises that *new work habits* are essential. In another handbook, he provides these ground rules for worker success in our changing world:

- Become a quick-change artist—be flexible and adaptable.
- Commit fully to your job—it makes work satisfying and ensures success.

- Speed up—accelerate with the organization.
- Accept ambiguity and uncertainty—change is the only certainty.
- Behave like you are in business for yourself—assume personal responsibility.
- Stay in school—lifelong learning is essential.
- Hold yourself accountable for outcomes—set goals and targets.
- Add value—contribute more than you cost.
- See yourself as a service center—customers are a source of job security.
- Manage your own morale—be responsible for your attitude control.
- Continuously strive for performance improvement.
- Be a fixer, not a finger-pointer—assume ownership of problems.
- Alter your expectations—rely on yourself to develop work skills for success in the information age!

## CONCLUSIONS

In this chapter, we have presented the idea that all global leaders must be, first and foremost, learners. Hopefully, readers will be increasingly convinced of the importance of learning from others in a global business world.

Culture is a dynamic concept that changes, as does the way we communicate it. Those with the mindset and skills of a global manager exercise proactive leadership in altering both the macro- and microlevels of culture. To cope effectively with today's accelerating change, effective leaders continuously revise their images of self, role, and organization, and assist their personnel to do the same. Thus, attitudes and behavior are modified to become more relevant.

Although our outlooks on change and leadership are culturally conditioned, we must realize that we must be open to change. We best meet human needs by creating new technologies, markets, processes, products, and services.

Successful leadership styles are dependent to a degree on the people and their cultures at a given point in time. Generally, the contemporary work environment calls for more participative, team-oriented management that responds rapidly and synergistically to changing situations. In the emerging knowledge culture, leadership opportunities are shared with competent knowledge workers, regardless of gender, race, religion, or nationality. The aim is to empower people, so that they will, in turn, develop their own as well as the organization's potential. To meet that challenge, the underlying assumption of this chapter is that global leaders should be planned change makers, beginning with one's self.

## MIND STRETCHING

1. Is the "westernization of the world" happening as a function of globalization?
2. Have we lost our "curiosity" about other people and nations? Curiosity has been demonstrated to be an important trait of skillful global leaders.
3. Do less-developed countries always desire industrialization?
4. If you could be a person from another culture, what culture would it be? Why?

# REFERENCES

1. Isaacson, W. *Einstein: His Life and Universe*. New York: Simon and Schuster Paperbacks, 2007.
2. Bennett, J. M. "Cultivating Intercultural Competence," *The Sage Handbook of Intercultural Competence*, Deardorff, D. (ed.). Thousand Oaks, CA: Sage Publications, 2009.
3. Hamel, G. and Prahalad, C. K. *Competing for the Future*, Boston, MA: Harvard Business School Press, 1994.
4. Ouchi, W. G. and Jaeger, A. M. "Made in America under Japanese Management," *Harvard Business Review*, Vol. 52, No. 5, 1974, pp. 61–69. See also Chen, M. *Asian Management Systems*. London: Routledge, 1995; and Funakawa, A. *Transcultural Management*. San Francisco: Jossey-Bass, 1997.
5. Goldman, H. H. "The Origins and Development of Quality Initiatives in American Business," *The TQM Magazine*, Vol. 17, No. 3, 2005, pp. 217–225.
6. Moran, R. T. "Cross-Cultural Management," *International Management*, March 1985.
7. Ohmae, K. "The Global Logic Strategic Alliances," *Harvard Business Review*, March-April 1989.
8. Ashkenas, R. N., DeMonaco, L. J., and Francis, S. C. "Making the Deal Real: How GE Capital Integrates Acquisitions," *Harvard Business Review*, January-February 1998.
9. Edwards, T., Almond, P., Clark, I., and Colling, T., et al. "Reverse Diffusion in U.S. Multinationals: Barriers from the American Business System," *The Journal of Management Studies*, Vol. 42, No. 6, September 2005, 1261–1286.
10. Drucker, P. F. *Managing in the Next Society*. Oxford: Elsevier/Butter-worth-Heinemann/Elsevier Science, 2002, pp. 74–75. www.books@elsevier.com/management.
11. Donadio, R. "Abuse Crisis Explores Flaws in Vatican's Ancient Ways of Management," *New York Times*, April 7, 2010, Section A p. 11.

12. Harris, P. R. *The New Work Culture—HRD Transformational Management Strategies.* Amherst, MA: HRD Press, 1998. Republished as *The Work Culture Handbook.* Mumbai, India: Jaico Publishing House, 2003. www.jaicobooks.com.

13. Moran, R. T. and Riesenberger, J. R. *The Global Challenge: Building New Worldwide Enterprises.* London: McGraw-Hill, 1994; Harris, P. R. *Managing the Knowledge Culture.* Amherst, MA: HRD Press, 2005.

14. Abbott, J. D. and Moran, R. T. "Uniting North American Business—NAFTA Best Practices," *Eurodiversity—A Business Guide to Managing Differences,* Simons, G. D. et al., Oxford: Elsevier/Butterworth-Heinemann, 2002.

15. Grove, A. S. *Only the Paranoid Survive.* New York: Currency/Doubleday, 1996; also refer to Peterson, B. *Cultural Intelligence—A Guide to Working with People from Other Cultures.* Boston, MA: Nicholas Brealey/ Intercultural Press, 2004.

16. Symonds, E. "When Companies Connect—How the Internet Will Change Business," *The Economist,* June 26-July 2 1999, pp. 1–40, Special Survey Insert also refer to Benson, L.K. *The Power of eCommunication* and Carliner, S.*An Overview of Online Learning.* Amherst, MA: HRD Press, 2004.

17. Young, S. "Micro-Inequities: The Power of Small," *Workforce Diversity Reader,* Vol. 1, No. 1, Winter 2003, pp. 88–93. [Quarterly published by The Learning Institute of Workforce Diversity, 30095 Persimmon Dr., Cleveland, OH 44145, USA, Tel: 1–800/573–2867; www.workforcediversity.org.]. Kirton, G. and Greene, A-M. *The Dynamics of Managing Diversity.* Burlington, MA: Elsevier/Butterworth-Heinemann, 2004.

18. Beatty, R. W. and Ulrich, D. *Re-Energizing the Mature Organization. Organizational Dynamics,* Vol. 20, New York: American Management Association, Summer 1991; Refer to Armstrong, C. and Saint-Onge, H. *The Conducive Organization-Building Sustainability.* Burlington, MA: Elsevier/Butterworth-Heinemann, 2004.

19. Developed by the author's late wife, Dr. Dorothy Lipp Harris, when she was a professor at the School of Business and Management, United States (now Alliant) University in San Diego, California. For update, refer to Holbeche, L. *Understanding Change—Theory, Implementation, and Success.* Burlington, MA: Elsevier/Butterworth-Heinemann, 2005.

20. Pritchett, P. and Pound, R. *Employee Handbook for Organizational Change;* Pritchett, P. *The Employee Handbook of New Work Habits for a Radically Changing World.,* 1994. (Both available from Pritchett and Associates. PO Box 802889, Dallas, TX 75380, USA.) Refer to Hubbard, E. E. *The Manager's Pocket Guide to Diversity Management.* Amherst, MA: HRD Press, 2005.

# TRANSCENDING CULTURE: WOMEN LEADERS IN GLOBAL BUSINESS

"Dear Ms. Moran:
Thank you for your e-mail.
We do not carry women's pilot shirts.
I did check online and found a Web site that lists this item:
www.mypilotstore.com.
Please let me know if I can be of further assistance.
Sincerely,
Customer Service"

"Dear Customer Service,
Thanks for your response; it is appreciated. I was able to do a search and was initially excited to find "girls are pilots, too" Web sites, only to be disappointed in finding they sell pink tank tops with "I love my pilot" written on them, with a link to "dogs are pilots, too" (selling stuffed animals).

After further searching, I was able to find one that sells proper professional women's pilot shirts. The search was a bit of a disappointment (in more ways than one), but if I ever need aviation cookware, I know where to find it online now. I guess one has to have a sense of humor...

May I suggest you (being one of the most popular pilot supply Web sites) sell women's pilot shirts?
Thank you,

Rebecca,
Pilot in Tanzania, East Africa"

In July 2007, it is estimated that the world's population is about 6,602,224,175, with about 3,278,616,036 (or 49.66%) females, and 3,323,608,139 (or 50.34%) of the males.[2] The proportion of women relative to men, both working in employed positions, varies globally, and ranges from 20% in Arab countries like Bahrain, Iraq, Qatar, Oman, Saudi Arabia, and the United Arab Emirates, to 50% in countries like Cambodia, Ghana, and Latvia.[3] Worldwide, more men than women are found in the upper echelons of government and business, and it is these leaders who hold the greatest influence in shaping their country's policies and corporate HR management structures and behaviors.[4]

Collectively, women are not culturally distinct, which raises the question of our purpose for including this chapter. We are aware of the fact that historically and currently, there remains a significant gap of female representation and compensation in the upper echelons of the global work force. It is this disparity, and the societal and cultural influences upon this gap, that we address in this chapter.

## LEARNING OBJECTIVES

We believe that culture counts. Culture provides definitions for expected female and male roles, and, as such, provides the values and the subsequent expected behavioral norms for men and women within each culture.[5] Gender norms vary across cultures, and can influence how women combine the expected roles of a female leader with the general role expectations of their culture.[6] These cultural gender norms also influence how men respond to their family roles.

Culture sets the expected norms and values of gender-related behaviors, and there are many differences within nations and cultures with how these play out.[7]

While culture can set the standard for expected behaviors, this does not mean that all men, and all women, will automatically respond to these cultural norms accordingly. However, culture does have an influence on gender roles, and this reality influences both men and women. For example, Egyptian women collectively stood up for their rights and were legally allowed to not wear a veil in the 1920s and to vote in 1956; however, in 2009, a survey of 15,000 youth revealed that 67% of female respondents still believed that a woman deserves to be beaten by her husband if she speaks to another man.[8] In another example, a global study of 62 women with families and prominent leadership work-related positions found that "the American women leaders pride themselves on never missing their children's school play or soccer games; mothers in Hong Kong put more emphasis in helping their children with their school work; the Chinese mothers across the different societies emphasize family dinners, describing how they eat with their children before they go to their business dinners or go back to work in the office at night."[9]

From an organizational perspective, we contend that companies that use and build on an increasingly diverse workforce that include women will have the competitive advantage. While the number of international businesswomen has grown over the years, this number has not increased at a rate consistent with the number of women in the workforce of their respective countries. Globalization has transformed worldwide organizational culture and the workforce, and this has created an increased need for enhanced workforce collaboration and support. Since national corporations have expanded to global corporations, companies have had to account for an increasingly diverse workplace of varying ethnicities, nationalities, and languages.

Over the last 50 years, an increasing number of professional women have entered and remain in the global workforce. For all workforce professionals to perform to their potential, they need support, training, and mentoring. Often, for women and minorities, the challenge can go well beyond this. If women are less than 25% of the total directors in highly developed countries, progress for women is still far from accomplished.

In this chapter, we address the opportunities and challenges faced by women as global businesspeople. In no manner are we forgetting the contributions that many men have made for the benefits of their wives' careers, and for their children to create and maintain the work-family balance. Therefore, our first objective is to raise some awareness about the status of women in global organizations. The second objective is to suggest some ideas about women as global leaders and specific issues women may be confronted with in managing cultural differences.

## CURRENT STATUS OF GLOBAL WOMEN MANAGERS

Although globally women have considerably increased their presence in all industries, Exhibits 5.1–5.3 are researched examples illustrating that progress is yet to be made.

Meyerson and Fletcher[10] wrote of an outdated, but prevalent, practice of women still tending to be responsible for the "softer" aspects of work, while corporate culture is predisposed to highly value the traits of toughness, aggressiveness, and decisiveness—all stereotypically associated with men. Nevertheless, this isn't to say that men are to blame and that all men benefit because corporate culture is primarily male dominated.

Many organizations are working hard to leverage workforce diversity and gender equality so that all people can succeed. The key to making concrete changes in organizations is the leadership, which must have a keen interest in recruiting and *retaining* a diverse workforce while promoting qualified women. Unfortunately, statistics demonstrate that companies are falling short of the goal of gender equity in the workplace. Meyerson and Fletcher stated that, "Women at the highest levels of business are still rare.

## EXHIBIT 5.1

### STATUS OF GLOBAL WOMEN MANAGERS IN 2002

| Facts | Women | Men |
|---|---|---|
| CEOs of *Fortune* 500 companies | 6%, or 1.2% (Carleton S. Fiorina, former CEO, Hewlett-Packard Company; S. Marce Fuller, Mirant; Andrea Jung, Avon Products, Inc.; Anne M. Mulcahy, Xerox; Marion Sandler, Golden West Financial Corporation; Patricia Russo, Lucent) | 494 |
| CEOs of *Fortune* 1000 companies | 11 | 989 |
| Number among top corporate officers | 2140 (15.6%) | 11,533 |
| Number holding "clout" titles | 191 (7.9%) | 2221 |
| Representation among top earners | 118 (5.2%) | 2141 |

*Source*: Catalyst 2002 Census of Women Corporate Officers and Top Earners of the Fortune 500. Retrieved April 27, 2010, from http://www.catalyst.org/publication/174/2002-catalyst-census-of-women-corporate-officers-and-top-earners-of-the-fortune-500.

## EXHIBIT 5.2

### STATUS OF GLOBAL WOMEN EXECUTIVE OFFICERS IN 2009

| Facts | Women | Men |
|---|---|---|
| 2009 Executive Officers | 13.5% | 86.5% |
| 2009 Top Earners | 6.3% | 93.7% |

Less than 1/5 of companies were found to have three or more women executive officers. About 1/3 of all companies have no women executive officers.

*Source*: 2009 Catalyst Census: Fortune 500 Women Executive Officers and Top Earners, retrieved March 2nd, 2010 from http://www.catalyst.org/publication/358/2009-catalyst-census-fortune-500-women-executive-officers-and-top-earners.

They comprise only 10% of senior managers in *Fortune* 500 companies; less than 4% of the uppermost ranks of CEO, president, vice president, and COO; and less than 3% of top corporate earners."[11] Likewise, tied to the challenge of leveraging a diverse workforce with equal opportunity and compensation, the statistics for women of minority ethnicities are even worse: "Although women of color make up 23% of the U.S. women's workforce, they account for only 14% of women in managerial roles. African-American women comprise only 6% of the women in managerial roles."[12]

## EXHIBIT 5.3

## SELECT SURVEY RESULTS OF THE CORPORATE GENDER GAP REPORT 2010

A select group of over 3000 companies responded to this survey of about 25 questions in each of the 30 member countries of the OECD (Organizataion for Economic Cooperation and Development) and Brazil, China, Russia, and India. In each economy, a minimum of 20 completed surveys of 100 companies were completed.

The following are some selected results:

| | | | |
|---|---|---|---|
| Percentage of Female Employees | India<br>Japan<br>Turkey<br>Austria<br>Finland<br>Canada<br>Spain<br>United States | 23%<br>24%<br>26%<br>29%<br>44%<br>46%<br>48%<br>52% | Female employees were found to be concentrated in entry level to middle level positions |
| Average number of women holding the CEO position | Italy<br>Brazil<br>Norway<br>Turkey<br>Finland | 11%<br>11%<br>12%<br>12%<br>13% | Among the following survey respondents—Belgium, Canada, Czech Republic, France, India, Greece, Mexico, Netherlands Switzerland, United States, and United Kingdom—there were no female CEOs |
| Corporate Measurement and Target Setting | Of the sample, 64% of the companies surveyed did not set any specific targets, quotas, or affirmative goals. | | 72% of the companies surveyed did not monitor salary gaps between women and men or implement counteractive procedures |
| Maternity Leave Practices | 13% of surveyed companies offered no maternity leave. | | India, Mexico, and the United States offered the minimum leave time, and 33% of companies in Mexico offered less than the minimum leave time. |

*Source:* Tesfachew, T., Zahidi, S., and Ibarra, H. "Measuring the Corporate Gender Gap." *The Corporate Gender Gap Report 2010*, Zahidi, S. and Ibarra, H. World Economic Forum, Geneva, Switzerland, 2010. Retrieved April 27, 2010 from http://www.weforum.org/pdf/gendergap/corporate2010.pdf

In 2005, *The Economist*[13] reported the following:

- In Japan, 20-30 years ago, it was unacceptable for a woman to stay in the office past 5 p.m. There has been some progress since, with two women being appointed in 2005 as the head of two big Japanese companies:
  - Fumiko Hayashi is now the chairman and CEO of Daiei.
  - Tomoyo Nonaka has been appointed CEO of Sanyo Electric.
    - In France, Corinne Maier, an economist at EDF, a French energy group, said that 5% of French executives are women and that "Equality in the French workplace…is a far-off dream."
- In Britain, a large research sample of British companies found that 65% had no women on their board at all in 2003. Though 44%of the British workforce is female, no British woman has ever been the head of a large British company.

Five years later, in 2010, *The Economist*[14] published an article discussing the position of women in the workplace. While this is not intended to be compared to their article published in 2005, the purpose is to look at working women relative to men worldwide:

- There is an increase in the number of women in the workplace, women in the United States and in Spain now make up 49.9% of all U.S. workers, and in the U.S., women earn almost 60% of all university degrees.
- The unemployment rates for men in Japan and in Italy are more than 20% higher than for women, and even though women's employment has risen in the last decade significantly, it is still 50% below that of men, and more than 20% below that of Denmark and Sweden.
- Women, on average, still earn significantly less than men, and are underrepresented at the top of organizations.
- Women are often still forced to choose between motherhood and careers, and, as a response, in Switzerland, more than 40% of women are childless or delay having children for so long that they are prime candidates for fertility treatment.

However,

- Finland and Hungary provide up to three years of paid leave for women, and Germany has introduced a parent salary to encourage mothers to stay home for a time while keeping their careers.
- And more than 90% of organizations in Germany and Sweden allow for flexible working, dividing the work week in new ways to allow for improved work-family balance.

According to a 2006 report by the BBC, 75% of women work in the five lowest paid sectors; women hold less than 10% of top positions in FTSE 100 companies, the police, the judiciary, and trade unions.[15]

Retired women have on average a little over half the income of retired men. Barriers to women's entry into senior management, otherwise known as the "glass ceiling," exist across the globe, and it is worse in some areas of the world than in others. An article on the most influential women in business highlighted that it is easier to find ethnic British and Chinese women in positions of power, but much more difficult to find Korean or German women at the same level.[16] And although women represent 43% of the European workforce, they are still largely underrepresented in top management—in the UK, women represent slightly over 30% of managers and senior executives.[17]

One of the best examples of a society that promotes gender equality is Norway.[18] Here, 80% of Norwegian women work outside of the house, and half of the current government ministers are women. Scandinavian countries have the highest level of female employment in the world, and the fewest social problems, as the state has been closely involved in promoting gender equality. For example, Norway has used quota threats to increase female representation—and the result is that about 40% of the legislators are now women.[19] In 2002, a law was instated requiring that 40% of all company board members be women, and gave time until 2006 for companies to comply.[20]

Yet, while representation has increased, the expected link between women and performance in the board room was found to still be questionable. This is possibly because of the fact that the boards chiefly supervise and give advice to executives and top managers who are mostly men. Global representation in the board room and among executives and top managers still has a long way to go: "In the United States, roughly 15% of the board members of the *Fortune 500* companies are women, while at the top of Asian companies, women remain scarce: in China and India, they hold roughly 5% of board seats, and in Japan, just 1.4%…" While "women represent 27-32% of managers in Nordic countries, against 34% to 43% in Australia, Britain, Canada, and the United States, where maternity leave is more limited."[21]

Creating opportunities for female representation in the global workplace is only part of the matter. Biases or stereotypes are beliefs that influence behavior, and, often, these beliefs can lead to unequal treatment and representation. Stereotypes often hinder—although women and men are equal in their managerial abilities and overall ability to succeed—the promotion of women to senior positions.

## GLOBAL CULTURAL STEREOTYPES ABOUT WOMEN LEADERS

Psychological research has found that there are two types of sexist ideologies; one, benevolent sexism, is rooted in the belief that the gender differences are complementary and that women should be protected and taken care of; the other, hostile sexism, is rooted in the belief that women are inferior to men.[22] These sexist ideologies are rooted in each culture's stereotypic views about how women "should" behave. When women behave differently from prescribed stereotypes, often there are penalties that are administered.[23] "For example, women who are viewed as self-promoting or as 'acting like men'...are judged as deficient in social skills, are less liked and socially accepted, and receive fewer recommendations for employment."[24]

From Asia to the Americas to Europe, some of the unfortunate and disturbing *global stereotypes* include, but are not limited to the following:

*Women's behavior at work*

■ Women are fundamentally different and too "soft" to handle hard-nosed managerial decisions. Women cannot be aggressive enough, and will therefore lose business or do not have the competitive edge needed to win.

■ Contrary to the stereotype that women are too "soft," when women behave in accordance with the behaviors expected of their male counterparts, then the stereotype changes to the following: women overcompensate when in male environments, and become too masculine when managing, alienating employees and often alarming clients.

■ Yet in China, especially after the Cultural Revolution, women are expected to behave more aggressively.

■ Women lack quantitative skills, and therefore cannot hold technical positions or understand the numbers required in a profit-and-loss environment. Women possess "soft" skills such as communication and team building.

*Women and mothers*

■ Women are not as dedicated or as committed as their male counterparts, and therefore are not "executive material."

■ Once a woman becomes a mother, her priorities change completely, and she can no longer be counted on as before. Women often opt to quit working and become full-time mothers. How can a company promote someone who they know will ultimately leave? Companies cannot afford to have women coming and going whenever they wish.

*Women in an international context*

■ Women are not interested in an international career, and therefore should not be considered for international positions. In addition, women can't handle the cultural differences that occur outside their home country.

■ When companies send women abroad, their image will be less credible in male-dominated societies.

■ Other men won't take the woman manager seriously.

■ Because of current sexual harassment laws, nothing can be said to women without getting it blown out of proportion, and the result is that all interaction becomes suspect.

■ Women cause problems by looking for love in the workplace, and this will disrupt the workplace and ultimately lead to greater problems.

■ There aren't enough qualified women to promote. No matter how hard the company has tried, there just aren't any women with the exact qualifications they are looking for.

Such stereotypes are extremely counterproductive in the workplace. Blind stereotypes inhibit women and men from working effectively together, and inhibit women from working to their potential because they are active in keeping women "in their place." Overall, whether they are benevolent forms of sexism, or hostile, they inhibit the advancement of women in business around the world, and obscure women's skills.[25]

## Stereotypes Can Hinder the Advancement of Women

Quite often, these stereotypes go unnoticed by both men and women, as they are so deeply rooted within a culture. Other times, even when aware of these stereotypes, some women might choose to behave according to the stereotype in order to avoid dealing with strong attitudinal obstructions while at work. There are a variety of global issues that confront women in the workplace. A few are highlighted to gain a greater understanding of the obstacles women must still overcome.

*Women are more likely to be pigeonholed into less challenging positions than men.* Women are often tracked into separate, and less promising, career paths. As upper management positions require broad and varied experience among other skills and talents, as well as a sense of responsibility, many potential executives are "pipelined" through certain high-visibility and high-responsibility areas such as marketing, finance, and production.[26] These are often referred to as "line" positions, in preparation for upper-management promotion. Women "tend to be in supporting, 'staff' function areas—personnel/human resources, communications, public relations, and customer relations. Movement between these positions and 'line' positions is rare in most major companies. Furthermore, career ladders in staff functions are generally shorter than those in line functions, offering fewer possibilities to gain varied experience."[27]

This is a stereotype that can be found across the globe; women are seen as more "human" and therefore better suited for a specific type of job, such as human resources, communications, public relations, and marketing. Management, especially in the areas of finance and information services, continues to often be seen as a job better suited for men.

This stereotype could be linked to the global expectation of a woman's role as mother or primary caretaker in the family. This common stereotype is as follows: if a woman's focus is on bearing children, she would subsequently be taking time off, and could not be considered an effective front-line executive. In Chile, a woman's marital status can be an important consideration during the hiring process; it is generally featured at the top of a resume with other essentials such as name, address, and phone number, along with a photograph. A young, married woman with no children can be considered a "risky investment" because the perception is that she will soon have children, leave her job, and the company will have to pay for pregnancy expenses. Although times may be changing in Chile, it is still generally expected that women will relinquish their career aspirations and stay at home when children arrive. For some women, this can begin immediately after marriage.

During the 1980s, in the United States, the "mommy track" was designed to facilitate having children and maintaining a professional life. Nevertheless, many women who choose to have children still maintain high career aspirations and get stuck in less-challenging or demanding jobs. While this stereotype tends to be focused upon the role of women, it is also evolving into a parental stereotype, as a number of male partners and husbands of working women are staying home to care for children.[28]

*Significant pay gaps exist between women and men in the same position.* Despite significant progress and a variety of laws designed to prevent wage discrimination, women are still earning less than their male counterparts for the same job. According to Catalyst, in the United States, "The nation's highest-paid female corporate executives earn 68 cents to every dollar earned by the highest paid [male] corporate executives. The median total compensation of men in the study was $765,000; the median for women was $518,696."[29] The BBC reported that, according to the Equal Opportunities Commission (EOC), there is a 19% pay gap between men and women in the UK.[30]

*Exclusive corporate cultures.* One influential factor still affecting women's advancement in business, and this is true in many areas across the globe, is that most of today's existing work environments were designed by men. Women, functioning in sometimes a more male-oriented corporate culture, are under constant pressure to adapt or transform their styles of working. This, however, is slowly changing. In Japan, for example, women face a challenge to adapt to the expectation that management requires mixing work and play, often by drinking and bar-hopping until late hours. Women colleagues are nowadays invited to join in on such social activities, although a married woman with a family might find it very difficult to meet, on a consistent basis, such a time commitment. In some South American countries, strong, unspoken norms exist about what is appropriate or inappropriate for a woman to do, regardless of career position; as such, higher-level female executives can be excluded from after-work activities and/or can exclude themselves in fear of the backlash in breaching these norms.

In some American corporate environments, younger generations of women have almost eradicated the "male only" designated corporate culture by joining in, and instigating, happy hours, golf games, and softball tournaments. In some cases, these women have even redefined the culture itself by adding new twists like cultural outings or joining in on the "male only" outings.

*Limited access to information, contacts, and high-level networking opportunities.* While the term "old boys' network" was coined long ago, in many companies the institution itself is thriving. The "old boys' network" refers primarily to a group of white male executives who have an informal yet somewhat exclusive club that manifests itself in the upper echelons of management. Women and people of color are generally not included. Communication within these exclusive informal networks can perpetuate gender stereotyping and bias through jokes, stories, and slurs. Whether it is on the golf course, hunting, having late night drinks, or in the men's room, women can often be excluded from this high-level interaction, when it is often these informal networks that can improve chances of promotion and success.

According to *The Economist*, few women are able to reach the higher management levels because of exclusion from informal networks, which across the globe can include late-night boozing and a common tradition for sales teams to take potential clients to strip clubs.[31] Executives and upper-level managers like to hire who they know, and the more contact with an individual the better. Unfortunately for women, many of the "bonding" experiences take place in venues that are not necessarily women-friendly, such as strip clubs, or where women are simply not invited out of habit. In Israel, women are almost completely excluded from the senior ranks of the military. This exclusion from what is considered by many in the corporate world as an invaluable learning experience for managing large organizations limits women as choices for future senior executives.[32]

As a result, women often are not informed of advancement opportunities, are not as visible as male colleagues, and are not given additional opportunities to prove their credibility for promotion. According to Wernick,[33] "Managers and executives look for 'signals' from those they will select to advance. Those signals found to be most significant indicate credibility and provide increased access to visibility to decision makers. Access to information, which is critical to advancement, is often limited to selected groups or individuals within the managerial ranks or workplace." This can be exacerbated when the company does not have a formal executive development program or tracking program that explicitly monitors promotions and pay increases for employees.

*Fewer women participate in executive development programs, employer-sponsored training programs, or "fast-track" programs.* As evidenced through a variety of studies, women are often not given as many opportunities as their male colleagues for education, training, or special high-profile programs. This could emanate from the stereotype that women will eventually leave their jobs to have children, so why invest the money in enhancing their skills when a man would be a better "investment" opportunity? Without proper corporate intervention to increase women's participation in such programs and opportunities, the result would be that women remain in their positions with little to no overall growth.

*Fewer women are asked to take on risky positions.* One area where this is particularly evident is in expatriate work, where the position and results tend to be highly visible. Fewer women are asked to fill expatriate positions, although just as many women as men request these positions abroad. A prominent researcher on the role of women in global business, Adler interviewed many people to determine whether MBAs from seven management schools in the United States, Canada, and Europe would like to pursue an international assignment during their career.[34] The overall response was 84% favorable, with little difference between male and female responses. Adler conducted another survey of 686 Canadian and American firms to determine the number of women sent abroad.[35] Of 13,338 expatriates, only 3% were women, when women actually accounted for 37% of domestic management positions. One other obstacle exists for women who would like to hold international assignments; the cultural biases in certain countries against women, both native and foreign, are such that it is very difficult for women to work, to live, and overall to succeed in that particular country.

## BALANCING WORK AND FAMILY

Balancing life outside of work and life at work is a major concern of most working professionals. It is also a major concern for working couples who, when working equally together, balance work and family to the benefit of both partners. Here we define balancing work and family "...as the degree to which an individual is able to simultaneously balance the temporal, emotional, and behavioral demands of both paid work and family responsibilities."[36] Though in the past, women were required to make a clear choice as to whether they wanted to have a career or a family, today a professional career and motherhood are no longer considered mutually exclusive, as the concept of fatherhood has also evolved.

Nevertheless, working mothers who are not married to men who partake equally in the family responsibilities tend to have to juggle two full-time jobs. When national cultural norms still promote a more traditional model of "parenthood," the work-family balance debate is relegated as an issue that women face. Even though in some cases, this can conceal a male belief that household and child-related work are primarily women's responsibilities,[37] it is also an issue that men face in an effort to find work-family balance.

A series of women were interviewed who were either middle or senior managers and who had recently become new mothers,[38] and all of the women interviewed stated that motherhood had given them a new perspective on their work, and that this was, in general, very positive. They also felt that motherhood had given them a new sense of confidence, enabling them to let their personalities become apparent in the workplace. Planning was critical to juggle the daily demands of family and work. Nevertheless, many women, particularly in Europe and Asia, choose to take a break from professional work once they begin a family. Furthermore, more research should be done to look at how men balance work and family as well, for as long as the stereotype that caring for children and the home is an expected female role is encouraged worldwide, and relevant research tends to focus on women's attitudes toward work-family balance, this stereotype is reinforced.

## Challenges Faced with Trying to Balance Work and Family

It is certainly a strain to balance one's personal and professional responsibilities. In the United States, for example, there is still a lingering belief that it is the woman's responsibility to take care of children. Separating work and family into two different domains tends to be found in current Western thinking, and it supports a popular myth that women can choose one or the other, but having both is extremely difficult—when, in reality, women have almost always worked and had families, and only the context has shifted and changed over the years.[39] In the United States, many American businesses are addressing the bottom-line implications of employees' need for affordable and high-quality child and elder care. Wiley Harris of GE Capital Services states that, "Every employee is important to our company's health, and when employees are distracted by family issues, we lose productivity."[40] The Family and Medical Leave Act of 1993 was a response to concerns from men and women about being able to care for family members at critical life stages without the risk of job loss. Even with its enactment, the United States continues to compare poorly with other developed countries such as France, Sweden, Canada, and Finland, where family care is institutionalized.

## Research on Work-Family Balance

Lately, research on work-family started to include things like "positive spillover, balance, interface, mutual facilitation," and can incorporate an international perspective.[41] For example, in the Chinese society, where work and family are seen as interdependent,[42] and roles tend to be more nebulous, as work is seen as having a long-term benefit for the family. Furthermore, the Maoist ideology of gender equality and the one-child-per-family *policy* have greatly contributed to women's promotion and motivation in the workplace without having to focus on finding day care.[43] However, Chinese Confucian principles of governance and morality still lend to women being seen by some as less than men.[44] This being said, however, this study[45] found that Chinese women's work motivation was just as high as that of Chinese men, and managerial motivation was found to be positively related to the hierarchical job level. Among their findings was that intrinsic motivation, standing out from the group, and exercising power might be factors that enable women to supersede negative work-related prejudices about work-family dynamics that could hamper job advancement.

In Europe, a study[46] of managers from twenty different EU countries analyzed the intersection of, and among, three variables: (1) the degree of each country's national gender equality, (2) the degree of organizational support for family-work balance, and (3) individual qualities, such as individual manager's work-family balance characteristics. This study noted correctly that a country's national gender equality and context are very relevant. Work-family balance can be supported by national government regulations and programs, such as Sweden's policy on subsidized childcare programs and required parental leave.

Furthermore, it was found that organizations are more likely to follow through if their external environment enforces compliance, thus reflecting the relationship between national context and organizational practice. This study underscored how important national context is to gender equality in the areas of parents being able to have work-life balance, and women's life expectancy, education, and standard of living. Overall, parents who have positive work-family balance tend to be more satisfied with their job, are more committed to their organization, and are more satisfied with their family dynamics as well.[48]

While in locations like many European countries, states provide childcare support and have national programs to facilitate work-family balance, in the United States, the individual employers are expected to be the principal purveyor of family assistance, even though they often feel that it is not their responsibility but the family's.[49] However, these programs of the employers are successful only if top management is committed to their implementation.[50] A very recent study[51] of U.S. personnel analyzed supervisors' perceptions of family-work conflict and the ability to balance expectations of both, through investigating two aspects of promotability: (1) the manager's perceptions of the promotability of their employees, and (2) employee statements of whether they had been nominated for promotion or not. They[52] found that managers had the propensity to pigeonhole women as the gender that experienced more work-family conflict, even after the researchers controlled for family responsibilities and the women's own perceptions of work-family balance. The main contribution of this study is the finding that even though women's work-family conflict may impact their career progress, the perceptions of their work-family conflict that their superiors may have also can influence their career advancement, and these perceptions can unwittingly create the "glass ceiling" effect.

# THE GLASS CEILING

The "glass ceiling" refers to barriers to reaching the upper echelons of organizations. These barriers to the advancement of women and minorities are often very subtle. For example, a very interesting study[53] in 2008 looked at HR personnel records of a *Fortune 500* company from 1967 to 1993, drawing a random sample of more than 5000 managers of both genders. After dividing the sample into four work levels (entry, middle, upper middle, and upper), the analysis revealed that women tended to be hired at lower levels and lower salaries than their male complement, and were more likely to be located in support positions. The result was that women were less likely to be on the path to the top of the organization, and even by 1993, while 40% of the women hired were in entry-level positions, in the higher echelons, they were only 20% of the middle managers, and 10% of the upper middle and upper levels.

Further research[54] has found that there are subtleties that influence the "glass ceiling" barriers, and consist of gender stereotypes, a deficiency of opportunities for women to acquire the necessary work experience and knowledge to excel, a scarcity of top management dedication to initiatives for gender equality and equal opportunity, and a male wealth stereotype that men deserve greater salaries than women.[55]

Exhibit 5.4 presents the findings of research about women and wages worldwide.[56] It provides us with one way to understand the impact of female worker proportion relative to men, with *special attention to* merit pay and strikes, on payment within and across organizations and occupations. This interesting study concluded that many employees are underpaid relative to their country's level of wealth, and points toward sociopsychological forces that impact economic compensation.

## EXHIBIT 5.4

### A STUDY OF WOMEN AND WAGES WORLDWIDE

- 59 countries which had estimates for wages from the World Economic Forum of 1999 Global Competitive Report were included in the study. The survey measured the perceptions of 3934 government officials and senior business leaders working in these 59 countries.
- The factors used to determine the objective size of the gender contrast (the national proportion of working women) included the country's:
  - Overall male/female ratio (0.52 in Qatar $< x <$ 1.19 in Latvia)
  - Fertility rate (1.2 in Italy $< x <$ 7.6 in Yemen)
  - Economic growth rate ($-0.09$ in Georgia $< x <$ 0.09 in China)
  - Socioeconomic necessity of families having a dual income
  - War and emigration

continued

*Findings*

1. Workers in countries with larger proportions of working women *were found to be underpaid*.
2. neither payroll taxes, merit pay, nor strikes could substitute working women as the main predictor of underpayment, *however,* they did appear to account partially, in a curvilinear fashion, for *this* underpayment.
3. Both previous results appeared to be driven by the following economic and sociopsychological forces:
   a. The proportion of working women is a demographic and sociopsychological factor.
   b. Underpayment across countries with little merit pay or strikes can be tied to men's higher status relative to women.
   c. Underpayment across countries where merit pay or strikes are more common can be better tied to the absence of salient gender contrasts.

*Source*: Van de Vliert, E. and Van der Vegt, G. "Women and Wages Worldwide: How the National Proportion of Working Women Brings Underpayment into the Organization." *Organization Studies*, Vol. 25, No. 6, 2004, pp. 969-986.

# COMPANY INITIATIVES TO BREAK THE GLASS CEILING

Most companies have put into place specific programs to assist in breaking down barriers impeding a woman's progression. Many include a combination of flexible work arrangements, mentoring, women's support groups, and leadership development. Various companies have also developed support and structures designed to advance women.

## *Quality Management Models: Audits*

Even though a lot of research, conferences, meetings, and workshops have been conducted in the area of gender and diversity, and there are an increasing number of qualified and career-oriented women in industry, there appears to still be limited progress within industry in Europe. This is because, in Europe, resistance is found through low commitment by top managers, weak gender or diversity marketing campaigns, and no incentives or systemic planned methods to improve the diversity and gender policy.[57] In order to improve processes such that women in corporations become a source of productivity and high performance, audits help to provide documented, systemic examination of this topic and can assist industry to improve its gender-related policies. Rather than looking simply at the number of men or women involved in an industry, audits help to examine the contributions of different areas and groups within industry. Audits help to provide instruments to verify management and information on the efficiency of a company's performance, and provide mechanisms to display how strategic decisions play out, as well as a benchmark to compare with other companies.[58]

## A Tracking System

Accenture is the winner of the "2003 Catalyst Award for Innovative Programs to Help Women Advance in the Workplace." Accenture developed a global "Great Place to Work for Women" initiative, and uses a variety of innovative processes such as geographic scorecards, global surveys, and performance appraisals to guarantee that company leadership remains accountable for the initiative's results. Joe Forehand, Accenture's chairman and CEO, states that, "Empowerment without opportunity is useless. At Accenture, we've focused on fostering a more inclusive work environment. Our Great Place to Work for Women program is one way we're enabling women to take charge of their careers and move into broader leadership roles."

## A Support Structure: Mentoring Programs

IBM, Kodak, and 3M have women's networks in place to help promote women's careers. Apparently, one-third of all *Fortune 100* companies have such networks aimed at developing skills, building careers, and supporting women. Research has demonstrated that mentoring is a critical part of career success. Mentoring is defined as "a cooperative and nurturing relationship between a more experienced businessperson and a less-experienced person who wants to learn about a particular business and gain valuable insight into some of the unspoken subtleties of doing business."[59] Many experts claim that it is beneficial to have more than one mentor present within an organization, and that these mentors should be at different levels. Mentoring comes into play at crucial points in an individual's career and can be an effective source of advice and encouragement.

Burke and McKeen found, however, that men and women view mentoring in different ways.[60] It is often more difficult for women than men to find appropriate mentors. Many Internet sites have popped up in the past few years offering women the opportunity to network with each other in a nontraditional setting. The U.S. Small Business Administration has set up a specific program, open to all women, specifically focused on helping women entrepreneurs and those considering to becoming entrepreneurs.

## Work Still to Be Done

Although women have achieved significant advances since entering the workplace, much remains to be done for women to be considered as qualified and talented as men. Companies need to take more responsibilities and initiatives to fully integrate women into their environments at all levels of the corporate hierarchy. Companies that champion diversity champion women. Some issues to consider include the following:

*Increasing the flow of information and educating women about current issues.* It is only with concrete facts and information about women's position in the workplace that any calibration of gains can be measured. Catalyst, a nonprofit organization focused on women's issues in the workplace, has taken a wonderful role in initiating this process. When women appreciate where they have been and understand the issues that confront them, they can see and decide where the future lies.

*Demonstrating CEO commitment.* As the corporate leader, the CEO has the most significant influence on the direction and vision of the firm. It is through her or his direction that a "persistent campaign of incremental changes that discover and destroy the deeply embedded roots of discrimination" will occur.[61]

*Closing the pay gap.* A true merit system distinguishes individuals on the basis of their effort and skills, and rewards each person for his or her work regardless of gender. Men and women work equally hard in the same positions; their pay should reflect this equality.

*Increasing recruitment, providing training opportunities, and placing women in high-profile positions.* Companies should step up their efforts to recruit and train qualified women, and ensure that more women get access to "line" positions versus being immediately segmented into "staff" positions. "Recruiting the right potential very much depends on the individual employer attractiveness. Besides challenging projects and job security, equality and family-friendly policy belong to the most important motivation factors. This means that...for a company, it is a must to implement gender mainstreaming activities within the concept of high-qualified diversity management."[62]

# WOMEN AND OVERSEAS, EXPATRIATE ASSIGNMENTS

Women's representation in the global arena has grown (albeit slowly) to 17% of the expatriate population, though in some industry sections, the percentage is considerably higher.[63] Although the percentage of women expatriates is rising, many companies fail to send women overseas, in particular to areas of the world where the demarcation between male and female roles is clearly defined. Global women managers often talk about the "double-take" or stares they receive in Asia, South America, or the Middle East when they are first introduced. For example, in Latin America, women report having been mistaken for the wife or the secretary during important high-level business meetings and social events. However, most women who were sent abroad say that the first reaction of surprise is quickly replaced by professionalism and respect.

## The Expatriate Glass Ceiling (The Glass Border)

In multinational companies, a foreign assignment is often the stepping stone into a higher-level management position. A recent study[64] found that employees who exhibited greater personal agency and had less family obligations were more willing to go on expatriate assignments, search for expatriate jobs, and leave their home countries. This same study found that women with partners and/or children were most restrained in their willingness to expatriate. Even with willingness to expatriate, there is still a strong disparity between the number of male and female managers, not only in home country operations, but also in expatriate assignments.[65] This expatriate "glass ceiling" has three implications: (1) there is a greater challenge to filling expatriate assignments, as nowadays, men are often opting out because of family and dual-career concerns, (2) a lack of diversity of the top management group can lead to homogeneity, and thus weaker leadership decision-making, and (3) if lower-level women feel that the opportunity is limited, they may be less motivated to compete for higher-level jobs.[66]

## Breaking the Glass Border to Succeed in an Expatriate Assignment

From 2000 on, women's participation in international assignments has been on the rise, as data from Europe, Australia, and the United States have found a rise of 16.5% of women in expatriate assignments in 2005.[67] Nevertheless, there is an underrepresentation of women on international assignments. "These barriers are informed, predicated, and reinforced by organizational and societal conventions, including the lack of women mentors and role models, the weakness of female organizational networking, and lack of social support that influence promotion to, and acceptance at, the top."[68] Breaking this ceiling requires concerted corporate programs, as well as determined efforts by women, to actively engage in self promotion and networking.

Three strategies are recommended[69] to assist women to advance toward top-level positions and into foreign assignments. One, *preassignment strategies:* It is recommended that women be proactive agents of change in their own career, and recognize their cultural values that might influence their behavior. Companies should reevaluate and change policies and procedures related to selection, training, and repatriation of female expatriates. They should improve the training of the selection's decision makers as well, to avoid antiwomen bias, while assisting couples who have dual careers to collectively manage both their careers so that a woman can take an international assignment. Two, *on-assignment strategies:* It is recommended for women to proactively find a mentor and take advantage of reverse learning and hindsight. Companies should match assignments to assist with the expatriate adjustment, and continue training and mentoring programs. Three, *postassignment strategies:* It is recommended for women to volunteer to be a mentor. Doing so, they also take responsibility to manage their own career. Companies should have women, who were on assignments internationally, become mentors for future female expatriates.

When many women have been nominated for an international business assignment in what the company thought would be a hostile culture, most of these women have succeeded with flying colors. Why? This is because expatriate women are not expected to behave according to the same social guidelines as natives of that particular culture, and women can be "…especially adept at cross-cultural management skills because they use behavior patterns emphasizing sensitivity, communication skills, community, and relationships. This personal orientation is valuable in globalization."[70] Women are often seen as foreigners first, and thus can be beholden to different rules of conduct than the local women. Here are some words of advice for women to help lay the groundwork[71]:

1. *Establish credibility.* Have strong support from senior management in the organization, and make sure that your expertise is communicated to the destination location.
2. *Have a higher-ranking person* who knows the people in the culture with whom you will be working, and openly talk about your credentials.
3. *Present yourself* as sincere, professional, and confident.
4. *Act reserved* with male colleagues (and formal).
5. *Wear tasteful conservative clothing*, especially in male hierarchical cultures.
6. *Express your opinions* politely, diplomatically, and tactfully.

Adler, a leading expert in women and management, emphasizes the following words of advice: "If a woman is going to work in a society with culturally based sexism, when asked about your marital status, it is helpful to have prepared answers so that you answer with grace. In more 'macho' cultures, be culturally sensitive. Allow men to pay for your drinks, food, and cab. It also helps to include a businessman in your work dinners to ensure the message is sent that the dinner is work only. In hierarchical cultures, respect peoples' titles, and introduce your educational background and accomplishments."

The difficulties that women may encounter when working on a foreign assignment depend to a certain extent on the social and economic context of the country in which they are conducting business, and on the individuals with whom they come into contact. Both the woman international manager and the company she represents can take steps to minimize any negative aspects.

*Companies and managers should lay the groundwork.* Do not surprise a client. While this recommendation is not only specific to a foreign assignment, before any meeting, regardless of the gender of the participants, it is important to provide adequate information about the agenda and who will be present.

*Practice what is preached.* If a corporation empowers women managers and treats them equally and seriously in business dealings abroad, it should ensure that women are also treated equally and fairly in the organization. Success begins at home.

*Consider both women and men for international positions.* Do not rely on the assumption that women will not want to accept the position.

*Provide proper cross-cultural training and preparation courses.* Training is vital to all managers to be successful abroad. Specific assistance should also include what to expect from male superiors, peers, clients, and subordinates, and how to handle uncomfortable situations, such as discrimination.

*Be realistic.* Women managers abroad suffer from the same culture shock as men. It is important to keep expectations reasonable, build trust, and create professional relationships.

## HOW HAVE SEVERAL SPECIFIC WOMEN SUCCEEDED? ARE THEY GOING ABOUT BUSINESS DIFFERENTLY?

### Selected Women Managers' Views

The August 5, 1996, edition of *Fortune* ran an article titled "Women, Sex, and Power." Contrary to what the title might suggest, the article focused on seven women who are the best of the best in their fields of business. Among these were Charlotte Beers (Ogilvy & Mather) and Jill Barad (Mattel). These women are part of the new female elite who are changing the way women reach the top. The following recommendations are still relevant today:

*Have confidence in yourself.* In the past, many women felt obliged to hide their femininity so as to be seen as managers first and women second. Many women in today's business world no longer view their sexuality as a hindrance. Despite the fact that the office is often still male dominated, they are no longer attempting to become more male-like or androgynous in order to be promoted.

*Survive and overcome difficult working conditions.* Most women, especially of older generations, have had to face discrimination from men and women alike. Charlotte Beers remembers, "Early in my career, during my first week at J. Walter Thomson in Chicago, I had a secretary who asked the company for a transfer. She told me, 'No offense, but I want to work for a man who's going to move ahead.'" The story goes that two years later, the secretary, impressed by Beers' stellar career path, asked to come back, and Beers, who liked her honesty, accepted.[72] Many successful businesswomen have had to overcome adverse working conditions and have been able to build their careers during these tough moments.

*Do things differently.* Many women are successful by incorporating aspects of their personality into their work or by daring to do things differently. In the end, many of them drastically change the way business in their field is done. Linda Marcelli, of Merrill Lynch, started selling stocks by setting up personal meetings instead of cold calling. Anita Roddick was an international hit with her "Body Shop" that brought environmental consciousness to a new level.

*Have your own leadership style—neither "feminine" nor "masculine."* Women are often described as having a more "open" approach to management, relying on consensus building as opposed to the old style of command and control. Recent research demonstrates that women and men executives in similar positions demonstrate more similar behaviors than dissimilar. This research has shown that, "women who have made it into senior positions are in most respects indistinguishable from the men in equivalent positions. In fact, the similarities between women and men far outweigh the differences between women and men as groups."[73]

Many women are concerned that the debate as to whether men and women exhibit different leadership styles continues to perpetuate typical stereotypes of women as "soft" managers. As Adler and Izraeli point out, managers (male and female) in the United States have tended to identify stereotypically "masculine" (aggressive) characteristics as managerial and stereotypically "feminine" (cooperative and communicative) characteristics as "unmanagerial."[74]

More and more companies are assertively trying to advance women's issues. "Woman-friendly" companies have been proven to provide a more beneficial environment to both *men* and *women*.[75]

## THE FUTURE OF WOMEN IN LEADERSHIP POSITIONS

The obvious long-term goal is gender equality in the workplace: equal job opportunity, equal pay, and equal advancement. Once gender parity and equality are achieved, management can redirect its additional time and energy to further enhance corporate objectives.

*Increased emphasis on strategic alliances between women.* The May 10, 1999, *Wall Street Journal* reported on a new conference, "Women & Co.," designed for high-level, high-powered women executives from across the nation. The conference not only facilitated female-specific networking and alliance-building opportunities, but also educated the women on current hot topics such as crisis management, the media, dealing with investors, risk management, and selecting CEOs and directors.[76] With the steady increase of women in management, woman-to-woman mentoring systems and extended support networks and associations will gain significant power in lobbying for change and making significant inroads in the boardroom.

*More women and men working out of the home.* Advances in technology, combined with more family-friendly businesses, will allow women and men to easily work out of the home and spend quality time with their children or elder relatives. E-mail, fax, and tele- and video-conferencing capabilities are just a few of the high-tech conveniences that enable all workers to create an office and work productively for their firm at home. New advances are surely in the pipeline to further facilitate working out of the home. As a result, both the mother and father will have more time to devote to raising the children and sharing family duties.

*More women-owned businesses.* Often, women who get discouraged with the traditional workplace create their own businesses. If companies are slow to respond to women's needs, we can expect more women-owned businesses that will change the fabric of today's workplace. Women-owned businesses have already doubled as women are recognizing the value of creating one's own work environment, calling the shots, making the hours, and reaping the monetary rewards. Furthermore, with their comprehensive workplace knowledge, these women will design a workplace that is woman friendly.

*Changed roles within the home.* With more and more couples working full time, duties in the home should become equally divided. Equality at home will be a fundamental factor that can assist in opening the doors fully to equality in the workplace. Couples can distribute tasks equally, including chores, child rearing, and elder care, and in the process this might mean paying more for services such as house cleaning, shopping, laundry, prepared meals, etc. As women continue to make more money, it will be more acceptable and common to see a "househusband" as the couple together decides the payoff with one breadwinner in the family.

*Heightened development of family-friendly policies.* As companies value their human capital more, policies could include allowing for two-year "sabbaticals" for either parent to raise children, with computerized "update" training and a guaranteed job upon return. "A few employers, including Eli Lilly and IBM, guarantee a job after a three-year leave. Such policies take the heat off parents."[77] Via Internet education, companies could update these employees on current corporate issues or the latest technology in order to ensure that the employee transitions effectively back into the company.

*Acceptance of paid paternity leave designed for new fathers.* When companies offer paid paternity leave, they are further encouraging the active role of the father in the family unit. While many women get paid time off after the birth of a child, most fathers are left out of the loop, with only evenings and weekends to help out with the child rearing. While some companies offer time off for the new parent, paid paternity leave is rare. Nevertheless, in France, the government recently offered two weeks of paid paternity leave to all new fathers.

*Growth of part-time, contract, temporary, or freelance career paths.* If companies do not adequately respond to working parents' needs, the part-time, contract, temporary, and freelance career options will boom. These types of careers give parents the flexibility to combine work and family life, yet without the responsibility of a full-fledged, self-owned business. Many intelligent and educated women choose to stay home with their families because they are forced to choose between work and a family; these types of careers can offer a lucrative middle ground. *The Wall Street Journal* reported an increase in the profitable temporary executive business, where an individual is hired to do high-powered work for a short period of time.[78]

*New markets will emerge to support the career woman's work/life balance.* Changes in the workforce and consumer demographics inevitably lead to increased opportunity for new markets. This could translate into increased opportunities in the service industry, retail, food, health care, child care, and elder care to meet the needs of working women. Convenience, portability, and ease of use will become more vital as people have less and less time for complicated items.

Women who choose to be full-time mothers and homemakers should be respected for their choice. However, we recognize and believe that the role of nurturer within the home is increasingly being seen and acknowledged as a role both men and women fulfill.

## CONCLUSIONS

Careful observation reveals a rapidly increasing number of countries and companies moving away, for the first time, from their historical men-only pattern of senior leadership. The question is no longer "is the pattern changing?" but rather "which companies will take advantage of the trend, and which will fall behind?" Which companies and countries will lead in recognizing and understanding the talents that women bring to leadership, and which will limit their potential by clinging to historic men-only patterns....[79]

Depending on the country, different societal forces have contributed to increasing female presence in high-level positions within corporations. Women in the United States have benefited from affirmative action and equal opportunity laws that hold employers accountable for promoting women. In Germany, women are becoming increasingly present in the political arena. Nevertheless, despite recent progress in most countries, women's advancement in the business arena has been steady but slow. As we move into the twenty-first century, companies will need to increasingly reflect this diversity in all levels of their workforce.

The problem of how to get women in those positions of great importance throughout the enterprise still remains. Numerous barriers still exist for women across the globe. Women have made incredible advances, yet one of their next great challenges will be to assure proportional representation in senior management positions. A strong business imperative can be made that companies who do not address the needs of their women employees (as well as employees of minority cultures) in terms of recruiting, promotion, and career development will suffer the following long-term consequences:

■ Not being viewed as an employer of choice.
■ Undervaluing top performers; therefore, not using employees' full potential.
■ Losing a competitive edge.

In today's competitive world, ignoring the potential of the greatest (in number and in potential) group of your workforce is more than just an oversight—it is extremely costly.

## MIND STRETCHING

"The most important determinant of a country's competitiveness is its human talent—the skills, education, and productivity of its workforce. Women account for one-half of the potential talent base throughout the world and, therefore, over time, a nation's competitiveness depends significantly on whether and how it educates and utilizes its female talent."[1]

1. What are the cultural expectations of women in your culture?
2. What are the stereotypes about women that are believed and communicated in your culture?
3. What is your personal view of men and women's role:
   ■ In relationships?
   ■ In family?
   ■ In business?
   ■ In politics?
4. How do your personal views of men and your personal views of women influence how you relate to, communicate with, and interact with men and women in each of the above contexts?
5. What are the specific issues women may experience in business in specific countries in North America, Central America, South America, Europe, Asia, the Middle East, and Africa?
6. What are some methods to address negative gender stereotypes, and redefine them such that they are changed into positive?
7. How does religion influence the expected role of men and women? To what extent is this expectation flexible?

# REFERENCES

1. Tesfachew, T., Zahidi, S., and Ibarra, H. "Measuring the Corporate Gender Gap," *The Corporate Gender Gap Report 2010*, Zahidi, S. and Ibarra, H. (eds.). Geneva, Switzerland: World Economic Forum, 2010, Retrieved April 27, 2010, from http://www.weforum.org/pdf/gendergap/corporate2010.pdf.

2. https://www.cia.gov/library/publications/the-world-factbook/geos/xx.html# People, Retrieved, February 4, 2010.

3. Van de Vliert, E. and Van der Vegt, G. "Women and Wages Worldwide: How the National Proportion of Working Women Brings Underpayment into the Organization," *Organization Studies*, Vol. 25, No. 6, 2004, pp. 969–986.

4. Ibid.

5. Halpern, D. and Cheung, F. *Women at the Top; Powerful Leaders Tell Us How to Combine Work and Family*, Malden, MA: Wiley-Blackwell, 2008.

6. Ibid.

7. Ibid.

8. "Arab Women Rights, Some Say They Don't Want Them," *The Economist*, March 27, 2010, p. 53.

9. Ibid, p. 171.

10. Meyerson, D. E. and Fletcher, J.K. "A Modest Manifesto for Shattering the Glass Ceiling," *Harvard Business Review on Women in Business*, Sylvia Ann Hewlett and Carolyn Buck Luce (eds.), Boston: Harvard Business School Press, 2005, pp. 69–94.

11. Ibid., p. 70.

12. Ibid., p. 94.

13. "The Conundrum of the 'Glass Ceiling,'" *The Economist*, July 23, 2005, pp. 63–65.

14. "Female Power," *The Economist*, January, 2, 2010, pp. 49–51.

15. "Britons 'Accept' Pay Sexism," *BBC NEWS*, 2/28/06, www.newsvote.bbc.co.uk/1/hi/business/3038394.stm.

16. "Most Powerful Women in Business, the Power 50, Why are Some Women More Successful in Some Countries than in Others?" *Fortune*, September 27, 2002.

17. www.AdvancingWomen2003.org.

18. Clark, N. "Getting Women into Boardrooms, by Law," *The International Herald Tribune*, Thursday, January 28, 2010, p. 1.

19. "We Did It!" *The Economist*, January 2, 2010, p. 7.

20. Clark, N. "Getting Women into Boardrooms, by Law," *The International Herald Tribune*, Thursday, January 28, 2010.

21. Ibid., p. 9.

22. Halpern, D. and Cheung, F. *Women at the Top; Powerful Leaders Tell Us How to Combine Work and Family*. Malden, MA: Wiley-Blackwell, 2008.

23. Tyler, J. and McCullough, J. "Violating Prescriptive Stereotypes on Job Resumes: A Self-Presentational Perspective," *Management Communication Quarterly*, Vol. 23, No. 2, 2009, pp. 272–287.

24. Ibid., p. 273.

25. Mihail, D. "Gender-Based Stereotypes in the Workplace: The Case of Greece," *Equal Opportunities International*, Vol. 25, No. 5, pp. 373–388.

26. Glanton, E. "Pay Gap Endures at Highest Levels," *AP News*, womenconnect.com, November 10, 1998.

27. Glass Ceiling Commission. The Glass Ceiling Fact-Finding Report. "Good Business: Making Full Use of the Nation's Human Capital," 1995.

28. "She Works, He Doesn't," *Newsweek*, May 12, 2003.

29. Catalyst 2002 Census of Women Corporate Officers and Top Earners of the Fortune 500.

30. "Britons 'Accept' Pay Sexism," *BBC NEWS*, 2/28/06, www.newsvote.bbc.co.uk/1/hi/business/3038394.stm.

31. "The Conundrum of the 'Glass Ceiling'," *The Economist*, July 23, 2005, pp. 63–65.

32. Adler, N. and Izraeli, D. "Where in the World Are the Women Executives?" *The Business Quarterly, London*, 1994.

33. Wernick, E. "Preparedness, Career Advancement, and the 'Glass Ceiling'," *Glass Ceiling Commission*, May 1994.

34. Adler, N. J. and Izraeli, D. (eds.). *Competitive Frontiers: Women Managing Across Border*, Cambridge, MA: Blackwell Publishers, 1994, p. 28.

35. Ibid., p. 27.

36. Lyness, K. and Kropf, M. "The Relationships of National Gender Equality and Organizational Support with Work-Family Balance: A Study of European Manager," *Human Relations*, Vol. 58, No. 1, 2005, pp. 33–60.

37. Yegisu, C. "Can Men Stomach Marrying Wealthier Women?" *Daily News and Economic Review, Istanbul*, January 23–24, 2010, p. 10.

38. Tanton, M. *Women in Management: A Developing Presence*, London: Rutledge, 1994, p. 82.

39. Halpern, D. and Cheung, F. *Women at the Top: Powerful Leaders Tell us How to Combine Work and Family*. Malden, MA: Wiley-Blackwell, 2008.

40. http://www.pathfinder.com/ParentTime/workfamily/workcare.html.

41. Halpern, D., and Cheung, F. *Women at the Top: Powerful Leaders Tell us How to Combine Work and Family*, Malden, MA: Wiley- Blackwell, 2008, p. 176.

42. Ibid.

43. Chen, C., Yu, K., and Miner, J. "Motivation to Manage: A Study of Women in Chinese State-Owned Enterprises," *Journal of Applied Behavioral Science*, Vol. 33, No. 2, pp. 160–173.

44. Ibid.

45. Ibid.

46. Lyness, K. and Kropf, M. "The Relationships of National Gender Equality and Organizational Support with Work-Family Balance: A Study of European Manager," *Human Relations*, Vol. 58, No. 1, 2005, pp. 33–60.

47. Ibid.

48. Carlson, D., Grzywacz, J., and Zivnuska, S. "Is Work-Family Balance More than Conflict and Enrichment," *Human Relations*, Vol. 62, No. 10, 2009, pp. 1459–1486.

49. Halpern, D. and Cheung, F. *Women at the Top: Powerful Leaders Tell us How to Combine Work and Family*. Malden, MA: Wiley-Blackwell, 2008.

50. Ibid.

51. Hoobler, J., Wayne, S., and Lemmon, G. "Bosses' Perceptions of Family-Work Conflict and Women's Promotability: 'Glass Ceiling' Effects," *Academy of Management Journal*, Vol. 52, No. 5, 2009, pp. 939–957.

52. Ibid.

53. Wyld, D. "How Do Women Fare When the Promotion Rules Change?" *The Academy of Management Perspectives*, Vol. 22, No. 4, 2008, pp. 83–85.

54. Bell, M., McLaughlin, M., and Sequeira, J. "Discrimination, Harassment, and the 'Glass Ceiling': Women Executives as Change Agents," *Journal of Business Ethics*, Vol. 37, 2002, pp. 65–76.

55. Williams, M., Paluck, E., and Spencer-Rodgers, J. "The Masculinity of Money: Automatic Stereotypes Predict Gender Differences in Estimated Salaries," *Psychology of Women Quarterly*, Vol. 34, 2010, pp. 7–20.

56. Van de Vliert, E., and Van der Vegt, G. "Women and Wages Worldwide: How the National Proportion of Working Women Brings Underpayment into the Organization," *Organization Studies*, Vol. 25, No. 6, 2004, pp. 969–986.

57. Domsch, M. "Quality Management in Gender and Diversity: The Role of Auditing." *European Commission, Women in Science and Technology: The Business Perspective*, Belgium: European Communities, 2006, pp. 37–47.

58. Ibid.

59. www.sysop@advancingwomen.com.

60. Karsten, M. F. *Management and Gender: Issues and Attitudes*. Westport, CT: Praeger Publishers, 1994.

61. Meyerson, D. E. and Fletcher, J. K. "A Modest Manifesto for Shattering the 'Glass Ceiling'," *Harvard Business Review on Women in Business*, Harvard Business School Press, 2005, p. 70.

62. Domsch, M. "Quality Management in Gender and Diversity: The Role of Auditing," *European Commission, Women in Science and Technology, The Business Perspective*, Belgium: European Communities, 2006, p. 38.

63. Solomon, C. M. *Women Managers in the Global Workplace: Success through Intercultural Understanding*, Mobility, January 2006.

64. Tharenou, P. "Disruptive Decisions to Leave Home: Gender and Family Differences in Expatriation Choices," *Organizational Behavior and Human Decision Processes*, Vol. 105, 2008, pp. 183–200.

65. Inch, G., McIntyre, N., and Napier, N. "The Expatriate 'Glass Ceiling': The Second Layer of Glass," *Journal of Business Ethics*, Vol. 83, 2008, pp. 19–28.

66. Ibid.

67. Altman, Y. and Shortland, S. "Women and International Assignments: Taking Stock—A 25-Year Review," *Human Resource Management*, Vol. 47, No. 2, 2008, pp. 199–216.

68. Ibid, p. 207.

69. Inch, G., McIntyre, N., and Napier, N. "The Expatriate 'Glass Ceiling': The Second Layer of Glass," *Journal of Business Ethics*, Vol. 83, 2008, pp. 19–28.

70. Adler, N. J. *Organizational Behavior*, Third edition. Cincinnati, OH: South-Western Publishing, 1997, pp. 308–309.

71. Adler, N. J. *International Dimensions of Organizational Behavior*, Fourth edition. Canada: Southwestern/Thomson Learning, 2002.

72. "Women, Sex and Power," *Fortune*, August 5, 1996.

73. Wajcman, J. *Managing Like a Man*, University Park, PA: Pennsylvania State University Press, 1998.

74. Adler, N. J. and Izraeli, D. J. (eds.). *Women in Management Worldwide*, London: M.E. Sharpe, Inc., 1988, pp. 20–24.

75. Wilkof, M. V. "Is Your Company and Its Culture Women-Friendly?" *The Journal for Quality and Participation*, June 1995.
76. Beatty, S. "A Power Confab for Exclusive Businesswomen," *The Wall Street Journal*, May 10, 1999.
77. Shellenberger, A. "Work & Family: The New Pace of Work Makes Taking a Break for Child Care Scarier," *The Wall Street Journal*, May 19, 1999.
78. "Work Week," *The Wall Street Journal*, May 11, 1999.
79. Adler, N. J. *International Dimensions of Organizational Behavior*, Fourth Edition. Canada: Southwestern/Thomson Learning, 2002, pp. 173–174.

# MOTIVATING THE GLOBAL WORKFORCE: The Case for Diversity and Inclusion

"At the level of international management pressures, as well as urgency of diversity management, interventions vary more extensively than at the level of domestic operations. This means that global diversity approaches are informed by the pressures both at the domestic and international level. The international level pressures are the increased convergence of legal pressures to combat different forms of inequality; the regional influences are those such as the case of the Social Charter of the European Union and the influence of incipient international campaigns and organizations."[1]

## LEARNING OBJECTIVES

The effective utilization of the talents of all employees is stated by most executives as the organization's greatest asset, but these executives often do not know how to accomplish this with an increasing multicultural workforce. "In recent years, diversity management has been considered both an issue of employment relations and an issue for all sections of the organization, from financing and accounting to customer relations and from strategy to marketing."[2] To unleash the talent and potential of this changing workforce, the public and private sectors are assessing their organizational systems to capitalize on the prevailing benefits of a diverse workforce and clientele.

The process of leveraging workforce diversity has many applications, and this chapter focuses on a few of them. We do want to emphasize that the strategy and subsequent actions of managing a diverse workforce should be considered from a standpoint that takes into account the corporate systems within which employees work. This standpoint helps a company attain the end goal of maximizing employee potential, whether the employee belongs to the majority or minority group. By valuing differences, companies are acknowledging the historic shifts in the makeup of the labor market. They realize that it is a business and bottom-line issue, for it involves motivating and communicating with diverse employees so that the collective work output reflects each employee's highest potential.

This chapter will provide a basis and some implementation strategies on effectively managing a diverse workforce.

## DESCRIBING GLOBAL DIVERSITY

All in all, diversity is related to the vast range of differences that requires attention to facilitate living and working together effectively. Human diversity has been popularly understood to refer to differences of color, ethnic origin, gender, sexual or religious preferences, age, and disabilities. In academic research, diversity has been characterized by either surface-level demographics such as gender, age, race, and nationality, and task-related and cognitive diversity such as educational and functional background.[3] Stated definitions of *organizational* diversity recognize a wider range of characteristics. According to American Express Financial Advisors, they include:

> race, gender, age, physical ability, physical appearance, nationality, cultural heritage, personal background, functional experience, position in the organization, mental and physical challenges, family responsibilities, sexual orientation, military experience, educational background, style differences, economic status, thinking patterns, political backgrounds, city/state/region of residence, IQ level, smoking preference, weight, marital status, nontraditional job, religion, white collar, language, blue collar, and height.[4]

Historically and currently, the movement of people from one locale to another has encouraged the formation of our diversity.

### *People on the move*

In the late 1980s, Allan Wilson and his colleagues used mtDNA to determine human ancestry. By comparing mtDNA and Y chromosomes from people of diverse populations, they were able to map human migration originating in Africa many years ago.[5] "Migration has helped to create humans, drove us to conquer a planet, shaped our societies, and promises to reshape them again.... If they [people] had not moved and intermingled as they did, they probably would have evolved into a different species."[6]

## Categories of people on the move

In addition to business, government, global travelers, as well as tourists, there are also three other categories of people on the move[7]:

- *Refugees.* People living outside their country of nationality, afraid to return for reasons of race, religion, social affiliation, or political opinion.
- *Internally displaced persons.* People forced to flee their homes because of armed conflict, but who have not yet crossed international boundaries. Like refugees, they have generally lost all they own and are not protected by their national governments. Today, we estimate that there are an estimated 41.9 million refugees and internally displaced persons, many of whom sought asylum from some kind of persecution or discrimination.[8]
- *Migrant workers.* People, both skilled and unskilled, who work outside their home country, including employed migrants without legal permission to work, and undocumented immigrants. It is estimated that there are about 214 million international migrant workers and their families worldwide, and an estimated 20-30 million of them are unauthorized.[9]

The social fabric in the host countries are often reconfigured and strained by massive waves of immigrants, legal or illegal, who migrate to live and work permanently or temporarily in another country. The demographic changes are often from developing economies to industrialized nations. These mass migrations are usually in pursuit of a better way of life; however, this movement of people from different cultures and backgrounds has frequently caused costly, complex social and financial problems for the host culture struggling to absorb the new arrivals.[10] Exhibit 6.1 summarizes the dual impact of the ongoing push and pull of immigration.

These recent arrivals bring new energy, talent, and enthusiasm to their new homes and their new work, while adding both human and financial capital. The mix of citizenry, ethnicity, and tribal backgrounds is like a mosaic. We believe that the global work culture is best characterized by two words—*change* and *diversity*. It is well to remind ourselves that, just as in nature, diversity makes for adaptation.

## Exhibit 6.1
## Root Causes of Immigration

When people leave their homes, generally there is a "push" factor from the sending country and a "pull" factor from the receiving country. Of course, individual, religious, political, or economic reasons play a critical role.

| Principal "push" factors include: | "Pull" factors in receiving countries include: |
|---|---|
| ■ War and civil strife, including religious conflicts | ■ Substantial immigration markets and channels opened up in the West |
| ■ Economic decline and rising poverty | ■ Family reunion with workers already living in Europe |
| ■ Rising unemployment | ■ Safety |
| ■ Population pressures (more specifically, burgeoning numbers of unemployed youth) | ■ Freedom from fear or violence, persecution, hunger, and poverty |
| ■ Political instability | ■ Economic opportunity |
| ■ Large-scale natural disasters and ecological degradation | ■ Education |
| ■ Human rights violations | ■ Maintaining ethnic identity |
| ■ Denial of education and health care for selected minorities, and other kinds of persecution | ■ Access to advances in communication and technology |
| ■ Government resettlement policies that threaten ethnic integrity | |
| ■ Resurgent nationalism | |

Adapted from: Stalker, P. "The Work of Strangers: A Survey of International Migration," *Aids in Place of Migration*, Bohning, W. R. and Schloeter, M. L. (eds.). Geneva, Switzerland: International Labour Office, 1994. (Also available from ILO Publications Center, 49 Sheridan Ave., Albany, NY 12210, USA.)

## *Three Additional Global Trends*

As the twenty-first century begins, global leaders who understand what is happening to societies and work places should also be aware of two other trends impacting world development.

■ Resurgence of the world's attention to peoples' interest in their ethnic identities, religious roots, and ancient affiliations as related to conflict. "One-sixth, at most, of the world's population identifies with politically active cultural groups. More precisely a survey…has identified 268 politically significant national and minority peoples in the larger countries of the world. The outer bound of potential supporters for these ethnopolitical movements is slightly more than one billion, or 17.7% of the global population."[11]

■ An emergence of transnational ethnic groups or global tribes who have a major influence on international trade and the economy. The latter, whatever their origin, are frequently venture capitalists, financiers, arbitrageurs, and entrepreneurs who benefit by the discipline of their traditions.

A third trend to recognize is the desire of peoples everywhere for the protection of their human rights, including at work. This means that leadership should always be committed to resolving any conflicts that arise, with full respect toward the rights of all individuals involved. The United Nations has best articulated their aspirations in its Declaration of Human Rights. Those who would be competent and nondiscriminatory global leaders recognize that both society and the corporate work environment must follow the declaration's guidance.

## Global Diversity and Conflict

"In the real world, relations between most groups have a history; they are often influenced by complex socio-cultural factors that extend their influence over long periods of time. The history of slavery in the United States is likely to be relevant to the present relations in that country; the history of European colonialism is likely to be relevant to the present relations between newly arrived Third World immigrants and indigenous European populations; and the past history of English domination in Canada is likely to influence the present state of relations between English and French Canadians."[12]

Because of technological and human advancement, our world is deeply interconnected, and we are in constant contact with our differences, characterized by varying cultures, ethnicities, religions, fundamental beliefs, and values. When in conflict, it is difficult for individuals to perform to their potential. Human discord results from many factors and, throughout history, there are examples of forced assimilation of minority cultures into the dominant culture, in both nations and organizations. However, consistently, history has shown that few cultures can be completely assimilated into another. There are many current and historical global examples of the differential treatment of various ethnic groups in political, social, and economic areas.

"Disadvantages" means socially derived inequalities in material well-being or political access in comparison with other social groups. In chaos theory, or "the butterfly effect," events in one part of the world can significantly affect the other side of the world. Likewise, events in the political arena spill into the business arena, and political oppression is linked to social and economic oppression. "Traditional concepts, like the balance of power or ideology, are...not as useful as they once were in explaining the sources of...conflict, particularly when conflicts are rooted in a complex and rich brew of ethno nationalism, religion, socio-economic grievances,...globalized markets, and geopolitical shifts."[13]

We must learn to appreciate the fact that our common survival and the satisfaction of our universal needs and concerns are interdependently linked. All must work toward our common survival through multilateral action that reflects appreciation and acceptance of differences, with mutual respect for each other. In order to do so effectively, learning conflict analysis and resolution skills are necessary in today's world.

Bartos and Wehr[14] define conflict as something that occurs when actors utilize conflict behavior against each other to achieve incompatible goals. While this is defined in the more extreme sense, they believe that determining the operational causes for conflict should help us in understanding the conflict, as this is the first step toward finding ways to resolve it. Understanding why individuals or groups are in conflict behavior requires us to learn what these individual grievances, goals, and motivations are with regard to the conflict, and then determining ways to find an equitable solution. One of the greatest causes of conflict is when one group or all groups involved in the dispute remain inflexible and see only their own perspective as valid. Through refusing to comprehend, acknowledge, and appreciate the perspective of another, while holding on to stereotypical assumptions of the other party, conflict behavior is almost an assured outcome.

An example of one organization that seeks to address this need is Stirling University. This school has recently developed a course for leaders, students, writers, and politicians to learn skills in conflict resolution, management, and prevention. Course director Vassilis Fouskas states:

> Although we would all wish otherwise, there is little likelihood that the world in the twenty-first century will be a better place to live in, or that it will be without conflict, war, dictatorship, terrorism, genocide, or poverty. The least we can do as academics and teachers is to try to produce serious-minded, prospective leaders able to understand the past, intervene in the present, and shape a more just, fair, and equitable world.[15]

# ETHICS, LEADERSHIP, AND DIVERSITY

The valuing of diversity is not only a means to improve employee performance through encouraging employees to find optimum ways to work together harmoniously, or customer satisfaction and marketing tactics, it is also a moral assertion. While some would assert that valuing diversity in organizations is a performance concern, others would say that it is also a moral one. Subordinates tend to watch very carefully the nonverbal and verbal behaviors of their leaders, and they make assessments of their leaders' moral character. This, in turn, depending on the moral character of the subordinate, and how similar or dissimilar their moral character is to the leader, can influence the nature of the relationship between leader and subordinate, as well as employee performance.

Ethics comes from the Greek word *ethos,* which means character. The study of ethics is concerned with morality, or what is deemed "right" and "wrong." In each society, a leader's character has to do with their moral fiber, and is usually analyzed as "good" or "bad," which is relative to their culture's value set. A "good" leader can be considered good on the technical level, where a leader is described and rewarded based upon his or her technical deeds and successes.[16] A good leader can also be considered "good" on the moral level, who looks at how those deeds were accomplished and whether it was through proper behavior. Here, intentions, goals, and methods to reach goals are analyzed from the ethical standpoint.[17]

## Ethical Issues and Leadership

Howell and Costley[18] discuss one main ethical issue, *power,* and how this is correlated to a leader's influence upon, and relationship with, subordinates. As cited by Howell and Costley, there are three psychological debasing influences of power: (1) some people might have the goal to have power and will seek it regardless of the obstacles; (2) due to power disparities, subordinates may give a leader artificially positive feedback, and this positive feedback can lead to the leader thinking unrealistically highly of themselves; (3) this in turn, can influence a leader to devalue the worth of their subordinates, and this can be reflected in negative leadership behavior. As is well known, power can be used in many different ways, some of which are[19]:

1. Threat power: which has to do with reciprocating bad behavior toward another;
2. Trading power: which has to do with reciprocating good behavior, but may lead to stalemate if parties involved do not act;
3. Giving power: which has to do with giving behavior with no agenda to receive anything in return.

The first form of power, when used, tends to creates additional conflict, while the latter two have more positive outcomes.

Howell and Costley note that leaders should be held to the same moral standards everyone else is held to, should demonstrate moral stability, should be effective leaders, while at the same time acting ethically, own up to making any moral mistakes, and demonstrate responsible leadership with respect to the power that they do have. These five issues are not only at the micro level of interpersonal behavior, but can also be seen at the organizational level. If an organizational mandate has a directive to value diversity, and employees are knowledgeable of this, then employees will see this, experience it, and when there are digressions, will see that those responsible for devaluing diversity *should* be reprimanded and reminded that they should demonstrate in actions valuing diversity.

## The Global Challenge of Ethical Relativity

Although there is much controversy over the definitions of diversity and the organizational processes that may result, Thomas states that:

> People want to act like diversity is synonymous with differences. They talk about diversity fracturing the country, fracturing the organization. For me, diversity refers to both differences and similarities. So diversity, as opposed to fracturing, becomes the context within which you can talk about the ties that bind and also the differences that make us unique.... We can be different and still united.... Now, it remains to be seen if we can come together and move forward in a united way around similarities and still be very different.[20]

Evanoff[21] analyzed the ethical dimensions of intercultural relations, comparing and contrasting two traditional approaches: universalist and relativist, and proposed a third approach—constructivism. The universalist approach takes as assumption that ethics can be supported by universal principles and norms, that are true for all people, regardless of time or place or any differences that can be found culturally, between individuals or certain periods of history. On the other hand, the relativist approach takes as assumption any cultural human reality is not universal and thus has marked discrepancies across cultures.

While the universalist approach assumes rigid global norms, it is often viewed as intolerant and an attempt to enforce imperialistic norms (in our times, Western countries) upon others; the other assumes comparative norms, and is based upon the notion of tolerance and respect, but can be rigid and is criticized as a means to enforce the status quo.[22] Notably missing is the strategy needed for how to develop new ethical configurations, when cultures are in constant contact with each other, and there are differences that need to be resolved. Thus, Evanoff's analysis concludes with the constructivist notion of co-created norms. This notion proposes that dialogue and interaction both assist in resolving any cross-cultural problems that present themselves when parties with different cultures, and who exhibit different behaviors and ethics, interact together. Through constructing an agreed-upon, shared norm, we can build bridges across differences through not only learning from other cultures, but also from the adoption of shared values and behaviors to improve positive interaction. This is one of the primary objectives in effective management of diversity in global organizations.

# GLOBALIZATION, DIVERSITY, AND MANAGEMENT

Globalization is shaping our world today, and cross-cultural conflict is only one of the byproducts. Advances in telecommunications, mass transportation, technology, and changes in the global political arena have led to the emergence of a global, information-oriented culture. With the expansion of globalization, awareness of the global complexities involved in cross-cultural interactions has been expanding. Globalization has greatly increased interaction at both the macrolevel, exempified by the expansion of technology through business, and at the microlevel, exemplified by the individual use of laptops, cellular phones, and the Internet. Though it can be said that at the macrolevel there is a form of global culture around the use of technology, communication advances, and the practice of business, at the microlevel, the experiences, values, perceptions, and behaviors of individuals vary within and across national and ethnic cultures.

## Capitalizing on Human Diversity

As a concept, diversity has different meanings and applications, depending on where you are in the world. Within our information society, it is important to recognize that increasing *globalism* enormously impacts the workforce worldwide. For leading-edge organizations, this denotes the creation of an organizational cultural norm to embrace diversity to maximize the potential of personnel, especially through cohesive work teams.[23]

Research[24] has demonstrated that as the length of time increases when diverse group members work together, the negative effects of surface-level diversity (i.e., age, sex and ethnicity) decrease such that stereotypes have a lower degree of salience. Furthermore, in this research,[25] the effects of deep-level diversity (attitudes, beliefs, values) led to increased information about each group member. These deep-level diversity characteristics at the group level, as mediated by time, meant that as time increased, the richness of information exchange augmented, which allowed for more profound mutual understanding and greater satisfaction among members.

For global managers, the challenge is to innovate ways to improve human commitment and performance at work. Since so many people aim to achieve their full potential through their work and career, the new work culture fosters values such as empowerment and character development, gauging success not in terms of organizational status but in the quality of work life. There is very strong empirical confirmation that successful diversity management and a resulting improvement in organizational performance are positively correlated.[26] Furthermore, for meta-industrial workers, Nair suggests that the quest for personal/professional excellence and meaningful business relationships takes precedence over climbing the corporate ladder and the pursuit of external rewards.[27]

## A Global Illustration: European Union Diversity and E-Europe

An excellent example of working together for a common good is the European Union (EU). In business today, people are the most important source of sustainable competitive advantage. Every person brings a unique combination of background, heritage, gender, religion, education, and experience to the workplace. This diversity represents a noteworthy source of new ideas and vitality.

The phenomenon of growing diversity in the work environment is worldwide. But Europe today is a prime example as 27 national cultures now work together to integrate as members of the EU. The last two members, Bulgaria and Romania, were admitted to the EU in January 2007. At this time, candidate countries include Turkey, Croatia, and the former Yugoslav country of Macedonia. What began as a smaller economic community seeking a greater share of the global market has evolved into a grand plan of sociopolitical and even military association with its own unique constitution. Simons has articulated the challenge of diversity and globalization:

> Our present diversity challenges are being determined by forces shaping the economy and business world generally and cannot be discussed in isolation from them. Diversity is about globalization, organizational learning, and the growing importance of knowledge management, just as much as it is about recruitment, equal opportunity, workforce demographics, and social integration. It concerns the information technology that is almost daily revolutionizing communication. It affects interactive networking and transport. It is perhaps the critical issue in many mergers and acquisitions—and often the least attended to! It is at the root of how organizations transform themselves....
>
> Historically, Europe, or the "Old World," is different from the lands in which European emigrants settled and made their own. Europe has always been very diverse, and Europeans have always been conscious of their diversity. They differ from North Americans in what they do about it. In the best of times, Europeans believe that "good fences make good neighbors." In the worst of times, those who attempt to shape or create or reshape those borders are painted in blood.... Diverse by nature, the European Union got its start in the search for peace and prosperity after history's most devastating war (World War II, 1938-1945).... In Europe, economic cooperation among its diverse peoples was the starting point. Only later did this cooperative enterprise begin to take responsibility for a social and cultural integration whose necessity, utility, and desirability continue to be questioned every step of the way[28].

The Cultural Diversity Market Study reported that the European Committee for Standardization (CEN) has been focusing its activities on cultural diversity and e-business.[29] "E-Europe feels that global issues increasingly demand global response, and that is the reason that there is a strong need for a collective European approach. Globalization, enlargement, and internationalization are keywords in E-Europe. This requires consideration of the cultural and linguistic diversity of Europe, thereby giving equal chances to all businesses and citizens in Europe to benefit from the Information Society." This study[30] had three main conclusions:

1. An identified lack of awareness regarding the importance of cultural diversity was apparent. Diversity was not a high priority of EU industry or its consumers; however, there were many activities handled in a multicultural manner.

2. Issues surrounding cultural diversity are addressed primarily from a technical perspective, with little or no quantitative look at the costs and benefits.
3. The study recognizes the need for cooperation within the international environment and within each industry.

The EU has had to overcome periodic conflicts in the past by working together across cultural differences to build a multinational, multicultural, multilingual powerhouse. The subject of increasing immigration, especially in Europe, is also discussed in Chapters 10 and 14.

# THE GLOBAL MANAGEMENT OF DIVERSITY

Global diversity management practices tend to have three varying approaches.[31] One approach is localized, in which the global organization would have each subsidiary determine a diversity management strategy unique to themselves. This would allow for the consideration of each subsidiary's unique diversity needs. However, this approach does not address what can happen if different diversity management techniques across the network allows for too much leeway that can ultimately lead to insufficient diversity management measures in specific subsidiaries. To address this shortcoming, the universal approach provides a means to standardize across subsidiaries and throughout the global firm. Once more, this generates the question about whether this approach is then insensitive to local customs and diversity challenges. A third method, the transversal approach, necessitates a negotiation in which each subsidiary takes into account their local situation when engaging a global diversity management policy. This method is more constructivist, and allows for variation of diversity practice across subsidiaries, through adapting to each local situation, while shaping policy and practice globally. Exhibit 6.2 presents some key constructivist competencies for both the organization, the group, and for the individual.

## EXHIBIT 6.2
### SOME KEY ORGANIZATIONAL COMPETENCIES

The following competencies are recommended to be adopted by organizations to help create the conditions that recognizes the human factor and demonstrates value for diversity.

Each nation is unique, each national system is relative to its unique culture, and each organization has a distinctive culture as well. Therefore:

■ Analyze employee work environments and staffing mechanisms through the lens of multiple legal systems.

■ Be culturally sensitive to each employee's motivational dynamics.
■ Be culturally sensitive to each organization's unique administrative systems.

Create mechanisms for employees to identify cultural differences, and provide ways to connect across those differences.

■ Provide technical support (i.e., language translation), cross-cultural training, and network support.
■ Enable flexible system designs to create interlinking modules to work across different organizational systems.
■ Create a learning environment with a focus on knowledge management where mistakes are a source of information and allow for continuous learning.
■ Create a network of communication that through technology provides nonverbal and verbal exchanges of information.
■ Create a flexible system whereby conflict is recognized and resolved in the direct or indirect manner that demonstrates respect for cultural protocols.

Adapted from: Barrett, G. "Cultivating Global Teams: Diversity Management Square (DM$^2$)." *Borderless Business, Managing the Far-Flung Enterprise*, Mann, C. and Gotz, K. (eds.). Westport, CN: Praeger, 2006, pp. 275-294.

## A MACROSYSTEMIC PERSPECTIVE

World leaders understand that global business can be complex, and are always studying it from multiple perspectives. They understand that there are many ways to perceive a particular situation, and that each perspective helps create the larger picture. The talented global leader oversees an organizational system that seeks to enable each employee to reach her or his potential. These leaders understand that to influence the macrosystem through the interaction of each individual, the microsystemic aspect, the whole organization is efficiently empowered.

In the event of an international merger or acquisition, cultural variance can have enormous negative effects if the differences and systemic discrepancies are not properly addressed. For example, in 1996, Ericsson bought a company based in California, called Raynet, and in taking its usual integration approach, quickly discovered that a majority of the staff whose skills were crucial to Raynet had left. Subsequently, Ericsson took a more hands-off approach in the acquisition, allowing the organizational culture to maintain its arrangement, which then eased the merger process.

However, taking too much of a hands-off approach after a merger or acquisition can prove to be risky as well. "Such failures of management reflect cultural differences."[32] Culturally, synergistic leaders address the whole cultural organizational system, thus allowing for the *highest level of competence*, building on diversity reflected at all levels of the organization.

We believe that the challenge lies in establishing a diversity mission that is flexible enough to take into account subsidiary differences, yet tangible enough to be communicated company-wide, and is consistently enforced system-wide, both behaviorally and communicatively. Changing the attitudes and behaviors of any workforce is challenging, but changing them in an unreceptive environment is an enormous task. This requires a strong visionary, blessed not only with persistence and stamina, but also with the foresight to realize that it takes consistent enforcement of its policies. It is unrealistic to expect upper management, middle managers, and employees to dismiss any of their deeply embedded perceptions and embrace diversity overnight—no matter how charismatic or persuasive the leader. Rethinking diversity and establishing a companywide-enforced strategy will positively affect every aspect of organizational culture. Exhibit 6.3

## EXHIBIT 6.3

### EXAMPLES OF COMMON PERFORMANCE INDICATORS USED BY COMPANIES TO GUIDE THEIR PROGRESS

The European Commission Directorate General for Employment, Social Affairs, and Equal Opportunity commissioned an extensive study to understand better the business case for diversity and assess what future policies and recommendations are needed at the national, organizational, and individual levels. The following are examples of performance indicators that some companies have set to support their diversity approaches:

- An increase in the number of women, disabled people, and ethnic minorities, at all levels of the organization, but with a special focus on senior levels. Specific targets are set for each.
- High-quality managers (especially women and ethnic minorities) are retained.
- The perception of minority and majority groups within the organization are improved, especially around diversity concerns. This is measured against an employee satisfaction rating (through employee attitude surveys) that the company targets.
- Use of business standard and quality models that assist the company to implement management benchmarks and structures to set corporate requirements to help reach diversity and employee performance objectives.

Adapted from: European Commission, "The Business Case for Diversity: Good Practices in the Workplace." Luxembourg: Office for Official Publications of the European Communities, 2005, 62 pp. Retrieved April 14, 2010 from http://ec.europa.eu/social/BlobServlet?docId=1428&langId=en.

provides performance indicators that some companies have used to support their diversity approaches.

## Macroorganizational Leveraging of Diversity: A Study

Thomas and Ely conducted a 6-year study that researched the process of solving the system-wide challenge of leveraging the full potential of a diverse workforce.[33] Their research was undertaken from the standpoint of the average employee. The results of, and the recommendations from, this study are worth noting in some detail, offering a global leadership framework to gain knowledge of how to effectively and comprehensively leverage cultural organizational diversity. In this study, the simple assumption of increasing the number representation of diversity was used to investigate its link to organizational effectiveness. It was found that, in fact, it (i.e., number representation) inhibited organizational effectiveness as employees were unable to bring their "whole" self to the workplace.

In general, companies tend to use two paradigms to address workforce diversity. In this research, however, they were found to be counterproductive, creating more problems and inferior employee performance. A third paradigm emerged from this study, which portrayed an organization in which leadership plays a fundamental role through systemic analysis of the whole organization, while, at the same time, redefining cultural variance or diversity and its subsequent actions, thus enabling each "individual to work to her or his potential." This type of organization can actualize its goal of improving organizational processes for the company and cultivating a high level of productivity at all levels of the organization.

A short synopsis of the three paradigms is as follows:

- The Discrimination-and-Fairness Paradigm, characterized by leadership that values the equality of all employees. These are often bureaucratic, controlled structures that have easily observable cultures. Its benefits are demographic diversity and promotion of fair treatment; however, the limitations of this paradigm were significant. Disagreements, wrongly interpreted, often did not generate multiple ways of leading, working, or viewing the market. The result is a workforce unable to be open about new ideas or work to their full potential, and the inability of the organization to improve its own strategies, procedures, and performances.
- The Access-and-Legitimacy Paradigm, which emerged between the 1980s and 1990s, is based on the acceptance and the honoring of diversity, with the main push towards a more diverse clientele by matching workplace demographics. The company focuses on matching diversity among its employees with the diversity of its clientele, focusing on difference but without assessing how those differences affect work-related procedures. In this system, workers tend to be placed into pigeonholed positions.

■ These researchers found that the third emerging paradigm illustrated an organization that makes the most of its diverse employee and customer base. This paradigm surpasses the previous paradigms in promoting equal opportunity and acknowledging cultural differences as a valuable asset. These organizations tended to "incorporate employees' perspectives into the main work of the organization, and to enhance work by rethinking primary tasks and redefining markets, products, strategies, missions, business practices, and even cultures. Such companies are using the learning-and-effectiveness paradigm for managing diversity and, by doing so, are tapping diversity's true benefits."[34]

There are eight preconditions for making a paradigm shift.

1. Leaders appreciate the perspectives and approaches of a diverse workforce and value the diversity of opinions.
2. Leaders acknowledge that with this diversity of perspective and approaches comes conflict and learning opportunities.
3. The culture of the organization reflects high standards of performance from each employee.
4. With high standards of performance comes the need for the organization to continuously inspire the personal development of all employees, and brings out each employee's full potential.
5. The organizational culture must encourage openness through a high tolerance for differences of opinion. The organization understands the value of organizational learning that comes out of conflict.
6. All workers must feel valued by the organization. Workers must feel empowered and committed to the organization to feel comfortable in taking full advantage of their resourcefulness to enhance their job performance.
7. The mission of the organization must not only be well articulated and widely understood, but it must also be followed by each individual in the organization and enforced by all leadership. This organization understands that hypocrisy has severely negative consequences for employee performance and retention.
8. This organization must have a structure that is egalitarian and non-bureaucratic, but still gets things done. At the same time, it promotes an exchange of ideas and welcomes constructive challenges to the status quo.

## A MICROSYSTEMIC PERSPECTIVE

Globalization has prompted domestic business to seek diverse partners abroad, sometimes as part of the process of "de-verticalizing" an organization in which manufacturing is left to others.[35] Likewise, international competition is another powerful force behind the diverse work culture. Thus, the firm must (a) seek workers, regardless of gender, race, or ethnic origin, who possess these core competencies; (b) create a work community in which these high performers freely exchange information and knowledge about optimum work practices, and (c) share collective knowledge to keep ahead of competition.[36]

Exhibit 6.4 provides monitoring activities that global organizational leaders can utilize to effectively assist the improvement of performance for all employees. Exhibit 6.5 provides knowledge, skills, and abilities that all individuals can learn to help improve their own performance when working with individuals who are of a different culture than themselves.

## Diversity and Work Team Performance

We know that diversity management is directly linked to team functioning, and can either improve or upset team performance.[37] As organizations rely on teams to accomplish a vast amount of tasks, the question of how teams should be composed and managed has come under greater scrutiny.[38] The composition of teams should take into account the salience of diversity in a team, and the levels of interdependence and longevity that a team will have to deal with,[39] along with the reward structure associated with team output. For example, in a recent research Homan et al.[40] found that a high degree of diversity in both high-performing and low-performing teams influenced performance. It was also found that the reward structure greatly influenced the highest performing teams, while the teams in which diversity was most salient and had the lowest level of openness, also were the lowest performing teams.

---

### EXHIBIT 6.4

### EXAMPLES OF INDICATORS THAT COMPANIES CAN USE TO MONITOR EMPLOYEE PERFORMANCE

---

- ■ The implementation of employee surveys to evaluate employee attitudes and degrees of satisfaction and identify areas in need of improvement.
- ■ Ongoing discussions with employee networks and their resource groups.
- ■ The use of workforce profiling to summarize nationalities, religions, gender, languages, and age to understand demographics and determine where there might be underrepresentation.
- ■ Setting up a database of employee skills to monitor employee development and progression.
- ■ Providing for diverse perspectives in standard business reviews, and provisions for equal pay evaluations.

continued

EXHIBIT 6.4

■ Examining the complaints registered with regard to bullying, harassment and the nature of which, the speed by which, and how solutions are found.

■ Examining business costs due to illness and court hearings.

■ Monitoring employee responses to exit interviews and organizing comments by gender and ethnicity to determine if there are patterns.

Adapted from: European Commission. "The Business Case for Diversity: Good Practices in the Workplace." Luxembourg: Office for Official Publications of the European Communities, 2005, 62 pp. Retrieved April 14, 2010 from http://ec.europa.eu/social/BlobServlet?docId=1428&langId=en

EXHIBIT 6.5

SOME KEY INDIVIDUAL COMPETENCIES

Barrett encourages individuals and teams who are working within the global arena to cultivate the following competencies. Some of which are learned through life experiences, others through education and training, yet most can be developed with enough concerted effort.

*Knowledge to Cultivate*

■ Learn about other nations' histories, cultures, national systems, values, customs, and the many ethnic groups that live within these other nations.

■ Learn how different systems, organizations, groups, and individuals discover how to work together through understanding change management practices and philosophies.

■ Learn about group development and group dynamics to understand how groups interact.

■ Learn how to simultaneously understand how the macrolevel (the nation, the organization) and more microlevels (the group, the individual) of interaction are cocreated.

*Abilities to Cultivate*

■ Learn how to be at ease with the unfamiliar.

■ Learn how to think like people who are remarkably different from the self. This helps discourage ethnocentrism.

■ Learn how to *learn*, and be open to continuous learning and to rapidly adapting.

- Learn how to cultivate meaningful relationships, based upon respect and trust, with people who are very different from the self, both culturally and personally.
- Learn how to manage one's stress, and learn to see difficulties as a part of an experience and as opportunities to *learn*.
- Learn to be aware of one's self; learn to accept feedback, both positive and negative.

Adapted from: Barrett, G. "Cultivating Global Teams: Diversity Management Square (DM²)," *Borderless Business, Managing the Far-Flung Enterprise*, Mann, C. and Gotz, K. (eds.). Westport, CN: Praeger, 2006, pp. 275-294.

Furthermore, the degree to which team members' need for cognitive stimulation also impacts diverse teams' performance. In a recent study, team members' need for cognition[41] was researched in a study of 83 teams from eight organizations. The researchers determined that two types of diversity, age and education, were positively correlated to team identification. In this research, team performance increased when the teams' need for cognition was high. The implications of this research are that the "…need for cognition…is a more specific variable that can be more easily linked to the demands entailed by diverse teams performing knowledge-based tasks, but also lends itself well to drawing managerial implications. Need for cognition represents a staple, but not invariant, intrinsic motivation to process a wide range of information."[42]

Improving the performance of individuals and teams within organizations should be a company-wide initiative. This ought to be an ongoing process that is integrated throughout the corporate system. One way to impart corporate initiatives and expectations of manager and employee behavior is through training.

## Cross-Cultural and Diversity Training

While the leadership must also approach diversity from a macrosystemic perspective, all employees must be made aware of company-wide efforts to leverage employee potential through the microsystemic efforts of enforced behavior and consistency. Pedagogically well-rounded training programs should include the following components:

- A cultural general section
- A section that emphasizes mastering cross-cultural communication
- A section that teaches cultural self-awareness
- A section that has cultural specifics
- A section that teaches how to resolve conflict

■ A section that focuses on developing cross-cultural skills
■ A section that addresses specific (and current) employee-requested concerns, such as "I have a meeting with a manager from Russia, how do I market our product in their culture?" or "How do I improve my customer service skills when interacting with customers from Brazil?"

Nevertheless, if employees are subject to cross-cultural or diversity training that is mere "lip service," while at the same time these employees are experiencing negative micromessages that insinuate subtle discrimination in the workplace, then all training efforts are in vain.[43] When negative micromessages are focused on employees who are of specific ethnic backgrounds, and these messages are allowed to fester in the workplace, then the end result is a workplace where certain employees cannot work to their full potential.

Young wrote about the impact of "small" communicated messages on the entire organization.[44] From a 10-min conversation, he estimated that two people can send from 40 to 120 micromessages to each other. Though small isolated messages might not have a significant effect, continuously repeated micromessages do. "Negative micromessages, 'micro-inequities,' erode organizations. They are a cumulative pattern of subtle, semiconscious, devaluing messages, which discourage and impair performance, possibly leading to damaged self-esteem and withdrawal. For example, micro-inequities can occur within a team when a manager or a colleague communicates different messages to team members, often linked to differences between them."[45] Within the organization, one challenge that companies face is encouraging peak performance from every employee.

The following are results of a study that researched the negative effects of organizational communicated messages on team members and on employees' performance.

## Microorganizational Communication: The Impact of Mixed Messages

Moran conducted a study that looked at a *Fortune 100* company's diversity training from the perspective of expressed employee needs determined from focus group data.[46] It was found that this organization does have some characteristics determined to be within the first two paradigms identified by Thomas and Ely.[47] The study analyzed focus group data from four different ethnic groups regarding their organizational experiences in the company of their managers, mentors, and team members. It also looked at employees' perceived ability to progress and utilize their potential, all as related to organizational diversity. The second aspect of this study was a comparative look at employee-expressed needs regarding diversity in the organization (determined through focus groups) and the yearly, strictly adhered-to diversity training offered to, and required of, employees. Although this company has been consistently ranked in the top 25 of companies that are deemed to highly value diversity, the results of the study have shown otherwise. The findings were as follows:

- Employees had specific requests for the company to address precise issues around employee relations, mentor relationships, team leader communications, customer service strategies, and team interaction. Employees believed the company ignored these requests and did not properly address them.
- This company endorsed a "diversity training" that was rigid in form and practice. Diversity trainers were required to follow word for word, page by page, an 8-h training session, which employees were required to attend yearly.
- The content of the training encompassed American legal reasons why diversity is required of this company, why prejudice and stereotypes are 'bad' and specific activities that enforced political correctness in the workplace.
- Employees had the genuine desire to learn concrete strategies to improve their productivity within their culturally diverse teams, international customer relations, and improving mentor/manager to employee relationships. This was not addressed nor recognized by the diversity training offered by this company.
- By the same token, the leadership was striving for and had accomplished excellent outside recognition of their diversity efforts. The result was that employees found the training and organizational system practiced by this company to be wholly contradictory to the recognition and rewards endowed on the company for its diversity efforts.
- As this company operates through the custom of team management, a phenomenon emerged that was found to be explained by focus groups and diversity training. A majority of the focus group members, who were employees of color, expressed an overwhelming experience of being disconnected from their mentors and were unable to succeed to their potential. Likewise, work group and team member relationships were strained as employees were unable to effectively work together, for their differences created more conflict than harmony. Negative micro-communications had a profound effect on these employees, resulting in a communication breakdown cycle that had the likely results of inferior team performance and substandard employee productivity.[48]

In the Industrial Age, much emphasis was placed on loyalty to the organization, and many employees stayed with the same department or work unit throughout their career. As the old system disappears, the new work culture calls for dynamic, flexible, and responsible adults committed to personal and professional excellence. In the diverse work environment previously described, loyalty is now transferred from the organization to the work team and to individual career enhancement. We recommend that leadership enforce a diversity mission that is consistently acted upon throughout the organization. It must be inescapable for the organization's leaders, and for the lower-level managers to the highest level executive. All employees must be able to see and experience this enforcement.

## EMPOWERING WORKERS

The concept of empowerment refers to altering management style and transforming organizational arrangements from hierarchical to more participatory, sharing authority and responsibility with workers in a variety of ways. To empower means that leaders, be they heads of organizations, groups, or families, give individual members more freedom to act and therefore have more control over their own lives. Inclusion, rather than exclusion, particularly with regard to women and minorities, becomes the organizational norm based on the competence of the individual. This approach is more open and decentralized.

This form of team management is spreading across Asia and Europe. The Japanese, who are culturally group-oriented, have been slow to empower women and minorities. Meanwhile, in some countries in Asia and Eastern Europe, empowerment is manifesting itself in political restructuring from authoritarianism to democracy and free enterprise, in which managers are freed from government or party controls and are beginning to involve their coworkers in the process of reshaping factories, cooperatives, and businesses. As globalization bridges the gap between national economies and peoples, empowerment does the same between management and labor.

Kouzes and Posner state that there is one clear and consistent message about empowerment: "feeling powerful—literally feeling "able"—comes from a deep sense of being in control of our own lives."[49] When we feel we can determine our destiny, and we have the assurance that the resources and individuals needed to support us are available, we can persist in our efforts. Conversely, when an individual is controlled by others, he or she may comply but not excel. Leadership is enhancing the individual's self-confidence and personal effectiveness. Kouzes and Posner(ibid) have identified five fundamental strategies for empowering others.

1. *Ensure self-leadership by putting people in control of their lives.* When leaders share power and control with others, they demonstrate trust and respect in others' abilities. They, in essence, make a covenant with them that is reciprocal and mutually beneficial. Individuals who can influence their leaders are more attached to them and committed to the give-and-take of the shared power of their responsibilities.
2. *Provide choice.* Providing individuals with options and discretion in the day-to-day operation of their jobs increases creativity and flexibility as one is freed from the standard set of rules and procedures. Jobs that are broadly designed and defined encourage this. Choice without skill can leave many employees overwhelmed.

3. *Develop competence.* Leaders must invest in developing individuals' skills and competencies. Giving employees opportunities to grow in their area of expertise, as well as in general business knowledge, enables them to act in the best interest of the corporation and the customer.

4. *Assign critical tasks.* Critical problems in an organization are usually addressed by those who have the most power. However, in innovative corporations like Chaparral Steel, research and development, for example, is brought to the factory floor. Empowerment encourages involvement and responsibility regarding tasks that employees can own and make excellent critical judgments about.

5. *Offer visible support.* Leaders who want to empower are highly visible and make conscientious efforts to have employees gain recognition and validation. Making connections and building strong networks and relationships is empowering. A leader should introduce employees to others in the corporation or community who may help them along their career path as well. Individuals take responsibility for their own career development, while leaders create a work environment that encourages others to achieve their human potential.

Employees who feel powerless often hoard whatever shreds of power they possess, reinforcing the organizational cultures that are often hierarchical and bureaucratic. Leaders who share power help to build profound trust and shared responsibility. Employees view improvements and communication as a two-way street, with the leader being as influenced by his or her workforce as the workforce is by management. Each is committed to effectively doing their part.

With a multicultural workforce and customer base, leadership must provide the vision, motivation, and reasons for commitment. For contemporary organizations and their workers, knowledge and innovation lead to global marketplace power. To that end, we hope that we have shared some constructive information about how to transform organizational systems into structures that value diverse personnel for their competency rather than establishing barriers based on race, gender, or handicaps.

## CONCLUSIONS

Modern psychology has demonstrated repeatedly that stimulus-response models are inaccurate representations of human behavior. Insofar as the same stimulus is interpreted differently by different individuals or groups, beliefs matter. The identity of individuals and groups, in part, shapes how they see the world; the way people see the world shapes how and when they perceive threat, as well as how they formulate their goals, assess constraints, process information, and choose strategies. Individuals are not passive receptors of environmental stimuli, but they actively construct representations of their environment.[50]

Diversity of all kinds has always been a significant feature of all societies. However, diversity has been addressed in the past and today in our globally interconnected world, and it cannot be ignored or pushed to the side. In culturally diverse societies and organizations, it is imperative that leadership expects that all individuals learn to value diversity. The challenge that remains is enforcing this expectation through macro- and microsystemic changes into true, consistent action. The following statements about diversity are a good summary[51]:

1. People who are part of the minority culture do not want to be tolerated. Neither do other employees. They want to be valued. If they are valued, they can be more effective.[52]
2. The "inventor" of racism is not present in any society or organization, but we all need to learn how to work with one another more effectively.
3. When power is shared, people are able to devote tremendous energy to the work at hand.
4. Human beings are the most important asset of any organization. They are the only sustainable competitive advantage for the future.
5. There is a great deal of information on the subject of human diversity, and much of it is overlapping.
6. There is no simple model for effective cross-cultural and diversity training. However, it should address the specific needs of the organization's employees. Prewritten generic training programs are generally ineffective.
7. Diversity initiatives should be system-wide but with enough flexibility to adjust to specific regional needs. If effective, they impact positively on an organization's productivity.
8. Diversity initiatives should focus on information, management, processes, and results.
9. Diversity initiatives are not a replacement for Equal Employment Opportunity (EEO) or Affirmative Action (AA).
10. Diversity is to be cherished, for it enriches life and advances the actualization of human potential.

## MIND STRETCHING

1. In what ways does a multicultural workforce impact an organization's productivity?
2. Why is it important to take a systems approach to improve employee performance within global organizations?
3. Provide an example of a cross-cultural organizational experience that you were involved in that was difficult for you. How was it difficult? How would you improve the situation?
4. Do you believe your organization or educational institution values diversity? Explain why or why not, and give specific examples.

# REFERENCES

1. Ozbilgin, M. and Tatli, A. *Global Diversity Management: An Evidence-Based Approach*. Houndsmills, Basingstoke, Hampshire, UK: Palgrave MacMillan, 2008, p. 18.

2. Ozbilgin, M. "Global Diversity Management,"pp. 395–396 *The Handbook of Cross-Cultural Management Research*, Smith, P., Peterson, M., and Thomas, D. (eds.). Los Angeles, CA: Sage Publications, 2008, pp. 379–380.

3. Kearney, E., Gebert, D., and Voelpel, S. "When and How Diversity Benefits Teams: The Importance of Team Members' Need for Cognition," *The Academy of Management Journal*, Vol. 52, No. 3: 2009, pp. 581–598.

4. American Express Financial Advisors. "Diversity: Report to Benchmark Partners," *Cultural Diversity Sourcebook*, Abramms, B. and Simons, G. F. (eds.). Amherst, MA: ODT, 1996.

5. Ibid.

6. Parfit, M. "Human Migration," *National Geographic*, October 1998, pp. 11–14.

7. "A Global Pursuit of Happiness," World Report, *Los Angeles Times*, October 1 1991, H13.

8. http://www.refugeesinternational.org/who-we-are.

9. http://www.iom.int/jahia/Jahia/global-estimates-and-trends.

10. Stalker, P. "The Work of Strangers: A Survey of International Migration." *Aids in Place of Migration*, Bohning, W. R. and Schloeter, M. L. (eds.). Geneva, Switzerland: International Labour Office, 1994 (Also available from ILO Publications Center, 49 Sheridan Ave., Albany, NY 12210, USA.)

11. Gurr, T. R. "Minorities, Nationalists, and Ethnopolitical Conflict." *Managing Global Chaos; Sources of and Responses to International Conflict*, Cocker, C. A., Hampson, F. O., and Aall, P. (eds.). Washington, DC: International Institute of Peace Press, 1999.

12. Taylor, D. M. and Moghaddam, F. M. *Theories of Intergroup Relations; International Social Psychological Perspectives*, Second edition. Westport, CN: Praeger, 1994, pp. 197–198.

13. Crocker, C. A., Hampson, F. O., and Aall, P. (eds.). *Managing Global Chaos: Sources of and Responses to International Conflict*. Washington, DC: United States Institute of Peace Press, 1999.

14. Bartos, O. and Wehr, P. *Using Conflict Theory*. Cambridge, UK: Cambridge University Press, 2002.

15. "Course Teaches Conflict Solving." Published 2006/04/04, http://news.bbc.co.uk/2/hi/uk_news/scotland/4876028.stm.

16. Howell, J. and Costley, D. *Understanding Behaviors for Effective Leadership*. Upper Saddle River, NJ: Pearson Prentice Hall, 2006.

17. Ibid.

18. Ibid.

19. Bartos, O. and Wehr, P. *Using Conflict Theory*. Cambridge, UK: Cambridge University Press, 2002.

20. Thomas, R. R. "Diversity Is a Business Issue," *Cultural Diversity Fieldbook*, Simons, G., Abramms, B., Hopkins, L. A., and Johnson, D. J. (eds.). Princeton, NJ: Peterson's/Pacesetter Books, 1996, pp. 197–198.

21. Evanoff, R. "Universalist, Relativist, and Constructivist Approaches to Intercultural Ethics," *International Journal of Intercultural Relations*, Vol. 28, 2004, pp. 439–458.

22. Ibid.

23. Gardenswartz, L. and Rowe, A. *Managing Diversity—A Complete Desk Reference*. San Diego, CA: Pfeiffer & Company, 1993. The same publisher offers numerous diversity games, profiles, and training activities.

24. Harrison, D., Price, K., and Bell, M. "Beyond Relational Demography: Time and the Effects of Surface- and Deep-Level Diversity on Work Group Cohesion," *The Academy of Management Journal*, Vol. 41, No. 1, 1998, pp. 96–107.

25. Ibid.

26. Ozbilgin, M. "Global Diversity Management," *The Handbook of Cross-Cultural Management Research*, Smith, P, Peterson, M, and Thomas, D. (eds.). Los Angeles, CA: Sage Publications, 2008, pp. 379–396.

27. Nair, K. A. *Higher Standard of Leadership—Lessons from the Life of Gandhi*. San Francisco, CA: Berrett-Koehler Publishers, 1994.

28. Simons, G. *EuroDiversity—A Business Guide to Managing Differences*. Burlington, MA: Butterworth-Heinemann/Elsevier, 2002, pp. xviii, 1, 2.

29. "Cultural Diversity Market Study," *Luxembourg: Pricewaterhouse Coopers*, Draft Final Report, February 14, 2001.

30. Ibid., p. 2.

31. Ozbilgin, M. "Global Diversity Management," *The Handbook of Cross-Cultural Management Research*, Smith, P., Peterson, M., and Thomas, D. (eds.). Los Angeles, CA: Sage Publications, 2008, pp. 379–396.

32. Willman, J. "In European Countries, there are Three or Four Competitors. In the U.S., there are 10 or 20," *Financial Times*, February 25, 2003.

33. Thomas, D. A. and Ely, R. J. "Making Difference Matter, New Parading for Managing Diversity," *Harvard Business Review on Women in Business*. Boston, MA: Harvard Business School Publishing Corporation, 2005, pp. 125–158. See also Moran, S. "Comprehensive Evaluation of a Diversity Training Initiative in a Global Company," Unpublished master's Thesis, Arizona State University, May 2000.

34. Ibid., p. 40.

35. Pueik, V., Tichy, N. M., and Barnett, C. K. *Globalizing Management: Creating and Leading the Competitive Organization*. New York: John Wiley & Sons, 1993. See also CPC/Rand Report, *Developing the Global Work Force*. Bethlehem, PA: CPC I, 1994.

36. Prahalad, C. K. and Hamel, G. *Competing for the Future: Breakthrough Strategies for Seizing Control of Your Industry and Creating the Markets of Tomorrow*. Boston, MA: Harvard Business School Press, 1994.

37. Homan, A., Hollenbeck, J., Humphrey, S., Knippenberg, D., Ilgen, D., and Van Kleef, G. "Facing Differences with an Open Mind: Openness to Experience, Salience of Intragroup Differences, and Performance of Diverse Work Groups," *Academy of Management Journal*, Vol. 51, No. 6, 2008, pp. 1204–1222.

38. Kearney, E., Gebert, D., and Voehpel, S. "When and How Diversity Benefits Teams: The Importance of Team Members' Need for Cognition," *The Academy Of Management Journal*, Vol. 52, No. 3, 2009, pp. 581–598.

39. Joshi, A. and Roh, H. "The Role of Context in Work Team Diversity Research: A Meta-Analytic Review," *The Academy of Management Journal*, Vol. 52, No. 3, 2009, pp. 533–627.

40. Homan, A., Hollenbeck, J., Humphrey, S., Knippenberg, D., Ilgen, D. and Van Kleef, G. "Facing Differences with an Open Mind: Openness to Experience, Salience of Intragroup Differences, and Performance of Diverse Work Groups," *Academy of Management Journal*, Vol. 51, No. 6, 2008, pp. 1204–1222.

41. Kearney, E., Gebert, D., and Voehpel, S. "When and How Diversity Benefits Teams: The Importance of Team Members' Need for Cognition," *The Academy of Management Journal*, Vol. 52, No. 3, 2009, pp. 581–598.

42. Ibid., p. 595.

43. Moran, S. "Comprehensive Evaluation of a Diversity Training Initiative in a Global Company," Arizona State University Unpublished master's Thesis, May 2000.

44. Young, S. "Micro-Inequities: The Power of Small," *Workforce Diversity Reader*, Vol. 1, No. 1, Winter 2003, pp. 88–93.

45. Ibid., p. 89.

46. Moran, S. "Comprehensive Evaluation of a Diversity Training Initiative in a Global Company," Unpublished master's Thesis, Arizona State University, May 2000.

47. Thomas, D. A. and Ely, R. J. "Making Difference Matter, a New Parading for Managing Diversity," *Harvard Business Review on Women in Business*. Boston, MA: Harvard Business School Publishing Corporation, 2005, pp. 125–158.

48. Moran, S. "Comprehensive Evaluation of a Diversity Training Initiative in a Global Company," Unpublished master's Thesis, Arizona State University, May 2000.

49. Kouzes, J. M. and Posner, B. Z. *The Leadership Challenge*. San Francisco, CA: Jossey-Bass, 1995.

50. Stein, J. G. "Image, Identity, and Conflict Resolution." *Managing Global Chaos; Sources of and Responses to International Conflict*, Crocker, C. A., Hampson, F. O., and Aall, P. (eds.). Washington, DC: United States Institute of Peace Press, 1999.

51. Moran, R. T. and Stockton, J. L. "Diversity Training, What Works: Training and Development Practices," *American Society for Training and Development*. 1997.

52. Bassi, L. J. and Russ-Eft, D. (eds.). *What Works: Assessment, Development, and Measurement*. Alexandria, VA: American Society for Training and Development, 1997.

# EFFECTIVE PERFORMANCE IN THE GLOBAL MARKETPLACE

During the last fifty years, leadership scholars have conducted more than 1,000 studies in an attempt to determine the definitive styles, characteristics, or personality traits of great leaders. <u>None</u> of the studies have produced a clear profile of an ideal leader.[1]

## LEARNING OBJECTIVES

This chapter offers some ideas and models on what we know about the skills and behavior of individuals who perform skillfully in today's global marketplace. We begin with three quotations:

Fifteen people are seated around the table, each representing one of our businesses in Asia-Pacific.... The outgoing president of Asia-Pacific formerly ran our business in South Africa. The new president comes from Australia. There are Americans at the table, an Australian, a New Zealander, and a Brit...and they're attending this business meeting in Beijing...home of one of our most recent joint ventures.[2]

We are considering opening an office in Dubai, and none of us know anything about that country.

A Global Executive

The most common reason that organizations do not have exceptional global leadership is a lack of commitment to the process of developing it.[3]

The implication of these quotations is that global leadership skills are essential for effective global performance. *Leadership* remains a hot topic among best-selling business books. Some world leaders share their insight into leadership and performance in a political context.

*Jimmy Carter*, 39th president of the United States, commented about leadership in conflict resolution: "All too often, conflicts and wars arise when we fail to consider the views of others or to communicate with them about differences between us."[4] The Carter Center Principles for Peacemakers amplifies their vision of what a global leader should do, which provides useful guidance for corporate executives:

- Strive to have the international community and all sides in any conflict agree to the basic premise that military force should be used only as a last resort.
- Study the history and causes of the dispute thoroughly.
- Seek help from other mediators, especially those who know the region and are known and respected there.
- Be prepared to go back and forth between adversaries who cannot or will not confront each other.
- Be willing to deal with the key people in any dispute, even if they have been isolated or condemned by other parties or organizations.
- Insist that human rights be protected, that international law be honored.
- Tell the truth, even when it may not contribute to a quick agreement.
- Never despair, even when the situation seems hopeless.

*Mikhail Gorbachev*, former President of the Soviet Union, observed this on leadership: "The world is becoming ever more integrated.... The real leaders of today are capable of integrating the interests of their countries and peoples into the interests of the entire world community....[A] leader combines a political and a moral authority."[5]

*Desmond Tutu*, the South-African Archbishop who received the Nobel Peace Prize in 1984, writes: "The authentic leader has a solidarity with those he or she is leading.... The good leader is one who is affirming of others, nurturing their best selves, coaxing them to become the best they are capable of becoming...[has] the capacity to read the signs of the times...knows when to make concessions."[6]

*L. D. Schaeffer*, when CEO of Blue Cross of California, described leadership not as a "...state, but as a journey, requiring different styles that are determined in part by the demands of the marketplace."[7]

## The Challenge of Measuring Effectiveness and Predicting Global Performance

In an earlier survey[8] of over 100 executives of global organizations, we found that along a continuum of 0-100%, over 60% agreed that "global managers are made, not born" and 72% agreed "in global organizations, a new kind of leader is required."

Many business school professors and executives of global organizations know what the key positions are in organizations, but most are less successful in predicting who will be a star performer in that position. And when star performers are identified, they find it difficult to articulate what makes them the best.

Wilson Learning Corporation[9] has developed a global competency model based on an examination of the literature and interviews with organizations in the airline, high-tech, telecommunications, and consumer goods industries. They have identified the following themes related to global leadership:

- Understanding the business from a global perspective
- Assimilating and acting on large amounts of complex or ambiguous information
- Driving change based on global strategy
- Commitment to learning
- Effective cross-cultural communication
- Establishing personal connections readily across cultural boundaries

Moran and Riesenberger[10] developed a straightforward model of globalization related to performance based on research and experience. The framework is presented in Exhibit 7.1

External factors such as the economies of scale, global sourcing opportunities, exchange rate exposure risks, and other factors are presenting increasing opportunities for organizations to become global.

As a result, the vision, mission, and structure of the organization change. However, to benefit from organizations becoming "global," new and different leadership competencies are required. When the competencies possessed by the leaders are marginal, the benefits are minimal. When leaders possess these competencies to a high degree, the benefits are significant. "Making It Overseas," a recent *Harvard Business Review* article,[11] suggests similar skills continue to be required today.

## EXHIBIT 7.1
### MORAN/RIESENBERGER FRAMEWORK

**External Forces**

| | | |
|---|---|---|
| ■ Economies of scale | ■ Economies of scale | ■ Economies of scale |
| ■ New and evolving markets | ■ New and evolving markets | ■ New and evolving markets |
| ■ Global sourcing opportunities | ■ Global sourcing opportunities | ■ Global sourcing opportunities |
| ■ Reduced tariffs/ customs barriers and tax advantages in many countries | ■ Reduced tariffs/ customs barriers and tax advantages in many countries | ■ Reduced tariffs/ customs barriers and tax advantages in many countries |
| ↓ | ↓                    ↑ | ↑ |

## EXHIBIT 7.1
## MORAN/RIESENBERGER FRAMEWORK (CONTINUED)

### GLOBALIZATION

| Vision | Strategy | Structure | |
|---|---|---|---|
| ↑ | ↑ | ↑ | ↑ ↑ |

Competencies required to make it work

| Attitudes | Leadership | Interaction Leadership | Cultural Leadership |
|---|---|---|---|
| ■ Possesses a global mindset<br>■ Has the ability to work as equals with persons of diverse background<br>■ Has a long-term orientation | ■ Facilitates organizational change<br>■ Creates learning systems<br>■ Motivates employees to excellence | ■ Negotiates and approaches conflicts in a collaborative mode<br>■ Manages skillfully the foreign deployment cycle<br>■ Leads and participates effectively in multicultural teams | ■ Understands their own culture values and assumptions<br>■ Accurately profiles organizational culture and national culture of others<br>■ Avoids cultural mistakes and behaves in a manner that demonstrates knowledge and respect for the way of conducting business in other countries |

*Source*: Moran, R. T. and Riesenberger, J. R. *The Global Challenge: Building the New Worldwide Enterprise*. London: McGraw-Hill Book Co., 1994.

## DESCRIPTION OF COMPETENCIES

## *Leadership Attitudes*

### Possess a Global Mindset

In the play *South Pacific*, Rogers and Hammerstein wrote:[12]

> You've got to be taught to hate and fear
> You've got to be taught from year to year,

It's got to be drummed in your dear little ear,
You've got to be carefully taught.
You've got to be taught to be afraid
of peoples whose eyes are oddly made,
And people whose skin is a different shade,
You've got to be carefully taught.
You've got to be taught before it's too late,
Before you are six or seven or eight,
To hate all the people your relatives hate,
You've got to be carefully taught.
You've got to be carefully taught.

The lyrics state eloquently what we have known for a long time: namely, a fundamental vehicle for learning has always been, and will continue to be, other humans. At birth, infants are completely dependent on others for survival. In maturing and throughout the socialization process, children learn that the gratification of needs is, to a large extent, dependent on demonstrating "appropriate" behavior. In groups, whether family, business, or other, individual social needs become suggestive to the influence of others, especially those in authority.

Attitudes are learned, and therefore can be unlearned. A *global mindset* is an attitude; it is not knowledge or information. We learn to be ethnocentric, and we can learn to be global in our perspective.

## Global Mindsets

Stephen Rhinesmith postulates that a "global mindset" is a requirement of a global leader who will guide institutions and organizations into the future. He defines a mindset as:

> a predisposition to see the world in a particular way that sets boundaries and provides explanations for why things are the way they are, while at the same time establishing guidance for ways in which we should behave. In other words, a mindset is a filter through which we look at the world.[13]

Rhinesmith states that people with global mindsets approach the world in a number of particular ways. Specifically, they:

1. Look for the "big picture"; that is, they look for multiple possibilities for any event or occurrence—they aren't satisfied with the obvious.
2. Understand that the rapidly changing, interdependent world in which we are living is indeed complex, and that working in these environments where conflicts need to be managed skillfully is the norm rather than the exception.
3. Are "process"-oriented; in our experience, this is the most important dimension, and the one that is most lacking in individuals

who are not globally oriented. Many individuals are unable to understand or are unwilling to learn to "process"; namely, to reflect on the "how" as opposed to the "what."

4. Consider diversity as a resource and know how to work effectively in multicultural teams; an ability to collaborate instead of competing is also integral to the person with a global mindset.
5. Are not uncomfortable with change or ambiguity.
6. Are open to new experiences.

With globalization, contact between persons from different cultures increases. What happens when this occurs? Do individuals become more global or more ethnocentric?

Following a review of the literature on intergroup contact, Amir concluded that the direction of attitude change, following contact with people who are different, depends largely on the conditions under which the contact has taken place.[14] He indicates that there are "favorable" conditions, which reduce prejudice, and "unfavorable" ones, which may increase prejudice.

The favorable condition of "equal status" as a factor in reducing prejudice was reported by Allport.[15] He pointed out that, for contact between groups to be an element in reducing prejudice, it must be based on "equal status contact between majority and minority groups in the pursuit of common goals." Organizations that are globalizing must have common goals.

## Works as an Equal with Persons from Diverse Backgrounds

In Chapters 5 and 6, we have emphasised the importance of this leadership skill. The ascendance of people from minority groups to leadership positions offers the organization an opportunity to explore new ideas and approaches. Companies that find new, innovative approaches are the ones that are experiencing success today—not the ones that have maintained the status quo. Tom Peters, coauthor of *In Search of Excellence*, declares: "Gone are the days of women succeeding by learning to play men's games. Instead, the time has come for men on the move to learn to play women's games."[16]

## Has a Long-Term Orientation

There are many reasons why companies have not been successful in competing in the global marketplace. One of these reasons is "short-termism." Dick Ferry, president and cofounder of Korn/Ferry, addresses this issue:

Corporate America may talk, on an intellectual level, about what it'll take to succeed in the twenty-first century, but when it gets right down to decision-making, all that matters is the next quarterly earnings report.

That's what's driving much of the system. With that mindset, everything else becomes secondary to the ability to deliver the next quarterly earnings push-up. We're on a treadmill. The reward system in this country is geared to the short term."[17]

Why do our foreign competitors take a long view? In Germany and Japan, "cross-ownership'" is the norm. *Stakeholders* (customers, suppliers, and banks) are closely involved in the operations of the business.

The short-term view also has other implications. For total quality management to work, organizations must take a long-term view and exercise patience. Few dispute the importance of total quality. However, several recent studies on total quality management have questioned the short-term "quick-fix" mentality of individuals who do not recognize the need for long-term approaches in the implementation of total quality management.

The orientation to short-termism is almost an addiction, and is present in most corporations. Long-term orientation is a critical competency to make globalization work.

## The Global Leader Facilitating Change

Most global leaders believe managing organization change is a serious challenge. This was true in the 1990s when the *Harvard Business Review* World Leadership Survey of approximately 12,000 global managers from 25 countries[18] concluded that change is a part of corporate life.

Percy Barnevik, the former CEO of Asea Brown Boveri (ABB) Ltd., puts it this way:

> I try to make people accept that change is a way of life. I often got the question from Swiss and Germans: 'Mr. Barnevik, aren't you happy now? Can't we relax a bit?' They see new targets as a threat or an inconvenience. But I say, you must get used to the idea that we are changing all the time.[19]

Why do most change initiatives fail to reach their full potential? Steve Gambrell and Craig Stevens suggest there are three phases of organizational change: what occurs before, during, and after changes.[20] They believe that for the change process to be successful, an organized plan is necessary throughout each phase of the change process. Part of this action plan includes understanding motivations for resistance, differences in employee/management perceptions, and the importance of ongoing communication.

Gambrell and Stevens state that to maximize the chances of positive outcome, it is important that the following skills of leaders are developed:

■ Unbiased open-mindedness
■ Good strategic planning abilities

■ Good team-building skills
■ Effective communications skills

Global leaders need these skills to effectively facilitate and lead organizational change.

## Creates Learning Systems

Peter Senge said it best in his book, *The Fifth Discipline*: "The organizations that will truly excel in the future will be the organizations that discover how to tap people's commitment and capacity to learn at *all* levels in an organization."[21]

The following is a case study of a nonlearning organization in a global context.[22]

---

### CASE STUDY

Several long conversations I've had recently with a European executive have made me acutely aware of two major cross-cultural organizational problems. The first is the inability of many companies to make use of new expertise developed by individuals in the firm. The second is the rather serious reentry problems experienced by many expatriates following a successful international experience.

My friend is 51 years old. He has worked for one of the largest chemical companies in Europe for more than 25 years. He joined the company as a young chemical engineer, completed his apprenticeship, and accepted a position as a sales representative in Australia. He lived there until his return to Europe 5 years ago.

After his first 5 years in Australia, he was appointed president of a small subsidiary. Though the European parent company has a policy of job rotation every 3 years, no replacements were available, so he was happy to stay on in Australia working for various subsidiary companies.

By the end of his Australian stint, he was a member of many of the most important boards in the country. By all obvious measures, he was a success. The companies he managed flourished, and several of them were sold at considerable profit. Yet during his long spell in Australia, he never once had a performance appraisal, and never knew clearly how his work was viewed by his superiors in Europe.

When he was eventually replaced in Australia by another European, he was brought home and given a job that he has found to be neither satisfying nor challenging. He has specific responsibilities related to overseas assignments in one country. Ironically, his immediate boss has never lived outside his native country.

continued

The executive's case highlights the tragic inability of many large organizations to handle their people well, and to integrate their individual learning into the organization. What is most surprising to me is the executive's claim that since his return, he has never been consulted about Australia by anyone in his company.

He knows the country well—his company has large investments there, not all of them going so well today. He believes that his replacement is not doing well, and that two or three of the Europeans assigned there should be reassigned. The trouble is that all are "being propped up," he says, by someone in the European headquarters.

But the real problem, as this case illustrates, is what to do with these people when they eventually return to Europe or their home country.

In creating learning systems, the leader must be the teacher. Senge believes that "leaders of learning organizations must do more than just formulate strategies to exploit emerging trends. They must be able to help people understand the systemic forces that shape change. It is not enough to intuitively grasp these forces." Leaders must help others see the bigger picture, and cannot just impose their strategies and vision. Concurrently, and perhaps most importantly, leaders must "foster learning" continually for all employees.

### Motivates Employees to Excellence

George Land and Beth Jarman address the challenge of getting a large organization to pull its employees together to work toward a common goal.[23] They recommend following the principles of "Future Pull." The task will then become easier, and should result in greater trust and loyalty of the employees. Future Pull has several components:

1. *Know your purpose and vision.* A vision is the bigger picture. In other words, what is the company's ultimate goal and purpose for its employees? This should relate to the employees and not to the product.
2. *Commit to achieve your vision and purpose.* "Actions speak louder than words." The leader and members of top management must be committed to the vision, and must reinforce it on a daily basis with their actions.
3. *Abundance is nature's natural state.* When the vision is embraced and the employees have been empowered, it follows that the rewards will also be there.
4. *Make the world a better place by living according to shared values.* Team-building is almost always a key component. Expand the vision externally to customers—not just employees.

In global companies, the complexity of motivating employees to excellence is increased. To whom do they give their allegiance? Robert Reich asks, "Who is them?"[24] He defines "them" as the growing group of global managers. Their allegiance is not to any particular nation or culture, but to the success of their company. Motivating employees to excellence is a task of the leaders of global organizations.

## Negotiates and Approaches Conflicts in a Collaborative Mode

To make globalization work, we need to negotiate and approach conflicts collaboratively. Skillful international business negotiators *know* more than, and *behave* (act) differently from, nonskillful negotiators. This leadership skill is covered in detail in Chapter 3.

## Manages Skillfully the Foreign Deployment Cycle

The necessity to prepare for global assignments and a successful global deployment process is demonstrated by research on Canadian technical advisors by the Canadian International Development Agency. The book, *Cross-Cultural Effectiveness*,[25] found an important interaction between overseas effectiveness and overseas satisfaction.

In terms of overseas effectiveness, the study found that 65% of the technical advisors were neither effective nor ineffective, 20% were highly effective, and 10%were very ineffective. However, no matter how effective or ineffective they were, 75% were satisfied, 10% were neutral, and 15% were highly dissatisfied with their assignments.

This competency is covered in detail in Chapter 8.

## Leads and Participates Effectively in Multicultural Teams

My worst experiences at Thunderbird were the project teams I had to participate in.

Recent Master of International Management Graduate

The teams I was a member of were the best learning experiences I've ever had.

Another Recent Master of International Management Graduate

Every morning in Africa, when a gazelle wakes up, it knows that it must run faster than the fastest lion or it will be killed. Every morning that a lion wakes up, it knows that it must run faster than the slowest gazelle or it will starve.

Moral: It doesn't matter whether you are a lion or a gazelle. When the sun comes up, you had better be running.

"High performance teams," "team work," "worldwide global product teams," and other words expressing similar ideas are commonplace in management literature today. Stories of teams producing remarkable accomplishments are well known. Well-functioning teams can increase productivity and creativity.

However, functioning skillfully on a team is a learned skill. We have covered aspects of effective teams in several chapters.

## Understands Their Own Culture, Values, and Assumptions

"Know thyself"

Socrates

Global managers from one country have to work and negotiate with their global counterparts regularly. A common requirement is that they must each be able to communicate effectively and work with individuals who have been socialized in a different cultural environment, and whose customs, values, lifestyles, beliefs, management practices, and other important aspects of their personal and professional lives are different.

A European executive during a personal conversation said, "I -can't think of any situation in my 25 years of international experience when international business was made easier because people from more than one country were participating." A global manager must be aware of the many beliefs and values that underlie his or her own country's business practices, management techniques, and strategies.

"The journey to authentic leadership begins with understanding the story of your life."[26] When the seventy-five members of the Stanford Graduate School of Business Advisory Council were asked to recommend the most important capability for leaders to develop, their answer was nearly unanimous: self-awareness.

## Accurately Profiles the Organizational Culture and National Culture of Others

Corporate culture is the way of life of an organization. The best recent book on the subject is John Kotter and James Heskett's *Corporate Culture and Performance*. From their recent studies of many large organizations, they conclude that:

1. Corporate culture can have a significant impact on a firm's long-term economic performance.
2. Corporate culture will probably be an even more important factor in determining the success or failure of firms in the next decade.
3. Corporate cultures that inhibit strong long-term financial performance are not rare; they develop easily, even in firms that are full of reasonable and intelligent people.
4. Although tough to change, corporate cultures can be made more performance-enhancing.[27]

Hofstede's research on aspects of national culture is covered in Chapter 1.

## Avoids Cultural Mistakes and Behaves in a Manner that Demonstrates Knowledge of and Respect for Other Countries

Many years ago Jack Condon and Fathi Yousef wrote:

> Many people believe that the language of gestures is universal. Many people believe that one picture is worth a thousand words, the implication being that what we see is ever so much clearer than what is said. Many people believe that communication means speaking, and that misunderstandings only occur with speaking. Many people believe that smiling and frowning and clapping are purely natural expressions. Many people believe that the world is flat.[28]

### Examples of cultural mistakes/cultural counts

In February 1977, U.S. President Jimmy Carter was in Mexico to "build bridges" and "mend fences." Mexico had recently discovered large amounts of oil. President Jose Lopez Portillo was the first speaker. "Let us seek only lasting solutions—good faith and fair play. Nothing that would make us lose the respect of our children," he said. On hearing Lopez Portillo's remarks, Carter didn't use his prepared speech, but chose to answer spontaneously. He said:

> We both have beautiful and interesting wives, and we both run several kilometers everyday. As a matter of fact, I told President Lopez Portillo that I first acquired my habit of running here in Mexico City. My first running course was from the Palace of Fine Arts to the Majestic Hotel where me and my family were staying. In the midst of the Folklorico performance, I discovered that I was afflicted with Montezuma's revenge.[29]

As it turned out, stating that he had Montezuma's revenge (diarrhea) was not funny at all. In light of what he wanted to accomplish—"building bridges"—the remark was entirely inappropriate.

When United Airlines bought the Asia-Pacific routes from Pan Am, John Zeeman, the executive vice-president for marketing and planning, acknowledged in a speech examples of the numerous cultural mistakes that United Airlines made and learned from:

- The map we inserted into our sales promotion brochure left out one of Japan's main islands.
- Our magazine ad campaign, "We Know the Orient," listed the names of Far Eastern countries below pictures of local coins. Unfortunately, the coins didn't match up with the countries.
- I leave to your imagination how Chinese businessmen felt taking off from Hong Kong during the inauguration of our concierge services

for first-class passengers. To mark the occasion, each concierge was proudly wearing a white carnation...a well-known oriental symbol of death.

■ Perhaps the most embarrassing mistake was our inflight magazine cover that showed an Australian actor, Paul Hogan, wandering through the Outback. The caption read, "Paul Hogan Camps It Up." Hogan's lawyer was kind enough to phone us long distance from Sydney to let us know that "camps it up" is Australian slang for "flaunts his homosexuality."[30]

U.S. baseball players in Japan also experience the difficulty of communication as related by Robert Whiting. The story is told about a U.S. player in Japan who was knocked down by the opposing pitcher of the Orions:

> Tony Solaita of the Nippon Ham Fighters paid a call on the Lions' catcher during pregame batting practice. The catcher was Japanese, so Solaita was forced to converse with him through the interpreter assigned to him by his employers.
> "Listen, you no good SOB," Solaita growled, "if you have a pitcher throw at my head again, I'll bleeping kill you!"
> The interpreter did not turn a hair. "Mr. Solaita asks that you please not throw at his head anymore," he translated. "It makes his wife and children worry."[31]

It is important to state loudly and clearly that it is our experience, supported by long discussions with many global managers, as well as research, that *not only American globals make mistakes; Japanese, French, German, Swedes, Chinese, Mexicans, and globals from all other countries also make cultural errors.*

## REUBEN'S GLOBAL SKILLS REQUIRED TO TRANSFER KNOWLEDGE

Ruben has identified the following skills as being associated with effective transferring of knowledge in a multicultural environment.[32] We shall refer to these skills as abilities. Most of them are common sense skills, but often not demonstrated by global leaders or supervisors of minority employees in one's own culture.

■ *Respect.* The ability to express respect for others is an important part of effective relations in every country. All people like to believe and feel that others respect them, their ideas, and their accomplishments. However, it is difficult to know how to communicate respect to persons from another culture. The following questions should be considered by people working in another culture with persons from that culture. What is the importance of age in communicating respect? What is the significance of a manner of speaking? Do you speak only when spoken to? What gestures express respect? What kind of eye contact expresses respect? What constitutes "personal questions" as an invasion of privacy and a lack of respect? These are only a few of the many questions that could be generated relating to the important question, "How do I demonstrate that I respect the people I am working with?"

■ *Tolerating Ambiguity*. This refers to the ability to react to new, different, and at times, unpredictable situations with little visible discomfort or irritation. Excessive discomfort often leads to frustration and hostility, which are not conducive to effective interpersonal relationships with persons from other cultures. Learning to manage the feelings associated with ambiguity is a skill associated with adaptation to a new environment and effectively working with managers who have a different set of values.

■ *Relating to People*. Many leaders, concerned with getting the job done, are overly concerned with the task side of their jobs. Transferring skills and knowledge to persons in another culture requires getting the job done, but in such a way that people feel they are a part of the completed project and have benefited from being involved. Too much concern for getting the job done and neglect of "people maintenance" can lead to failure in transferring skills.

■ *Being Nonjudgmental*. Most people do not like to feel judged by others in what they say and do without the opportunity of fully explaining themselves. The ability to withhold judgment and remain objective until one has enough information requires an understanding of the other's point of view, and is an important skill.

■ *Personalizing One's Observations*. As previously indicated, different people explain the world around them in different terms. The global leader should realize that his or her knowledge and perceptions may be valid only for him- or herself and not for the rest of the world. Thus, one would be able to personalize observations, be more tentative in conclusions, and demonstrate a communication competence showing that what is "right" or "true" in one culture is not "right" or "true" in another. As one author said, "this is my way, what is your way?"

■ *Empathy*. This is the ability to "put yourself in another's shoes." In this context, most people are attracted to and work well with leaders who seem to be able to understand things from their point of view.

■ *Persistence*. The global leader may not be successful at getting things done immediately, but with patience and perseverance, the task can be accomplished.

In the *Sage Handbook of Intercultural Competence*,[33] there are many additional contemporary and traditional theories and models of leadership and effective global performance.

## Global Entrepreneurs

Furthermore, in knowledge-based economies and industries that cross cultures, creativity is a critical factor for remaining on the leading edge of any business or field. The entrepreneurial spirit can manifest itself within existing world organizations through *intrapreneurs*. The entrepreneurial personality reflects creativity, risk-taking, self-confidence, optimism, venture commitment, high performance, and effective management of both change and resources.

The entrepreneur aims to control his or her own destiny; anticipates people and market needs; avoids excessive expenditures and bureaucracy; seeks greater freedom and rewards. Like innovators, entrepreneurs work for self-fulfillment by high performance. Backed by venture capitalists, such men and women are adventurers, inventors, and discoverers. Their strategic orientation is driven by the perceptions of opportunities that they are committed to seize. To control resources effectively and flexibly, they create a flat management structure with multidisciplinary project teams and multiple informal networks. Exhibit 7.2 contrasts their entrepreneurial mindset with the more staid manager or *trustee*.

### EXHIBIT 7.2
### CONTRAST IN ENTREPRENEUR'S MINDSET

| The Promoter | The Trustee |
|---|---|
| ■ Perceives opportunity. | ■ Controls current resources. |
| ■ Has short-term orientation. | ■ Has an evolutionary outlook. |
| ■ Makes minimal commitment of resources when decisions are made to pursue business opportunities. | ■ Makes maximal commitment of resources when decisions of resources when decisions are made to pursue business opportunities. |
| ■ Prefers minimal overhead, seeking to borrow, barter, or lease. | ■ Prefers to own or control contractually. |
| ■ Is comfortable with a flat, lean organization that emphasizes team management and networking—knows who to call upon. | ■ Is comfortable with organized hierarchy, levels of responsibility, and position management; is dependent on staff. |
| ■ Creates high-potential ventures to meet human needs, using varied management systems/styles— manages for ultrastability. | ■ Manages for stability and steady growth, seeking annual bottom-line profitability and quantifiable results. |

*Source*: Harris, P. R. *Managing the Knowledge Culture*. Amherst, MA: HRD Press, 2005, p. 207.

## Developing Human Resources

Throughout this book, we have underscored the pervasive impact of culture on our lives in general, as well as on management and work practice in particular. Some cultures inhibit people and constrain their creativity and intellectual activities. These cultures exclude whole segments of their populations because they are *different*, whether their prescriptions are against ethnic or religious minorities, youth, or women. In such cultures, females, for example, are not permitted to be free and independent human beings; their minds, voices, and desires are locked inside social prisons; their lives are dedicated to the service of males and their families—women's personal rights are minimal, their contributions to the advancements of society and themselves are aborted.

In some developing countries, human development is further curtailed by the misuse of child labor. Rather than a childhood experience of education and play, youth are abused by being recruited into labor-intensive occupations or into the military as "child soldiers."

Even in developed nations, schooling of the young is undermined by violence and racism on campus, prejudice toward women, minorities, homosexuals, and the disabled. Hate crimes are perpetuated in schools as well as the community. Moreover, such deviant behavior is also found within institutions of higher education, those supposedly dedicated to the pursuit of knowledge and enlightenment. Hence, cross-cultural education at all levels, including elementary, becomes important so that the young are taught *tolerance*—that is, to respect each other and accept differences in people. As societies and workplaces become more multicultural or diverse, learning intercultural sensitivity and skills is essential at all levels of human resource development (HRD).

In today's knowledge culture, continuous, lifetime learning is necessary for all people. The scope of such preparation has been outlined somewhat by the American Society for Training and Development in Exhibit 7.3.

## Mentoring and Coaching

In earlier times, the apprentice system was used to train craftsmen and workers. In this knowledge culture, such one-to-one guidance is given by experts to newcomers, formally or informally, through mentoring and coaching. A *mentor* is an experienced and wise counselor to a student or new employee for the purpose of personal or professional advancement. The two form a relationship in which the older person shares knowledge and expertise with the younger individual seeking to learn and advance. This communication may take place in a variety of ways from personal to electronic encounters, from meetings to e-mail, chat rooms, and conference calls.

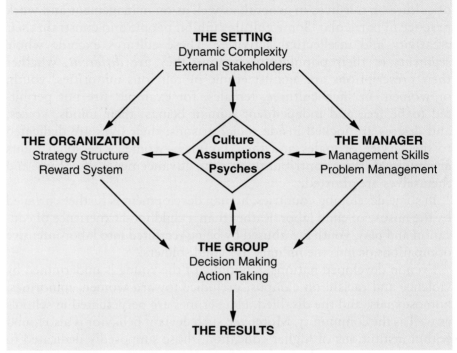

*Source*: American Society for Training and Development, Washington, D.C. Reprinted with permission.

Another strategy to improve human performance is coaching. A *coach* is a competent and experienced person who trains, tutors, or teaches a beginner, individually or in groups, to improve performance in a specific skill. Sometimes the learner is designated an *intern*, staying in that role for a specific time period until a measure of mastery is attained. Teams, whether at work or at sport, may benefit from the coach's guidance.

Contemporary institutions have to become *learning organizations*, establishing knowledge management and HRD systems that ensure continuous growth in member knowledge and skills. That may translate to establishing formal mentoring and/or coaching systems so that new generations of workers benefit from the wisdom gained by their predecessors. When formalized as part of ongoing HRD, consider requiring a written agreement between the learner and the mentor or coach. This clarifies the relationship, especially relative to purposes, processes, resources, and measurement of progress. For global organizations, a mentoring or coaching system abroad might include expatriates assisting locals, or older indigenous personnel helping the newly hired. Whatever approach is adopted, it makes good policy to utilize the brain power and expertise of high-performing, mature workers, or even retired ones, to help the younger members develop their potential.

# ETHICAL BEHAVIOR IN THE GLOBAL WORKPLACE

Worldwide issues of character and honesty in human exchanges are critical. Witness what has happened recently in the political, business, religious, and virtually every center of power. One observes lying, cover-ups, lack of integrity, accountability, and stewardship together with unfocused, narrow, and self-serving visions of the future. Cases abound in the newspaper and in business journals. Interestingly, among 2002 *Time* magazine's *Persons of the Year* were whistle-blowers: Cynthia Cooper of World-Com, Coleen Rowley of the FBI, and Sherron Watkins of Enron. All are women who had the courage to take risks to identify executive behavior that lacked integrity.[34] Daimler Benz is reported to have agreed to pay $185 million in U.S. funds for bribing officials in other countries.

## Bribery and Ethics in a Global Context

Corruption and bribery are present in most, if not all, societies; more so in some cultures than others. Truth and honesty are noble ideals, but they are also relative. As managers operate globally, they must be aware of the *relativism* in each culture regarding acceptance of a tip, bribe, incentive, etc. Different criteria and values between Eastern and Western cultures, for example, determine what is acceptable or appropriate. In developing countries where people struggle to survive, bribes and corruption, especially in the public sector, are endemic to the system; in industrialized countries, the practice is often more sophisticated, less visible, but prevalent. Payoffs to public officials, especially the police, have been reported in the media, e.g. from Mexico City to the New York Police Department.

## Ethical Relativism

As indicated earlier, the perception of bribery is culturally relative and one's *conscience* is "culturally conditioned." In some countries, the same action condemned as *bribery* might be considered a *tip* (to ensure promptness or service), especially when dealing with the bureaucracy. Among government officials in many lands, the ethical dilemma has also been labeled "influence peddling." Here, there is a fine line between legal and illegal, or even moral and immoral behavior. The spread of questionable and inappropriate behavior in both business and government within the so-called advanced countries has led to a demand by the public for more character education in the schools, especially university courses in ethics at business and professional schools. What is ethical or standard in one culture may not be so in another.[35]

Hooker[36] makes three distinctions regarding cross-cultural ethics:

■ *Contextualism* which allows for different obligations in different cultural contexts, though they may flow from the same universal principles. *Cronyism and nepotism* may be unacceptable if one's culture is built on transparency and merit, but acceptable in a culture that is relationship-based. People tend to support the cultural system on which they rely.

■ *Ethical relativism* claims that fundamentally incompatible ethical principles rule in different cultures. Western individualism leads to ideas such as equality and human rights, while Hindu pantheism recognizes the connectedness of all beings, and permits a stratified society based on *karma* (fate or destiny). On the other hand, *ethical universalism* holds that world cultures ultimately agree on basic values.

■ *Metaethical relativism* states that value statements are inherently relative—judgments based on prevailing conditions. Thus, in this analysis, ethical assertions, as opposed to normative ethics, mean investigating the circumstances in which decisions or behavior occur. For example, corruption in Western societies is criminal behavior because this is a rule-of-law-based culture that perceives rules as fair and justly enforced; people generally play by those rules. In Chinese culture, *guanxi,* or the giving of favors, contributes to stable and trusting relationships important in their trade and negotiations.

## Corporate Social Responsibility

In today's global marketplace, there is a positive trend toward good corporate citizenship and business ethics. Thus, global leaders at all levels of management are concerned that neither the organization nor its personnel engage in behavior that harms society. The proper goal of business is still maximizing owner value, but within the constraints of ethical conduct. That means leaders recognize that some actions may be legal, but unethical; also, that many things required by ethics are not required by law. Owner value, however, implies respect of other's property rights, especially "intellectual property." Edith Sternberg, a business philosopher, maintains that "ordinary decency" excludes behavior in commerce such as lying, cheating, coercion, violence, spying, stealing, and killing. Normally, honesty and fairness are good for business, and crime does not pay. Corruption and intimidation, as well as subversion of politics and law enforcement, not only undermine business, but also society. "Distributive justice," on the other hand, implies that performance and promotion are based on merit, not influence; benefits are distributed in return for helping the organization achieve its goals. In too many corporate scandals, managers acted as if they were accountable to nobody.

Thus, the movement toward *corporate social responsibility* (CSR)— that is, good management and accountability for the benefit of stakeholders and society—means that ethical behavior, like ordinary decency and distributed justice, are adhered to by organizational leaders.[37] It is up to government to be guardians of public interest by reasonable legislation and enforcement, mediating among diverse interests, collecting taxes to provide public goods and services, and, when necessary, to organize resources in cases of disaster.

## High-Performing Global Leadership

To ensure top performance, the global leader continually updates and broadens his or her understanding of culture and its impact on our lives. Although there may be few management theories that can be universally applied across all cultures, there are many principles and practices of leadership that can be adapted to various countries. Despite the cultural differences in managerial approaches, it is possible to produce cultural synergy in the pragmatic operations of management.

Elashmawi and Harris,[38] in their research into global joint ventures, focused on clashes within multicultural work environments, such as establishing a plant overseas. These offshore enterprises require the hiring, training, and management of local in-country personnel of differing cultural and technical backgrounds. Our late colleague identified cultural clashes arising from language and nonverbal communication, time and space orientation, decision-making and information systems, conduct of meetings and training, as well as motivation. On the other hand, Hampden-Turner and Trompenaars[39] urge transforming conflicting values into complementary values.

Technology transfer in the twenty-first century has seen accelerated growth in *outsourcing/insourcing/nearsourcing*, especially in the fields of information technology and services.

# CONCLUSIONS

Global business is a learning laboratory. Peaceful and cooperative free enterprise on an international basis contributes to world economic development, while reducing disparities in terms of poverty and population. The export/import exchange, particularly of information and new technologies, fosters political and social stability, as well as developing human resources and potential.

The global market and workplace are the forum for satisfying human needs, while building a multicultural environment where high performance and productivity flourish. As Alvin Toffler wisely observed, "Nobody knows the future." However, twenty-first century global leaders can have a constructive impact on this new millennium—they can make a difference in achieving human potential. Integrity, courage, cultural sensitivity, and a global mindset are prerequisites for making a positive difference.

## MIND STRETCHING

1. Why are cross-cultural sensitivity and skills so important for the success of global leaders?
2. What other personal and professional qualities should global leaders cultivate?
3. How does the global marketplace benefit from the activities of innovators and entrepreneurs?
4. How is global work performance improved by the practice of HRD management, mentoring and coaching, ethical behavior, and appropriate technology transfer?

## REFERENCES

1. George, B., Sims, P., McLean, A. N., and Mauyer, D. "Discovering Your Authentic Leadership," *Harvard Business Review*, February 2007.
2. Bonsignore, M. Chairman CEO Honeywell Inc., The Conference Board, 1995, presentation at the Strategic Alliances Conference, March 29, 1995. Also refer to Gundling, E. *Working Global Smart: 12 People Skills for Doing Business Across Borders*. Palo Altos, CA: Davies-Black, 2003.
3. McCall, M. W. and Hollenbeck, G. P. *Developing Global Executives*. Boston, MA: Harvard Business School Press, 2002. Also refer to *Leadership in Diverse and Multicultural Environments*, Pedersen, P. and Connerley, M. (eds.). Thousand Oaks, CA: Sage Publications, 2005.
4. Carter, J. "Searching for Peace," *Essays on Leadership*. Washington, DC: Carnegie Commission on Preventing Deadly Conflict, 1998, pp. 26, 36–36.
5. Gorbachev, M. "On Non-Violent Leadership," *Essays on Leadership*. Washington, DC: Carnegie Commission on Preventing Deadly Conflict, 1998, pp. 64–65.
6. Tutu, D. "Leadership," *Essays on Leadership*. Washington, DC: Carnegie Commission on Preventing Deadly Conflict, 1998, pp. 70–71.
7. Schaeffer, L. D. "The Leadership Journey," *Harvard Business Review*, October 2002.
8. Moran, R. T. and Riesenberger, J. R. *The Global Challenge: Building the New World Enterprise*. New York: McGraw-Hill, 1994. And more strongly supported in interviews by Robert Moran in 2009 and 2010.
9. Leimbach, M. and Muller, A. *Winning the War for Talent: Global Leadership Competencies*. Wilson Learning Corporation, Version 1.0, 2001.
10. Moran, R. T. and Riesenberger, J. R. *The Global Challenge: Building the New World Enterprise*. New York: McGraw-Hill, 1994. And more strongly supported in interviews by Robert Moran in 2009 and 2010.

11. Javidan, M., Teagarden, M., Bowen, D. "Making It Overseas: Developing the Skills You Need to Succeed as an International Leader," *Harvard Business Review*, April 2010.

12. Song "You've Got To Be Taught," in the play *South Pacific*, music by Richard Rogers, lyrics by Oscar Hammerstein II, 1949.

13. Rhinesmith, S. *A Manager's Guide to Globalization*. Homewood, IL: Business One Irwin, 1993.

14. Amir, Y. "Contact Hypotheses in Ethnic Relation," *Psychological Bulletin*, Vol. 71, 1969, pp. 319–342.

15. Allport, G. *The Nature of Prejudice*. Reading, MA: Addison-Wesley, 1954.

16. Peters, T. and Waterman, R. *In Search of Excellence*. New York: Harper Row, 1982.

17. Quoted byBennis, W. *On Becoming a Leader*. Reading, MA: Addison-Wesley, 1989, p. 23.

18. Kantor, R. "Transcending Business Boundaries: 12,000 World Managers View Change," *Harvard Business Review*, May-June, 1991.

19. Barnevik, P. "Mr. Barnevik, Aren't You Happy Now?" *Business Week*, September 27, 1993, p. 128.

20. Gambrell, S. W. and Stevens, C. A. "Moving through the Three Phases of Organizational Change," *International Management*, July/August 1992, pp. 4–6.

21. Senge, P. M. *The Fifth Discipline*, New York: Doubleday Currency, 1990.

22. Moran, R. T. "Cross-Cultural Contact," *International Management*, January 1988, modified 2010.

23. Land, G. and Jarman, B. "Future Pull," *The Futurist*, July/August 1992, pp. 25–27.

24. Reich, R. B. "Who Is Them?" *Harvard Business Review*, March/April 1991, pp. 77–88.

25. Kealy, D. J. *Cross-Cultural Effectiveness: A Study of Canadian Technical Advisors Overseas*, Quebec: Canadian International Development Agency, 1990.

26. George, B., Sims, P. McLean, A. N., Mauyer, D. "Discovering Your Authentic Leadership," *Harvard Business Review*, February 2007.

27. Kotter, J. P. and Heskett, J. L. *Corporate Culture and Performance*. New York, Free Press, 1992.

28. Condon, J. and Yousef, F. *An introduction to Intercultural Communication*, Indianapolis, IN: Bobbs-Merrill, 1988.

29. *New York Times*, February 15, 1977.

30. Zeeman, J. "What United Airlines is Learning in the Pacific," speech given before the Academy of International Business, Chicago, November 14, 1987.

31. Whiting, R. *You Gotta Have Wa*. New York: Macmillan, 1989.

32. Ruben, B. *Handbook of Intercultural Skills*. Vol. 1, New York: Pergamon Press, 1983. See also Kenton, S. B. and Valentine, D. (eds.). *Crosstalk: Communicating in a Multicultural Workplace*. Upper Saddle River, NJ: Prentice-Hall, 1997.

33. Deardorff, D. K. *The Sage Handbook of Intercultural Competence*. Thousand Oaks, CA: Sage, 2009.

34. Lacayo, R. and Ripley, A. "Persons of the Year," *Time*, January 6, 2003.

35. Daly, M. "The Ethical Implications of Globalization of the Legal Profession," *Fordham International Law School Journal*, New York: Fordham University, 1998.

36. Hooker, J. *Working Across Cultures*. Stanford, CA: Stanford University Press, 2003, pp. 314–330.

37. Beniff, M. and Southwick, K. *Compassionate Capitalism: Can Corporations Make Doing Good an Integral Part of Doing Well?* London, UK: Career Press, 2004.

38. Elashmawi, F. and Harris, P. R. *Multicultural Management 2000: Essential Skills for Global Business Success*, 1998. Also refer to Elashmawi, F. (ed.). *Competing Globally: Mastering Multicultural Management and Negotiations*. Burlington, MA: Elsevier/Butterworth-Heinemann, 2001.

39. Hampden-Turner, C. M. and Trompenaars, F. *Building Cross-Cultural Competence: How to Create Wealth from Conflicting Values*. New Haven, CT: Yale University Press, 2002.

# MANAGING GLOBAL TRANSITIONS AND RELOCATIONS

A hero ventures forth from the world of the common day into a region of supernatural wonder; fabulous forces are there encountered, and a decisive victory is won; the hero comes back from this mysterious adventure with the power to bestow boons on his fellowmen.

Joseph Campbell, *The Hero with a Thousand Faces*.

We need to throw our hats far away to make retrieving them interesting.

French Saying

## LEARNING OBJECTIVES

This chapter has several objectives: first, to appreciate the challenges inherent in transitional experiences and relocations; second, to examine ways for fostering acculturation when abroad, especially through customized deployment systems that train expatriates in proper business etiquette and protocols for living and working appropriately in an alien environment.

## SAGA OF MY BRAZILIAN ADVENTURE

The adventure was finally started. The airplane landed smoothly in Guarulhos Airport in São Paulo, Brazil, early in the morning on January 2, 2004. This was to be about the last smooth experience I would have for a long while.

Many times, I wondered how I was so lucky to have found my way into the position that I was in. Here I was, a person from the rural midwestern United States, being charged with upgrading the breadth and depth of a major multinational company's corn-breeding organization in Brazil. I was to do this from a base in Central Brazil, right on the frontier of the Cerrados, the vast Brazilian savannah. This must have been what it was like when my grandfather emigrated from Europe to southwest Minnesota about 100 years ago. He was moving to the land of Crazy Horse, the famous Sioux Indian Chief, big sky, and horse races by the pool hall. I was moving to the land of Rondon, Amazonia, big-time agricultural entrepreneurs, and the best football (soccer) in the world.

At Customs, I immediately noticed things were different. People from the United States were being segregated into a separate line. This had never happened before. Fortunately, I was at the head of the line, since there were only a few people on the flight from the United States, and only a very small group of them were U.S. citizens. As I walked up to the tables, I noticed they were manned by the Federal Police, and the tables were in addition to the customary immigration booths that one passes through to enter the country. It all seemed rather haphazard but very police-like.

As I handed the tall, brasiliera in a Federal Police uniform my passport, I inquired:

> "What is going on?"
> "What do you think of your president?" she growled.
> "What is the right response?"

She gave me an attractive smile and eased off. She then explained "that some judge in Mato Grosso" had ordered her to come to the airport and provide the same scrutiny to the incoming people from the United States as the United States was giving to the brasilieros. This was done at the last minute, and this guy was doing this only for political reasons.

She then proceeded to fingerprint me, all 10 fingers dipped into ink and pressed onto a card. I then had numbers somehow arranged onto a card, maybe it was my passport number, and held this against my chest while the other policeman "photographed" me. Both were a source of amusement, as I was the first one for them, and they were somewhat shocked at the process once they actually did it, especially for an *ianqui* who, they learned, enjoyed their country.

Finally, I was appropriately documented, and allowed to go to the other line for the normal immigration and behind all the other foreigners in my flight and another much fuller flight. Eventually, I passed through immigration and went to retrieve my luggage.

I was coming into the country with only what I was carrying, so I was traveling heavy. After filling my luggage cart with the four bags I was carrying, two quite large and heavy, plus my carry-on bag and briefcase, I headed out the door, finally!

No sooner had I passed through the door than a very smartly dressed man with a perfect haircut and smile came up to me and asked me if I was an American. I indicated I was, and only then noticed the person with the television camera coming up. He introduced himself as working for a television station in São Paulo, and he asked if he could interview me regarding my thoughts on the revised immigration procedure for U.S. citizens.

My immediate thought was, "This is trouble." I had some experience with the press in the past and had an inherent distrust of their appetite for controversy. I politely responded, "No, but I am sure there are others that would be happy to respond to your questions."

With that I turned away and began to make my way through the crowded airport. Guarulhos is one of the few airports that I travel to that can be crowded on January 2.

I must have looked like a beleaguered American with lots of heavy baggage, tired from 18 h of traveling, needing to change clothes, wanting to brush my teeth, needing a cup of coffee, and working my way through the crowd. Before I went 20 ft, the television reporter again asked for an interview, only this time the man with the camera appeared to have it running. Again, I politely declined.

By the time I reached the center of the main hallway in the airport, the crowd thinned, but once again, my shadow, the television news personality, was there to ask for an interview. This time, I reconsidered. I decided he was not going to go away, and I did not want to be cast as the ugly American. The best approach was to give him a brief interview, and then I would be able to have some peace.

"How did you feel about the new immigration procedures, fingerprinting and photographing of everyone from the U.S.?"
"I like Brazil so much that it is worth the effort."
A noticeably perplexed look began to appear on his face.
"Was the line long, and did you have to wait a long time?"
"Yes, the line was long, but so was the other line."

By this time, the interviewer realized this would be a rather boring interview, so he stopped asking questions and thanked me for my time.

I was sure I had escaped unscathed and went on to my destination, Brasilia, which required another 6 h of travel time.

Two weeks later, I traveled back to São Paulo to participate in a weeklong Portuguese immersion course. No sooner had I been introduced to my first professor than she recognized me from television. She was shocked.

Apparently, the news program had found a U.S. citizen who was sufficiently angry that they obtained the desired emotion. They ran my interview along with the other one as a measure of the range in response. About this time, widely publicized reports began to appear of an incident involving a pilot of a U.S. commercial airline. Apparently, the pilot became angry with the delays on entering the country; flight crews normally do not have to stand in line with all the passengers and get preferential treatment at immigrations. So he very publically insulted the federal police. He was arrested and fined quite a considerable amount of money.[1]

## CROSS-BORDER GLOBAL TRAVEL

Today, people move across the planet or beyond in person, or electronically for short or long time periods. Such travel may be for pleasure, professional development and education, or for business and military service. Humans have the capacity to move their bodies and/or their brains. The latter is evident in unmanned, automated space missions to the far corners of the universe. Electronic travel may range from telephone, radio, and television, to computer exchanges via the Internet in the form of mail, Web sites, chat rooms, podcasts, blogs, and wikis. In all cases, cross-cultural sensitivity and skills can facilitate global communications. Perhaps it would be wise to heed the advice of humorist Mark Twain: "20 years from now, you will be more disappointed by the things you didn't do, than by the things that you did. So throw off the bowline, sail away from the safe harbor. Catch the trade winds in your sails. Explore, Dream, Discover…. Travel is fatal to prejudice, bigotry, and narrow-mindedness."

In today's global village, the number of people living in another country for lengthy periods is increasing. Virtually everyone comes in contact with individuals who speak a different language or who were reared in another culture. In this twenty-first century, cultural homogeneity and isolation exist in very few places—heterogeneity, or diversity, is the reality everywhere. Within our shrinking world, everyone, from executives to entertainers, soldiers to humanitarian volunteers, needs skills in managing both cultural differences and synergy.[2] Furthermore, we are transitioning into an emerging *knowledge culture* that offers new applications for such competencies. Richard Lewis suggests that it is a risk-taking, electronic culture that (1) encourages entrepreneurialism, Western-style individualism, and rapid decision cycles; (2) responds quickly and flexibly to end-user needs; (3) allows for greater customization of brands and services; and (4) communicates interactively for "communities of families and friends."[3]

Embarking on a "hero's journey" is the way the late anthropologist Joseph Campbell describes the challenge of living outside one's culture, while Osland reports on adventures abroad as "hero's tales."[4]

Furthermore, we have not even to risk the adventure alone, for the heroes of all time have gone before us. The labyrinth is thoroughly known. We have only to follow the thread of the hero path, and where we have thought to find an abomination, we shall find a god. And where we have thought to slay another, we shall slay ourselves. Where we had thought to travel outward, we will come to the center of our own existence. And where we had thought to be alone, we will be one with the world.

Early researchers in cross-cultural studies were concerned primarily with what happened when a person transitioned from home culture to a host culture. Today, interdependence between nations has facilitated the cross-border flow of people, ideas, and information. But we have a broader view of *transition trauma* associated with life's turning points, be they relocation or other personal and professional challenges. The trauma may simply be triggered by multiple career assignments or opportunities, whether experienced domestically or internationally. In addition to the ordinary lifestyle transitions that everyone faces, contemporaries must cope with rapid alterations in their work, environments, and cultures.

Increasingly, we interact with people who are very different from us, or in situations that are unfamiliar. Even when we share a common nationality, we may have to deal with citizens who are indeed "foreign" to us in their thinking, attitudes, vocabulary, and background. Individuals may face challenges within their environment due to their upbringing or local cultural conditioning. These challenges present opportunities either for growth or disruption. Such life-turning points may range from married couples who divorce; to families who move from one geographic area to another, whether at home or abroad; to those who have major alterations in careers, jobs, or roles; to personally confronting issues of serious illness or even death.

To get a sense of transitional experience that can cause culture shock, consider the following scenarios (Exhibit 8.1).

## EXHIBIT 8.1

## U.N. STUDY CITES VALUE OF GLOBAL MIGRATION

A recent United Nations study reports a surge in global migration at the turn of this century that is keeping populations from declining in Europe, as well as stimulating economic growth in North America by increased foreign income and workers.

### *Majority to Minority Culture*

Your company transfers you and your family to a section of your country where you feel like an alien. From the Northeast, you come to this Sunbelt state that is so different and unique. Your boss suggests you enroll at the local university to take a course entitled "Living Texas" to introduce you to the myths and mannerisms of Texans.

continued

EXHIBIT 8.1
U.N. STUDY CITES VALUE OF GLOBAL
MIGRATION (CONTINUED)

### Transitions in the Global Marketplace

You are a North American marketing consultant worldwide for a high technology company worldwide. Because of your expertise, you are much in demand, traveling beyond your home culture on short assignments. Your professional activities take you to a variety of host cultures. Typically, you are there for 1-2 weeks, consulting with local executives, many of whom are quite different in their approach to you as a woman. Most of your clients are men from cultures as diverse as Indonesia, Malaysia, Mexico, India, Hungary, and Russia.

### Technology Transfer

You are an engineer from a highly industrialized nation. Your overseas assignments are mainly to less-developed countries. You realize that the indigenous population is not ready for sophisticated technologies. To help them in their transition to modern economies, and rather than sell them expensive equipment that they cannot afford or maintain, you prefer to design appropriate machines that pump water, cook food, and meet their real and practical needs.

### Adjusting to New Immigrants

You live in east San Diego near a local Somali community and have been a leader, helping new arrivals to acculturate. You have been notified that some 10,000 more Somali Bantu refugees are being relocated to the United States with your government's assistance. Two hundred of these tribal people, descendants of slaves, are coming to "America's Finest City."

### Deployment for War and Peacekeeping

As a U.S. Marine sergeant, you are a veteran of the Iraq War. You were one of those marines who went off to fight in the last decade and returned forever changed by your brief, intense experience with death and privation. You came back a driven and changed man, worrying if your marriage would also become a casualty.

All of the above incidents are *real, transitional experiences*. Each is an example of a life challenge that can be perceived as either devastating or a new chance. Having in-depth, intercultural encounters can be stimulating or psychologically disturbing, depending on your preparation and approach to them. Acculturation, or the process of adjustment to new experiences or living environment, takes time, possibly months and even years, while one learns new skills for responding and adapting to the unfamiliar. The extent of the trauma depends on the situation, such as whether one lives abroad among the native population or in a protected compound, be it a military, diplomatic, corporate, or religious enclave. The experience of coping with global diversity can be renewing or debilitating. When we are strangers in a place where the traditions and customs are foreign and unexpected, we may lose our balance and become unsure of ourselves. The same thing can happen within our own society when change happens so rapidly that the old traditions, the cues we live by, are suddenly undermined and irrelevant, threatening our sense of self.

Transitional experiences offer two alternatives—to cope or to "cop out." One can learn to comprehend, survive in, and grow through immersion in a different culture. The positive result can be increased self-development. Whenever we leave home for the unfamiliar, it involves basic changes in habits, relationships, and sources of satisfaction. Inherent in cultural change is the opportunity to leave behind, perhaps temporarily, one set of relationships and living patterns and to enrich one's life by experimenting with new ones. Implicit in the personal conflict and discontinuity produced by such experiences is the possible transcendence from environment or family support to self support. Intercultural situations of psychological, social, or cultural stress also stimulate us to review and redefine our lives—to see our own country and people in a new perspective. Or, we may reject the changes or new culture and lose a possible growth opportunity.[5]

## Culture Impacts Identity

One reason the transitional experience is so significant is that it may alter our sense of identity. Fearn[6] writing on the subject of philosophy makes the point that all humans are faced with three critical questions. One, *who am I?* (mind and body); two, *what do I know?* (language and knowledge); three, *what should I do?* (morals and meaning of life). Major turning points in our lives often force us to rethink our answers to these inquiries which affect our self-perception, and the image we project to others.

All transitions influence one's sense of identity—some strengthen this sense of self, while others may threaten that identity or even change it. That is why we should deal with this matter before departure overseas. When we go outside our home culture into a foreign culture, we may, for example, experience an identity crisis abroad. As a result, personal development occurs when we redefine our answers to the above questions, thereby expanding our perceptual field.

Perhaps the most important lesson for the cross-cultural sojourner is to understand one's cultural baggage.

When we relocate within our own country or abroad, we may be subject to culture shock. Although scholars have only researched this phenomenon during the past 50 years or so, its impact on people has been written about in works of fiction as early as 1862, including Tolstoy in his book *The Cossacks*. Again, Jack London, in a 1900 story, described what it felt like to be a "foreigner," but in a literary, not scientific, way. London describes what a sojourner should expect:

> He must be prepared to forget many of the things he learned, and to acquire such customs as are inherent with existence in the new land; he must abandon the old ideals and the old gods, and oftentimes he must reverse the very code by which his conduct has hitherto been shaped.... The pressures of the altered environment are almost unbearable, and they chafe in body and spirit under the new restrictions which are not understood. This chafing is bound to act and react, producing diverse evils and leading to various misfortunes.[7]

Essentially, culture shock, as described by London, is our psychological reaction to a totally unfamiliar or alien environment, which often occurs with any major transitional experience.[8] Culture shock is neither good nor bad, necessary nor unnecessary. It is a reality that many people face when in strange and unexpected situations that makes it difficult for automatic coping, as we do in our home culture. Oberg referred to culture shock as a generalized trauma one experiences in a new and different culture because of having to learn and cope with a vast array of new cultural cues and expectations, while discovering that your old ones probably do not fit or work. More precisely, he notes:

> Culture shock is precipitated by the anxiety that results from losing all our familiar signs and symbols of social intercourse. These signs or cues include the thousand and one ways in which we orient ourselves to the situations of daily life—how to give orders, how to make purchases, when and when not to respond. Now these cues, which may be words, gestures, facial expressions, customs, or norms, are acquired by all of us in the course of growing up, and are as much a part of our culture as the language we speak, or the beliefs we accept. All of us depend for our peace of mind and efficiency on hundreds of these cues, most of which we are not consciously aware of.[9]

## *Myriad forms of Culture Shock*

A new form of this trauma, growing exponentially throughout the world, is *future shock*, of which Alvin Toffler warned in his 1970 book by that title and again in a 1980 volume, *The Third Wave*. Essentially, this mass culture shock is being experienced by whole groups and nations because of the inability to transition rapidly from a previous stage of human development (e.g., agricultural or industrial) into our present Information Society, or knowledge culture. The technological, scientific, and knowledge advances have been so large and so accelerated that many people cannot cope with the pace of these changes. They opt out or are bypassed by the mainstream of civilizations; many end up in an underclass position in modern society. Furthermore, today, countries and institutions—such as religious, educational, and political systems—are resisting modernization, suffering from culture lag, and living in the past, unable to cope with present and future challenges. For institutions, the same phenomenon is referred to as *organization shock*.

According to Klopf,[10] there are six stages of culture shock resulting from relocation.

1. The *preliminary stage* involves preparation for the experience. During this stage, anticipation and excitement build as one packs, makes reservations, and plans for departure with many unrealistic expectations.
2. Arrival at the destination marks the *spectator stage*, during which there are many strange sights and different people. All of this newness produces fascination with the culture. This honeymoon stage may last from a few days to 6 months.
3. The *participation stage* occurs when the individual must do the hard work of living in the culture and learning about it, especially its language—the honeymoon has ended. The sights have been visited and, now, coping with everyday life must occur.
4. When problems begin to arise that are difficult to handle, usually the *shock stage* sets in. Irritability, lethargy, depression, and loneliness are symptoms. One must find ways to confront and adjust to the differences in culture.
5. If the individual reaches the *adjustment stage*, identification with the host culture has progressed satisfactorily. Relationships with locals develop, along with a sense of belonging and acceptance.
6. For individuals living permanently in a culture, the adjustment stage finishes the transition period—one may assimilate or become bicultural in mindset. For those who are temporarily living in a host culture, the return to the home culture introduces the *reentry stage*. Culture shock in reverse may set in, with individuals again going through the above five stages, but this time in their native land. A sense of discomfort, disorientation, and even frustration may be experienced, often up to 6 or more months.

The pace at which one advances through these stages is different for each individual. For those who are experienced in international travel, it may quicken and perhaps lessen the trauma.

However, for the *long-term expatriate* exposed to a very different culture from one's own, physical and psychological concerns may be real or imagined. Those experiencing culture shock manifest the obvious symptoms, such as excessive anxiety over cleanliness and sanitary conditions, feeling that what is new and strange may be "dirty." This may be seen with reference to water, food, dishes, and bedding, or evident in unreasonable fear of servants and shopkeepers because of disease they might bear. Other indications of such traumatic behavior are feelings of helplessness and confusion, growing dependence on long-term residents of one's own nationality, constant irritations over delays and minor frustrations, and undue worry about being cheated, robbed, or injured. Some may exhibit symptoms of mild hypochondria, expressing apprehension about minor pains, skin eruptions, and other ailments, real or imagined—it may even get to the point of actual psychosomatic illnesses. Often, individuals experiencing culture shock postpone learning the local language and customs, dwelling instead on their loneliness and longing for back home, to be with one's own, and to talk to people who "make sense." However, persons who seek international assignments as a means of escaping "back-home problems" with career, marriage, or substance abuse will probably only exacerbate personal problems that would be better resolved in their home culture.

Osland[11] uses the concept of "learning to live with paradox" instead of emphasizing the shock that may come from experiences in an alien society. Such paradox occurs when we have to hold ideas in mind that are seemingly opposite to the home perspectives. Osland calls this the "road of trials" when we are confronted with obstacles and tests on our way to "normally" perceiving and functioning. To deal with such paradoxes more effectively, she proposes we learn from expatriates who have gone before us, which can begin before departure and continue on-site.

To facilitate acculturation, organizations responsible for sending others abroad should be careful in their recruitment and selection of individuals for international assignments. Surveys have shown that those who adjust and work well outside their own culture are usually well-integrated personalities, with qualities such as *flexibility, personal stability, social maturity, and social inventiveness*. Such candidates for overseas work are not given to unrealistic expectations, irrational concepts of self or others, nor do they have tendencies toward excessive depression, discouragement, criticism, or hostility. Global corporations, government agencies, and international organizations that sponsor people abroad have a responsibility to prevent or reduce culture shock among their representatives. It is not only necessary for individual acculturation, but is more cost effective, while promoting out-of-country productivity and improving client or customer relations with host nationals. This will be discussed further in the section on deployment systems.

One should also be realistic about the difficulties that may be experienced when living abroad. Intestinal disorders and exotic diseases are real, and may not always be avoided by inoculations or new antibiotics. In some countries, water, power, transportation, and housing shortages are facts, and one's physical comfort may be seriously inconvenienced.

Political instability, ethnic feuds, and social breakdown may make an assignment unacceptable. Adjustment may also be slowed because of not knowing the local language, or in trying to cope with strange climates and customs. But we are born with the ability to learn, to adapt, to survive, to enjoy. After all, human beings do create culture, so the shocks caused by such differences are not unbearable or without value. The intercultural experience can be more satisfying, contributing much to, personal and professional satisfaction. One can discover friends everywhere. The expatriate experience has always meant accepting risk implicit in living and traveling beyond your own borders.

As nongovernmental organizations (NGOs) increase in number and influence, *global humanitarians* are more prevalent. But today, their service abroad on behalf of others may often place them in "harm's way." Civil strife may cause them to shut down operations, or they may face kidnapping, bodily harm, and even death.

## Role Shock

The phenomenon and process of culture shock have applications to other life crises. For instance, there is also role shock. Each of us chooses, or is assigned, or is conditioned to a variety of roles in society and its institutions—man or woman, family member, son or daughter, parent or child, husband or wife (single/married/divorced), teacher or engineer, manager or union organizer, amateur or professional. In these positions, people have expectations of us, as we do of their varied positions. These role opportunities or constraints often differ in another culture. A woman, for instance, may do in one culture what is forbidden in another. In some societies, senior citizens are revered, and in others ignored. In some cultures, the youth regard teachers with awe, while others treat them as inferiors or "buddies."

Role perception is subject to change according to time, place, and circumstances. But for the past 60 years, our defined roles have changed at an accelerating rate. In the past, our roles were fairly stable, clear, and predictable. Today, our roles are fuzzy, more unpredictable, and fluid. The person who has a particular understanding of what a manager is and does may be upset when he or she finally achieves that role, only to discover it to be altered considerably! Our traditional views of such functions are suddenly obsolete. All this role uncertainty can be very disconcerting; the resulting shock to our psyche may be severe and long lasting. Role shock can lead to an identity crisis, especially if one's sense of self and life are tightly linked to a career or work role. Consider the trauma an older person experiences when suddenly there is a reduction in the workforce, and unemployment lines are long, while jobs are scarce. Furthermore, a cross-cultural assignment can accentuate role shock. Many individuals sent abroad find themselves adjusting to totally different role requirements than back home.

Role shock may be apparent as a result of organizational mergers or acquisition, or of reorganization or redesign of a system. The outcome may cause a person's position to be combined with others, downsized, or even lost. In the past decade, many middle managers were simply eliminated in corporations trying to cope with new economic conditions. Even when one retains his or her post within a newly acquired company, the organization and its culture may perceive "your role" in an entirely different way. Role transformation or elimination may come from new technologies, new research, new markets, or new crises.

## Reentry Shock

When expatriates return from foreign deployment, they face another form of reverse culture shock. Reentry research and its impact on the individual and the organization has been largely neglected.[12]

Having objectively perceived his or her culture from abroad, one can have a more severe and sustained jolt through reentry into a home culture. The intercultural experience widens perceptions and broadens constructs, so the person is less myopic in the homeland and more cosmopolitan. Some returning "expats," or those returning from long service overseas, feel a subtle downgrading and loss of prestige and benefits. Others bemoan the loss of household help and social contacts, as well as other "perks." This is especially evident with members of the military who come home after a lengthy deployment in other parts of the world. Many feel uncomfortable for 6 months or more in their native land, frustrated with their organization and bored with their "narrow-minded" colleagues who never left home. Some returnees seem out of touch with what has happened in their country or corporation during their absence, and no longer seem to fit into the domestic organization.

The coming home phenomenon described here can be temporary and less intense if the expatriate is helped by a professional reorientation program. For some, culture and reentry shocks may be the catalysts for major choices and transitions, such as a new locale and new relationships, pursuit of additional education or training, a change in job or career, and generally an improved lifestyle. While some expatriates never make the necessary readjustments, living as strangers in their home cultures, for the majority, the intercultural experience is very positive, a turning point toward an enriched quality of life.

## FOSTERING ACCULTURATION

After culture shock subsides, with hope, real acculturation settles in. Anyone who has gone from home to live, work, or study in a foreign country must learn about and adapt to another quite distinct cultural environment. As early as the 1930s, *acculturation* was being formally researched by scholars. The definition developed then is just as valid today—when groups of individuals having different cultures come into continuous firsthand contact with subsequent changes in the original cultural patterns of either or both groups.[13]

Most obviously, one must assimilate to fulfill practical needs for survival and accommodation in strange situations, like finding grocery stores, doctors, schools, banks, etc. Integration into a different society produces more personal changes, as one moves beyond the familiar patterns and institutions of the old, while attempting to absorb and understand the new. Value systems and attitudes also undergo alteration in this process. Furthermore, there may be biological changes as one adjusts to a different climate, bacteria and viruses, or unknown food and plant life. Also, social changes occur as the visitor seeks to find and form new relationships and friendships. All of these happenings may result in stress or tension.

Sociologists point out that stable, healthy family relationships can make the difference between success and failure in the foreign assignment. Families who interact in mutually supportive ways can be their own resource for acculturation into another environment. As ambassadors of your native culture, do endeavor to establish wholesome intercultural relations with the local people. Such behavior not only contributes to creating a favorable image of your own country, but facilitates your adjustment as well. Extending culture shock can be a hindrance to forming friendships and effective business relations abroad. Travelers abroad have to reach out and create a friendly, positive impression, lest we be perceived as arrogant and imperious.

The following 10 recommendations will help to deflate the stress and tension overseas, while advancing successful acculturation:

*Be Culturally Prepared*. Forewarned is forearmed. Individual or group study and training are necessary to understand cultural factors and cultural specifics. Public libraries and the Internet provide a variety of resource material. Also, the Public Health Service will advise about required inoculations, dietary clues, and other sanitary data. Before departure, the person scheduled for overseas service can experiment with the food in restaurants representative of the second culture. Furthermore, one might establish contact in his or her homeland with foreign émigrés, students, or visitors from the area to which he or she is going. A helpful approach is to seek out your own *cultural mentor*—a wise friend or counselor who has lived in the host country, or who is there upon arrival. The expatriate's mentor is capable of guidance, encouragement, and help in mastering the intricacies of a new culture. Sometimes your organizational sponsor abroad may link you to such a resource or even provide a *cultural coach*.

*Learn Local Communication Complexities*. Study the language of the place to which one is assigned. At least, learn some of the basics that will help in exchanging greetings and shopping. In addition to courses and books on the country, audio or videocassettes and discs can advance your communication skills in the host culture. Published guides can be helpful in learning expected courtesies and customs.

*Interact with the Host Nationals.* Meeting with people from the country you are going to is helpful. There are many such foreign nationals within your own organization or local community who may provide introductions to relatives and friends abroad, as well as useful information regarding their native culture and its unique customs. If one lives overseas within a corporate or military colony, avoid the "compound mentality." Immerse oneself in the host culture. Whenever feasible, join in on the artistic and community functions, the carnivals and rites, the international fraternal or professional associations. Offer to teach students or businesspeople one's language in exchange for knowledge of their language; share skills from skiing to tennis, from the performing to intellectual arts—all means for making friends worldwide.

*Be creative and experimental.* Innovating abroad may mean taking risks to get around barriers of bureaucracy and communication to lessen social distance. This principal extends from experimenting with the local food to keeping a diary as an escape to record one's adventures and frustrations. Tours, hobbies, and a variety of cultural pursuits can produce positive results. One needs to be existential and open to the daily opportunities that will be presented. Consider preparing a newsletter for the "folks back home" in which you share your cross-cultural adventures and insights, either by regular or electronic mail.

*Be culturally sensitive.* Be aware of the special customs and traditions that, if followed by a visitor, will make one more acceptable. Recognize that in some cultures, such as in Asia and the Middle East, saving face and not giving offense is considered quite important. Certainly, avoid stereotyping the natives and criticizing their local practices and procedures, while using the standard of one's own country for comparison. Americans are dynamic and pragmatic, generally liking to organize things "better," so it may be a challenge for them to relax and adjust to a different rhythm of the place and people they are visiting.

*Recognize complexities in host cultures.* Counteract the tendency to make quick, simplistic assessments of situations. Most complex societies comprise different ethnic or religious groups, stratified into social classes or castes, differentiated by regions or geographical factors, separated into rural and urban settlements. Each of these may have distinct subcultural characteristics over which is superimposed an official language, national institutions, and peculiar customs or history that tie a people together. Avoid pat generalizations and quick assumptions. Instead, be tentative when drawing conclusions, realizing one's point of contact is a limited sample within a multifaceted society.

*Understand oneself as a culture bearer.* When going abroad, each person brings his or her own culture, conditioning, and distortions. Thus, one views everything in the host culture through the unique filter of his or her own cultural background. For example, if one is raised in democratic traditions, it may be unsettling to live in a society that values the authority of the head male in the family and extends this reverence to national leaders. But with locals, quiet conversations and behavior may persuade others to appreciate your cultural perspectives.

*Be patient, understanding, and accepting of self and hosts.* In an unfamiliar environment, one must be more tolerant and flexible. An attitude of healthy curiosity, a willingness to bear inconveniences, and patience when answers or solutions are not forthcoming or difficult to obtain are valuable ways to maintain mental balance. Such patience may also extend to other compatriots who struggle with cultural adjustment.

*Be realistic in expectations.* Avoid overestimating oneself, your hosts, or the cross-cultural experience. Disappointments can be lessened if one scales down expectations. This applies to everything from airline schedules to renting rooms. Global managers, especially, must be careful in new cultures not to set unreasonable work expectations for themselves or others until both are acclimated.

*Accept the challenge of intercultural experiences.* Anticipate, savor, and confront the psychological challenge of adapting and changing as a result of a new cross-cultural opportunity. Be prepared to alter one's habits, attitudes, values, tastes, relationships, or sources of satisfaction. Such flexibility can become a means for personal growth, and the transnational experience can be more fulfilling. Of course, a deep interest and commitment to your work—professionalism—can be marvelous therapy in intercultural situations, counteracting isolation and strangeness when living outside your home culture.

## Deployment Systems

When an organization is sending people out of the country as its representatives, it has an obligation to ensure that such persons are adequately selected, prepared, and supported, as well as assisted when they return to the homeland. The sponsors need to have a *system* for relocating their personnel or members. Behavioral scientists have been investigating the whole phenomenon of people exchanges, especially for those who live and work in isolated and confined environments (ICE).[14] The latter experience may range from offshore oil rigs and polar research stations to undersea submarines, orbiting space stations, and a lunar base. The following describes the four major components in a relocation or deployment system, whether terrestrial or in space. The extent to which these guidelines are followed depends on the length of the assignment.

The *Sage Handbook of Intercultural Competence*[15] has many chapters that are especially relevant for anyone who wishes to explore this topic in more detail (especially Chapters 1, 3, 6, 14, 28, and 29).

# STAGE ONE: PERSONNEL AND PROGRAM ASSESSMENT

The first major component in a relocation or foreign deployment system involves assessing individual candidates for service abroad or in ICE, and later evaluating their on-site performance. In addition, the sponsor should periodically and objectively evaluate its relocation services and training, including transfer and reentry process.

*Predeparture assessment*—From the perspective of the sponsoring organization's responsibilities, a complete foreign deployment evaluation system needs to:

- Ascertain the adaptability of key personnel for foreign service, including their ability to deal with the host nationals effectively.
- Develop a psychological profile for the candidate—summarize a psychological evaluation of the candidate's skills in human relations within an intercultural context, as well as determine the candidate's ability to cope with changes and differences, and the candidate's susceptibility to severe culture shock.
- Identify specific physical and intellectual barriers to successful adjustment in the foreign environment, if possible, to correct any deficiencies before departure.
- Highlight any specific technical or management factors that need strengthening before the cross-cultural assignment.
- Seek out any personal or family problems that would undermine employee effectiveness abroad.
- Develop a performance review plan for the individual when abroad, as well as assessment of the support services to be rendered.
- Adapt the above evaluation process to foreign nationals brought on assignment into domestic operations.
- Involve expatriate employees who have returned from foreign sites or host country nationals in predeparture training of émigrés.
- Provide instruments for data gathering about the candidates' attitudes and competencies regarding change, intercultural knowledge and relations, and communication skills. These may involve commercial or homemade questionnaires, inventories, checklists, and culture shock tests.
- Use, assessment and training, simulations, case studies, and critical incidents that approximate life abroad.
- Employ a reality check on individual expectations regarding the foreign post, as to living conditions, job requirements, opportunities, and incongruities.

*On-site assessment*—When the individual is sent overseas, the continuing performance review might further investigate:

- The actual tasks or activities the expatriate engages in, and the person's ability to accomplish them.
- The people with whom the individual interacts—his or her ability to deal with the indigenous or local population.
- The extent to which the official posting requires social interactions with host and third-country nationals, as well as expatriates from other organizations—capacity of the sojourner to deal with such variety of human relationships.
- The work duties required, whether by an individual or team collaboration, especially with persons outside the company.
- The language skills required (English or a foreign language), and the capacity of that employee to meet them.
- The individual's outlook abroad, whether provincial or cosmopolitan. Has that person demonstrated interest in the local culture and its manifestations? Has the organization's representative made satisfactory progress in the foreign culture?
- The expatriate's self-reporting—his or her sense of how the international experience is affecting personal and family life, including impact of absence from the homeland while on foreign assignment (i.e., influence on personal life and that of dependents, as well as on career development and life plans).
- The overall rating of the individual's performance and adjustment in the foreign assignment and its society.

*Continuing system improvements*—Findings and insights obtained from both the predeparture and on-site assessment programs should be viewed as feedback to further improve the relocation system with the next group of candidates. For example, a survey of employees on foreign assignment or of expatriates who have returned may reveal special needs and problems that the organization's foreign deployment system is, or is not, addressing satisfactorily.

The selection systems of organizations vary, but some use the following techniques:

- Within the HRD division or department, establish an assessment center that has the responsibility for recruitment and selection of overseas personnel.
- Outsource for services by contracting an external relocation resource, such as intercultural consultants and/or an international executive/management/technical search firm.
- Set up a selection review board made up of an organization's own employees or members, qualified volunteers who have served abroad, especially in the target culture; include company specialists in corporate health and personnel services.
- Limit selection for overseas assignments to expatriates who have previously demonstrated their effectiveness abroad, whether within the organization or hired from outside.

*Selection criteria*—Overall, seek candidates for overseas service who are capable of empathy, openness, persistence, sensitivity to intercultural factors, respect for others, role flexibility, tolerance for ambiguity, and who possess two-way communication skills. Research indicates that possession of these characteristics is correlated to adaptation and effectiveness outside an individual's home culture.

# STAGE TWO: PERSONNEL ORIENTATION AND TRAINING

The second component in a foreign deployment system is some type of self- or group-learning experience or training about culture generally, as well as specifics about the target area's culture. This can be accomplished electronically or in live sessions with *PowerPoint* briefings. The general content can include learning modules on cross-cultural communications and change, understanding culture and its influence on behavior, culture shock and cross-cultural relations, improving organizational relations, and intercultural effectiveness. To increase cultural awareness and skills, several alternative methods are possible. These have amply been reviewed in our accompanying *Instructor's Manual for Managing Cultural Differences*.

Today, an increasingly popular means of cross-cultural learning is electronic, especially by means of the computer and television. To supplement or replace formal group instruction, individualized learning packages can be provided for the employee and his or her family. Such programmed learning and media systems can educate on cultural differences in general, as well as on the specific country to be visited. This type of learning can occur in a company learning center or at home with one's family. It might also serve as preparation for classroom instruction.

Culture-specific briefing programs can be developed for a particular geographical region or country, such as is provided in Unit 2 of this volume. For example, the Middle East could be a subject of study, with particular emphasis on Egypt, Saudi Arabia, and Turkey, or even Israel/Palestine, Iraq, and Iran. A learning program of 12 or more hours can be designed with a self-instruction manual for individual study, or the materials used for group training. Obviously, no relocation orientation is complete without adequate language and technical training. However, the focus here is on cultural training and preparation.

Current thinking on this second stage of foreign deployment leads us to these recommendations for dividing the preparation for service abroad into four phases. In other words, the predeparture program would involve the following components. The time and scope of each activity would again depend on whether it was a long- or short-term assignment out of country:

*Phase one—general culture/area orientation:*

1. Become aware of the factors that make a culture unique and the characteristics of the home culture that most influence employee behavior abroad.
2. Seek local cross-cultural experience, and engage in intercultural communication with minority cultures within the homeland so as to sensitize oneself to cultural differences.
3. Foster more global attitudes and tolerance within the candidate family, while counteracting prejudice and ethnocentrism. For example, cook national dishes of other countries, attend cultural weeks or exhibits of foreign or ethnic groups, or invite a foreigner to your home.

*Phase two—language orientation:*

1. Undertake 60-80 h of formal training in the language of the host country.
2. Supplement classroom experience with 132-180 h of self-learning in the language, by listening to the foreign tongue via audio/videocassettes or radio; by watching television or Internet shows and films; by reading newspapers, magazines, or books in the new language; by speaking to others who have this language proficiency.
3. Build a 500-word survival vocabulary in the target language.
4. Develop specialized vocabularies for the job, marketplace, etc.
5. Practice the language at every opportunity, especially with family members.
6. Seek further education in the language upon arrival in the host country.

*Phase three—culture-specific orientation:*

1. Learn and gather data about culture specifics of the host country.
2. Understand and prepare to counteract "culture shock."
3. Check out specific company policies about the assigned country. These policies are related to allowances for transportation, housing, education, expense accounts, and provisions for salaries, taxes, and other fringe benefits, including medical service and emergency leave.
4. Obtain necessary transfer documents (passports, visas, etc.), and learn customs, policies, and regulations, as well as currency restrictions, for entry and exit to host country.

5. Interview, in person or electronically, fellow employees who have returned from the host country. Get practical information about banking, shopping, currency, climate, mail, and law enforcement.
6. Read travel books and other information about the country and culture.

*Phase four—job environment/organization orientation:*

1. Obtain information about the overseas job environment and organization.
2. Be aware of the government's customs, restrictions, and attitudes regarding business, and your local corporation or project.
3. Arrange for necessary technical training to assure high performance abroad; seek a local mentor or coach.

Relocation strategies should encompass the staff engaged in recruiting, selecting, and training; the employee and dependents assigned abroad; as well as the host culture managers who are responsible for expatriate personnel in the new environment. The focus should be on the opportunities afforded by the international assignment for personal growth, professional exchange and development, and effective representation of country and corporation.

# STAGE THREE: SUPPORT SERVICE: ON-SITE SUPPORT AND MONITORING

Once employees have been recruited, selected, trained, and transported abroad, the organizational responsibility to personnel should be to:

1. Facilitate their integration into a different work environment and host culture.
2. Evaluate their needs and performance abroad.
3. Encourage morale and career development, especially through homeland communications.

As a follow-up to the predeparture training and after the employee or family arrives in the host country, some type of on-site orientation and briefing should be arranged. Back home, there might have been a lack of readiness to listen to details about the job and new community. Now that the expatriates are faced with the daily realities of life abroad, they may have many questions. Periodically, the newcomers should be provided opportunities to come together socially and share as a group.

The in-country orientation should be pragmatic and meet the needs of the expatriate family. It should demonstrate that the organization cares about its people. It should aid the employee and his or her family to resolve immediate living problems; to meet the challenge of the host culture and the opportunities it offers for travel, personal growth, and intercultural exchange; to reduce the culture shock and to grow from that experience; and to provide communication links to the local community and the home organization. Much of this can be accomplished in a systematic, informal, friendly group setting, or even electronically.

# STAGE FOUR: REACCULTURATION: REENTRY PROGRAM

The last component in the foreign deployment system involves reintegrating the expatriate into the home society and domestic organization. The person or family who has been abroad for some time will discover when they return that the homeland and the organizational cultures will have changed. The reentry process begins overseas with the psychological withdrawal the expatriate faces with returning home. Upon return, reentry shock may occur for 6 months or more, as the person struggles to readjust to the lifestyle and tempo of the changed home and organizational cultures. Apart from the challenge of reestablishing home and family life is the issue of reassignment in the parent company or agency.

For many expatriates, the last stage of the culture shock process is a time of crises and trauma. Such personnel may experience mild or severe *reentry shock*. The experience abroad for those who are sensitive and who become involved in the host culture is profound. It causes many people to reexamine their lives, values, attitudes, to assess how they became what they are. It is a turning point, prompting lifestyle changes when they get back. The reentry process becomes the opportunity to carry out these aspirations. Individuals may not be satisfied to return to old neighborhoods, old friends, or the same job or company affiliation. Many wish to apply the new self-insights and to seek new ways of personal growth. The organization that sent them abroad in the first place should be empathetic to this reality and be prepared to deal with it, including by providing severance benefit packages or even outplacement services. The relocation system is incomplete unless it helps returning employees to fit comfortably into their home culture and organization. Closing the deployment loop may involve group counseling with personnel specialists, psychologists, and former expatriates. Always consider expatriates coming back from an overseas assignment as a valuable resource. The corporation can learn much from their cross-cultural experience.

An example of the reentry complexity is described by Chang,[16] demonstrating how the interaction between mothers and their children changed when the student returned. The research demonstrated that the mothers' confusion about their children's cultural identity resulted in a confusion about their motherhood identity. One of the coauthors of this book remembers overhearing his mother on the telephone with one of her friends after he returned from working overseas for 5 years. "I don't know what happened to Bob when he was in China." However, I wasn't in China; I was in Japan.

## BUSINESS ETIQUETTE AND PROTOCOL ABROAD

Cooperation in world trade and commerce is considered by many to be humanity's best chance to maintain global peace and prosperity. Training in managing change, interpersonal skills, cultural difference, and creating synergy can improve not only human relations, but the "bottom line."

Webster's dictionary defines protocol as *a code prescribing adherence to correct etiquette and procedures*. While modern management, the Internet, and mass communications are forming new protocols for the global marketplace, we still cannot ignore the local expectations for business and professional activities. Nelson[17] advises these basic protocols be observed.

1. Remembering and pronouncing people's names correctly.
2. Using appropriate rank and titles when required.
3. Knowing the local variables of time and punctuality.
4. Creating the right impression with suitable dress.
5. Practicing behavior that demonstrates concern for others, tact and discretion, and knowledge of what constitutes good manners and ethics locally.
6. Communicating with intercultural sensitivity, verbally and nonverbally, whether in person, electronically, or in writing or printing.
7. Giving and receiving gifts and favors appropriate to local traditions.
8. Enjoying social events while conscious of local customs relative to food and drink, such as regarding prohibitions, the use of utensils, dining out and entertaining, and seating arrangements.

According to Lewis,[18] a *psychological contract* is forged between the individual and the institution which employs that person. This represents unwritten, unexpressed needs and expectations on the part of both parties. For an employee or member, it is a highly subjective perspective, and is the glue that binds that person to the organization. In the disappearing industrial work culture, the psychological contract focused on job security in return for loyalty and hard work. Currently, the emphasis is for employees to give their organizational support in return for compensation, plus opportunities to learn and acquire new skills. Employability, rather than stability, is the centerpiece of the contract. And the contract varies somewhat when personnel are posted outside their homelands.

For expatriate workers, the employer has more influence in terms of provisions for housing, education, welfare, recreation, and social events. Because of this, perceived contractual violations may provoke intense reactions from employees overseas. This dissatisfaction may be expressed in a variety of ways from negative communications and damage to company reputation, to misconduct, hostility, and even sabotage. Continued exposure abroad to a stressful environment may cause alterations in sleeping patterns, high anxiety, neurotic defense mechanisms, and other manifestations of culture shock.

## ASSESSMENT INSTRUMENTS[19]

Most global leaders have received feedback from completing a variety of questionnaires and instruments designed to measure skills and attitudes, such as linguistic ability, which is easy to access, and global mindset attitudes,[20] which are very difficult to measure.

Over the years, we have found the following instruments to be valuable from the list of Fantini in the *Sage Handbook on Intercultural Competence.*[21]

■ Assessment of Intercultural Competence (AIC)
   *Measures*: Intercultural competence, including language proficiency
   *Description*: This questionnaire, designed in a YOGA format ("Your Objectives, Guidelines, and Assessment") is used for self-assessment and assessment by peers and teachers. The tool monitors the development of the intercultural competence of sojourners (and hosts) over time, providing valid and reliable indicators.
■ Cross-Cultural Adaptability Inventory (CCAI)
   *Measures*: Individual potential for cross-cultural adaptability
   *Description*: A culture-general instrument designed to assess individual potential for cross-cultural adaptability.
■ Cross-Cultural Assessor (CCA)
   *Measures*: Individual understanding of self and others
   *Description*: This tool is designed to improve people's understanding of themselves and others, as well as to promote positive attitudes to cultural difference.
■ Cultural Orientations Indicator® (COI®)
   *Measures*: Cultural preferences
   *Description*: A Web-based cross-cultural assessment tool that allows individuals to assess their personal cultural preferences and compare them with generalized profiles of other cultures.

- Global Literacy Survey
  *Measures*: World knowledge
  *Description*: A self-test used to measure the degree of knowledge young Americans have about the world.
- Global Team Process Questionnaire™ (GTPQ)
  *Measures*: Effectiveness of global teams
  *Description*: A proprietary instrument designed to help global teams improve their effectiveness and productivity.
- GlobeSmart
  *Measures*: Effectiveness of global teams
  *Description*: A Web-based tool that investigates how to conduct business effectively in 35 countries.

## CONCLUSIONS

Life is filled with crises, some of which can be turned into challenges for personal and professional growth.[22] Some happen by going abroad into another culture, or even in making the passage from an industrial to knowledge work environment. The trauma experienced in this adjustment process can take many forms, whether it is called culture or reentry shock, role or organization shock, or even future shock. Essentially, cross-cultural transitions threaten our sense of identity. Such transitions force us to rethink and reevaluate the way we read meaning into our private worlds. They are opportunities to learn and develop, causing a transformation in our behavior and lifestyle, as well as in our management or leadership.

Organizations can reduce such shocks to their personnel by coaching, counseling, and training. The stress and anxiety that may result need not lead to severe disorientation, depression, and unhealthy behavior. These can be countered by increasing awareness and information that provides more enjoyable intercultural experiences.

When considered in the context of sending employees overseas on assignment, the return on organizational investment in cross-cultural preparation and continuing support services can be considerable. We recommend that sponsoring multinational corporations or agencies institute a foreign deployment *system*. This approach to relocation activities will not only reduce premature return costs and much unhappiness among expatriates and overseas customers, but it can improve performance, productivity, and profitability in the world market. Furthermore, observing and practicing both national and international protocol facilitates human performance and cooperation, especially in development projects. Such counsel becomes even more meaningful in the context of technology transfer, whether within a nation or across borders.

## MIND STRETCHING

1. Explain the concept of the transitional experience and its many manifestations. Apply these insights to the university graduate going into the world of work, or civilian and military personnel assigned overseas.
2. Why are so many workers leaving their culture of origin to work abroad, despite the many difficulties encountered? What are the responsibilities of communities and organizations in facilitating the acculturation of foreign newcomers?
3. Why does a relocation assignment pose a challenge to one's sense of identity? What are culture and reentry shock? How can these phenomena be avoided or delimited?
4. What is your understanding of being "global"?
5. Why should world-class corporations have a foreign deployment system? Overall, what does such a system entail?

## REFERENCES

1. Shoper, J. April 18, 2006. e-mail to Robert Moran from John Shoper. Used with permission.
2. Peterson, B. *Cultural Intelligence—A Guide to Working with People from Other Cultures.* 2004; Comes, A. *Culture from Inside Out—Travel and Meet Yourself*; Storti, C. *Figuring Foreigners Out.* Boston, MA: Nicholas Brealey/Intercultural Press, 1999.
3. Lewis, R. D. *The Cultural Imperative-Global Trends in the 21st Century.* Boston, MA: Nicholas Brealey, 2002, p. 228; Lewis, R. D. *When Cultures Collide—Managing Successfully Across Cultures.* Boston, MA: Nicholas Brealey, 2000.
4. Campbell, J. *Hero with a Thousand Faces.* Princeton, NJ: Princeton University Press, 1968; Osland, J. S. *The Adventure of Working Abroad—Hero Tales from the Global Frontier.* San Francisco, CA: Jossey-Bass, 1995; Hofstede, G. J., Peterson, P. B., and Hofstede, G. *Exploring Culture—Exercises, Stories, and Synthetic Cultures.* Boston, MA: Nicholas Brealey/Intercultural Press, 2002.
5. Spencer, S. A. and Adams, J. D. *Life Changes—Growing Through Personal Transition*; Bridges, W. *Transitions—Make Sense of Life's Changes*; Biracress, T., and Biracress, N. *Over Fifty—Resource Book for the Better Half of Your Life*; Cort-VanArsdale, D. *Transitions—A Woman's Guide to Successful Retirement.* These books on lifestyle transitions are available from Knowledge Systems, Inc., 7777 W. Morris St., Indianapolis, IN 46231.
6. Fearn, N. *Philosophy: The Latest Answers to the Oldest Questions.* New York: Atlanta Books, 2005.

7. Lewis, T., and Jungman, R. (eds.). *On Being Foreign: Culture Shock in Short Fiction*; Kols, L. R. *Survival Kit for Intercultural Living*; Storti, C., *The Art of Coming Home*. Boston, MA: Nicholas Brealey/Intercultural Press, 1986, 2001.

8. Furnham, A. and Bochner, S. *Culture Shock—Psychological Reactions to an Unfamiliar Environment*. New York: Methuen & Co., 1986.

9. Oberg, K. *Culture Shock and the Problem of Adjustment to New Cultural Environments*. Washington, DC: Foreign Service Institute, 1958; Storti, C. *The Art of Crossing Cultures*; Sichel, E. F. and Sichel, N. (eds.). *Uprooted Childhoods: Memories of Growing Up Global*. Boston: Nicholas Brealey/Intercultural Press, 2001, 2004.

10. Klopf, D. W. *Intercultural Encounters*, Third Edition. Englewood, CO: Morton Publishing Company, 1995. Also refer to Gundling, E. *Working Global Smart—12 People Skills for Doing Business Across Borders*. Palo Alto, CA: Davies-Black, 2003; Ember, C. R. (ed.). *Cultures of the World*. New York, NY: Macmillan, 1999.

11. Osland, J. S. "The Hero's Adventure: The Overseas Experience of Expatriate Business People," unpublished doctoral dissertation, Case Western University, 1990. Available through University Microfilms International, 300 N. Zeeb Road, Ann Arbor, MI 48106; Also refer to Dr. Eileen Sheridan (Wibbeke), more recent doctoral dissertation on this subject in 2005 at the University of Phoenix Online (e-mail: docwibbeke@gmail.com).

12. Szkudlarek, B. "Reentry—A Review of the Literature," *International Journal of Intercultural Relations* 34, 2010.

13. Berry, J. W. "Psychology of Acculturation," *Applied Cross-Cultural Psychology*, Brislin, R. W. (ed.). Newbury Park, CA: Sage Publications, 1990; Laroche, L. *Managing Cultural Diversity in Technical Professions*. Burlington, MA: Elsevier/Butterworth-Heinemann, 2002.

14. Relative to *deployment systems*, refer to Haines, S. G. *The Manager's Pocket Guide to Systems Thinking and Learning*. Amherst, MA: HRD Press, 2004. Also contact the Society for Human Performance in Extreme Environments for information and publications (e-mail: Society@HPPE.org or Web site www.hpee.org). Relative to a *space deployment system*, Harrison, A. A. *Spacefaring—The Human Dimension*. Berkeley, CA: University of California Press, 2001; Harris, P. R. *Launch Out—A Science-Based Novel about Lunar Industrialization*, 2003; Freeman, M. *Challenges of Human Space Exploration*, 2000; Harris, P. R. *Living and Working in Space—Human Behavior, Culture, and Organization*, 1996. These space books are available from Univelt Inc., Escondido, CA (www.univelt.com or EM: roberthjacobs@compuserve.com).

15. Deardorff, D. K. (ed.). *The Sage Handbook of Intercultural Competence*. Newbury Park, CA: Sage Publications, Inc., 2009.

16. Chang, Y. "A Qualitative Study of Temporary Reentry from Significant Others' Perspective," *International Journal of Intercultural Relations*, Vol. 33, 2009, pp. 259–263.

17. Nelson, C. A. *Protocol for Profit—A Manager's Guide to Competing Worldwide*. London: International Thomas Business Press, 1998; Olafsson, G. *When in Rome or Rio or Riyadh—Cultural Q&A's for Successful Business Behavior Around the World*, 2004; Mole, J. *Mind*

*Your Manners—Managing Business Cultures in the New Global Europe*, Boston, MA: Nicholas Brealey/Intercultural Press, 2004.

18. Lewis, K. G. "Breakdown—A Psychological Contract for Expatriates," *European Business Review*, Vol. 97, No. 6, 1997, pp. 279–293. Also refer to Rampersad, H. K. *Total Performance Scorecard—Redefining Management to Achieve Performance with Integrity*. Burlington, MA: Elsevier/Butterworth-Heinemann, 2003.

19. Deardorff, D. K. (ed.). *The Sage Handbook of Intercultural Competence*. Newbury Park, CA: Sage Publications, Inc., 2009.

20. Javidan, M., Teagarden, M., and Bowen, D. "Making It Overseas: Developing the Skills You Need to Succeed as an International Leader," *Harvard Business Review*, April 2010.

21. Deardorff, D. K. (ed.). *The Sage Handbook of Intercultural Competence*. Thousand Oaks, CA: Sage Publications, Inc., 2009.

22. Sheehy, G. *New Passages, Mapping Your Life Across Time*. New York: Random House, 1995.

# LEADERSHIP IN CREATING CULTURAL SYNERGY

Multinational organizations have a special role not only in building cross-cultural bridges, but in innovating synergies through their practical knowledge of putting together human and natural resources with the know-how of managing both in the most effective ways.[1]

Given our interdependence, any world order that elevates one nation or group of people over another will inevitably fail. So whatever we think of the past, we must not be prisoners to it.

U.S. President Barack Obama, Cairo, Egypt, 2009

Linda Zhou, Alice Wei Zhao, Lori Ying, Angela Yu-Yun Yeung, Lynnelle Lin Ye, Kevin Young Xu, Benjamin Chang Sun, Jane Yoonhae Suh, Katheryn Cheng Shi, Sunanda Sharma, Sarine Gayaneh Shahmirian, Arjun Ranganath Puranik, Raman Venkat Nelakant, Akhil Mathew, Paul Masih Das, David Chienyun Liu, Elisa Bisi Lin, Yifan Li, Lanair Amaad Lett, Ruoyi Jiang, Otana Agape Jakpor, Peter Danming Hu, Yale Wang Fan, Yuval Yaacov Calev, Levent Alpoge, John Vincenzo Capodilupo and Namrata Anand.[2]

## LEARNING OBJECTIVES

*Synergy* is a difficult word to understand, and even more challenging to implement. It implies a belief that we can learn from others and others can learn from us. Ways to understand synergy are presented in this chapter.

If we are able to learn from others (Chapter 4), we have the possibility of creating synergy. Consider the differences that would take place in the quality of life in the twenty-first century if we were to take the time to develop the mechanisms of working together to create synergy.

Fareed Zakaria said it well: "If, on the one hand, we come together and work on common problems of humanity, imagine the opportunities it would create for everyone."[3]

Cultural synergy is a dynamic approach to managing cultural diversity in a variety of contexts. Nations and organizations as systems are continuously affected by the dynamics of globalization. Global economic trends have shown increasing enchantment with globalization. The universal proliferation of services and technology opens markets and accelerates global business opportunities. Globalization has also shown that attempts to effect international deregulation and economic integration have elicited strong protectionist measures stemming from economic, ideological, cultural differences, and the simple desire to retain autonomy.

Cultural synergy builds on common ground, transcending mere awareness of difference, to form multifaceted strategic alliances and partnerships. In this manner, people who represent disparate perspectives and needs find ways through working together to seek a solution where all parties are content with the outcome and therefore together succeed. This is the essence of effective cross-cultural management.

## UNDERSTANDING SYNERGY'S IMPLICATIONS

Synergy comes from the Greek word meaning *working together*. This powerful concept:

1. Represents a dynamic process.
2. Involves adapting and learning.
3. Involves joint action in which the total effect is greater than the sum of effects when acting independently.
4. Creates an integrated solution.
5. Does not signify compromise, yet in true synergy nothing is given up or lost.
6. Develops the potential of members by facilitating the release of team energies.

Synergy is a cooperative or combined action, and occurs when diverse or disparate individuals or groups collaborate for a common cause. The objective is to increase effectiveness by sharing perceptions and experiences, insights, and knowledge.

Synergy begins between colleagues, then extends to their organizations, and finally involves countries. The differences in the world's people can lead to mutual growth and accomplishment that is more than the single contribution of each party. As people, we can go beyond awareness of our own cultural heritage to produce something greater through synergistic actions. The sharing of dissimilar perceptions and cultural backgrounds can be used to enhance problem solving and improve decision making. Using information and technology to promote cooperation among disparate elements in human systems creates something better than existed by separate endeavors.

Some cultures are synergistic and inclined toward cooperation, while other cultures tend toward individualism and competition. The late anthropologist Ruth Benedict studied this phenomenon. Her research was amplified by groundbreaking humanistic psychologist Abraham Maslow. A summary of their characterizations of high-synergy and low-synergy societies is presented in Exhibit 9.1. This model analyzes various cultures throughout the world as to their synergistic relations or the lack of the same. Japan and Sweden are two national cultures that are seemingly high synergistically, while Serbia and Iraq would seem

## EXHIBIT 9.1
## CHARACTERIZATIONS OF HIGH-SYNERGY AND LOW-SYNERGY SOCIETIES

| High-Synergy Society | Low-Synergy Society |
| --- | --- |
| ■ Emphasis is on cooperation for mutual advantage. | ■ Uncooperative, very competitive culture; enhances rugged individualistic and "dog-eat-dog" attitudes. |
| ■ Conspicuous for a nonaggressive social order. | ■ Aggressive and antagonistic behavior toward one another, leading to either psychological or physical violence toward the other. |
| ■ Social institutions promote individual and group development. | ■ Social arrangements self-centered; collaboration is not reinforced as desired behavior. |
| ■ Society idealizes win-win situation. | ■ Society adheres to win-lose approach. |
| ■ Leadership fosters sharing wealth and advantage for the common good. Cooperatives are encouraged, and poverty is fought. | ■ Leadership encourages private or individual gain and advantage, especially by the power elite; poverty is tolerated, even ignored. |
| ■ Society seeks to use community resources and talents for the commonwealth, and encourages development of human potential of all citizenry. | ■ Society permits exploitation of poor and minorities, and tolerates the siphoning of its wealth by privileged few; develops power elites and leaves undeveloped the powerless. |

## EXHIBIT 9.1

## CHARACTERIZATIONS OF HIGH-SYNERGY AND LOW-SYNERGY SOCIETIES (CONTINUED)

| High-Synergy Society | Low-Synergy Society |
|---|---|
| ■ Open system of secure people who tend to be benevolent, helpful, friendly, and generous; its heroes are altruistic and philanthropic. | ■ Closed system with insecure people who tend toward suspiciousness, ruthlessness, and clannishness; idealizes the "strong man" concerned with greed and acquisition. |
| ■ Belief system, religion, or philosophy is comforting and life is consoling; emphasis is on the god of love; power is to be used for benefit of whole community; individuals/groups are helped to work out hurt and humiliations. | ■ Belief system is frightening, punishing, terrifying; members are psychologically beaten or humiliated by the strong; power is for personal profit; emphasis is on the god of vengeance; hatreds go deep and "blood feuds" abound; violence is the means for compensation for hurt and humiliation. |
| ■ Generally, the citizenry is psychologically healthy, and mutual reciprocity is evident in relationships; open to change; low rate of crime and mental illness. | ■ Generally, the citizenry tend to be defensive, jealous; mass paranoia and hostility; fears change and advocates status quo; high rate of crime and mental illness. |

*Source*: Ruth Benedict, Anthropologist; Abraham Maslow, Psychologist.

less so. While Japan and Sweden are highly synergistic, they are also highly monocultural. When one group makes up the majority of all people within a system, finding common ground is far easier than when multiple groups, who often have different and conflicting beliefs, values, religions, and cultures, live in proximity with each other. Iraq and Serbia represent such highly complex and multicultural societies, whose history has shown internal, conflict due to fundamental differences and historical grievances.

# CROSS-CULTURAL CONFLICT AND CULTURAL SYNERGY

What comprises a conflict in one culture is a daily difference of opinion in another. A serious insult in one setting—crossing one's legs or showing the sole of one's foot, for example—is a matter of comfort in another.

An arrogant challenge in one culture—putting one's hands on one's hips—is a sign of openness in another. A normal pathway for de-escalating a conflict in one society—fleeing the scene of an accident—constitutes a serious offense in another. Human boundaries are cultural creations; social boundaries, legal boundaries, and emotional boundaries are all drawn according to each culture's values, myths, and preferences.[4]

According to Adler:

> Cultural synergy, as an approach to managing the impact of cultural diversity, involves a process in which managers form organizational policies, strategies, structures, and practices based on, but not limited to, the cultural patterns of individual organizational members and clients....This approach recognizes both the similarities and differences among the cultures that compose a global organization, and suggests that we neither ignore nor minimize cultural diversity, but rather view it as a resource in designing and developing organizational systems.[5]

Conflict is a fact of life. When humans interact, whether or not cultural differences are a factor, it is inevitable that conflict will arise and must be resolved. In the workplace, managers must learn how to manage conflict successfully; if it is left unresolved, the negative effects extend far beyond the conflicting parties.[6] "If the executive director of a non-profit agency and her board cannot get along, employees tend to take sides, fear for their jobs, and, like those above them, wage a campaign discrediting the other group....Ignoring workplace conflict sets destructive forces in motion that decrease productivity, spread the conflict to others, and lead to lessened morale."[7]

According to Wilmot and Hocker, if employees study organizational conflict, they can learn how to get along with their colleagues, their manager, and the public better; supervisors can learn how to predict the onset of conflict, learn how to utilize a productive response to conflict, and help employees resolve their differences, while keeping conflict from spreading to other parts of the organization.[8] In cross-cultural conflict, it is difficult to predict an individual's behavior toward conflict by his or her country of origin. However, here are some guidelines to help you to acquire an approximate idea of a likely behavior toward conflict from a dualistic perspective. As noted in an earlier chapter, cultural traits fall along the continuum of individualistic at one end and collectivistic at the other end. The following guidelines have been adapted from Wilmot and Hocker.[9]

*Patterns of behavior toward conflict from individualistic cultures:*

- Individualistic cultures tend to emphasize analytic, linear logic, and view a difference between the conflict and the conflicting parties involved.
- Conflict tends to ensue when individual expectations are violated.
- People from individualistic cultures are very direct and tend to be confrontational.
- Individualistic cultures tend to enforce the following approaches to dealing with conflict:

- ■ Solution and action orientation.
- ■ Open and direct communication.
- ■ Linear logic with the use of rational and factual rhetoric.

*Patterns of behavior toward conflict from collectivistic cultures*:

- ■ Collectivistic cultures tend to emphasize holistic logic with group-oriented, collective normative expectations.
- ■ There is an integration of the conflict and the conflicting parties; no separation is seen.
- ■ Conflict tends to ensue when collective expectations are violated.
- ■ People from collective cultures tend to conceal their conflict and be indirect, nonconfrontational, and passively aggressive.
- ■ Collective cultures tend to enforce the following approaches to dealing with conflict:
  - ■ Saving face and one's relations as a priority.
  - ■ Intuitive, affective, ambiguous, and indirect rhetoric strategies to resolve conflict.
  - ■ Point-logic styles of communication.

## Global Complexity and Cultural Synergy

It is theorized that the flap of one butterfly's wings, flying over the Great Wall of China, has a direct link to the substantial dust storm that forms over Marrakesh, Morocco, some time later, severely disrupting all forms of travel from air traffic to ground travel for a full day. A nontheoretical example, many might remember, is the eruption of the Eyjafjallajokull volcano in Iceland that created havoc for air travelers around the world and incalculable business losses.[10] The Butterfly Effect came out of chaos theory, in which seemingly small local events have the distinct potential to cause systemwide disruptions.[11] The idea behind this theory is that global societies and global, multicultural organizations can be analogous to a living creature that adapts and learns, in which the individual person is influenced by many factors, including governmental policies, religious creeds, societal influences of others around them, and cultural pressures.[12]

For each action, there is a reaction and, often, several diverse reactions. On the human front, from each perspective, there lies a way of seeing the world and reacting to it, which then determines behavior and actions. The following quote illustrates the perspective from the standpoint of two people interacting presumably from the same culture. After reading it, imagine the complexity and potential for conflict when different cultural groups interact within the context of organizations.

> *You* can see things behind my back that *I* cannot see, and *I* can see things behind *your* back that are denied to your vision. We are both doing essentially the same thing, but from different places; although we are in the same

event, that event is different for each of us. Our places are different not only because our bodies occupy different positions in the exterior, physical space, but also because we regard each other from different centres.[13]

Just as there are high- and low-synergy societies, there are high- and low-synergy organizations. A high-synergy corporation is one in which employees cooperate for mutual advantage because the customs and traditions of the corporation or organization support such behavior. In this noncompetitive atmosphere, the individual works toward his or her betterment as well as that of the group. Employees work to ensure that mutual benefits are derived from their common undertakings. The same high/low-synergy dimensions may also be applied to group activities.

A low-synergy business is one that is ruggedly individualistic, insisting on going it alone. It avoids partnerships and agreements with other entities, and finds it difficult to adapt quickly to change. Employees are not empowered—often systems and policies are more important than the customer or the people. Managers impose "their way" or organizational culture upon others, often to their mutual detriment. The business focus is on getting ahead at any cost, without regard to the human needs of workers or customers or long-term effective solutions.

## Synergistic Leadership

Synergistic organizations also encourage self-actualization. But, throughout this process, human systems must educate and train their members in new interpersonal and organizational skills so that adherents can communicate and cooperate across cultures and act together for mutual benefit. Such leadership also implies helping participants to conserve and develop human and natural resources for the common good. Finally, it means that leaders must acquire and practice a partnership form of power; namely, that of group initiative and cooperative action for mutual learning. Those with management responsibility are challenged to act as mentors or coaches for their members, so as to earn their commitment. Empowerment is the key.

Another change indicator in human resource development today is increasing emphasis on use of left- and right-brain learning activities. It appears that certain capacities are associated with either side of the cortex. Similarly, every person has qualities that are associated with both the female and male psyche. Holistic learning of males would include cultivation of those aspects commonly associated with the feminine character, and vice versa for the female. Furthermore, it has also been observed that one of the major problems with global leadership, whether political or corporate, is its male domination. Many decision-makers tend to be chauvinistic and skewed toward the male perception of "reality" and the male approach to problem solving. If we are to have synergistic leadership, male/female thinking and powers must be integrated. Perhaps the world's persistent, unsolved problems—mass unemployment, hunger, violence, aggression, underutilization of human capital, among others—exist partly because our attempts to manage them have been so lopsided. That is, over one-half of the human race, women, are too frequently excluded from power and the decision-making process. Synergy is thwarted as long as outmoded cultural beliefs, attitudes, and traditions make false distinctions of a person's intrinsic worth based on gender. Such misconceptions have led to a human resource development movement worldwide toward diversity management and training.

Synergistic leaders in a knowledge economy promote planned change in the work culture that:

- Emphasizes quality of life, rather than just quantity of goods/services.
- Promotes concepts of interdependence and cooperation, rather than just competition.
- Encourages work and technology in harmony with nature, ever conscious of environmental/ecological considerations.
- Is conscious of corporate social responsibility goals, rather than just technical efficiency and production.
- Creates an organizational culture that encourages self-achievement and fulfillment through participation, in contrast to dogmatism and dependency.
- Restates relevant traditional values, such as personal integrity, work ethic, respect for other's property, individual responsibility, and social cohesion.
- Encourages the capacity for intuition, creativity, flexibility, openness, group sensitivity, and goal-oriented planning for change.

The exercise of leadership in today's complex systems in transition is a challenge. It is an illusion that a single leader or decision-maker can alone make the difference. Contemporary leadership failures, especially in the political or corporate arenas, stemming from incompetence or corruption, disillusion the average citizen. In the twenty-first century, only the combined brainpower of multiple knowledge workers or teams is appropriate, so that many become involved with their unique resources and mobilized toward complex solutions. Contemporary changes in markets and workers call for a new type of management development.

Innovative leaders assist people and their social institutions to build upon, yet to transcend, their cultural past. Anthropologist Edward Hall recalled that formerly one stayed relatively close to home, so behaviors around us were fairly predictable. But today, we constantly interact personally or through electronic media with strangers, often at great distances from our home, even at the other side of the globe. Such extensions have widened our range of human contact and caused our "world" to shrink, especially because of the twin impacts of mass communications and transportation. Today, global leaders require *transcultural insights and skills* for coping with such changed circumstances, shared readily with their colleagues. To be comfortable with changing cultural diversity and dissonance, we must literally move beyond the perceptions, imprints, and instructions of our own culture and personally change our mindsets.

Cultures worldwide are in the midst of profound change, but nowhere is this change more evident than in the workplaces of free-market economies. So, while the pace of change varies around the world its focus and challenges differ by region, community, and institution. But wherever the change occurs, it requires leaders who will create a culture of innovation and entrepreneurship. Then, people will be open to continuous change, seeking creative solutions that contribute the next wave in human advancement.

"Developing countries are competing on creativity as well as cost."[14] "The emerging world, long known as a source of cheap labor, now rivals the rich countries for business innovation."[15] *The Economist* article presents a perspective that many emerging economies are being "hotbeds" of business innovation. They are producing US$300.00 computers and US$30.00 cell phones, and involving new systems of production, distribution, supply chain management, and recruitment and retention of employees. These innovations are being accepted by many organizations at the more developed countries, and synergy results. We are learning to learn from others.

## SYNERGY IN GLOBAL ORGANIZATIONS

To facilitate understanding of this key concept, imagine the following scenarios, for which we will later provide examples, of how synergistic relations can be fostered in acquisitions, relocation, structural change, personnel change, role change, consortium formation, and global consultation.

- The chief executive officer of a large global corporation visits the facilities of a newly acquired subsidiary to determine which of the parent company's policies, procedures, and personnel should be utilized in the merged firm, and which approaches or strategies of the acquisition should be retained.
- A New England plant is being relocated to Alabama. Its Northern employees have been given the opportunity to move to the South, so as to join an enlarged workforce of local Southerners. The plant manager at the Alabama plant is a technocrat from England who immigrated to the United States 5 years ago.
- A major retailer is in the midst of profound organizational change. A traditional company with branches throughout the country, it is proud of its 75 years of customer service and long records of faithful employees. Declining sales, fierce competition, and inflation led to the election of a new chairman of the board, who has hired some new competent managers. Together, they have begun to shake up the corporation to ensure its survival.

- A European conglomerate has purchased controlling rights of an American steel manufacturer. Key management positions have been filled with French, Italian, and German specialists in downsizing and mergers, though most of the effective American management has been retained. Plans are under way to improve operations and turn the company into a profitable venture.
- As employees become more sophisticated at computers and information processing, doing business electronically in the global marketplace is critical. Thus, competent information technology personnel begin a retraining program in new systems and networking.
- European partners are successfully involved in producing innovative aircrafts at Airbus Industries. It began with three major companies from three different countries, and eventually a fourth company/country entered into the agreement.
- A Canadian consulting firm agreed to assist a Mexican corporation in the use of advanced technology. It is part of a larger deal between the governments of both countries, in which Mexican energy is to be supplied in return for Canadian expertise and equipment.
- A Japanese auto manufacturer seeks to penetrate the EU market, so it buys existing automobile plants in England and Poland.
- Sixteen nations and their space agencies join forces in constructing and maintaining a macroproject, called the International Space Station.

The common element in each of these scenarios is the opportunity to exercise leadership in cultural synergy. In these situations, differences in organizational cultures can either weaken the intended actions or they can be used to enhance goal achievement.

Leaders can either impose their corporate policies, procedures, and cultures on others, often to their mutual detriment, or simply be aware of the other's institutional culture, its strengths, and limitations. But a better approach is to objectively evaluate what is of "value" in each of the existing enterprises and build upon such foundations, being sensitive to cultural differences and opportunities for synergy that result in mutual growth and development.

## Transforming the Work Culture

High-synergy organizations are essential in a knowledge culture. Promoting synergy in and through the organization is one strategy for transitioning into this twenty-first century work environment. It is impossible to fully describe here this new work culture.

For the past 50 years, a wide range of behavioral scientists, in cooperation with executives and other organizational leaders have been engaged, in transforming the work environment from that of the Industrial Age toward the postindustrial directions. Our research has identified 10 general characteristics of this emerging work culture. In the future, workers at all levels will generally manifest:

- Enhanced quality of work life
- More autonomy and control over their work space
- Improved organizational communication and information dissemination
- Participation and involvement in the enterprise and its decision making
- Relevant, creative organizational norms or standards
- High performance and productivity
- Skill in using new communications and robotic technologies
- More research and development activities
- More personal entrepreneurialism and organizational intrapreneurialism
- More utilization of informal and synergistic relationships

Such should be the goals of global leaders who seek to transform the work culture.

# SYNERGISTIC TEAM MANAGEMENT

Traditional organization models and management styles are gradually being replaced or reworked because they are inadequate and unproductive within the knowledge culture. A major transition is under way in social systems from "disappearing bureaucracies" to "emerging ad hocracies." Global leaders facilitate the transition from past to futuristic operations by promoting team management practices. This approach may operate under various designations, such as a project, task force, product, business systems team, or an ad hoc planning committee. The point is that work is organized around a "temporary" group that involves permanent (functional) and impermanent lines of authority.

## Understanding the Team Strategy

The dictionary defines a *team* as a number of persons associated in some joint action, while *teamwork* is described as a cooperative or coordinated effort by persons working together. Teams are collections of people who must rely on group collaboration if each member is to experience the optimum of success and goal achievement.

Changing technology and markets have stimulated the team approach to management, because temporary groups can function across organizational divisions and better cope with diversity of membership. Multicultural and multifunctional teams are becoming commonplace. Furthermore, the complexity of society and the human systems devised to meet new and continuing needs require a pooling of resources and talents. Inflation, resource scarcity, reduced personnel levels, budget cuts, and similar constraints have underscored the demands for better coordination and synergy in the use of "brainpower."

In effect, the team management model alters organizational culture. The term used currently is *self-managed teams*, which contribute to employee empowerment and problem solving. Such work units evolve their own unique *team culture*. As noted previously, high-technology corporations excel with project teams consisting of a variety of skilled specialists from management information systems, accounting, and new technologies. With the team approach, obsolete business separations give way to synergistic, functional arrangements among those employed in manufacturing, marketing, and administration; line and staff activities overlap and often merge.

## Team Building for Success and Synergy

Astute HRD executives make provisions for team building or training within their organizations by qualified internal or external consultants. In such human-relations training, leaders seek to cultivate a *team environment* that facilitates the group's performance. However, these guidelines might be questioned in whole or in part by readers from other national or cultural backgrounds. In essence, in team building, members learn:

- Tolerance of ambiguity, uncertainty, and seeming lack of structure.
- To take interest in each member's achievement, as well as the group's.
- The ability to give and accept feedback in a nondefensive manner.
- Openness to change, innovation, group consensus, team decision making, and creative problem solving.
- To create a team atmosphere that is informal, relaxed, comfortable, and nonjudgmental.
- The capacity to establish intense, short-term member relations, and to disconnect for the next project.
- To keep group communication on target and schedule, while permitting disagreement and valuing effective listening.
- To urge a spirit of constructive criticism, and authentic, nonevaluative feedback.
- To encourage members to express feelings and to be concerned about group morale/maintenance.
- To clarify roles, relationships, assignments, and responsibilities.
- To share leadership functions within a group and to use total member resources.
- To pause periodically from task pursuits to reexamine and reevaluate team progress and communications.
- To foster trust, confidence, and commitment within the group.
- Sensitivity to the team's linking function with other work units.
- To foster a norm that members will be supportive and respectful of one another, and realistic in their expectations of each other.
- To promote an approach that is goal-directed, seeks group participation, divides the labor fairly, and synchronizes effort.

■ To set high performance standards for the group.
■ To cultivate listening skills.

Since each team experience is different, uniqueness and flexibility should be encouraged. Yet, at the same time, coordination and integration of team effort with other units and the whole enterprise are essential if the sum is to be greater than its parts. When team cultures contain the elements previously outlined and are reflective of the whole organizational environment, then they become closely knit and productive. The more team participation is provided and employees are included in team decision making, the healthier and more relevant is that human system.

## Improving Performance Through Team Culture

Just like the organization in general, we might have an image of the team as a smaller "energy exchange system." When the group functions well, human psychic and physical energy is used effectively. Team interaction is an energy exchange. As the group seeks to achieve its goals, members energize or motivate themselves and one another by example. Team planning and changes become projections on energy use and its alteration. Every aspect of the group process can be analyzed in terms of this human energy paradigm. The key issue, then, is how the team manages its energies most productively and avoids underutilizing or even wasting the group energies. There are ways that members can analyze their functions and performance in projects, task forces, or product teams.

Team behavior can be examined from the viewpoint of task functions, which initiate, give, or seek information, clarify or elaborate on member ideas, and summarize or synthesize. It can also be seen from the angle of group maintenance or morale building, such as encouraging, expressing group feeling, harmonizing, and compromising. It is the last element that builds group cohesion and camaraderie.

Such periodic behavioral review and data gathering can be useful to improve the group's effectiveness. Not only can the information help a member to change his or her team behavior, but when such findings are combined into a visual profile, they offer a diagnosis of team health from time to time. It is recommended that teams pause on occasion for such self-examination. Sometimes a third-person facilitator, such as an internal or external consultant, can be most helpful in this analysis of team culture and progress. When the group's assessment is summarized, the team can then view its implications for more effective use of member energies.

Team participation is an intensive learning experience. When members voluntarily involve themselves and fully participate, personal and professional growth is fostered. The team is like a laboratory of the larger organizational world in which it operates. Although a temporary experience, it is an opportunity for individual and team development. Each participant shares self and insights from the basis of unique life and organizational experiences. Synergy occurs when the members listen to each other and enter into the private worlds of the others. Total team perception and wisdom then become more than the sum of the parts.

If the organization's culture emphasizes employee participation through team management, the group microcultures are likely to reflect that system's macroculture. Thus, collaborative management should be evident not only within an individual team, but in intergroup relations. There is an implicit assumption that the team culture exerts a significant influence on an individual member's behavior. As a team member, one functions beyond the individual level, becoming representative of the group "persona." Those who serve in two or more interlocking groups are expected to act as linking pins in the accomplishment of organizational mission through these separate but interdependent entities.

Everything that anthropologists would examine in the culture of people in a national or organizational group can be analyzed in the miniature environment of the team. That can range from the group's beliefs and attitudes, to procedures and practices, to priorities and technologies. The team atmosphere, task orientation or processes, communication patterns, role clarification or negotiation, conflict resolution, decision making, action planning, intragroup and intergroup relations, all can be scrutinized for better diagnosis of the group's dynamics. When a global manager or consultant engages in such analysis, the team can become more effective in the use of its energies.

## Transcultural Teams

Social scientists are conducting research on what people can do in small multinational groups to facilitate a meaningful experience and productive outcome. One exciting example of this occurred at the East-West Center in Honolulu, Hawaii.

At its Culture Learning Institute, Dr. Kathleen K. Wilson spearheaded an investigation with 15 other distinguished colleagues on the factors influencing the management of International Cooperative Research and Development projects. Their ICRD findings still have implications for any professional seeking to improve human performance and collaboration. Although the researchers are examining project team effectiveness among internationals, their insights can be extrapolated to other forms of inter- and intragroup behavior, whether it is a matrix organization, product team, task force, or any work unit.

The contexts in which international cooperative groups operate may vary, but there are similar factors present that affect performance. These external factors affect the environment within the project itself, and include such diverse elements as political, organizational, and cultural aspects, the size and scope of the endeavor, the disciplinary background of team members, and individual characteristics, research, and development policies and problems. A summary of factors that foster or hinder professional synergy follows in Exhibit 9.2. Certainly, the exhaustive list of situations that influence a project's effectiveness points up the

## Exhibit 9.2

## Human Factors That Foster or Hinder Professional Synergy Within a Project

- How project business is planned
- Consideration of other problem-solving viewpoints
- How the work should be organized
- Approach to R&D tasks
- Definition of R&D problems
- Ambiguity resolution and problem formulation
- Methods and procedures
- Decision making relative to recurring problems
- Allocation of resources to team members
- Accountability procedures relative to resource use
- Timing and sequencing approaches
- Determining objectives for an R&D effort
- Affiliation and liaison with external groups and degree of formality in their work relations
- Quantity and type of project human resources
- Qualifications, recruitment, and selection of new members
- New member orientation and training on the project
- Management of responsibilities
- Underutilization of workers relative to skill competencies
- Motivating behavior and reward expectations
- Coordination of long/short-term members
- Agreement on degree of innovation required
- Experience with cooperation especially relative to international R&D tasks
- Official language(s) to use on projects
- Method of reporting every one's involvement in the project
- Coping with internal demands and visitors
- Meeting face-to-face and having to resort to other forms of more impersonal communication
- Involvement in making viewpoints known
- Power differences because of institution resources brought to the project
- Prestige, risk-taking, tolerance of uncertainty, and perceptions
- Project leadership and/or organizational policies changing unexpectedly
- Quality of work presented in evaluation methods
- What constituted success in project work, and what to do when members fail to meet group expectations
- Clarification of roles on the relationships

need for strategies to manage the many cultural differences existing between and among professionals attempting to work together. One can apply these observations to real-time group situations, such as teams functioning:

■ within the United Nations or UNESCO, the World Health Organization, World Bank, or International Monetary Fund;
■ within a global corporation that spans many countries and includes multinational membership;
■ within the International Space Station, both on the ground and in orbit, with its sponsorship of some 16 nations; and
■ within the European Union as it moves from 15 members to include 10 more from Central and East Europe.

The East-West research on international cooperation projects offers some criteria that can be used in recruiting, selecting, and assessing professionals. *Team member characteristics* that foster group synergy are also implied in Exhibit 9.2. Such benchmarks can be helpful in interviewing potential team members, choosing collaborators, and setting goals for self-improvement in organizational relations.

Finally, these ICRD researchers offered some indications for ensuring synergy within global teams. First, they established these criteria for evaluating international project effectiveness and management competence:

1. Individual team member satisfaction
2. Group satisfaction and morale
3. Work progress relative to intended goal statements
4. Social and cultural impact of the endeavor on people

Second, the East-West Center's researchers also identified interpersonal skills that influence a professional group's situation and accomplishments. These international team competencies and capacities are summarized in Exhibit 9.3.

## EXHIBIT 9.3

### SELF-MANAGEMENT COMPETENCIES AND EFFECTIVE TEAM MEMBERS

**Self-Management Competencies Permit the Project Member to:**

■ Recognize other members' participation in ways they find rewarding.
■ Avoid unnecessary conflicts among other team members, as well as resolve unavoidable ones to mutual satisfaction.
■ Integrate different team members' skills to achieve project goals.

continued

- Negotiate acceptable working arrangements with other team members and their organizations.
- Regard others' feelings and exercise tactfulness.
- Develop equitable benefits for other team members.
- Accept suggestions/feedback to improve his or her participation.
- Provide useful specific suggestions and appropriate feedback.
- Facilitate positive interaction among culturally different members, whether in terms of macrodifferences (national/political), or microdifferences (discipline or training).
- Gain acceptance because of empathy expressed and sensitivity to end users.
- Encourage dissemination of project outcomes throughout its life.
- Recognize national/international differences in problem statements and procedures, so as to create appropriate project organizational responses.
- Anticipate and plan for probable difficulties in project implementation.
- Recognize discrete functions, coordinating discrete tasks with overall project goals.
- Coordinate transitions among different kinds of activities within the project.

**The Effective Team Member Has the Capacity for:**

- Flexibility and openness to change and others' viewpoints.
- Exercising patience, perseverance, and professional security.
- Thinking in multidimensional terms and considering different sides of issues.
- Dealing with ambiguity, role shifts, and differences in personal and professional styles or social and political systems.
- Managing stress and tension well, while scheduling tasks systematically.
- Cross-cultural communication and demonstrating sensitivity to language problems among colleagues.
- Anticipating consequences of one's own behavior.
- Dealing with unfamiliar situations and lifestyle changes.
- Dealing well with different organizational structures and policies.
- Gathering useful information related to future projects.

These insights, offer a compendium of the shared leadership skills that professionals should expect to contribute in the course of group collaboration. For organizations that provide project management training or team building for their members, these are the skills to be sought in team development, especially when members represent multicultural backgrounds.

In the pursuit of our interests and careers, we have numerous opportunities to form professional relationships. They may occur through the Internet by means of electronic mail and chat rooms. Or they may come about by joining a professional association or an organization, such as the Rotary or Kiwanis Club, which have worldwide branches. For those engaged in international business, for example, local *world trade centers* are "passports to opportunity." Usually operating in conjunction with the Chamber of Commerce in major cities, they offer global managers a chance for synergistic networking and career development. Often, they sponsor a World Trade Day dealing with such subjects as business opportunities on the Internet, overseas markets, tips for importing/exporting, gathering competitive intelligence, and forming strategic alliances.

## CONCLUSIONS

After explaining the concept of cultural synergy, this chapter provided a contrast of societies that could be characterized as having high or low synergy, as well as organizational culture that reflects high and low synergy.

Within organizations, the research insights reported here centered on behaviors and practices that contribute to synergy and success among teams, particularly in terms of international projects. The concluding section described people who are truly "professional" in their attitude toward their career and work and in how they can mutually benefit by synergy. Global leaders actively create a better future through synergistic efforts with fellow professionals.

Contemporary global leaders, then, seek to be effective bridge builders between the cultural realities or worlds of both past and future. Cultivating a synergistic mindset, accelerates this process.

### MIND STRETCHING

1. Why is it difficult to achieve cultural synergy in multinational organizations?
2. What are some best strategies global business leaders should take to mitigate these difficulties?
3. There are many examples of cross-cultural organizational conflicts and problems. Think of one and determine the root causes of the conflict. Then answer: How would you create a culturally synergistic solution to this challenge?

continued

4. What basic skills must a global leader have to build up a culturally synergistic organization?
5. Why is it insufficient for global leaders to be global-minded thinkers?
6. How is the concept and practice of leadership changing?

# REFERENCES

1. Freeman, O. L. "'Foreword' by former president of Business International Corporation, Governor of Minnesota, and U.S. Secretary of Agriculture," *Managing Cultural Synergy*, Moran, R. T. and Harris, P. R. (eds.). Houston, TX: Gulf Publishing, 1982.
2. Friedman, T. "America's Real Dream Team," *New York Times*, March 22, 2010, listing the majority of high school finalists in the 2010 Intel Science Talent Search.
3. Zakaria, F. *The Post-American World*. New York: W. W. Norton and Company, 2009.
4. Augsburger, D. W. *Conflict Mediation Across Cultures: Pathways and Patterns*. Louisville, KY: Westminster/John Knox Press, 1992, p. 23.
5. Adler, N. J. *International Dimensions of Organizational Behavior*, Fourth edition. Canada: South-Western Thomson Learning, 2002, p. 116.
6. Wilmot, W. W. and Hocker, J. L. *Interpersonal Conflict*, Seventh edition. Boston, MA: McGraw-Hill, 2006.
7. Ibid., p. 6.
8. Ibid. Original source is Gudykunst, W. and Ting-Toomey, S. *Culture and Interpersonal Communication*. Beverly Hills, CA: Sage, 1988, p. 158.
9. Ibid.
10. *New York Times International*, April 17, 2010, p. A6.
11. Crocker, C., Hampson, F. O., and Aall, P. (eds.). *Introduction: Managing Global Chaos*. Washington, DC: United States Institute of Peace Press, 1999.
12. Ormerod, P. *The New General Theory of Social and Economic Behavior: Butterfly Economics*. New York: Pantheon Books, 2000.
13. Wheatcroft, A. *Infidels, A History of the Conflict between Christendom and Islam*. New York: Random House Trade Paperbacks, 2005, p. 295.
14. *The Economist*, April 17, 2010.
15. Ibid.

# Unit 2

## Regional Cultural Specifics*

*Culture hides much more than it reveals.*
Edward T. Hall, Anthropologist

Some 80,000 years ago or less, a great human migration out of Africa occurred. The first long journey south went from Africa to Asia. Some 50,000 years or less, a second wave pushed north through the Middle East and Central Asia, then west to Europe or east to the Americas.[1] Along the way, humanity acculturated differently to the local environment and circumstances, thus creating differences in culture specifics. Their cave art and myths reveal the continuing development of consciousness. Between birth and death, our ancestors coped in astonishing and diverse ways. As is true today, their adaptive innovations are revealed not only in art and decorations, but also in language and stories, beliefs and rituals, traditions and practices, economic and social organization, tools, and technologies.

While Homo Sapiens became defined by ecology and geography, ethnology and ethos show the myriad variations in cultures. Although 7000 languages are presently spoken, their number constantly diminishes. Yet research into the human genome underscores our common genetic heritage. But the one constant in the history of the human family is our capacity to cope with *change*, even as its pace accelerates in contemporary times. For millennia, our peoples have used *culture* to make sense of changes and challenges, and thus build human civilization.

To appreciate human diversity and potential, the next five chapters enable readers to be more effective as they live and work beyond the borders of their homelands!

---

*Notes on the material in Unit 2.

Every effort has been made to ensure the accuracy of the information in Unit 2. Each country profile has been reviewed by at least one credible resource from that country, and much of the material has been reviewed by several.

Economic and demographic information is also available on the Internet. We especially recommend the following:

www.economist.com/countries

www.cia.gov (then check on link World Factbook)

Of course, many other sources are available in English and other languages. Some are listed in specific chapters.

# 10

# DOING BUSINESS WITH MIDDLE EASTERNERS

## Egypt, Saudi Arabia, and Regional Countries

## LEARNING OBJECTIVES

This chapter is dedicated to a better understanding of the cultures and complexities of that region of the world known to geographers as the Middle East. Specifics will be shared on the Arab culture, plus in-depth contrasts in the cultures of Egypt and Saudi Arabia. In addition, cultural capsules of other nations in the region will offer a more comprehensive overview of the region's peoples.

The Middle East commonly refers to the lands from the eastern shores of the Mediterranean and Aegean Seas to India. Geographically, it encompasses areas of the eastern Mediterranean and central Asia. To many of its inhabitants, it is known as the Arab homeland, *Al-waton Al-Araby*, which refers to those areas in which Arabic is spoken.

The Middle East is a region where the geography and ecology are important architects of history and cultures; it is where three continents meet, a focal point in the development of civilization. After the Ice Age, its topography was gradually transformed from a climate that supported grasslands and waterways into vast steppes and desert. This landmass has been considered a strategic location, a crossroad for trade, faith, and conflict. Generally, the term Middle East refers the Arabian Peninsula, a dry desert, and Asia Minor.

## *The Historical Perspective*

In ancient times, the Middle East was referred to as Mesopotamia, the Fertile Crescent from which agriculture and settlements would emerge. In those days, what is today called Libya was rich in olives, wine, and livestock, and Egypt was a marshland teeming with wildlife and reed forests. It was here that farming and irrigation were first developed along the Nile Valley, that the original dwellers of the Tigris-Euphrates Valley brought forth civilization in Sumer, today's southern Iraq. The Sumerians were largely Semites and spoke a Semitic language from which evolved the major languages spoken by Middle Easterners, such as Aramaic, Syriac, Hebrew, and Arabic. Here, the first few cities that flourished were founded with exotic names like Ur, Babylon, and Gaza. This ancient land became the center of world civilization—its cultures first produced wheeled vehicles; the pottery wheel and pottery making; written records and codes of law in cuneiform; art, monumental architecture, and urbanization; and multiple religions, along with complex political and trading systems.[2]

From its very beginning, as a site for human settlement until now, the Middle East has been marked by *diversity*. For thousands of years, the waves of migration into the area have extended from the Sumerians, possibly from central Asia, to the latest Filipino, Korean, or Indian immigrant searching for work. In the latter part of the twentieth century, more than 3 million Asian and Indian laborers were imported into the area to help build modern infrastructure. Although there is much today that is shared by the majority of Middle Easterners, such as the Arab culture, language, and religion, there are also distinct ethnic minorities in every country of the region. Since the seventh century, Islam is the principal binder among the peoples of this area—it is a *way of life*, not just a religion. *Islam* is an Arabic word that means surrender or submission to Allah or God; a person who so behaves and follows the teachings of Islam is called a Muslim. Non-Arabs, such as the Iranians, are linked to their Muslim brothers and sisters throughout the world through their religion of Islam.[3]

This is the same place from which the religions of Judaism and Christianity arose; all three faiths revere the prophet Abraham. Islam began later, in A.D. 570, with the birth of Muhammad the Prophet in Mecca. In the century following the Prophet's death in 632, zealous Bedouin forces swept out of the Arabian Peninsula to impose Islam on vast areas stretching from Spain to China. They were inspired by this great leader, a combination of general, statesman, social reformer, empire builder, and visionary. As both a religion and a philosophy, Islam owes its origin to Muhammad's teachings, which he encapsulated in the *Qur'an* (Koran), the sacred book of Muslims, as precious to them as the Torahs are to Jews and the Bible to Christians. Islam means the act of giving one's self to Allah or God, and this faith has worldwide followers. The Koran contains the discourses Allah revealed to his prophet Muhammad. Yet, as a religion, Islam is diverse in terms of having different interpretations of its teachings; for instance, by Sunni Muslims in Algeria and Saudi Arabia, or Shi'is Muslims in Iran and Iraq (where most believers are Shi'ites). Neither visitor nor business or military person traveling to the Middle East can hope to comprehend its peoples without understanding the powerful religious and cultural force of Islam. Its primary tenets are summarized in Exhibit 10.1.

The teachings in the Koran, like those in the Bible, can be taken out of context and distorted to serve a particular cause—such as ultra-militants twisting the interpretation of *jihad*, a verse prescribing struggle against the enemies of God for spiritual purity and enlightenment.

---

### EXHIBIT 10.1
### PILLARS OF ISLAMIC BELIEF

*Profession of Faith* (Shahadah)—open proclamation of submission that "there is no God but Allah and Muhammad is the messenger of God"—at mosques this is chanted five times a day.

*Prayer* (Salah)—at prescribed hours, worship or ritual prayer five times daily, individually if not preferably in groups—the bowing or kneeling for this is toward Mecca; the Muslim doing this must be pure, hence newly washed and not dirty; Friday is the traditional day of rest, when the congregational prayers of men at midday should ordinarily be performed in the mosque.

*Almsgiving* (Zakah)—the Koran teaches that all believers must give to the needy and today this is normally a personal act ranging from 2 to 10% of one's yearly income.

*Fasting* (Sawm)—throughout the 30-day lunar month of Ramadan, a Muslim abstains from food and drink, while practicing continence in other respects, from dawn to sunset; in some Muslim countries, such as Saudi Arabia, the obligation is legally enforced.

*Pilgrimage* (Haj)—at least once in a lifetime, if one is financially and physically able, a Muslim is expected to perform this act of piety by going to Mecca as a pilgrim during the month of Haj; merit is great for those who go there and perform the rites and ceremonies for 8-13 days.

*Note:* Some Muslims believe in a sixth pillar, *Holy War* or *Al-Jihad*, which offers the reward of salvation. This effort to promote Islamic doctrine among nonbelievers is not necessarily done through actual war as occurred in past ages. All observant Muslims are expected to practice hospitality toward strangers, even "infidels," as well as to enhance family relationships.

---

Contemporary analysts argue that the concept of jihad as practiced today by the al-Qaeda followers is a departure from traditional Islam. At its height, Islam's empire was larger than that of Rome at its zenith. Islam produced great civilizations that made enormous contributions to art, architecture, astronomy, literature, mathematics, medicine, and other intellectual pursuits which we still benefit from today.[4]

To appreciate Islam's origins in the Middle East, consider the many other countries outside the region to which it spread. For example, the Muslim culture and way of life is global in scope. Parts of Europe have large Muslim populations, including Albania, Bosnia, France, Spain, and Russia with its neighbors in the Commonwealth of Independent States. In North America, there are large Muslim communities in both the United States and Canada. But in Asia (e.g., Bangladesh, Pakistan, and Indonesia) as well as in Africa (e.g., Gambia, Morocco, and Nigeria), entire nations are Muslim. In the twenty-first century, Indonesia is the largest Muslim nation. Throughout the world, there are 42 Muslim majority nations, and Iran, Sudan, and Mauritania are officially Islamic states ruled by Islamic law. In Chapter 14, the continent of Africa is discussed, which alone contains 11 countries with majority Muslim populations, only one of which, Egypt, is considered Middle Eastern. Religious diversity is also evident in all Middle Eastern nations because of varied religious minorities, including Christians and Jews of many persuasions or sects, as well as myriad other believers. With more than a billion followers and growing fast, it is not difficult to visualize the worldwide influence of Islam with 1,200,000,000 adherents—approximately 20% of the world's population.

Egyptian hotel entrepreneur Teymour Adham rightly maintains that most of his fellow believers are "Spiritual Muslims" who identify themselves by their faith. It is a personal and spiritual thing, so they do not talk or preach about their religion, just live it. Unfortunately, some people develop Muslim stereotypes, particularly because of the Islamic terrorist fringe, conveniently forgetting the great diversity within this global religious culture. Like their counterparts in other religions, Muslims have their inflexible ultra conservatives, as well as tolerant, open-minded progressives. Islam is a vast mosaic.

## The Modern Middle East

The word *caldron* describes this region because, for a very long time, the Middle East has been embroiled in different forms of conflict and violence. The seeds of contemporary turmoil there were largely sown in the past, so one should analyze current events in the region within that larger context. When the indigenous tribes and religious sects were not confronting one another, their crossroad location became the battleground for warring invaders, some of whom were called Crusaders in medieval times. From the sixteenth to nineteenth century, the Muslims of the Middle East were under the domination of the Ottoman Turks. In the twentieth century alone, we witnessed a series of external wars extending to the region, resulting in European colonial occupiers with League of Nations' mandates taking over as "protectors." At that time, new nations were created after World War I, with land divided without respect for tribal differences, or promises made to Arabs for their aid during that war. This resulted in unresolved issues to this day. To comprehend somewhat Middle Eastern complexities, history has much to tell us about current issues within this region in the twenty-first century. Further, the recreation of the nation of Israel in 1948 divided the Arab world, leading to several wars between Israelis, Egypt, Syria, and Palestinians which involved neighboring countries. That conflict goes on over 60 years later as these two Semitic peoples still struggle for peaceful coexistence. Late in the last century, American and Allied invasions triggered by controversy between Iraq and Kuwait led to the Gulf War and United Nations' sanctions. In this century, the United States and its coalition partners not only went to war again in Iraq, supposedly to topple a wretched dictator while searching for weapons of mass destruction, but invaded Afghanistan to replace the Taliban fundamentalists with a more democratic government.

Sometimes the conflicts are within countries where Muslim extremists oppose established governments, as in Algeria, Egypt, and Saudi Arabia. At other times, the fighting occurs because local groups, with outside assistance, oppose the occupiers, as in Palestine's West Bank and Gaza, Kuwait, and Afghanistan. Often, there have been outright civil wars, as in Yemen, Somalia, and possibly Iraq in the near future. Currently, the hope for the region is that the battles between Israel and her Muslim neighbors give way to peaceful negotiations, conflict resolution, and economic development, such as is happening with Egypt and Jordan. Because of economic setbacks, even Syria shows signs of negotiating with the Israelis and Americans. Yet many are alarmed when countries like Iran invest in violent movements like Hezbollah in Lebanon, Hamas in the Palestinian territories, and Shia extremists in Iraq. However, some are more concerned about the larger clash of civilizations due in part to culture and economic lag in Moslem societies, with fears of Western-style modernization and way of life.

To put events within the Middle East in context, an observer of Islam today, R. D. Lewis, reminds us that[5]:


■ A persistent historical characteristic of the Muslim religion has been open tolerance for other faiths....
■ Western civilization is indebted to Arabic translations in the Middle Ages of Hellenistic knowledge and tradition, especially in science and medicine....
■ Mutually enriching coexistence of Muslims and Westerners has been the rule, rather than the exception, over the centuries....
■ Islamic scholars maintain they are not against the West, but fear its power and influence within their own societies, particularly with reference to materialism and cultural imperialism....

- More than half of the 1 billion Muslims are not Arab, and most Muslims are moderates who admire piety and devoutness....
- Muslims are divided among themselves with a multiplicity of interests and agendas, especially in their Sunni and Shi'ite communities....
- Many Muslims are concerned about the slowness of democratic reforms, and the inequality in distribution of wealth in their countries, not about supporting violent Islamic radicalism and its call for jihad.

A watershed event occurred on September 11, 2001, which rudely brought the problems of the Middle East into global consciousness. On that day, a terrorist network under the leadership of wealthy Osama bin Laden crashed three hijacked airliners into New York's World Trade Center, Washington, D.C.'s Pentagon buildings, and a Pennsylvania field, killing over 3000 people. Fifty-six Muslim states immediately condemned the attack, pointing out that such behavior was against the basic tenets of Islam. These atrocities against humanity generated a global war against terrorism, accompanied by Western invasions, occupations, and reforms in both Afghanistan and Iraq.

In a *Discovery Channel* television broadcast on the root causes of the 9/11 catastrophes, commentator Thomas L. Friedman summarized the problems of the contemporary Arab world that might prompt individuals to commit such misguided acts (March 26, 2006). Primarily, they seemingly result from frustration of people's needs because of the challenges faced within contemporary Arab societies, such as: corruption of their leaders, some of whom become dictators; poverty and economic powerlessness of the majority, despite some oil riches; male oppression of women by exclusion and underdevelopment of their potential; radicalization of their youth in *mosquesdia* by fundamentalists and extremists; double standards used by the West in support of Israel over Palestinian human rights and welfare. Friedman emphasized that the younger Arab generation, including those educated abroad, often has a sense of being oppressed and humiliated by Westerners. Some of these disillusioned young people have been recruited into militant, terrorist networks (see section at end of this chapter on the "Subculture of Terrorism). Economic factors almost beyond their control are sweeping the Muslim nations and peoples into the global marketplace. In general, the Middle East today can be described as a region in the midst of profound cultural, social, political, and economic transition![6]

## CHARACTERISTICS OF ARAB CULTURE

For outsiders, the key to a better comprehension of the contemporary Middle East is understanding Arab culture. We stress the point that not all Middle Easterners are Arab, as Iranians, Turks, and Israelis will remind us. Over 20 Arab countries can be identified as members of the League of Arab States. Arab countries include: Algeria,

Bahrain, Comoros Islands, Djibouti, Egypt, Iraq, Jordan, Kuwait, Lebanon, Libya, Mauritania, Morocco, Oman, Palestine, Qatar, Saudi Arabia, Somalia, Sudan, Syria, Tunisia, United Arab Emirates, and Yemen. To say that member countries have similar cultural attitudes, behaviors, and communication is very misleading. For example, in the Muslim countries of Sudan, Somalia, and Mauritania, tribal languages, rather than Arabic, are spoken, and there are cultural practices that favor their African heritage. Not all Arabs believe in Islam, as Christian Arabs will confirm. But Arab peoples have a Muslim majority in the Middle East—outside the region, they represent only 20% of the Muslim population. As a rule, *Arab* is an ethnic reference to a Semite, whereas *Muslim* signifies religious belief and grouping.

What are some generalities about this distinctive Arab culture? Simply that it is a varied tapestry of religious and socio-political configurations, causing the Arabs to recast and revise themselves as circumstances around them also change. Exhibit 10.2 confirms this in the dimension of world finance.

## EXHIBIT 10.2
### ISLAMIC FINANCE

Normally, Islamic law scholars would explain that *sharia-compliant* products and services should adhere to these two principles—interest must not be paid; and wealth shall not be generated from means considered improper (e.g., alcohol, gambling, tobacco). But the market is changing, especially in the Middle East, because of the wealth obtained from oil and gas production. Rich Muslims invest their petrodollars abroad, especially in countries with a Muslim majority, such as Malaysia and Bahrain, and in ventures that are *sharia-compliant*. But Sameer Abdi of Ernst and Young estimates that many will invest in global market undertakings that are commercially competitive. In the Middle East, big corporations are shifting to both public and private financing, complying with Islamic traditions only within their own countries. As international investors look to Islamic financing for big infrastructure projects, the global banking system seeks to offer *sharia-compliant* products and services. But there is a dearth of credit ratings for regional products, while accounting and reporting must be better aligned.

Foreign investment bankers use terms like *riba* in place of "interest." Islamic finance, once considered an oddity, is now viewed as an opportunity. Standard and Poor, a rating agency, estimates the market for Islamic financial products to be about $400 billion (e.g., banking, mortgages, equity funds, fixed income, insurance, underwriting projects, private equity, and derivatives). When Dubai

continued

EXHIBIT 10.2

ISLAMIC FINANCE (CONTINUED)

World issued an $800 million *sukuk*, 40% of the investors came from Europe. At the same time, another Dubai developer, Nakheel, offered a $2.5 billion *sukuk*. it is no wonder that Islamic finance has gone mainstream. With a little innovation in the risk arena, cultural barriers can be crossed, even in the world of finance.

*Source*: Adapted from "Calling the Faithful," *The Economist*, December 9, 2006, pp. 77-79 (www.economist.com/freeexchange).

Here are five key distinguishing characteristics of Islamic culture:

*Arab Language*[7]—For Arabs, their language is sacred because it was the means by which God revealed the Koran to Muhammad. Classical Arabic is used not only by religious scholars, but also the educated and the media. But there are many forms of colloquial Arabic which may be incomprehensible to those speakers from the Arabian Peninsula. Today, radio, television, computers, and mobile telephones are spreading these other dialects. The Bedouins excel in oral verse, filled with emotion and evocative forms of poetry that are used to express strong feelings. Literature is most prized in this culture, contributing to group solidarity.

*Arab Values*—In traditional societies, the paramount virtues are considered to be dignity, honor, and reputation. A shared honor code frequently dictates certain behaviors, especially to preserve the family's reputation. The expression of gender roles differ in Arab societies which may be ultra-conservative. Foreigners at all costs should avoid causing an Arab to lose face or to be shamed. Loyalty to family, as well as courteous and harmonious communications, is emphasized. Arabs are noted for their love of family and its privacy, as well as for their hospitality. In tribal and traditional communities, Arab priorities are first to one's self, then kinsman, townsman, or tribesman, and those who share the same religion and country.

*Arab Personal Distance*—Arabs seek close personal relationships, preferably without great distance or intermediaries. Thus, olfaction is prominent in Arab life. For many Arabs, smells are necessary and a way to be involved with each other. Body and food odors are used to enhance human relationships; the former is even important in the choice of a mate. This cultural difference also extends to an Arab facing or not facing another person; to view another peripherally is impolite, so to sit or stand back to back is rude. Although Arabs may be very involved when interacting with friends, they may not seek a close distance in conversations with strangers or mere acquaintances. On such social occasions, they may sit on opposite sides of a room and talk across to one another. Yet, they are generally a warm and expressive people, both verbally and nonverbally.

*Arab Sociability and Equality*—Cordiality is at the core of this culture, and is evident from such occasions as feasting at a lamb banquet to drinking strong black coffee. It extends also to business meetings when the first session is devoted to getting acquainted with little regard for schedule or appointments. The traditional greeting is to place one's right hand on the chest near the heart as an indication of sincerity and warmth, though modern Arabs may precede this with a long, limp handshake. The custom is for men to kiss one another on both cheeks. For those Arabs who are Muslims, there are Islamic teachings that affect social relations, such as taboos against eating pork, drinking alcohol, gambling, and prostitution.

*Arab Women*—The Arab patriarchal culture places the male in the dominant role, while protecting and respecting the female. In an Arab household, for example, the man is overtly the head with a strong role and influence; the mother "behind the scenes" is often the authority on family matters. Honorable female behavior implies being loving mothers and daughters, acting in modest and respectful ways, such as by running efficient and generous households. Publicly, the woman defers to her husband, but privately she may be more assertive. Paradoxically, Islam does not advance the notion of women's inherent inferiority, only her difference; it does not perceive biological inferiority and affirms potential equality between the sexes. During an interview, Dr. Fatima Mernissi stated: "The whole Muslim system is based on the assumption that the woman is a powerful and dangerous being."[8]

In some Arab countries, women enjoy equality with men, while in others there are limitations on their role. In more traditional Arab communities, where mullahs control marriage laws, men are allowed to marry more than one woman, including the foreign born. Women may marry only one husband, excluding foreigners. Husbands may divorce without stating a cause, whereas a wife must specify grounds to the satisfaction of the court, and in a courtroom, it takes the testimony of two females to equal one male.

The Koran, for instance, does not say that women must be veiled, only that they must be modest in appearance by covering their arms and hair, which are considered very sensual. Scholars see the use of the veil as symbolic with sociological meaning. The veil's use depends on time period and circumstances. Some Arab countries are without dress restrictions for women, so they may wear the latest fashion; whereas others, which are more traditional, may require a long cloak of black gauze or chiffon—an *abaya*—which is to cover from crown to ankle. The cultural contrasts within Arab societies on this matter are considerable. In some Arab countries, most females are illiterate, whereas in others they are well educated; in some, they are not allowed outside their home alone nor permitted to drive an automobile, whereas in other states, women may hold jobs and drive cars. In many Arab states, women are not allowed to vote, whereas in others they have that franchise; in most Arab societies, marriages are arranged, whereas in a growing number, freedom of marital choice is respected. Within an Arab world in turmoil and change, one may observe both resurgent

Islamic fundamentalism and an emerging feminist movement. In the traditional societies, such medieval codes of female behavior may be enforced by a Committee to Prevent Vice and Promote Virtue—the *matawa*, or religious police. In more conservative Arab communities, when a woman disobeys these rulings, such as on being modestly cloaked in the *abaya*, not entering a bus by a separate rear door, and sitting in a segregated section, she may be flogged or caned by these religious police. Yet, there is great diversity within the Arab world on the status of women. Contrast a women's role in Saudi Arabia with that in the Muslim country of Brunei, Southeast Asia; there, women outnumber men at the university, drive automobiles, hold senior offices in both the public and private sectors, and can even serve as ambassadors and airline pilots. Some Muslim women are protesting and working toward greater emancipation for their gender against stifling morality.[9]

However, foreign females visiting Arab countries must exercise great sensitivity to what is acceptable or unacceptable in the local situation. Women from outside the culture who do not heed this counsel may have unhappy experiences. Whether female or male, those who would engage in successful commercial or professional exchanges within the Arab world should be aware of such proprieties.

## CULTURAL ASPECTS OF EGYPT AND SAUDI ARABIA

By focusing on two similar but distinctly different cultural targets, one may gain insight into the cultural dimensions of these and other remarkable peoples in the region. Both Egypt and Saudi Arabia are part of the Arab world, but Egypt originates from an ancient civilization and is more liberal, whereas Saudi Arabia is a traditional nation created in the last century, propelled by vast oil discoveries. Geographically, Saudi Arabia is located on the Arabian Peninsula, Egypt lies on the continent of North Africa, but we include it here as culturally part of the Middle East.

## EGYPT

The Old Kingdom was a civilization that built the first great nation-state, flourishing for five-and-a-half centuries before its collapse. It is a culture that produced *hieroglyphics*—one of the world's first written languages—and humanity's first macroprojects—construction of monumental pyramids dating from 2630 to 2250 B.C. Whether tombs of predynastic kings or, later, Pharaohs, these magnificent structures reveal a culture whose leaders and builders were obsessed with preparing for the afterlife. In the mineral-rich eastern desert of Upper Egypt, the hub was Thebes, with its awesome funerary temples and rock-cut tombs. The building of pyramids and tombs became a central force for the organization and mobilization of townspeople, a means for creating a national state, and a magnet for early Middle Eastern trade. Then, as now, the Nile River with its network of hand-dug canals ties the country together geographically. By 2200 B.C., climatic crises arose when Nile flooding became unpredictable, and drought seized the land. Although Egyptians identify with their pharaonic past, since the seventh century (A.D.) they are concerned about their Islamic present. Their country has become a center of learning for the Arab world. This is a land which has suffered many foreign invasions which impacted the culture and formed the basis of modern Egyptians.[10]

## The People and Their Homeland

Most of Egypt is high dry plains, rugged hills, and mountains, stretching along the Red Sea Coast to the valley of the Nile. The population of the Old Kingdom was less than 2 million while today's Egypt has more than 79 million inhabitants. This most populous of Arab states has one of the highest population densities in the world. Cairo, for instance, has approximately 16 million people for a city originally designed for 3 million—this capital is the largest city in Africa and the Arab world. Today, Egypt's citizens are mostly a Hamitic people practicing the Sunni form of the Muslim religion.

In northern Egypt, there is a mixture of peoples from the Mediterranean and other Arab countries, whereas the south consists mainly of black African Nubians (see Exhibit 10.3). In addition to thousands of the latter, this region also includes two other minorities—about 5 million Coptic Christians, descendants of whom did not convert to Islam, who have their own language. In the desert areas, there are some 50,000 nomadic Bedouins who are transitioning to a more settled life in oasis, Cairo, and Alexandria. The major language spoken is Arabic, with some French and English, reflecting the heritage of previous European colonialists. Immigrants from all over the Middle East also live and work in this country.

## Geographic Features and Cities

Although a Middle Eastern nation, it is located on the African continent at the crossroads of the Mediterranean Basin, Africa, and Asia. Less than 5% of the country is cultivated; with the climate permitting several crops a year, but the potential exists for increased agricultural production. Beside its great north-south Nile River, the following are other notable geographic features further influencing the culture:

■ The Suez Canal links the Mediterranean Sea on the north with the Gulf of Suez and Red Sea on southeast.

EXHIBIT 10.3

THE NUBIAN HERITAGE

These non-Arab Egyptians traditionally occupied Nubia, an unbounded valley in the south that borders on Sudan. They spoke Nobin, first converted to Coptic Christianity, and eventually to Islam beginning in the 14th century. In 1960, their lives were altered by the Aswan Dam, built to prevent the annual flooding of the Nile. Thus, this displaced people lost their homeland and way of life, centered on villages along the Nile banks. Presently, some 873,000 Nubians live in Egypt and adjoining Sudan.

By 1500 B.C., their sophisticated settlements stretched from the Second to Third cataract of the Nile. The Nubians sprang from a robust African civilization that flourished for 2500 years on the Banks of the Nile, going back as far as the first Egyptian dynasty. This ancient people provided Egypt with the "Black Pharaohs" beginning in 730 B.C., when the King of Nubia, Pye, invaded the land to the north and became its pharaoh. The dark-skin Nubians ruled from the capital of Upper Egypt, Memphis, for three quarters of a century as the 25th dynasty. These black leaders reunited a tattered Egypt, built glorious monuments, and created an empire from present-day Khartoum north to the Mediterranean Sea. In 701 B.C, their forces saved Jerusalem from Assyrian armies.

But in 2009, the Sudanese government completed the massive, hydroelectric Merowe Dam 600 miles upstream from the Aswan Dam. Its 106-mile lake called *Nasser* by Egyptians and *Nubia* by Sudanese will flood thousands of unexplored archaeological sites.

*Source*: Adapted from Robert Draper's "Black Pharaohs," *National Geographic*, February 2008, pp. 35-59 (www.ngm.com).

■ The northeastern Sinai Peninsula is desert area that abuts Israel and the Gulf of Aqaba.
■ The Aswan High Dam in the southeast includes Lake Nasser, which extends down into the Nubian desert and the southern border with Sudan.

## Political and Social Conditions

The foundations of governance were laid by twenty dynasties when Pharaohs and kings reigned from 3000 to 715 B.C., extending their rule as far as Lower Nubia, Palestine, and Syria. Invasions in that period brought in temporary rulers and settlers from Asian Hyksos, Libya, Persia, and Nubia. Since 333 B.C., Egypt's heritage reflects the presence of a series of conquerors—from Alexander the Great and the Roman Empire, to Arabs and the Turkish Ottoman Empire, to the establishment of a British presence (1882-1952), during which a monarchy was formed in 1922 under King Fouad I. Because of worsening economic and social conditions, military officers staged a coup d'état on July 23, 1952, under the leadership of Lt. Colonel Gamel Abdel Nasser—that date is now celebrated there as National Day. On June 18, 1953, this junta declared Egypt a republic. This became a turning point for modern Egyptians, who then felt more independent and spearheaded a resurgence of Arab nationalism throughout the Middle East. In 1971, a new constitution was adopted for the Arab Republic of Egypt that guarantees the individual rights of its citizens. Subsequently, two more presidents have led the country—former General Anwar Sadat, who was assassinated, and, currently, former General Hosni Mubarak, who has served several terms in that office. There is also a National Assembly with four political parties.

During the closing four decades of the twentieth century, Egypt struggled internally to restructure its socioeconomic system, including reapportioning wealth and some land reform. Moving away from earlier experiments with socialism, contemporary Egypt espouses democracy and a market economy, providing incentives for both domestic and foreign investment. Yet, this is a developing economy, plagued by uncontrolled population growth, poverty, and insufficient food. With 94% of its people Muslim adherents, it is understandable that civil law is influenced by *Shariah* or Islamic law. But it is economic degradation among the masses that fuels Islamic militants seeking to establish a Muslim government, often leading to terrorist acts against both the leadership and foreigners.

Since the late President Sadat signed a Peace Treaty with Israel (March 25, 1979), Egypt for many years was both the target of Arab economic reprisals and the recipient of significant foreign aid from the United States. To curb attacks of Islamic militants in the area, President Mubarak hosted a summit in Cairo at the beginning of Ramadan in 1995. Prime Minister Yitzhak Rabin of Israel, PLO leader Yasser Arafat, and King Hussein of Jordan joined him in the elusive pursuit of peace and prosperity for the Middle East. In a collective communiqué, "The four parties condemned all outbreaks of bloodshed, terror, and violence in the region and reaffirmed their intentions to stand staunchly against and put an end to all such acts."[11] Ironically, Rabin was later assassinated that same year by a Jewish fundamentalist who opposed this reconciliation. But Egypt continues to cooperate as a peace broker in a region where nations have more to gain by peaceful collaboration than from continuing conflict.

The governance and political system have undergone some liberalization in recent times. The constitution provides for a strong president, vice presidents, prime minister, cabinet, and governors for 26 provinces. The single legislature is the People's Assembly with 444 elected delegates and 10 appointed by the president; 50% reserved for farmers and workers. The *Shura* is a consultative council for advising on public policy but with little legislative power. The governing National Democratic Party (NDP) dominates politics. Today, Egyptians are intensely nationalistic and Arab sensitive. Although a secular state and somewhat Westernized, especially with reference to international business, traditional Arab patterns are also present. Realistically, Egypt has a long way to go before it can be designated as a fully functional democracy that protects human rights.

*The Economy and Business*—The change and diversification still under way are evident in its exports—a shift from the traditional cultivation of cotton and rice, to the rising production of petroleum, cotton textiles, and metal products, as well as increasing tourism, construction, and mining. Europe, followed by the United States, is a growing importer of Egypt's exports. With the gradual dismantling of bureaucratic regulations, foreign investment increases, as do reclamation projects. The currency is the Egyptian pound divided into 100 piasters, or 1000 millimes.

*Investments*—Law 43 and subsequent amendments liberalize foreign investment, providing incentives, particularly with reference to new technologies, and exemptions (from nationalization, custom duties, some regulations and taxes, etc.), plus guarantees for repatriation of capital. For potential traders and investors, the most significant developments have been in the banking system that now allows joint ventures with foreign banks and improvements in transportation, hotels, and resorts.

*Workforce*—Since 1974, there have been significant changes in the business environment, encouraging the private sector in an economy still dominated by the public sector. The 10 million plus people that comprise the available workforce are well trained. Egyptian skilled labor and entrepreneurial talent is sought by other nations in the area. Basic Labor Law 91 protects workers' rights and sets work policy; foreign firms may be exempt from some of these regulations.

*Social Life*—This is oriented toward extended families and public gatherings, with a close sense of distance. Prepare for a slower way of life, including decision making, and a lack of punctuality in keeping appointments. People follow the Islamic calendar. Five national holiday dates are fixed, whereas Ramadan and Islamic New Year are approximate depending on lunar observations.

*Work Practices*—The workweek is from Saturday through Wednesday, with no business conducted on Thursday and Friday (Muslim Holy Day). Business hours vary, but typically in summer are 8 a.m. to 2 p.m.; in winter, 9 a.m. to 1 p.m., and 5 to 7 p.m. Paperwork includes two dates—Gregorian or Western, and Hijrah or Arabic. (Coptic Christians have a different calendar, but Christmas has been designated a national holiday.)

Modernization is evident in many ways, such as the grand Al-Azhar Park on the outskirts of Cairo. This historic district was founded by the Aga Khan, whose ancestor founded the oldest university in the world, just a mile way and after which this development is named. Today, it is a garden paradise with spectacular views of Egypt's monuments, plus fountains, walkways, restaurants, and remains of twelfth century city walls.

As in all Muslin societies, the *hajj* is an important annual event, which Exhibit 10.4 explains.

EXHIBIT 10.4

## EXHIBIT 10.4
## THE HAJJ: JOURNEY OF FATIH

This is the annual holy pilgrimage to the heart of Islam, Mecca in Saudi Arabia. Called Makkah in Arabic, the "City of God" where the Prophet Muhammad is buried. Considered the fifth pillar of Islamic belief, performing the Hajj at least once in a lifetime is required of every Muslim who is able. A deeply spiritual undertaking, it underscores the historical continuity of Islam's 14 centuries. By returning to the site of *Kabah* to pray and commemorate Abraham's willingness to sacrifice his son to God's command, the rites of *Id al-Adha*, Muslims reenforce the links that bind them to each other, to the Prophet Muhammad, and to the beginnings of monotheism.

As a result of journeying to Mecca, pilgrims have opened up trade routes across the world, developing in the process an Afro-European free trade zone. In the name of charity, other Muslims facilitate their travels by building rest sites, supplying water, providing protection, and giving pious donations to assist with expenses. The Hajj has also become important as a social phenomenon, contributing to the forging of Islamic culture worldwide, while bridging differences of nationality, ethnicity and custom. Hajj is the heartbeat of the Earth's first genuinely transcontinental culture, nurturing and expanding science, commerce, politics, and religion. Millions of pilgrims learn of their commonality during prayer five times each day facing Makkah, fasting together during Ramadan, observing the injunctions of the Qur'an, and sharing hospitality. Over centuries, the desire to assist pilgrim travel spurred Muslim advances in mathematics, optics, astronomy, navigation, transportation, geography, education, medicine, finance, culture, and even politics. Despite the arduous journey and multiple risks, the constant flow of these pilgrims is channels of cultural and intellectual ferment.

*Source*: Adapted from David W. Tschnaz's "Journeys of Faith, Roads of Civilization," *Saudi Aramco World*, September/October 2004, pp. 2-5.

## SAUDI ARABIA

The Arabian Peninsula is the heartland of Islamic culture, which is 14 centuries old, originating in Mecca. Arabia's inhabitants were the primary source of Arab expansion throughout the Middle East and Europe from A.D.570-1258, the Golden Age of the Arab empire. But Saudi Arabia as a nation is a product of the twentieth century, particularly because of oil discoveries and development. In decades, its citizens have transitioned from a Bedouin tribal culture to a modern urban culture. After hundreds of years of subsistence living, a nomadic, patriarchal, and impoverished society has been transformed suddenly into a more prosperous, educated, and internationally oriented one. Within this whirlwind clash between tradition and modernization, the affluent kingdom founded on Islamic principles has experienced cataclysmic change. Popular magazines have described the nation as a desert super-state—a rich, vulnerable, feudal monarchy being hurdled into the space age.[12] In 2007, Saudi Arabia celebrated its 75th anniversary as a modern state, and Exhibit 10.5 highlights some of the milestones of its remarkable growth in the context of its major oil company, Saudi Aramco.

## The People and Their Homeland

Approximately 90% of the Saudi people are Arabs, with a 10% minority of Afro-Asians. The kingdom's population has risen rapidly to almost 28 million, and is growing. The country occupies four-fifths of the Arabian Peninsula, a landmass of 850,000 square miles, making it geographically one of the largest countries in the region. Geographically, it is a harsh, rugged plateau reaching from the Red Sea on the west toward the Gulf on the east (called "Arabian" by the Saudis and "Persian" by

---

### EXHIBIT 10.5

### 75 YEARS OF SAUDI ARAMCO

1932. Abd al'Sa'ud proclaims the Kingdom of Saudi Arabia

1933. Saudi government signs concession agreements with Standard Oil of California. Prospecting begins and 2 years later first test well is drilled; in 1935, Texaco buys 50% interest in SoCal's concession.

1938. Damman Well #7 discovers commercial oil, so barges begin to export it to Bahrain; the following year, the first tanker load of oil is shipped.

1944. Company name of California Arabian Standard Oil is changed to Arabian American Oil Company (ARAMCO), and the next year the Ras Tanura refinery begins production.

1950. Trans-Arabian pipeline completed from Eastern Province to Mediterranean Sea coast.

1951. Corporate headquarters moved from New York to Dhahran, and the following year the company begins building government schools; first for girls opened in 1964.

1973. Saudi government buys 25% participation in ARAMCO; the next years increased this to 60% interest, and in 1980, 100% participation.

1983. First Saudi, elected ARAMCO president, and by 1988 the company is established as Saudi Arabian Oil Company which now owned East West crude oil pipeline, off-shore loading terminal, and four supertankers.

the Iranians on the opposite side). Other Gulf states sharing that peninsula from north to south are Kuwait, Bahrain, Qatar, and the United Arab Emirates. The Saudi's northern frontier abuts Jordan, Iraq, and Kuwait, and, in the south, Yemen and Oman. There is wide variation in the Saudi citizens, ranging from desert dwellers to, increasingly, city dwellers. Bedouin tribesmen in origin are a keen, alert, astute people, never to be underestimated. Saudi Arabians live in an entirely Muslim country with oil reserves of some 261.8 billion barrels.

Today, the country has 300 modern hospitals, as well as 5 million students enrolled in 24,000 schools, eight universities, and numerous colleges and training centers. But too many Saudi youths in higher education are not being realistically prepared for the present-day job market because their studies are not in line with market realities. Thus, one of every five workers in the kingdom is foreign born. Approximately 1 million immigrants and technicians are in Saudi Arabia to help build the infrastructure and defense, as well as to provide new technologies and services. This influx includes Americans, Europeans, Japanese, and third-world laborers and servants, such as Filipinos, Africans, and other Middle Easterners.

With a literacy rate of over 62%, rapid Saudi modernization and affluence has brought increased educational opportunities both at home and abroad for males and some females. Throughout history, Arabic has been a source of a great literary communication. Although this language, with its three forms (classic, standard, and dialects), is principally used by Saudis, English is widely spoken or understood among the educated commercial class. The citizens' three most common symbols are the date palm emblematic of growth and vitality, the unsheathed sword of strength rooted in faith, and the Muslim reed. Although the unique flowing robes and headdress of the Arabs are preferred, cosmopolitan Saudis are equally at home in Western dress when appropriate.

The kingdom follows a form of strict Islamic conservatism called *Hanabalism* (or *Wahhabism* by detractors)—it is among the most restrictive of Sunni Muslim jurisprudence. Although it has been criticized by outsiders as rigid, uncompromising, and self-righteous, most Saudi people follow a hybrid that mixes local traditions with modern developments. The ordinary Saudi is known for exercising generosity and hospitality.

## Geographic and Economic Features

This country has four major topographical regions:

- *Asir*, a relatively fertile strip of coastal mountains in the southwest with peaks up to 10,000 feet and terraced farming.
- *Hijaz*, a mountain chain encompassing the rest of the west coast along the Red Sea.
- *Nejd*, the arid peninsula plateau with the Rub-al Khali or Empty Quarter, the largest continuous sand desert in the world, a place of oases in the north as well as shifting sand dunes and untapped oil fields—the capital city of Al-Riyadh at its center is a "garden" because of springs and well water.
- *Al Hasa*, the eastern province where the principal oil and gas production occurs, along with agriculture in numerous oases, such as Haradh and Hofuf.

Saudi Arabia has 14 principal population centers and several major cities. Riyadh, the royal capital of some 3.5 million, is a modern desert city with new freeways, hospitals, schools, shopping malls, and one of the largest airports in the world. The Red Sea port city of Jeddah is the nation's leading commercial center and hub of the country's 8000-mile highway system. Jeddah's huge $10 billion airport handles the 2 million Muslim guests annually en route to its holy places. Assembling on the Plains of Arafat, the *hajj* or pilgrim caravan, move to Mecca some 50 miles away.

## Political and Social Conditions

The nation's history parallels the House of Saud, founded in the eighteenth century, which recaptured the traditional family seat of Riyadh in 1902, then extending their control over what is modern Saudi Arabia. This was accomplished under the leadership of Abdul

Aziz ibn-Abd ar-Rahman. Called ibn-Saud, he was proclaimed king of the entire region in 1927; the new nation was named The Kingdom of Saudi Arabia in 1932, and by 1945 was a founding member of the United Nations and the Arab League. With the help of American petroleum engineers, King Abdul Aziz in 1939 launched the country's and the Aramco Company's future by opening the valves for oil production at 4 million barrels a day; over time, hundreds of billions of barrels have been extracted, and it is still flowing. Aramco, a leader in OPEC, is now entirely state-owned under Saudi control and management, producing 95% of the nation's oil. The country is a member of the World Trade Organization.

The sixth king, Abdullah bin Abdul Aziz, rules today with assistance from a royal family of some 30,000, of whom 7000 are "princes"; about 5000 princes are in government service, but only 60 are thought to be involved in decision-making. Tribal connections are maintained through the Saudi National Guard. The combined wealth of the Al Saud family is estimated to be in the hundreds of billions of dollars.

In Saudi Arabia, the *Sharia* governs national life and behavior. A judiciary interprets and advises the king on this law and in other matters not stated. The *Sharia* courts consist of 7000 judges, the backbone of the legal system, but the bane of reformers. The *Majlis al-Shura* is a consultative council of 100 appointed members, broadly representative of the kingdom's diversity, except that it excludes women. Although there are no elections or legislature, the king and his governors of provinces, as well as the royal princes, govern by consensus but with absolute authority. In a system based on trust, they hold regular *majlis*, or audiences, where citizen petitioners may approach in open court to make requests, to lodge complaints, or to adjudicate grievances. Internationally, the king opposes Western democracy and its institutions, while gently nudging his country forward on social matters without unduly offending conservatives.

Islam permeates Saudi life—Allah is always present, controls everything, and is frequently referred to in conversation; that name appears in Arabic script on the nation's flag. Everything written in the preceding sections on Islam and Arab culture is fervently present in this traditional society, now on the verge of even greater change.

*The Role of Women*: Islamic tenets limit the number of wives a man may have by imposing restrictions on divorce, and ensure a woman's rights to property and inheritance from husband or father. Men may divorce their wives with a simple oath, while women must plead before an all-male, extremist Wahhabist judiciary, and mothers have no right to custody of the children. Further, husbands may deny wives the right to travel, work, or study at university. Following the impact of the first Gulf War with Iraq, women began a quiet revolution. For centuries, women in Saudi Arabia lived in extreme privacy, wore the long veil or *abaya*, and were protected by the males. Today, Saudi women are still socially segregated, constrained in their movements and dress. The many successful female entrepreneurs resent having to have a male agent to represent them. Yet with advanced education, Saudi women have begun to enter the business world and the professions, especially teaching, along with social and public services. Though women today make up over half of university enrollment, they number only a fraction of the work force. The so-called invisible women are said now to control as much as 40% of private wealth, much of it inherited under the law. Despite social limitations on women, as well as bans on their driving, travel, and political activity—all enforced by the *mutawa* or religious police—cosmopolitan female Saudis slowly forge ahead. Their growing economic assets are increasingly used to invest in property and to engage in business ownership—over 2000 of the latter are registered with the Riyadh Chamber of Commerce. Despite the establishment of a National Human Rights Commission, a 2008 report by the International Human Rights Watch based in New York observes that there are obstacles to female advancement and utilization of this great human resource. Major ones are the obligatory requirements for a male guardian when females go out in public, and that women may be legally responsible for a supposed crime while deemed not to have full legal capacity.

The royal family, controlling the top government positions and a large share of the nation's wealth, struggles to maintain some balance between modern global influences, and insular, ultraconservative clerics of Wahhabism who seek to return Islamic practices to the seventh and eighth century versions. But in this twenty-first century, they face a time bomb, with 70% of its population under 21, incomes falling, unemployment rising, and external Middle Eastern conflicts impacting their society.

The Saudi government is under great pressure to change faster because of events such as these in the opening of the twenty-first century:

■ *The global war on terrorism, and attacks by Islamic militants upon Western targets*, such as New York City and Washington, D.C.; Madrid, Spain; and London, England. Many of the youths involved had been born and raised in Saudi Arabia, often from affluent families. They had become radicalized in fundamentalist Mosque schools at home or abroad funded by wealthy Saudis and taught by fiery mullahs who were narrow-minded, religious zealots. Furthermore, some of the Islamic charities supported by Saudi funding were found to be the source of financial support for extremist groups. Yet many Saudi donors claim they did not know their contributions were being so misdirected. In any event, this internal terrorism has prompted intense introspection and debate.
■ *Their ally, the United States, undertook a second invasion of Muslim Iraq, thus destabilizing the whole Middle East.* While many American troops have since been removed from Saudi Arabia, the country is criticized by fellow Muslim nations because of its close ties for eight decades to the USA.
■ *Human rights abuses seemingly exist*, especially among foreign workers who face petty discrimination and have little recourse to justice.

There is apparently some persecution of religious minorities, such as non-Wahhabi Muslims and visiting Christians.

■ *Increasing quiet agitation by an affluent middle class for political reforms*, including liberalization of strict religious constraints, especially upon women, and allowing more democratic institutions. The *Islahi* or reformist movement performed best in the first municipal elections. A, progressive elite has a strong voice in the local Saudi press and on satellite television channels. Thus, the Al Sauds family, representing a broad spectrum of opinion, strives to preserve between liberal demands and strident preachers among the *mutawaa*.

■ *While maintaining orthodox Islamic teachings and supporting Arab world ambitions, the Saudis play a pivotal role within global Islam*, both in Muslim countries, as well as with Muslim minorities seeking to reconcile their faith with life in the West. Saudi Arabians have invested in building mosques anywhere from Los Angeles to Kula Lampur, influencing the architecture, reading matter, training, and style of the imam, or spiritual leader. Some critics see this version of Islam as intolerant and puritanical, neglecting the artistic, literary, and diverse scholarly traditions of Islam. Yet in 2008, King Abdullah tried to be a cultural and religious bridge builder in Madrid by convening with the Muslim World League, a "World Conference on Dialogue." As "Custodian of the Two Holy Mosques," the king is concerned for Muslims everywhere, while decrying extremism among adherents. Yet his kingdom still bans all other non-Muslim places of worship, discriminates against Islamic and Shia minorities, and supports an obscurant religious establishment. Though pious with some creditability as an interfaith conciliator, this king has yet to confront reactionary clerics while guiding Islam in more moderate directions worldwide.[a]

## The Economy and Business

Beginning in the twentieth century, Saudi Arabia's financial situation skyrocketed from the subsistence level based on herding and farming to wealth from oil and gas development. Over the past 85 years, this developing economy has been transformed from a desert backwater with nomadic trade and barter to a rich, complex, global system. By the mid-1970s, the energy production accounted for 74.5% of the domestic gross product, thus enabling the country to become the world's largest exporter of petroleum. Large-scale diversification into hydrocarbon-based industries is vigorously pursued. Provision of new infrastructure also spurred the growth of the non-oil economic sector, expanding

---

[a] "Global Islam—Unusual Guests, A Most Unusual Host," *The Economist,* July 26, 2008, p. 71.

private enterprise as well. A series of 5-year development plans and over $95 billion in government expenditures on ports and roads have spurred commerce.

Sheep, goats, and camels have given way to automobiles, jets, and supertankers, making for a new mobility for both the populace and their products. By the 1980s, with a proven oil reserve for the next 60 years, the country was producing 9.5 million barrels of oil per day.

Other trends within the kingdom are the following:

- A foreign investment law in 2000 that permits 100% ownership of in-country projects, and reduced corporate taxes to 30%; agreements signed with eight international companies to invest in three integrated natural gas development ventures.
- Encouraging privatization within a state-run economy, establishing a public stock market, and building of the futuristic Al Faisalah complex with modern stores, hotel, and apartments.
- In the past 10 years, the kingdom has issued forty laws to streamline commerce. The country's regulatory bodies are well regarded in their governance of capital markets, telecoms, and industrial standards, while the patent office is under reform. SAGIA, the government's business-promotion entity, is competent and seeks foreign investment.
- Active support, loans ($14 billion), and contributions to numerous international and humanitarian organizations and causes, especially to Middle Eastern peace and development. The King Faisal Foundation alone has contributed millions of dollars to global philanthropic projects promoting Islamic values. It also assists the world's 1.2 billion Muslims in making global religious pilgrimages to the holy sites of Mecca and Medina, with the government providing support to the needy making the *hajj*.
- Reduction of income polarization, so that 3 million Saudis now hold local equities. With 23 million people and rising, the market for trade is promising. This population growth necessitates huge investments in infrastructure. Thus, in 2005, the World Bank ranked Saudi Arabia as the best place in the region to do business!

To balance such positive development, consider these observations of Madawi al-Rasheed, a Saudi scholar, that the family which unified the kingdom some 80 years ago now has become a "headless tribe" with at least five factions: "Supposedly, this gerontocracy sits atop a society in stress, where money, in the absence of constitutional tools or intellectual freedom, has been the only buffer against wrenching and rapid change" (*The Economist*, Nov. 19, 2005, p. 88).

*IRAN*—Inheritor of the ancient Persian empire and culture, this country is a Shiite giant of over 71 million people. In 1979, an Islamic revolution overthrew the Shah to install a government called the "Islamic Republic." A modern constitutional theocracy ruled by religious clerics, it engaged in a brutal war with Iraq which cost a million lives. It permitted the take-over and closure of the American Embassy by radicalized students who then took the staff there as hostages. A sworn enemy of Israel, it has sponsored Hamas and Hezbollah terrorism in that country and Lebanon, while supporting Shiite extremists in Iraq. An important player in the region, Iran faces U.N. sanctions for its development of nuclear power that possibly may become atomic weapons. Currently, its leaders reinforce a fiery rhetoric and fanaticism against the West. How long this regime will endure is uncertain, given that two out of three people are below the age of 30. These youth yearn for modernization and freedom, so are bored with tired slogans from a long-ago revolution. Its educated population clamor for social, economic, and political reforms. Exhibit 10.6 provides more perspective on this nation of increasing importance in world affairs.[13]

*IRAQ*—The land of ancient Mesopotamia, between the Tigris and Euphrates rivers, was home to the luxurious city of Babylon, with a population now estimated as high as 28 million. In 1921, the British established it as a monarchy with a figurehead king. The new political entity was created out of three Ottoman, ethnically diverse provinces centered in Basra, Baghdad, and Mosul.[14] Then an army coup installed dictator Saddam Hussein, who fought a war with the Iranians, practiced genocide on his own citizens, and invaded Kuwait in 1990. This provoked United Nation sanctions, and two invasions by the United States and its collation partners—first the Gulf War in 1991 and again

---

### EXHIBIT 10.6

### IMPRINTS ON MODERN IRAN'S CHARACTER

The recorded history of the present-day people called Iranians spans 2500 years. Their Persian ancestors built a conquering empire, stretching from the Mediterranean Sea to the Indus River—one that was more glorious and benevolent then most civilizations of antiquity. It encompassed the present-day countries of Iraq, Pakistan, Afghanistan, Turkmenistan, Uzbekistan, Tajikistan, Turkey, Jordan, Syria, Israel, Lebanon, Egypt, and the Caucasus region. It is evident in the magnificent remains of Persepolis, the capital built by Dairus the Great who reigned from 522 to 486 B.C. Their ancient religion of Zoroastrian's teachings centered on clarifying good and evil, free will, final judgment, and one almighty God—all of which in turn influenced Judaism, Christianity, and Islam. Persian principles of governance were enshrined in their Cyrus the Great Cylinder—it resembles a clay corncob inscribed in cuneiform with the first chanter of human rights. This exalted artifact, now the London's British Museum calls for religious and ethnic freedom, bans slavery and oppression, opposes the taking of another's property by force or without compensation, allow states voluntarily to become members of the empire.

continued

EXHIBIT 10.6

IMPRINTS ON MODERN IRAN'S CHARACTER (CONTINUED)

Today's Iran's identity has been shaped in part by this Persian heritage, forged by living at the crossroads of migration, invasion, and trade. Located at the eastern end of a Turkish-Iranian plateau, this somewhat arid region is homeland to people who live mainly in cities which in earlier times were on the historic Silk Road. In these foothills of great mountain ranges, Iranians now live with proven oil reserves (135 billion barrels) that are exceeded only by Saudi Arabia and Russia. On their western border are Iraq and what they call the Persian Gulf; to the north is the Caspian Sea and Turkmenistan, while to the their east are Afghanistan, Pakistan, and Baluchistan; to the south is the Gulf of Oman and the United Arab Emirates.

Their culture favors hospitality, courting, family affairs, and political negotiations. Their Farsi language, one of the oldest in the world, has the word *taarof* which signifies the unwritten code of how people should treat one another, with a system of ritual politeness aimed at acquiring knowledge from the other party. Over 26 centuries of being in the middle of trade, cultural exchange and friction, the country's long history of wars, invasions and martyrs culminated in the Iran-Iraq War if the 1980's. But in the seventh century, the Arab invaders brought Islam, but the Persians adopted the Shiite form of this religion. Iranians are proud of their capacity to assimilate foreign ways without surrendering their own. Since their first human settlement 10,000 years ago to the bustling capital of modern Tehran, the Iranian psyche is nostalgic about their thousand-year heritage as the world's first superpower. The people here want to be judged for the greatness of their civilization and not just for the last 30 years of the Islamic revolution. The soul of this nation is evident in citizen pride in their antiquity, so evident in archeological sites. In addition to Persians, the population includes Arabs, Azeris, Baluchis, Kurds, and Turkmen.

*Source*: Adapted from Maguerite Del Giudice, "Ancient Soul of Iran," *National Geographic*, August 2008, pp. 34-67, "Iran-Born at the Crossroads" (www.nationalgeographic.com).

in 2005, in which the regime and its large armed forces were quickly defeated both times. Although the present occupation by American and allied troops failed to uncover "weapons of mass destruction" as expected, it did trigger a serious insurgency by locals and foreign terrorists, resulting in much loss of life and property so that many fear a civil war. Hussein was captured, put on trial, and executed. Efforts are still under way to formulate a more effective and democratic form of government. Elections have been held for the first time in the country's history to pass a constitution and install a parliament. Under the previous Baath Party totalitarian rule, the 36% Sunni Muslims dominated the government, so are resisting participation in the new regime. Its majority are Shiite Muslims who share power with the minority Kurdish Islamic parties and some Sunnis who together govern along ethnic and sectarian lines. Whether these three factions can ever cooperate in establishing a balanced government of national unity is an open question. But by 2008, then-prime minister Nuri al-Maliki attempted to build some national, nonsectarian consensus and a viable army, trained largely by the Americans. The economy is improving fueled by oil revenue, as well as sales of consumer and durable goods.

Reconstruction and rehabilitation projects have been hampered by security problems, with the fanatical insurgents engaged in bombings, kidnappings, and intimidation. Increase in female suicide bombers are most troubling for the population tired of chaos and ethnic violence. The main terrorists undermining essential order are al-Qaeda external extremists, Sunni insurgents, and Shiite militias; the last mentioned seem to be funded and supported by Iran. At the moment, the people fear their safety, complain about water scarcity, electricity failures, high unemployment, and the struggle to create a democratic market economy. Foreign contractors and business persons, as well as humanitarian volunteers, operate in "harm's way," undermining efforts to rejuvenate commerce, the infrastructure, and oil production. An Iraq Study Group of 10 prominent Americans made recommendations for restoring order in a moderate Iraq society. Whether these strategies will be implemented and become policy both in the United States and Iraq remains to be seen. In 2009, the new U.S. Presidential Administration began a policy of American troop withdrawal from this beleaguered country.

The Kurds in Iraq have gained a measure of autonomy and peace for their mountainous northern region, and are currently cooperating with the central government in Baghdad. Their goal is to control some 9 billion barrels of crude oil in Iraqi Kurdistan, and eventually gain independence to form a new state with the Kurds living within the borders of Syria, Turkey, and Iran—something vehemently opposed by those three nations. Having 100,000 of their people killed under Saddam's administration and experienced freedom for the last 15 years, the Iraqi Kurds will not give it up without a fight. With foreign aid and smuggling, these fierce warriors and builders now experience a measure of prosperity, despite no native industry. The deep ethnic and sectarian divides in the region are evident in Kirkuk, where fighting between Kurds and Turkman continues.

*ISRAEL*—Although the Hebrews lived on this ancient land during Biblical times, they did not regain a state until 1948 with the help of the United Nations when the British left Palestine. Since then, Israel had turned these 20,277 sq. km. into a prosperous garden, economy, and refuge for over 6 million Jews from all over the world. But its successes with agriculture, industry, technology, trade, and tourism have been eclipsed by conflict and terrorism. In the process, its superbly trained, equipped, and motivated military forces have had to fight six wars over six decades with 750,000 displaced Palestinian Arabs and their allies. There have been numerous violent reprisals by both parties, along with ongoing peace negotiations involving the United Nations and many countries. Frequent Israeli military incursions and illegal settlements within Palestinian territories in the West Bank and Gaza only add to the region's instability and feelings of frustration and hopelessness among Arab neighbors.

The global Jewish population is about 14 million, or 2% of the world's peoples. Despite having developed a new homeland in modern Israel with a common religion and language, the world Jewish community is quite culturally diverse given the national origins of its members. In the Middle East, there is much commonality in Jewish beliefs, laws, and family life with their Semite brothers in Arab communities. In the twentieth century alone, Jews have won over 120 Nobel Prizes (Exhibit 10.7).

Prestigious international universities have opened campuses in the Gulf States. For example, in Abu Dhabi, Imperial College London has a new gleaming diabetes center in a brand new hospital that can care

---

## EXHIBIT 10.7

## DUBAI: A FUTURISTIC CITY

This is a zany, ambitious, and modernistic boomtown on the Persian Gulf. Salem Moosa is developing skyscrapers and other marvels built on man-made islands in the shape of palm trees. He is creating replicas of great monuments, such as the Eiffel Tower, the Pyramids, the Taj Mahal and the Lost City of Atlantis. Dubai also boasts of its indoor ski resort, its underwater hotel, the world's largest shopping mall, and largest skyscraper. Suffering from construction fever, it is afloat in fantasy, ambition, and rivers of cash. This city is at the forefront of the Emirates push to the sky, as it reinvents a once sleepy port of pearl traders and pirates. Perched at the crossroads of Europe, Africa, and India, the sheikdom has relatively little oil while becoming a global trading hub and a center of Arab investment. Dubai is also a bewildering stew of nationalities, a place where natives are less than 20% of the 1 million population, politics are played down and spending is played up. Among its many development projects are Internet City which 5 years ago was only sand; a tall encased ski run; the world's most treasured diving sites recreating the Maldives, the Barrier Reef, the Caymans, and the Red Sea. The man-made islands were the vision of Crown Prince Sheik Mohammed ibn Rashid al Maktum, which started the innovation process in Dubai.

*Source*: Adapted from Megan K. Stack's "In Dubai, the Sky's No Limit," *Los Angeles Times*, October 13, 2005, pp. A1 and 6.

for 6000 patients (prosperity has brought a sedentary lifestyle, triggering a genetic predisposition toward diabetes among Arabs). Before this economic transformation, this UAE capital lacked paved roads in 1961. Now, like other countries in the region, its economy struggles to absorb petrodollars and avoid inflation. The six nations who are members of the Gulf Cooperation Council earn over $400 billion annually from their exports. The Institute of International Finances predicts that at the present rate of a $100 barrel of oil, the GCC could reap a cumulative of $9 trillion by year 2020! This hoard of profits is not all ingested internally, as in its central banks, but also in overseas' investments. The Gulf states are now a financial "superpower" with great domestic ambitions.

## MIDDLE EAST BUSINESS CUSTOMS AND PROTOCOL

Consider this case in point:

A Midwestern banker is invited by an Arab sheik to meet him at the Dorchester Hotel in London. A friend of both arranges the get-together, and facilitates the introduction. Dark sweet coffee is served. No business of consequence is discussed, but there is a sociable exchange…. Subsequently, the American is invited to a series of meetings in Riyadh. The Saudi greets the banker with, "There is no god but Allah, and Muhammad is his messenger." More strong coffee is served, and sometimes others are present in the meeting room…. In time, a mutually beneficial business relationship is established.[15]

This short episode encapsulates several important points for succeeding in Middle Eastern business ventures. First, nothing happens quickly and patience is a virtue. Second, trust is paramount, and it is cultivated over a period of time, often with the assistance of a third-party acquaintance. Although business customs will vary somewhat in the region, by trying to understand Islam and Arab culture, an individual is in a better position to be effective. In this section, insights from the write-up on Saudi Arabia may be adapted and selectively applied elsewhere in the Middle East, but are subject to change.

Among the modern institutions of higher education recently established within Saudi Arabia, King Fahd University of Petroleum and Minerals is among the best. There, Dr. Mohammed I. Al-Twaijri has conducted and published studies comparing Saudi and American managers, purchasing agents, and negotiators. Some of his research findings and comments are:

■ There is a trend toward "Westernization" of Middle East managers, and Saudi managers are becoming less paternalistic.

- There are significant differences in the way Arab managers respond to questionnaire items in their native Arabic language, as opposed to the English version of the same instrument.
- In negotiations, the Saudis have two dominant styles, competitive and collaborative, both of which are expressed within the Arab cultural context.
- In joint ventures under way with Saudi Arabia, foreigners are required to build extensive training programs for the locals into their project management, increasingly the trend in most Middle Eastern countries.

Apart from what has already been described about Middle Easterners and their cultures, Arabs are a people of great emotion and sentimentality—and sometimes of excess and extremes. They hold in high regard friendship, loyalty, and justice. When events and behavior go against that sense of justice, Arabs will likely be morally outraged and indignant. Generally, Arabs tend to be warm, hospitable, generous, and courteous. Like many Middle Eastern persons in commerce, the stereotype is that they are either very sincere and trustworthy, or the opposite, insincere and sly. It is dangerous to stereotype any culture, so one is advised to deal with each Middle Easterner individually as a person, and to treat him or her with respect and dignity. Semites, whether Arab, Christian, or Jew, also have reputations as effective traders and salespeople.

Furthermore, Arab society places great emphasis on honor. Its concept of shame is somewhat alien to Western mind-sets. Shame must be feared, avoided, or hidden, so one prays to Allah for protection from others (public exposure). Thus, foreigners should avoid embarrassing Arabs. Because of the society's powerful identification between the individual and the group, shame means a loss of power and influence, particularly for the family. In addition, the tribal heritage influences and values a high degree of deference and conformity, often expressed in a somewhat authoritarian tone. In return, the individual has a strong sense of place, and shares in the group's social prestige. That is why Arabs typically worry about how their decisions, acts, and behavior reflect on their family, clan, tribe, and then country. In a traditional society, honor is important, and to admit "I don't know" may be difficult; constructive criticism can be taken for an insult. For an Arab, the "self" is buried deep within the individual. This relates, then, to the previously explained sense of distance—because the "self" is personal and private, yet in public touching and jostling among males is quite evident .

## Business Tips

To an Arab, commerce is a most blessed career—the prophet Muhammad, after all, was a man of commerce who also married a lady of commerce. Thus, business and trade are highly respected, so one is expected to be sound, shrewd, and knowledgeable. Some Middle Eastern business practices to observe are noted below:

- *Business relationships* are facilitated by establishing personal rapport, mutual respect, and trust—business is done between people, not merely with a company or contract.
- *Connections* and *networking* are most important—vital to gaining access to both private and public decision-makers, so maintain good relations with people of influence.
- *Negotiating* and *bargaining* are commonplace processes, and somewhat of an art in these ancient lands, so expect some old-fashioned "haggling."
- *Decision-making* is traditionally done in person, thus requiring an organization's representative of suitable rank; decisions are usually made by the top person in the government agency or corporation, and normally are not accomplished by correspondence, fax, or telephone.
- *Time is flexible*, according to the concept of "tomorrow if God wills"; it is an expression of the cultural pattern of fatalism. Avoid imposing Western time frames and schedules, though as such modern business practices become customary, appointments may be set and kept. Arabs may be prompt, or not, and appointments will likely not be exact or may start late. Their day is divided into five prayer times, and meetings are scheduled accordingly.
- *Marketing* should be focused on specific customer-client segments; because centralized governments in many Arab countries hold the economic power and are the principal buyers, one must learn the public sector development plans for obtaining goods and services, then develop contacts and relationships with senior officials in appropriate ministries.
- *Socialization* in business is traditional, and social gestures, courtesies, and invitations are commonplace, but deals are not usually concluded under such circumstances. Traditionally, Arab women are not part of this scene, but mixed social gatherings in private are becoming more common.
- *Communication* is especially complex in the Middle East, and outsiders should show harmony and agreement, following the host's lead. Arabic as a language is high context, manifested with raised voices and much nonverbal body language (wide gestures, animated facial expressions, eyebrow raising, tongue clicking, standing close, eye contact, and, except with strangers on first meeting, a side nod of the head is often given as affirmation). Hyperbole is normal, and a *yes* may really mean *maybe* or even, *probably not*.
- *Taboos* are many, so caution is advised in unfamiliar circumstances. Exhibit 10.8 offers some further information for appropriate business behavior in the region.

EXHIBIT 10.8

IN THE MIDDLE EAST, AVOID:

- Bringing up business subjects until you get to know your host or you will be considered rude.
- Commenting on a man's wife or female children over 12 years of age.
- Raising colloquial questions that may be common in your country but possibly misunderstood here as an invasion of privacy.
- Using disparaging or swear words and off-color or obscene attempts at humor.
- Engaging in conversations about religion, politics, or Israel.
- Bringing gifts of alcohol or using alcohol, which is prohibited in some countries, such as Saudi Arabia.
- Requesting favors from those in authority or esteem, for it is considered impolite for Arabs to say "no."
- Shaking hands too firmly or pumping—gentle or limp handshakes are preferred.
- Pointing your finger at someone or showing the soles of your feet when seated.

In light of the above advice, it is interesting to note that among U.S. troops in Iraq, the Marine Corps Intelligence Activity issued *Iraq Culture Smart Cards* with cultural tips to help American military stay out of trouble in that Arab country. It contains pointers on gestures to use (right hand over the heart as a sign of respect; right hand palm up, fingers touching to mean slow down or be patient; quick upward head snap with tongue click to signify "no"; avoid using the left hand in contacting others; do not show women attention by touching or staring; slouching as a sign of indifference).

## Global Managers Alert

Nineteen states in the Middle East share the common Arab culture and practice of Islam, but there are differences in interpretations and practices. Saudi Arabia is stricter in this regard as the Gulf's elder statesmen and protector of Muslim traditions, especially as perceived by the Wahhabi sect. Elsewhere, social and business life may be more relaxed as in Bahrain or Dubai. There is a continuum between a country like Iran, now under a fundamentalist religious regime, and Jordan, which is under a progressive monarchy greatly influenced by former British presence and customs. Business ethos in one country may frown upon *baksheesh* or payments for favors received, whereas elsewhere it may be tolerated, even encouraged. In some Arab countries, a local sponsor or partner is essential for a successful joint venture, whereas in others it is not.

## Middle Eastern Reactions to Westerners

Peoples from ancient civilizations, like Egypt, Persia, Turkey, and Arabia, are proud of their past—its history, art, poetry, literature, and cultural accomplishments. Unfortunately, many Westerners and Asians carry distorted cultural images or stereotypes about Middle Easterners and their contributions to human development. North American and European media has been particularly inept, slanted and at times false in their presentations about the Middle East and Arabs.

There is deep underlying suspicion in the Middle East against former European colonial powers, especially the British and French who once ruled much of the area. But insensitive American behavior toward Middle Eastern peoples and their religion explain, in part, reactive "anti-American" campaigns abroad that undermine both political and business relationships. That happened in Iran, a non-Arab country, in 1979 when American influence and actions threatened Persian identity and culture to the point of a violent takeover of and hostage-taking at the U.S. Embassy. Currently, resentment centers on America as the only superpower capable of military intervention in their region, especially the U.S. coalitions that went to war against terrorism twice in Iraq, as well as against the Taliban in Afghanistan. Both Arabs and Westerners are given to distorting each other's actions, behavior, and beliefs, thus promoting mutual xenophobia. The global terrorist movement among Islamic militants rose partially out of fear for Western culture and values destroying or undermining traditional Arab culture.

## As They See Us

Seventy percent of the world's oil reserves are in the Middle East. This results in an influx of Europeans, Americans, and even Asians into the region, bringing repercussions from the indigenous peoples about these guests who come to engage in business and development. Here is a summary of the feedback about foreigners from the Arab perspective:

- Many foreigners express superiority and arrogance; they know the answers to everything.
- Many do not want to share the credit for what is accomplished by joint efforts.

- Many are frequently unable or unwilling to respect and adjust to local customs and culture.
- Some fail to innovate to meet the needs of local culture, preferring to seek easy solutions based on the situation in their homeland.
- Some individuals refuse to work through the normal administrative channels of the country, and do not respect local legal and contractual procedures.
- Some tend to lose their democratic ways when on foreign assignments, becoming instead more autocratic and managing by instilling fear in subordinates.
- Westerners are often too imposing, aggressive, pushy, and rude.
- Frustration over American and European imbalance in support and aid for Israel, in contrast to the Palestinian cause and human rights.

# THE SUBCULTURE OF TERRORISM[16]

What is unique in this twenty-first century is the globalization of terrorism. Terrorists strike fear and cause reprisals everywhere—Asia, Africa, Europe, Latin America, Middle East, and North America. As to preferred means or weapons for expressing this hatred through destruction are bombs, often by suicide bombers, both male and female. Sometimes the Internet is used to spread this terrorism. Often, the terrorism and xenophobia is launched in the name of patriotism or religion. Michael Buleigh, author of *Blood and Rage*, maintains that the West must wage a more effective cultural war against jihadist ideology and their human bombers.

Currently, too many such evildoers seem to come from the Middle East and fundamentalist Islam. Some are poor, unemployed, and deeply frustrated. The West largely perceives these Muslim radicals as semiliterate extremists, brainwashed by their mullahs, or spiritual counselors. That is what the uninformed mistakenly thought of Osama bin Laden and his al-Qaeda followers who were involved in America's 9/11 mass killings. But some of the suicide attackers are educated, middle-class, often from good families in Saudi Arabia, Yemen, or Egypt. Seemingly, the Islamic militants want to unify the Muslim world under the rule of the holy law or *sharia*. Sometimes they commit crimes against humanity as they seek to promote communal hostility, such as in India where the Mujaheddin terrorist group tries to split the Muslim and Hindu communities by bombing attacks, such as happened in Bangalore. At other European sites, as in London and Madrid, the zealots sought to cause widespread panic by bombing transportation infrastructure, and innocent commuters panic. Others, as in Indonesia, aimed at nightclubs where tourists gathered. Some

Islamic radicals, like Hamas and Hezbollah, prosper because of injustice against some 5 million Palestinian Arabs.

In the twenty-first century, al-Qaeda has expanded upon decades of Middle Eastern terrorism. Now, these global *jihadists* seek to maximize their civilian casualties for spectacular effects. Despite significant set-backs, the movement has learned how to operate worldwide, particularly by using the Internet for transfer of funds, recruitment, and propaganda (as illustrated by their manipulations of Arab media to transmit their distorted views). They have created a "virtual caliphate" in cyberspace which binds together amorphous groups seeking to spread chaos and destruction. Although only hundreds in a core group, they have enlisted thousands of disaffected fighters into the subculture of rebellion. This hydra-headed monster aids and abets the Taliban and Pushtan warriors in Afghanistan, along with religious fanatics in Pakistan, India, Indonesia, and the Philippines. In Iraq, the people and their allies are showing that these wanton slaughterers can be curtailed, particularly when killing innocent Muslims alienates the populace. As author Peter Begen has observed, "Self-destruction is encoded in the DNA of groups like al-Qaeda." That group was delivered a blow in 2007 when one of al-Qaeda founders and chief ideologist wrote from an Egyptian jail: "There is nothing that invokes the anger of God and His wrath like the unwarranted spilling of blood and wrecking of property." It is a battle for hearts and minds, especially within the Islamic world. Counter-terrorism strategies, humanitarian assistance, economic development, and improved cross-cultural relations help undermine terrorism. When Western nations permit human and legal rights for their terrorist prisoners, or with the 21,000 prisoners held by American forces in Iraq, then Muslims will believe democracy practices what it preaches. When the Islamic world hears the story of Muslims in the United States who benefit from freedom of religion, speech, and other rights, then the war of ideas may be reversed.

## SYNERGY: MIDDLE EAST HOPE

Slowly and painfully, a new cooperative relationship is emerging among the states and inhabitants of the Middle East. In addition to Arab unity efforts among themselves, peace accords have included neighbors in the area, such as between Egypt and Israel. Peaceful negotiations, mediation, and problem-solving skills are needed to resolve long-standing conflicts, instead of using weapons and violence. Gradually, this approach reached agreements between Israelis and Jordanians, while the search continues for comparable accords with the Palestinians, Syrians, and Lebanese. Exhibit 10.9 underscores the type of skills necessary to advance such a peaceful approach.

To realize the economic potential of their region, more Middle Easterners of all types are beginning to prefer collaboration with one another, even former enemies. Since they are only a short jet hop away from Europe, the interchange with peoples on both continents has increased. Arabs fly regularly to EU countries for study, investment, commerce, medical assistance, vacations, or even to reside. Europeans in greater numbers go to the Middle East seeking new markets and as tourists. In place of former colonial dominance, the present and future offer opportunities for more synergistic relationships if Arabs, Europeans, as well as Americans, Asians, and Africans appreciate each other's cultural heritages and differences, while seeking mutual benefits from interchanges. Practicing synergy is the key to peace and prosperity in the twenty-first century, both for that region and the world.

Efforts promoting cultural synergy need to be widely extended at all levels of education, as well as through churches and community forums. Indeed, knowledge of foreign languages and culture are keys to successful interaction and security in today's globally interconnected world—cultural skills are necessary to help peoples comprehend what is actually meant when they communicate with or about one another. If bridges are to be built across cultural divides, all must reach out to learn about other religions and countries. Only in such peaceful cooperation can the world community, especially through the United Nations, contribute to solutions of current Middle Eastern challenges, such as these:

- The reconstruction of Afghanistan and Iraq, so that their peoples may meet basic human needs in freedom and dignity.
- The resolution of conflict and violence between Israel and the Palestinian Authority.
- The restoration of harmony in Iran's internal struggle between the elected representatives of the people and the elected representative of God.
- The modernization of socio-political-economic systems in this region.

Through the practice of cultural synergy, then the Middle East has prospects for security, prosperity, and peace for its inhabitants.

# CONCLUSIONS

The Middle East is critical for world peace and prosperity, so global organizations will continue to seek commercial opportunities and relationships there. The material in this chapter is an introduction to the area in terms of its ancient glories, diversity, and current difficulties. Particular attention was devoted to increasing understanding of both Islam and Arab culture, the dominant factors in the vast majority of populace in the area.

While each country in the Middle East is unique and different, we provided an overview of business customs and protocols. We concluded with a call for cultural synergy, not only within the region, but also between the Middle East and Europe, Africa, America, and Asia, because so many of its former inhabitants now live and work in these other areas.

*Some Western commentators go to great length to portray Arab societies as backward or feeble.... But the West's inability to deal productively with the allegedly simplistic Arab culture actually highlights the weakness of the West's own condescending logic. In reality, there is no naiveté in the Arab world about its centrality in future success or failure of globalization, both geographically and geologically. It will not be, as some commentators claim, left behind.*

Parag Khanna, *The Second World: Empires and Influence in the Global Order.*

New York, NY: Random House, 2008.

*What is taking place now in the Muslim world is an internal conflict between Muslims, not an external battle between Islam and the West.... The centuries-old struggle is between the traditionalists and the rationalists over proper interpretation of the Quran, and the outcome is in doubt.... The fact is that the vast majority of one billion Muslims in the world are committed to genuine Islamic values, like pluralism, freedom, justice, human rights, and above all, democracy.*

Reza Aslan, *No God but God: The Origins, Evolution and Future of Islam.*

New York, NY: Random House, 2005:

## REFERENCES

1. Wade, D., Harris, K. D., and Howell, C. H.(eds.). *Book of Peoples of the World—A Guide to Cultures.* Washington, D.C.: National Geographic, 2008.
2. Felton, J. *The Contemporary Middle East.* Washington, DC: CQ Press, 2008; Gelvin, J. L. *The Modern Middle East: A History.* New York, NY:

Oxford University Press, 2008; Milton-Edwards, B. and Hinchcliffe, P. *Conflicts in the Middle East since 1945*. London, UK: Routledge, 2008; Fisk, R. *The Great War for Civilization—The Conquest of the Middle East*. New York, NY: Knopf, 2005; Khashan, N. and Bowen, J.(eds.). *Encounters with the Middle East*. London, UK: Solas House, 2007; Norwich, J. J. *Byzantium: Decline and Fall*. New York: Alfred Knopf, 1996; *Atlas of the Middle East*. Washington, DC: National Geographic, 2005; Nawwab, I. I., Speers, P. C., and Hoye, P. F.(eds.). *Aramco and Its World—Arabia and the Middle East*. Houston, TX: Aramco Services Company, 1981. [For information on Middle Eastern publications, visual aids, and exhibits, contact *Saudi Aramco World*, Box 2160, Houston, Texas 77252, USA. www.aramcoservices.com. For a complimentary DVD of *Saudi Aramco World* archives of back issues, contact Aramco Services Co., Public Affairs, 9009 West Loop South, Houston, TX 77096, USA.]

3. Esposito, J. L. *The Oxford History of Islam*. Oxford UK: Oxford University Press, 2000; Armstrong, K. *Islam: A Short History*. New York: Modern Library, 2000; Lunde, P. *Islam: Faith, Culture, and History*. Fremont, CA: DK Publishing/Rumi Bookstore, 2002; Aslan, R., *No God but God: The Origins, Evolution, and Future of Islam*. New York, NY: Random House, 2005; Brown, B. A. *Noah's Other Son: Bridging the Gap Between the Bible and the Quar'an*. London, UK: Continuum International, 2005.

4. Kennedy, H. *The Great Arab Conquests: How the Spread of Islam Changed the World We Live In*. London, UK: Weidenfeld & Nicholson, 2007; Roy, O. *Secularism Confronts Islam*. New York, NY: Columbia University Press, 2007; Roy, O. *Globalized Islam: The Search for a New Umah*. New York, NY: Columbia University Press, 2005; Kepel, G. *The War for Muslim Minds: Islam and the West*. London, UK: Belnap Press, 2005; Zaytuna Institute and Al-Qalam Institute. *Islam in the Balance: Toward a Better Understanding of Islam and Its Followers*. Fremont, CA: Rumi Bookstore, 2001. [For further information, visit these Web sites: www.rumibookstore.com; www.islaminthebalance.org.]

5. Lewis, R. D. "Epilogue: After September 11," *The Cultural Imperative— Global Trends of the 21st Century*. Boston, MA: Nicholas Brealey/ Intercultural Press, 2003.

6. Devji, F. *Landscapes of Jihad: Militancy, Morality, Modernity*. Ithica, NY: Cornell University Press, 2005; Little, D. *American Orientalism: The United States and the Middle East Since 1945*. Chapel Hill, NC: University of North Carolina Press, 2002; Reeves, M. *Muhammad in Europe: A Thousand Tears in Western Myth-Making*. New York: New York University Press, 2000; Lewis, B. *The Crisis of Islam: Holy War and Unholy Terror*. New York: Modern Library, 2003; Lewis, R. D. *When Cultures Collide: Managing Successfully Across Cultures*. Boston, MA: Nicolas Brealey Publishing, 2000.

7. Conover, D. L. (Skip), *Tsunami of Blood—How Fear-Mongering Politicians, Hate-Mongering Theologians, and Irresponsible Press Are Guiding Us to an Age of Horrors*. Annapolis, MD: Words Matter, LLC, 2007. www.wordsmatterradiio.net; www.tsunamiofblood.com.

8. Mernissi, F. *Los Angeles Times*, June 8, 1990, p. VII/25.

9. Ali, A. H. *The Caged Virgin—An Emancipation Proclamation Women and Islam*. New York, NY: Free Press, 2006; AlMunajjed, M. *Saudi Women Speak: 24 Remarkable Women Tell Their Success Stories*. Saudi Arabia: Institute for Research and Publishing, 2007.

10. Goldsmith, A. *Brief History of Egypt*. New York, NY: Checkmate Books, 2008; Bradley, J. R. *Inside Egypt: The Land of the Pharaohs on the Eve of a Revolution*. New York, NY: Palgrave Macmillan, 2008; Sayyid-Marsot, A. L. *A History of Egypt—From Arab Conquest to the Present*. Cambridge, UK: Cambridge University Press, 2007; Brewer, D. J. *Egypt and the Egyptians*. Cambridge, UK: Cambridge University Press, 2007.

11. *San Diego Union Tribune*, February 3, 1995, pp. A1 and 12.

12. Bowen, W. H. *The History of Saudi Arabia*. Westport, CT: Greenwood Press, 2007; Vivano, F. "Saudi Arabia on the Edger," *National Geographic*, October 2003, pp. 22–23. www.ngs.com; Al-Rasheed, M. *Contesting the Saudi State: Islamic Voices from a New Generation*. Cambridge, UK: Cambridge University Press, 2006; Rodenbeck, M. "A Long Walk—A Survey of Saudi Arabia," January 7, 2006, p. 12. www.economist.com/surveys.

13. Del Guidice, M. "Ancient Soul of Iran," *National Geographic*, August 2008, pp. 34–57; "The Revolution Strikes Back—A Special Report on Iran. *The Economist*, July 21, 2007, p. 16. www.economist.com/specialreports; Grimond, J. "God's Rule or Man?—A Survey of Iran," *The Economist*, January 18, 2003, p. 16. www.economist.com/surveys.

14. Davis, E. *Memories of State: Politics, History and Collective Identity in Modern Iraq*. Berkeley, CA: University of California Press, 2006.

15. Elashmawi, F. and Harris, P. R. "Managing Intercultural Business Negotiations," *Multicultural Management*, 1993; Elashmawi, F. *Competing Globally-Mastering Multicultural Management and Negotiations*, 2001. Burlington, MA: Elsevier/Butterworth-Heineman.

16. LaGuarida, A. "Winning or Losing: A Special Report on al-Qaeda," *The Economist*, July 19, 2008, p. 12. www.economist.com/specialreports; Burleigh, M. *Blood and Rage: A Cultural History of Terrorism*. New York, NY: HarperCollins, 2009; Sageman, M. *Leaderless Jihad: Terror Networks in the Twenty-First Century*. Philadelphia, PA: University of Pennsylvania Press, 2008; Ollapally, D. M. *The Politics of Extremism in South Asia*. Cambridge, UK: Cambridge University Press, 2008; Wittes, B. *Law and the Long War: The Future of Justice in an Age of Terror*. New York, NY: Penguin Press, 2008; Mayer, J. *The Dark Side: The Inside Story of How the War on Terror Turned into a War on American Ideals*. New York, NY: Doubleday, 2008; D'Souza, D. *The Enemy at Home: The Cultural Left and Its Responsibility for 9/11*. New York, NY: Doubleday, 2007.

# WEB SITE RESOURCES

www.amazon.com/books.
www.Brint.com/opinion.
www.cia.gov/cia/publications/factbook/ (country).
www.cs.org (cultural survival).
www.En.wikipedia.org/Saudi_Arabia.
www.hrdpress.com.
www.hunews.hui.ac.
www.mideastinfo.com/Saudi.htm.
www.Saudiaramcoworld.com (Request 1950–2997 PDF Archive).
www.springer.com.
www.wfs.org/worldviewsforum.htm.

# DOING BUSINESS IN CENTRAL AND SOUTH AMERICA

The debate over the causes of Latin America's failures relative to the success of Canada and the United States has been a recurrent focus of Latin American intellectuals, and there are enough explanations to suit anyone. At the beginning of the nineteenth century, they put the blame on the Iberian inheritance with its intolerant Catholicism. Around the middle of that century, the shortcomings were attributed to the demographic weight of an apparently indolent native population opposed to progress. At the beginning of the twentieth century, and particularly with the Mexican Revolution in 1910, it was said that poverty and underdevelopment were caused by an unfair distribution of wealth, above all by the peasants' lack of access to land. Starting in the twenties and accelerating thereafter, "exploitative imperialism," mainly "Yankee imperialism," was blamed. During the thirties and forties, the view was espoused that Latin America's weakness was a consequence of the weakness of its governments. All these diagnoses and proposals reached the crisis point in the eighties—"the lost decade"—when experience demonstrated that all the arguments were false, although each may have contained a grain of truth. Who is responsible? One possible, although partial, answer is "the elites": the groups that lead and managed the principal sectors of a society—those who act in the name of certain values, attitudes, and ideologies that, in the Latin American case, do not favor collective progress.[1]

Now, in the twenty-first century, there has been no serious conflict between any two South American countries for decades; it is a continent where the concept of interstate war is obsolete. At the same time, almost every Latin American country is constantly at war with itself over its raison d'être, leadership, resources, and social stability.[2]

# LEARNING OBJECTIVES

This chapter presents an overview of Latin America, including specifics principally about Brazil and Argentina on the South American continent. In addition, information will be presented on the principal cultural themes and conditions that   doing business in or visiting this part of the global market. Finally, we examine some of the challenges for Pan-American cooperation in the decades ahead. In previous editions of this book, we included a section on Mexico, which is geographically in North America. The material on Mexico is now available on the Managing Cultural Differences Web site.

# LATIN AMERICAN OVERVIEW

The map above will help you visualize the geographic area of those people designated as "Latin Americans." The term extends from Mexico to Puerto Rico, Cuba, and the Dominican Republic, which are within North America, through Central America, and on to that huge continent called South America.

Many countries in part of the world differ widely in history, socioeconomic status, education, governance, and society; so, too, the behavior and values of the people there are diverse. Nevertheless, there are commonalties and overlapping cultural themes in Latin American countries, such as the influence of the Catholic Church, the value of the family, the separate but distinct male and female roles, and, for many inhabitants, the Spanish language.

Pan-America has been inhabited for thousands of years. Archaeologists are unsure from where early inhabitants came. However, we will begin our examination of the diverse cultures in the southern parts of the Americas with their aboriginal descendants, the so-called "Amerindians." Many are descendents of ancient, highly developed people and civilizations, such as Aztecs, Inca, and Maya. Indigenous people make up a high proportion of the populations of many Latin countries, including Mexico and Bolivia. In some parts of the southern hemisphere, they have integrated into modern civilization. In other localities, they have chosen to remain more traditional, living somewhat as their ancestors did.

Global and local developers frequently impinge upon the rights and lands of such native people in the name of economic development, often with destructive results. Agencies like the World Bank are now demanding inclusion of programs that protect the rights of 200,000 aborigines before they will fund economic development projects in the Amazon region. In Central America, Indians try to survive the ravages and clutches of civil and guerrilla warfare. The Hispano-Indians are caught in conflicts between the political and military forces of both left and right.

Sometimes the rebels seek haven or recruits among the Indians, while the government troops destroy the native villages. The Amerindians are often caught in the middle of various socio-political revolutionary struggles currently taking place regionally, as in Venezuela.

As the original European colonies of the last six centuries were gradually replaced by the contemporary nation-states, these southern countries of the Americas have failed to keep up with their rich neighbors to the north, the United States and Canada. Despite their natural beauty and resources, the Latin countries have been plagued by poverty, despotic governments, bloody revolutions, and profound social unrest. Part of this has been caused by financial mismanagement of enormous natural and human resources; and part from the unequal distribution of wealth and power that is concentrated among less than 5% of the total population—the upper-class educated "elites." In the last century, some progress has been made in the growth of a middle class, the adoption of democracy, and free enterprise, the latter especially because of NAFTA, Andean Group, and MERCOSUR (Mercado Comun del Sur)—all regional trade and border agreements among neighboring countries seeking to promote the free enterprise markets and greater prosperity.[3] The latest attempt at some hemispheric integration is called CAFTA—the Central American Free Trade Agreement lowered United States tariffs on area imports. The general U.S. neglect of this region and the Caribbean has allowed other foreigners to prosper here, as we shall see later with reference to China. Today, smaller Latin countries can attract the attention of other players in the global marketplace.

In the past, a convenient way to designate economic development in countries throughout the planet was to label them First, Second, or Third World. The First World was the rich nations, such as those that attend the G8 meetings. The Third World was simply the poor, somewhat unstable nations, now referred to as emerging economies. The Second World had been the socialist states, such as the European East bloc nations under Soviet communist domination. With the demise of the Soviet empire, many of these postcommunist states are transitioning into the first category, especially those who have become members of the European Union. In the geopolitical marketplace, Paraga Khanna suggests a redefinition of the label Second World, now the undeveloped swing states that are determining global order.[2] He sees such nations as the tipping point that will determine the twenty-first century balance of power. There is a North-South shift of influence to the East-West, especially in the Far East. Many of these new Second World states are found in Latin America. They include resource-rich nations like Bolivia, Columbia, and Venezuela, as well as the Andean bloc of countries. The big power investors in these states now involve China, Japan, and the European Union, in addition to the United States.[4]

We end this opening section with a profile of Latin America (Exhibit 11.1) with its diverse people and culture.

# EXHIBIT 11.1

## LATIN AMERICA—PROFILE

| Population | Land Mass |
|---|---|
| More than 400,000,000 | 8 million square miles |

### National Cultures

- Twenty countries
- One commonwealth (PR)
- Twelve island countries of West Indies
- Many Indian cultures

### Major Cultural Inputs

- Native Indians—descended from ancient, highly developed civilization that flourished prior to European arrival (Mayan, Incas, Aztecs)
- European—in most countries, largely Spanish with lesser influences of Germans and Italians, except in Brazil where dominant influence was Portuguese
- African
- Asian—ancient Polynesian influence and some Japanese influence, particularly in Brazil

### Socio-political Developments

- Napoleonic Code of Laws
- Feudalistic societies of Spain/Portugal imposed by conquerors on developed Indian civilizations
- French/Austrian royalty/empire imposed on Mexico, the latter being the center of revolutions in 1821, 1824, and 1838 that impacted South America
- Family oriented with authority centered in the father and often extended to the "father of the nation"
- Universities and republics from the nineteenth century, with great dependence on military institution controls
- Problems of social class integration—although there was much intermarriage of the races, the powerful elites from an economical/social/political standpoint control and dominate the poor, often peasants of Indian heritage. The disenfranchised have moved beyond political/military protest for social justice to terrorism as a means of changing the status quo
- Economically and technically developing, and in the process of moving from the agricultural through the industrial stage of development; energy discoveries and development in Mexico can dramatically forge a new relationship with its neighbors.
- Despite significant growth in spiritualism and Protestantism, the Roman Catholic tradition is still dominant, but undergoing a profound role change—instead of traditional support for the oligarchy, many clergy provide some leadership in a revolution for social justice

continued

In summary, the Latin American people are transitioning in this twenty-first century, caught between their pasts and possible futures. They are in the process of modernizing their economies, social institutions, and infrastructures. Because of their cultural heritage and architecture, many of these countries are popular as tourist destinations, where visitors may view a wide spectrum of human development—from ancient cities like Machu Picchu in the Peruvian Andes, to Galapagos Islands off the coast of Ecuador, to nascent space programs in Mexico and Brazil.

## CENTRAL AMERICAN COUNTRIES

On the western side of the Caribbean Sea is a land bridge between the northern and southern continents of the Americas that also fronts on the west with the Pacific Ocean. The seven nations located between Mexico and Colombia are usually referred to as Central America—all but Belize are primarily Latin in culture. The future of these countries depends on whether they can capitalize on their geographical position to become a corridor of intercontinental globalization!

If ever there was a need and case for synergy, it is in these Central American states, with some 35 million people. The nineteenth-century federation called the United Provinces of Central America may have been premature, but it provided a cooperative model for the future—if not politically, at least economically. Only by collaboration can this block of countries overcome their chronic poverty, illiteracy, and violence. Perhaps where political and military power types have failed, local business leaders and global managers may succeed in raising the standards and quality of living for the populace. Sandwiched between North and South America, this strategic area cries out for new solutions and contributions from its neighboring nations, with their Anglo and Latin cultures.[4] Adjoining to the east are the many small island nations scattered across the Caribbean Sea, the largest of which is Cuba.

A hopeful Central American trend is toward greater integration of the nation-states there. The region is finally moving toward some form of federal get-together, ala the dream of Simon Bolivar. The isthmus five current free market governments have a Central American Free Trade Agreement. CAFTA includes Costa Rica, Nicaragua, Honduras, El Salvador, and possibly Panama, with the United States and Canada as participants to lower their tariffs on CAFTA exports. Since 1821, the isthmus seven small countries have been trying to become more unified. What is different at this time is the unstoppable trend toward economic integration from the bottom up, along with regional business consolidation. The area's growth in financial services and tourism is stimulating modernization of infrastructure, such as joint national projects, like the new container port of La Union in El Salvador. Regional law enforcement is improving in its battle against the *maras*—dangerous, well-organized regional gangs. (See "Together Again, After All These Years?" *The Economist*, May 14, 2005, p. 41.)

Panama, which has never considered itself a part of Central America, has been spared regional strife and might become a laboratory, along with Costa Rica, for creation of models that would influence the other states to join in a regional entity for self-improvement. Application of new techniques to promote social peace and reduce internal political violence, as in El Salvador and Guatemala, should become the concern of Pan-American social scientists. Simplistic, anticommunist, and military approaches will not solve the region's problems or tap its vast, undeveloped human and natural resources. China appreciates such resources, so is very active in the region with investment, trade, and building factories.

## Other Latin American Trends

Apart from Puerto Rico, which is a U.S. commonwealth, there are two other Latin American states in the Greater Antilles. Both are island nations in the Caribbean seas that share the Spanish language and culture. Cuba is 110,861 square kilometers with a population of 11,322,000, and has a communist dictatorship, despite the influence of Roman Catholicism. It has a literacy rate of 96%, a life expectancy of 76 years, and a GDP per capita of $1700. The Dominican Republic shares with strife-torn Haiti, the island of Hispaniola, which consists of 48,734 square kilometers. This relatively peaceful country, largely Roman Catholic, has a literacy rate of 82%, a 73-year life expectancy, and $5700 annual per capita income. Although Latin in culture, its neighbor Haiti is influenced by French culture and language, as well as African. Presently, the presence of U.N. peacekeepers from China, Chile, and Brazil are keeping this country from relapsing into anarchy.

# SOUTH AMERICAN CULTURAL DEVELOPMENT

As the global manager flies over the 12 countries that compose the southern continent of the Americas, he or she is struck by the immensity of this land mass and the potential resources down below, especially in Brazil and Argentina. Among the 350 million people living on this continent, nine countries have, in addition to their ancient native heritages, descendents from Africa and Asia, and a European cultural base (Spanish, French, British, Italian, or Dutch). One nation, Brazil, has both Portuguese and African languages and cultural influences. Centered between the Atlantic and Pacific Oceans, South America is shaped like an elongated triangle of some 6.0 million square miles that extends down to the apex of Cape Horn.

South America is a place where we can simultaneously be amazed at the beauty of the pre-Columbian artifacts and civilization, or the very modern and colorful artworks and high-rise architecture. Yet, visitors are also appalled by the poverty of the masses and the great wealth of the few, by the violence and terrorism, and by the dominance of a powerful military or dictators. But outsiders are also encouraged by the progress in democratic institutions, education and literacy, health services and population control, changing images, and aspirations of South Americans.

Despite the great diversity in Latin America, there are common themes and patterns. After the development of fairly sophisticated Amerindian civilizations, there was a period of European colonization and exploitation from the fifteenth through eighteenth centuries, followed by wars of independence and attempts at federation during the nineteenth century. Since the early twentieth century, Latin American nations have been engaged in internal and external conflicts. But the last half of that century saw relative peace and significant economic progress among many nations of Central and South America.

With the exception of Suriname in South America's northeast, these countries also share another factor—a Roman Catholic cultural tradition that pervades not only their history but also their way of life and thinking. At first, the clergy protected and educated the indigenous people.

Their network of Franciscan, Dominican, and Jesuit missions became agricultural and trading centers and, eventually, the great cities of South, Central, and North America's southwest. With the passage of time and increase in wealth, the Church became part of the establishment, despite the notable successes of priest revolutionaries, like Father Miguel Hidalgo, who espoused the causes of nationalism and freedom for the peasants. As a major landowner itself, the Church has not only supported the oligarchy but also opposed population control, divorce, and social change. The growth of the militant theology and activities in the Latin American Church caused the late Pope John Paul during his visits to the western hemisphere to protest social inequities, while warning the clergy to concentrate on their spiritual mission. In any event, no modern manager operating in Latin America can afford to ignore the Catholic Church as a cultural force. Cooperation and collaboration for social improvement in Latin America will be significantly advanced when business cooperates with all institutions for human development. The new brand of Christianity on the rise there is "Evangelico," principally Pentecostal, with a fundamentalist view of scriptural teachings. In the twenty-first century, Protestants have now risen to 50 million on that continent. With a conversion rate of 400 per hour, demographers predict Latin American will be newly evangelical before the end of the century. The "born again" movement matches the transition toward industrialization and urbanization. The religious cultural shift is toward self-reform, spiritual empowerment, and responsibility for improving your own life now, not just in the hereafter. A powerful tool for this religious revolution is satellite television beamed southward from what is left of Protestant America's "Bible Belt." Four hundred years of authoritarian Christianity may be overturned in a single generation, and Latin American people will never quite be the same again.

A positive development within South America has been the creation of a partial common market, called MERCOSUR. It originated in 1985 when Argentina and Brazil signed an economic integration agreement. This trade bloc was expanded in 1991 by the Treaty of Asuncion, which added Paraguay and Uruguay. In 2006, Venezuela became a full member, while Chile, Bolivia, Columbia, Ecuador, and Peru are associate members without full access and voting rights. This restriction is because these nations are also members of CAN, the Andean Community of Nations, which is a smaller trade bloc. Presently, some 250 million people benefit from this trading security, which has a collective output of $1.1 trillion. Ultimately, it is hoped that all the nations in South America will become associated with this trade and business network.[5] Whether this common market will ever evolve as the European Union did is an open question.

A president of Mexico, Felipe Calderdon, stated the continental challenge well: "Latin America faces a critical choice between the past and the future, between returning to authoritarian rule or strengthening democratic systems, between protectionism and more open markets, between the wastefulness of populist measures and a responsible balance in public finances."[6] There is also a growing global interest in the Latin American market, both for exports and imports. Exhibit 11.2 provides one indicator of this trend.

## EXHIBIT 11.2

## CHINA'S ROLE IN LATIN AMERICA

While the United States is losing its influence in Latin America, former outsiders, such as China, are assuming a greater role in hemispheric affairs. Their economies have been growing at a reasonably healthy rate. In 2005, the U.S. Presidential Administration, opposed by Venezuela and Bolivia, failed again to get a majority for its candidates in the Organization of American States, a 34-country entity. While Washington did succeed in signing a free trade deal with Central America and the Dominican Republic at the Mar del Plata Summit, the presidents of both Argentina and Venezuela made speeches against the United States, blaming it for the region's ills. Although the region's forecasts are for modest economic growth, Brazil and other Latin countries are becoming successful players in the global economy, thereby reducing the region's poverty somewhat.

Meantime, China is emerging as one of the largest trading partners of South American countries. Press reports claim that PRC has already invested some $50 billion and plans a $100 billion trade exchange by 2010 in Pan-America. China is developing a commercial and strategic presence in the region. It seeks Latin American resources—raw materials, like iron ore, minerals, oil, soy beans—which have significantly impacted the economic growth of Brazil and Argentina. A Chinese firm now operates port facilities at both ends of the Panama Canal and essentially controls that waterway relinquished by the United States. Further, to accommodate its huge tankers, it signed an agreement with Panama to expand the canal. China has also renovated Central American ports and factories to expedite delivery of its goods to the United States. It assists Latin states with infrastructure improvements and export revenues, so that the local government can improve social safety nets and empowerment provisions. This Asian superpower is offering Latin countries a new way of doing business without a ticket of codes and regulations. Imperialistic *El Norte* no longer rules the hemisphere.

*Source*: Adapted from Parag Khanna's *The Second World*, New York, NY: Random House, 2008; Andres Oppenheimer, "China Topping U.S. in Latin America," *Miami Herald*, reproduced in the *San Diego Union-Tribune*, December 30, 2005, p. B8.

# BRAZIL[a]

Since it is impossible to cover all countries in South America, we have first selected Brazil for a detailed cultural analysis because it is the largest in terms of population, land mass, and economy.

## Historical, Political, and Economic Overview

Brazil is a federated republic of more than 3 million square miles. First inhabited by nomads from Asia millennia ago, the indigenous people evolved into tribal groups, which today are called Amerindians. The civilizations they developed included empires, such as the Inca, which stretched from Columbia to Argentina. The first Europeans to discover Brazil may have been Jean Cousins in 1488 or Christopher Columbus in 1498. But Portuguese claimed the land in 1500 when their fleet of some dozen ships under the command of Pedro Alvarez Cabral arrived mistakenly in what is called today the state of Bahia!

For almost four centuries, Portugal maintained control of Brazil, exploiting many of its resources. Gold, gems, rubber, cocoa, cattle, and other products were shipped to the homeland or abroad. Portuguese noblemen ruled in 12 areas of the colony, and established a plantation economy. This led to the import of some 4 million African slaves to work in the land. In 1615, Brazil became the seat of the entire Portuguese empire. When the emperor returned to Portugal, his son Pedro II declared Brazil an independent nation in 1822. In 1865-1870, the country engaged in a ruinous war with Paraguay. His 49-year reign transformed the country into a modern state, including the freeing of the African slaves in 1888.

When the military overthrew his monarchy, they declared Brazil a republic in 1889. By the twentieth century, the nation has experimented with various forms of governance—from military rule to dictator to democracy, which prevails today. Between 1955 and 1960, the president, Jucelino Kubitcheck, undertook major construction projects, including building a new capital, Brazilia, in the middle of this vast country. From 1964 to 1945, a military coup took over the government and produced the "Brazilian Miracle," when the economy grew by as much as 11% a year. The sinister side was that this regime arrested, imprisoned, and killed its supposed opponents, forcing many into exile, especially artists and academics. Finally, the military dictatorship was replaced by election of a new president in 1990. After he was later impeached, Fernando Cardoso, a sociologist and former minister of the

[a]The material on Brazil was originally written by Kristine Elaine Menn. She has lived in Sao Paulo, Brazil, since 1992, where she works as a consultant and teacher of cross-cultural communication and English. Subsequently, the authors have updated and added material to this section.

economy, was chosen as head of state. During his term from 1995 to 2001, many economic and social reforms were undertaken, some of which still benefit the society and its citizens.

Today's federated republic has a bicameral National Congress with a Federal Senate and Chamber of Deputies. The latter's 513 members are elected by proportional representation and serve 4-year terms. Besides this legislative branch, the judiciary consists of the Supreme Federal Tribunal with 11 members appointed by the president for life and confirmed by vote of the Senate. There are many political parties, and passing reforms is difficult; governance is by coalitions and concessions. The country has formal relationships with many international organizations, such as the United Nations, World Trade Organization, World Bank, and economic partnership with its neighbors through MERCOSUR, a regional trade group.

The Brazilian presidential election on October 27, 2002, was a milestone. For the first time, a simple man from a poor family was successfully elected to the highest position in Brazilian politics. Luiz Ignácio Lula da Silva, known as "Lula," was one of the founders and foremost leader of the metallurgical union and the Workers' Party (PT). Historically, Brazilian presidents have come from the elite class. Because of his origins, and because 22% of the population lives below the official poverty level, President Lula chose to focus his administration upon the "Zero Hunger" program, while seeking solutions to critical social problems: improving education; century-long land reform problems; cleaning up rampant corruption and crime; reducing unemployment and reformulating the pension, benefit system; curbing inflation, and national debt problems; jump-starting a stagnant economy. His first term had some accomplishments, but was hampered by corruption scandals within the Workers' Party. As a result, changes are occurring now, which have never before been seen in the country's long history. The battle is between progress and inertia, especially in a stifling government bureaucracy and regulations. The country is in the midst of a slow economic metamorphosis from unequal and hierarchical to more universal and equalitarian conditions. Brazil will host the 2016 Summer Olympic games.

In the twenty-first century, Brazil is a large democratic and stable society, rich in resources, with a strong economy. Yet, having won a second term until 2010, President Lula is trying to expand upon the stability and predictability his administration has established. Two economic programs have been successful. The consolidation of sugar and ethanol production has alleviated energy needs and powers automobiles, while creating a new export business. Biofuels and flex-fuel cars, operating on both ethanol and gasoline, are now big businesses. Biotech laboratories are springing up everywhere, and researchers are studying new possibilities from drought-resistant soya to new energy sources. Brazil is learning to capitalize on nature's sun, water, and soil, and its corporations are becoming multinationals. The other success story is *Bolsa Familia*—a benefit program that gives federal cash (95 reais a month) to poor parents who ensure that their children stay in school and take them to clinics for health tests. This conditional cash plan now reaches 46 million people.

In 2008, Petrobas, the state oil giant, announced development of a new field containing $5-8 billion barrels of light, sweet crude oil. Known as *tupi*, this offshore rich resource is located under a layer of salt deep beneath the floor of the Atlantic Ocean. Since it sits up to 7 km below sea level, with some fields 350 km off the coast, pumping this oil will be a complex technological challenge. In the waning days of his administration, President Lula seeks to have income from this new enterprise devoted to education.

### Protecting the Amazon

Brazil's 3.3 million square miles of Amazon rain forest, 40% of its national territory, is a world resource in need of careful management. Unregulated agriculture, mining, and logging threaten this green belt—destruction in the Amazon forests contributes to pollution and three-quarters of the country's carbon emissions. So those who would preserve this rich environment and its indigenous people are contributing to the government's new Amazon Fund. Size and accomplishments make Brazil the continent's natural leader, but it could lead the environmental movement by preserving the earth's largest ecosystem in the Amazon Basin.[7] This could be the capstone in the energy leadership Brazil already demonstrates!

The Amazon forests are shared with several of Brazil's neighbors, including Peru and Columbia. Here, as elsewhere in Latin America, the government owns the subsoil and any oil, gas, and minerals found there. All these Amazon nations are attempting to use the rainforest for oil and gas exploration. In all cases, an improved policy is needed to reconcile national interests with those of the environment and local inhabitants, usually Amerindians. NGOs are urging industries to watch over the jungle as they would for the ocean, using helicopters and aero imaging, instead of building logging roads or pouring waste into the rivers.

## *The People*

### Social Structure, Race, Values, and Religion

Brazil is a spectacular country in both social contrasts and geographical size. First-world living conditions are seen in upper-class neighborhoods; across the street from the massive electronically operated skyscrapers, people live in *favelas* (shantytowns), sometimes with not even the most basic of services. An estimated 4 million people live in these shantytowns in the cities of Rio de Janeiro and São Paulo alone. Another contrast is in the people's skin tone—a complete spectrum of skin colors, from black to white, and all skin tones in between. Although 55% of the people consider themselves to be "white" (primarily descendants of Portuguese, German, Italian, Spanish, and Polish, as well as Lebanese and Japanese).While only 6% consider themselves to be "black," it is estimated that about 45% of the population has some degree of African ancestry. With 50% of its total population under 20 years of age, Brazil is a very "young" and diversified country. Here, segregation is more class based than race based.

A prevalent cultural generalization concerning the people of Brazil is that they are a warm, friendly, and emotionally sensitive people who are generous and receptive to foreigners. The Brazilian class structure is based on economics. While the highest 10% of the population enjoys 47% of the country's consumption share, the lowest 10% only has 1%. The rich in Brazil consists of both the old wealthy class and a new affluent class made up of mainly the descendants of poor immigrants from Europe who built up empires of riches.

Perhaps more important in Brazil than in any other Latin American country, the family has been the single most significant institution in the formation of Brazilian society. The meaning of family in Brazil is not limited to the immediate family, but instead includes the entire *parentela*, or extended family, from both the mother and father's side. This group can consist of hundreds of people, and it gives the foundation of the individual's social structure. It is not unusual to see many generations living together under one roof, or at least in the same town or city. It is customary for children to live with their parents until they marry, although this has been changing, especially in the big cities. Loyalty to one's family is the individual's highest ranking obligation. Although the traditional family is usually male dominated, for economic reasons many women work outside the home, and single-parent families are common. Other traditional dominant values in the Brazilian society include community, collectivism, procreation, and a hierarchical society. As anthropologist Roberto DaMatta has commented, in hierarchical society, the attitude is one of "Don't you know who you're talking to?"

A traditional value that has its basis in the Catholic Church is one of fatalism. Evidence of this can be found in expressions that are very common in everyday conversations, such as "*se Deus quiser*" ("the Lord willing"). The Brazilian attitude is the result of a history full of unpredictable changes and circumstances over which the individual has had little control. Some examples of more recent circumstances of this type include electricity and water shortages that have resulted in periods of blackouts and lack of water supplies.

Even though the Catholic Church has had a profound effect in the formation of the dominant values found in Brazil, a large part of Brazilians are only nominally Catholic. Brazilians are very accepting of different religions, and some even practice more than one type of religion. Additionally, though they profess to have at least some alliance to the Catholic Church, Brazilian Catholics have adopted many traditions of Afro-Brazilian religions as well, offerings made at intersections, even on the busiest of streets in the largest of cities. Brazilians' religious tolerance is evident in the rapid growth of Protestant evangelism.

## Cultural Characteristics of Business

Brazil is rich in both natural and human resources. However, doing business in Brazil can be a challenging experience due to economic uncertainties involving inflation, currency exchange, and interest rates, among other things. At the same time, working in Brazil can be enjoyable and exciting because of the immense economic opportunities that the country offers. Brazil's diverse economy produces everything from automobiles and airplanes to shoes and orange juice. The service and high-tech industries are rapidly growing.

By trying to understand this culture better, it is easier to avoid committing blunders that could potentially lead to negative results in business situations. One of the biggest mistakes that can be made is to consider Brazil to be just another country in Latin America, and to assume that what works in Chile or Mexico or Panama will also work in Brazil. One of the most blatant examples is that it is the only country in Latin America in which Portuguese is the official language. In addition to this example, there are innumerable subtler cultural differences.

### Greetings

Handshakes are the appropriate form of greeting between men and women in a business setting. However, because Brazilians are warm and friendly people who feel free to show their affection in public, one or two kisses on the cheeks are common between a man and a woman as well as between two women. Women sometimes will kiss three times if one of the women is not married. This is said to bring good luck in finding a husband. Men do not kiss, but it is normal for acquaintances to pat each other on the back or on the arm while shaking hands. It is usual for men and women who are friends to hug each other when they meet. Brazilians touch each other more and for longer periods of time than is acceptable in some other cultures. Upon arriving and before leaving, it is important to greet and say goodbye to each individual, while refraining from use of impersonal statements, like "Hi/ Bye, everyone!"

### Names and Titles

Most Brazilians are less formal than people in the other Latin American countries; consequently, titles are not always used. First names are used routinely, but it is a good idea to let the Brazilian ask you to call him by his or her first name before doing so. Often, a title is used with a first name, such as *Dona* (Lady) Maria or *Senhor* (Mister) John. *Doutor* or *Doutora* (Doctor) is commonly used to express respect even if the person is not a doctor or Ph.D. (especially with older folks). First and last names may be made up of two or more names. Take the example, *Luis Henrique Meirelles Reis*. In this case, it appears that *Henrique* is the middle name, but friends and family will call him by *Luis Henrique*. Furthermore, a first name may be a combination of the mother and father's first names. An example of this is *Carlene*, which is a combination of *Carlos* and *Marlene*. A person's compound last name may be a combination of the mother's maiden name followed by the father's last name. This order is different from the order used in Spanish-speaking countries. It is not uncommon for a person's full name to be made up of five or six individual names! Another interesting point is that in the Portuguese language, there are two words for the English word *you*. The use of *o senhor* or *a senhora* denotes more respect than the use of the casual *você*.

## Hospitality and Entertaining

Brazilians are well known for being courteous and hospitable. They endeavor to make visitors feel welcomed and comfortable. Expect to be offered limitless cups of very small, but very strong, coffee, both in the office and while visiting someone's home. It is polite to accept the coffee, but it is not considered rude to politely refuse it. Brazilians will often keep offering even if they think that you don't want any more. Do not feel that it is necessary to keep accepting more food or drinks just because your host continues offering! It is just a way of being polite. It is also usual for a person who is about to begin eating to offer some of his food to others. This is only done to show consideration to those around him, and the person offering the food probably has no intention of sharing, but instead expects a polite "No, thank you" in return.

Although Brazilians do entertain in their home, among coworkers it is more common to go out for lunch, drinks, or dinner. It is normal for the person who invites to pay, but it is just as normal for the bill to be split equally among all present, regardless of who ate what. Toasts are common in Brazil, but they are not an elaborate ceremony as they are in some cultures. To make a toast, simply lift your glass and say, "*Saúde!*" ("Health!"). Never tap your glass with a piece of silverware to get your group's attention before making a toast. Another form of behavior that is not considered polite is to snap your fingers or hiss to get a waiter's attention. Even though this action might be seen in some restaurants, it is not typical behavior.

## Appearance, Hygiene, and Dress

Considered by many to be very beautiful people, Brazilians in general are extremely concerned about their appearance. They go to great pains to keep in good physical condition by working out in clubs, running in parks or along the beaches, and undergoing plastic surgery. It is usual for both women and men to keep their fingernails and toenails neatly manicured, and a visitor doing business in Brazil should do the same. Due to the typically hot weather, it is not uncommon for Brazilians to take two showers a day, one in the morning and another before going to sleep at night. Brazilians also like to brush their teeth after every meal, so it is not unusual to see people brushing their teeth in the restrooms of restaurants or companies.

Dressing for work in Brazil depends on the employer codes, but the standard dress for men is a dark- or light-colored two-piece suit, shirt, and tie. Many companies have adopted the casual Friday concept, and some have casual day every day. While men in the Brazilian workplace dress in much the same way as their American counterparts do in general, the same may not be true for the Brazilian women. While many Brazilian businesswomen do wear suits, they also dress in a variety of other ways. For example, it is not unusual to see women dressed in low-cut, tight, transparent tops, even with spaghetti straps (or no straps) in the office. Sundresses are also common. Often, women will wear sandals without pantyhose. One important point is that a woman's purse and shoes should always match. Brazilian women in general prefer a more natural look, and little if any make-up is worn. It is also not uncommon to see a woman come to work without drying her hair. Usually, visiting businesswomen from abroad dress more conservatively than what has been described above. Outside the workplace, dressing is usually casual. During the weekends, even at some fine restaurants in São Paulo and Rio de Janeiro, men wear khaki shorts, slacks, or jeans, and either a button-down or polo-type shirt. Keep in mind when traveling to Brazil that the seasons are opposite, and when it is freezing cold in the northern hemisphere, it is quite hot in Brazil.

## Gifts and Bribes

Doing business in Brazil does not require gift giving, but since Brazilians regard business relationships as personal relationships, they value all acts of generosity, including receiving presents from their visitors. It's a good idea to try to personalize the gift as much as possible, due to the fact that Brazilians appreciate the attention and thought that goes into selecting the right present. Some appropriate gifts include calendars, chocolate, wine, top-quality scotch whiskey, name-brand perfume, or anything unique from the visitor's country that may not be available in Brazil.

When does a "gift" become a "bribe"? This is a difficult line to determine, so it is best for a visitor to err on the safe side and not participate in this practice. Although it is traditionally true that bribes are sometimes given in Brazil, things are changing. If you are not familiar with the culture's subtleties, you could get into trouble either by offending someone by offering the bribe or by not offering the right thing. For this reason, it may be beneficial to hire a *despachante* to help you. *Despachantes* are specialists in knowing what is appropriate and cutting through the endless bureaucracy that can be found at any level of government. A tool that is very useful in Brazil is the *jeitinho*, which is a term that means "getting around obstacles in order to obtain what you want." Another Brazilian tradition is the *cafezinho*, literally meaning "little coffee." This is a small tip that you give someone when they help you out. If you offer to pay someone for doing a favor for you and he tells you that a *cafezinho* would be fine, he really is not asking for coffee!

## Time

Brazilians' idea of time is more flexible than it is in some cultures. Although in the workplace punctuality is considered important in theory, in reality it is common for meetings to start 5-20 min late (or more). One reason for this (or maybe more of an excuse) is the unpredictable traffic found in the big cities. Once the meeting does start, it is important to spend some time with small talk. Some topics appropriate for small talk include family (only if you have met the family previously), current events, the weather, any positive topic, and sometimes soccer, depending on the person you are talking to. In general, negative and controversial subjects should be avoided because they could lead to feelings of embarrassment and an uncomfortable situation. Expect to spend a long time in meetings before any results are produced. Brazilians are not always very direct; in their opinion, it is important to establish personal relationships and a sense of trust before doing business with someone.

Time in social situations is seen in a different way. Parties always start later than the time shown on the invitation. If you receive an invitation for dinner at someone's home, you should arrive no more than 15 min late; do not come early or exactly on time because the host may not be ready to receive you.

## Communication: Verbal and Nonverbal

While Portuguese is the official language, many distinct dialects exist in different parts of the country. Accents and even the meaning given to words vary from region to region. Moreover, there are many subcultures in Brazil who still use the language of their ancestors. It is common to hear German and Polish spoken in the South, Italian and Japanese spoken in São Paulo, and Spanish spoken along the borders of neighboring countries. Among the members of the "international business subculture," English is definitely the official language. It is more the exception than the rule for people in managerial positions at multinational companies not to speak some degree of English.

Brazilian communication style is very expressive and animated. The norm is to speak fast, without much time between words. Due to variations in the pitch and volume of the voices, a dialogue may resemble more a song than a conversation. Depending on the topic, it may even appear that a fight is about to break out, but, more often than not, it is just an emotionally friendly discourse. Furthermore, Brazilians like to say one thing, give examples or details, and then rephrase the sentences many times, repeating the same idea over and over again. Foreigners may find this style of communication to be confusing, unorganized, or misleading.

The Brazilian writing style shares many characteristics with their oral communication style. Comma splices and run-on sentences, considered incorrect in English, are common in Portuguese writing. Brazilians also use the indirect style of digression more than other cultures do. This sometimes can make it difficult to understand the writer's line of thought.

The concept of low- and high-context communication styles involves both verbal and nonverbal communication aspects. While Brazilians generally are more low context than the eastern and middle-eastern countries, they are usually more high context than the United States and northern European countries. Although Brazilians use words profusely, at times they can be very indirect in expressing their feelings. Therefore, it is imperative that the visitor be aware of the possible underlying meanings in communicative exchanges in order to avoid serious misunderstandings.

While it has been said that nonverbal communication accounts for about 70% of all communication, this percentage can be even higher when members of different cultures try to exchange information, especially if one does not speak the local language. At times, the nonverbal forms of communication carry more weight in a conversation than the actual words do. One form of nonverbal communication is eye contact. Brazilians in general, and especially among individuals who hold the same status level, look each other in the eye when speaking. However, it is also common for a person from a lower class to look down when speaking to someone he considers his superior. This is a form of showing respect, and should not be looked on with suspicion. In public places, it is not unusual for people to stare at others for lengths of time that may make members of different cultures uncomfortable.

Silence during conversations has no room whatsoever in Brazilian communication, and the use of interruptions in discussions is common in Brazil. While this may be considered rude in some cultures, there are situations when a person might use interruptions to show enthusiasm and interest in the conversations.

In this country, close physical contact is the norm. An individual's personal distance is short, and touching during a conversation is considered normal. It is common for pedestrians walking on crowded city streets to brush or even run into each other without apologizing. Brazilians like to talk with their hands; it is almost impossible for them to have a conversation without moving their hands to help express themselves. Consequently, the use of hand gestures is widespread. The following is a description of some of the most commonly seen gestures in Brazil:

- The "OK" sign used in the United States is considered extremely vulgar, especially when the three extended fingers are held parallel to the ground, close to the chest, with the palm up.
- Extending the middle finger upward is also vulgar.
- Hitting an open palm into a clenched fist sends the same message as the two examples above.
- Extending the index and little finger upward while making a fist with the other fingers means, "Your wife/girlfriend is cheating on you."
- Opening and closing all fingers together many times with the palm up means that a place is crowded or full.
- Pulling the lower eyelid down with the index finger means "pay attention!," "watch out!," or "I am watching and paying attention."
- Brushing the fingertips of one hand under the chin and continuing to move the hand out in an outward direction, palm facing inward, means "I don't know."
- Snapping all fingers on each other while moving the hand up and down quickly adds emphasis to what is being said.
- Snapping the thumb and middle finger, pointing the fingers inward while moving the hand from the chest to the shoulder at ear height means "a long time ago."
- Wiping the fingers of one hand with the fingers of the other hand, in a downward direction in front of the chest with palms facing upward, means "it doesn't matter."

## Women's Role in Business

Though traditionally Brazil shares the *machismo* characteristic that is common throughout Latin America, the reality in Brazil today is very different. In many situations, women need to work outside the home to help support the family. This is especially common in big cities. More and more, women are achieving upper-management positions, and even directorships. However, it is still rare to see women presidents in large companies, both domestic and international. Women are also gaining greater roles in political areas, such as obtaining the position of city mayor or state governor. Women also are serving at the national level of government as cabinet and Supreme Court members.

## Negotiating in Brazil

Although a sense of fatalism exists in Brazil due to a feeling of lack of control over one's own future, and the "get rich quick and get out quick" philosophy can still be found, the general attitude while doing business and negotiating in Brazil is more along the lines of "take your time." Negotiations cannot be rushed in this country. Business is done with friends, and friendships take a long time to build. Because personal relationships form the basis of trust in business deals, nepotism and giving preference to friends is common in both companies and government. The following are some characteristics of negotiating styles in Brazil:

- *Particular over Universal.* When making decisions, Brazilians like to look at the details involved in each particular situation, instead of applying universal rules or patterns of behavior to all situations.
- *Relationship over Task.* Brazilians feel that a good relationship must be in place before anything can be accomplished, and it is never a good idea to damage a relationship that is intact, even if it means not completing a task.
- *Polychronic over Monochronic.* Brazilians tend to view the concept of time in a polychronic way, often discussing the details of a proposal in a random order instead of in a sequential manner.
- *Indirect over Direct.* Seemly a contradiction, Brazilians are a very emotional and affective people, but their style in both personal and business affairs is very indirect. Brazilians are usually nonconfrontational and believe in face saving.
- *Group over Individual.* Although this depends on the circumstances, Brazilians feel the group and relationships within the group are more important than individual aspirations. This has implications concerning methods of motivation. Sometimes an individual manager would prefer to share a bonus with his subordinates or coworkers instead of keeping it all for himself.
- *Flexible over Inflexible.* Due to constant changes in Brazilian laws, as well as the uncertainty brought by fluctuations in exchange rates, interest rates, and inflation rates, Brazilians have become very adept at "rolling with the flow." They consider people who always follow standard procedures to be unimaginative and lacking intelligence.

# ARGENTINA

The second largest nation on the continent of South America is Argentina, in terms of population, land mass, and economy. Geographically, it is bounded by five other Latin countries—Bolivia and Paraguay to the north, Uruguay and Brazil to the east, and Chile to the west. This most southern country extends with its neighbor Chile to the tip of Cape Horn, where the Atlantic and Pacific Oceans converge. It is the eighth largest national state in the world; its people dance to the *tango* and the tune of free market enterprise. It is a founding member of a South American trading group known as MERCOSUR, previously discussed. Buenos Aires in the northeast is its beautiful capital city. Beside this federal city, the country is divided into 26 provinces (www.infoplease.com/ipa/AO107288.html).

Although Spanish is the principal language, the upper classes are also English speakers because of historical British influences there. With the shift from military to civilian political leadership, recent government reforms have fostered not only free enterprise and deregulation but control of a volatile economy and inflation, so as to encourage external investment in this resource-rich land (oil, natural gas, hydroelectricity, ranching, grain, oil seeds, etc.).

## Cultural Influences

■ *Inhabitants.* About 3% of the population descends from the original "Amerindian" people, who now live largely in remote areas. This percentage includes *mestizo* (mixed) and other nonwhite groups. The remaining 97% are of European stock, largely Spanish and Italian ancestry. Argentina's cosmopolitan and progressive citizens express intensive opinion about world affairs, their government, its police, politics, and taxes, but usually avoid personal public criticism, except among trusted friends. Gregarious by nature, Argentineans are noted for their respect of the individual, acceptance of failure, and lack of punctuality.

■ *Geography.* Argentina, over a million square miles, has a large plain that rises above the Atlantic Ocean and extends to the towering Andes Mountains to the west. The northwest is home to *chaco*, or swamp land, and the great rivers of the *Plata* system. The rolling *pampas*, or prairies, are in the central part, featuring ranches, cowboys, and famous for wheat growing and cattle raising. Sheep raising occurs in the southern tableland of Patagonia. Although its climate is generally temperate, the *Chicao* region is subtropical, while in southern Patagonia, the winters are quite cold. The country's expansive capital is the largest in Latin America, with the world's largest boulevard, elegant retail shops, and 150 parks!

■ *History and Governance.* After the Amerindian civilizations flourished, the Europeans entered this land's Rio de la Plata area by way of the Spanish influx in 1516. By 1580, they had established Buenos Aires as the center of their government on the central east coast, adjoining Uruguay on the Atlantic Ocean. In 1810, a tradition of revolutionary revolts and military *juntas* began as a continuing struggle for governmental control. By 1816, Argentina gained independence from Spanish colonial rule under the leadership of its national hero, Gen. José de San Martin. The economy prospered because of rubber plantations and beef production until the end of World War II, when Argentina's unique position of neutrality ended. After decades of instability, Col. Juan Peron became president in 1946. Under his dictatorship, and with the help of his wife, Evita, the poor supposedly benefited, while the unions, military, and the economy declined. So much so that Peron was forced into exile in 1955. When a provisional military government fared no better, he managed to return to rule with the assistance of the Peronist party, which still has influence there—Peron was elected president along with his second wife, Maria, as vice president. Within a year, he was dead from natural causes, and his widow became the first woman to head a national government in the western hemisphere. In 1976, her administration ended with a bloodless coup and the establishment of martial law.

Then the ruling military *juntas* were responsible for a campaign supposedly against terrorism, which itself resulted in thousands of kidnappings, arrests, assassinations, and executions. The military's loss of war against the British over possession of the Falkland Islands brought a return to civilian rule and democracy in 1983 with the election of President Carlos Menem. Sweeping economic reforms and various international agreements brought a measure of prosperity. But in 2001, defaults on $95 billion in bonds led the subsequent administration of President Nestor Kirchner into conflict with the International Monetary Fund over international loans and repayment of a $14.8 billion debt with the IMF. As industrial production shrunk in 2003, Argentina was forced to restructure debt and promote economic reforms, despite $12.3 billion in foreign reserves. In 2007, Nestor's wife, Cristina Fernandez de Kirchner, was elected chief of state for 4 years. Presently, a bicameral National Congress consists of the Senate—72 members elected by direct vote to serve a 6-year term—and a Chamber of Deputies elected by popular vote for 4-year terms. The Supreme Court includes nine justices appointed by the President and elected by the Senate. The nation also is a member of numerous international and regional associations, including the World Trade Organization.

Argentina continues to claim Islas Mavinas off its southeast coast, which the United Kingdom continues to administer under the name of Falkland Islands.

## Religious and Social Life

The observations made elsewhere in this chapter on Latin America also apply, for the most part, to spiritual and social life most evident in Argentina. For example, 95% of the people are nominally Roman Catholic, but only a fourth are regular practitioners, while the remaining limit their participation to special occasions. Foreigners and minorities are free to practice their preferred religions.

Again, Latin social customs are prevalent here, such as those described in the next section. The *Senors* (men), *Senoritas* (unmarried, usually younger women), and the *Senoras* (married, usually older females) typically shake hands while nodding to show respect. Close friends among males may embrace, while females will kiss one another on the cheeks and shake with both hands. First names are only used with close acquaintances. Ordinarily, females do not speak to strange males without an introduction. Normally, Argentineans do not yell at one another from a distance, but simply raise a hand and smile.

Upper-class Argentineans are proper, with reserved manners, yet friendly. Social etiquette in this country requires one not to open a conversation with a question, but to start with a greeting. Wait for an invitation to be seated in an office or home. The locals appreciate compliments about their children, décor, and gardens. They also eat in the European style, with knife in the right hand and fork in the left. It is considered bad manners at the dinner table to place your hands in the lap, to use a toothpick, to clear your throat, or blow your nose—rather, you should excuse yourself and go outside the dining area for such purposes. Beef is a favorite dish. Waiters will respond if you raise your hand and index finger. Dress is elegant but conservative—men's hats are removed when in buildings, elevators, or the presence of women. In families, the elderly are respected, the wife is the household manager, and deference is shown to the father as the head of the family. When meeting an Argentinean, it is advisable not to question the person as to his/her career or how he or she earns a living; their occupation will be revealed when they are ready.

Generally, in Argentina, business hours are 8 a.m. until noon; then 3-9 p.m. Retail stores usually are closed on Sundays. Soccer is a favorite sport, followed by racing, boating, basketball, and horseback riding.

*Social Challenges.* Like other countries in both North and South America, Argentina has its social inequities and difficulties. Approximately 23% of the population lives below the poverty line, and there is no strategy to reduce that percentage. It is also a transshipment center for illegal drugs to Europe, along with money laundering in the Tri-Border Area. There is also a lack of vigorous confrontation with law enforcement corruption. Argentina is also a source, transit, and destination country for trafficking of people in forced labor and sexual exploitation. However, their Congress enacted new federal antitraffic legislation aimed at protecting human rights. Despite its advantageous climate and resources, Peter Khana views Argentina as a new second world entity.[2]

However, this nation, so rich in natural resources, is a world leader in environmental protection, especially in the setting of voluntary greenhouse targets. It is also an active participant in numerous international conservation programs. Argentina now has much to gain in emulating and cooperating more with Chile, its neighbor, with a Pacific coastline of some 3000 miles that is a gateway to oversees markets. Today, Chile consistently demonstrates 5% annual economic growth. It is governed by a successful center-led coalition and a progressive female president, Michelle Bachelet. In the twenty-first century, Argentina continues to be a land of promise with enormous potential!

Central and South America are made up of many nations and cultures. In addition to the Amerindians' cultures and languages, the Spanish heritage and language dominate, except for Brazil, where the Portuguese language and culture are prevalent. Across the Americas, other European cultural inputs are German, Irish, Italian, as well as African and some Asian influences. Some countries, such as Mexico, Bolivia, Colombia, and Brazil, have strong manifestations of ancient cultures of indigenous tribes. The latter people are growing in influences with improved education and economic opportunities. For example, in 2005, the newly elected president of Bolivia, Evo Morales, had a powerful mandate because of his indigenous origins. He gained political support from the poor, the Andean Indians, and the *meztizos* (mixed race).

Global managers realize that all the countries and people south of the U.S. border are not basically the same. Communication and business practice have to be adapted to local circumstances.

Generalizations regarding Latin America are dangerous. Many of the countries differ greatly in socioeconomic status, educational levels, governance, and composition of the population. However, the following observations from the late Alison Lanier's classic, *Living in Latin America*, and others may prove helpful.[8,9]

## Social Customs

*Shaking Hands.* This is the same as in Europe. If there are several people in the room, with a little bow, go around to each person and shake hands. The "Hi, everybody" is considered rude and brash. "So long; see you tomorrow" is equally poor. The *abrazo* (embrace) is a greeting used with individuals one knows well.

*Pleasantries.* Nobody rushes into business. As a foreign businessperson, take your time and ask about your colleague's family's health, the weather, or perhaps the local sports team.

*Expressing Gratitude.* Send "thank you" notes promptly after any courtesy. Flowers are often presented as an expression of appreciation.

*Time.* Latin Americans may appear often to be late for appointments, according to North American standards, but they expect North Americans to be on time. Business hours normally begin about 8 or 9 a.m., depending on local custom. A lunch break or *siesta* may extend from 12 to 3 p.m. Their offices and stores usually close about 6-8 p.m. Dinner may begin at 8-9 p.m. As a guest, arrive about a half-an hour late, never exactly on time.

*Party Traditions.* Traditionally, women congregate on one side of the room and men on the other, but that is changing. For large formal affairs, invitations are written by hand. Flowers are often sent before a large affair. At a smaller party, you should take them to your host or hostess.

*Privacy*. There are often closed doors, fences, and high walls around homes, especially of the more affluent. Knock, and wait to be invited in. Do not drop in on neighbors, for this is not customary. Personal security is very important, so the more affluent may have bodyguards and security system.

*Questioning*. Some North Americans get to know people by asking questions. However, in Latin America, it is safer to talk about local issues of interest. Personal questions are often interpreted as prying.

*Space*. Latin-speaking distance is closer than North American-speaking distance. Instead of handshakes, men often embrace.

*Class and Status*. People may not be served on a first-come, first-served basis. Their place in society may determine the order of preference as to serving and seating.

*Business Practices*. The pace in Latin America is traditionally slow, relaxed, and less frenetic, especially when negotiations are under way. Normally, decisions are made at the top. Brazilians, for example, do not like quick, infrequent visits. They like relationships that continue. This implies a long-term commitment in Brazil. Deals are usually concluded in person, not finalized over the telephone or by letter or electronic mail. Again, do not call anyone by his or her first name unless the person has invited you to do so. When in doubt, be formal. Dress conservatively, and use business cards of good quality and in the local language.

## Cultural Themes and Patterns

Themes are basic orientations that are shared by many or most of the people in the region. They are beginning points for understanding, and they sometimes form a pattern of behavior.

*Personalismo*. For the most part, a Latin's concerns are family, personal friends, hobbies, political party, and possibly athletics, such as the local bullfight. But transcending all these is the concern for oneself. So, to reach a Latin, relate everything to him or her in personalized terms.

*Machismo*. It means "maleness" and is an attitude that men have toward women. The macho is aggressive and sometimes insensitive; machismo represents power. Machismo is made up of virility, zest for action, daring, competitiveness, and the will to conquer. How is it translated into daily business life? A man must demonstrate forcefulness, self-confidence, visible courage, and leadership with a flourish. The machismo concept is implanted early in childhood and varies from country to country. Saving face and honor are important concepts for Latin males. Never criticize family or friends.

*Femaleness*. Traditionally, women were "up on a pedestal" to be carefully protected by the male who was in charge. Yet, the female may actually control the home, children, and husband. As women in Latin

America get better educated and pursue careers, their historical role in the family and society as wife and mother is changing. For example, in 2005, Michelle Bachelet was elected President of Chile, only the third woman to be so elected to national office in Latin America—the first who was not the widow of an illustrious husband. Instead, this moderate socialist was a twice-separated mother of three children. In her socially conservative country, she previously served in the national government as Minister of Health and Defense. Realize that in some countries, like Venezuela, there is the "public" wife who runs the home and its finances, as well as raises the children, and the "private" wife, or mistress, who is for male pleasure.

*Desires to Get Rich Quick—Fatalism.* There is instability in many Latin American economies, and, as a result, there is a boom-or-bust attitude. Many desire to make it rich by speculation, manipulation, or gambling. As a result, some Latin businesspeople are less interested in stable growth as U.S. businesspersons. Related to this is the Latin American tendency to let chance guide their destiny. Most are convinced that outside forces govern their lives. They are willing to "accept the inevitable." Don Quixote, who followed his quest whether or not it appeared hopeless, seems like a foolish man to many foreigners. To most Latin Americans, he is heroic. He was "bowing to fate, " "taking what comes," and "resigned to the inevitable." Their attitude is, "what will be, will be, God willing."

*Good Manners, Dignity, and Hospitality.* Latin Americans are much like Europeans in this respect. They are more formal and more elaborate. They shake hands on meeting and departing. In Latin America, the work one does is directly related to the social class one is in, "high" or "low." Latin Americans are, by and large, stratified societies. Latin Americans are born with a sense of place, but the two classes of very rich and very poor is giving way to a growing and more affluent middle class. Latin people have enriched cultures because of their skills in music, art, and architecture. At the same time, Latin Americans are warm, friendly, and hospitable. They like to talk and want to know about a visitor's family and interests.

*Human Resources.* Aristocratic values, late industrialization, and strong central governments have combined to create an imbalance in manpower needs of South America and the supply. Large numbers of South American workers have no industrial skills, but there is an oversupply of professional and white-collar workers, especially an acute shortage of trained managers. Part of the problem lies in a centuries-old university curriculum with an overemphasis on lawyers and engineers, which is very much in need of modernization. The global market, foreign investments, and increase in high technologies are facilitating the emergence of a knowledge culture in Pan-America.

*Authoritarianism and Egalitarianism.* Signs of respect can be determined in both tone of voice and manner that denote grades of inferiority and superiority in a hierarchical society. The *patron* is the man of power or wealth who sustains loyalty from those of lesser status. He can be the employer, the politico, the landowner, and in other cases, the money lender or merchant. Authoritarianism does not allow for questioning. The *patron* knows everything and is all powerful. To play these roles, one has to be respectful in a subservient position. As the middle class continues to grow in size and strength, authoritarianism is less prevalent.

Latin America is going through a social revolution in which agricultural and traditional societies are giving way to modern industrial and technological economies. The impact of Roman Catholicism is strong in the Latin cultures, but lessening as a force in the daily lives of people, especially in the urban areas. The profound social, economic, and political changes under way are altering many of the above customs and influences, especially among the younger generation. Democratization, world communications, international exchanges, and contemporary realities are transforming Latin America. Its global managers are sophisticated in the ways of international business, and may not illustrate, at least on the surface, the typical social or cultural characteristics of the region.

## Latin Cross-cultural Communications

Gordon has done extensive research to improve cross-cultural communications throughout the Americas, as the following excerpt emphasizes:

> The real difficulties in cross-cultural communications may be occurring because value systems are in conflict. While North and South Americans at a Pan-American conference, for instance, may be in agreement on general goals, the conflict might be anticipated in the means to achieve such goals; that is, the time, place, division of labor, sequence of actions, and other factors. When one is not open to consideration of the other's values, then emotions may rise and disagreements increase.

For successful Pan-American exchanges and collaboration, Gordon's research indicates that each party in the cross-cultural encounter must learn (a) to recognize symptoms of miscommunication in oneself and the other; (b) to separate fact, interpretation, and conclusion; (c) to derive silent assumptions about major premises in the interpretive process from the foreigner's minor premises and conclusions; and (d) to request information from the host country citizen in such a way as not to bias or inhibit the response.

# CHALLENGES FOR PAN-AMERICAN COOPERATION[10]

The prospects for Pan-American synergy in the twenty-first century are encouraging. Inflation is still a major problem, coordination of economic policies is distant, but barriers to trade are being reduced, and governments are committed to cutting fiscal deficits. There has also been relative peace between the nations of the western hemisphere, despite internal upheavals within various Latin American states. Yet, political factions do often block hemispheric efforts toward shared energy and trade exchanges.

There have also been some noble efforts toward economic cooperation that lay the groundwork for real collaboration in the future. It takes time for such diverse cultures to learn the value and skills of joint endeavors. But the ground for synergy has been broken in such undertakings as the Organization of American States, the former Alliance for Progress, the Central American Common Market, the Andean Pact, the North American Free Trade Agreement, and MERCOSUR. All such cooperative arrangements seek to collaborate in common economic and trade policies that are more market friendly, while reducing protectionism. Another hopeful sign is the shift away from unilateral foreign aid to sharing of resources through multilateral institutions, such as the World Bank and the Inter-American Development Bank. Lately, the concerns of the various Latin American nations have shifted more to the social arena with the establishment of such entities as the Inter-American Commission on Human Rights. Another reason for optimism about the future of relationships is the Pan-American Development Foundation (PADF). Its objective is to help the lowest income people in Latin America and the Caribbean to participate productively in the socioeconomic and cultural development of their societies. PADF activates the involvement of the local private sector, especially the business community, through the formation of national development foundations in the various countries.

Underlying all of Latin America's difficulties is the need for integral development in the areas of education, health care, and opportunities for self-development. The interdependence of North and Latin America and the need for the other are obvious. Economic development is now more horizontal in the Americas, and not just vertical. Those with vision will set goals to close the Pan-American poverty gap within the next 50 years.

Achieving synergy within Latin America requires leaders able to:

■ Better manage the national resources of all states in the hemisphere by more effective collaboration of public and private sectors in each country, and between north/south regional relations.

■ Manage the transfer of technology and information for mutual development of North and Latin American people.
■ Contribute to economic and social development of Latin America through the exercise of corporate social responsibility by multinational enterprises on both continents.

Meeting the challengers of globalization has increased support for the proposed South American Community of Nations (SACN), perhaps as a replacement for the less-effective Organization of American States (OAS).

## CONCLUSIONS

Chapter 11 provided global managers an overview of doing business in Brazil and Argentina. To improve the quality of life for all the America's inhabitants, effective and ecologically controlled utilization of resources on these twin continents is a major management challenge. Trained and experienced managers in transnational enterprises throughout Pan-America may be able to accomplish in the decades ahead what politicians, dictators, revolutionaries, and soldiers have failed to accomplish in the past centuries—cooperation and collaboration for the common good. The potential of Latin America is finally beginning to be actualized.

### MIND STRETCHING

1. What is most striking to you in the contemporary development of Mexico? (See Mexico section on Web site.)
2. Why do the Central American states need to implement their negotiations for regional economic trade and development?
3. What is the significance of Portuguese culture and language in Brazil, in contrast to Spanish culture and language elsewhere in Latin America?
4. How do you envision the future of indigenous people or Amerindians in Latin America?
5. Why are North America, Europe, China, and Japan so interested in Latin America?
6. What are the implications of so many Latin Americans migrating to the United States and Canada?
7. Why does Latin America have to act as a trading bloc with Asia, Europe, and North America?
8. How can Latin Americans expand their business relationships with Africa, the Middle East, and Russia?

# REFERENCES

1. Montaner, C. A. "Culture and the Behavior of Elites in Latin America," *Culture Matters*, Harrison, L. E. and Huntington, S. P. (eds.). New York: Basic Books, 2000, pp. 57–58. Also refer to Chong, N. and Baez, F. *Latino Culture—A Dynamic Force in the Changing American Workplace*. Boston, MA: Nicholas Brealey/Intercultural Press, 2005.

2. Khanna, P. *The Second World—Empires and Influence in the New World Order*. New York, NY: Random House, 2008.

3. Abbott, J. and Moran, R. T. *Uniting North American Business—NAFTA Best Practice*. Burlington, MA: Elsevier/Butterworth-Heinemann, 2002.

4. Cardoso, F. and Bell, P. *A Break in the Clouds: Latin America and the Caribbean in 2005*. Washington, DC: Inter-American Dialogue, 2006; Fay, M. (ed.) *The Urban Poor in Latin America*; de Ferranti, D. et al. (eds.), *Inequality in Latin American and the Caribbean*. Washington, DC: IBRD, World Bank, 2005; Paige, J. *Democracy in Central America*. Cambridge, MA: Harvard University Press, 1998.

5. Klonsky, J. and Hanson, S. *Mercosur: South America's Fractious Trading Bloc*. Washington, DC: Council on Foreign Relations, 2008. www.cfr.org/publications/12752/mercosur.html.

6. Calderon, F. "Mexico's Road," *The World in 2008*, *The Economist*, 2008. www.economist.com or www.theworldin.com.

7. Unger, B. "Dreaming of Glory—A Special Report on Brazil," *The Economist*, April 14 2007, 16 pp. www.economist.com/specialreports.

8. Council on Foreign Relations, Barshefsky, C. et al. (eds.). *U.S.-Latin American Relations—A New Direction for a New Reality*. Washington, DC: CFR Publication, 2008 (Task Force Report #60) www.dfr.org/publication/16279; Morrison, T., Conway, W. A., and Douress, J. J. *Dun & Bradstreet Guide to Doing Business Around the World*. Paramus, NJ: Prentice Hall Press, 2008; Axtell, R. E. *Gestures: The Do's and Taboo's of Body Language Around the World*. White Plains, NY: John Wiley & Sons, Inc., 2008; Stephenson, S. *Understanding Spanish-Speaking South Americans*. Boston, MA: Nicholas Brealey/Intercultural Press, 2003.

9. Lanier, A. *Living in Latin America*. Boston, MA: Nicholas Brealey/Intercultural Press, 1988; Gordon, R. *Living in Latin America*. Skokie, IL: National Textbook, 1976; Stephenson, S. *Understanding Spanish-Speaking South Americans*. Yarmouth, ME: Intercultural Press; 2003.

10. Skidmore, T. E. and Smith, P. H. *Modern Latin America*. New York, NY: Oxford University Press, 2005; Burns, E. B. and Charlip, J. A. *A Concise Interpretive History of Latin America*, Eighth edition. Upper Saddle River, NJ: Prentice Hall, 2006; Goodwin, P. B. *Global Studies: Latin America*, Thirteenth edition. 2008.

## USEFUL INTERNET WEB SITES

tradeport.org/ts/ (enter name of Latin American country for trade information).
mera.com (country business guides).

eiu.com (country name).

living.abroad.com (country profiles).

businessculture.com.

expatexchange.com.

cia.gov/LatinAmerica.

ibge.gov.br.

lanic.utexas.edu.

economist.com/guliver (businesstravelips on Latin America)..../countries..../
management.

google.com (enter name of Latin American country).

# 12

# DOING BUSINESS WITH ASIANS AND AUSTRALIANS

Australia, China, India, Indonesia, Japan, Malaysia, Singapore, New Zealand, Pakistan, Philippines, South Korea, Taiwan, Thailand, Vietnam*

Home to nearly two-fifths of humanity; two neighboring countries, India and China, are two of the world's fastest growing economies. The world is taking notice. But India and China, always different, have followed different paths to growth.

Simon Long[1]

## LEARNING OBJECTIVES

To appreciate the scope, diversity, and opportunities within the Asian or Pacific Rim region, this chapter begins with an overview of Pacific Basin countries, plus demographics on six Central Asian nations of growing economic importance. Then, we examine in some depth, a dozen cultures and business climates of the principal Asia "players" within the global marketplace, especially China, India, and Japan. China, India, and Indonesia have 40% of the earth's inhabitants.

---

*The material on Australia, Indonesia, Malaysia, Singapore, Taiwan, and Thailand is available on the *Managing Cultural Differences* Web site.

Asia is the world's largest continent bounded by Europe, and the Arctic, Pacific, and Indian Oceans. Sometimes referred to as the Far East, its almost 2 billion inhabitants are dispersed over 16 million square miles. Geographically, the term "Asia" covers from Japan to Georgia, from Malaysia to Mongolia. It is a place of increasing importance to global managers as a trade shift occurs from the Atlantic to the Pacific. Many Asian countries over the past several decades have increasingly experienced the benefits of a market economy over ideology. For some, such as China and Vietnam, this change is new. For others, like Australia and Japan, it is not.

The twenty-first century has been called "The Century of the Pacific," led by China.[2] If that forecast is valid, then the information in this chapter takes on increasing importance. For example, at the end of the twentieth century, China and India were classified as developing countries and economies. By the end of the twenty-first century, expect China to become an economic superpower, with India not far beyond. One indicator is that by year 2020, China's GNP will exceed the United States' GNP by 40%. Another prediction is that in the emerging world economy, the balance of power will shift to the East, as China and India evolve. Globalization also underscores the importance of the Chinese diaspora—55 million Chinese live overseas, principally in Asia.

However, there are regional realities to be confronted before such optimistic scenarios can be realized. In the early 1990s, many Asian countries achieved spectacular economic growth as their affluence and middle-class population increased. However, many of these same nations were facing social instability as a result of an "economic meltdown" caused by an undermining of their financial and political systems. In the early twenty-first century, there are again positive economic signs in most Asian countries, but political uncertainty remains, such as between North and South Korea, between India and Pakistan, and in smaller countries where there is internal conflict, like Burma (Myanmar) and Thailand. Matlock offers this insight, which is still timely:[3]

> What brought rapid economic development to the "Asian tigers" was the same thing that brought it to countries elsewhere: capitalism, hard work, frugality, and limited government. There was no Asian miracle; if economic development was more rapid in some Asian countries than it had been in the West, that was because modern technology and communication have accelerated the process of change and because these countries were playing catch-up. It takes longer for pioneers to clear the way than for late starters to follow a well-marked trail.

As United States influence diminishes somewhat in Asia, Europe is playing a larger role there, particularly because the European Union (EU) represents a large market for imports. Thus, Asia-Euro cultural, trade, business, and scholarly exchange has increased. Economically, the middle class is growing dramatically in Asia, along with organized crime and ruthless gangs engaged in money laundering and drug sales.

A critical factor distinguishing Asian cultures from that of other people is their ancient philosophies and religions. For example, Buddhism, developed originally in India some 2500 years ago, still is a major influence in the region. Confucianism, a code of conduct developed by its Chinese founder in 551 B.C., impacts many areas' cultures as an ethical system to guide social relations, with special emphasis on meritocracy. Hinduism, on the other hand, is centered on India and some neighboring countries. To lesser degrees, Christianity from the West and Islam from the Middle East also have significant sway on large numbers of Asian people.

# CHINA

Those responsible for managing China's industry have had their world turned upside down. Old certainties have been eroded, new challenges have emerged. China's accession to the Word Trade Organization in December 2001, a milestone in its reintegration with the global economy, is beginning to change the economic landscape of East Asia and has a profound impact not only on China and East Asia but on the rest of the world as well. China and India—rarely has the ascent of two relatively poor nations been watched with such a mixture of awe, opportunism, and trepidation. By contrast, they possess the weight and dynamism to transform the twenty-first century global economy.[4]

## Geographic Perspective

China is on the western seaboard of the Pacific Ocean, south of Russia, with the Himalayan Mountains separating it from India. Almost 10 million square kilometers in land mass, the country is dominated by mountain ranges, broad plains, expansive deserts, and numerous rivers—the Huang He (Yellow River) in the north, Yangtze in the central area, and Xijiang River in the south. The huge country has 4000 miles of coastline, and the Gobi Desert of some 500,000 square miles.

To comprehend the vastness of this country, divide it into four quadrants—the southeast contains 60% of the population; the northeast includes the capital Beijing and is known now for impressive industrialization and infrastructure; and its two western quadrants, including interior provinces of Tibet and Xinjiang, developing economies with immense natural resources. Other major cities are Shanghai, Tianjin, Guangzhou, and Shenzhen. China's revolution in urbanization is everywhere—there are now a hundred midsize cities with over a million residents, many with skyscraper skylines and serious air pollution. Chongqing near the center of the country in Sichuan province is the world's largest municipal area with 30 million inhabitants. Offshore, the 11-square mile outpost of Macau has in 4 years eclipsed La Vegas as the gambling capital of the world. By 2011, seven new mega resorts with 20,000 more hotel rooms will go up in this city alone, costing some $16 billion. It is the largest development project in Asia and will move 3 million cubic meters of sand from the Pearl River to create more land on this island. This old Portuguese enclave seeks to become a world-class tourist center for sophisticated travelers.

With modernization and the velocity of economic growth come problems on a scale much bigger than elsewhere, especially relative to the environment. So, China is now the second largest global polluter behind the United States—something against its ancient culture of cleanliness and order. When it comes to energy, China uses more solar power for heating water than the rest of the world, has more hydroelectric and nuclear power projects, as well as natural gas terminals than any other nation. Now, clusters of wind farms are appearing in its western provinces near the Kazakh border. These are just some indicators of how China today is transitioning from a third world to first-world economy. The population of over 1 billion people includes a peasantry of 700 million. The growing middle class wants to improve the quality of life and enjoy a healthy great outdoors.[5]

Just as the ancient Silk Road was once China's land route to the West, today the South China Sea and the Straits of Malacca are its maritime passageway to the resources and markets of Europe, Latin America, Persian Gulf, and Africa. Another indicator of this new reality is that while China produces a third of the world's steel, it now consumes twice as much as the United States and EU.

## Chinese Pride[6]

For millennia, the Chinese have always held themselves in high esteem. The name of their ancient country translates as "center of the world"— their image of themselves, their country, and culture has long been viewed as the center of human civilization. For past centuries, they expected that all other people and nations would pay tribute to the Chinese and their unique culture so influenced by Confucianism, Taoism, and Buddhism.

Throughout the history of this civilization, Chinese agriculture and handicrafts have been renowned for their high level of development, producing notable thinkers, scientists, inventors, statesmen, authors, and artists. There, the art of papermaking was discovered 1800 years ago; printing was invented over 1300 years ago. The Chinese writing system, which has lasted for more than 3000 years, spanning generations, has helped unify China, its culture, and tradition. China is one of the oldest civilizations in the world, and has also influenced countless others, including Japan, Korea, and Vietnam. People of Chinese descent live all over the planet. They represent a culture that transcends the individual and favors group initiative.

Within this context, foreigners do business within a modern and changing China. For example, its entry into world organization and agreements expanded business opportunities and increased trade volume. Progress can be seen in macroprojects like the Three Gorges Dam on the Yangtze River; the world's largest bridge (36 km), across the Gulf of Hangzhou from Ningbo to Shanghai; and very modern industrial parks, as well as affluent home developments around its major cities. In 2008, Beijing's Olympic Games redefined the country's international image. In 2010, ambitious Shanghai hosted the World Expo in its futuristic Urban Planning Exhibition Hall. This is a new dynamic urban area that hopes to "become a global Mecca of knowledge workers" with its nine planned communities for 800,000 residents. Thus, the Chinese demonstrate their historical long view, as well as a futuristic perspective. They encourage multinationals to come there, who will bring leading-edge technology. For example, Siemans was required to build a Maglev research institute to get the contract helping the Chinese to build a Maglev high-speed train system to connect Shanghai to Beijing.

## Historical Perspective[4]

China's history can be traced to many centuries "B.C.," beginning with its first emperor, Fu XI. The history that followed included feudalism, which hindered China's economic and political development. Once a leader in ocean-going exploration and trade, Zheng Ho, a Muslim of Mongolian ancestry, had led the largest fleet ever assembled on seven expeditions from 1405 to 1433 throughout the Indian Ocean. With some 317 huge ships with up to 30,000 diplomats and troops, he projected China's power, wealth, and influence for political and trade purposes as far as India until a new emperor, Hung-shi, put an end to these voyages. For many years, China generally isolated itself behind the Great Wall, forcing most traders and merchants to remain outside. From the Ming Dynasty (fourteenth century) until the 1950s, it sought to close itself to the rest of the world, despite incursions by Western and Japanese imperialism, sources of great humiliation for the Chinese.

In 1949, following the revolution and establishment of the People's Republic of China (PRC), the Communist Party attempted to change basic attitudes, values, and behavior of the Chinese people, including both verbal and written language. Its chairman, Mao Zedong, and his reformers gave the country a new direction, transforming a traditional feudalistic society into a modern socialistic one. With his death in 1976, China's new leader, Deng Xiaoping, realized that economic progress required infusions of Western technology and skills, opening possibilities for investors who would move China economically forward. On January 1, 1979, full diplomatic relations between the PRC and the United States were established; soon, embassies of the United States and the PRC opened in Peking and Washington, respectively. The first U.S. ambassador to the PRC was Leonard Woodcock, former United Auto Workers president. Since that time, a great deal of water has flowed along the Yangtze River, while the number of businesspeople and others visiting mainland China has steadily increased.

Since 1949, two major events in Chinese history occurred: the Great Leap Forward in the late 1950s and the Cultural Revolution in the late 1960s. During these two periods, economic efficiency and social order were forsaken as the country embarked on major new programs that were designed to eliminate "revisionist" elements and to illustrate to the people the importance of their role. By mid-1985, the late Deng Xiaoping had inaugurated campaigns for modernization and economic reform, even encouraging entrepreneurialism and replacing senior party leaders with younger officials. To deter democratization, sad and traumatic events of suppression occurred in 1989, including the riots in Tiananmen Square that have been described as the "great leap backward." In the twenty-first century, the Chinese leadership is moving quickly toward a market economy, where individual enterprise is becoming a norm. Increasingly, state-controlled entities are becoming consumer driven and market oriented. Necessary legal supports and financial reforms incur too slowly, thus inhibiting economic development and personal initiative.

Seemingly, the political and military leadership operates by consensus, especially to ensure economic reforms and political stability. In practice, the CCP officials make the major decisions. Ministries and/or standing committees of the National People's Congress (NPC), the legislature, formulate policy on long-term and daily issues. Some provincial governors, especially in fast-growing coastal regions, may adopt policy variations. Despite a strong president, who is also the head of the party, it would appear that China is moving toward collective leadership rather than one predominant figure.

## Sociopolitical Insights[5]

Presently, PRC is governed under a constitution formally adopted in 1982. Under its provisions, the highest order of state power is the NPC. Deputies are elected from every region in China for 5-year terms. The NPC then elects the head of state, the president of China. They also elect the State Council that administers the country. The State Council comprises the premier, two vice premiers, ministers, and heads of various state agencies. The Chinese Communist Party controls all government functions. Recently, the people are permitted to elect local town officials. Although the country's political leaders call themselves communists, they are increasingly acting like capitalists, as Exhibit 12.1 indicates.

Today, China's priority is to restructure state-owned enterprises (SOEs) established in the 1960s. Many entities seek to make a mark on world commerce. One indicator is that senior executives in publically owned companies earn on average $180,000 annually, plus stock options up to $140,000 in equity stakes that are rarely exercised. Still, the aim is to ensure the state's more effective control over the economy;

## Exhibit 12.1

## Lenovo—A Chinese Global Corporation

Today, world-class corporations are more globally integrated and oriented toward resource productivity for effective use of energy and water, as well as material and human resources. One such enterprise in an emerging market country is Lenovo, a Chinese company with a global brand. Its personal computer business produces revenues of $16 billion or more annually, and is now listed in the *Fortune 500*! In 2005, it purchased IBM's personal computer division for $1.75 billion, with rights to the IBM logo for 5 years. Despite being a state-owned company, it enjoys remarkable independence to pursue the developing world's rural markets.

Its chairman, Yang Yuanqing, has been the leader behind Lenovo growth and unique management style. It hires competent international managers, like chief executive Bill Amelio, with a distinguished career history at IBM and Dell. Although proud of the company's Chinese roots, Yang sought to make it global by having its headquarters worldwide, so senior managers rotate among corporate bases abroad. Its development teams are made up of diverse people from these various centers, such as its market department in Bangalore, India, and often working virtually by telecommunications.

To buttress this management philosophy, Yang has sought to integrate its organizational culture and promote cross-cultural teamwork. One corporate policy reads: *In all situations, assume good intentions; be international about understanding others, and being understood; respect cultural differences*. To confirm this approach, Yang has moved himself and his family to North Carolina, so as to deepen their understanding of American culture. He himself speaks English well, while encouraging all employees to improve their command of this global business language. Lenovo, for instance, encourages its Chinese employees, who are normally reticent at management meetings, to speak candidly with their American colleagues.

*Source*: Adapted from "A Bigger World—A Special Report on Globalization," *The Economist*, September 20, 2008, 26-page insert (www.economist.com/specialreports or/rights). See also this London magazine's reports on "The World Economy," October 11, 2008; "Corporate IT," October 25, 2008.

so political, not management, skills are more important in these undertakings. Thus, only 11 such Chinese organizations have made it into the *Forbes 500* list of top global firms measured in terms of revenues produced. Eighty-three mostly state-controlled corporations account for more than half of the stock market value of all Chinese firms! Within an intensively political culture, Chinese banks are an appendage to SOEs and have reorganized as commercial, stock-holding companies.

However, because of this change, SOE employees have dropped by 20 million in a shift to private enterprise. Because China's economic future is so dependent on SOE reform, the government is giving this top priority for the next 5 years, as state business government, seen as massive, bureaucratic, and more supportive of state companies (half of their loans go to them). Therefore, the SOEs virtually crowd out the private business sector, threatening the entire financial system. Yet within that business climate, entrepreneurial activities continue to emerge and expand, as well as efforts to transform some into global entities.

While the northeast is home to hulking state industries and socialism, the south along the coast is a capitalist heartland, especially Zhejiang, where the per capita annual income is the third highest in the country and its inhabitants earn twice as much as those in the north. Sixty-two of China's wealthiest citizens have homes here. Ninety-one percent of its 240,000 enterprises are privately owned with annual revenues of 700 billion yuan. There, an entrepreneurial trading heritage combines with family-controlled businesses, which are taking the global markets by storm. The City of Wenzhou alone is home to 3000 small firms that club together in flexible production, and create real wealth. People here believe in Chairman Deng's exhortation—*to get rich is glorious, and to be a wealth creator is morally uplifting!* No wonder this is a culture that rarely transcends the individual. Exhibit 12.2 tells another story of Chinese entrepreneurs.

## EXHIBIT 12.2
### PIONEERING ENTREPRENEUR AND CAPITALIST

The 2005 obituary of Rong Yiren was a unique account of a Chinese anomaly about the scion of a family commercial empire founded in 1902. His death at 69 raised the question of how this Chinese billionaire, who was not a known member of the Communist Party, ever became vice president of the People's Republic and twice chairman of the National People's Congress. More intriguing is how he managed to regain his wealth after ceding his family's business holdings after the 1949 revolution, and losing the rest during the Cultural Revolution of 1966-1976. Yet, within a decade or so, he arose as one of the 50 most charismatic businessmen in the world, and one of its richest by a 1999 reckoning of *Fortune* magazine. All this despite his family fleeing to Taiwan and the United States, leaving him in mid-century to run 24 flour mills, textile, and printing plants employing 80,000.

Mr. Rong presented himself as a "patriotic" capitalist who remained to help China end its poverty by shifting to a market economy. When he gave the Party what it wanted, he subtly asked

EXHIBIT 12.2

PIONEERING ENTREPRENEUR AND CAPITALIST (CONTINUED)

for a favor in return. The astute and handsome executive not only survived, but along the way became vice mayor of Shanghai, and in 1959, vice minister for the textile industry. Through *guanxi*, or personal connections, he positioned himself to creatively help Deng Xiaoping open windows to the capitalist world. Educated under the British system at Shanghai's St. John's University, this graduate became Deng's symbol of the new Chinese entrepreneur.

In 1979, at the Party's behest, he founded CITIC as an investment arm of the state to acquire telecoms, utilities, and highways. When a Special Economic Zone was established in southern China for foreign investments, CITIC was there to exploit the property boom. Rong, roving extensively, found the foreign concerns willing to invest in China, and lured them to the Zone. This handsome, sophisticated executive did well for his country and himself. In 2000, *Forbes* estimated the wealth of Rong and his son, Larry Yung, now head of CITC-Pacific, to be $1.9 billion. Their conglomerate boasts global assets of $6.3 billion, and includes two hundred affiliated enterprises. And, in the process, China has been moving steadily toward a free enterprise system!

*Source*: Adapted from "Obituary—Rong Yiren," *The Economist*, November 5, 2005, p. 94.

There is a big income disparity between rural and urban areas in China, which the government is trying hard to address. Several coastal cities have a GDP per capita of almost US$5000 per year, whereas the interior of China, which is more underdeveloped, remains below US$400 per year. With the mass migration of peasants to urban area, their income has risen dramatically. Now, as a member of the World Trade Organization, the government is also encouraging private companies to compete with SOEs for markets and resources. China's main exporters are to the United States, Hong Kong, and Japan, while their leading suppliers are Japan, the EU, and Taiwan. Sixty percent of China's wealth seems to be due to Hong Kong, Shanghai, and even Taiwan.

Furthermore, the Economist Intelligence Unit ranks Shanghai as the best city in mainland China for doing business, followed by fast-growing Guangzhou, and then Beijing (www.economist.com). No wonder that China now attracts more financial investment from outside its borders than any other country, while seeking multinationals that are prepared to top-tier technologies to further their mega-economy. Further, it has now become the world's most trade-oriented nation, using its $1 trillion currency reserve to invest widely in foreign markets so as to acquire more know-how (Exhibit 12.3).

## Cultural Guidelines for Business in China

China is a hierarchical society that often makes it difficult to practice Western management theories of empowerment and delegation. Chinese tend to think in terms of "role fulfillment": give me a role or title and I will perform the job. This Confucian culture is pragmatic—people prefer to learn by doing. However, the Western assumption is "prove that you can do your job well and more responsibility will be added." Western managers can misconstrue this difference as a lack of initiative on the part of the Chinese. They usually have a "role expectation" for their bosses and maintain a certain distance with them. The leadership traits they admire are determination, calmness, strength, intelligence, honor, and reserve.

China is a group-oriented, high-context culture that reflects the Confucian philosophy that values the collective over the individual. Chinese are not comfortable in making recommendations or suggestions publicly. By using one-on-one communication and understanding nonverbal signals, one can usually determine the true meaning of a conversation over time.

Yet, personal development and growth, as well as monetary reward, are important motivators for Chinese employees. Good training programs are very attractive to them, and often they are willing to take less pay for educational and career opportunities. In any bonus plan or performance award system, both team and individual performance are considered. A detailed and clear reward system is important to such workers.

Experienced China traders advise that when it comes to doing business, *throw away the rule book, and expect the Chinese to be one step ahead of you!* The local business environment is eccentric and often nonrational, causing managers and negotiators from abroad to make false assessments of the situation. Foreigners are further puzzled by the cultural challenge in the Chinese game to *save face*, so that deception with an opponent is acceptable. Appearance and scoring points often seem more important than substance or making a good deal.

Despite reforms in China, foreign investors and managers are still concerned about inadequate protection of intellectual property and human rights, rapid price inflation, and corruption. They have to act defensively, such as by trying to avoid joint ventures with government entities, and monitoring carefully the native who hires staff. Some outsiders play the role of the "dumb foreigner" by asking detailed questions, supposedly to better understand the system. Reality is that many Chinese government officials live in fear of being criticized for not upholding the state's interests. Avoid being overanxious and giving too many concessions, lest an unfair deal is forced upon you in the local expectation that foreigners will give anything in order to operate in China.

Managing in China requires introduction of effective human resource programs. Too many ordinary workers prefer not to think creatively, and avoid taking responsibility for decisions. The rote education that conditions them needs to be countered by training that increases the power of analysis and leadership. Furthermore, among China's 800 million workers, there is a shortage today of qualified surplus labor. While the shift of workers from agriculture to industry has been significant, there is an acute need to train migrant workers in new factory skills.

To uplift the 800 million Chinese, China has a vigorous program under way, including a $40 billion social investment program. The government is also building 50,000 miles of new roads that will connect remote villages with existing highways, in addition to its spending on fiber-optic cables so as to connect the people of the countryside to the information superhighway. Furthermore, China's culture values knowledge and education. Nowhere is this more evident than in the

Chinese Academy of Social Sciences, the world's largest think tank, where intellectual debate has increasing impact on global social order. Like the timeless character of its language, Chinese leaders take a long view of current events, while pursuing harmony and economic coprosperity!

## Corruption

Some outsiders who have lived and worked within China claim it is among the most corrupt countries in the world. In 1993, China officially began an anticorruption campaign. Although some progress has been made, fraud is endemic.

Corruption, counterfeiting, and even blackmail are also thought to be rampant in China, especially when dealing with import taxes and kickbacks to get contracts. Often, to avoid bribery, many MNCs use creative ways to build relationships. One way is partnering with other local companies, or with top business schools to launch special executive education programs, inviting local businesses to participate. The expatriate executive confronts a culture in which business is about survival—someone has to win or lose! Also, be aware that the Chinese executives today are not only very competent but also increasingly sophisticated as executives. Never underestimate them.

Foreign firms in China are well advised to:

■ carefully investigate and vigilantly supervise the quality and safety of products;
■ avoid bully suppliers to cut costs, nor make complex logical demands;
■ maintain a product review system, especially with brand development; and
■ assist in management development.

But in developing economies like China, leaders of would-be world-class corporations would do well to heed these words: *It is true that multinationals shop around for taxes, but in other ways they are usually sticklers for good behavior. Encouragingly, firms from emerging markets are finding that a globally integrated company needs a single culture, and that the best way to foster this is to make the highest ethics anywhere in the firm, the norm for everyone wherever they are working. Anything less tends to corrode the culture.* ("Global Business—In Praise of the Stateless Multinational," *The Economist*, September 20, 2008, p. 20.)

## Negotiating in China

China, being a group-oriented society, implies that negotiation must cover the interests of many different parties. In meetings, Chinese will examine a counterpart's attitude and speech and apply it to the problem solving. Technical competence is critical, and some negotiators have requested more seasoned technical people join their negotiating team midway through negotiations.

The Chinese rank among the toughest negotiators in the world, but they are normally reputable and honorable with outsiders. In addition, China is probably one of the most difficult countries to understand and adapt to. Foreigners are advised of the following, regarding Chinese negotiators:

- Emphasis is placed on trust and mutual connections.
- Chinese usually stick to their word.
- Long-range benefits are preferred.
- Utilize global consultants who understand the workings of the PRC.
- Consider national sensitivities, while being wary of propagandistic slogans and codes.

So as not to lose face, Chinese often prefer to negotiate through an intermediary. Initially, a business meeting is devoted to pleasantries (e.g., serving tea, chit-chat), while waiting for the right opening to begin serious discussions. An early key signal of the intensity of Chinese interest in doing business with you is the caliber of the Chinese assigned to the sessions. Chinese posture becomes rigid whenever they feel their goals are seemingly being compromised.

Many outsiders are convinced that the Chinese consciously use slow-down techniques as bargaining ploys (e.g., exploit a natural American tendency for impatience to get things done quickly). During first encounters, the Chinese usually seem to be bound by their traditional nonlegalistic practices. Businesspersons soon appreciate that they operate only at the tolerance of the Chinese. Those of Chinese origin, who live and work outside the homeland, are more flexible and attuned to global business expectations.

Chinese seem to have a compelling need to dwell on the subject of friendship, convincing foreigners that reciprocity in this spirit was a prerequisite for doing business with China. However, once Chinese decide who and what is the best, they show great steadfastness. Sometimes, their strategy is to put pressure on visitors when discussing final arrangements for an agreement (e.g., suggesting that the spirit of friendship, in which the business relationship was originally established, has been undermined or strained). In Chinese negotiations, nothing should be considered final or complete until it has been actually realized. Chinese do not treat the signing of a contract as a completed agreement. They conceive of the relationship in longer and more continuous terms and will not hesitate to suggest modifications immediately on the heels of an agreement. For this purpose, it is wise not to inform people of your departure date. Recognize China has an inadequate system for dispute resolution.

## Business Courtesies

Without a business card, a visitor on business is a nonperson—have an ample supply with information on one side in English, and in Mandarin Chinese on the other side. Remember, when using colors that gold is considered prestigious, while red is considered lucky. Since Confucianism gives rank to everyone in society, deference to those in higher rank is expected, so at a business conference, the highest in authority leads the delegation. Thus, take time with these people and be patient, anticipating speeches. Despite official disapproval, expect locals to resort to traditional beliefs, even in making a business deal (e.g., astrology and geomancy).

When a foreign visitor has an appointment with a Chinese official, one will generally be introduced and offered some tea and cigarettes. Prior to your entrance, your Chinese host will be briefed on who you are and why you are there. Polite questions about your trip and about the United States may be initiated, generally in the area of pleasantries, and perhaps even about your family. If your call is merely a courtesy call, it may not go beyond this. If this were more than a courtesy call, it would be appropriate to begin discussion of a business nature at this time. The Chinese host will generally indicate when it is time for a person to leave.

Seating arrangements during formal meetings are a critical issue. Guests are seated according to their business or social status. The head of the meeting will be seated at the "master table," in the "master seat." The most important counterparts will be seated at the master table to the right and left of the head. Generally, there will be a key Chinese member at each table to facilitate discussion.

It is also important to reciprocate invitations when they are given in the PRC, especially with a government representative. For example, if a banquet is given in the honor of the foreign team, they should reciprocate by giving a banquet for the Chinese team. Small company souvenirs or picture books often make good presents, but expensive gifts should not be given.

## Business Cautions

The Chinese are sensitive about foreigners' comments on Chinese politics. Even a joke about the late Chairman Mao, or any of their other political leaders, is extremely *inappropriate*. It is best to listen, ask questions related to your particular business reason for being in the PRC, and leave it at that.

The Chinese are punctual, and you should arrive promptly on time for each meeting.

These people do not like to be touched or slapped on the back, or at times even shake hands. A slight bow and a brief shake of the hands is more appropriate.

In business meetings, the Chinese expect businesspeople to dress formally. In addressing another, the family name is always mentioned first. For example, Teng Hsiao-ping should be addressed as Mr. Teng.

During one's stay in the PRC, a visitor may be invited to a dinner in a restaurant by the organization that is sponsoring the visit. The guest should arrive on time, or even perhaps a little early. The host would normally toast the guest at an early stage of the meal, with the guest reciprocating after a short interval. During the meal, alcoholic beverages should not be consumed until a toast has been made. It is a custom to toast other persons at the table throughout the meal. At the end of the dinner, the guest of honor makes the initial move to depart. The usual procedure is to leave shortly after the meal is finished. Most dinner parties usually end by 8:30 or 9:00 in the evening.

The Chinese generally believe that foreign businesspersons will be highly qualified technically in their specific areas of expertise. The Chinese counterpart does not need to show his or her intellectual expertise or to make an impression on the foreign guest. The foreign businessperson, who is a true professional, will have discreet but lavish attention showered on him or her while in China. Remember, your Chinese counterpart may be well qualified in engineering, science, and mathematics, but less astute in the ways of Western business and management practices.

The Chinese representative traditionally places much emphasis on proper etiquette. It is recommended that the qualities that foreign businesspersons possess going to the PRC are dignity, reserve, patience, persistence, and a sensitivity to and respect for Chinese customs and temperament. Cultural and basic language preparation is essential

The Chinese generally prefer companies with longstanding relationships with state trading companies or large companies with financial strength and/or political clout. Newcomers and new business organizations have to adjust to the Chinese style of arranging and negotiating contracts. Very often, several visits to the PRC are necessary to consummate any business transaction, and be prepared for long-term follow-up actions.

Privacy is not highly regarded due to the strong emphasis on personal relationships and living together in extended families. Personal information that Westerners consider private, like salary, is openly discussed in China, since in most state-owned companies it is common knowledge what individuals earn. Yet with economic development, the concept of privacy is growing, and modern Chinese are beginning to resent intrusions of nosy employers, data-gathering marketers, ubiquitous security, and officious government inquiries into personal and family life. Generally, better-educated people are taking charge of their own lives as central planning yields to the market system. Although Orwellian controls over politics, news media, religion, and free expression remain in place and legal protections for privacy are limited, times are changing and the trends support the concept of personal privacy.

## Facilitating Cross-Cultural Communications

Usually, foreigners should not focus on the individual Chinese person, but rather on the group of individuals who are working for a particular goal. If a Chinese individual is singled out as possessing unique qualities, this could very well embarrass the person. People from the PRC have had their negative experience in the past with Western imperialism and superiority. Generally, in discussions with Chinese, the foreigner should avoid "self-centered" conversation in which "I" is excessively used.

Generally, the Chinese are somewhat more reticent, retiring, reserved, or shy when compared with North Americans and Europeans. They also avoid open displays of affection, and the speaking distance between two people in nonintimate relationships is greater than that in the West. Mobile telephone calls, fax machines, Internet, and other forms of modern telecommunications are a vital part of business, but Chinese prefer that important business be conducted face to face.

The insights shared in this section also have some applications with (1) territories over which the PRC has gained national control, such as the formerly European colonies of Macao (Portuguese) and Hong Kong (British), as well as in the Buddhist kingdom of Tibet; (2) overseas Chinese communities around the world—more so cultural and business practices than political. Since Hong Kong is such an international and financial center in Asia, there is additional information below on this prosperous and more democratic entity. Since China is an emerging economic superpower, business savvy and cultural sensitivity are essential for business success everywhere.[7]

Chinese have a great love for gambling and sport. Perhaps Exhibit 12.4 will underscore the challenges in dealing with the new China.

Those who seek success in their negotiations with Chinese would do well to remember that a thousand years ago, China was a leader in globalization, giving the world the printing press, compass, and gunpowder! Finally, consider Exhibit 12.5 regarding globalization of the workforce that is altering business in all countries.

---

EXHIBIT 12.4

OYMPIC MILESTONE IN TRANFORMING CHINA'S IMAGE

---

In August 2008, something happened in China's 5000-year history that was akin to building the 4000-mile Great Wall to keep out invaders. This time, the country hosted an international sporting event, the XXIX Summer Olympic Games which welcomed the world to the New China! Its success was a turning point in the global perception of a modern nation and its people, while changing the Chinese image of their place on the planet! It gave the people

EXHIBIT 12.4

OYMPIC MILESTONE IN TRANFORMING
CHINA'S IMAGE (CONTINUED)

of this ancient civilization a sense of national pride and identity in modern times. By means of television and computers, an audience of 4 billion worldwide watched the spectacle. Humanity was awed by the scope of the Chinese preparations and presentations, as well as of their management of this momentous undertaking. It was confirmation of the transformation under way from a backward, communist, third-world nation, to an emerging economic superpower—in one generation, China has pulled 300 million inhabitants out of poverty!

Both visitors and viewers were stunned by changes in the country's infrastructure. To provide facilities and housing for their Olympic guests, some $40 billion was invested by the government and local planners over a 7-year period. Top architects came from across borders to design many of the unique buildings, including the huge stadium dubbed *The Birdsnest*, with 91,000 seats in its concrete bowl; the *T3* new $3.8 billion airport, the world's largest with its 10.6 square feet; the newest Beijing subway line from the airport to the city center (now the area has eight such lines with 120 miles of track, and by 2015 plans call for 19 lines and 350 miles of track); the 49-story masterpiece for CCTV headquarters; the National Center for the performing arts, a giant titanium egg surrounded by a moat, so visitors can enter through tunnels under water. Then there were the many Olympic venues provided the athletes, including the *Water Cube* for aquatic events.

Eleven thousand athletes from 205 nations, plus 80 heads of states from across the globe attended the spectacular opening or closing ceremonies, which inspired viewers in many nations. Hundreds of drummers greeted guests in a 2500-year-old performance, while thousands engaged in a musical extravaganza with colorful, oriental dances and acrobatics. For this "coming out party," the Chinese spruced up their *Forbidden City*, even managing to curb pollution and improve the air quality, as well as to cause a little needed rain to fall! And, to top this off, Chinese athletes won the largest number of gold medals for the sporting contest.

The lucky-numbered 8/8/08 Olympic opening and closing ceremonies boosted citizen morale, while the whole feat indicated that China was on its way to having the most influential culture in today's world. All this in a historical context was a turning point to help 1.3 billion Chinese forget the past humiliations of the nineteenth-century colonialist powers who occupied their land; the

continued

## EXHIBIT 12.4
### OYMPIC MILESTONE IN TRANFORMING CHINA'S IMAGE (CONTINUED)

painful Long March to unite the country; the chaotic and damaging Cultural Revolution; the traumatic Tiananmen Square crackdown in 1989 on youthful reformers; the destruction of recent earthquakes, which killed some 50,000 citizens; the 8/7/08 rebuke of the U.S. president to their Communist government over repression of human rights and freedoms. Now that their space program has put Chinese astronauts in orbit, no one doubts their accomplish plans to put some of their own on the moon by 2024!

*Source*: Adapted from Mark Ziegler's "China Emerges from the Chairman's Shadow," *The San Diego-Union Tribune*, August 7, 2008, pp. Al & 8; international television broadcast commentary by NBC, August 7-24, 2008. For further insights, read Professor Susan L. Shirk's *China: Fragile Superpower*. New York, NY: Oxford University Press, 2008.

## EXHIBIT 12.5
### WORKFORCE GLOBALIZATION: BRAZILIANS IN CHINA

Not only do Chinese travel all over the world to invest and work, but in this global market, foreign professionals and businesspersons come to China in increasing numbers. Look at Dongguan, a city of 7 million people situated 56 miles north of Hong Kong. There you will find a community of some 3000 Brazilians contributing to the country's economic boom through the footwear industry. In 2007, Brazil exported 177 million pairs of shoes, but China powered ahead to be the world's biggest footwear exporter. China's lower costs in production enticed skilled Brazilians to go there, providing know-how and craftsmanship. The Chinese eagerly sought their knowledge and expertise in high-quality shoe production.

Since 1995, for instance, Richard Correa, the owner of Paramount Asia, relocated to Dongguan to share his competence in product and quality development. His workforce of 800 includes 100 Brazilians and the remainder Chinese; business is conducted in English! Most of the shoes manufactured are shipped to the United States. Other Brazilian professionals have followed the show specialists to provide support services.

*Source*: Adapted from "Brazilians in China—Footloose Capitalism," *The Economist*, September 13, 2008.

We are all prisoners of our own time and place, and we inevitably judge the new and strange in terms of the old and familiar. For millennia, humans in the West have sought passage to the East, especially to obtain its spices and precious metals. Herodotus, a Greek who lived 484-425 B.C. and known as the "father of history," regarded India as the richest and most populous place in the world. From 580 to 480 B.C., these fabled riches first attracted the Persians, Carthaginians, and Egyptians; the latter originally found a way around Africa, as well as to Europe, to facilitate voyages of exploration. India became the destination of the monsoon trading system that took classical form in Islamic times, 750-1500 A.D. The Indian Ocean defines a region of great linguistic, ethnic, cultural, and religious variety, with a single unifying factor—the monsoon winds of Southeast Asia. As the Occident reached out to the Orient, a wide variety of countries benefited from this ocean-going trading network. The seas of the ancient trade routes led to wealth and invasions, in what was almost a forerunner of today's global economy.

> Adapted from Paul Lunde, "The Indian Ocean and Global Trade,"
> *Saudi Aramco World*, July/August 2000
> (www.saudiaramcoworld.com).

The Indian economy is sometimes likened to an elephant, which is not capable of running as swiftly as some of the smaller "tiger-like" Asian countries, but has the advantage of being stable and less affected by shocks and disturbances. These elephantine qualities were severely tested during the recent years when political and economic problems were aplenty. These included the global economic slowdown (exacerbated by the terrorist attacks of September 11), increased political tension with neighboring Pakistan (especially after the terrorist attack on the Indian Parliament), a poorly performing industrial sector, stagnant exports, and a capital market that remained in the doldrums....But today, India is suddenly an emerging superpower, a center of high and information technology, as of global off-shore business activities.

> Robert T. Moran[8]

## Historical Perspective[8]

The ancient land of India began in prehistoric times. Around 1500 B.C., Aryans descended from the north and integrated with the native Dravidians to form the basis of classical Indian society. The earliest inhabitants settled along the banks of great rivers. Archaeological discoveries reveal that some 500 years ago, a high-level civilization flourished in the western and northwestern parts of India.

As in Asia, the sixteenth century saw the Western European nations establishing trading posts in India. The Portuguese efforts were focused upon Goa/Cochin on the west coast, and the French in Pondicherry on the east coast. However, the British were the most successful and expanded their influence and power throughout the subcontinent. They built a colonial infrastructure that remains today in large part, including the heritage of English in a *land of many tongues*. After World War I, nationalism grew in India. Mahatma Gandhi organized a series of passive-resistance campaigns and civil disobedience to British rule. The British reign ended on August 15, 1947. On January 26, 1950, the Indian constitution was promulgated, and the country became a sovereign republic and the world's largest democracy.

Hinduism, believing birth is destiny, perpetuates the caste system, which separates the social classes by occupations, so that privileges or disadvantages are transmitted by inheritance. For over 5000 years, the caste system with its thousands of subsystems divides people into four divisions—priests, warriors, traders, and workers. Then there are the untouchables, or *dalits*, excluded because of the nature of their crafts, such as working with leather. However, when industrialization began in twentieth-century India, many of this underclass were recruited by foreign investors to learn new skills for factory work. An example of how this injustice is breaking down for some 200 million so classified is the late K. R. Narayanan. Born of a poor southern Indian family and educated by Christian missionaries, he won scholarships to college and proved to be a very talented student. Upon his return, India's first prime minister, Jawaharlal Nehru, found Narayanan a job in the diplomatic service where he ended up an ambassador to Thailand, Turkey, China, and the United States. In 1984, he was elected to Parliament from his native Kerala. To the surprise of the elite, he subsequently was elected vice president and then president, saying: "My life encapsulates the ability of the democratic system to accommodate and empower marginalized sections of society." Today, discrimination on the grounds of caste is illegal, and affirmative action programs are under way.

## Business Insights in India

### Governance

The government of India is based on the British parliamentary system with a bicameral legislature and executive and judicial branches. India is governed by a council of ministers led by the prime minister (appointed by the president). The ministers and prime minister are responsible to the House of People, the Lok Sabha, which is elected by universal adult franchise. There is an upper house called the Rajya Sabha, that is, the senate bills submitted by the prime minister have to be passed by both the Lok Sabha and the Rajya Sabha before being signed by the president. The bills only become law on the president's signature. The president may return the bills to the legislature for changes that he or she may suggest. The powers of the government are, in fact, vested in the prime minister, who is generally the leader of the majority party in Parliament and usually the lower house, Lok Sabha. Nevertheless, the president is the commander-in-chief of the armed forces, and also has the right to fire the prime minister in cases of national emergency or lack of confidence. The president has very little executive power.

## Economics

Money supply is managed by the Reserve Bank of India, which is the country's central bank. The unit of currency is the rupee. The Reserve Bank acts as banker to the government, the commercial banks, and some of the financial institutions. The banking system is deeply involved in the industrialization of the country through financing of both fixed assets and working capital. The State Bank of India is the largest commercial bank in the country, and it also carries out some of the functions of the Reserve Bank of India.

The industrial economy of India has a public sector and a private sector. The public sector companies are government-run industrial and commercial undertakings, while the private sector is composed of profit-oriented business organizations run increasingly by professional managers. The country has made rapid industrial growth in recent years, with capabilities increasing in almost every sphere of industry, especially information technologies. Exports have become much more diversified from just agricultural products to textiles, tea, iron ore, spices, and light engineering products. Exhibit 12.6 below is an indication of why India is becoming an "economic tiger."

---

### EXHIBIT 12.6
### THE HIGH HIGH-TECH REVOLUTION

Bangalore is the center of India's booming information technology (IT) industry. Yet, it is something of a paradox—inside its modern industrial parks, business and living conditions operate at a higher level; while outside, its surrounding urban area suffers from deteriorating infrastructure and attempts at renewal. But this city is a global and national hub of sophisticated software and remote services, such as business processing outsourcing (BPOs, or call centers). But the old city and local government are straining to keep up with the demands of its economic drivers, companies like Wipro and Infosys. These high-tech endeavors employ some 260,000 workers, and leading firms are hiring 1000 new staff per month; foreign firms are arriving to set up business at the rate of three a week. No wonder the economic forecasts for this dynamic ecosystem are 25% or more annually. However, this city, known for its beauty, lush parks, greenery, and mild climate, struggles to cope with a population that has grown from 800,000 in 1951 to 7 million today!

continued

EXHIBIT 12.6

THE HIGH HIGH-TECH REVOLUTION (CONTINUED)

This municipality has also become a knowledge center that attracts technical and scientific institutes. Their leaders are the Indian Institute of Science, a world-class university known for its excellence, plus Karnataka, whose 77 engineering colleges alone produce 29,000 graduates per year and spearhead India's space program. A few miles out of town is "Electronics City," a cosmopolitan oasis with amenities to suit the needs of these knowledge workers—from "state-of-the-art" remote network management systems and cappuccino bars to lively nightlife.

With urban chaos and commuter nightmares in major cities, like Bangalore, Delhi, and Mumbai, second-tier cities are growing fast as postindustrial corporations are attracted to Gurgaib and Noida on the edges of New Delhi; Mumbai's new town; Chennai, formerly Madras; Hyderabad in the south; Pune in the west; Mohali in the north. Even old Calcutta, now called Kolkata, is trying to woo investments for its IT and BPO firms. As successful companies expand aggressively, many move out to less-congested areas of the country.

Within attractive IT and BPO campuses, the R&D is either outsourced or extended to new global market niches—for example, processing insurance claims; desktop publishing; remote management and maintenance; backup navigation systems; compiling audits and completing tax returns; transcribing medical records; financial research and analysis. Predications are that in a few years, many multinationals will have up to 25% of their staff in India. Also, security and data protection at these advanced facilities are tight! In 2008, IT and its enabling services employed some 4 million people who earned up to $65 billion from exports, accounting for 7% of GDP.

Part of this success is attributed to keeping government out of this new business. Also, India has a big competitive edge in its annual production of 2 million English-speaking graduates, many of whom benefit from a quality education.

*Source*: Adapted from "Special Report on Outsourcing and IT in India—The Bangalore Paradox," *The Economist*, April 23, 2005, pp. 67-69 (report updated).

## Human and Capital Resources

There is a large pool of managerial, skilled, and semiskilled labor. There is also a good and developed capital market and a large domestic market. Over the past 10 years, Bangalore, a beautiful city in south central India, has emerged as the Silicon Valley of India. In fact, two-thirds of all custom software programming for the United States is done in India.

## Communications

India has a great variety of languages, customs, beliefs, and cultures. There are 15 official languages including English, plus more than 1400 dialects. Language reflects regional differences and is a problem in achieving national unity. Most languages find their origin in an ancient Indian language called Sanskrit. Radio, television, mobile telephones, and the computer, especially the Internet, are advancing internal communications within India and with the outside world.

## Religions

India is a land of the gods—over 230,000 such deities. The subcontinent reflects great spirituality, most evident in ashrams, meditation, swamis, and gurus. Over millennia, it has suffered numerous invasions and assimilated the invaders' beliefs. It is also a place of great religious discord, even in modern times.

Hinduism is not only the principal religion of India but its philosophy dominates the entire culture and relationships. It can also be a source of serious ethnic conflict with Muslims and Christians. It determines a woman's role in society. Although the Hindu woman's legal position has greatly improved over the years, she is still bound by ancient traditions of behavior that emphasize her dedication, submission, and obedience to her husband and his wishes. This may not be so strictly adhered to in the big cities and Westernized circles, where Indian women are increasing in the workforce, especially in the professions (doctors, engineers, lawyers) and in government.

## Corruption and Ethics

While honesty is esteemed in this vast and poor country, corruption and fraud are endemic in all levels of society. Corruption, bribes, or payments for "fixing" exist in everyday life and are something that must be dealt with, even accepted, to get things accomplished. In India, business is based on personal contacts, and it is crucial to know the right person in order to get contracts. As India's global corporations become more integrated with a single organization behavior worldwide, expect ethical standards to rise.

Eileen S. Wibbeke examines the issue of ethics from a cross-cultural perspective, urging managers abroad to look beyond Western traditions.[9] For example, her analysis of Hindu ethics points out its complexity due to historical and cultural tradition. There are a number of ways a believer may seek spiritual liberation, and there are many Hindu scriptures from which to choose. This religion is flexible, tolerant, and socially important. Some Hindu philosophers teach that an act is *amoral* only if it is taken out of informed choices that are freely made. Hindus live by two principles—*karma*, or act morally and you affect your future life for good; *dharma*, or choose right and appropriate actions, including moral ones. The latter virtues include honesty, patience, temperance, hospitality, and kindness. Other religious traditions in India express their attitudes toward ethics in different ways, adding to the country's diversity.

To appreciate the new business environment in India, consider the implications of Exhibit 12.7.

---

### EXHIBIT 12.7

### INDIA'S TATA ENTERPRISES

One of India's most successful global corporations originated in 1858 with a Parsi family named "Tata." Now, this diversified enterprise operates in 85 countries, and is continually acquiring high-profile businesses, like purchasing in 2000 the iconic tea company "Tetley," which is London based. In 2007, it spent $2 billion for Corus, a European steel maker, and in that same year bought two legendary car companies from Ford. In this deal, it paid $2.3 billion for Land Rover and Jaguar, along with its British plants. Tata Industries reflects great financial strength from both domestic and foreign markets and looks upon these acquisitions as long-term investments. Alan Rosling, the company's chief British strategist, believes Tata will reap the benefits of Ford's previous efforts with these venerable automobiles. Due to its Indian origins, he is optimistic about Tata's increasing global research because of its sensitivity to cultural differences and seeks to imitate some of the world's best corporations.

The Tata group is an Indian conglomerate that spans countries and products, such as automobile and steel manufacturing, along with software and tea production. An example of its innovations in emerging markets is Tata's Consulting Services, which specializes in the outsourcing business processes of higher value. Perhaps one of Tata's most exciting ventures is the building of a small, inexpensive automobile with better fuel mileage. It is intended not only for the massive Indian market but also for emerging markets everywhere. An example of frugal engineering, this *Nano* is to be a "people's car," selling for around US$2500. State-of-the-art virtual design technology is being used in this undertaking. Global teams are driving such innovations. Mr. Tata sees these endeavors as safe and less-expensive alternatives for consumers in both developing and mature economies.

*Source*: Adapted from "A Bigger World—A Special Report on Globalization," *The Economist*, September 20, 2008, 26-page insert (www.economist.com/specialreports).

# Cultural Guidelines for Business in India

The people of India are very friendly, hard working, and diverse. Extended family living is the norm and somewhat hierarchical. A friend's role is to "sense" a person's need and to do something about it. Young, educated urban youth have more modern clothing and attitudes that are far different from their counterparts in rural villages.

Astrologers still play an important role in India, as most people believe that nothing is accidental, and the universe and all living components have a fundamental order. Two types of managers are likely to be encountered in India—the more traditional and bureaucratic, loyal to British traditions and systems; and modern, progressive, entrepreneurial business leaders, technologically sophisticated and attuned to the global market.

## Social Customs

Social amenities and practices vary in this huge country, depending on location. Those of the Braham elite are in urban areas, as compared to village peasants or Christian communities in Goa or Kerala. Generally, here are some guidelines that may prove helpful in India:

- Social freedom between the sexes is not appreciated very much, except within more progressive communities; normally among traditionalists, a stranger should not speak to a woman if he is not acquainted with her or her family. For a young woman to take the hand of a man who is not her husband is usually objectionable. Bold, emancipated women may dare to indulge in dancing with their husbands, but to dance with anyone who is not her husband would be improper.
- Use of first name in addressing someone should be avoided. It is customary to add to the names of the Hindus the affix "ji" as a mark of respect. For instance, Ravi in polite speech becomes Raviji. Here, Ravi is the first name, but by adding the affix "ji," you are calling the person with respect and, in this instance, use of the first name will not be improper. In Bengal, mister is replaced by "Babu." Thus, Ravi Babu means Mr. Ravi. In much of India, in correspondence or invitation cards, the classic Sanskrit prefixes "Shriman" for men and "Shrimati" for women are used.
- The method of greeting depends on the social status of the persons meeting. A son greets his father usually by bowing down and touching his feet. A foreign businessperson will be considered an equal, so among equals the usual method used will be to press one's palms together in front of the chest and say *namaste*, meaning, "greetings to you." Among the other classes of people, educated in Western style, shaking hands is acceptable. Hindu women who have been educated usually would not mind shaking hands with men when introduced. However, it is safer not to extend one's hand to a Hindu woman until

she takes the initiative and extends her hand first. It is safer to stick with "namaste." This actually is the universal form of greeting in India.

- Indian food varies from state to state, and is usually spicy because of the curry used in preparation. Fish and tandoori chicken from the north are popular dishes. Hindus are normally vegetarians and beef is prohibited for them, while for Muslims and Jews pork is forbidden. Among Hindus, the drinking of alcoholic beverages of any kind is considered degrading, and in some states prohibition is legally enforced. Traditionally, Hindus are a nation of water drinkers. While entertaining at home, it is purely with nonalcoholic beverages like tea or coffee. However, in upper middle class and upper class homes, alcoholic drinks are not uncommon. A variety of desserts made out of fruits or milk are also available. Betel leaf (*paan* in Hindi) is usually taken after a meal to aid digestion and freshen one's mouth. International cuisine is available in all the major hotels and select restaurants.

- Hospitality is universal in India, and Indians are tolerant of the social *faux pas* of a foreigner. A well-mannered Hindu will not eat without asking his guest to join him. It is said that satisfaction of a guest will assuredly bring the housekeeper wealth, reputation, long life, and a place in heaven. One is not required to take any gift if invited for supper but, if one did, it would be accepted graciously.

  Do not be surprised if you have your meal only with your business partner and not the whole family; wives and children usually help from the kitchen to make sure that the guest is treated well. At Indian homes, eating without knives, forks, and spoons is not uncommon. People eat with their hands at home. If dining with the whole family, wait until everybody is at the table before you start eating. Let the host start eating first before you do or start when you are asked to go ahead. Do not get upset if your host asks you several times to have some more food. Simply refuse politely if you don't want more. It is Indian custom to ask repeatedly to make sure their guest does not get up hungry from the table.

- For the businessperson visiting India, shirt, trousers, tie, and suit will be proper attire, but lightweight in fabric and white or light tan color. The Indian climate is hot; therefore, a very light suit in winter is recommended. If a person is in the north during winter, he or she will find it a little cooler and, again, a light sweater and a jacket will be sufficient. In public places, women visitors avoid wearing shorts or revealing dresses, as it draws unneeded attention. Though Western business dress is commonplace, in this climate, coats are often eliminated and hats are worn for protection from the sun. Indian businessmen, in many situations, wear "dhotis"—a single piece of white cloth about five yards long and three to 4 feet broad. It is passed round the waist up to half its length, and the other half is drawn between the legs and tucked at the waist. For the upper part of the body, they wear long shirts. Sikhs from Punjab wear turbans, which have a religious significance. Well-to-do Hindus who wish to appear aristocratic wear long coats like the Rajahs. The long coat, known as *sherwani*, has been standardized and is the dress recognized by the government of India for official and ceremonial wear. Many modernized Hindu males have adopted the European costume in their outdoor life and Indian dress at home. The Hindu lady is extremely loyal to her *sari*, while female dress may vary in ethnic communities (e.g., Punjabi women may feature scarfs and shawls, with loose-fitting blouse and bellowing pants). The modern sari compares favorably with fashionable clothes of Western women.

■ The noble teachings of Mahatma Gandhi on nonviolence and tolerance are frequently ignored today. Hindu nationalism dominates the government, often to the exclusion of Muslims.

## Nonverbal Communication and Social Tips

To succeed in business or socially, here are a few do's and don'ts for India:

■ Grasping one's own ears expresses repentance or sincerity.
■ Beckoning is done with the palm turned down; pointing is often done with the chin.
■ Backslapping is not a sign of affection.
■ The *namaste* gesture can be used to signal you have had enough food.
■ Foreign men should not touch women in public, nor talk to a lone woman in public.
■ The left hand is considered unclean. Use the right hand for eating with the fingers, or for giving or accepting things, for handshakes.
■ Do not lick postage stamps.
■ Eat willingly with your right hand if the occasion calls for it.
■ Do not ask personal questions until you are friends.
■ Use titles such as doctor and professor.
■ Whistling is considered impolite.
■ Public displays of affection are inappropriate.
■ Bargain for goods and services.
■ Gift giving is important, but such gifts are not opened in the presence of the giver.
■ Business relationships are based on personal relationships.

Indians are very tolerant and will completely accept the fact that you are unfamiliar with their customs and procedures. There is no need to conform to Indian behavior. For example, the body gestures (shaking of the head) for "yes" and "no" are just the opposite for North Americans and Indians.

Exhibit 12.8 will provide current insights on the subcontinent of India.

EXHIBIT 12.8

INDIA ON A FAST LANE TO FUTURE

What is startling to visitors in India is the mixture of the ancient with the modern. For example, on a new superhighway, cows, scared to Hindus, have the right of way! The Golden Quadrilater (GQ) is a state-of-the-art expressway of 3633 miles linking the major population centers of New Delhi, Mumbai, Chennai, Kolkata, and Bangalore. It provides hope to a billion people from the Arabian Sea to the Bay of Bengal. This grand infrastructure project pushes the country's economic engine into overdrive, while allowing inhabitants of impoverished villages' access to booming cities. The GQ is the most elaborately conceived highway system in the world, a masterpiece of high-tech ingenuity. Yet, this mechanical and social engineering feat is bringing old and new India into jarring proximity, challenging the moral and cultural underpinnings of the society.

A nation founded on the Gandhian principles of austerity and brotherhood, today its people's appetite tends toward acquiring material possessions, especially autos. The GQ is a metaphor for modern India speeding a hundred miles an hour toward greater prosperity for all citizens. It is a $30 billion macroproject going north to south, and east to west on this subcontinent. Yet on its six lanes, you will find not only motorcycles, cars, and trucks but also oxcarts, water buffalo, and goats grazing on the median strip. Crossing a busy intersection reveals the Indian character—enterprising, pushy, relentless, and surprisingly good natured. Nearby may be old villages and gleaming new suburbs reflecting the country's booming economy and entrepreneurial zeal. The GQ leads to Special Economic Zones (SEZs) with thousands of skilled workers demonstrating creative, energetic zeal for new ideas and technologies. These ecosystems are home to international and domestic corporations, like Hyundai, surrounded by numerous smaller companies as suppliers. But with the building of these industrial centers, even home-grown companies like Tata find themselves in the midst of clashes between the highway authority and local farmers over land acquisitions for these new economic ventures.

Many of these upwardly mobile workers would ascribe to the teachings of the nineteenth-century Swami Viveknanada: *Education is the perfection already in man.* Their high-tech employers provide opportunity, training, and experience that free millions of rural Indians from the bonds of caste and poverty, as the GQ and the old British railway system enable them to move beyond the bounds of geography. This rising middle class manifests the national zeigest of Gandhi—courage, competence, and willingness to change.

*Source*: Adapted from Don Belt's "Fastlane to the Future," *The National Geographic*, October 2008, pp. 72-99.

Contemporary Japanese culture is considerably different from previous, traditional notions of it and from most people's current stereotypes, including those of the Japanese themselves. Japan is commonly and stereotypically known as a land of nobility and chivalry, with values such as honor, pride, and perseverance. These form a moral code of everyday living that has permeated Japanese society for generations, even centuries. Yet contemporary Japanese culture (especially for younger Japanese) seems to operate from different values, attitudes, beliefs, norms, and behaviors. In short, Japan is evolving into a society with a different culture.

D. Matsumoto[10]

No country in modern history has moved so swiftly from worldwide adulation to dismissal contempt as did Japan. In the past fifteen years, amid crushing stock and property markets, mountains of dud debt, scores of corruptions scandals, vast government deficits, and stagnant economic growth, Japan mutated from a giver of lessons to a recipient of lectures, all of which offers recipes for its reform and revival. Now, however, the time for lectures is over. Japan is back. It is being reformed. It is revising. Really?

Bill Emmott[10]

The Prius is a Japanese hybrid car propelled by a combination of a petrol engine (for range) and an electric motor (for energy efficiency). But the Prius also symbolizes another transformation: that of Japan itself. Japan has been developing a new hybrid model of capitalism that brings together aspects of the Japanese model, which ran into trouble in the early 1990s, with carefully chosen elements of more dynamic American or Anglo-Saxon variety of capitalism. The resulting hybrid model has been adopted by many firms, and has already helped to transform Japan's fortunes. After wrenching political and corporate reforms, the country emerged in 2002 from over a decade of economic stagnation.

Tom Standage[10]

Asia is a potpourri of nations and cultures, so it is difficult to generalize about its diverse people and their mindsets. Japanese behavior may seem puzzling and be a source of both confusion and wonderment. For North Americans, perched on the Pacific Rim, Japan is the epitome of the Far East and its enigmas. Because Japan is going through profound economic and social transformation within a generation or so, its cultural specifics must be viewed in that context. Realities of their participation in the global market and media are only two of the driving forces altering cultural preferences in that traditional society, especially among the new generation.

Japanese markets are indeed hard, but not impossible, to penetrate, as McDonald's, Coca-Cola, IBM, and many others have demonstrated. Informal protection, in the form of close linkages between supplier and customer, is a handicap to outsiders.

## Historical Perspective[10]

Geographically, the Japanese archipelago in located on Asia's east coast, consisting of four large islands (Honshu, Hokkaido, Kyushu, and Shikoku), plus approximately 4000 small islands—they are spread in a 2000-mile arc in the Western Pacific. Honshu, the largest island and cultural center, has about 50% of the population, including five major cities, the capital of Tokyo, as well as Yokohama, Osaka, Nagoya, and Kyoto (its ancient capital). Steep mountains run through the centers of these islands, so that the flat terrain is only along the coasts and valleys. Only about 15% of the terrain is suitable for agriculture—their growing staple is rice, fruit, and vegetables, plus extensive fishing. This relatively small landmass has contributed to a collective mindset of paradox, insularity, and expansionism of a relatively homogenous population.

Indeed, Japan is an ancient society—myth indicates its founding in 660 B.C. by Emperor Jimmu, but records on this country do not appear until 3 A.D. Seemingly, the majority of its people are descendents of migrating Mongolians from the northeast; its minority population of *Ainu* inhabitants concentrated in the north supposedly are descendents of Caucasoid types from northern Asia.

Since its beginnings, Japan has been influenced by both Chinese and Korean cultures, as well as by Shinto, a dominant philosophy here that is entwined with the state. This "way of the gods" details rituals and customs, which foreigners perceive as religious ceremonies. From the fifth century onward, there is evidence of development of a clan-based society on the Yamato plains. It is here that the myth originated of the clan leaders' divine descent from the sun goddess, continued through the imperial line down the centuries until Emperor Hirohito in 1946 denied his divinity, a traumatic postwar experience for his subjects.

The clan system of governance gave way in 1192 A.D. to military overlord rule and establishment of the feudal system. Emperors were relegated to ceremonial roles, power shifted to powerful noble family control holding the title of *shogun*. This was the period of family lineage and honor, self-discipline and bravery epitomized in the warrior retainer or *samurai*. Various shogun dynasties rose to rule. This agrarian economy changed slowly as a result of encounters with Westerners, starting with the Portuguese in 1542. By the mid-1600s, foreign missionaries were expelled, and Japan cut itself off from the world for 200 years. For most of its modern history, the Japanese were influenced by feudalistic concepts of absolute obedience and loyalty to their superiors.

Japanese feudal society lasted until the nineteenth century, when Commodore Perry's voyage forced open Japan to the West. Typically, a series of changing images about the Japanese people and culture emerged and can be grouped around stages. The first is pre-World

War II, when the Japanese were admired for their ambitious effort to catch up to European and American industrialization. At this stage and the next, many viewed Japanese diplomatic endeavors as devious and were threatened by assertions of hegemony over Korea, annexing Taiwan, war with Russia (1904–1905), which it won, gaining not only control of Korea but also the southern tip of Manchuria until it gained total control there by 1931. As it sought further modernization, it became a major colonial power, invading even China in this process. Before World War II, the nation aligned itself with Nazi Germany and Fascist Italy; its imperialism compelled the United States to impose limited economic sanctions in 1940. America and its allies were abashed by the daring and destructive Japanese attack upon Pearl Harbor in 1941, which forced the United States to declare war on Japan. During WWII, it continued to expand in China, Vietnam, and elsewhere in Asia until Allied military successfully forced a retreat. The use of the atomic bomb finally caused the Japanese government to surrender and accept American occupation of their homeland. The victors then proceeded to demilitarize the nation, democratize the government, and reform the Japanese society and economy. The Allied peace terms stripped Japan of all territories acquired since 1894 in East Asia.

During the postwar period, the foundations were laid for today's economic and political society, and the occupation ended in 1952 when Japan was declared an independent state. Since then, in the late twentieth century, Japan transformed itself into an industrial superpower—by 1960, it had the third largest economy in the world. Interestingly, in the twenty-first century, its old enemy, Russia, is building an oil pipeline passing north of Lake Baikal to the Sea of Japan to supply both the Japanese and Koreans. Today, Japan seeks to be both a world leader in climate change and environmental matters, as well as a cooperator in the international space program.

Although there are eight political parties, the Liberal Democratic Party (LDP) until 2009 has dominated the government since its founding in 1955, despite corruption, other scandals, and economic reverses. In 2007, it lost its majority in the upper house of the Diet (Parliament), and the opposition Democratic Party (DPJ), which is challenging the ruling LDP coalition which has had a series of short-term prime ministers. Yet, Japan is a strong democracy where human rights are respected and militarization is avoided. Under the new constitution, the parliamentary form of government has been retained and the Emperor's role is symbolic. The head of government, the prime minister, is elected by the Parliament or National Diet. The Upper and Lower Houses are elected by the public.

Despite its economic "miracles" and leadership in the global marketplace, Japan is still a highly insular culture with an entrenched bureaucracy and protectionist trade policies. It suffers today from economic setbacks and political confusion. Yet, the nation has trade agreements throughout the world with various countries, such as Chile, while also investing in other economies, such as India. Like China, it holds over $1 trillion currency reserves in the United States. Also, many people of Japanese heritage are to be found in the United States, Peru, and Brazil.

## Cultural Guidelines for Business in Japan

Japan is a "high-context" culture that thrives on subtlety and consensus. Its people manifest high educational abilities, formidable technological skills, and powerful social coordination.[11] Since 20% of the world's earthquakes occur here as a result of three interacting tectonic plates, the citizenry live in a state of perpetual preparedness for 10,000 annual tremors. With national motives directed to success and status, the acquiring of credentials through education is a high priority. At anything undertaken, most Japanese are usually meticulous and methodical. The following general insights may prove helpful when dealing with the Japanese, whether at home or abroad.

### Language and Communication

The Japanese language is complex, subtle, and predictable. By the time a native speaker is halfway through a statement, a Japanese will translate simultaneously and likely know how the sentence will end. Whereas that same person interpreting from English will wait until the foreigner has finished before beginning the translation into Japanese. Communications there are usually marked by these characteristics:

■ Indirect and vague are more acceptable than direct and specific references—ambiguous terminology is preferred. Sentences frequently are left unfinished, so that another may make a conclusion. Conversation transpires within an ill-defined and shadowy context, never quite definite, so as not to preclude personal interpretation.
■ Language is capable of delicate nuances regarding states of mind and relationships; while rich in imagination, it can be clumsy for science and business. There are layers of soft language with various degrees of courtesy and respect. The female is especially affected by this; "plain" or "coarse" language is considered improper for her.
■ The listener makes little noises of tentative suggestion, understanding, and encouragement—"*hai*" may mean more than "yes" and imply, "I'm listening," or, "I understand."
■ Nonverbal communications are subtle, and Japanese are disconcerted by broad expressions and gestures of Americans.

There is a formal politeness for official negotiation and ordinary business communication, while an informal approach may be used while socializing. Frequently, while entertaining, the real business and political deals are concluded.

The Japanese require more information about the person with whom they interact, so as to determine which form to use in their complex language. Thus, they are given to asking questions about your job, title, responsibilities, etc. When a business meeting is scheduled, they prefer advance information in the form of electronic mail, brochures, and even proposals.

These people appreciate it when outsiders seek to learn more about their unique culture and language, even if it is only a few phrases or expressions in Japanese.

## Dress and Appearance

Neat, orderly, and conservative for managers; ordinary workers and students frequently wear a distinctive uniform and even a company pin, which managers also may sport (a holdover from feudal days when a kimono carried a lord's symbol). The ancient, classical dress, the kimono is becoming less common even in the privacy of the home and is retained for ceremonial events. Western formal dress is used for important state occasions. Traditional native dress is sexless, although the shape of the garment is different. The colors are often neutral with women sometimes tending toward flowery patterns.

Japanese youth prefer to wear contemporary clothes and hairstyles—they want to look like teenagers seen elsewhere. Also, with changes in diet, the young appear to be physically larger than their parents, and obesity is a growing problem with this affluent generation.

Colors have different significance in Japanese culture (e.g., white for sorrow, black for joy).

## Food and Eating Habits

Eating here is ritualistic, communal, and time-consuming. The interaction is considered important as the food. While the traditional diet emphasizes rice, noodles, and fish, youths tend toward popular Western foods. The alcoholic beverage of *sake* often accompanies the main or ceremonial meal so as to facilitate conversation. Tokyo is said to have a restaurant, bar, or cabaret for every 110 members of the population, with many international foods represented. Fast-food establishments are everywhere and popular.

## Time, Age, and Rewards

Japanese are punctual, and need time for connections to make proper contacts. Yet, they expect you to wait for group decisions that also take time to arrive at consensus.

Traditionally, they respect seniority and the elderly. There is a sense of order, propriety, and appropriate behavior between inferiors and superiors.

In the past, young managers, recruited from the universities after stiff examinations, are expected to stay with a company until they are 60 years of age, conforming, doing what is expected of them, and showing respect and deference to senior or older employees. Then, the crucial decision is made as to whether the 60-year-old manager is to become a company director; if he or she makes it, he or she can stay beyond the normal Western retirement age and may work into his or her eighties. The remainder of the managerial group not so selected become department or subsidiary directors and are expected to retire between 55 and 60, though even then they can be retained in a temporary capacity. These customs are now changing. Yet, there is a tendency to reward and recognize the group or organization rather than the individual in Japanese organizations. One achieves and is recognized through the group in ever-widening circles: family, team, department, division, company, nation.

Great emphasis is placed on security and the social need for "belonging." Notice that when traveling abroad, Japanese stay within their own group, generally avoiding individual contact with the locals. However, Japanese managers abroad are more inclined to be engaged with their foreign workers.

## Relationships

Japan, a nation of the size of California, is cohesive and crowded, which accounts for its rituals of bowing and politeness in crowded urban areas. Japanese relationships are familial and group oriented, instead of individualistic. Japanese value group relations and harmony. Group leadership is more highly regarded than individual initiative. There is a tendency toward clannishness based on family or group connections—know your place and be comfortable with it. Thus, the drive toward agglomeration, combines, and clustering of organizational relationships.

Personal relationships score high with Japanese, and future relationships depend on how you respond in the first encounter. Cut-and-dried relationships with business contacts are inadequate and must be supplemented by a social relationship for maximum effect. This usually means entertaining the client with a "night on the town" and not at one's home. Part of the Japanese manager's reward is a generous budget for entertaining. When away from home on business, the Japanese businessperson expects to be entertained lavishly (meals, theater tickets, etc.), but repays this kindness manifold.

With regard to international relationships, Japan has close emotional and economic ties to the United States, but is suspicious of aggressive Americans. The Japanese fear China, yet they are emotionally allied and identify with the Chinese.

In business relationships, there are two Japans—officialdom and the intellectuals (e.g., politicians and businesspersons). In both, decisions tend to be group mulling for consensus, give and take inconclusiveness, and the traditional authority pyramid. There is a symbiotic relationship between government and business—cozy but not constricting. This is still an unsolved issue.

In context of social relations, Japanese tend to be clean, polite, and disciplined. Social and self-control disguise a highly emotional quality of the Japanese character and relationships; the mesh of binding social relationships is weakening and hard to comprehend. While the Japanese are sensitive to what others think or expect of them, and have a sharp sense of right and wrong, they find it difficult to deal with the unexpected and strange, and so may laugh inappropriately.

Again, youth epitomize the culture in transition. They are energetic and productive, yet anxious for change, gaining a new sense of "I my me-ness," while the pattern for their elders is "we-ness." The general gap between the generations is very wide. For example, younger university graduates are more open to entrepreneurship, especially in information technologies.

In business organization, the "bridge" for the young manager is an elder, upper middle manager assigned as a guide or facilitator. This senior person is rarely the direct superior of the young manager, but is expected to know him or her, meet regularly, and be available for advice and counsel, and to assist in transfers and discipline, when necessary. This respected elder manager is always consulted on promotions and other personnel matters concerning that young person's career. He or she is the human contact for the organization with the young manager, the listener and guide who provides a significant human relationship.

## Attitudes and Beliefs

The typical Japanese character is diverse with a sense of poetry and ephemeral. There is a concern for the transitory, inconclusive qualities of life, for nature, and its observation. It is actively curious, energetic, and quick, with a sense of delicacy and wistfulness. One manifestation is in the art of flower arrangements.

Although many Japanese will not admit to being religious, there are two philosophies of life that are pervasive and influence their behavior. Confucianism introduced in fifth century A.D. and Shintoism which is native to people of this island. Shinto teaches respect for nature and counsels harmony between man and nature. Shinto minor deities are found in shrines (*jinja* distinguished by red wooden archways, and in nature itself, for example, mountains and rivers). The dominant religious thrust is the convergence of Shintoism and Buddhism (married Shinto, buried Buddhist). Buddhism is the largest conventional religion in Japan, whereas Christianity has made limited impact (except with Christmas celebrations and decorations in retail stores). The crusading Soka Gakkai sect is also a political party that fights inequalities of the social structure, while enshrining the idealistic, self-denial, and the espousal of the underdog.

## Values and Standards

The dominant ethos of Japanese are familial relationships, loyalty, conformity, and the collective good. Their personality is generally self-confident and flexible, demonstrating a sense of order, propriety, and appropriate behavior; there is a tendency toward diligence and thrift, balanced by a fun-loving approach, which, at times, seems almost frivolous and extravagant.

In outlook, the Japanese are cautious and given to stalling tactics. They are also insular, which is manifested by the in-group tendency. The rigid, ossified Japanese class system is disappearing; each person has his or her place as superior or inferior.

Japanese value peace and economic progress, ensured somewhat by the fact that only 1% of the nation's gross national product is devoted to defense spending. This culture highly regards new ideas and technologies, swallowing them up until they are Japanized (internalized) after careful, detailed examination—the success of Japanese communications and automotive industries confirm this value. Today, there is a subtle shift in emphasis under way from copying others to creating one's own by innovation.

Japanese society also values training and education, especially of the young. It also values a spirit of intensity and craftsmanship manifested by a quality of deep penetration and pride in work no matter how humble. This has been expressed not only in arts and crafts, but also in graphic novels and animation.

Japanese prefer congenial, known surroundings, and seek to create an atmosphere of well-focused energy and disciplined good cheer. A basic standard of Japanese life is work and play hard—work particularly for the good of the family or company family, and maintain controlled competition and cooperation in the process. Then play hard—modern Japanese devote more time to leisure and recreational activities.

Postwar Japanese fear foreign military involvement, but are willing to engage in humanitarian endeavors sponsored by the United Nations.

The younger generation seeks more control over their lives. A minority of radical, revolutionary Japanese youth have an entirely different set of values from the majority—some can be vicious and violent, yet espouse a spirit of self-denial, self-correction, and self-dedication to what they consider a higher cause. Even criminal gangs will publicly apologize in press conferences to the public when they cause too much violence and disruption in society. Youths are transforming this traditional society and are more globally attuned because of telecommunications and travel. Also, a falling birthrate may force Japan to seek ever more foreign workers, causing even greater ethnic diversity in the future. Globalization and acquisitions have also brought more foreign managers and professionals into this rather closed society.

Essentially, in the twenty-first century, this is a society concerned about national economic welfare, market penetration; and humanitarian endeavors. Increasingly, Japanese companies are giving a percentage of profits to promote education, social welfare, culture, and protection of the environment.

## Managing in Japan

The old industrial model of management, which produced initially a "Japanese miracle" in the last half of the twentieth century, is undergoing rapid change. It was based on (1) lifetime employment by the same organization; (2) workers spend their entire career working their way up in the same firm to gain seniority-based pay; (3) company-based unions that promote cooperation between labor and management; (4) close relationship of the company with its bank and other corporate groups bound together in cross-share holdings—called a *keiretsu*. This model once ensured social stability and cohesion, as well as rapid economic growth abroad. To remain globally competitive, a new model is emerging: (1) effective redeployment of labor, including proper use of women and the elderly; (2) encouraging entrepreneurship and innovation; (3) greater integration in the global economy by accessing fast-growing foreign markets and meeting international competition. As the third quote above indicates, a more hybrid model is developing closer to Western ways of managing, while still utilizing some of the old ways that work in this culture. Japan is searching for its own capitalistic in a market economy, so that both shareholders and stakeholders are protected. Thus, the traditional "salarymen system" is giving way to a more flexible labor market that is performance based. There is also greater use of part-time, temporary, and contract workers. The challenge is for improvement in conditions of "nonregular workers," women, and immigrants. Rigidity in the Japanese workforce is slowly moving away from cultural factors like group conformity to creative individualism. Today, young professionals are not afraid of moving between companies or to work for foreign firms. The "now" generation refuses to make work the center of their lives and are unwilling to accept corporate paternalism.

Japanese continue to pursue the acquisition of Western management skill, not simply technical knowledge of products or manufacturing, but sophisticated management theory and concepts transferred to the Japanese environment. This is forcing changes in the way of dealing with foreigners. A more competitive climate is developing for foreigners or *gaijin* that permits more direct investment in Japanese enterprises.

Furthermore, when expatriate managers return from working in Japanese operations abroad, they introduce some of their new learnings from that experience into local management.

In their organizations, the goals are product quality and superiority; team work and consensus; corporate growth and social responsibility. Yet, too many managers there avoid saying what they think because it disrupts harmony, seems to be immodest. Subordinates are usually reluctant to challenge their ideas, lest the boss loses face. Risk taking and initiative are stifled, and seeking consensus can become an excuse for compromise and avoiding hard decisions. Mental health problems are rising in the workplace, and the country's suicide rate is among the highest in the world. The work environment needs to provide more individual incentives, responsibility, and rewards based on performance, not age or seniority.

Here are some observations about this unique but changing business culture:

- Japanese will try to achieve sales and profits without harming face and harmony or creating a poor standing in the business community.
- Third party or indirect introductions are important for creating trust between individuals who come together through a mutual friend, go-between, or arbitrator. This person may be involved until the conclusion of the negotiation.
- Whomever you approach in the organization, do so at the highest level; the first person contacted is also involved throughout the negotiation.
- Avoid direct communication on money; leave this to the go-between or lower echelon staff. Money, if passed to a Japanese businessperson, should be in an envelope.
- For social visiting, a guest is frequently given a present or small gift, such as a hand towel beautifully wrapped; however, on the next exchange of visit, you are expected to offer a gift in kind.
- Avoid publicly putting a Japanese in a position where he or she must admit failure.
- Play down praise of your product or services; let your literature or go-between do that.
- Use business cards with your titles in both Japanese and English.
- Logical, cognitive, or intellectual approach is insufficient; the emotional level of communication is considered important (e.g., as in dealing with a known business associate versus a stranger).
- Formality prevails in senior staff meetings with interpreters present. The more important the meeting, the more senior executives present.
- Wait patiently for meetings to move beyond preliminary tea and sometimes long formalities.

## Decision Making

Again, the Japanese value decision by consensus. Before action is taken, much time is spent on defining the question. They decide first if there is a need for a decision and what it is all about. The focus is on what the decision is really about, not what it should be; once agreement is reached, the Japanese move with great speed to the action stage. Referral of the question is made to the appropriate people, in effect, indicating top management's answer to the question. The system forces the Japanese to make big decisions, and to avoid the Western tendency toward small decisions that are easy to make (minutia). For example, instead of making a decision on a particular joint venture, the Japanese might consider the direction the business should go, and this joint venture is then only a small aspect of the larger issue.

## Terms of Employment

As noted above, the traditional corporate policy of long-term or lifetime employments is changing. First, not all workers are considered permanent. A substantial body of employees (perhaps 20%) is not subject to this job security. Some positions are hired and paid for by the hour; women are generally considered in the temporary work category, and some who retire at 55 may be kept on in that temporary capacity: adjustments in workforce can be readily made among these "temporaries."

For full-time employees, pay as a rule is on the basis of seniority, and doubles every 15 years. Retirement is a 2-year salary, severance bonus, usually at 55. Western pension plans are beginning to come into companies slowly, and are low in benefits. In the past, permanent employees who left an employer had a very difficult time obtaining permanent positions with another employer. However, the new work environment places more emphasis on competence and performance. Another standard of Japanese work life seems to be *continuous training*. It is performance focused in contrast to promotion focus; in scope, it involves training not only in one's own job but also in all jobs at one's level. The emphasis is on productivity, and the real burden of training is on the learner—"What have we learned to help us do the job better?"

On the whole, Japanese believe that the older worker is more productive, and output per man-hour is invariably higher in a plant with an older work population. With the new knowledge workers, that attitude is also being altered. Recognize also that the Japanese labor force is both aging and diminishing today. This has promoted the trend toward more women in the work force, and giving them a greater role, as well as increasing the use of robots! Realize that birth rates have plummeted, the population is shrinking drastically—possibly from 128 now to 100 million by 2050. This will affect the nation's GDP which is also on the decline. Expect Japan in the near future to become a major leader in pan-Asian cooperation, while remaining a close ally of the United States.

The Japanese are a remarkable and unique people. Their subtle, complex culture, in particular, illustrates the differences and diversity of Asian cultures, in general. The Japanese have also learned and successfully applied many lessons from other countries, so other nations should be learning from their culture, especially in terms of management and organizational behvior!

Japan is not a superpower, like the United States, EU, and China, but a balance country that can either support or not support those three countries. The Japanese constantly reinvent themselves with technological breakthroughs, such as in robotics and nanotechnologies. But their companies must improve in collaboration with other firms around the world, like the global alliance of Renault-Nissan and Sony-Ericsson. On the other hand, foreign firms going into Japan need to understand that distinctive, local market, as Starbucks did when it crafted its strategy for doing business there. Patience and determination are the keys to success in this culture. Just remember that Japan is still the world's second-biggest economy, representing half of the Asian market.

# PAKISTAN

Modern Pakistan has the Arabian Sea to its southwest, India in the southeast, Afghanistan to the north (which adjoins Turkmenistan, Tajikistan, and Kyrgyzstan), and China on the east. In addition to its own Balochi and Burusho groups, it shares tribal people with other nations—90 million Punjabis in Pakistan and India; 27 million Pashtuns in Pakistan and Afghanistan.

## Historical Perspective[12]

The recorded history of the people now living in this land goes back to 3000 B.C. Here in the Indu Valley, the Indo-Aryan civilizations developed a mixed culture resulting from numerous invasions of nomadic tribes from the west, including Persians. Located on a number of major trade routes, the region also attracted Arab, Mongol, and Europeans; more recently, Afghan refugees have arrived in great numbers. Today, the inhabitants are primarily Punjabis, but the other four groups include Pathan, Sindhi, Mujhair, and the Balucchi—all named after provinces from which they originated. Given such ethnic divisions, the society is split along tribal, caste, and economic lines. Although 97% are Sunni Muslim.

The Islamic Republic of Pakistan was founded in 1947, when Britain divided the subcontinent into two nations. Religion was the main divider, as the Hindus were predominantly in India and the Muslims in Pakistan. At that time, Pakistan was also divided, whereby Muslim districts were in West Pakistan, and East Pakistan consisted of a single province; in 1971, the latter gained independence, and is known today as Bangladesh. Since its founding, the two sides could not come to an agreement about the states of Jammu and Kashmir. The status of Kashmir is in dispute still and the cause of much hostility with India, although its population is largely Muslim.

In the twenty-first century, Pakistan has assumed a strategic role in the war on terrorism, especially with the Taliban and al-Qaeda in Afghanistan—many of the latter seem to be hidden from the American and allied NATO forces in the mountains of northwest Pakistan. This region consists of seven semiautonomous tribal agencies that provide refuge and a supply route for the insurgents. Seemingly, Pakistan has been unable to bring order to this frontier, and is reluctant to abandon jihadst proxies. In areas where tribal elders still rule, Islamic militants have been resisted and given little support. In 2005, the country also suffered from massive volcanic eruptions that prompted significant international aid to flow into this poor country. Increased terrorism has also struck in the capital.

Today, Pakistan is a federal republic with the prime minister and president presiding. President General Musharraf's military takeover as head of the National Security Council, composed of military chiefs, lasted from 1999 to 2008. Civilian rule was then restored in this very volatile society with the election of Asif Zardari in 2008.

## Cultural Guidelines for Business in Pakistan

The official language of Pakistan is Urdu; however, this is only spoken by 9% of the population; 48% speak Punjabi, 12% Sindhi, and 27% speak other languages including Pushtu, Saraiki, Baloch, and Brahui. English is used by the government and military. The state religion is Islam, which 97% follow. Minority religions include Christianity, Hinduism, and Parsi. Ethnically, Pakistan is composed of Punjabis, Sindhis, Pashtuns, Afghans, Balochs, and Muhajirs.

Pakistan is still behind many countries with similar per capita income. There is also a big gender discrepancy, whereby boys will usually complete 5 years of school and girls only 2.5. Similarly, 55% of males and only 29% of females are literate. Muslim fundamentalism is partially responsible for women failing to achieve their full potential in this traditional society, but gender restrictions are lessening. In urban areas, women have moved ahead in government and the professions.

Pakistan faces another development problem, where 25% of the population falls below the poverty line. GDP growth is low, and agriculture accounts for 24.7% of GDP. Pakistan is one of the world's largest producers of raw cotton. The United States is Pakistan's biggest export market, representing 24%. The two biggest suppliers to Pakistan are the UAE (13.1%) and Saudi Arabia (11.3%).

The United States imposed sanctions on Pakistan following nuclear tests conducted in 1998. However, following the terrorist attacks on September 11, 2001, the United States needed Pakistan's help to achieve military action in Afghanistan. The situation changed overnight for Pakistan, with over a billion dollars in loans from the United States. Pakistan ended ties with the Taliban in December 2002 and has cooperated reluctantly with the West in seeking out terrorists, even within its own borders.

Recently, Pakistan indicated that it would eliminate its nuclear weapons if India does so as well. Pakistan has also been implementing a strategy to end its conflict with India, especially over Kashmir. Better relations and negotiations between these two great nations of the subcontinent are proceeding.

### Tips for Doing Business in Pakistan

The family and the clan is the basis of this culture, and such connections influence business and political relationships. Unfortunately, economic gains have benefited the few wealthy families who control commerce and government; some large landowners have become regional officials in the public sector. Two-thirds of the masses live in rural villages with limited opportunities. There is some social mobility, particularly in urban areas. After family, friends are important. Pakistanis are straightforward, honest, hospitable, and tolerant of foreigners.

■ *Work Practices*—During winter, business and government offices normally operate from 9 a.m. to 5 p.m.; during summer (April 15-October 15) from 8:30 a.m. to 5 p.m. Hours differ for retail shops and banks and for Ramadan, when normal work is from 8:30 a.m. to 11:30 a.m. The work week is Sunday to Thursday, with time off on Friday for the Islamic holy day of rest; some businesses open on Saturday morning. Prayer time is 1 p.m.

■ *Business Relationships*—Foreigners are well advised to have an introduction to key persons they seek to contact. They should verify references and anticipate boasting about capabilities. Maintaining personal honor is critical. The government has two investment agencies that produce helpful publications for the company and exporting. To facilitate export, 57 industrial estates have been established throughout the country to provide infrastructure and various concessions that encourage investment. Expect handshakes, business cards, and tardiness. This people have a relaxed sense of time and deadlines.

■ *Social Customs*—Since this is a strict Muslim society, act accordingly; the locals do not eat pork or drink alcohol. The left hand is unclean, so do not touch food with it. The culture is very protective of women, so their head is covered or veiled, and many wear the *burqah*, the dark tent-like garb. Business entertaining is usually done with dinner in a restaurant or by an invitation to a home. If so invited, remove shoes before entering, and bring a small gift. Pakistanis are generous, hospitable, and will ensure you have plenty of food to eat.

Pakistan is known for its love of religion, arts, festivals, and poetry. Annually, for instance, upwards of 15,000 people will gather for *Musaira*, an all-night celebration in Karachi of regional poets and their works. Wisely, a 12-year-old girl poet at the event wrote in her diary: *I write a poetry of love, and I want the world to know that we Pakistanis are about more than terror.* Similarly, the poet Wasi Shah spoke passionately when he observed: *Our poetry does not produce violence.*

# THE PHILIPPINES

The Philippines' 7000 islands cover approximately 116,000 square miles in the South China Sea. The 11 largest islands comprise over 95% of the total land area and population, with Luzon being the largest island and Mindanao being the second largest. Although Quezon City was declared the capital in 1948, most government activity still remains in Manila on the island of Luzon.

## Historical Perspective[13]

In this island chain, the prehistoric evidence of humans goes back 22,000 years. By the ninth century A.D., trade with China was vigorously under way, and continues to this day. In the twelfth century, traders and clergy from Indonesia brought Islam to the Philippines. In 1521, Ferdinand Magellan became the first European to visit in Cebu, claiming the lands for the King of Spain. In 1565, the Spanish began to settle, and named the archipelago *Philippines* in honor of their king, Philip II. Spain was so successful in converting the natives to Christianity that it remains the majority religion even today. Their missionaries in religious orders impacted the culture, especially education, social life, art, and architecture. By the eighteenth century, these orders were the largest landowners. However, Muslims in the southern islands resisted these conversion efforts. Many of the nation's modern problems stem from its colonial past.

Spain exploited the country's wealth. Spanish prestige was undermined when the British won the Seven Years' War and captured the Philippines. Though returned in 1764, English and American influence emerged from then on. By the nineteenth century, many Filipino elite had visited Europe, and nationalists began to advocate independence. When the United States won a war with Spain over Cuba in 1898, it took over the Philippines. This foreign regime was subject to wars and sporadic fighting with the nationalists, until the Japanese occupation from 1942 to 1945. After WWII ended, the Americans established a new political structure, known as the Commonwealth of the Philippines. The United States granted the country independence on July 4, 1946, partially in appreciation for Filipino help during the war. While the Americans retained military bases, these were a source of contention with the locals until Clark Air Force Base was closed in 1991 and Subic Bay Naval Base in 1992.

Ferdinand Marcos was elected president in 1965; by 1972, he declared martial law and ruled as a dictator until overthrown in 1986. Cronyism has always permitted the well connected to profit illegitimately. A series of unstable governments have further weakened the government.

Historically, power in this land belongs to an oligarchy of powerful landed gentry and extended families, as seen in Exhibit 12.9. In 1987, a new constitution was adopted modeled on that of the United States, and the nation returned to a constitutional democracy, with elections of a president and vice president by popular vote, along with bicameral legislature, plus an independent judiciary headed by the Supreme Court. For governance, the country is divided into three geographic regions—Luzon, Visayas, and Mindanao, in addition to 15 administrative regions.

## EXHIBIT 12.9

## CONFRONTING POWER AND WEALTH

A crippled woman is leading the way to greater democracy in the Philippines. "My weakness is my strength," declared Grace Padaca, a recently elected governor of Isabela, a poor northern province. She referred not only to a childhood bout with polio that requires her to use crutches, but also her lack of political connections and financial muscle. To promote reforms that benefit the average poor citizen, she confronts influential political clans. Despite their elections as President, both Corazon Aquino and Gloria Arroyo came from the elite class and had such family connections. The reality, especially at the national level, is that Philippine politics is more dynastic now. Province Isabela is a case in point—when Ms. Padaca won the election against a rival, she ended the Dy family's 41-year monopoly as local governors and mayors, representatives in Congress.

EXHIBIT 12.9
CONFRONTING POWER AND WEALTH (CONTINUED)

Such wealthy families perpetuate themselves in power by patronage networks that function as political parties elsewhere. Those in public office use their positions to channel money, jobs, and other benefits to their supporters. In this province, Chinese-Filipinos dominate business, as with the Dy clan's heritage. Padaca, a popular radio crusader, was able to counter such alliances to get elected, but as she tries to promote necessary social change, her efforts are frustrated by the Dys, one of whom was the former governor who left the public treasury heavily in debt. This valiant female governor's 3-year term is threatened by a recall election engineered by the Dy opposition. Sheila Coronel, of the Philippine Center for Investigative Journalism, argues that it is almost impossible for independent candidates to break political dynasties' lock on high office. But democracy is fighting back in mayoral and local elections. Joel Rocamora, of the Institute for Popular Democracy, maintains that there are more first-generation candidates emerging and winning lower offices. The hope is that political dynasties will be undermined as the people move to the cities where they become better educated and more independent minded in their voting.

*Source*: "Asia—The Philippines, Limping Forward," *The Economist*, March 19, 2005, pp. 47-8.

## Cultural Guidelines for Business in the Philippines

Whereas its neighbors became bywords for economic dynamism, the Philippines became famous for the excess of its rules and for the poverty in major cities. The government's budget now is seemingly on course with a surplus, and the infrastructure bottlenecks that throttled growth for so long are gradually being tackled. At last, the Philippines looks ready to emulate sustained rapid growth, enjoyed by much of the region.

In this multicultural society, Filipino, or Philipino, is the principal language, but English is also spoken, as well as Chinese. Hospitality, friendliness, and sincerity are prominent aspects of the Filipino culture. An ambience filled with gaiety may be the result of over 300 years of the Spanish culture. Filipinos are predominantly of Malay stock, with Chinese, Spanish, and American cultural influences.

Great contrasts in terrain and climate exist throughout the Philippines. Northern Luzon is mountainous, the southern islands comparatively dry, while other parts are dense jungle areas. In addition, there are a number of volcanoes throughout the islands. The Philippines are located within the tropic zone with the low areas having a warm, humid climate and only slight variations from the average temperature of 80°F. The monsoon season lasts from June to November, and periodic typhoons pass over the island causing immense floods and damage to crops and homes.

The foreign policy of the Philippines is based on a close alliance with many other Asian countries, principally through ASEAN—the Association of South East Asia Nations. Contacts in high places of government are essential in cutting through the bureaucratic red tape. The people basically work on the "mañana" system, but things do get done.

*Utang na loob*, literally meaning "debt on the inside," is another trait of some Filipinos. A Filipino remains indebted for a favor for a long period of time. One may even be asked to respond to a favor that was bestowed upon an ancestor many years ago.

The nation's economy is based on agriculture, forestry, and fishing, which employ more than half of the total labor force and account for more than 50% of all exports. The agricultural sector consists of the production of food crops essentially for domestic consumption (rice and corn) and cash crops for export. The country's major exports are sugar, copra, copra meal, coconut oil, pineapple, tobacco, and abaca. The Philippines is also one of the world's leading producers of wood and wood products. Although fishing contributes to the economy, the fertile fishing area has not been developed to its full potential. The Philippines is rich in mineral resources, with nickel, copper, and other mineral deposits among the largest in the world. However, only a small portion of these have been surveyed and exploited. Government programs have recently been initiated to strengthen the industrial development and have included protective import duties and taxes. The United States has been a leading trading partner of the Philippines, purchasing about 30% of the country's exports. Japan is second with about 18%, and the EU purchases about 7%. Imports consist mainly of fuel and manufactured goods, particularly machinery. Of the 32 million people in the labor force, nearly 10% are unemployed or underemployed. Over the past years, the Philippines has been recovering from an economic slowdown, but unemployment still remains high. The administration is trying to restore confidence, both domestically and internationally, in an attempt to regain economic stability.

The Philippines' population has more than doubled since independence was obtained over 60 years ago, and contributes to the poverty of the masses. With a population numbering approximately 84 million, the Philippines has one of the highest birth rates in the world. Further, émigrés have come to the Philippines from many Southeast Asian countries, such as Indonesia, Malaysia, and China. The blend of these cultures has formed the Filipino culture. The most significant alien ethnic group residing in the Philippines are the Chinese, who have played an important role in commerce since their arrival in the fourteenth century.

The present culture strongly reflects all these inputs. The education system was impacted by the presence and relationship here of the United States from 1898 to 1946. Education is highly valued, and there is free, though not compulsory, education through the secondary level. The literacy rate is approximately 95%, with a large portion of the nation's budget being spent on education. The Philippines prides itself on its educational system, and many of its graduates become professionals who work overseas, particularly in health care.

The standard of living in the Philippines varies, with only a few families owning a large percentage of the rural and urban real estate. These wealthy few control profitable businesses and the universities, while living in luxury. Reform, especially in land ownership, progresses very slowly.

## Business and Social Tips

■ *Harmony*—Filipinos believe in *pakiksama*, which literally means the ability to get along with people, emphasizing their attitude of conceding with the majority rather than strongly standing up for one's personal opinion. Confrontation is usually avoided. The consequences of an insult or crime are quick, often violent, retaliation. True feelings of the Filipinos are often subtle, behind an agreeing facade, and the foreign businessperson in the Philippines should attempt to read hidden signals.

■ *Social Forces*—*Hiya*, or shame, is important for Filipinos, and the idea is instilled in their children at an early age. To accuse a person of not having this *hiya* trait is a gross insult, because it indicates that a person is unable to feel shame as well as all other emotions. Therefore, in this society, avoid criticizing another person in public or in front of his friends because it shames him or her, and is thus the greatest of insults.

The negative ramifications of *hiya* are that the Filipinos avoid change, innovation, or competition simply because if the result is failure, it would cause him to shame his family. Consequently, the Filipino family and the Filipino businessperson will "save face" at any cost.

■ *Fatalism*—Success in the mind of the Filipino is often a function of fate rather than individual merit, and, therefore, most people are content in their social position only because they feel fate has placed them there. Expressions such as "never mind," "it doesn't matter," or "it was my fate" are common reactions to problems such as typhoons, epidemics, and crop failures. Another demonstration of their belief in fate is that the Filipinos frequently gamble and play games of chance.

- *Sensitivity*—Due to their heritage, Filipinos are a somewhat emotional people, and very sensitive. They are loyal friends and demand the same kind of loyalty in return. This aspect is reflected in social situations, as well as business interactions. They are reluctant to share or to do business with a person unless there is a mutual sincerity. This has been a great obstacle in the past, as Filipinos have described American businesspeople as being overly aggressive and insensitive to feelings.

- *Hospitality*—Filipinos enjoy entertaining others. When accepting invitations, one should inquire if the starting time is "American time" or "Filipino time." In the case of American time, one should arrive at the hour requested. However, if the arrival time is on Filipino time, it is not necessary to arrive until an hour or two later than requested. However, for sit-down dinners with a limited number of guests, one is expected to be on time. Filipino food may be eaten in the *kamayan* way, or with the hands.

- *Individualism*—Individualism is much valued by the Filipinos so much so that If a foreign businessperson fails to treat a Filipino as an individual, the visitor may be refused help. It is important to take time to talk with adults and children, avoid being judgmental. The Filipinos will make every effort to maintain their reputation as being hospitable people. In return, foreign businesspeople should be mutually polite and respectful toward them, avoiding superiority.

- *Female Roles*—Although a moral double standard for males and females is still prevalent in the Philippines, the country prides itself on being one of the few Asian countries with a large percentage of women in government and politics. Women as well as men inherit property here, in contrast to other Asian countries.

- *Nonverbal Communication*—Such techniques used in the Philippines include raising of the eyebrows, which indicates an affirmative reply, namely a "yes." A jerk of the head downward means "I don't know," while a jerk upward means "yes." Like the Japanese, the Filipinos rarely say "no" like Americans do. They resist confrontation and may say "yes" verbally while putting their head downward, namely a nonverbal signal for "I don't know." To indicate "come here," one would extend the hand out with the palm down moving the fingers in and out.

- *Religion*—The Philippines is the only predominantly Christian country in the Far East, primarily due to the previous Spanish influence. Over 83% of all Filipinos are Roman Catholic, which affects their culture and daily activities. The second largest church in the country is the Protestant *Iglesia ni Cristo,* or Church of Christ. There is a growing revival of fundamentalism in the country. A significant minority striving for human and religious rights is the one-and-a-half million Filipinos who are Muslims. In southern areas of the islands, Islamic practices and militants dominate, and violence, kidnapping, and clashes with the government continue.

- *Morality and Ethics*—What is "correct" behavior is more likely to be defined by tradition and related to the family and other reciprocal obligations. Failure to measure up in terms of family expectations and traditions produces feelings of shame. As in most developing nations, including the Philippines, corruption is prevalent in the public services, government, and business. It is not uncommon for many complications in business and government bureaucracy to be speedily resolved by the payment of a favor. Such practices are the result of long historical and cultural development, rooted in the Spanish tradition. Also, as in the case of many developing countries, a foreign businessperson should be aware that an informal business sector operates underground, parallel to the formal sector.

- *Family Corporations*—These are numerous with management composed of the nuclear family, and all the stockholders are relatives. Trust is not easily given to those who do not belong. The *palakasan* system refers to going through connections instead of through the proper channels. Having the right connections can facilitate a deal or employment. Note that Filipinos have produced an extraordinary synergy among their diverse cultural groups, so are open to cooperation and collaboration.

- *Work Relations*—Filipinos see no reason why conflict should be courted when silence or evasive speech will preserve peace. Filipinos' excessive attention to recognition sometimes results in preoccupation with form over substance, and people tend to say what they do not mean to maintain appearances. The business card, as far as Filipinos are concerned, is a handy reference and could be exchanged at the end of a meeting. In a business negotiation, every detail, however insignificant, should be negotiated to avoid misunderstanding and renegotiation. A Filipino business partner has to be cultivated, and then this development may result in a reliable business relationship. These people place greater importance on personal relations than on a written contract.

## SOUTH KOREA

Today's South Korea's business landscape stands radically transformed. Of the 30 biggest chaebol, 16 have been shut down or radically downsized. The survivors—companies such as Samsung Group and LG—barely resemble their former selves. Of the 2100 financial institutions cluttering the banking industry in 1998, just 1600 are now standing. Of 24 major city banks, only half remain. Imagine such ruthless restructuring in Japan. The average income per person is half that of Japan. So unification with North Korea, if and when it comes, will require South Korea to field huge resources expended on integration of the two Koreas.[14]

The Korean Peninsula lies south of China, with the Yellow Sea to the west, and the Sea of Japan to the east. Manchuria and Russia border on the north. The total land mass for this peninsula, including islands, is about 85,500 square miles. Today, the Communists in North Korea occupy about 55% of the land, while the democratic Republic of Korea in the south controls the remaining 45%. The two political entities are separated by the Demilitarized Zone, an outcome of Korean War in 1953. This DMZ is a 4-km wide strip of land that runs along the 38th parallel for 243 km, or 150 miles.

In 688 A.D., the Paekche people were in the southwest and Silla in the southeast when the latter conquered the other two kingdoms to found a state that was the foundation of modern Korea. Over their long history, Koreans clashed with many neighbors until the Monguls conquered them in 1259 to set up a reign that lasted a hundred years. In 1392, the Korean throne was seized by General Yi-Song-gye, whose Choson Dynasty ruled until 1910. Previously, the country, afraid of Christian missionaries, isolated itself from the rest of the world and was known as the "Hermit Kingdom" until it opened itself to trading with the West in the 1860s. In the nineteenth century, both Japan and China vied for control of Korea, so the king turned to Russia for assistance, but the latter sought to control the nation's warm water ports. When Koreans staged protests for independence, it lead to the Sino-Japanese War of 1984-1995, which resulted in Japan assuming control on the peninsula, something confirmed again when Japan won a war with Russia in 1905. By 1910, the Japanese abolished the Korean monarchy and treated the country as a dependent colony, ruling ruthlessly. When Japan again went to war with China from 1937 to 1945, it mobilized the country as a military base. The Koreans were forced to adopt the Japanese language and names, as well as belief in Shintoism and the divinity of the Japanese emperor.

Korea and its sufferings were virtually ignored by the rest of the world until WWII ended. Then Russia assumed control of the peninsula north of the 38th parallel, while Americans occupied the rest of Korea in the south. In 1948, the Soviets established a Communist state in their zone and withdrew from the country—this "Democratic Republic of Korea" (DPRK) in the north is still the center of international tension in the twenty-first century. The next year, the Americans also withdrew, leaving in place the "Republic of Korea" (RFK), known today as South Korea. Efforts by the United Nations to reunite the two entities were blocked by Communist nations. At that time, Korea became a focus of world attention in a clash between the East and the West; a battleground of communist and democratic ideologies. When North Korea invaded South Korea in 1950, it led to war with both UN, led by the Americans, and China's intervention. With a stalemate in this conflict, an armistice was signed in 1953, leaving Korea divided by the DMZ in two states of suspended hostilities.

Syngman Rhee was elected first president of South Korea, serving in that role from 1948 to 1960. After a period of political disorganization and rule by military junta led by Park Chung Hee, a new constitution obtained widespread public support. When Park was officially elected president in 1963, his authoritarian regime was successful in promoting the country's development. South Korea's economic transformation was then the wonder of the world. It took South Korea only three decades to transition from a farming nation to an industrial giant. Its quality products and energetic workers are exported around the globe, along with eager-to-learn technicians. South Korea has begun to open its market in a bid to join the big league of global competition, but some say it is difficult to shed its protectionist ways. With an economic growth rate of 4.4% annually, this country has a highly productive export market.

South Korea has renewed its cities and built satellite cities around Seoul, as well as renewing the country's west coast. While northern relatives stagnate under totalitarianism, this dynamic society produced first-class Olympic Games and facilities in 1988. It has experienced relatively peaceful elections as the nation transformed itself into a constitutional democracy. Its population is restless for more freedom, improved working conditions, and benefits, plus progress toward national reunification with the North. The Korea Development Institute reports that the country is restructuring toward a domestic-driven economy, especially with citizens having more disposable income. There is a growing demand for domestic goods and services, along with the desire for improved housing and tourism abroad. Doing business here requires great care and sensitivity in a land of Confucian family structure. Koreans have a passion for work and self-improvement and are respected for their disciplined determination and entrepreneurship.

And to the north, a ruthless regime abuses 23 million inhabitants, denying them freedom and food, while undermining international relations. In this failed state, with the worst human rights record in the world, one in 40 spend time in a *gulag*, one in 20 are in the military;, famine stalks and malnutrition spreads. Mobile phones and the Internet are forbidden, and refugees flee to China or South Korea. The dictator, Kim Jong II, pushed toward a global showdown over his nuclear weapons program until economic deterioration forced him to dismantle his atomic bomb facilities in exchange for outside aid (Exhibit 12.10).

## Cultural Guidelines for Business in South Korea[a]

The business environment in this country is slowly changing from some of what is described below. However, given the large number of Koreans living or working abroad, especially in the United States, this information should prove useful in cross-cultural communication with such expatriates.

---

[a]The authors are grateful for the insights in this section provided by Dr. Paul S. Crane's *Korean Patterns*, published by the Royal Asiatic Society in 1974.

In the twenty-first century, the international community has been concerned about North Korea's ability to create nuclear power and weapons. Numerous six-party negotiations by America, South Korea, Japan, China, and Russia with this rogue regime ended in discord. Despite promises of food and other aid, Kim Jong II and his militarists resisted, until recently, attempts to coax better behavior. But that is not the only problem neighbors have with this wily and cruel administration, which permits its own population to starve. There are a range of other complaints about its criminal activities, ranging from kidnappings of other nationals and production of fake drugs, to money counterfeiting and laundering, to illegal trade in endangered species, missiles, and other weapons. This racketeering state, responsible for tons of illicit goods and fake currency throughout Asia, has seen its diplomats expelled from a variety of countries. The United States slapped sanctions on North Korea for illicit weapons proliferation. Up to 40% of the state's exports result from its criminal sector, earning up to $1 billion in ill-gotten gains. Meanwhile, South Korea has quietly negotiated with northern officials to provide material assistance, while lessening restrictions on the exchange of citizens throughout the peninsula. For a protein society in flux, harsh realities force northerners toward improvisation in order to survive, while some elites even manage to thrive despite government mismanagement.

But South Korea is ill prepared for the collapse of its northern neighbor, and eventual integration of the two Koreas will challenge the South to provide huge resources to the North. Further, their compatriots from the North will face severe culture shock when they try to acculturate to the modern world. A positive development is that the DMZ has become a wilderness zone with flower and fauna that the Peace Forum wants to keep undeveloped as a "Peace Park."

*Source*: Adapted from "Asia—North Korea and Those Six-party Talks: A Frustrating Game of Carrots and Sticks," *The Economist*, February 11, 2006, pp. 39-40. Dominic Ziegler's "The Odd Couple: A Special Report on the Koreas," September 28, 2008, 19-page insert.

## Cultural Characteristics

If one were seeking a national characteristic for these people, choose *resiliency* to describe their ability to survive hardship and to sacrifice. A vital concept to understand in Korea is *kibun*, which is one of the most important factors influencing the conduct and the relationship with others. The word literally means *inner feelings*. If one's *kibun* is good, then one functions smoothly and with ease. If one's *kibun* is upset or bad, then things may come to a complete halt, and one feels depressed. The word has no true English equivalent, but "mood" is close. In interpersonal relationships, keeping the *kibun* in good order often takes precedence over all other considerations.

In business situations, individuals try to operate in a manner that will enhance the *kibun* of both persons. To damage the *kibun* may effectively cut off relationships and create an enemy. One does not tend to do business with a person who has damaged one's *kibun*. Much of the disturbance of *kibun* in interpersonal relationships has to do with lower class persons disturbing higher class persons. Thus, for example, a teacher can scold a student in the class and no individual feels hurt, so no one's *kibun* is especially disturbed.

Proper interpersonal relationships are all important among Koreans, and there is little concept of equality in relationships. Relationships tend to be vertical rather than horizontal, and each person is in a relatively higher or lower position. It is essential for one to know the levels of society and to know one's place in the scheme of things. In relationships, it is often necessary to appear to lower oneself in selfless humility and give honor to other people. To put oneself forward is considered arrogance and worthy of scorn.

Confucianism's emphasis on hierarchy has also influenced relationships. Confucian thought is that one should rank the public higher than the private; one's business or government duties come before one's personal consideration. Protocol is also important to Koreans. When meeting others, if you do not appreciate a person's actual position and give it due recognition, then one might as well withdraw on some pretext and try to avoid future contacts. A representative of another person or group at a meeting is treated with great care because the substitute may be sensitive to slights, either real or imagined, and report it back to his or her colleagues. This is very difficult for Westerners to understand, but a Korean who fails to observe the basic rules of social exchange is considered by other Koreans to not even be a person—he or she is an "unperson" or "unable." Koreans show very little concern for an unperson's feelings or comfort; thus, such an unperson is not worthy of much consideration; however, every effort must be made to remain within the framework of polite relation

## Religion and Spirituality

The underlying ethic of Korea is Shamanism, but the people have also been strongly influenced by Buddhism and Confucianism. Shamanism, the religion of ancient Koreans, venerates the spirit and ancestors, and considers elements of earth, mountains, rivers, etc., as sacred. Buddhism was introduced in Korea in the fourth century and has the longest history among the organized religions in Korea—27% identify themselves as Buddhists. Confucianism also has been a strong force and the reason behind this people's appreciation of knowledge and education. The most influential of the newer native Korean religions is *Ch-ondo-gyo*, which was founded in the mid-nineteenth century on the belief that every person represents heaven.

Koreans are proud that Christianity was not introduced there by missionaries. Instead, in 1777, a Korean scholar in Peking had himself baptized as Catholic and introduced his new religion to his homeland. Protestantism gained a foothold in 1984 via a Korean doctor who became a royal physician diplomatic and spread this religious version. Today, Christianity has the second largest constituency (about 24%), of which the majority adhere to Protestant denominations.

Be aware that fortunetellers are consulted by Koreans in all walks of life. Called a *mudang*, even executives resort to their forecasts, and a bad report may undermine a business undertaking.

## Deference and Respect for Elders

Elders in Korean society are always honored, respected, pampered, and appeased. To engender the anger of an elder means serious damage, because age allows an older person to influence the opinions of others, regardless of the right or wrong of the situation. Like children, elders must be given special delicacies at meals, and their every wish and desire is catered to whenever possible. The custom and manner in which elderly people are sometimes sent to elder-care facilities in the United States is extremely barbarous and shocking to the Koreans. Every home in Korea, no matter how poor, allocates the best room in the house to the honored grandfather or grandmother.

## Etiquette

Koreans are considered by others to be among the most naturally polite people in the world when the proper rules of etiquette are followed. In personal relationships with strangers or associates, Koreans avoid touching another person physically. This is considered an affront to his or her person, unless there is a well-established bond of close friendship or childhood ties.

In modern Korean society, many businesspersons now shake hands. However, they will very often bow at the same time that they shake a person's hand. To slap someone on the back or to put one's arms around a casual acquaintance or to be too familiar with someone in public is a serious breach that may effectively cool future relations.

To embarrass someone by making a joke at his or her expense is highly resented, even if done by a foreigner who does not understand the customs. After a few drinks, businessmen often become very affectionate, but at the same time apologize for being a bit drunk. The next day they will tell their colleagues that they are sorry for imposing on one's good nature while being a little tipsy.

When appearing in public to speak, one bows first toward the audience and then toward the chairman of the meeting. Businesspeople should learn the proper bowing procedures and etiquette expected here. Korean businesspersons do not seem to worry about keeping time, being on time, beginning on time, or leaving on time to the same extent that Western businesspersons do. However, this is changing now, and there is more of a tendency to follow the same time schedule as in the West.

## Introductions

Traditionally, it is not the custom among the Koreans to introduce one person to another. Instead, one would say to another, "I have never seen you before" or "I am seeing you for the first time." The other person repeats the same thing, and then usually the elder of the two persons in age or rank says, "Let us introduce ourselves." Each person then steps back a little, bows from the waist, states his or her own name, or the elder initiates a handshake. They are then formally introduced. Names are stated in a low, humble voice, and then calling cards are exchanged. One may learn the new person's name and position at leisure. Do not say, "Sorry, I did not get your name. Would you tell me again?" Business cards are very necessary in Korea and should be used by foreign or Western businesspeople at all times, beginning with the first visit.

The use of names in Korea has an entirely different connotation than in most Western cultures. To the Confucian, using a name is presumptuous and impolite, as a name is something to be honored and respected, and it should not be used casually. In Shamanism, to write a name calls up the spirit world and is considered bad luck. One's name, whether it is written or spoken, has its own special meaning and is that person's personal property. To call someone directly by his name is an affront in most social circumstances.

In Korea there are approximately 300 surnames, but more than half are Kims, Lees, and Parks. When a Western businessperson uses a Korean's name to his face, one can usually observe a slight wince around the eyes of the Korean. It is almost always there. A Korean is addressed by his title, position, trade, profession, or some other honorific title such as teacher. As opposed to our U.S. training of saying, "Good morning, Mr. Kim," a polite "Good morning" is better or "Good morning, teacher" is acceptable. Many Koreans live next to each other for years without even knowing their full names. A Korean's name is usually made up of three characters—the family's surname is placed first, and then the given name, which is made up of one character. It is used by all members of the same generation. By knowing this name, a person's generation in the family tree can be recognized.

## Privacy and Propriety

South Korea has one of the most densely populated, crowded nations on earth, so personal space is limited. On the street, this may result in standing or sitting close together, unintentional bumping into one another, or treading on another's foot without apology. Privacy is a luxury that few can afford in Korea, so the people have learned to make imaginary walls about themselves. A visitor calling on a hot day may find this person with his feet on the desk, fanning himself. The visitor coughs to announce his arrival, but he does not knock. This person does not "see" the person he has come to visit, nor does this individual "see" the visitor until he has risen. Then they "see" each other and begin the formality of greeting. To have privacy, a Korean withdraws behind an imaginary curtain, or does what he or she has to do, not seeing or being seen by those who, by the literal Western eye, are in plain view. It is considered discourteous to violate this screen of privacy once it is drawn about a person. A discreet cough is intended to notify the person behind the screen that an interruption is impending.

Table manners are based on making the guest feel comfortable. The attitude of a servant is proper for a host with his guest. Traditionally, at meals, the hostess is at the lowest place, the farthest from the place of honor, and often will not even eat in the presence of a guest. Before beginning to eat, the host will often make a formal welcome speech, stating the purpose of the gathering and paying his respects to his guest. Often, food is served on small individual tables, each with many side dishes of food, a bowl of soup, and a bowl of rice. Korean food tends to be highly seasoned with red pepper, thus a careful sip of the soups is advisable before taking a large mouthful. To lay the chopsticks or spoon on the table is to indicate that you have finished eating. To put them on top of a dish or bowl means that you are merely resting. A guest may show his appreciation for the meal by slurping soup or smacking one's lips. The host will continue to urge his guest to eat more, but a courteous refusal can be accepted. A good healthy belch after a meal is a sign that one has eaten well and enjoyed it.

Avoid writing or printing a Korean's name in red ink—this is the color that Buddhist reserve to announce death or its anniversary.

## Gift Giving

Koreans give gifts on many occasions, and the appropriate etiquette surrounding the giving of gifts is often a problem to Western business-people. In this context, every gift expects something in return, and one rarely gives an expensive gift without a purpose. The purpose may be to establish an obligation, to gain a certain advantage, or merely to create an atmosphere in which the recipient will be more pliable to the request of the donor. To return a gift is considered an affront, but in some instances, it may be better to return the gift than to accept it with no intention of doing a favor in return. Some Koreans have a special ability to work their way into the affection of foreigners and form personal relationships that may later prove embarrassing and/or difficult to handle when some impossible or very often illegal and unlawful request is made. In Korean, "yes" may merely mean "I heard you," and not agreement or intention of complying. To say "no" is an affront and could hurt the feelings, and thus is poor etiquette. Many Koreans often say "yes" to each other and to foreigners, and then go their own way doing quite the opposite with little sense of breaking a promise or agreement.

## Business Attitudes

In business, praise is a way of life, and without subtle praise, business would come to a halt. One must begin on the periphery in business relationships and gradually zero in on the main business in narrowing circles. To directly begin a discussion of some delicate business matter or new business venture is considered by Koreans to be the height of stupidity and dooms the project to almost certain failure. Impatience to a Korean is a major fault. A highly skilled businessperson moves with deliberation, dignity, and studied motions, and senses the impressions and nuances being sent by the other businesspeople.

To Korean businessmen, Western businesspersons often appear to make contracts on the assumptions that all the factors will remain inventively the same. In Korea, a written contract is becoming as important as in the West. A change in the economy, the political situation, or personal reasons of one of the contractors may invalidate the completion of the contract without any sense of misdeed. To navigate business here, an outsider needs a Korean intermediary, as well as the help of the chamber of commerce and embassy.

The economy and corporate structure here is still dominated by *chaebols*, or large business conglomerates, which are closely related to the government. Some of these entities are family owned and managed, and employees tend to stay a long time with one employer. *Chaebols'* dominance is under challenge, for these big corporations have been accused of keeping wages low, sending jobs overseas, and suffocating the myriad small and middle-sized enterprises.

In the twenty-first century, their emphasis is upon design as a driver of economic growth and social progress. Seoul has been called "The World Design Capital," and is redeveloping its old Yongsan district into a "Dream Hub" for international business, along with a "Digital Media City" in Jamsil, a complex for information technology innovations.

Korea is a male-oriented society, and a man rules at work and at home. The "boss" is all important in this hierarchical culture, and all is deferred to him. The "supervisor" is therefore treated with much respect. This trait is reflected in eye contact—persons of lower rank will avert his or her eyes during conversation with a higher ranking individual. Foreigners should avoid eye contact with Koreans, for this is often associated with anger or aggression. Korean managers are also very territorial about their desks—visitors never would put information or sales literature on that desk, but give it to a lower intermediary for transfer upward. Korean society accepts centralized control, and makes a clear distinction between the ruler and subordinates.

Gradually, educated women are moving into middle management within business. Family household, financial, and child management are the female's responsibility. In public, this gender may appear quiet and submissive, but behind the scenes, women may exert great power. Public displays of her power or affection are unacceptable.

Because there are similarities between Korean and other Asian cultures, cross-cultural skills that are effective in this society have application elsewhere. For example, there is a large minority population of Koreans in Los Angeles, and their native language is the third largest spoken in that California city. In many ways, Korean is also a synergistic culture, except for the political division of the peninsula. Fortunately, North and South Korea have begun a positive dialogue to permit further exchanges among the divided families; this may eventually lead to improvement in their political and economic relationships.

# VIETNAM

Vietnam is located in Southeast Asia, bordered by Laos and Cambodia to the west, China to the north, and the South China Sea to the east and south. It lies on the eastern side of Indonesian peninsula of the Gulf of Thailand. The land mass is 331,688 square kilometers (128,065 square miles)—this long, narrow country has a coastline of over 2000 miles, plus sovereignty over numerous islands. Divided into three main geographical regions, the north is mountainous with its Red River Delta, central highlands in the center, the coastal highlands and Mekong River Delta in the south. The capital of Hanoi is located in the north, while its commercial center, Ho Chi Minh City (old Saigon), is in the south. The climate is humid in both the summer and winter seasons, with temperatures in Hanoi ranging between 13°C (55 °F) and 33 °C (91 °F). Monsoon rains are present throughout the year, contributing to the average rainfall of 60-80 inches.

## Historical Perspective[15]

The earliest known inhabitants of this land lived in the north some 500,000 years ago. In the thirteenth century B.C., Bronze Age Don Son culture appeared, and the descendents of modern Vietnamese can be traced to Red River Delta settlers, 500-200 B.C. Always a crossroads for migrants, these ancestors were a mix of Australoid, Austronesian, and Mongoloid people. For over a thousand years from 111 B.C. to 939 A.D., Vietnam was ruled by China as a province called Giao Chia. Even after throwing out the Chinese, inhabitants had to resist numerous Chinese attacks, so allied themselves with their neighbors with whom they maintained close political and military ties. As the population expanded southward, Vietnam came into conflict with a number of ruling dynasties from Cambodia and India. From the first to sixth century A.D., the southern part was under the control of Hindu kingdom of Funan, which influenced art and architecture, as well as religious beliefs. However, the people succeeded in overthrowing the Hindu Kingdom, Khmer empire, and Le dynasty. While the first Europeans landed here in 166 A.D., it was not until 1516 that their influence became significant with the arrival of the Portuguese. By 1630, Spanish missionaries from the Philippines had perfected a romanized system for writing the Vietnamese language. In 1637, the Dutch were among the many traders coming there from abroad.

By the eighteenth century, the ruling Vietnamese families were beset by a number of peasant rebellions for better distribution of wealth from rich to poor. Meanwhile, French missionaries in the north were lobbying their own government for greater political and military presence in Vietnam. A combination of Vietnam and French forces defeated the Tay Son rebels, and the Nguyen dynasty took over the whole country in 1802, becoming the first to rule Vietnam until 1945. But back in 1867, France had brought Vietnam directly under its rule, dividing the country into three parts—forming protectorates in Tonkin and Annam in the North, the Central area of Vietnam, and then directly administering "Cochinchina" in the South. Thus, the French dominated Vietnam until World War II, when the Japanese occupied parts of the country. After Japan was defeated, the Allies divided the country into two parts: the North and the South. France gained power in the South, while China chose a new emperor in the North, Boa Dai, who stepped down in favor of Ho Chi Minh, founder of Vietnam's Communist Party. By September 2, 1945, this astute and powerful leader proclaimed the independence of the Provisional Democratic Republic of Vietnam (DRV). Then this political and military genius proceeded to lead an invasion of the French-ruled South, ultimately winning this war in 1954 with the defeat of the French at Dien Bien Phu.

After terms for an agreement were signed in Geneva in 1954, Ngo Dinh Diem became the prime minister of the South, and, following a referendum in 1955, he proclaimed himself president of the Republic of Vietnam. He refused to hold 1956 elections under the new peace agreement. Therefore, the North approved a strategy for the communist-based National Liberation Front (NLF) to oppose Diem and move to control South Vietnam. This prompted the United States to expand military support for Diem and his government in 1961. The struggle turned into an American war following an incident involving U.S. warships. American troops and supplies were sent in to fight against the Viet

Cong guerrillas (Southern communists fighting the South Vietnamese government) and North Vietnamese troops (Viet Minh). The war spread to Laos and Cambodia, and eventually to North Vietnam itself. The Americans increased troop deployment to 500,000, bombing extensively areas held by the Viet Cong. When the Communists launched the Tet offensive in 1968, U.S. public opinion diminished support for war that could not be won. Peace talks in January 1973 included a ceasefire in the South, the withdrawal of U.S. forces by the beginning of 1975. In that year, the peaceful reunification of Vietnam began when the PRG (Provisional Revolutionary Government formed by the NLF in the South), combined with North Vietnamese troops, attacked the South, ultimately leading to the fall of Saigon in April.

Effective control of Vietnam was placed in the hands of Hanoi, which renamed the city of Saigon to Ho Chi Minh City in 1976. In an attempt to neutralize opposition, thousands of officials were summoned to "reeducation" camps. All three Indochinese countries, Vietnam, Laos, and Cambodia, came under the communist governance. Thousands of families fled these countries at that time, becoming refugees in numerous countries, including North America. In 1976, the reunited country's name was changed to the Socialist Republic of Vietnam, while the ruling party adopted the designation of Communist Party of Vietnam (CPV). The United States refused to acknowledge the new government and severed all diplomatic relations. After the war, troops under Cambodia's Pol Pot government attacked Southern Vietnam. This led to an all-out Vietnamese invasion of Cambodia in December 1978, installing a new government loyal to Hanoi. In the same period, the Chinese launched an unsuccessful attack against the Vietnamese and ultimately withdrew from Vietnam.[b]

Since then, Vietnam has focused on internal matters. In 1986, Nguyen Van Linh, Communist Party General Secretary, introduced the concept of *doi moi*, or renovation. This term includes private enterprise and the approval of 100% foreign ownership of firms and joint ventures, openness to overseas Vietnamese, an interest in tourism, and greater individual freedoms. It took 3 years, however, for the South to start implementing these reforms, along with the withdrawal of Vietnamese troops from Cambodia in 1989. Since then, the government has been fully committed to the idea of *doi moi*, as is evidenced by new investors from Japan, Taiwan, Hong Kong, and Australia. These countries already know they would not have to wait long for the emerging, thriving Vietnamese economy. Australia has targeted Vietnam as its "Asian Business Success Program," while billboards with ads for Minolta and Hitachi dominate intersections in Hanoi and Ho Chi Minh City. For the rest of the non-Asian countries who did not jump at the early opportunities, competition will be even stiffer now.

---

[b]The authors acknowledge the research performed in the above section by Laurel Cool when she was a graduate student at The Thunderbird Graduate School of International Management.

It was also the 1989 peace treaty with Cambodia that opened up diplomatic talks with the United States and the countries of Western Europe. In fact, the treaty was the turning point for Vietnam. Within months, diplomatic ties had been fully reestablished with China and the above-mentioned countries. Washington opened a diplomatic office in Hanoi in 1991 to coordinate the search for American MIAs (soldiers missing in action). After cooperation from the Vietnamese in this search, the United States lifted some economic sanctions in 1992 and 1993. President Clinton then lifted the trade and investment embargo in February 1994, and since then the United States has established itself as a significant investor in Vietnam. The Vietnamese people heralded the removal of the trade embargo as the end of the "American War," rejoicing in total independence from foreign invaders for the first time in centuries.

The year 2000 was significant for Vietnam, as it marked 55 years of independence and 25 years since the end of the Vietnam War. The main changes now are more openness than before; founding of the first stock exchange center in Ho Chi Minh City; membership in the World Trade Organization; and reduction of the poverty level to below 10%. Under the administration of technocrats, a top priority of Vietnam is to fix the corruption that has been widespread in government. Inventory in coal, cement, steel, and paper has increased due to foreign competition. Near the end of 2001, the United States-Vietnam Bilateral Trade Agreement was launched in an effort to increase Vietnam's exports. Currently, Japan receives about 18% of Vietnam's exports, while the United States receives some 8%.

## Cultural Guidelines for Business in Vietnam

Vietnam has a population of 81 million, of which 87% are ethnic Vietnamese. The largest minority group is Chinese. There are also approximately fifty small ethnic groups who live primarily in the mountain areas. Since independence in 1945, Vietnam gradually began to use Vietnamese, which is the official language today and is taught in schools. However, there exist distinct northern, central, and southern dialects. Furthermore, many minority groups speak their own language at home. The most popular foreign languages to study include English, Russian, and French. Most government officials understand some English.

## Sociopolitical-Economic Context

Although the new constitution adopted on April 15, 1992, confirmed the omnipotence of the Communist Party, the spirit and practice of free enterprise expands rapidly. The National Assembly, consisting of 400 members and elected to 5-year terms by universal adult suffrage, holds all legislative powers. The president, elected by the Ninth

National Assembly, is also the head of state and commander-in-chief of the armed forces. The president then appoints a prime minister with the approval of the National Assembly, who in turn forms a government consisting of a vice president and a council of ministers. The National Assembly must approve all appointments. The country is divided into provinces, which are under tight control of the central government. On a local level, citizens are elected to a People's Council, which runs the local government.

The Vietnamese economy is based on the agriculture, forestry, and fishing industries, which employ 73% of the workforce and account for 60% of all exports. The agricultural sector consists of a staple crop of rice, which provides about 15% of export earnings, as well as other cash crops of rubber, coffee, tea, cotton, and soybeans. A ban was imposed on logs and timber in 1992, in order to preserve the heavily depleted forests. Fishing is also very important; seafood, including shrimp, crabs, and cuttle fish, is exported along with petroleum and coal. Vietnam's principle trading partner is Singapore; others include France, Germany, Japan, and Hong Kong.

Education, which is free to all, begins at age 6 and continues to age 18. University education is also free, but there is tough competition for admittance. The literacy rate is 94%, and approximately 10% of the nation's budget is spent on education. The state operates a system of social security, in which health care is provided to everyone, free of cost. However, in 1991, there was only one practicing doctor for 3140 inhabitants, and facilities are often inadequate, especially in rural areas.

The Vietnamese have lived 1000 years under Chinese domination; French colonialism from 1867 to 1954; a civil war ensued for 30 years, which included the war against the United States. This has left the Vietnamese people with a strong sense of national pride. They are more future oriented than past oriented. Because the *American War* was relatively short compared to Vietnam's past, and since two wars have been fought thereafter against China and Cambodia, the Vietnamese today do not harbor animosity toward Americans. They view that conflict already as past history, and are very curious toward all Americans, anxious to conduct business and tourism with their former enemy.

Great social and economic change is taking place now in Vietnam, and with it are the struggles to get ahead. People in the urban areas are generally happy, due to improved basic services, and a more open political and cultural environment. However, people in the rural areas, who constitute 75% of the Vietnamese population, are currently very unhappy and frustrated. This malaise is due to a dearth of cultural opportunities, lack of electricity and other basic services, and neglect of the poor. Party officials still take advantage of the peasants, who do not hold much weight in voting matters. For Vietnam to obtain prosperity, the inequalities that exist between urban and rural citizens must disappear.

## Customs and Courtesies

In Vietnam, people shake hands when greeting and saying goodbye to someone. Also common is the use of both hands, which indicates respect. A slight bow of the head also shows respect. Elderly people in rural areas may also nod their head upon greeting someone, and women are more inclined to bow their head than to shake hands.

Here, names begin with the family name followed by the given name. For example, in the name Nguyen Van Duc, Nguyen is the family name and Van Duc is the given name. Although they address each other by given name, the Vietnamese add titles, which show their relationship to the other person. These titles tend to be used more personally, in one's family, than professionally. Among coworkers, the younger of the two might call the other *ahn*, or older brother. To say hello to someone using the given name and title, they would say "Xin chao," or hello. However, "Xin chao" could have one of six other meanings, since Vietnamese is a tonal language. Therefore, it is important to stress the proper syllable. International visitors who can properly say "Xin chao" are met with delight by the Vietnamese. In business settings, business cards may be exchanged in greetings and should be in both Vietnamese and English.

The following gestures should be noted when in the company of the Vietnamese:

- Do not touch the head of a young child, as it is considered a sensitive spiritual point.
- Do not use your index finger to call someone over; it is considered rude.
- When calling someone, wave all four fingers with the palm down.
- Men and women do not show affection in public.
- Members of the same sex may hold hands in public. This is normal.
- Vietnamese use both hands to give an object to another person.

The Vietnamese place a great deal of importance on visiting people. Therefore, one should not just "drop by" someone's house without first being invited. They also show a strong sense of hospitality and prepare well in advance of the guest's arrival. Gifts for the hostess are not required but greatly appreciated. A small gift for the children or elderly parent is also much appreciated. Acceptable gifts include flowers, tea, or incense.

The traditional Vietnamese family is an extended one, including parents, unmarried children, and married sons with their families. The extended family still predominates in rural regions; however, there is a trend toward singly-family homes in urban locations. Families maintain strong ties with each other and provide financial and emotional support as needed.

As the world's thirteenth largest country, the government has shown a strong interest in becoming a market economy and opening itself to outsiders. Furthermore, with the reestablishment of diplomatic relations with the United States and other major economic players, business opportunities have increased dramatically over the past years. Those companies who take advantage of conducting business in Vietnam now will be rewarded with a high-growth market of consumers that is estimated to reach 600 million by 2010 (Exhibit 12.11).

---

## EXHIBIT 12.11

## TRANSFORMING VIETNAM

Today, Vietnamese welcome the tourist dollar, even for excursions to their war-time Cu Chi tunnels. Such excursions demonstrate their ingenuity, adaptability, perseverance, and determination to resist foreign invaders down through the centuries.

The past two decades have transformed Vietnam by rapid and equitable development in a free-enterprise environment. You can see this in vibrant Ho Chi Minh City, especially downtown at the smart Dong Khoi Street where young, prosperous, confident Vietnamese shop. In what was a poor country, the quality of life has dramatically improved, despite choking traffic and constant construction work. With a switch from a command economy, gradual financial liberalization and market reforms have been fostering rapid poverty-reducing growth. Multinational aid and investment of $5.4 billion in 2008 have pushed annual economic growth to 7.5%. The country is still handicapped by legislative and bureaucratic processes, especially with regard to the justice system and countering Communist Party corruption. Other problems to be confronted are rising inflation, slumping stock market, need for greater trade, and political liberalization, as well as improvement of corporate governance.

A positive aspect of Vietnamese culture is its flexibility to seek better role models, which are melded then into something uniquely their own. Vietnam is active in Asia-Pacific Summit, World Trade Organization, and ASEAN, all of which provide insights for social and economic change. This is a syncretistic society with increasing entrepreneurs and booming business. Further, foreign multinations have been permitted to undertake a huge range of projects throughout the land. Refugees who left as boat people are either returning or sending back funds for their families or investments. Nothing reveals Vietnam's remarkable turnaround than agriculture—the countryside with 70% of the people now provides 21% in exports. But climate change could endanger this progress down on the farms. The Party with 3.7 million members has a congress policy "to be friends with all people." And this has contributed to a rise in tourism, along with a lessening of restrictions against religious groups

EXHIBIT 12.11

TRANSFORMING VIETNAM (CONTINUED)

and ethnic minorities. With the selling of public assets to private enterprise, the state becomes less important as employer and provider, while the Party also matters less. As Vietnam continues to open its economy to business and strive to meet the UN Millennium Development goals in poverty reduction, its youthful population becomes the most optimistic in Asia.

*Source*: Adapted from Peter Collins, "Half-way from Rages to Riches—A Special Report on Vietnam," *The Economist*, April 25, 2008 (www.economist.com/specialreport).

## CONCLUSIONS

Asia is a demonstration model of the complexity and multidimensional aspects of culture. Although we have provided cultural specifics on only a dozen countries, perhaps it is enough to convince global managers of the important distinctions that exist between the people of this region and Westerners in critical matters like physical appearance, language, religion, family, social attitudes, and other assumptions that influence business practice and relationships. The new market opportunities and diversity in the Pacific Basin alone should motivate us to seek further cultural information, whether we are dealing with Australians who are seemingly similar, or with Vietnamese who are so obviously different.

The social situation in Asia is normally peaceful, but also very dynamic, often volatile. Traditional societies are in transition to a technological and knowledge culture. Unfortunately, Asia, like the world, is now being threatened by global terrorism and insurgencies, some of which is coming from the Middle East and Islamic extremists. However, in these ancient lands and cultures, peaceful exchange and trade have always been the way to promote well-being, commerce, and prosperity. International trade is already transforming Asian societies, such as in the emerging superpowers of China and India.

The area also benefits from the global cooperation of nations to curb negative behaviors endangering the world community, such as coping with natural disasters, limiting drug trafficking, as well as containing infectious disease, unequal distribution of wealth and opportunity for the planet's inhabitants! Two examples of synergistic relationships in this region are South Asian Free Trade Alliance and the Asian Development Bank. Their leaders are in agreement that by 2020, the "new Asia," as well as their own organizations, will need radically different strategies with a global focus.

# REFERENCES

1. For all Asian countries, see Metcalf, J. *Essential Atlas of the World*, Sixth edition, London, UK: DK Publishing, 2008; Long, S. "The Tiger in Front—A Survey of India and China," *The Economist*, March 2, 2005, p. 16. www.economist.com/surveys. For historical perspective from 500 to 1500 A.D., we recommend Stewart Gordon's *When Asia Was the World,* published in 2007 by Da Capo. Shambaugh, D. (ed.). *Power Shifts—China and Asia's New Dynamics*. Berkeley, CA: University of California Press, 2005; Mahbubuni, K. *The New Asian Hemisphere—The Irresistible Shift of Global Power to the East*. New York: Public Affairs/Perseus Books, 2008; Pempel, T. J. *Remapping East Asia: The Construction of a Region*. Ithaca, NY: Cornell University Press, 2005.

2. Smambaugh, D. (ed.). *Power Shifts—China and Asia's New Dynamics*. Berkeley, CA: University of California Press, 2005; Kleveman, L. *The New Great Game: Blood and Oil in Central Asia*. New York: Atlantic Monthly Press, 2003; Ringmar, E. *The Mechanics of Modernity in Europe and East Asia: The Institutional Origins of Social Change and Stagnation*. London, UK: Routledge, 2004; Covington, R. "Hearts of the New Silk Road," *Saudi Aramco World*, January-February 2008, pp. 18–33.

3. Matlock, J. W. "Chinese Checkers," *The New York Times Book Review*, September 13, 1998.

4. Gifford, R. *China Road: A Journey into the Future of a Rising Power*. New York, NY: Random House, 2008; Shenkar, O. *The Chinese Century: The Rising Chinese Economy and Its Impact on the Global Economy, the Balance of Power, and Your Job*. Philadelphia, PA: Wharton School Publishing, 2005; Bell, D. *Beyond Liberal Democracy: Political Thinking for an East Asian Context*. Princeton, NJ: Princeton University Press, 2006; Ringmar, E. *The Mechanics of Modernity in Europe and East Asia*.

London, UK: Routledge, 2004; Menkhoff, T. *Chinese Entrepreneurship and Asian Business Networks*. London, UK: Routledge, 2002.

5. Fishman, T. C. *China Inc.: How the Rise of the Next Superpower Challenges America and the World*. New York, NY: Scribner/Simon & Shuster, 2005; McGregor, J. *One Billion Customers: Lessons from the Front Lines of Doing Business in China*. New York, NY: Free Press, 2005; Zinzius, B. *Doing Business in China—A Handbook and Guide*. New York, NY: Praeger, 2004.

6. Tang, J. and Ward, A. *The Changing Face of Chinese Management*. London: Routledge, 2003; Ghosal, A. "Some Implications of China Joining the WTO," *InSight*, 2003, Vol. 3, No. 1; Engardio, O. 2003, www.businessweek.com/go/china-india; Ziegler, D. "Reaching for the Renaissance—Special Report on China," *The Economist*, March 13, 2007, www.economist.com/specialreports; Darling, A. M. and Gladney, D. C. "China's Nu Ahong," *Saudi Aramco World*, July–August, 2008, pp. 24–33.

7. Adapted with permission from Robert T. Moran's *Venturing Abroad in Asia*, London: McGraw-Hill, 1988; For Hindu culture anywhere, see Knapp, S. *Proof of Vedic Culture's Global Experience*. Detroit, MI: The World Relief Network, 2000.

8. Panagariya, A. *India: The Emerging Giant*. Oxford, UK: Oxford University Press, 2008; Luce, E. *In Spite of the Gods: The Rise of Modern India*. New York, NY: Doubleday Broadway/Random House, 2008; Grihault, N. *India—Culture Smart: Quick Guide to Etiquette and Customs*. London, UK: Kuperard. 2006; Singh, S., Bindloss, J., Wlodarski, R., and Kavalin, A. *India Country Guide*. New York, NY: Lonely Planet, www.lonelyplanet.com; Long, S. "The Tiger in Front—A Survey of India and China," *The Economist*, March 5, 2005, www.economist.com/surveys; *Business Week*, a collection of pertinent articles by multiple authors on "China & India," April 22/29, 2005, www.businessweek.com/go/china-india; Davies, P. *What's this India Business? Offshoring, Outsourcing, and the Global Services Revolution*. Boston, MA: Nicholas Brealey/Intercultural Press, 2004.

9. Wibbeke, E. S. *Global Business Leadership*. Burlington, MA: Elsevier/Butterworth-Heinemann, 2009; pp. 55–71, www.elsevierdirect/alerts; Moran, R. T. and Youngdahl, W. E. *Leading Global Projects—For Professional and Accidental Project Leaders*. Burlington, MA: Elsevier/Butterworth-Heinemann, 2008.

10. Standage, T. "Going Hybrid: A Special Report on Japan," *The Economist*, December 1, 2007, www.economist.com/specialreports; Emmott, W. "The Sun Also Rises—A Survey of Japan," *The Economist*, October 8, 2005, p. 18, www.economist.com/surveys; See also Gordon, A. *A Modern History of Japan*. Oxford, UK: Oxford University Press, 2008; Reiber, B. and Spencer, J. *Frommer's Japan*. Hoboken, NJ: John Wiley, 2008; Matsumoto, D. *The New Japan*. Boston, MA: Nicholas Brealey/Intercultural Press, 2002; Hall, E. T. and Hall, M. R. *Hidden Differences—Doing Business with the Japanese*. Garden City, NJ: Anchor/Doubleday, 1987.

11. De Kavanagh Boulger, D. E. *Central Asian Questions: Essays on Afghanistan, China, and Central Asia*. London, UK: Adamant Media Corp./Elibron Classic Series, 2005; Evans, M. *Afghanistan: A Short*

*History of its People and Politics.* New York, NY: Harper Collins, 2002; Chayes, S. *The Punishment of Virtue: Inside Afghanistan after the Taliban.* New York, NY: Penguin Books, 2007; Crews, R. T., and Tarzi, A. *The Taliban and the Crisis of Afghanistan.* New York, NY: Amazon Books. Hiebert, A. *Afghanistan: Hidden Treasures.* New York, NY: Amazon Books, 2008; Sageman, M. *Leaderless Jihad: Terrorist Networks in the Twenty-First Century.* Philadelphia, PA: University of Pennsylvania Press, 2008; Lollapally, D. *The Politics of Extremism in South Asia.* Cambridge, UK: Cambridge University Press, 2006; Post, J. *The Mind of the Terrorist.* New York, NY: Palgrave Macmillan, 2007.

12. Jaffrelot, C. (ed.). *A History of Pakistan and Its Origins.* London, UK: Anthem Press, 2004; Hussain, H. Z. *Frontline Pakistan: The Struggle with Militant Islam.* New York, NY: Columbia University Press, 2008; Riedal, B. *The Search for Al Qaeda: Its Leadership, Ideology, and Future.* Washington, DC: Brookings Institution Press, 2008; Cohen, S. P. *The Idea of Pakistan.* Washington, DC: Brookings Institution Press, 2006; Rushid, A. *A Descent into Chaos—The United States and the Failure of Nation Building.* New York, NY: Viking Penguin, 2008.

13. DeMarga, A., Blair, E. H., and Robertson, J. A. *History of the Philippines Islands.* New York, NY: BiblioBazaar, 2 Vols., 2006; Roces, A. and Roces, G. *Culture Shock! Philippines: A Survival Guide to Customs & Etiquette.* New York, NY, 2006, Amazon.com; "Staying Ahead in the Philippines," *The Economist,* November 16, 1996, pp. 18/33.

14. Ziegler, D. "The Odd Couple—A Special Report on the Koreas," *The Economist,* September 27, 2008, www.economist.com/specialreports; "Cool Korea," *Business Week,* June 10, 2002; "How Dangerous Is North Korea," *Time,* January 13, 2003; Hoare, J. *Korea—Culture Smart: A Quick Guide to Customs and Etiquette.* London, UK: Kuperard, 2006; Ungoon, G. R., Sters, R. M., and Park, S. *Korean Enterprise: The Quest for Globalization,* Boston, MA: Harvard Business Press, 1997.

15. Collins, P. "Half-way from Rags to Riches—A Special Report on Vietnam," *The Economist,* April 26, 2008, p. 16, www.economist.com/specialreports; Karnow, S. *Vietnam—A History.* New York, NY: Penguin Group, 1997; Ray, N. *Vietnam (Country Guide).* London, UK: Lonely Planet, 2007.

## INTERNET WEB SITES

After http:// and/or www, add: cia.com/ (insert name of a specific country). economist.com/countries/ (insert name of a country, city, surveys, briefing). investaustralia.com. hup.havard.edu. nationalgeographic.com. cambridgeuniversitypress.com.

RECOMMENDED: The National Geographic catalog also lists country packages with music CD, a visual DVD, map, and brochure on various locales in the world (www.ngm.com/catalog). REMEMBER, most Asian nations have diplomatic and tourist offices in your country, as well as Web sites, which will provide further information about their country. Also consider an Internet country search.

# DOING BUSINESS WITH EUROPEANS

## European Union: Principally France, Germany, Great Britain, Greece, Ireland, Italy, Poland, Russia, Spain, and Turkey*

Those fusty old Europeans are engaged in a radical experiment to reinvent themselves—this bid to create a "New Europe" is more than a collection of countries, but less than a unified state. The Maastricht treaty is not yet a teenager, the common currency is barely out of its nappies, a new constitution is being debated, new members have been admitted, and new candidates are under consideration. There is agreement on a united financial recovery strategy, and still talk of a common foreign policy. The Euro is doing better than expected as a means of financial exchange. Now their European Space Agency is planning lunar missions.

*The Economist*, January 22, 2003.

## LEARNING OBJECTIVES

The principal objective of this chapter is to understand some of the cultural complexities and diversities in the European Union members. Specifically, a number of European countries will be examined in some depth, providing historical perspective and cultural guidelines, while combined profiles will be presented for 18 other nations. So as to appreciate the continent's differences and prospects, this treatment is

---

*Cultural profiles of France, Germany, Italy, and Russia are included in the book. Additional country profiles are on the Managing Cultural Differences Web site.

divided into five geographical areas—western, central, northern, south-eastern, and eastern, including Eurasia.

Europe is the world's second smallest continent, bounded to the west by the Atlantic Ocean, to its east by Russia, and to the southeast by Turkey. It ambles from Iceland to Gibraltar—in the north, this landmass is set apart by the Arctic Ocean and in the south by the Mediterranean, Black, and Caspian Seas. Amidst its landmass, peninsulas, and islands, it is home to more than 40 countries. Between two major mountain systems, a rolling, fertile plane stretches from the Pyrenees to the Urals. Herein are located some of the world's greatest urban centers, such as London, Paris, Berlin, and Moscow. Although set in a northern location, thanks to the influence of the Gulf Stream, Europe generally enjoys a mild climate, except for occasional winter and ice storms. The whole region, including the European part of Russia, represents 7% of the Earth's landmass, but is only half the size of North America.

The continent has some 728 million people, three-fourths of whom live in urban areas. Home to multiple ethnic groups, some 230 indigenous languages are spoken (the eight major branches today include Italic, Thracon-Ikkyrian, Uralic, Basque). For millennia, Europeans have been providing humanity with ideas, ideals, and information that have nurtured the world's cultures and societies.

## Historical Perspective[1]

According to the latest scientific research, human migration from Africa to what is known today as Europe likely occurred from 50,000 to 35,000 years ago. For hundreds of thousands years, the Neanderthals had preceded these modern humans, and shared the continent for several thousand years with them before those prehistoric people were replaced. Recently, hominid fossils, a species of our ancestors, were uncovered in the Atapuerca hills of northern Spain; carbon dating indicates that they were living there some 800,000 years ago—these Europeans may be the last common connection to both the Neanderthals and *Homo sapiens*. The wall art and artifacts in caves of northern Spain and southern France confirm the aesthetic sense and tool technology of Stone Age cultures. Migration of pastoralists from Central Asia some 5000 years ago brought the Indo-European language groups into the region. The first known civilization in the area dates back to 2000 B.C. in Crete where Minoans produced an impressive culture, trading with Egypt and Asia Minor. In the eighth century B.C., classical Greeks enriched the world, especially future European civilization, through philosophy, mathematics, natural sciences, political thought, arts, and architecture. This legacy was bequeathed to the Romans who became masters of architecture, engineering, law, and military strategy. Their empire was the first attempt at uniting the continent's peoples, even extending beyond its borders into the Middle East. Although lasting only 500 years, their Latin language, infrastructure, and heritage continue to influence mankind.

As the Roman Empire declined, Christianity, coming out of western Asia, entered Europe and became a binding force in Europe until modern times. Throughout the Middle Ages, monasteries were centers of learning, spirituality, and agriculture. The first major religious split on this continent occurred in the eleventh century; as a result, Roman Catholicism under the popes dominated the west, whereas Orthodox Christianity under the patriarchs reigned in the east. European religious unity was further undermined in the fourteenth and fifteenth centuries with the introduction of Islam by the Ottoman Turks into the Balkans, and later into Spain via North Africa. Both religious and political powers were further fractured by the sixteenth century with the Protestant Reformation. As medieval feudalism diminished, powerful kings and nations arose, especially in Western Europe. In the second millennium, provincial allegiances gave way to rising nationalism that helped to create modern states, inspiring the concepts of common language, economy, and governance so prevalent now.

By the eighteenth century, modern Europe arose in the aftermath of two revolutions, in the British colonies of the New World and in France. The powers of aristocracy and royalty lessened, while for the next two centuries, nationalism, socialism, and democracy flourished. Since the sixteenth century, European powers sought to colonize America, Africa, and the Middle East, as well as parts of Asia. Beginning in England some 400 years ago, the impact of the Industrial Revolution extended throughout the planet until present times. In the twentieth century, after two world wars and a cold war, Europe was divided into two geopolitical spheres between Western Europe and the East Bloc countries under Soviet control. Business practices varied according to whether the capitalist or socialist system was used. The demise of communism blurred that demarcation, but complicated the situation. Despite their totalitarian conditioning for 70 years or less, nations from Central and Eastern Europe began to seek entry into the free enterprise system established in 1952 as the European Common Market. In this twenty-first century, Europe is a dynamic and exciting place to do business, although it is undergoing profound transition. The winds of economic, social, and political change are sweeping throughout the entire continent. Since 1957, the member nations of the European community (EC), now called *union*, have striven together to improve their standard of living and to foster closer relations among their countries. Their collaboration has facilitated more unified continental activities, while attempting to preserve local cultures and languages.[2]

Thus, Europeans today have a long cultural history, representing a highly diverse mixture of peoples and their governance, making generalizations difficult. Demographically, Europe's population of some 728 million is dropping, and by 2050, that figure may be only 653 million in countries where the populations are aging. Although immigration helps in resolving these problems, many inhabitants resist that solution and the EU efforts toward free movements of people, capital, goods, and services! The next section will provide further context to understand Europe of the future.

## EUROPEAN DIVERSITY AND SYNERGY

Late in the twentieth century, the multinational entities of Europe sought ways to unify their economic efforts through the formation of a European Common Market. As the scope of cooperation increased among the participants (e.g., European Space Agency), the term *EC* came into use. In 1991, member countries signed the Maastricht Treaty, a road map for establishing an economic and monetary union. Renamed the EU, three key institutions were created—a European Council, Commission, and Parliament. By 2002, a common currency called the *euro* was put into circulation and originally adopted by eleven member states (Denmark, Great Britain, Greece, and Sweden have yet to use it officially).[2] The EU spends more than a billion dollars a year to maintain language equality by translating documents into 20 official documents!

These synergistic endeavors toward a EC resulted in formal agreements that allow goods, people, services, information, and capital to move freely among member countries.[3] In 2010, EU membership is expanded to 27 nations. There are three candidate countries who have applied for admission. The original members are Austria, Belgium, Denmark, Finland, France, Germany, Greece, Ireland, Italy, Luxembourg, the Netherlands, Portugal, Spain, Sweden, and the United Kingdom. With the admission of the former group, President Jacques Chirac of France observed, "For nearly 50 years, the heart of our continent was split between democracy and dictatorship in a balance of terror. The fracture that started in Europe spread across the planet."[3] Now, the forces for unity and inclusion on this continent are spreading. Despite Turkey being a member of NATO and a leading EU applicant, it has yet to be officially admitted. Russia has sought membership, and has developed special working relationships with both NATO and the EU. The two latter countries are located in Eurasia, and will be discussed in the last section of this chapter.

Currently, the EU encompasses almost 500 million people, and has an annual GDP of about $14 trillion. Now, the central EU themes are to (1) attain a single market economy of consumers that offers peaceful stability and wealth, as well as political and economic clout; (2) establish European-wide institutions and policies; plus (3) respect, and not fight about differences within this voluntary union. Although Europeans still cherish their diversity, not all is smooth sailing as different and competing visions emerge. The EU's rapid expansion has raised tensions over ethnic, religious, and cultural identity. However, many of the following issues have been solved or are in the process of resolution:

- Technical—differing national standards and regulations, conflicting business laws, and protected public procurements.
- Free flow of goods once they have cleared customs in the EU, as if national boundaries did not exist.
- Free movement of workers, so that citizens of one state may seek employment in another without discrimination relative to type of job, remunerations, or other employment conditions.
- Freedom of establishment, so a citizen or business from one state has the right to locate and conduct business elsewhere in the EU.
- Freedom to provide services to persons throughout the EU.

The efforts toward European integration and standardization have successfully led to greater economic and currency unification, as well as respect for the rule of law. Some of the benefits the new EU policies are intended to accomplish include the following:

- Ensure cost savings by removal of internal border controls.
- Increase competition and consumer demand.
- Facilitate economies of scale in production.
- Foster greater expenditures on combined research and development.
- Promote more efficient use of continental human resources.
- Decrease unemployment.
- Lower prices while increasing economic growth throughout the EU.

To manage the EU and achieve such goals, the European Commission has 27 commissioners appointed by national governments for a 5-year term. With headquarters in Brussels, the EU executives consist of 20,000 officials. Political matters are left to the European Council made up of 27 heads of government; law and budgetary matters are the concern of the Council of Ministers under a 6-month rotating chair under a head of a member state. These are supplemented by a very imperfect European Parliament in Strasbourg of 785 members, and a Council of Justice based in Luxembourg which acts as a supreme court. The EU has a plethora of other agencies to advance its social partnership by the four freedoms of movement for goods, services, labor, and capital.

To take advantage of the single market opportunities, global corporations are establishing EU-based companies, and the Japanese are most prominent in this strategy. Many foreign enterprises are acquiring or merging with European industrial units, increasing the cross-cultural challenges at both the national and corporate levels. In addition to knowing about EU policies and regulations, global managers assigned to Europe will have to be more competitive, as well as better trained and more culturally sensitive. They also must deal with various economies and monetary systems, particularly the euro currency, which is not utilized everywhere. But they face new consumer opportunities, for Europeans increasingly buy beyond national borders, whether it is for insurance policies, bank accounts, mutual funds, or euro bonds.

Europe's efforts toward synergy are not without other problems and challenges because of its very diversity, as the next section demonstrates. In 2000, the EU's Lisbon Agenda sought to promote liberalized reforms, increase R&D spending, and encourage deregulation of labor and product markets across member countries. To transform Europe by 2010, their aim is to turn the EU *into the most competitive and dynamic knowledge-based economy in the world.*

## The European Union Today[3]

In the opening decade of a new millennia, the optimist would declare the EU somewhat a success in achieving many of the above goals, but still is a work in progress. In his book, *Why Europe Will Run the 21st Century,* Mark Leonard argues that the EU is now the world's biggest market, exporter, and foreign investor. This author points out that Europe is now home to many of the largest and most successful companies; some member countries, such as Finland and Ireland, rank at the top of global competitiveness, while new Central Europe members are mainly fast-growing economies. For the past 60 years, Europe has experienced relative peace, except in the Balkans, after rising from economic ruins in 1945. But Gideon Rachman, in his 2004 survey of the EU, cites critics who say that far from promoting peace, prosperity, and freedom, it now threatens these achievements. Many of the unnecessary laws and regulations emanating from EU institutions in Brussels weaken some members' self-government and democracy, while engulfing the European economy. Eurosceptics fear that continuing EU enlargement distracts from the formation of an effective federation by increasing diversity of political interests and views. Further, Europe still lacks a common language, national media, and national identity. Half of the people in EU still speak only their mother tongue. Some contend that further European integration undermines their country's nationalism, for citizens interact mainly with their own governments, not the EU. The recent failure to ratify the proposed constitution deterred the development of a multitiered union.[4]

Yet at its fiftieth anniversary, the EU has emerged at the heart of the continent's economic life, and increasingly impacts social and foreign policy. The candidates for membership, like the Balkan countries, find the benefits of EU membership so attractive that they are even willing to make peace and introduce democratic reforms—Croatia being a case in point. Negotiations are under way to admit Turkey, a large Muslim nation; such memberships would confirm that Islam is not incompatible with Western values. Euronationalists think that there is a distinctive European approach to global needs, such as support for multilateral institutions and antiwar demonstrations. A half-century after its birth, the EU has yet to obtain genuine popular support for "ever-closer union" which contributes to the gradual emergence of a euroculture. What may result is a more diverse EU which allows members and their inhabitants to adopt different levels of integration more attuned to their national preferences. EU expansion has been a tool for stabilizing the continent, creating new markets, and promoting interdependence through free trade and movement. The hope is that its very diversity may stimulate competition between different economic and social models within Europe! With reference to the Muslim impact on Europe, Exhibit 13.1 provides further insights. All this and more is also changing relations with North America.

---

## EXHIBIT 13.1
## INTEGRATING EUROPE'S MUSLIMS

Arabist scholar, Bernard Lewis, forecasts that by the end of this century, Europe would turn Muslim, thereby creating an Arab West. The EU now is coping with twin challenges—acculturating a massive immigrant flow, and Islamofacist extremists (Spain, Great Britain, and France have already suffered the latter's destructive violence). Both Islamic populations and religiosity are growing rapidly throughout the continent and the UK—in some cities, more go to mosques each week than churches. European countries differ on how to manage this new reality. France is strict about the integration of outsiders into their culture, and tends to keep the Muslim migrants in separate poor communities that breed radical youths; the Netherlands and Britain favor multiculturalism.

Already, with 20 million Muslims in the EU, debates go on about the admittance of Turkey with its 71 million Muslims. And the predictions are that a 10th of Europe's population will be Muslim by 2025! Currently, there is not only economic progress among this minority, but also a rapid rise of Muslims in the workforce, including in business, politics, law enforcement, universities, as well as an increase in interracial marriages. While the average Muslim is a hard-working, peaceful, and moderate, it is the *jihadists* who alarm the average citizen. Yet Euro-Muslims are changing because of their experiences in a new homeland, so they are building coalitions with non-Muslims.

Even Russia's fastest growing religious group is its Muslims, and many of its important neighbors from the ex-Soviet bloc are Islam adherents. Actually, Russia has more Muslims than any other European state but Turkey; some 23 million, over 10% of its population, are followers of Mohammed. With 1300 mosques, Russian Muslims are concentrated in Moscow, as well as Bashkoratan and Tatarstan (www.islam.ru). Thus, Euro-Islam is a factor to carefully consider in any pan-Europe analysis.

*Source*: Adapted from special report, "Look Out Europe," *The Economist*, June 24, 2006, pp. 29-34. "Russia's Muslims—Benign Growth," *The Economist*, April 7, 2007, pp. 47-48.

# Cultural Guidelines for Doing Business in Europe

As Europe moves beyond national borders and national cultures toward regional cooperation, a new European identity is developing. EU youth, such as in Ireland, envision themselves as the *New Europeans*. While assimilation takes place within the Union, the cultural identity of each member country needs to be preserved as the basis for a diverse and enriched European cultural future. Latin verve and British pragmatism, for example, are viewed as strengths within the EU, rather than as divisive elements. However, the distinct cultures and enormous differences in values and outlooks among member countries must be addressed to overcome impediments to deeper unity. That being said, among the EU's burgeoning bureaucracy of approximately 26,000 personnel, no organized research is ongoing to study the impact of cultural diversity and ways to promote more cultural synergy.

Nowhere is the latter collaboration more evident than in the field of management. Managers readily cross national boundaries not only on business, but for professional development as well. Furthermore, European managers attend courses and workshops at one another's universities, and read one another's management journals and business publications. Perhaps the transnational aspects of European management are best demonstrated in matters of partnerships, joint ventures, and acquisitions. For example, the Republic of Ireland boasts not only of its more than 200 British industries and many new American and European firms, but also of the young, well-educated workforce available for service throughout the EU.

The "internationalization" of the European workforce has been progressing for at least five decades, accelerated by the multinational corporation. Since World War II, more than 30 million workers—mostly from countries in southern Europe and North Africa—have flowed into western and northern Europe (the foreign-born population is now 33 million). European businesspeople have always excelled at multilingual skills. These trends are some of the reasons that cross-cultural management training is increasing within Europe.

*So who is European?* It is no longer the typical inhabitants of the last two centuries on that continent. The enlargement of the EU changes demographic factors, such as affluence, poverty, and fertility. Also, the ongoing mass immigration into Europe is altering the composition and culture of its peoples. Many of the new arrivals face not only discrimination, but also civil disorder caused by anti-immigrationists. The EU estimates that 500,000 illegals are being absorbed yearly. Add to that the 400,000 refugees claiming political asylum, and harmony in Europe is threatened. At present, there is no common EU policy on asylum, and refugees are subject to the national regulations of member regimes. And while this influx goes on, the EU is still debating about establishing a policy on Pan-European border policing to replace national frontier controls. Furthermore, there is not a consensus in Europe as to *who is an immigrant*? The EU has not adopted the UN definition: a short-term migrant is anyone who moves to a new country and stays for 2-12 months; long-term is considered a year or more. The EU member states not only have differing policies regarding those who emigrate to their countries, but also record the numbers differently. In Switzerland, for instance, one may receive "temporary" resident permits of a year or more; whereas in Britain, acceptance or rejection of those seeking entry may take years. In Germany, automatic citizenship is bestowed on children born to foreign parents in that country. Because there may be 500,000 migrants in Italy alone, its parliament is working on proposed legislation for controlling immigration, which may include the deportation of illegals. The country's extensive coastline has large landings of Albanians, Kurds, Africans, and some Asians. The new law requires legal immigrants from non-EU nations to have job contracts before leaving their homelands and to be fingerprinted upon arrival.

## European Perceptions

When we analyze Europe, it is not easy to define a cultural set of beliefs, customs, values, practices, and feelings. While each country therein has its own distinctive culture, there are still commonalities that distinguish the "old world" from other regions. Below is an overview of principal themes on that continent that may alter outsiders' perceptions of them:

■ Europeans have an inherent interest in the quality of life, at all levels of society. There is a predominant humanist belief that people are to be served by progress, and not the reverse. They enjoy socialization with family and friends over beverage and meals.
■ Europeans generally have an inordinate sense of reality. When one reflects on the wars and disruptions in Europe in the twentieth century alone, one can understand how Europeans know that tragedy can be just a breath away, and that perhaps only this moment is real.
■ Europeans historically have had to fight their neighbor, whereas Americans have had to conquer the elements to develop their country. European heritage is such that they think in the context of centuries, whereas Americans' historical sense is in terms of decades.
■ Europeans have endured. They have survived plagues, atrocities, great wars, and border and government changes. They have lived through many ambiguities, and have the threads of ancient customs and traditions in the fabric of their cultures. They know the fragility of their civilization. On the one hand, it is the sense of survival, but the balance is that disaster is often not far off.

However, such perspectives may have a disadvantage in that Europeans may be less willing to take a risk on a new idea or venture with a possibly good future. For them, the concept of simply making money is not the foundation of a company; the long-term survival of the business is also important. The following are the characteristics that are representative of the overall European cultural outlook:

- An almost cynical realism schooled by history.
- A belief that individuals should be at the center of life.
- A sense of social responsibility.
- A mistrust of authority.
- A feeling that all people have weaknesses, and sometimes one has to "muddle through" life.
- A desire for security and continuity.
- A belief that maximum profit is not the primary aim of business.

It has also been observed that relationships between the individual and authority in Europe are accented by differences in educational and political attitudes within the continent. The reports below would seem to substantiate this.

## Education/Schooling

Educational systems in Europe tend to be very traditional, somewhat rigid in offerings and organization, and resistant to change. While strong in science, engineering, literature, and languages, courses in business, management, and entrepreneurship were only recently and slowly introduced. In a recent OCED survey of Euro educational standards, only young Estonians and Solvenes performed above average in reading, science, and mathematics; Bulgarian and Romanian students were way below average. Here is a sampling of some trends in schooling the next generation:

- Teachers in the Netherlands and Scandinavia have far less "distance" between themselves and their pupils than their counterparts in Mediterranean countries have.
- In one of the world's most egalitarian societies, Dutch children are taught to keep low profiles, and that being "first" at something is not necessarily a virtue; whereas in Mediterranean countries, such as Greece and Italy, children tend to be nurtured as special, unique, and implicitly superior individuals. In Britain, it is acceptable to finish first, but only if one can do it without seeming to work harder.
- In many European countries, such as in the United Kingdom, their educational systems suffer from culture lag and need updating of their instructional systems for an "information society" and a "knowledge culture."
- Germany's first woman chancellor, Angela Merkel, announced a plan in 2008 to modernize and renew that country's educational system at all levels.

## Politics/Economics

While there is diversity within Europe's political and economic systems, the EU is a force for standardization. Very gradually, the EU is fostering political integration, as demonstrated by the *euro* currency. Here are trends to observe there:

- Countries like Britain and Denmark, with long traditions of relatively nonintrusive government but with respect for the law, have tended to resist proposals for new regulations from EU administrators in Brussels. Yet, once agreement is reached, they have the best record of implementation. But the newest EU members are less resistive and more cooperative so as to retain EU benefits.
- On the other hand, Belgium, where bureaucracy is oppressive and evading laws/regulations is widespread, ranks among the quickest to propose new EU rules, but has the worst record for implementing adopted regulations.
- In France, over 700,000 Arab citizens are now eligible to vote in presidential elections, thus influencing the outcome of future governmental policies.
- While some complain that there are too many national entities in Europe, it is also home to many supranational organizations, such as NATO, UNESCO, OECD, and the European Court of Human Rights.

Kagan argues that Europe is trying to find a "post-historical paradise"—a self-contained world built on transnational rules and negotiations.[5] His point is that the fundamental cleavage is all about power. The Americans believe that world order ultimately rests on military power, whereas the Europeans envision an orderly world based on international law and multilateral institutions. The New Europe seemingly wants a more independent relationship from America, drawing on the wisdom of the old continent, while forging ahead with a more united destiny of its own creation.

Currently, Europeans are divided in their viewpoint of their world role with regard to transatlantic relations. Some argue that the EU's main weakness lies in inflexible political and economic structures that make it less capable of responding adequately to both globalization and its own enlargement challenges.[6] Yet the EU leaders announced at the turn of this century their goals to create *the most competitive and dynamic knowledge-driven economy in the world by 2010*. With its expansion in membership, the EU's gross domestic product is some $13.8 trillion, better than that of the United States. Exhibit 13.2 offers one insight into the growing Pan-Europe commercial activities and their impact on the environment.

EXHIBIT 13.2

CROSS-BORDER ALPINE BUSINESS

A recent magazine feature bewailed how the Alps mountain chain is under pressure from the heavy toll of tourism, commerce, pollution, and global warming on Europe's winter playground. Along with artificial snow-making machines, synthetic blankets which reflect solar radiation are being used to slow summer melting. If current temperature trends hold, 50-80% of the remaining Alpine glacier ice could vanish by 2100! The whole Tyrolean culture and way of life is under threat. Arrayed across the heart of Europe, the Alps have been intensely used for centuries, but only 17% of its 74,000 square miles are protected. Fourteen million people live there, but usable space in Alpine valleys is limited, yet there is an orgy of multitasks under way there by humans—factories, train tracks, hotels, houses, churches, ski lifts, farms, parking lots, stores, boutiques, and restaurants, all bounded together by concrete roads. Every day, 4000 tractor trailers thunder through the Mount Blanc tunnel connecting France and Italy. With the cars and buses for thousands of tourists, the small village roads are clogged, and pollution results from all that traffic. The Alps are big business, a sort of factory producing 1.6 million gallons of liquid water; millions of cubic meters of lumber; tons of iron and salt; spectacular cheese, wines, and apples; amusements, athletic challenges, and artistic inspiration; plus mining and fishing. Seventy-seven million tons of cargo move through these mountains in an average year, and trans-Alpine commercial transport is likely to double by 2020!

The Alps stretch 650 miles across eight European nations, housing some 650 ski resorts. Scientists predict that as the permanent snow line rises along with temperatures, half of these resorts will go out of business. Furthermore, less snow and ice cover means less runoff to feed Europe's major rivers; melting permafrost destabilizes steep slopes and the structures built upon them. The mountains also concentrate fumes and noise from all the vehicle traffic, and their carbon dioxide contributes to the global warming, while the valley walls carry the maddening noise upward. Moderns are negatively impacting this unique environment and culture. Alpine people—known for their stoicism and individualism, crafted for a world of isolation and avalanches—are now coping with a host of modern problems. As the awesome mountains with their beauty and tranquility are the central reality of Alpine life, humanity should cherish and protect them.

*Source*: Earla Zwingle, "Meltdown—The Alps Under Pressure," *National Geographic*, February 2006, Vol. 209: 2, pp. 96-115.

## Immigration and Labor Exchange

The new EU immigration regulations and job opportunities have attracted to this continent a host of external migrants, legal and illegal. The émigrés come largely from Africa, the Middle East, and Turkey. Destination Europe now accounts for over 33 million immigrants from abroad. Though the new arrivals ease labor shortages, they increase the anxieties of Europeans about cultural identities and values. EU countries have dealt with the challenge in various ways—from integrating them into society to legal containment or expulsion. For example, Austria will fine and expel immigrants who fail to attend mandated classes in the German language, while Britain requires those seeking citizenship to pass a test. As émigrés swarm into Western Europe, the nations there are tightening their immigration laws. Many of these "visitors" live together in ghettos, forming new ethnic minorities. So far, European policy has been inadequate, not facilitating integration into their societies and not encouraging assimilation. On the other hand, some of the new arrivals have resisted acculturation, refusing to learn the language and culture of the host country, and not letting their children marry the locals or outside their religious faith. When second and third generation children of immigrants are unable to enter the mainstream society, they often resort to protests and riots, such as that happening in France. Unemployment among such youths is usually higher than average, and obstacles are often in place against home ownership and adequate education.

Under the EU policies, internal migrants seeking work outside their own country in other member nations are free to do so. But such labor exchange, especially from the East, finds an open market that is curtailed, except in Britain, Ireland, and Sweden, who only delimit benefit-seekers. Most of the other original 12 members impose transitional arrangements to curb "freedom of movement," which is supposedly a right of all EU citizens. Their governments fear that Eastern Europeans will steal jobs from the locals, but in actuality, more often they take work that the locals shun. Germany and Austria are most chary of opening their labor market, because their countries are on the border of former communist countries whose workers go west for higher wages (e.g., Austria's wages are five times higher than those of Slovakia). Globalization and an aging workforce in Europe will eventually cause greater labor mobility that will prove beneficial, forcing more workforce flexibility among the EU member states.

## Multiculturalism[7]

Another EU challenge is to promote multiculturalism among its 27 members, developing a continental wide application and understanding of Article 9 of the European Convention on Human Rights. While secularism is on the rise in Europe, and church attendance falls, new mosques are opening everywhere on the continent—the United Kingdom alone has over a thousand! The Islamic community now represents about 25% of the European populations, and so the term arose, *Eurabia*! In several member countries, violence has erupted between a swelling Muslim minority and the majority populations. Mosque and Muslim gravesites have been vandalized, and complaints rise about discrimination against them. The Muslim global backlash, as seen in the 2006 riots and burnings because of what they perceive as blasphemous, hurtful cartoons against their founder and beliefs originating in a Danish newspaper and reprinted elsewhere, is a case in point. The growing Muslim presence is changing the "face" of Europe, more than the military invasions of the Ottoman Empire in previous centuries.

Recent research with European Muslim elite revealed them to be secular in outlook and supportive of liberal values—such counterstereotypes of their coreligionist. These could become leaders in promoting integration of their communities with the mainstream culture, thwarting rising contention between Muslims and other Europeans. Euro leaders, in general, are also challenged to contain resurgent xenophobic behavior across the continent, from whatever source.

With the increasing activities of global terrorism networks, EU states have new concerns about foreign visitors and migrants. Further, Europe's Muslim minorities feel stigmatized for the actions of Osama bin Laden or other criminal Islamic fundamentalists. Although many Muslims assimilate into European cultures, others choose self-segregation, and many are forced, for economic reasons, to live in impoverished "ghettos." Often, they experience cultural chauvinism and discrimination, ranging from unemployment to outright racism and violence against their person and property. Most Muslims have come to Europe seeking the opportunity to improve their lives (Exhibit 13.3).

---

### EXHIBIT 13.3
### GENERAL TIPS FOR DOING BUSINESS IN EUROPE

---

- Customer service is the key to success. The standards of Europe in this regard are not up to that of the United States, especially in matters of rapid repairs and home service.
- Publish price lists in terms of local currency.
- Deploy Americans to Europe on the basis of a 2-year minimum commitment to establish meaningful customer relations; the staying power of expatriate personnel is a subtle indicator—whenever possible, hire locals and then train them.
- Lease office equipment and computers in Europe because of the electrical differences in power outlets.
- Ensure that sales personnel know their products. Europeans are sophisticated buyers of foreign merchandise.

- Europeans gauge the forethought and commitment of a foreign firm by the way it treats its sales representatives. They perceive the salesperson as a key role, which should be judged on long-term performance; select such representatives very carefully.
- Europeans do not like change, so it is important for the foreign company to project stability and long-range commitment, yet they are attracted to "new" products, processes, and services.
- When able to properly serve the primary market in Europe, remember geographic distances are not great. Assess the secondary markets (Spain and Portugal, Greece, and the eastern European countries), and respond carefully to all inquiries from such areas.
- Beside cultural, language, and political differences in Europe, be prepared to cope with technical differences (e.g., length of stationery and forms that do not fit standard copying machines, ink that does not reproduce well, different abbreviations).
- European nomenclature and honorific titles are to be observed in oral and written communication (especially spellings in English that differ between British and North American versions).
- Europeans value personal contacts and mementos, so the token gift may create a favorable impression, as may participation in a trade fair that is part of a centuries-old tradition.

## WESTERN EUROPE

In Western Europe, we will discuss, in some detail in the text or on the Web site, Great Britain, France, and Spain. There are eight other smaller countries in the area, a few of which we will profile briefly: Andorra, Belgium, Gibraltar, Ireland, Luxembourg, Monaco, Netherlands, and Portugal. Most are members of the EU. Further cultural information on all these countries is available from their embassies or on the Internet. Many books and magazines also contain cultural and country-specific information (e.g., www.economist.com/countries/cities).

## FRANCE

France is geographically the largest country in Western Europe. It lies south of Great Britain, separated by the English Channel, but connected now by an underwater tunnel, or "chunnel." This channel gives the nation access to the North Sea, as well as to the Celtic Sea and the Atlantic Ocean on its western coast, while to the southeast it is bounded by the Mediterranean Sea. On its northeastern border are Belgium, Luxembourg, and Germany; Switzerland and Italy to the east; and Spain in the south, separated by the Pyrenees, of which Mount Blanc is the high point. Its natural resources include coal, iron ore, bauxite, timber, zinc, and potash. Beautiful Paris is its capital, while other major cities include Marseille, Lyon, Toulouse, Strasbourg, Nice, and Bordeaux. Apart from its advanced postindustrial economy, France is also known for its farms and vineyards.

In medieval times, French royalty and troops moved back and forth from Normandy to the British Isles, exchanging feudal domains. In the late eighteenth and early nineteenth centuries under Napoleon Bonaparte, the *grande armee* extended its control across Europe to Russia. The empire's remnants reveal the scope of France's colonial power and help us appreciate the glory that was France. Begin by looking today at what was once French East Africa, and where the French language is still spoken (Burundi, Central African Republic, Congo, Djibouti, and, to a lesser extent, Rwanda). The same cultural impact is still evident in Northern Africa (Algeria, Chad, Egypt, Mali, Mauritania, Morocco, Niger, Tunisia, and Senegal); West Central Africa (Benin, Burkina Faso, Cameroon, Congo, Cote d'Ivoire, Gabon, Guinea, and Togo); and even in Southern Africa (Madagascar). Recall, too, the influence of French culture and cuisine in such widely separated locations as India (Pondicherry) and Indochina (Vietnam). Today, the Overseas Department of France governs somewhat the Caribbean islands, such as Guadeloupe and Martinique, and far into the Pacific Oceania on the French New Caledonia and Loyalty Islands, Iles de Horne, and Wallis. In addition, there are other French Polynesian islands (Bora-Bora, Gambier, Hiva Oa, Huahine, Manihi, Moorea, Raiatea/Tahaa, Rurutu, Society Islands, Tahiti, Tuamotu Archipelago, and Ua Huka).

## *Historical Perspectives*[8]

Many books have been written on the glorious history of France—from when it was known as Gaul under the Roman Empire, through the Middle Ages when France was gradually united under its own king, and then to its expansion across Europe under Emperor Napoleon. A great contribution toward the establishment of democracy came from its support of the American Revolution, and then through its own French Revolution. France helped to found both the European Common Market and Union, but with a diminished role in the world today.

The current Fifth Republic of France came into being in 1958, and has been governing by "cohabitation"—a sharing of power between the president with a 7-year term and the bicameral parliament of the National Assembly and Senate. The president appoints the prime minister, who runs the country on a daily basis, presides over the cabinet, commands the Armed Forces, and concludes treaties. He has the power to dissolve the National Assembly and assume full power. Two-fifths of members in that National Assembly are on leave from civil service. Fifty-seven percent of the adult population are either civil servants or their dependents. The various ministries of government employ some 2 million plus in public service. Confidence is eroding in the nation's lackluster economic formula of higher taxes and higher social charges, especially during the current slowdown in economic growth. Excessive spending on health care, continuing widespread strikes, and the country's limited role in world affairs have disillusioned the public. Although France's colonies have diminished, it still administers Tahiti in the Pacific, and has influence in its former possessions in East Africa.

France's entrancing countryside consists of vineyards and cornfields, pastures and picturesque villages, and superb cuisine and wines. After its world-class capital of Paris and the other major five cities, Strasbourg is home to the European parliament, high-tech industrial parks, and the International Space University. Experience of bitter defeat in three devastating wars (one in Indochina and two on its own soil) has produced a strong antiwar sentiment, plus a desire for peaceful cooperation with Germany, especially through the EU. Despite long positive relations with the United States, going back to the eighteenth century, its streak of Gaullist independence prompts French politicians to often disagree publicly with American policies, particularly those regarding the Middle East.

Living in the Elyse Palace, French presidents, like the late Francois Mitterrand, have used public monies for grand schemes while fostering a top-down bureaucratic approach to governance. The modern nobility, elite graduates of grand ecoles or universities, dominate civil service and business—all supposedly based on meritocracy. But the public sector mistrusts the private sector because it often hampers initiative, creativity, and entrepreneurialism. The French market is mature and sophisticated, open to global suppliers, especially to those from within the EU community. The commercial environment is dynamic and reflects consumer trends within a world marketplace (Exhibit 13.4).

## EXHIBIT 13.4

### PERCEPTIONS OF FRANCE

- The French constitute the most brilliant and the most dangerous nation in Europe, and the best qualified to become an object of admiration, hatred, pity, or terror, but never of indifference!
  —Alexis de Tocqueville
- The average Frenchmen is concerned about an elite of bureaucrats, businessmen, and politicians who seemingly run the country to benefit themselves amidst corruption and public scandals.
  —*New York Times*, August 1, 1999

continued

EXHIBIT 13.4

PERCEPTIONS OF FRANCE (CONTINUED)

■ The French themselves are horribly muddled over France's place in Europe, over the impact of globalization, and at root, over what it means to be French.... France has an identity problem. It needs the courage to redefine itself.

—*J. Andres, "A Divided Self—A Survey of France," The Economist,* November 16, 2002

■ The French have a passion for engineering and technology, for research and solutions that push back the boundaries. The Ecole Polytechnique is one of the best engineering schools in the world, and French technology tends to be very sophisticated.

—Nani Becalli, CEO, GE Europe (www.thenewfrance.com)

■ As an American living in France, I personally find the quality of day-to-day life far superior to anything I could afford back home in the USA.

—Richard Chessnoff, *The Arrogance of the French*

■ The biggest lesson of the French riots is that more jobs are needed. In the deprived suburbs, a kind of soft terror rules. When too many young people see nothing ahead but unemployment after they leave school, they end up rebelling. Thus, one rational analysis of the forces that lie behind the riots, car-burning, and street battles that have broken out, first in the banlieues of Paris and then right across France for two weeks. It points to a pressing case for action to build a greater sense of identity with French society among the rioters, most of whom are second-generation Muslims of north or west African origin. There are arguments over why 5-6m Muslims there feel alienated—one-third the total in the European Union and one-tenth of the country's population. But the answer surely lies in the toxic mix of poor housing, bad schools, inadequate transport, social exclusion, disaffection over discrimination, and, above all, high unemployment. French unemployment has hovered around ten percent; the average rate among youth is over twenty percent, one of the highest in Europe; among young Muslims in the banlieues, it has been twice as high again. Most of the French elite, on the left as well as the right, have simply ignored the festering problem. There are no black or brown mainland members of the National Assembly; hardly any on television. The yawning gap between the French elite and the ordinary people was a big cause of government's loss of the referendum on the European constitution.

EXHIBIT 13.4

PERCEPTIONS OF FRANCE (CONTINUED)

■ The unrest in French cities shows that social and policing policy has failed. France needs to acknowledge its multiracial complexion by adapting its vocabulary, rather than hiding behind "the myth of republican equality."

—"French Failure," *The Economist*, November 12, 2005, pp. 11-12; 24-26

■ France spends thirty percent of its budget on "social protection," and makes it possible for even an illiterate immigrant to live fairly well without having worked a day in his life. Yet shying away from reality by France's ruling class does not change the reality that one of the most civilized nations in Europe is sliding into barbarism. None of the violence was either surprising or unexpected. Indeed, it was easily predictable denouement of the gradual transformation of hundreds of Muslim enclaves into crime-ridden, self-isolated, anti-societies that have de-facto seceded from French society in virtually every aspect, except for continuing to depend upon the welfare state.

■ This is not merely a local situation, but has implications for much of Europe, in terms of socio-political and economic context. There seem to be three seemingly unstoppable trends: the implosion of the European social-market economy; an unprecedented demographic collapse of the native European populations; and the takeover of the burgeoning Muslim communities in Western Europe by radical Islam. The French and European socio-economic model had much to do with the rise of the Muslim ghetto, and its ongoing implosion will dramatically exacerbate its conflicts with society at large. The new tougher economic climate, combined with ever-present French xenophobia and racism, led to the high unemployment and progressive ghettoization of the second- generation Muslims. With a fertility rate twice that of the natives, the Muslim community in France and Western Europe is growing at fifty percent every decade. The European Union will lose nearly half its native population by 2050, while its Muslim community increases five-fold to 100 million. What is needed is a cultural revolution.

—Alex Alexiev, "France at the Brink,"
*The San Diego Union-Tribune*, 1/22/07, pp. G3/5

■ France is a stratified society in need of change, flexibility, and mobility.

—CBS Sunday Morning Report on the
Student Protests in Paris, April 2, 2006

continued

In July 2008, a Paris summit of 40 heads of states and the EU inaugurated an unprecedented Union of the Mediterranean to achieve the above goals for the benefit of southern and eastern nations bordering the Mediterranean Sea. The hope is to improve their trade with the EU members by joint programs to improve poor infrastructure, ill-educated workforce, and unemployment. The aim also is to upgrade the environment, climate, transport, immigration procedures, and policing in the region. The summit declaration committed the participants to preventing nuclear proliferation, countering terrorism in all its forms, and promoting democratic principles, human rights, and fundamental freedoms. The French led with Egypt in the effort to establish UM secretariat.

## Cultural Guidelines Doing Business in France

### Idealism

The French tend to believe that the basic truths on which life is based derive from principles and immutable or universal laws. They are concerned with the essence of values. The motto of the French Republic is "Liberty, Equality, and Fraternity." To the French, values such as these should transcend everything else in life. They behave in an individualistic manner. "*Chacun defend son beef-steak*" (everyone protects his own steak). Sometimes they are frustrated and find it difficult to live by these ideals in everyday life, yet the hunger for these altruistic ideals is still present and deeply ingrained in most French people. For example, contrast the French and the American views on sex and money. The French are not easily embarrassed by sex or nudity. But they are embarrassed talking about money, how you get it, or vocational positions and salaries. To them, your job, your income, and such are personal and not the business of others.

## Practicalities

Generally, except for lunch, the French time sense is casual, so people are often late and no offense is normally taken. Although the person in a subservient position is usually prompt, the executive is free to be late. Anticipate a reluctance to make commitments, leading to scheduling at the last minute. Also expect frequent rescheduling of meetings and appointments.

The French enjoy leisure and socialization, as can be seen in their 2-h luncheons, seven official holidays (www.getcustoms.com), and 4 or 5 weeks of vacations (usually in August, when the nation virtually shuts down). Although a land of great medieval cathedrals, over 75% of citizens who call themselves Roman Catholic do not see religion as playing a large part in their lives, and even may be slightly anticlerical. While giving lip service to religious toleration, the over 5 million Muslims in France are treated with mistrust and often only tolerated. Realistically, the country's far-right white extremists, influenced by a colonial past, are xenophobic and hostile toward Arabs. The intensely competitive French educational system puts immigrant children of non-French-speaking backgrounds at a real disadvantage, marooning them between two cultures, even when born in France. French education does impact business—schools are rigorous and value linguistic capability.

French society is stratified with sharply defined and competing classes, where diversity is just beginning to be appreciated. Despite some female prominence in public offices and the professions, women's rights have come late, and sexual harassment only became illegal in the past decade. Foreigners complain of inadequate customer service. Managers and employees are "family" who often unite against outsiders.[a]

## Social Structure and Status

The French are very status conscious. Social status in France depends on one's social origins. Outward signs of social status are the level of education, a beautiful house with a well-designed, tasteful facade (not a gaudy one), knowledge of literature and fine arts, and the social origins of one's ancestors.

Social standing and class are very important in France as well. The French social classes are the aristocracy, the upper bourgeoisie, the upper-middle bourgeoisie, the middle, the lower-middle, and lower classes (blue-collar workers, peasants). Social classes categorize people according to their professional activities (teachers, doctors, lawyers, craftsmen, foremen, and peasants), as well as their political opinions

---

[a]For the insights which follow, the authors express appreciation to Gerd-Peter E. Lotao, who first wrote on "Doing Business in France" in the World Trade Notes of *Credit and Financial Management Magazine* (June 1987, p. 10).

(conservative, left-oriented). The mass influx of immigrants, an under-class, into a relatively homogeneous society is altering the situation.

Social interactions are thus affected by these social stereotypes. It is extremely difficult for a French individual to be rid of social stereotypes. They affect personal identity. Unlike an American who can theoretically attain the highest levels of social consideration by working hard and being professionally successful, the French find it difficult to do so. If professionally successful, the French can expect to climb one or two stages of the social ladder in a lifetime, but often nothing more.[b]

## Cooperation and Competition

The French are not basically oriented toward competition. To them, the word *competition* has a very narrow meaning—practicing a sport at the highest level of international excellence. For example, the French consider superstar professional athletes as involved in competition. The average French person does not feel affected by competition, which can be dangerous to the country's economic welfare. Some years ago during a New Year's Eve television speech, then-President Giscard d'Estaing tried to educate the French and make them face the fact that competition really should affect their lives. He said competition is not just what the French soccer team experiences during the World Cup. The economic welfare of the French people actually depends on how competitive French goods are on international markets. He tried to awaken the French to the notion of competition, so that they would motivate themselves to work harder and be more productive.

When confronted with individuals with a competitive drive, the French may interpret them as being antagonistic, ruthless, and power-hungry. They may feel threatened, and overreact or withdraw from the discussion. Yet, the pyramidal structure of the French educational system exposes French children and adolescents to competition very early.

## Personal Characteristics

French people are friendly, humorous, and sardonic. The French wish to be admired. French people are more likely to be interested in a person who disagrees with them. Because they want to be liked, the French are very hard to impress and impatient with those who try. A French person, when trying to get a sense of another, looks for qualities within the person and for personality. French people tend to gain recognition and to develop their identity by thinking and acting against others.

---

[b]A previous edition of our book, *Managing Cultural Differences*, was translated into French under the title, *Au-Dela Des Cultures* in 1994 by InterEditions, Centre francaise d'exploitation du droit de copie, 3, Hautefeuille, 75006 Paris, France.

## Trust and Respect

Personal honor and integrity are valued in France. A French person trusts an individual according to an inner evaluation of the subject's personality and character. Because social stereotypes are so vivid, an average French person cannot earn respect from members of other social classes merely through work accomplishments and performance.

Regarding privacy, a foreign student living with a French family closed the door to his bedroom after dinner, not realizing that closed doors are considered rude and that the visitor was expected to socialize with the family. Furthermore, when shutters to the outside are closed, this is not a sign of distrustfulness by the French, but a desire for privacy from the passerby.

## Style of Conversation

French speakers seldom put themselves forward or try to make themselves look good in conversations. If they accidentally do, they will usually add, "Je ne cherche pas a me vanter mais..." ("I do not want to boast but..."). Boasting is often considered a weakness, a sign of self-satisfaction and immaturity. In conversations with the French, some may ask their French counterparts questions about themselves. The French will probably shun such questions and orient the conversation toward more general subjects. To them, it is not proper to show characteristics of self-centeredness.

Further, the French are so proud of their language that they expect everyone to be able to speak it—visitors not fluent in that language are advised to apologize for lack of that knowledge and to learn a few key phrases and pronounce the words correctly. Be sure to smile when you use them. Remember that for centuries, all Western diplomats spoke French, and it was the language of the Russian Czar's royal court. The French are very sensitive about the diminishment of their language in the global market and the introduction of English words into it.

The French, who may seem contentious, often criticize institutions, conditions, and people they live with. A disagreement can be considered stimulating to a French person. It is not uncommon to see two French people arguing with each other, their faces reddened with what seems to be anger, exchanging lively, heated, and irreconcilable arguments. Then later, they shake hands and comment, "That was a good discussion. We should do it again sometime!" The French tend to think that such arguments are interesting and stimulating. It is also a meaningful outlet for tension and appreciation of humor. They also often add a touch of cynicism to their humor and may not hesitate to make fun of institutions and people.

## Consistency and Contradictions

The French abound in contradictions and are not overly disturbed by them; instead, they relish their complexity. They profess lofty ideals of fraternity and equality, but at times show characteristics of utmost individualism and selfish materialism. On the political scene, they seem continuously restless, verbally criticizing the government and capitalism, yet they are basically conservative.

## Attitudes Toward Work

Typically, French attitudes toward work depend on whether they are employed in the public sector or in the private sector. In the French bureaucracy and in state-owned concerns, there is little incentive to be productive. Quotas are rarely assigned, and it is virtually impossible to lay off or dismiss employees on the basis of job performance. Massive strikes have caused difficulties when companies have attempted to reform or modernize, or when government tries to pass policies and legislation that many people object to. Strikes by university students have actually brought down the government in power because of the latter. In the private sector, the situation is different. It is true that French workers do not respect the work ethic. They are usually not motivated by competition or by the desire to emulate fellow workers. They frown on working overtime and have 4-5 weeks of vacation a year. However, they usually work hard in their allotted working time. French workers have the reputation of being productive. Part of the explanation for such productiveness may lie in the French tradition of craftsmanship. A large proportion of the French workforce has been traditionally employed in small, independent businesses where there is widespread respect for a job well done, and many French people take pride in such work. This may also be true as many have not been employed in huge, impersonal industrial concerns, where craftsmanship may not be so valued. Rather, they often have a direct stake in the work they are doing and are usually concerned with quality.

## Attitude Toward Authority

French companies contain many social reference groups that are mutually exclusive. Tight reins of authority are needed to ensure adequate job performance. The lesser emphasis on delegation of responsibility limits accountability and contributes to a more rigid organizational structure. As a consequence, decision-making is more centralized in French companies, and it may take longer before decisions are reached and applied. This may be a source of frustration for foreign executives (especially lower- and middle-management executives) who are working with

French executives from a comparable management level. The flow of communication is improved if American executives have direct access to two or three top executives of a French company. This is where the actual decision-making power is. French subordinates tend to view an attempt to track personal progress as an infringement on their territory. D'Iribane writes, "Factual data can play two roles: it can give an overview on how things are working, and it can provide a means to evaluate workers. In the French system, the confusion between these two roles is a source of resistance" (translated from the French). The following real example illustrates this point. A consultant on a project in the south of France reported the following:

> The main objective of our project was to increase sales of a high-tech product. One of the ideas to accelerate sales was to introduce the use of a daily chart to track each individual's sales progress. The goal was to focus management's and subordinates' attention on specific areas for improvement, as well as ask those who were doing well to share tips to help their colleagues' progress. Although management thought this idea was great, and many of the salespersons agreed that in theory it was a good idea, nine out of 10 salespersons loudly objected. The reason? They did not want management—or their colleagues—to be able to track their sales. This idea was never put into practice.

The highest executives of large French companies also have "different" management styles, as the French are judged on personal attributes as well as on performance. It takes poor performance for them to be challenged in their functions by a board of directors or by subordinates. Patterns of authority are stable in French industry. Therefore, because they do not need to justify their actions to the same extent, the very top French executives tend to be more autocratic in their managerial style. Executive functions also have more overtones of social leadership.

It is interesting to compare French and American business magazine interviews of executives. Along with professional experiences and activities, top French executives usually mention details concerning their personal lives, such as former professors who had an impact on them, enriching social and personal experiences, books that influenced their outlook on life, and what their convictions are on political and social issues. On the other hand, top American executives will more likely emphasize the progression of their career in terms of professional achievements. But in this arena of exercising power and authority, French management is also changing because of their involvement in the global marketplace and the foreign acquisitions, mergers, and alliances of French corporations. Obviously, there are considerable differences in the French management style as compared to the style of managers from other countries. Chapter 3 tries to explain some factors present in cross-cultural management.

## Organizational Structure and Style

The organizational structure of French companies tends to be rigid; the French put less emphasis on control of individual performance. The decision-making process is more centralized in French companies. Important decisions are made only by the top executives, but slowly there is a trend toward team management because of consortia formed with businesses outside the country, such as Airbus.

## Conflict

The mentally vigorous French have been aptly described as *combative libertarians;* that is, they appreciate strong argument and contradiction. The French, partly because they live in a more closed society with relatively little social mobility, are used to conflict. They are aware that some positions are irreconcilable, and that people must live with these irreconcilable opinions. They, therefore, tend not to mind conflict, and sometimes enjoy it. They even respect others who carry it off with style and get results. The French are also less concerned about negative reactions from those with whom they are in conflict.

French managers also report difficulties in adjusting to life in other countries. The French managers seem to experience problems caused by emphasis in the French culture on pride in their past cultural heritage, causing them to be too critical of people who do not benefit from that same cultural tradition. In their self-descriptions, the French managers feel handicapped by their conditioning to a formal way of thinking and a lack of actual knowledge of other cultures.

The atmosphere today in France is very diverse. There are some pessimists among the elite and intellectuals who are publishing articles and books forecasting the decline of France and its culture. For example, in 2003, Nicolas Bavez published a volume, *New World, Old France,* decrying French nihilism, which he predicts will lead to a *national crisis, unequaled since the agony of the fourth republic.* The increasing number of books and articles on such themes indicates a growing mood of melancholy, gloom, and discontent, evident in the May 2006 rejection in a national referendum of the EU constitution. The people's contrariness is reflected in a recent CSA poll when 70% reported that future generations would live less well than they do today, while 84% indicated that they were happy. More intriguing is the rise in French female fertility rate to 0.09 in 2004, the highest rate in Europe after Ireland—1.94 children per woman.

During this decade, the French have been gripped by antiliberalism, antiglobalization, and anti-Americanism. Though these attitudes are lessening, it would seem that the present disgruntlement of French citizens is caused by the country's political ecosystem whose past elite leaders were unwilling to promote necessary change in their society. Author Alfred Peyrefitte has suggested that his countrymen need a "mental revolution" to alter their mindset toward more risk-taking and innovation. Yet the French approach to citizenship has its strengths, with its unapologetic approach to national identity, and emphasis on secularism and equality (Exhibit 13.5).

---

### EXHIBIT 13.5
### BUSINESS TIPS WITH THE FRENCH

1. French handshake is FIRM, brief handclasp accompanied by short span of eye contact. When French employees arrive at work, they usually greet their colleagues with a quick handshake, and repeat the process when they leave. Some may kiss their friends of both genders on the cheeks, but this is the exception in a business setting. A French woman offers her hand first. It is considered vulgar to snap one's fingers.
2. French conversation is not linear, and frequent interruption of each other may occur. Conversation is meant to entertain, not just inform, so expect many references to art and argument, as every possibility is explored and articulated, opinions are expressed, and need not be refuted. The French complain that Americans lecture, not converse.
3. Food is important in France, so expect to share meals enthusiastically while doing business with the locals. Whoever initiates the meal is expected to pay, and to make restaurant reservations, except in hotels and brasseries. With an invitation to a person's home for a social occasion, it is polite to bring a gift of wine or flowers (not roses or chrysanthemums, which are more appropriate for funerals).
4. Respect privacy—close doors after you, and knock on them before entering.
5. Be attentive to voices—the French expect you to recognize the person over a telephone by voice alone. As a sign of closeness, avoid saying, "Who is this?" Regulate voice volume, lest you offend with loud or boisterous talk and braying laughter.
6. Neatness and good taste are important in this culture.

*Source: Dun & Bradstreet Guide to Doing Business Around the World,* Upper Saddle River, NJ: Prentice-Hall, 1997.

---

## CENTRAL EUROPE

Among the 11 nations in this geographic area, we will provide a cultural analysis of the two largest, Germany and Poland. However, we will profile selectively some of the remaining nine nations. With the exception of Switzerland, a global financial center, and the western part of Germany, all the others in this region were considered Eastern Bloc nations for the past half century or more. Thus, the majority of them were under the political and economic domination of the former USSR, meaning cultural conditioning in totalitarian and central planning. Though ravaged by war and occupations, Central Europe has a history of rich culture, democratic leanings, and relative prosperity now. Apart from stimulating their economies, the big problems center around coping with corruption and immigration issues, especially in former east bloc countries.[9]

# GERMANY

Geographically, this nation borders the Netherlands on the west, Belgium and France on the southwest, Switzerland and Austria on the south, and Czech Republic and Poland on the east.

## *Historical Perspective*[10]

The forerunner of today's Germans were the Saxons, whose trade and military excursions took them west into England (Anglo-Saxons), and south into what is now Romania. The foundation of Germany was laid by Teutonic feudal lords. From its Indo-European origins, the Germanic language was not only spoken in Germany, Austria, and Switzerland, but also impacted English, Dutch, Flemish, Scandinavian, and other languages. The culture became renowned for excelling in mathematics, natural science, and military science, as well as in the arts and music. Like most European powers in the sixteenth through nineteenth centuries, the Germans were late in becoming empire builders, eventually acquiring overseas colonies that spanned from the South Pacific to West Africa. Its former Kaiser was related to the British royal family. Prussian militarism led the emerging nation into a series of conflicts, beginning with the Franco-Prussian War, which it won, followed by World Wars I and II, which it lost. After temporary glories, the latter attempts at cross-border expansionism in the twentieth century resulted in much misery and deprivation for both the country and its people, as well as for many other nations and their citizens. The rise and fall of Adolph Hitler and his fascist Nazi party (1933-1945) negatively affected not only Germany, but also the millions of humans, both Jews and Christians, caught up in the fighting and purges, concentration camps, and the Holocaust. These horrible calamities laid waste to the continent and led to the Soviet invasion of East Germany with their establishment of a puppet state (German Democratic Republic) under the influence of the USSR. The former capital, Berlin, was divided temporarily among the occupying armies of the American, British, and Russian allies. In 1949, the west became the multiparty Federal Republic of Germany (FRG), adopting the *Grundgesetz* as its basic law, with Bonn then as its capital.

In time, the GDR communist government in the east built barriers to contain its German inhabitants from contamination by Western democracies and free enterprise. By November 9, 1989, irate Germans tore down that Berlin Wall, and its elimination marked the end of an era. On October 3, 1990, after 41 years of political division, Germany was reunified by the process of reintegration between its western and eastern populations. The unified FRG has evolved into a democratic, market-oriented, prosperous system. After 40 years of being apart, the two Germanys had developed differing cultural values, mindsets, and customs, in addition to opposing economic and political systems. However, by the twenty-first century, such divisions have been largely overcome in a united Germany, which again has its capital in a renewed Berlin. Modern Germans are allergic to militarism, anxious for positive international relations, and willing to aid other people in need.

In 2005, a physics professor, born in East Germany, was elected the first woman chancellor. Dr. Angela Merkel led a left-right political alliance and encouraged her countrymen to develop a more positive Germany as a world-class exporter with more competitive global corporations and improved investments, while serving domestic concerns. Merkel's leadership called for bold reforms in education and business. Within the EU, Germany accounts for almost 25% of its GDP. In the new Europe, it has become the biggest Western exporter to Iran and Russia, two nations that are also its biggest trading partners. Germany today has become the largest economy in Europe.

The priorities of the German government appear to center on the following goals:

■ Maintaining economic growth and competitiveness, especially by facilitating the growth of eastern Germany and attracting creative enterprise there.
■ Promoting peaceful security and commercial relationships with its neighbors, particularly those in the EU and NATO, as well as with Russia and its Commonwealth of Independent States.
■ Fostering international relations, both inside and outside the continent, while improving the integration of immigrants, especially the Turkish migrants.

As a parliamentary democracy with a bicameral legislature, there are two main governing bodies in Germany. The larger *Bundestag* (Parliament) consists of 672 deputies elected for 4-year terms from the states, and possesses legislative power. The upper house, the *Bundersrat* is composed of delegations from the 16 states that function under the *Laender* (state constitutions). Its 68 votes are based on the proportion of populations and power is limited, except in exercising vetoes over proposed legislation. Germany has a president, but the position is of honor and formality, not one of real power, which lies in the office of chancellor (*Bundeskanzler*). The chancellor is either the leading representative of the party with a majority of seats in the *Bundestag*, or the leader of the largest party in a coalition government.

There are presently five political parties, though the most influential have been the Christian Democratic Union (CDU) and the Social Democratic Party (SDP). Three critical challenges facing Germany today are reform of its educational, health care, and corporate governance systems. The present school system fails to make the most of its human capital by an inadequate three-tier infrastructure. Further, the university curriculum suffers from culture lag and lack of modernization. The health care system favors private insurers, while leaving the public sector with risks. Large public corporations are often unresponsive to stockholder wishes about expenditures and strategies.

Germany is losing its homogeneity with some 6.7 million immigrants, 8% of whom are naturalized citizens. The third generation Turks there are increasingly marginalized by a complicated school system and unresponsive labor market. Frankfurt is innovating with a city government Office of Multicultural Affairs, which offers new arrivals language training and translation services, as well as guidance on the educational and health care systems. Stuttgart assists foreign students through the thickets of German bureaucracy. Germany has to compete in a global search for talent in a knowledge culture requiring skilled and competent individuals. The new German environment will feature greater diversity and flexibility.

## Cultural Guidelines for Doing Business in Germany

Germans today are a more diverse people as a result of its immigrants. Traditionally, Germans have a reputation for being industrious, reserved, and seemingly "cold" in behavior. While the French are said to work to live, the Germans seem to live to work. Generally, they are perceived as meticulous and methodical, and precise in their actions (linear thinking). On the other hand, they have a reputation for quality and exactness—their bus, train, and plane schedules usually run on time. Detail in planning and project implementation is valued. Some of the world's greatest composers, writers, and philosophers are products of their German heritage.

It would appear that most Germans are not a spontaneous people. Their attitude is to organize the time allotted to its greatest efficiency, rather than wait and see what happens. Nor are the Germans normally an outward people; they tend to be very private. They maintain a slightly larger personal space around themselves, usually standing back 6 in. further than do North Americans. The German language is a key to understanding their national personality. The Germans make a strong distinction between an acquaintance (*bekannte*) and a friend (*freund*). Germans will only use *freund* when they really mean it; otherwise, it is a *bekannte*. Close family ties are also valued.

## Business Context

There are three things that heavily impact the structure of business in Germany today. These are the EU, codetermination, and government involvement. Germany is one of the original members of what was then known as the EC. Much of German business practices and laws are directly tied to the regulations and directives from that community or union in Brussels. The principle of collective good is important in the idea of codetermination (*mitbestimmung*). Codetermination allows for worker input into the management of the firm. Any firm with more than five employees should have a workers' council (*Betriebsrat*) that represents the employees and helps them solve various grievances with the firm's management. There is also a specially chosen labor representative on the management board of the company. All these illustrate an attempt to include a most important part of the economic structure, the worker. However, in the postindustrial work environment, such approaches are questionable.

German unions are very strong and provide workers with many more rights than some foreign counterparts. For example, they can become involved in decisions on dismissal. The process of codetermination gives management and workers the opportunity to work together to shape or define the firm's goals, objectives, and responsibilities. Employees are represented in five trade unions of professional organizations: German Trades Union Federation, German Salaried Staff Union, Christian Trade Union Federation, German Civil Servants' Federation, and the Union of Executive Employees.

The Germans are among the highest paid workers in the world, and enjoy a high standard of living. They are able to afford the luxuries and extras of life. An important part of this concept is the vast welfare state that supports the German worker. This includes liberal pensions, bonuses, medical and dental care, and 5-6 weeks of annual paid vacation. Though taxes are heavy, this system has relieved the typical German from many financial worries. But the above factors also contribute to driving up the costs of business and making Germany's products and services less competitive. Currently, Germany is known for its high quality of life and protection benefits for its citizens. But its current weak financial growth has been attributed not just to a downturn in the world's economy, but also to the need for restructuring what has become an overburdened welfare state. German politicians, given to compromise and consensus, are struggling with issues of federalism and decentralization. Without some radical socio-economic changes, the driving economy of the past decades may not be regained.

Germany is committed to a free enterprise economy. Government and business work very closely together, as can be seen in the extent of government control/participation in industry. The state holds control or equity participation in hundreds of firms. In the public service arena, the railroads and postal system are now privatized, with the state owning most of the shares. The state also owns a trade monopoly in alcohol. An area that is perhaps the fastest growing in Germany, as well as throughout Europe, is joint government and private business ventures. This means a partnership between private businesses and firms controlled by the government. With denationalization ongoing, this increase in joint partnership ventures is another indication of "collective interest" being an important part of the German business and economic community.

Trade plays a very important role in the German economy for sustaining growth and the standard of living because natural resources are very limited.

## Work Practices

The German sense of time requires punctuality for both business and social engagements, but does not seem to extend to delivery dates. Goods and services may be delivered late without explanation or apologies. There are 13 national plus regional holidays (see www. getcustoms.com). People take long vacations during July, August, and December. Little work is accomplished during regional festivals, such as Oktoberfest or Carnival prior to Lent. The work week is Monday to Friday, 8 or 9 a.m. to 4 or 5 p.m., but check on banking hours, which normally are 8:30 a.m. to 1 p.m.; 2-4 p.m., sometimes extended to 5:30 p.m. On Saturday, shops may close by 2 p.m., except for once a month when they may be open in the evening. The preferred time for business appointments is late morning or late afternoon, and these should be scheduled several weeks in advance.

## Social Customs

Germans are very knowledgeable and capable businesspeople. They pride themselves on having quality products to offer on the world markets. They are formal in their business dealings, not only with foreigners, but among themselves as well. For the foreigner, it is best to be conservative and subdued, unless you are given the indication to be more informal. The Germans do not like loud people, especially in business, and have little respect for the pushy or brassy businessperson. To them, such behavior reflects a weakness in the person or company. In this culture, business is taken seriously. Germans tend to be exact in their dealings and somewhat more distant in their business relationships.

The handshake is an important part of the German greeting. They shake hands often. The woman extends her hand first. Firm handshakes are preferred. If one is entering a room filled with many people, the person should proceed around the room shaking everyone's hands. Again, a friendly "good morning" or "good day" is appropriate.

In the German language, there are two forms of address, the polite and the familiar. The familiar form *du*, similar to "thou" in English, is used only for relatives, very close friends, children, and animals. The polite form *sie* is used on all other occasions, including in the business environment. Any foreigner addressing a German should use the polite form. Many Germans who have known each other for years still use the polite form. A German may initiate the usage of the *du* form, although this is not routine. Not only should you use the polite form of speech, but you should also refrain from using first names; *Herr* and *Frau* are more appropriate. In addition, women should always be called *Frau* regardless of their marital status.

The Germans are title conscious, and proper etiquette requires addressing them by their title. Also, those who have attained their Ph.D. are addressed by the term *doktor* (i.e., "Herr Doktor Schmidt" or "Frau Doktor Braun"). Women are called by their first names. The wife of Georg Meyer will not be Frau Georg Meyer, but rather Frau Ursula Meyer. A friend or associate should introduce the newcomer to the group, as Germans prefer third-party introductions.

In some countries, it is quite common to entertain a client for dinner at a fashionable restaurant. In Germany, particularly with large corporations dealing in multimillion-dollar contracts, the superiors will not allow their subordinates to accept the invitation. Many German firms would consider this to be a conflict of interest, and one could easily lose his objectivity, *verpflichtungen*. A good rule to follow is to conduct business during business hours.

The Germans like to discuss things and enjoy a good discussion on the topics of the day. Religion, politics, and nuclear power are freely discussed, but conversations relating to one's private life are only among friends. Bragging about personal achievements and finances should be avoided.

## Communications

*Gestures*—The Germans are generally restrained in their body movements. They do not wave their arms and hands a lot as in other cultures. It is impolite to talk to someone with your hands in your pockets. It is also considered rude to sit with the bottom of your shoes facing another person. For this reason, German men cross their legs at the knees, rather than with an ankle on the other knee. Most body movements could best be characterized as conservative. Whether sitting or standing, it is generally in a more upright and rigid position.

*Language*—German is the official language in Germany, although in border areas, other languages are spoken more often. There are hundreds of dialects and local variations spoken throughout the countryside, although dialects are generally only spoken in less formal situations with friends. *Hochdeutsch*, or the "high" German, is found in all magazines, newspapers, television, etc. In a business context, your counterpart will avoid the usage of dialects. English is the major foreign language taught in Germany, and most businesspeople are conversant in it. With the influx of Turkish workers during the past decade, Turkish is also spoken in some circles (Exhibit 13.6).

## EXHIBIT 13.6
## BUSINESS TIPS WITH GERMANS

1. Guests usually stand until a host enters the room, and then remain standing until offered a seat.
2. Avoid conversing with hands in pocket, or propping legs on desks or tables.
3. Germans are free-thinkers and have a wide variety of interests to discuss on social occasions, such as current events, politics, religion, sex, but avoid talking about work, private life, personal achievements, or American sports, unless you are friends.
4. Be formal in business deals, and avoid haggling.
5. Be aware that business responsibility is first to society and the environment, and then to maximize profitability.

## ITALY[c]

This portion of Europe has always been geographically distinctive because it is seemingly shaped like a human boot. In southeastern Europe, the country lies south of France, Switzerland, and Austria, with Slovenia and Croatia on its eastern borders. Apart from many small islands on its eastern coastline, the two largest are Sardinia and Sicily to the south. Generally temperate in climate, Italy's northern borders are separated from its neighbors by the snow-capped Alp mountain chain, thus enabling its city of Torino to host the 2006 Winter Olympic

[c]The authors are grateful to Maryellen Toffle, MIM, a graduate of the Thunderbird School of Global Management, who wrote the section on Italy. Her work resulted, in part, from interviews with Italian professionals, such as management consultant, Dr. Luigi Giannitrapani; managing director, Marina Zacco; and operations director, Dr. Annalisa Bardi. We have updated this material with special acknowledgment to "Audio, Dolce Vita—A Survey of Italy," *The Economist*, November 26, 2005, 16 pp. (www.economist.com/surveys).

Games. The rest of the peninsula is surrounded by water—to the east by the Adriatic Sea; while in the southeast, the Gulf of Taranto and the Ionian Sea; to the west, there is the Ligurian and Tyrrhenian Seas; and in the south, the Mediterranean Sea (Exhibit 13.7).

## Cultural Guidelines for Doing Business in Italy

Over millennia, this land was divided into so many independent political entities—each with autonomous governance, ruling families, language dialects, local customs and traditions, as well as cuisines—that the various parts of Italy today are unique in various ways while also sharing some common cultural values. By means of the mass

### EXHIBIT 13.7
### OBSERVATIONS ON ITALY

"The first thing to say about Italy is that, however grubby its politics or flaky its economics, it is still for most of its inhabitants and visitors, one of the most delightful countries of the world. Its confection of man-made and natural beauty, cultural heritage, and clement climate is second to none. Its people are blessed with charm, humor, and the ability to enjoy, let alone let others enjoy, life. Few have so brilliant a sense of style and fashion, so sumptuous a cuisine and cellar, so strong a tradition of melding hard work with pleasure."

This survey is filled with praise for the globe's sixth largest economy; its relatively strong family life and social cohesion; its top-flight universities and scientists; its manufacturing and high-tech pursuits. Then it points up Italy's continuing problems—government instability and turnovers; Western's Europe's worst performing economy; business failure to be competitive and to effectively use new communications technologies; slow pace of reform in labor markets and in overcoming the north-south income gap; inadequate probity in battling corruption and criminal behavior (e.g., the Mafia); lack of foreign investor trust because of the country's rickety and opaque legal system; need for faster decentralization and privatization, as well as for constitutional, electoral, and welfare reforms by the state.

But the report concludes that Italy is still one of the world's most dynamic, enjoyable, and, in many ways, admirable country.

*Source*: Jan Smiley, "A Survey of Italy—What a Lovely Odd Place," *The Economist*, July 7, 2001, p. 18. Also in the same publication, see the update by John Peet, "Addio, Dolce Vita—A Survey of Italy," November 26, 2005 (www.economist.com/surveys).

media and the education system, Italy today has grown closer together into a more united country, but it is still rare to find an Italian who will say he is Italian, and not Roman, or Florentine, or Genovese. This tendency demonstrates the strong cultural value of *campanilismo*. It centers on the campanile, or bell tower, that can be found in every village in Italy. Ordinary citizens feel comfortable when they can see the campanile of their own town. The implication is that Italians prefer to stay in their city of origin and will always consider the interests of their campanile in business situations. Yet as an EU member, many cosmopolitan Italian political and business leaders find themselves more involved today in European institutions, as well as the global market. Italians have served as president of the EU and CEOs of global corporations.

What can one say about Italy? Thousands of books have been written about its cultural treasures. Anyone who visits the country, falls in love with its picturesque villages and stunning countryside, its historic and beautiful cities, its poetic and dynamic language, and its incredible food and wine. It is the land of art, science, and passion, the land of "saints, scholars, and navigators" (Italian proverb). Apart from Italian contributions to art and architecture, music and literature, this creative people invented many current business practices (e.g., innovations in banking, insurance, and double-entry bookkeeping). Most people would agree that Italian fashion, food, and sports cars are the best in the world. There, we find *La Dolce Vita*, the ability to enjoy everything with art and style. But loving Italy and doing business there are two very different things.

One important thing to realize about Italy is that it has two faces, like the two-faced Roman god Janus—one looking forward and one looking backward. Italy is the vestige of the eternal Roman Empire, yet on the cutting edge of modern scientific research and many types of technology. It looks backward to its age-old traditions, and looks forward (painfully sometimes) to its position as a strong member of the EC. Italy is frequently in a state of social, economic, and political change. Such transitions attempt to cope with major challenges of immigration, European integration, globalization, and family breakdown. In addition to having two faces, Italy also has two halves. This is due in part to the historical occupations of the areas. The north is well developed into an industrial powerhouse and one of the richest areas of Europe. In contrast, the south (known as the *Mezzogiorno*), which is the southern half of Italy starting just below Rome, is one of the poorest areas of Europe. The south is economically depressed and primarily agricultural. It is perhaps Italy's greatest economic problem with social issues as well. The south embodies the stereotypes that foreigners have of Italy—chaotic streets, and violently honking horns with drivers shouting at each other. Mafia criminality also undermine Naples' and Sicily's progress, whereas the north exemplifies the best rendition of Italy as a modern industrial power.

Volumes have been written on the Italian contributions to Western civilization. The West owes its essence and structure to Italy in the many areas of science, economics, navigation, art, architecture, politics, and literature. In every area of study stand many Italian geniuses, including Dante, Galileo, Michelangelo, Leonardo da Vinci, Francis of Assisi, Verdi, and Marconi. Remember that Christopher Columbus (a Genovese navigator) "discovered" America, and don't forget that the name *America* comes from the Florentine cartographer, Amerigo Vespucci! Italians are very proud of their heritage, and it is advisable for businesspeople to know, appreciate, and respect it. Italians also have immigrated in large numbers abroad, especially to North America and Brazil.

The following are some insights about Italian sense of identity and cultural values that affect business. In a recent survey, Italians evaluated themselves in terms of their national character—the top three qualities reported were the art of *arrangiarsi*, creativity in art and the economy, and connection to the family. Interestingly enough, the feature that they reported as the least present was that of civic duty. Now to explain key concepts in the Italian mindset and lifestyle:

■ *Art of arrangiarsi* means to be able to make do, to get by, to work oneself out of any situation. This activity has been elevated to an art in Italy because of the fact that most systems do not function as expected. The cause of this has historical roots, owing to the numerous invaders, conquerors, and imposed systems of foreign government. In business terms, this could be called "creative problem solving." The Italians have learned to *arrangiarsi* as a reaction to the formidable system of government, laws, and taxes. It is hard for Americans to understand this idea because they are used to having systems that actually work as expected. Instead, Italians have developed ways to get around the system and accomplish what needs to be done in a creative way, via connections and family ties.

■ *Relationships with family and friends* emphasizes family ties, connections, and relationships as the bastions against the insecurities of life. Over the centuries, this value and system was a solution to problems imposed by foreign occupation. Today, everything flows from such relationships—from getting a job to opening a bank account; everything depends on connections. The successful foreign businessperson makes it a point to understand the connections and use them.

■ *La cordata* literally means rope or cord, referring to the practice of pulling along friends and family in the climb up the corporate ladder. It is an outgrowth of the relationship/family value explained above. People who find work in a company or government office immediately seek to be part of a *cordata,* or network. And if they also start their own enterprise, gradually their friends or relatives are involved some way in the undertaking, as the case may be. The practice is also used to form alliances between companies for buying materials or products. So Italians are very open to synergistic relationship.

■ *Bella figura* literally means *beautiful* figure, but it can make or break a business negotiation. *Bella figura* is the desire to make a good impression, to give a good appearance, and to convey a certain image. It is somewhat like the Asian value of saving face, but encompasses appearance as well as behavior. It is responsible for the fact that Italian fashion, art, and architecture are world renowned and sought after. Italians seek to make a *bella figura* through their appearance, both physical and economic, and their behavior. It is important for managers to remember this in all areas of interaction. Proposals and presentations must look good. Image is the key in all areas, including dress and behavior. Status and prestige also matter. The foreign businessperson is advised to imitate the Italians on this one. And be careful not to present a *brutta figura* (ugly figure)—that can mean being obviously drunk, looking slovenly, arriving late, being unprepared, giving an unattractive presentation.

■ *Furbo* is an Italian word that is very hard to translate. It can have negative or positive connotations. It has evolved as a concept that describes how to outsmart one's adversary or beat the system. A funny example is that of the seat belt law. Seat belts are now required everywhere in Italy, and the police will fine motorists if they aren't wearing them. Someone in Naples started producing a sweater that was made with a black diagonal stripe from the neck to the stomach, so that when you wear it, it appears that you are wearing a seat belt. So you outsmart the police. This is being a *furbo*. In business, it is very important to be on your guard, because often someone will try to outsmart you in some way. Beware of the well-developed *furbo*, because he is waiting to rip you off.

Foreigners also need to be aware of the following value orientations among the Italian people.

## Determinism

Italians are basically fatalistic, *che sarà, sarà*. Because of their long history of natural and political disasters, as well as their experiences with Catholicism, they tend to believe that nothing can be done to prevent things from happening the way they are destined to happen. Insecurity is viewed as a fact of life. This conviction may explain why they tend to live in the moment. Remember that the famous Latin quote *carpe diem* came from Italy; thus, they will take opportunities in the moment without thinking that they have control over their actual success. One source of frustration in business stems from this fatalism. Foreign managers will find it difficult to extract detailed objectives and plans from their Italian counterparts, as the practice of setting precise objectives goes against this deterministic philosophy. Besides believing that they do not control their destiny, they also hate to make mistakes (it causes *brutta figura*), so they do not like to pin themselves down too tightly to objectives they are not sure that they can complete.

## Time Sense

Italians are often multitasking. Conducting a meeting, taking a phone call, and signing papers all at the same time are quite common. It can be very stressful for foreigners to be in a meeting that is constantly being interrupted with knocks on the door and phone calls.

As far as punctuality is concerned, the north is much closer to Northern Europe in its adherence to meeting times and time allocation; but in the south, time flows at a slower pace, and people tend to be much more relaxed with appointments and schedules. It is common to have many changes of schedule, shifting, canceling, reinstating, and so forth. The best way to handle this is to be flexible and patient. Anticipate schedule changes as a matter of course. However, foreigners are expected to be on time for business and social engagements, while Italians have more latitude in this regard. Again, North Americans and northern Europeans will discover the business environment in the south to be less time conscious, even more relationship-oriented, and more relaxed.

Normal business hours range from 8 or 9 a.m. to 1 p.m., and then from 3 to 6 or 7 p.m. There are 12 national plus regional holidays; a city can shut down to celebrate the feast of the local patron saint. July and August are vacation months for firms, and many close during this period.

## Action Orientation

Italians tend more toward *being* than doing, because of their long past, their traditions, and their propensity to form relationships. They identify themselves with their region, their family, or their soccer team more than with their job. Italians define themselves also by their network of relationships and the connections they enjoy.

Again, there is a pronounced difference between north and south. The north has a greater focus on activity and is more dynamic; the south has an even greater focus on relationships and operates at a slower pace. The key difference between outsiders and the Italian is that individuals do not value themselves here by what they do, but by how well they, their families, and their friends can live on their financial and professional successes.

## Communication

Italian culture is high context, although the north is somewhat less than the south. The Italian language is very colorful and musical. One of the favorite pastimes of Italians is that of talking and engaging in polemic discussions. For visitors, the natives seem to waste a lot of time talking. They usually speak rapidly, in high volume, all at the same time, and in very heated discussions. They are known for their buoyant style, combining emotion, gestures, and volume that create an over-all impression of a theatrical presentation. One of their most admired abilities is that of being able to put on a spectacle or show. They tend to keep one eye on the other members of the group so that they can gauge their performance. They are very expressive, or *esternazione*, meaning *expressing* or *venting*, or *letting it all out*. *Esternazione* is reflected in every communication situation. In politics and the media, it means press releases. In private life, it means telling it all. There is no word for *privacy* in the Italian language. For some companies, this can pose a problem, because secret policies, etc., are never secret and are often discussed at the local cappuccino bar with the family, and even with the press. However, it must never be assumed that the Italian businessman will tell you everything. There is also another Italian quality, *omertà*, which means silence. Here are some communication behaviors to look for in Italians:

- *Indirect versus Direct*. In spite of *esternazione*, personal and business relationships can be quite indirect, on the basis of unspoken (high context) values that everyone (Italian) is supposed to know. Third parties are often used to communicate important messages, especially unpleasant ones. A foreign businessperson must be aware of the hidden cultural assumptions. The best solution for this is to have a bilingual, bicultural person to advise you.
- *Expressive*. Italians have an incredibly well-developed system of gestures. They also have an uncanny ability to yell at each other simultaneously, while somehow communicating a message.
- *Formal*. In spite of whatever stereotypes foreigners may have about the informality of Italians (i.e., drivers screaming and gesturing at each other in traffic jams), the Italians are initially quite formal, both in personal and business relationships. They adore the spectacle of form and ritual, even in business situations. Appropriate titles are always used, such as *Dottore/Dottoressa* (person with a university degree). The businessperson must be sure to know in advance the appropriate titles. When speaking in Italian, the *lei* form is always used unless otherwise specified. The above tendencies are evident in business cards, which may be of three kinds: formal with all the necessary business information, including titles and degrees; informal without extensive titles, but which indicates that one had formed a less formal professional relationship; social or visiting card with just the person's name.

## Physical Contact

Italians are very warm, and it is quite normal to see men hugging each other or sitting or leaning close. Women greet each other with a kiss on both cheeks, usually after the first time they meet. Men shake hands with men and will kiss women who they know on both cheeks. However, Italians have a smaller spatial radius than many foreigners. Part of this is due to the nature of the culture, very relationship-oriented, but also because in many areas space is actually very limited.

## Power Distance

Italians tend to follow more traditional roles of hierarchy. They seem to be very egalitarian in their communication style, but they respect hierarchical structure. Status and titles are important. Foreign managers who are more informal must remember to project themselves in terms of their perceived status.

## Individualism

Italians pride themselves on being highly individualistic. This comes out repeatedly as being a very important cultural value. But individualism does not mean independent. They are very social and prefer to be in groups, as long as they are still viewed as unique individuals. In negotiating, it often happens that each individual wants to speak, and basically repeats everything that has already been said. If the individuals are denied the opportunity to speak, they go away feeling resentful and undervalued. The result of this individualism is the fact that Italians find it difficult to truly work as part of a team.

## Competitiveness

Italians are competitive even though they put a high stress on relationships. Probably the biggest areas of competition are physical appearance and lifestyle. But Italian business does not have the same drive toward competition that many foreign businesses do, probably because business is based on relationships, which means that client relationships take precedence. It is not common practice in Italian business to give individual awards or single out one individual for commendation. This trait is very much evident in the field of sports.

## Structure

Italian life is seemingly highly chaotic, perhaps as a result of the bureaucracy and the lack of overall communication between government offices. Thousands of laws are made in the hope of imposing some sort of control. But as one writer said succinctly, the Italians are unpredictable, but they love routine. They are highly risk-aversive, but they go out of their way to circumvent regulations. Italian companies do not like to take risks. However, experience has shown that if a company is willing to take a risk, it will do very well in Italy.

## Thinking

Italians are *deductive* in academic situations, but pragmatic in business negotiations. They tend to decide on the basis of separate situations, and often refer back to other similar situations and results.

## *Italian Systems Orientation*

### Economy

Italy has the fifth largest economy in the world, despite its problems. The government seems to favor privatization and less state control of the economy, though it is required to meet EU standards and regulations. For all its attractions and successful firms, Italy is caught in a slow economic decline, requiring bold political leadership to push needed reforms. The single *euro* currency has broken the country's habit of frequent devaluation, but it is also forcing Italy to change its whole economic model while promoting structural reforms. Some of the biggest economic challenges facing Italy are the following:

- Living standards are falling in spite of increasing costs.
- Too many small, privately and family-owned companies, which contribute to low female participation in the workforce and are often in the wrong industries.
- Backward southern regional economy that is poorly performing and too dependent on the public sector.
- Corruption and violent crime (e.g., Naples), aided by Mafia activities somewhat delimited by prosecutions by dedicated magistrates.
- Underdeveloped tourism industry despite the gains the country can make from tourism.
- High unemployment rate, heavy business tax burden, and unwieldy government bureaucracy—the high rate of unemployment is caused by the heavy employment taxes that businesses must pay to employ people legally; high business taxes and red tape discourage foreign investment.
- A very strong black market, whose dimension is really not known. This means that the Italian economy is probably a lot stronger than it appears on paper because of the size of the *mercato nero*.

Further, the amount of foreign investment is significantly less than in other European countries, for several reasons. First, communism exerted a strong influence on the government after World War II, discouraging foreign business. Second, the distribution system of Italy has a long way to go before it can compete effectively with other European countries. Third, the practice of delayed payment discourages business in all areas. Italian companies usually pay on a 60- to 120-day basis, which ends up frequently translating into 120-160 days. This can cause a significant cash flow problem for foreign companies who are waiting for payment and must finance the delay. As can well be imagined, there is an ensuing snowball effect. Delayed payment is rampant in Italy. Currently, the government is trying to solve such problems, but it is unlikely that solutions will be found very soon.

## Sociopolitical Forces

The Catholic Church continues to be a significant political and cultural force in Italy, even though it has declined in power in the past few years. Italy is primarily Catholic, but a great percentage of the population does not actually regularly practice that ancient religion. However, the Vatican has a strong presence in the formation of government policy, especially in the moral and ethical areas.

## Government and Political Forces

Mussolini once said, "It is not impossible to govern Italians. It is merely useless." Italy is a multiparty parliamentary republic. Because of the large number of political parties (approximately 50 or more), Italy is basically governed by coalitions formed by various parties. One can only imagine the challenge of developing policies with so many parties. There is both a president and a prime minister. Government plays a heavy role in business, as do the labor unions. Foreign managers must be very aware of this added dimension to doing business in Italy, especially its complex justice system.

## Legal System

The Italian legal system and bureaucracy is infamously torturous and slow, as well as contradictory. It has been estimated that there are over 500,000 laws in Italy, many of which have never been cancelled since Roman and medieval times, as well as the hundreds of new ones that are made every year. This makes the law profession quite attractive and it is necessary for every business to have a competent lawyer on call. Similarly, tax codes are perilous. The situation is further complicated by the overlay of EU rules and regulations. Such a high number of laws, laughed one Italian businessman, and nobody follows any of them! Thus, the cultural value of *arrangiarsi* flourishes in response to an overloaded system.

## Women in Business

Traditionally, Italy and its business world were male-dominated, despite great respect for women and matriarchal figures. In the past two decades, the ladies have been challenging such attitudes. Although women in commerce and the professions are more prevalent and accepted, their salaries and perks usually are not yet comparable to their male colleagues, even when the women have superior education. However, their gender is making rapid progress, especially when such career women develop their own personalized management style.

## Business-Family Capitalism

As a great number of businesses in Italy are family-owned, many businesses lack management professionals. The head of the family wants to maintain control over the business. This widespread phenomenon weakens Italy because these businesses do not want to be publicly traded. Because they finance through debt, and because they want to maintain control at all costs, they limit their growth, and subsequently cannot compete in the global market (Exhibit 13.8). Yet the genial, amiable, and volatile Italian people will endure and move ahead in the twenty-first century—by most standards, they are wealthy, live long, and their families work together!

---

### EXHIBIT 13.8
### CONCLUDING TIPS FOR DOING BUSINESS IN ITALY

- Start-up: Be aware of possible problems—involving laws and taxes.
- Learn Italian.
- Try to find an Italian counterpart to help you through the bureaucracy.
- For the initial contact, a third-party introduction is very helpful; if you can't get that, write directly in Italian.
- Print materials in Italian.
- Meeting: Try to build a relationship. This is a relationship-oriented country, and if you form a relationship, you have a better chance. You do that by taking time, finding out about the other person, and building trust. It is perfectly acceptable to ask questions about the family, and expect to answer questions about yours. Dress code—look your best.
- Forms of address—Be formal until the other person indicates that you may speak in the familiar (that is, if you are speaking in Italian).
- Access the *cordata*.
- Get a good lawyer and a good *commercialista*.
- Be flexible.
- Make connections.
- Be patient (things go along at what seems to be a standstill, and suddenly the ball starts rolling).

In a sense, Europe borders on Russia and Turkey, both of which provide entry into Asia. In ancient times, they connected to a series of trade routes with multiple branches through the heart of Europe and Asia, such as the better-known Asian Silk Road.

The eastern region of the European continent tends to be landlocked, but for the European-Asian connection we consider in the section on Eurasia. However, this region is also punctuated by mountain systems like the Urals, and rivers known as the Deniester, Dnieper, and Don and Volga, which also empty into the Black Sea. The area also marks where Finland meets Russia, and where in past centuries, there were great westward migrations of peoples and their flocks.

From the geopolitical entity known as the USSR, the Russian Federation has emerged in the past decade, along with its neighbors in the Commonwealth of Independent States. Together, the CIS has sought to (1) repeal all Soviet laws and assume the powers of that former regime; (2) launch radical economic reforms, including the freeing of most prices; (3) retain the ruble, while allowing new currencies to be adopted in some countries; (4) establish a European-style free trade zone; (5) create joint control of all nuclear weapons; and (6) fulfil all foreign treaties and other obligations of the former communist regime.

Since the Soviet breakup, the countries immediately surrounding the Russian Federation have been in turmoil. Once part of the Czar's empire in the Caucasus, these entities struggle to be nations, like Belarus, Georgia, and the Ukraine. They seek a new identity and more independence, while coping with dictators, internal conflict, and serious economic problems. Besides the Russian Federation, the other key Commonwealth player is ancient Ukraine, populated with Slavic peoples from at least 2000 B.C. Its name means *borderland*, and its beautiful capital is Kiev, the mother city of the Old Russian Empire, Slavic Orthodox churches, and Cossacks.

## *Historical Perspective on Eastern Europe*[11]

To understand what is happening in contemporary Russia, its regions, and satellite countries, one has to comprehend that vast country's recent history, especially its 1918 revolution. Figes, who did a sweeping cultural survey of Russia for the past three centuries, raised an astute question: "How can this nation, whose elites have consistently looked to foreign countries for their cultural examples, be held together by the unseen threads of native sensibility?" Yet, for much of the last century, its totalitarian mindset and policies dominated political, social, and economic life throughout both Central Europe and Eurasia. When the Union of Soviet Socialist Republics was founded in 1922, Russia, and eventually its East Bloc allies, ensured that all major government and economic decision-making posts were filled by Communist Party members. These enforced its doctrine of centralism, requiring that decisions made at the top not be questioned by the lower echelons. This led to a situation in which a few people at the peak of the pyramid made almost every significant decision, and local initiative was practically nonexistent. The system restricted enterprise and meaningful contact with world market demand and supply. Its state monopoly sought to prevent capitalist countries from influencing the course of economic activities in the whole geographic area, except for what Western science and technologies its spies could steal.

Yet, under this repressive regime, the USSR did survive World War II, becoming a superpower that achieved some impressive accomplishments. These ranged from education and health care to industrialization and an innovative space program. Before its decline, the Soviet empire had 450 million inhabitants, including some 140 national groups with a mix of European/Asian cultures, and religions ranging from Christians to 50 million Muslims. The USSR's 31 so-called autonomous republics and regions stretched from the Gulf of Finland to the Pacific Ocean. As this great monolith disintegrated, the people of Russia and its satellite countries endured disruptions in their lives, such as the following:

■ Widespread unemployment and massive amounts of unpaid work.
■ Rapid rise in penury and beggary, stress and alcoholism, and corruption and crime.
■ Deterioration in public services and the economy, especially currency speculation.
■ Chaos in political, social, and family life.
■ Initial failure with capitalism, while the "new aristocracy" made up of greedy oligarchs or tycoons mainly prospered.

Since the collapse of the USSR in 1991, the peoples of Central and Eastern Europe identify themselves increasingly with Western culture and free-market enterprises. Their traditional institutions are trying to transform themselves, as new entities, missions, and roles are being formulated. There is growing emphasis on protection of freedom, human rights, and the rule of law, as well as on improving the environment and quality of life. Many of today's inhabitants are not only victims of communist cultural conditioning, but also suffered the effects from the former cold war between East and West.

The trends, depending on where you are in that area of Europe, are toward reviving the private sector, so that businesspeople can not only own property, but also get access to labor, capital, machinery, and raw materials. Increasingly, within their huge, inefficient public sector, governments have undertaken a number of reform experiments, such as the following:

- Downsizing bureaucracies to more efficient entities.
- Modernizing legal systems and procedures, especially regarding private property.
- Changing legislation to privatize state-owned businesses and to subsidize enterprises that are private or cooperatives.
- Permitting market forces, instead of the government, to set prices.
- Creating more flexible and open banking systems that lend money on the basis of fiscal soundness instead of merely connections.
- Innovating to attract Western investment, credit, and joint ventures.

Each of these countries is in transition, having troubles institutionalizing reforms and countering widespread corruption. But global managers with vision see new market possibilities in both Central and Eastern Europe, and seek to develop links there with representatives from governments, unions, businesses, churches, environmentalists, and students. Aware of the cultural and intellectual heritage of the region, as well as its potential, they network and encourage entrepreneurs, provide training and services, while promoting diversification and outside investment. Trade and education, especially involving the exchange of people, can be a powerful means of facilitating the reform of obsolete systems and practices. The twenty-first century provides a rare chance to work towards peaceful prosperity in this part of Europe for those bold enough to participate in the improvement process. To regain their dignity and enthusiasm for freedom and work, Dr. Woodrow Sears refers to this as the passing of the "sleepwalking culture"—dreams/ memories persist of Soviet work habits, lacking in real motivation and productivity.

To acculturate the peoples of former communist countries to real democracy and a market economy is a massive reeducation challenge that will take many decades. George Soros, investment broker, has made the case for this. Through his Soros Foundation, this billionaire funds practical projects in this region (and China) initiated by dissenters, journalists, educators, and entrepreneurs. He supports those seeking to bolster battered economies in their transition from socialism to free enterprise systems. In 1991, for example, at the start of an aborted Soviet coup, his foundation gave photocopiers to then-Russian President Boris Yeltsin, so they could print fliers to rally Moscow citizens to support the embattled reformers. Since then, this Quantum Fund founder spends both time and money in development of modern management within Central and Eastern Europe, cultivating entrepreneurial job skills, as well as basic market and consumer literacy. This philanthropist also founded and endowed Central European University, a private graduate school located in Budapest, Hungary, and Warsaw, Poland. Hopefully, it will inspire other Western institutions and foundations to emulate such endeavors.

## *Historical Perspective*

It is said that the very name "Russia" came from Viking invaders who called the inhabitants *Rus*. Over the course of the last seventeen centuries, many ethnic groups have come into this vast domain, some in peace and some by war. From the third to the seventh centuries, there were the nomadic Slavs, Turks, and Bulgars. By 1236, the Mongols came as conquerors. From the fourteenth to the fifteenth centuries, Moscow emerged as a center of power in the north. Then Tsars Ivan II (the Great) and Ivan IV (the Terrible) expelled the Tartars. Russian development was further impeded by internal conflicts among the feudal nobility, plus continuing border warfare with Poland and Sweden. Next, Russia progressed under Tsar Peter I (the Great) who opened the country to the West and its expertise. But the nation became a great power under Catherine II (the Great), who extended its borders in both the north and south. During the Crimean War and World War I, the Russian people and soldiers suffered severe setbacks. Then the Bolsheviks seized political power in 1917, and the Russian Revolution was launched. The monarchy ended, but a 5-year civil war ensued between two factions—the revolutionaries, or Reds; and the counterrevolutionaries, or Whites; aided by Western allied nations. The former prevailed, and a socialist, or communist, government, as previously noted, was established in 1922 as the Soviet Union (USSR).

The remainder of the twentieth century was marked by ups and downs—WWII and invasion of Nazi Germany; postwar expansion, and establishment of East Bloc sphere of influence and control; growth as a super power, significant accomplishments in the Soviet space program; a "Cold War" with the United States and Western allies. An unsuccessful invasion of Afghanistan proved costly in terms of deaths and finances, causing a loss in popular support for the government. By 1991, an independence movement arose, causing the USSR to implode and break up as a union of socialist "republics." Under the leadership of Boris Yeltsin, a new constitution was adopted in 1993, with a new type of governance constituted with a president, prime minister, and Federal Assembly, or state *Dumas*, consisting of 450 members, plus a Federation Council of 178 members. Furthermore, Russia led in the formation of a Commonwealth of Independent States, made up of neighboring nations who were once part of the old USSR. Both the Federation and CIS ostensibly aim toward democracy and free enterprise. Some of the ex-communist leaders from the old KBG managed to get "elected," such as Vladimir Putin, once President and now Prime Minister. But their actions have been mixed in consequences as they create a neo-KGB state. For example, a disastrous war, starting in 1994, was waged with a break-away region of Chechnya, and in 2008, Russia invaded Georgia for a short period. The Federation's Federal Security Service (FSB), successor to the old KBG, and its sister organizations now have undercover operatives who control the Kremlin government, the media, and large parts of the economy, as well as the military and security forces. These bureaucratic *siloviki* or "power guys" make important national decisions and control key state institutions, along with private security firms. From their ranks comes a Kremlin inner circle which actually manages the country and many agencies of government, while also consolidating political power and neutralizing other sources of influence. This brotherhood of secret servicemen consists of super nationalists who are not only loyal to one another, but entitled to break the law in pursuit of mission. Their children become graduates of the FSB Academy in Moscow, and are the new elite. Culturally, Russians have traditionally preferred rulers who are firm, reserved, and exercise authority with a degree of mystery.[d]

Although Russia had been reorganized into 89 regions with elected governors, Putin changed that so that these officials are now appointed by the President. Also, there has been much internal conflict within regions, causing severe crackdowns from the central government and their armed forces (e.g., Belsan, Chechnya, Ingushetta), or in others with large population fleeing elsewhere, such as in Chutkotka and Magadan. Still, other remote regions, like dismal Sakhalin, manage to attract the citizenry because of the jobs in the expanding oil and gas terminals there. In the twenty-first century, Russia has become a principal supplier of oil and gas to Europe, yet remains one of the most criminalized, corrupt, and bureaucratic countries in the world, most evident in its military forces. Russia is different, a work in progress, and not a full democracy or market economy in the Western understanding of such concepts.

Russia has yet to finalize its relationship with other European institutions. Fifteen years ago, it applied for EU membership, which has yet to be acted upon. Some argue that this nation is too big, too poor, and not European enough, while others make the case for admission as Russia has a democratic government and controls vast energy resources needed on the continent. Although it has associated agreements with NATO, Russia fears its expansion among neighboring states which once were under the old Soviet administration.

## Cultural Guidelines for Doing Business in Russia and the CIS

Whether the remodeled Russian Federation will be able to modernize further and peacefully meet the immense needs of its varied peoples is an open question. Obviously, this nation and its CIS partners are in the midst of a painful political, social, and economic transition. For centuries, the national cultures were autocratic and totalitarian, centered around bureaucratic centralized planning from Moscow. It was a culture with a very large underclass of poor peasants, led by a wealthy elite (first, aristocrats in the monarchy, and later, Communist Party insiders). The move toward a more open, democratic, free enterprise society is slow and disjointed. Apart from the weather, commercial efforts within Russia for

---

[d]"The Making of a Neo-KBG State," *The Economist*, August 25, 2007, pp. 25–28.

the uninitiated may prove difficult, if not dangerous. This is confirmed in the November 2008 "state of the nation" speech by Putin's hand-picked president. Dmitry Medvedev railed against bureaucracy and corruption, while also warning about state meddling into private business. In nationalist rhetoric, he said that business is frightened that it will do wrong. If this is true of domestic commerce, then envision the problems faced by foreign business representatives. Some of the challenges Russian citizens and expatriates face are analyzed in the following sections, insights essential if one seeks to do business there or negotiate agreements.

## Instability and Transformation

- Accelerating disintegration of the economy and need for reformed financial and legal systems, as well as more unfettered private enterprise.
- Deepening crises in food/consumer goods production and distribution, as well as in housing and health services.
- Breakdowns in traditional systems (e.g., legal, banking, business, fuel, and transportation), which hinder foreign investment and entrepreneurialism.
- Extensive job dislocation and rising unemployment.
- Political fragmentation and power-seeking by the republics, such as the independence movement in Chechnya and in other regions.
- Rising crime and political assassinations administered by a criminal underground *Mafia* that extends its power even to émigrés, such as in New York and Los Angeles.
- Remnants of very powerful "oligarchs" who once amassed their wealth by seizure or rigged purchasing of state assets, and still are to be found among the rich elite.

Yet the Russian and CIS transformation to a free-market system has many positives on which to capitalize, such as the following:

- Vast natural and material resources, much of which is yet to be developed.
- Incredible human resources of a literate people with a combination of unique traditions and contributions to the arts and sciences, from music and the ballet, to space technology, engineering, and physics.
- A sound educational system that provides high-level instruction in mathematics and sciences.
- Codependent economies that foster cooperative alliances, as in a compact signed among five Central Asian republics of Kazakhstan, Kyrgyzstan, Tajikistan, Turkmenistan, and Uzbekistan.
- Growing interest in preserving and protecting the environment and preventing disasters like nuclear accidents.
- Widespread movement toward divesting state industries to private enterprise and state landholdings to private ownership.

- Majority of the population demonstrating for conservative public decisions made in a democratic way, desiring order and discipline but not totalitarianism.
- Increasing interest in protecting individual and human rights, while moving in the direction of democratic freedoms and economic pragmatism.
- Resurgence of religion and religious tolerance.
- Expanding entrepreneurialism, even among academics and scientists.

Exhibit 13.9 puts the above observation in terms of one company transitioning from a totalitarian to free enterprise system.

---

## EXHIBIT 13.9

## THE SAGA OF THE RUSSIAN AUTO GIANT

KamAZ, an auto and truck manufacturing giant founded in 1969 at Kama in Central Russia, had developed hundreds of subsidiaries in the Ukraine, Kazakhstan, and Bashkiria. During the "detente" period of the 1970s, it benefited from a multinational consortium of American, West German, French, and Italian firms, which provided millions of dollars worth of equipment and 1000 foreign experts. By the 1980s, production of rugged, sophisticated trucks and engines had risen to 250,000 units annually. But with the communist state pocketing the profits, no modernization, and an acute shortage of equipment, the huge enterprise with 170,000 employees and a "company city" of 500,000 began to suffer from deterioration. In 1989, "perestroika" led to more privatization as workers approved lease-holding and empowered management to negotiate for them to take over the state-owned business. Under the innovative leadership of its general manager, Nikolai Beth, a joint stock company was established with shares purchased by its own personnel and 1200 other plans and organizations. In the 1990s, the KamAZ products won prizes at international rallies and competitions, and the worker-owners linked their higher living standards and social protection with growth of production and quality improvement.

Today, their corporate future depends upon penetrating foreign markets with their reliable, heavy-duty trucks, as sales in Saudi Arabia, Senegal, and Egypt prove. For that to happen, KamAZ seeks international partners in trading firms and automotive firms throughout the world. For global managers, this saga of the transformation and requirements of just one Russian business is both symbolic of what is happening throughout the republics within the CIS. There are many similar synergistic opportunities within Central and Eastern Europe for both investment and skill development by businesses from mature market economies.

## Negotiating Style and Protocol

During the ongoing change from centralized planning to market economies within the CIS, foreigners can expect much confusion, frustration, and uncertainty. In negotiations, the Russians are noted for patience and stalling, considering compromise a sign of weakness. They expect to "play hardball," continually seeking concessions, and revising "final offers"—the longer the foreigner holds out acceptance, the more attractive the offer. Emotional "walkouts" and dire proclamations are part of their process. So too, is the use of *blat*, or connections, who use influence on your behalf in exchange for favors, monetary or otherwise. Bribery and corruption are major problems, as are drinking bouts to solidify friendly relations.

There are two stages in actual business negotiations with the Russians. During the first stage, they try to get as many competitive offers as possible, and play one supplier against another, before making a final decision. Nothing may happen for a while after the Western firm has submitted its bid. Then, the Russians may notify the firm that they are still interested and resume negotiations. Potential suppliers are expected to provide detailed technical explanations of their products, so that the Russians can evaluate precisely what is being offered. Having collected several competitive offers, the Russians are adept at creating competition among the suppliers. Quotations from competitors are revealed to force bidding suppliers to cut their prices.

The second phase of negotiations begins when the supplier has been chosen. This phase is usually shorter than the initial one, but it still takes time to settle all of the various points in the final contract. Russian negotiators often negotiate with the weakest competitor first. After concessions are obtained from the weakest, the other companies are notified that they also must accept them.

Another maneuver used by Russian negotiators is to first fix the final price the supplier is willing to take for its product. Once this price is firmly quoted, the Russians may make additional demands for such extra services as free training of technicians or equipment maintenance, which were not originally included in the producer's description and price. Experienced foreign companies make it a standing rule to begin contract talks by discussing the articles of the purchasing agreement before any discussion begins on final price. It should also be made clear at the beginning on which points the supplier is willing to make concessions and on which it is not. The longer an executive postpones talking about demands that are of major importance to his or her company, the more forcefully the Russians may oppose them later.

Each agreement made with the Russians should stand on its own accord. Granting a price discount or making concessions to the Russians to win future business simply does not work. A common Russian tactic is to ask for a bulk price for a product, and then to apply the lower price per unit from the bulk price to a smaller lot. It is implied, and sometimes even promised verbally, that more purchases will follow. However, the Russians will honor only written agreements.

It is important to let the Russians know exactly where your firm stands on all issues. The Russians do not respect negotiators who make large concessions, because they then believe that initial proposals were inflated or deceptive. The proposer firm should be prepared to stand by its position, and to drop negotiations and cut its profits/losses if necessary. This will impress the Russians far more than slowly acquiescing to their demands. Although the "old" Soviet system may no longer exist, attitudes and cultural perceptions are much more resilient. Russians are very protocol conscious. Remember, just as everything else in Russia is being altered, so may be the above negotiating styles.

However, most of the CIS inhabitants are anxious to find international partners and to learn about Western business practices. No longer having to answer to a centralized government and wanting to move as quickly as possible toward "free enterprise," their business negotiators may be more flexible and accommodating than their Soviet predecessors.

## Work Environment

The work week is generally Monday through Friday, 9 a.m. to 5 p.m. Recently, some banks are opening on Saturdays and evenings. Retail stores may be open Monday through Saturdays from 8-9 a.m. to 8-9 p.m.; food stores are also open on Sunday. Although foreigners are expected to show up on time for business appointments, allowance is made to be 15-30 min late for social events. Your Russian counterpart may be tardy or not show up at all—the previous communist system conditioned people to lateness, not promptness, and endless waiting in lines. Now, foreign businesses are training their personnel in attitudes of punctuality and prompt customer service. Also allow for delays because of inadequate transportation and distances.

Typically, Russian and CIS officials expect to conduct business with only the highest-ranking executives. On the initial visit, the Western firm's representative is advised to send its top personnel to ensure a favorable first impression (e.g., a regional or East European manager). Final negotiations on larger deals should be handled by a key executive to demonstrate the importance the Western firm is placing on this business. Then the locals may be willing for their chairperson or deputy chairperson to enter the negotiations at some decisive stage.

The following are some additional cultural aspects of working in Russia:

■ *Consumers* are only beginning to get accustomed to higher quality for higher prices. In addition to a plentiful and consistent supply of quality food, they seek modern conveniences and entertainment. Having been subjected to substandard clothing and outdated styles, they hunger for Western adornments that are colorful, stylish, and practical in their climate. However, business dress is conservative (e.g., suit and tie).

■ *Business contacts*—Relative to foreign trade, the renamed Russian Market Institute can provide useful data and quotations. Outsiders will have to network and seek direct contacts with new factory owners and entrepreneurs. Emerging there and in the United States are consulting firms/publications to facilitate business in Eastern Europe. The Internet can be a prime source of this information.

■ *Currency challenges*—Innovative ways must be developed to convert the volatile ruble and other new monetary units into international hard currency, such as barter, exchange of services, or third-country transfer, as well as direct banking transfers to specific accounts.

■ *Attention to details*—Because of prior Soviet cultural conditioning for seven decades, visitors can expect local officials to give much attention to such matters as seating arrangements and invitations, business cards printed in both Cyrillic and one's own language or English, and the caliber of a technical presentation both written and oral. Continuity is an important factor, so the visiting team should designate one person as project manager or spokesman in all business dealings.

■ *Communication*—Facilitated when the foreigner can speak the local language, but many Russians, Ukrainians, and other republic representatives are comfortable speaking English, German, or French. The use of interpreters has both positives (clarifying meaning or building interpersonal relations) and negatives (perceptual slanting by the translator or lack of technical understanding). Orally, Russians may greet foreigners with *gospodin* (Mr.) or *gospozha* (Miss or Mrs.) and ask acquaintances for their *imya* (first name) or *ochestvo* (patronymic). Name listings are similar to those in the West, except for the use of the Russian middle name—a *patronymic* derived from the first name of one's father (e.g., the use of *Ivanovich*, meaning the son of Ivan). Women also add an "a" to their surname, as well as to their patronymic middle name (e.g., *Ivanova* for daughter of Ivan). Customarily, the use of the latter, or first name, is indicative of familiarity and friendship.

■ Get to know Russian body language. For example, to the Westerner, the traditional Russian official or executive may appear stiff. Gestures are usually kept to a minimum, and expressions may seem blank and uninterested. Smiles are rare, except between people who are very close. This is the public image Russians seem to convey. In private, they are much more expressive. The modest reserve that they publicly project breaks down under more personal surroundings and socialization.

■ *Time sense*—Quite different here, and the locals dislike the quick tempo of Western business or the attitude that time is money. They use the slower tempo to good advantage, especially in negotiations, business, or socializing. The inhabitants here quote old Russian proverbs like, "If you travel for a day, take bread for a week," or "Patience and work, and everything will work out." Part of this stoicism and slowness is due to inadequate telecommunications and transportation. Within this colossus of a country, even simple technological advances like fax machines can save much time and facilitate communication, while the computer may expedite matters, if the local has one that functions.

■ *National psyche*—Russians have long suffered from a sense of inferiority (for which they overcompensate); in the days of the aristocracy, the Czar's court turned to things French and German to show how civilized and sophisticated they were. Having been often cut off from outside contacts, the Russians also have manifested xenophobia periodically. Totalitarianism also made many citizens feel like prisoners in their own society. The younger generation is more educated, more open, and more cosmopolitan, as well as more disillusioned and cynical.

Russian leaders are generous hosts with food and beverage. Dinners are long and elaborate, and toasts are frequently and generously made to good business relationships and mutual friendships. The visiting foreign businessperson should be prepared to encounter some amiable "imbibing competition" stemming from the Russian prowess for drinking. To better comprehend these complex Slavic people, it helps to read their writers before traveling to Mother Russia. Remember, like other parts of this world, this is a risky, but highly profitable, place to do business today. Also realize that in many neighboring states, especially those in the old Soviet East countries, Russian culture, language, currency, and expatriates dominate; some, like Abkhazi, are even extended Russian passports. If Russia is to resurge, then its Kremlin leaders need to renounce their new imperialism and develop their economy, expected to be $5 trillion by 2020, to the benefit of its own people, so as to improve their living conditions. The promise of Russia is that it is likely to become the world's most prolific launchers of spacecraft, and a principal partner in the international quest to utilize space resources during this century.[12]

## CONCLUSIONS

In the opening section of this chapter, we have presented both a historical and a contemporary analysis of Europe as it enters the new millennium. The overview includes the ongoing developments within the EU expansion to 25 members, as well as its accomplishments and ambitions. Some countries who have expressed interest in EU membership have been given no timetable for admittance, such as the mini-Balkan states. Others, like Iceland, are conflicted about potential admittance—they would like the *euro* for currency stability, but are uncertain about other membership obligations. Yet Iceland has been one of Europe's richest countries and fastest growing economies until its financial meltdown in 2008.

Some key dimensions of European diversity and synergy have been examined here—from languages and demographics to immigration and identity. One new EU strategy for nonmembers is the *European Neighborhood Policy*—this offers countries of North Africa, the Mediterranean, the Caucasus, and Eastern Europe, graduated access to the single EU market. The aim is to provide financial and technical aid to these neighbors, in exchange for reforms that bring them closer to the Union's political and economic models.

To help global leaders become more effective on this important continent, the chapter then devoted its coverage to historical context, plus insights into diverse cultural and business practices in five separate geographic areas of Europe—the nations and peoples of the west, central, north, south, and east. Profiles were provided for most countries in these locations, while culture-specific information was shared about select countries. This sampling of the continent's complex cultural groupings and national entities may help readers avoid the trap of overgeneralized assumptions about Europeans. If more cooperative relationships are to be developed with their citizens and leaders, we recommend further data gathering, especially via the Internet. Information collection is the initial step in developing a personal file of business intelligence about countries and cultures if one wishes to perform well. Whether in Europe or elsewhere, such learning should be continually verified for validity in specific times and places, as well as with different individuals and organizations.

At this opening decade of the twenty-first century, profound economic, social, political, and cultural changes are under way throughout the whole of Europe. Peaceful trade, commerce, and travel there undergird that transformation process. But the EU is the key mechanism for furthering free enterprise and democracy, as well as the preservation of human rights while respecting diversity among all its inhabitants.

For the next 50 years, Europeans are likely to be engaged in struggles to (1) gain continental identity; (2) cope with fertility issues of lower birth rates among the traditional inhabitants, and higher ones among the immigrants; (3) control the flow and acculturate these new arrivals from abroad, especially among the Muslim populations; (4) transform their agricultural and industrial cultures to a continental knowledge culture; and (5) operate more effectively within the realities of the global market. At least over 16 European nations collaborate in space investment and exploration through the European Space Agency.

## MIND STRETCHING

1. Why is some understanding of European history so important to comprehending EU and related continental developments today?
2. What are the implications of changes in the balance of religious adherents within Europe (e.g., Christianity, Muslims, and Jews)?
3. How is the development of a single continental market strategy in Europe going to affect the global market?
4. Why are the nations in northern Europe concerned about the less economically developed countries in southern Europe?
5. What are some of the specific European countries whose cultures facilitate synergistic relations with their neighbors, and which ones are seemingly unsynergistic (e.g., more combative, less cooperative).
6. What impact do geography and climate in various parts of Europe have on a people's culture and economy?

## REFERENCES

1. *Europe in Transition—Reshaping a Continent* (a map insert). Washington, DC: National Geographic, 2008; *Family Reference Atlas of the World.* Washington, DC: National Geographic Society, 2002, "Europe," pp. 126–141; Davis, W., Harrison, K., and Howell, C. H. *Book of Peoples of the World—A Guide to Cultures.* Washington, DC: National Geographic, 2008, "Europe," pp. 192–255; Refer to Web site, www.nationalgeographic.com; Morrison, T., Conway, W. A., and Douress, J. J. *Dun & Bradstreet Guide to Doing Business Around the World.* Upper Saddle River, NJ: Prentice-Hall, 2009.
2. *Europe: The State of the Union.* New York, NY: Atlantic Monthly Press, 2008; Pinder, J. and Usherwood, S. *The European Union: A Very Short Guide.* Oxford, UK: Oxford University Press, 2007; *Guide to the European Union.* South Burlington, VT: Bloomberg Press/Economist Books, 2004, www.bloomberg.com/economistbooks; Beech, D. *The Dynamics of European Integration: Why and When EU Institutions Matter.* London, UK: Palgrave Macmillan, 2005.
3. Rennie, D. "In the Nick of Time—A Special Report on EU Enlargement," *The Economist*, May 31 2008, pp. 16; Peet, J. "Fit at 50—A Special Report on the European Union," *The Economist*, , March 17 2007, pp. 20, www.economst.com/specialreports. Richman, G., "Outgrowing the Union—Survey of European Union," *The Economist*, September 24 2004, www.economist.com/surveys.
4. Norman, P. *The Accidental Constitution—The Story of the European Convention.* London, UK: Palgrave Macmillan, 2005; Leonard, M. *Why Europe Will Run the 21st Century.* London, UK: Fourth Estate, 2006.
5. Kagan, R. *Of Paradise and Power: America versus Europe in the New World Order.* New York, NY: Knof Publishing, 2003; Simons, G. F.

Eurodiversity—A Business Guide to Managing Differences. Burlington, MA: Elsevier/Butterworth-Heinemann, 2002.

6. Storti, C. *Old World/New World-Bridging Cultural Differences: Britain, France, Germany, and the U.S.* Boston, MA: Nicholas Brealey/ Intercultural Press, 2003; Brittan, S. "Europe Is Not So Backward After All," *Financial Times*, July 30 2004; Roger, P. *The American Enemy: The History of French Anti-Americanism.* Chicago, IL: University of Chicago Press, 2005; Chesnoff, R. Z. *The Arrogance of the French—Why They Can't Stand Us and Why the Feeling is Mutual.* New York, NY: Sentinel Press, 2005; Ver Berkmoes, R. *Western Europe (Multi Country Guide).* New York, NY: Amazon.com/books, 2007.

7. Klausen, J. *The Islamic Challenge: Politics and Religion in Western Europe.* Oxford, UK: Oxford University Press, 2005; Burleigh, M. *Earthly Power—The Clash of Religion and Politics in Europe from the French Revolution to the Great War.* New York, NY: HarperCollins, 2006; Baker, R. W. *Islam without Fear—Egypt and the New Islamists, 2003.* Boston, MA: Harvard University Press, 2003.

8. Guizot, P. G. *A Popular History of France from Earliest Times*, Vol. 1. London, UK: BiblioBazaar, 2008; Porter, D. and Prince, D. *Frommer's France 2008.* Hoboken, NJ: Wiley Publishing Inc., 2007; Asselin, G. and Mastron, R. *Au Contraire! Figuring Out the French.* Boston, MA: Nicholas Brealey/Intercultural Press, 2001. "The Art of the Impossible—A Survey of France," *The Economist*, October 28 2006, pp. 16; "French Decline—Predators and Prophets," *The Economist*, February 4 2006, p. 6.

9. Howe, S. *Ireland and Empire: Colonial Legacies in Irish History and Culture.* Oxford, UK: Oxford University Press, 2002; Daugherty, C. *Frommer's Ireland 2008.* Hoboken, NJ: Wiley Publishing Inc., 2007; Golway, T. and Coffee, M. (eds.). *Irish America.* New York, NY: Hyperion, 1997.

10. Turner, H. (ed.). *Central Europe Profile: Essential Facts on Society, Business, and Politics.* New York, NY: Palgrave MacMillan, 2000; Sears, W. H. and Tamulionyte-Lentz, A. *Succeeding in Business in Central and Eastern Europe—Guide to Culture, Markets, and Practices.* Burlington, MA: Elsevier/Butterworth-Heinemann, 2001; Bateman, M. (ed.). *Business Cultures in Central and Eastern Europe.* Oxford, UK: Elsevier/Butterworth-Heinmann, 1996, www.books@elsevier.com/management.

11. Kitchen, M. *A History of Modern Germany 1800–2000.* Malden, MA: Blackwell Publishing, 2006; Porter, D. and Prince, D. *Frommer's Germany 2008.* Hoken, NJ: Wiley Publishing Inc, 2007; Bigham, G. *German Survival Guide.* Shell Rock, IA: World Prospect Press, 2008, www. worldprosectpress.com; "A Survey of Germany," *The Economist*, November 19 1996; "Waiting for Wunder—A Survey of Germany," *The Economist*, , February 11 2006, www.economist.com/surveys; "An Uncertain Giant," *The Economist*, December 7 2002, p. 20; Neiman, S. *Foreigners See It Differently.* Potsdam, Germany: Einstein Forum, 2005.

12. "Russia Resurgent and How the West Should Respond," *The Economist*, August 16–27 2008. pp. 1, 24–26; "Russia: A Special Report," *The Economist*, November 29, 2008; Service, R. *Commrades! A History of World Communism.* Cambridge, MA: Harvard University Press, 2007; Brown, A. *Seven Years That Changed the World: Perestroika to*

*Perspective*. Oxford, UK: Oxford University Press, 2007; Longworth, P. *Russia: The Once and Future Empire—From Pre-history to Putin*. New York, NY: St. Martin's Press, 2006; Neville, P. *A Travelers History of Russia*. New York, NY:Amazon.com, 2006; Figes, O. *Natasha's Dance: A Cultural History of Russia*. London, UK: Allen Lane/Penguin, 2002; Appelebaum, A. *Gulag: A History*. London: AllenLane/Penguin, 2003; Kotkin, S. *Armageddon Averted: The Soviet Collapse 1970–2000*. Oxford, UK: Oxford University Press, 2001; Aslund, A. *Building Capitalism: The Transformation of the Former Soviet East Bloc*. Cambridge, UK: Cambridge University Press, 2001; Holden, N., Cooper, G. and Carr, J. *Dealing with the New Russia—Management Cultures in Collision*. Chichester, UK: John Wiley & Sons, 1998; Granville, E. and Oppenheimer, P. *Russia's Post Communist Economy*. Oxford, UK: Oxford University Press, 2001; Tolstaya, T. *Pushkin's Children—Writings on Russia and Russians*. New York, NY: Houghton-Mifflin, 2002.

*Resources for the Future*: MCD8e readers concerned about the future of the world or a specific region or country will find useful these three sources of information:

1. The annual *State of the Future* report and CD (www.StateOfTheFuture.org; ). This is an outcome of The Millennium Project sponsored by the World Federation of UN Associations (e-mail:jglenn@igc.org).
2. The Foundation for the Future (www.futurefoundation.org; ). Request information about publications, proceedings, awards, and symposia (e-mail:info@ futurefoundation.org).
3. The World Future Society (www.worldfuturesociety.org; ). Request membership for access to their annual forecasts, publications, online exchanges, and conferences (e-mail:jcornish@wfs.org).

*Resources on Europe*: Periodically, *The Economist* magazine publishes special country surveys which are also available in reprints. Here are examples of relevant titles: EU Enlargement (June 2006, November 2003); EU's Eastern Borders (September 2005); European Business and the EURO (December 2001); Ireland (October 2004); France (October 2006, November 2002); Italy (November 2005, July 2001); Greece (October 2002); Germany (February 2006, December 2002); Netherlands (May 2002); Poland (May 2006); Portugal (December 2002); Spain (November 2008, June 2004); Switzerland (February 2004); Russia (November 2008, May 2004); Turkey (March 2005, June 2000). For latest surveys on any country, direct inquiries to www. economist.com/surveys.

# DOING BUSINESS
# WITH AFRICANS

### Northern Africa, East Africa, West Central Africa, and Southern Africa

Africa is often called the continent of beginnings. Fossil and bone records there of the earliest humans go back more than 4 million years. Perhaps our early upright ancestor, Homo erectus, departed Africa on the long journey that eventually peopled the Earth. It now seems likely that every person today comes from a lineage that goes back to an ancient African. Innumerable cave paintings and petroglyphs, from Sahara to South Africa, provide clues to the beliefs and way of life of these age-old hominids.[1]

## LEARNING OBJECTIVES

To appreciate Africa as the cradle of human civilization, not just as a continent of economically developing countries. After a Pan African overview, this chapter will examine the nations and peoples on this diverse continent, and culture specifics will be provided so as not only to facilitate communications and business with Africans, but also to better understand these remarkable inhabitants and some of their challenges.

## INSIGHTS INTO PAN AFRICA

Two hundred million years ago, this landmass split off from the ancient supercontinent of Pangea. Africa is the cradle of all humanity, for we all trace our DNA heritage to this area. *Homo sapiens* first appeared in Africa some 200,000 years ago, probably in what is today known as Omo Kibish, Ethiopia, where our ancestors' earliest fossils were found. Genetic data indicate that there were two human migrations out of this continent. The first group went no further than what is now Israel, dying out some 90,000 years ago. Descendents of modern humans left Africa some 70-50,000 years past. By 50,000 years ago, following a coastal route along southern Asia, they reached what is now Australia, a people known today as Aborigines. Some 40-30,000 years ago, human inland migration, apparently via Asia, seeded the continent known as Europe. About the same period, these humans pushed into Central Asia, arriving on the grassy steppes north of the Himalaya. They also traveled through Southeast Asia and China, eventually reaching Japan and Siberia. Genetic clues lead us to believe that humans in northern Asia eventually migrated to the Americas. Between 20 and 15,000 years ago, sea levels were low and lands connected Siberia to Alaska; the new arrivals trekked southward down the west coast. The DNA marker M168 among today's non-Africans proves that we all trace our origins to the *mother of the human family*—Africa! Our diverse faces and races come from these first hunter-gatherers.

Africa has largely remained a mystery to the outside world, marked perhaps more by its isolation than by any other feature. This stubborn reality can be traced to the earliest times, and is reflected in the hopelessly misrepresented images of ancient cartographers, whose graphic distortions were as errant as the half myths and false science that passed for knowledge about the "dark continent." Yet, ancient civilizations flourished in Africa from Carthage in the north to "empires" in the south. Among these indigenous kingdoms was Great Zimbabwe, which flourished in the eleventh to fifteenth centuries; and, in the Niger area, the grand states of Yoruba, Ashanti, and Hausa prospered, but only Benin survived the longest from the thirteenth to nineteenth centuries. From 900 A.D. onward, the coastal plains contained the Swahili culture and language that dominated from Somalia to Zanzibar, including a mix of local peoples, Arabs, and immigrants. From the sixteenth to nineteenth centuries, the search for riches and a route to India brought European explorers and occupiers, beginning with the Portuguese, and extending to the British, French, Belgians, and Germans. Unfortunately, few Europeans appreciated the civilizations and cultures already functioning there, imposing their own ways on the indigenous inhabitants. Although Africans dispersed by natural migration, they were also forcefully introduced into the Americas, Europe, Latin America, and the Middle East as a result of the inhumane slave trade. The last half of the twentieth century has been Africa's postcolonial period of independence. As the people of the world scramble to utilize African resources, may a mature continental civilization finally come into its own in this twenty-first century!

# Historical Perspective on Modern Pan Africa[2]

Approximately 53 countries share the African territory, from Algeria in the Islamic north to South Africa in the south. National identities are diverse for peoples assembled within borders imposed by departed European imperialists. The outsiders' partitioning of Africa in the past two centuries made little attempt to make national borders coincide with on-site ethnic groups and tribes. So, one uses the term *approximately*, for boundaries on this continent are continuously being reconfigured as new states emerge. Recently, Eritrea broke away from ancient Ethiopia, and the independent homelands of Swaziland and Lesotho someday soon may be reabsorbed back into South Africa. National names also change rapidly, as when Rhodesia became Zimbabwe, and Tanganyika became Tanzania.

Africa is home to one-third of the world's sovereign states, but only 19 of them here have democratic governments. At least four are classified failed states—Congo, Somalia, Sudan, and Zimbabwe. The World Bank-IMF classifies 38 nations worldwide as heavily indebted, poor nations—32 of these are on this continent! Most of these countries came into existence in the twentieth century, and currently about half of the governments were formed as the result of coups, principally by the military. In too many African states, the rule of law has been displaced by the rule of the big man who seizes power and control. The redrawing of former colonial boundaries need not mean smaller African states; it could simply mean more rational and viable political communities. The long-term scenario emerging from continuing crises may be the gradual change of boundaries between Zaire, Rwanda, and Burundi. Unless the Hutu and Tutsi are partitioned into separate countries or federated into a larger, stable, and democratic political community, they are likely to engage in endless conflict. One scenario calls for the international community to put together a large package of inducements and incentives to persuade Rwanda, Burundi, and Tanzania to create the United States of Central Africa; parts of Zaire could one day seek admission into the new federation. Currently, the Organization of African Unity acts as a coordinating medium for the continental countries, trying to encourage regional cooperation, trading, and political stability. Sovereign states with their bureaucratic controls are the hallmark of mass civilization. But such historical experience was largely absent in sub-Saharan kingdoms before the arrival of European colonialism during the past three centuries. Given this lack of the tradition of strong statehood on the continent, where tribal governance dominated, it is understandable why contemporary Africans struggle with the refinement and administration of government and political institutions.

Although Africans had learned to smelt iron by the year 1500 A.D., the industrial stage of development was missed by most Africans. They were mainly hunter-gatherers, farmers, and herders; only a small minority lived in organized states and urban areas. After a few hundred years of predatory slave-raiding and direct European influence or rule, most Africans only regained their independence and freedom within the past 50 years. Thus, a dynamic process is under way throughout Africa to develop modern mass societies with the accompanying political, economic, and technological systems. One needs an *afrocentric* approach to appreciate fully this heritage and experience. African expatriates may be found on every continent, but there are large populations of them in both North and Latin America, as well as in Europe. In 2009, the son of one from Kenya became President Barack Obama for the United States of America!

Africa is a land of great promise and potential, a continent of immense natural beauty and resources, most of which is still undeveloped. It is a region of contrasts between the primitive and the ultramodern, a place where new industries, technologies, and cities emerge gradually. Yet, in this postcolonial period, it is the misfortune of Africa, which birthed civilization, to remain mired in human suffering and carnage in this twenty-first century. Although this collective of countries is somewhat disconnected from the world by its unmatched sorrows, its rich mixture of people has a distinctly African sense of brotherhood and humor.

For global leaders to be effective in their trade and development efforts within Africa, they must be realistic in their analysis of its peoples and possibilities. First, there is great diversity to be found in terms of stages of human and institutional development, manifested in the multitude of tribes, languages, customs, religions, education, and governments. Second, most of the people here are generous and traditional, eager to learn, and hardworking. But in the past 40 years, their natural buoyancy and flexibility have been dampened by widespread famine, epidemics, exploitation, and social unrest. The world media often distorts the external image of Africa by its emphasis on African tragedies—the horror of the mass poverty, the AIDS epidemic, the extensive droughts, the many civil wars, and the millions of refugees. Often overlooked in these reports are the success stories—World Bank and UNESCO projects that work at the local levels, the green revolution that expands agricultural production, the many business enterprises that flourish, the African foreign students who return to apply their Western education, and the shift from failed socialism to democratic and market-oriented policies.

Africa entered this new millennium in a state of intense transition. The changes under way can also be summed up in three words: *tribalism*, *chaos*, and *developing*. To illustrate our choice of this terminology, consider the following observations.

## Tribalism

The tribe is the basic sociological unit of Africa that provides one's sense of identity, belonging, and responsibility. When tribal members leave rural areas to go to the city for a job or to study, traditionally their enhanced stature brings with it responsibility for assisting their tribal brothers and sisters at home. Such social pressure on successful Africans may impose a burden to augment income by any means, legal or otherwise. Tribal bonds also lead to intergroup conflict, destruction, and corruption. As the force of tribalism deteriorates in modern, urban environments, Africans search for other substitutes, new institutional loyalties such as membership in a religion, cooperatives, and political parties, often formed along ethnic lines.

For many, tribalism is the bane of independent Africa with its many tribes and clans involving 2000 language groups—Swahili, Zulu, and Hausa being the most prominent. Left over from the colonialists are areas where French, English, Portuguese, and a corruption of Dutch are widely spoken. National leaders seek to transform intertribal hostility into collaborative community endeavors. Tribalism is evident in elections when the voting favors the largest tribes, while the winners are only slowly learning that power should be shared with the minority losers. It also is behind failed attempts at ethnic cleansing, authoritarian regimes, and political corruption. The challenge for many Africans is to build upon tribal heritage, while moving beyond narrow tribal loyalties and constraints for the greater common good of the nation and its economic development.

This issue is closely connected to ethnicity, which is a source of identity for many people. Perhaps this definition will make our point: *An ethnic group is a distinct population whose members identify with each other based on a common ancestry. Such groups are distinguished by common cultural, linguistic, or religious traits.* Ethnicity is different from the concept of *race*, which divides people on the basis of physical or biological traits, such as skin color, which in Africa protects the inhabitants from a strong sun. The point for cosmopolitans to remember is that many African "leaders" exploit tribal and ethnic ties over national interests. Both are used by the "big boys" as a means of staying in power!

## Chaos

As Africans seek to move beyond their colonial dependency, while rapidly creating appropriate cultural institutions and opportunities, tumult abounds. The destabilization process is compounded by a combination of factors. Sometimes, it is caused by nature, when lack of rain triggers mass famine, or monkeys infect entire East African populations through the plague of Acquired Immune Deficiency Syndrome—the AIDS virus that has already killed 18 million on the continent, and continues to kill several thousand more each day. Because of poor or inadequate water systems, other diseases devastate Africans, such as malaria. In June 2003, a group of African presidents appealed for greater help from the rich G8 nations meeting in Evian, France. Foreign governments have spent billions to fight disease in Africa, mainly through the Global Fund, an organization supporting 150 programs to fight AIDS, tuberculosis, and malaria. But other nations have to match that commitment, which the G8 leaders promised to do. But in some African states, such as in South Africa, the governments have been unable to use the external resources effectively. Other countries on the continent lack a well-organized and functioning health care system. Many immature political entities do not use donor funds effectively because of a lack of medical personnel and inadequate road and communications infrastructure.

Sometimes, the disarray and obstacles to African development come from the following:

- The rise of extremist Muslim militants and terrorists as in North Africa, Sudan, Somalia, and more recently elsewhere, as in Kenya.
- Tribal conflicts in this past decade that escalated into civil wars, as in Rwanda when the Hutu army oversaw the murder of a million Tutsi; in Somalia where tribal warfare led to the collapse of the government and anarchy; and in the Congo and Sudan where genocide prevailed and millions died. Distorted ambitions and ideologies of local dictators and guerrillas to crush their opposition in other tribes have led to new tyrannies, such as that which occurred recently in Uganda, Nigeria, Liberia, Angola, and elsewhere.
- African infighting and destruction are sometimes attributed to religion, such as when brown-skinned, Muslim Arabs from the north of Somalia raid and destroy dark-skinned, Christians in the south of a country with hopeless governance.
- Incompetent strongmen who take political power through coups or rigged elections, and use their positions as head of state to benefit only themselves and their cronies. This lack of authentic leaders has contributed to undermining of national economies and exploitation of the citizenry. Hence, the rule of the "big man" replaces the rule of law, while the average person suffers. The deterioration of Rhodesia when it became Zimbabwe under its dictator, Robert Mugabe; Zaire when ruled by Mobutu Sese Seko; or Uganda under its despot, Idi Amin, are cases in point!
- Failure of the current states in terms of borders, governance, and infrastructure. Before the nineteenth century, Africa had been divided into thousands of kingdoms and chiefdoms whose systems of government developed over hundreds of years. For administrative purposes, European colonialists created a few dozen nation states whose borders often divided tribal lands. On all this was grafted European governance models, such as parliamentary democracy, that were alien to Africans, lacking in educated leadership, to make it all work. The new regimes proved unstable and dysfunctional, with elected governments giving way to authoritarianism, military take-overs, and assignations. The result has undermined any democratic free-enterprise system from growing, while incumbents became rich and powerful with their private militias and suppressed media, unless they were killed, jailed, or driven into exile.[4]

Often, such internal troubles get exacerbated by outside intervention, as when in past centuries, Europeans imposed their controls on the locals, so that today the influence of European cultures and dependency still may be found in former African colonies of Britain, France, Germany, and Portugal. In the twentieth century, Western powers have twice involved Africans in their world wars, as well as in the cold war between the United States and the former USSR. Africans have been involved again, when the United Nations sends relief efforts, but with inadequate peacekeeping troops to such places as the Sudan, Liberia, Rwanda, and Somalia.

The combination of such forces worsens because of overpopulation, the need for food because of disruption in farming and fishing, systemic corruption, and widespread unemployment. Mass poverty engenders desperation, which may feed political extremity. All of the above factors contribute to the displacement of millions of Africans from their homelands. Many end up as refugees amid poverty on a gigantic scale. One effect of this chaos is the threat it poses to the ecological environment of the continent. Deserts are widening, broad savannas and their communities struggle to survive. Sometimes the confusion is simply *future shock* as tribal cultures and rural peoples try to cope with the demands of an urban, postindustrial way of life. Finally, too many postcolonial nation-states and their political leaders in Africa are failing to liberate, protect, and service their own citizens, as well as their country's resources.

But the situation is not all bad—Africans are survivors with remarkable resilience and "make do" capacities. Entrepreneurs abound, humanitarian efforts progress, and some countries are justly and successfully ruled by elected leaders. Peacekeepers and peace enforcers do produce some positive results, as in Cote d'Ivoire, while the African Union is training regional brigades. Outside financial aid and other assistance from the UN, European Union, and other major nations, as well as from NGOs, are alleviating some of the problems which plague Africa.

## Developing

Africa has been classified as the Third World in economic terms—it contributes only 1% of the global economic output. This poor continent often is viewed as a land of tragedy or promise because of its rich natural and human resources that have not been fully developed. The nations here are being crippled by debt to foreign interests. The cause of the current woes goes well into the past with European colonialism and inadequate education of African people. Because of this historical influence, when the majority of Africa gained independence after the 1960s, many of its "leaders" were ill-prepared to lead their countries. They turned toward state socialism, favoring government intervention in the economy with bureaucratic controls that stifled initiative, killed incentive, and created chronic, artificial shortages. The situation represents a rejection of the continent's heritage of consensual and participatory democracy, which should embrace *free* markets, trade, and enterprise.

The full potential of Africa may be realized in this and the next century, if Africans are empowered to build an infrastructure on the basis of their own uniqueness and cultures. Development increases opportunity for people. But to actualize these prospects, Africans will have to learn how to (1) practice synergy among themselves; (2) control their populations; (3) advance their literacy, education, and productivity; (4) build infrastructure, especially roads and transportation; (5) promote conservation and ecotourism; and (6) connect with the information age and its technologies. Consider just one reality to be rectified—less than 10% of the continent's land is formally owned, and only one in 10 Africans lives in a house with formal deeds or titles. But Africa's biggest need is for effective, indigenous leadership at all levels of their society, yet no institution is effectively addressing this need.

There have been promising developments toward progress in Africa, as the next four reports indicate:

■ *Continental Synergy*: In the 1980s, 16 countries joined together to form the Economic Community of West African States while in the 1990s, nine more countries launched the Southern African Coordination Conference. In a sense, the current African Union (AU) is a case study illustrating in its short history the challenge and the promise of the future, as it evolved from prior attempts at unified action. First, there was the Organization of African States founded in 1963, then later the Organization of African Unity. Such institutions have been both a disappointment and modest success—too often their officials used their positions there for demagoguery, posturing, and travel junkets. Yet these unifying efforts also have achieved, through their economic and technical projects, the improvement of the continent's communication and banking systems and the maintenance of interstate peace. The hope is that the renewed African Union, with UN assistance, will become the forum and mechanism for continental recovery and renewal. Today, booming economies in Uganda, Mauritania, Ghana, and Mozambique demonstrate that African countries can thrive, given some measure of peace, stability, and governance. In the year 2000, total foreign investments in Africa were about $6 billion, only 3% of the $235 billion that flowed into Third-World economies. By 2006, that investment by outsiders had gone up considerably, thanks to establishment of the Millennium Fund. For this decade, the 48th sub-Saharan countries have been growing at a rate of 5% or more.

■ *Rebuilding Failed States*: The World Bank frets about 30 "low income countries under stress," while the U.K.'s Department of International Development worries about 46 "fragile states." Many of these today are in Africa, such as Angola, Central African Republic, both Congos, Nigeria, Somalia, Sudan, and Zimbabwe. For example, a third of the African countries are trapped in civil wars or cycles of unrest. But some are recovering—after a civil war, Liberia came back from misrule, violence, and famine a few years ago. While its former gangsterish president, Charles Taylor, along with other African warlords, is being tried by the International Criminal Court in The Hague, the Liberian electorate chose its first female head of state. A large UN peacekeeping force keeps the nation calm and safe while reconstruction goes forward with external humanitarian aid. Another failed state, Sierra Leone, again with UN help, is holding accountable those war criminals who despoiled it. Ultimately, restoring peace and a measure of prosperity is the responsibility of local citizens.[a] Following are some hopeful signs: two-thirds of African countries now limit presidential terms; multiparty political systems are growing; media coverage is improving, thanks to television and the Internet; the mobile phone revolution has helped many people, especially poor peasants and traders; banking systems are modernizing and attracting more international investment; mortgages are more available to a growing middle class; farmers are being helped by the issuance of individual land titles; creation of mechanisms like the Extractive Industries Transparency Initiative, a code for opening up agreements of governments and foreign investors; establishment of savings or sovereign funds in commodity-flush countries.

■ *Private Sector Initiatives*: If foreign aid, debt forgiveness, and trade reform are to help this continent, then a 2005 World Bank Annual, *Doing Business in Africa,* suggests the private sector must provide leadership. Public sector bureaucracy, ineptness, regulatory obstacles, and red tape contribute to undermining the business climate there. Investors, whether corporate or foundations, realize that if entrepreneurs are to flourish, programs must be undertaken to improve infrastructure, train skilled workers, provide capital support, and curb disease. Yet this report points to 14 sub-Saharan countries where healthy economic growth is under way, because their GNP has increased at least 5% a year since 1990. Botswana and South Africa are at the top when it comes to "best business environment." So, a group of multinational companies have formed "Business Action of Africa" to improve business conditions on that continent. In addition, 24 countries outside the region have signed on to a "New Partnership for Africa's Development," aimed at bringing together both the African public and private sectors to improve investment conditions on the continent. Yet, the UN Economic Commission on Africa calculates that already the foreign direct investment in Africa has on the average a four times better return than in G7 countries, and twice as much as in Asia![b]

---

[a]Refer to "Rebuilding Failed States—From Chaos, Order," *The Economist*, March 5, 2005, pp. 45-47.
[b]Refer to "Doing Business in Africa—Different Skills Required," *The Economist*, July 2, 2005, p. 61, and "African Optimism—The Hopeful Continent," *The Economist*, January 7, 2006, p. 50.

- *African Optimism*: They may not be the richest, but Africans remain the world's staunchest optimists. An annual world survey by Gallup International found that 60% of the African respondents think that the present year will be better than the last—twice as much as reported in Europe. Despite 2 million Africans killed by AIDS in 2005, these people are upbeat and hopeful. One speculation for this is that 9 out of 10 Africans are religious, and know how to transform suffering into recovery.

For foreigners to be more effective in their business and professional relationships with Africans, it is helpful to have some insights into the diverse cultures of this continent. In the previous chapter, we described the Islamic culture, which also dominates North Africa and the Muslim states elsewhere in this area. Within black Africa, there are some common cultural characteristics. The next section will review five dimensions of those African cultures—family, trust/friendship, time, corruption, and respect for elders. This selected analysis may increase awareness and improve interaction not only with Africans, but with the millions of descendants from this heritage who are found throughout North, Central, and South America, as well as in the Caribbean, the United Kingdom, and the Middle East. Be cautious with African generalizations, because African cultures are not only diverse, but dynamic, changing to ensure survival, as well as to adapt to new times and circumstances.

Exhibits 14.1 and 14.2 illustrates how quickly the situation can change in Africa, especially when private enterprise is allowed to work.

---

## EXHIBIT 14.1

### IMPACT OF TELECOMMUNICATIONS IN AFRICA

First radio, then television, and now mobile telephones are transforming African communications and business. The wireless age is overcoming the obstacles on this huge continent caused by poor roads, unreliable energy, political instability, and corruption that prevented the wiring of landline telephones. The new technologies bypass all this, giving regions and people access to phones they never had before. But Africans use this new communication tool for more than mere talking—shepherds in drought-ridden Sahel are using handheld GPS units and cell phones to alert others to good grazing; in Nairobi, customers avoid long lines at their bank by monitoring their accounts by text messaging; in Ethiopia, teachers are being trained to use solar-powered satellite radios to receive lessons broadcast to their classes; in South Africa, wives at home use mobile phones to talk in the evening with their husbands who work hundreds of miles away; health care

continued

EXHIBIT 14.1

IMPACT OF TELECOMMUNICATIONS IN AFRICA (CONTINUED)

workers use the phones to summon ambulances; fisherwomen who can't read tell their customers to call their cell numbers to order fish; and retailers in the slums can take delivery orders from affluent suburbanites. On a continent where some remote villages communicate by beating drums, cell phones are a technological revolution. Cell operators can't put up phone towers fast enough. This phenomenon is causing a sociological and economic godsend for Africans at large. Today, Africa is the world's fastest growing cell phone market—by 2004, 76.8 million mobile subscribers. Others simply buy cell phone time to make each call—buying wireless phone time is like using the grocery list. Used handsets are sold for $50 or less. All this from a people who typically live on $2 or less a day! Domestic cell companies, like MTB and Conteh, are not only building telecommunications networks, but providing much-needed jobs and national income.

International firms, like Vodacom, have 1.1 million subscribers in the Congo, adding a thousand new customers daily, and logging 10,000 calls a day. Bicycle-driven and battery chargers are being used in rural areas to provide sufficient electricity to charge the phones. It's all been a boon, not only to business throughout Africa, but also to families who want to connect with one another.

*Source*: "Making the Connection in Africa—Whatever You Thought, Think Again," *National Geographic*, September 2005. "Cell Phone Frenzy in Africa, World's To-Growth Market," *San Diego Union-Tribune*, pp. A1/12. "Africa Calling," *The Economist*, May 26, 2007, p. 74.

EXHIBIT 14.2

CHINA'S AFRICAN PARTNERSHIP

China takes a long view of its relationship to the continent of Africa and its people. It began in 1414 when Emperor Ming sent Admiral Zing He to East Africa. He took his vast fleet of 62 galleons for seven voyages there to engage in trade and establish diplomatic relations. After 1431, the Chinese did not return until the 1960s when Chairman Mao Zedong supported liberation movements and newly independent states. This time, the Chinese built roads, bridges, stadiums, water systems, and even the Tanzum railroad from Tanganyika to Zambia—all with thousands of Chinese laborers! They also established farms and factories, provided materials

EXHIBIT 14.2

CHINA'S AFRICAN PARTNERSHIP (CONTINUED)

and loans—all with a view of obtaining political support from Africa's 50 nations for China in the United Nations, World Trade Organization, et al. They also sent doctors, nurses, and medical aid. No wonder that, in 2000, governments in both China and Africa formed China-Africa Conference (POCAC). By the China-Africa Summit in 2003, China was writing off billions in Africa debts. Their managers in Africa live at the level of their workers, buying local products and selling their own wares made in China. Even traditional African fabrics are now made in Guangdong for export to Africa and elsewhere.

The center for Chinese Studies at Stellenbosch, South Africa, monitors considerable Chinese activities on the continent. China treats Africa as an equal, so their leaders appreciate that China presents itself as a neutral, nonimperialist, value-free outsider simply wanting a friendly trade relationship. Chinese there emphasize the best in Africa, avoiding references to its failures. Further, the Chinese keep their promises, building infrastructure on time and often under budget. But the Chinese employ their own, providing little training or limited jobs for the locals. In their African projects, the Chinese do not show much regard for environmental damage, human rights, combating poverty, nor the Charter of the African Union. The African governments have yet to successfully manage their business relationships with China, which views them as business opportunities. But it is the new professional middle class in Pan Africa that is taking control of the continent's development and transformation.

*Source*: Adapted from Richard Dowden's *Africa—Altered States and Ordinary Miracles*, London, UK: Portobellow Publishing, 2008, Ch. 17.

# CULTURAL CHARACTERISTICS OF AFRICANS[3]

We must always be cautious about cultural generalizations, and in Africa there is no one culture. The northern African states of Mauritania, Morocco, Algeria, Libya, and part of Sudan are closer to the Middle Eastern cultures. The descriptions that follow best apply to sub-Sahara, home of black Africans, like the peoples of Mali, Senegal, Ghana, Congo, Benin, Tanzania, and South Africa. Yet, even their music and musical instruments reflect the diversity of their culture. The African diaspora also brought to the West the popular music that is known today as blues, jazz, R&B, rumba, reggae, and even hip-hop![4]

## Family and Kinship

The basic unit of African society is the family, which includes the nuclear family and the extended family, or tribe. In traditional African society, the tribe is the ultimate community. No unit has more importance in society. There may be some loose confederations, but they are temporary and limited in scope. In political terms, the tribe is the equivalent of a nation. It does not have fixed boundaries, but on its sanction rests the law (customary law like the English Common Law). All wars were fought on the tribe's behalf, and the division between "them" and "us" lay in tribal boundaries.

Africans center their communities around villages for food gathering and cultivation. The village elders become judges, mediators, trade masters, and leaders within both religious and tribal life. In some ways, the tribe is more than a nation. In Europe and America, ethical and moral standards are not given by national sanctions, but rest on religious and cultural traditions common to the whole continent. But in traditional Africa, except for areas under Islamic control, the family tribe provides the guidelines for accepted behavior. The tribe bears a moral connotation and provides an emotional security. It is also a source of social and moral sanctions, as well as political and physical security. The tribe provides its members with rules governing responsibilities, explanations of the responsibilities, and guidelines for organizing the society, and, hence, the culture.

The tribe is broken down into different kinship lines. The concept of kinship is important to understanding African societies. It constitutes the primary basis for an individual's rights, duties, rules of residence, marriage, inheritance, and succession. Kinship refers to blood relationships between individuals, and is used to describe relationships in both a narrow and a broad sense. Parents and their children are a special kind of kin group. The social significance of kinship covers a wide social field in most African societies. In Western culture, its significance usually does not extend beyond the nuclear family, but in the African culture, it embraces a network of people, including those that left the village for urban areas.

The family—father, mother, children—is the ultimate basis of the tribe. But the tribal and family unit organization is being disrupted by changes in the economic organizational structure. The economic organization has tied reward to individual effort, and developed road, rail, water, and air communication networks that have increased the range and speed of contact—thereby increasing the rate of intercultural contact and change. The reorganization has also brought tribes together as territorial units, with greater opportunities for migration from one area to another, but with a corresponding weakening of family bonds and behavior control.

As this newfound mobility moves more people to the large urban areas, they try to maintain some family ties. This involves a responsibility to support family members still in the villages. It also affects Africans' business relationships with managers from abroad in terms of hiring practices and the need for extra income to support those at home. Earnings from business transactions are often used for this purpose.

## Trust and Friendship

Trust and confidence are essential elements needed for successful enterprise in Africa. It is very important to get to know coworkers as individuals before getting down to actual business activities. With Africans, after family, friendship comes next in importance. Often, a friendship continues after specific business activities end. Socializing outside of the office is common. It is under those relaxed conditions that managers talk politics, sports, and sometimes business.

In Africa, interpersonal relationships are based on sincerity. African societies are normally warm and friendly. People generally assume that everyone is a friend until proven otherwise. When Africans smile, it means they like you. When smiles are not seen, it is a clear sign of distrust. Once a person is accepted as a friend, that person is automatically an "adopted" member of the family. A friend can pop into a friend's place anytime. In African societies, formal invitations and appointment making are not common.

One of the most important factors to remember when doing business in Africa is the concept of friendship before business. Normally, before a meeting begins, there is general talk about events that have little or nothing to do with the business at hand. This can go on for some time. If the meeting involves people coming together who have never met, but who are trying to strike a deal (an African and a foreigner), the African will try to reach out for friendship first. If, in doing so, the African receives a cold response, he may become suspicious and lose interest in the deal.

In the traditional village culture, Africans share good fortune and food with other members of the community. This is an example of the wonderful values that modernization may unfortunately change. Society's predators—in the form of rebels and terrorists, greedy politicians, and abusive militias—undermine this cultural quality.

## Time and Time Consciousness

The way an individual views the concept of time has a major impact on any business relationship. If two businesspeople enter into a situation with complementary goals, abilities, and needs, a successful arrangement can be thwarted if each has different ideas about time. In Africa, time is viewed as flexible, not rigid or segmented. People come first, then time. Anyone in a hurry is viewed with suspicion and distrust. Because trust is very important, individuals who follow inflexible time schedules will have little success. The African wants to sit and talk—to get to know the person before discussing business. Normally, time is not seen as a limited commodity. What cannot be done today can always be accomplished tomorrow. Meetings are not held promptly, and people may arrive several hours late. Often, foreigners misinterpret this as laziness, untrustworthiness, lack of seriousness in doing business, or even lack of interest in the venture. However, lateness in meetings should be perceived as part of African life. It is understood among friends that even though everybody agrees to meet at a given time, they will not actually gather until much later.

However, when Africans are dealing with foreigners, they normally try to be on time out of respect for the non-Africans' concept of time. But in the larger cities of Africa, the concept of time is changing. Punctuality is becoming more important. Contact with Western businesspersons has brought an increasing awareness and acceptance of the segmentation of time and its consequent inflexibility. But away from the capital city, time is still viewed in a relaxed and easygoing manner.

## Corruption

Corruption in Africa sometimes is related to its poverty, and often results from tribal responsibilities that individuals carry with them when leaving the village for a job or schooling in the city. The enhanced stature of city life brings a responsibility of assisting one's tribal family. This obligation often imposes a financial burden on the successful member far in excess of income. The worker is unlikely to resist the pressures of society, and is thus forced to augment income, often by means regarded by foreigners as bribery or corruption. However, to the African, it is not. As long as great disparities in income and standards of living continue, the bribe system is likely to continue, as it has in many developing economies. In Africa, extra income is swiftly distributed through the extended family system to remote relations living in remote places. The tradition of sharing continues even as individuals move away from their tribal origins.

Corruption may arise because of inadequate compensation for work, causing laborers to seek additional income. Many African state governments have been corrupted by greedy political and military rulers who use public monies and offices to enrich themselves and their families at the expense of citizens and foreign business persons. Exhibit 14.3 on Jones & Smith Food Company gives readers some appreciation for the payment of gratuities.

## Respect for Elders

Age is another important factor to consider in Africa. It is believed that the older one gets, the wiser one becomes—life has seasoned the individual with varied experiences. Hence, in Africa, age is an asset. The

EXHIBIT 14.3

JONES & SMITH FOOD COMPANY

The Jones & Smith Food Company is located in the capital of a large African country. However, they want to expand their headquarters to another state capital. To do this, they need approval from both the federal and the state government. The company sent in a written application a few months ago, but did not get any response.

The manager of the project went several times to the Federal Ministry of Trade and Economic Development, but was always told to come back the next day. Mr. Jones became frustrated and mad at the clerks and officials involved. However, in the process of the argument, one of them said, "This is not America. It's Africa. If you want anything done on time, you've got to give a bribe. Kind of like a gratuity tendered before, rather than after, a service is performed."

Mr. Jones, who is not accustomed to such practices, angrily stormed out of the office. In the car, he narrated the incident to the driver, who advised him to give the "gratuity" or have the proposal denied.

In an emergency meeting, the company's board of directors decided to offer the gratuity. To the company's surprise, the proposal was approved the next day.

But back in Jones' home culture, a board of directors may frown upon such payments, and home country laws may consider such bribes illegal.

older the person, the more respect the person receives within the traditional community, especially from the young. Thus, if a foreigner is considerably younger than the African, the latter will have little confidence in the outsider. However, if sincerity, respect, and empathy are shown, the person will receive a positive response. Respect for elders tends to be the key for harmony in African cultures and village life.

Young Africans normally do not oppose the opinion of their elders. They may not agree, but they must respect the opinion. In some cases, especially in rural areas, young people are not expected to offer opinions in meetings. The informal and formal interpersonal relationships in Africa are on the basis of cultural norms of various African societies. As Africa modernizes—nearly 40 of its cities have over a million inhabitants—some of the old ways, such as respect and care for seniors, may unfortunately diminish, as is happening with other traditional cultures in transition. African cultural characteristics vary in an urban area, in contrast to classical village life.

# CULTURAL SPECIFICS BY GEOGRAPHIC REGIONS[8]

It is impossible here to cover all the cultural aspects of doing business or humanitarian work in all 50 African states. Instead, four major geographic areas of Africa will be profiled. In each region, we have selected one country for in-depth analysis for one or more of these reasons: (1) representative of a grouping; (2) economic implications for all of Africa; and (3) insights into what is happening in their societies. We will also consider a particular cultural dimension of Africa—business customs, protocols, and prospects.

## NORTH AFRICA[5]

Geographically, this region contains 11 nations: Algeria, Chad, Egypt, Gambia, Libya, Mali, Mauritania, Morocco, Niger, Senegal, and Tunisia. Nine classify themselves as republics; however, Libya is a Socialist Arab Jamahiriya, and was once a sphere of Italian influence. Morocco is the only kingdom. Except for the coastal countries, the area can be characterized as one of high temperatures, vast deserts, Muslim religious practice, and French colonial cultural influence. The economies are developing, centered on textiles, food processing, agriculture, and mining; several are better off for producing or processing crude oil and petroleum.

The history of North Africa has been impacted significantly by the Middle East, especially by the culture of the Arabs and the Muslim religion. The latter defines the region's ethnicity and languages, particularly among the Semitic-speaking Arabs. From Morocco to East Africa, Arabic is the unifying common cultural influence. Up to 10,000 years ago, we already learned that Egypt gave rise to agriculture and a civilization based upon it. The area has also been known in the past for its nomadic herding, with life centered around the oases, still evident in today's Libya. The sea and the camel became the means for development of North African trading routes. Since ancient times, the making and distribution of bread is a common factor which the Arabs call *aish*, or life. Other regional foods include rice, yogurt, and meat kebabs, along with Mediterranean dishes that feature eggplant, beans, olives, pickles, and pastries. Extended families with arranged marriages are traditional, but are changing with urbanization and modernization, especially with regard to the role of women in society. Oral verse, poetry, and literature are common here as ways of expressing feelings. Pan-Arab movements have occurred in both the past and present, but generally have not succeeded because Arab leaders prefer decentralized power, avoiding domination by others. Abdul Nasser's attempt in 1958 to found a United Arab Republic lasted about 4 years. The region resists national unity and federalism, as evident in Algeria, Libya, Yemen, and other parts of Africa, such as the Sudan and Somalia.

## Morocco

Europe and Africa are geographically nearest to each other in the narrow Strait of Gibraltar, the strategic passage between the Mediterranean Sea and the Atlantic Ocean. The two continents, once joined, are only 22 km apart and converge in the City of Ceuta, Spanish Morocco, often referred to as the gateway to Africa. Apart from its common coastline, North Africa spans some 3500 miles west to east, and contains the vast Sahara Desert, as well as the Atlas Mountains.

Some 50,000 years ago, there is evidence of the Neanderthals in this land, and 10,000 years ago, Stone Age humans dwelt in this place. From remotest antiquity, a panoply of peoples are represented here: Berbers, Phoenicians, Carthaginians, Romans, Mauritanians, Vandals, Visigoths, Byzantines, Arabs, Portuguese, Spanish, French, Jews, and Hindus. All have found a home in the region of Morocco over many centuries, and have left behind vestiges of their rich cultural heritage. For 2500 years, the inhabitants of what is now Spain and Morocco have traded cultures across a narrow channel. After the Carthaginians conquered Iberia, Hannibal brought African elephants over to help in his astonishing assault on Italy. When the Goths declined there, Islam swept across North Africa, leading in A.D. 711 to seven centuries of Moorish domination in Spain. Today, this relatively tolerant multicultural society features Muslim, Christian, Jewish, and Hindu citizens, and a semi-autonomous government. However, Morocco and Spain still dispute over the *Sebta* territory that maintains control over five plazas or North African enclaves, including Ceuta and Melilla. From this strategic location, one can easily travel to Casablanca, Morocco's largest and most important port city. Perched on Africa's northwest corner, today it is a cosmopolitan center for modern tourism. In 46 B.C., the Roman Empire annexed this region, calling it *Mauritania*. The province was eventually Christianized until the seventh century, when Islam became Morocco's official religion. In 1830, piracy along the coast led to the intervention of France; in 1912, its Sultan accepted a French protectorate, which lasted until the country gained its independence in 1956.

### Business Tips for Morocco

Moroccan business practices are more Arab and Mediterranean than typically African. The same business customs, protocols, and etiquette provided in Chapter 10 about Arab culture in the Middle East also apply in this society.

Business conferences are usually held in the office rather than over meals. Breakfast meetings are rare, and lunches are late and long. Appointments should be scheduled, and the foreigner is expected on time, but do not be surprised at delays. Although young local entrepreneurs may speak English because of a Western education, check if you will need an interpreter in Arabic or French. As there are some nine national holidays, plus four major religious celebrations, it is wise to determine on which days business will be set aside for a local feast or festival; many have dates that change each year because of the lunar calendar. Except for holidays, businesses normally operate Monday through Friday, and sometimes Saturday morning. Most will close for lunch from noon until 2 p.m. The currency is the dirham (DH).

Apart from flowing Arab dress, lightweight business attire is favored in this warm climate. Although Moroccan women are beginning to get involved in commerce and professions, foreign women usually have no difficulty here, though a conservative business dress is recommended; a head covering is advised when visiting mosques. Noted for their hospitality, Moroccans often entertain business contacts in their homes.

Finally, remember that the phrase, *in sha'allah*, as in other Arab countries, may mean *yes*, *no*, or *maybe*, depending on the intonation of the speaker. The message is, "if God wills or intends it." Other expressions to be heard in communications include *Bismilah-el-raham er rahim* (in the name of God, clement and merciful); *El-hamdu lilah* (praise to God), an expression of satisfaction; *Allah u akbar* (God is great); and *Allah y jib* (God will provide).

The subtle Arabic language is filled with rhetoric, intricacies, ambivalence, and contradictions in terminology.

## EAST AFRICA[6]

This eastern region encompasses a dozen states, just south of Libya and Egypt, and bordering on the Red Sea, Gulf of Aden, and Indian Ocean. The states include Burundi, Central African Republic, Congo, Djibouti, Eritrea, Ethiopia, Kenya, Rwanda, Somalia, Sudan, Tanzania, and Uganda. The area starts in the north with the Sahara Desert of Sudan and ends in the south with the Congo and Tanzania. Except for Eritrea and Somalia, the other 10 countries style themselves as "republics," despite the presence of dictators or military coup commanders. Although Ethiopia was an ancient empire, most East African states were created as national entities by Britain, France, Germany, and Italy during the nineteenth century. Their borders and names have frequently changed as a result of civil wars and other conflicts. Some geographers place Sudan as part of North Africa, but we prefer to consider it within East Africa, sometimes called the *Horn of Africa*.

East Africa is a landmass of great natural diversity and beauty, with its deserts and mountains, rivers, and lakes, as well as a long, stunning coastline. It has temperatures and precipitation—from 73 to 89 °F in the north, and from 64 to 69 °F in the south. Except for deserts and barren lands in five northeastern countries, the predominant land use is grassland, woodland, and forest, with some cropland and wetlands. Agriculture is the primary regional industry, along with mining of copper, gold, fluorite, and diamonds. Two manufacturing centers are in Khartoum, Sudan, and Kinshasa, Congo, as well as one processing plant near Lubumbashi, Congo. Resplendent with spectacular landscape, Tanzania has one of the largest populations in the area. The region boasts the natural wonders of Mount Kilimanjaro and Mount Kenya, Africa's highest peaks, as well as Lake Victoria, the second largest lake in the world and the largest on this continent. The latter is the source of the White Nile, the largest branch of the Nile River, which flows northward until it empties into the Mediterranean Sea.

Some of these countries are landlocked—Central African Republic, Congo, and Democratic Republic of Congo, but the latter does border on Lake Tanganyika. The remainder have coastlines along the Indian Ocean, Gulf of Aden, and the Red Sea. The land is defined by the Great Rift Valley, a 3000-mile-long fault that runs north to south, and was originally formed when massive tectonic plates shifted million of years ago.

It was from East Africa that humanity spread beyond its origins, moving to all five continents.

## Regional Insights

There are some commonalties among the nations in East Africa, such as the following: they are largely poor countries, but some have substantial, underdeveloped natural and mineral resources; most are dependent on international aid and humanitarian organizations (NGOs); the majority have very poor infrastructure, especially relative to roads and transportation; too many have heads of state who seized power by coup or otherwise with the help of the military, and some are dictators, even when there are staged "elections"; tendency toward too many political parties for effective governance; too many refugees from neighboring countries which require UN assistance; most have differing legal systems and are engaged in disputes with their neighboring states. There is an urgent need for outside forces, such as from the African Union, to disarming gunmen and rebels in the region. The area is also home to four failed states: Sudan with a weak central government given to genocide in Darfur; Somalia with no national government and strong piracy off its long coastline; Democratic Republic of the Congo with its constant strife and violence; Kenya with its tribal bloodletting and ethnic cleansing. Given these drawbacks, one can understand why, in the twenty-first century, the region has too many trouble spots lacking effective governments, as the following observations will indicate.

Since 1990, it is estimated that this continent has lost about $18 billion a year in useless conflicts and wars. But at the same time, there are huge swaths of Africa at peace where cows are tended, kids are going to school, songs are being sung, and things are just normal. We seldom hear of such places. For perspective, consider the next six countries:

- *Central African Republic* only gained its independence from France in 1960. Since then, there has been much misrule and factional fighting between the government and the opposition, leading to a coup in 2003 when General Francois Bozize took over as president. Although the people ratified a constitution in 2004, socio-political conditions have not improved very much, with lawlessness in the countryside. With 4 million recent deaths due to excessive mortality caused by AIDS and devastating wars, there is a desperate need for better health care and other relief services. Further massacres are expected in the eastern region near Kivu. The Tutsi rebels continue to fight with their neighbors in Rwanda, especially Hutu extremists.

- *Sudan* was devastated by a 20-year-old civil war between Muslims in the north, where the central government operates, and Christians in the south, where the oil is located. Since 2003, the Arab government has turned a blind eye to the Darfur conflict in the west, where a local Arab militia is engaging in monstrous "ethnic cleansing and genocide" against non-Arab peoples there. Despite both groups being Muslim, the origins of these clashes go back to the thirteenth century. But the result today is that up to some 300,000 have died, many from starvation, and 2 million have been displaced from their homeland—some 200,000 have fled east to neighboring Chad. Despite condemnation by world governments of the present regime, global politics have prevented the UN intervening there with a strong force of peacekeepers. The conflict originated over property rights, water shortages, and scarcity of grazing lands—all problems yet to be resolved (see http://en.wikipedia.org/wiki/Darfur_conflict).

- *Ethiopia* is an ancient civilization and empire whose capital is in Addis Ababa. Its 1 million plus square kilometers of land is bordered by the failed state of Sudan on the west, by rebellious Eritrea on the northeast, by Djibouti on the east central coast, and by lawless Somalia on its southeast. With a population of some 80 million, these tall, regal people are primarily Muslims, Ethiopian Orthodox Christians, and animists (most of its small Jewish community having emigrated to Israel). With six language groups (Amharic, Tigrinya, Orominga, Guarginga, Somali, and Arabic), this poor country has a literacy rate of only 42%. Inhabitants have a life expectancy of 45 years, and an annual GDP of approximately $600 per person. The economy centers around food and beverage processing; textiles, and chemicals; growing of cereals, coffee, and pulses; as well as the production of oilseed and leather products; plus some gold mining. Having a disastrous experiment in totalitarian Communism, today's failed leadership discourages private enterprise, commits human rights abuses against it own citizens, and engages in a ferocious counter-insurgency against separatist rebels. Famine again stalks the people because of drought, insect infections, and inadequate farming procedure and technology. To contain malnutrition, it is estimated that today 4.5 million people need emergency food aid.

- *Eritrea* is an alluring country with gentle people, whose land is strategically located on one of the world's busiest shipping lanes in the Red Sea. After a 30-year struggle with Ethiopia to gain its independence in 1993, the fledgling nation lost a senseless border war against Ethiopia in 1998, leaving it to face huge unemployment and near famine. Currently, UN peacekeepers protect their border to keep the two parties apart. Many citizens have fled abroad, such as to the USA.

- *Rwanda*, after staggering losses from genocide between the Hutu and Tutsi tribes, struggles to adopt a new constitution that ensures more democracy, but does not permit either ethnic group to dominate the country. To constrain the Hutu majority population, it attempts to introduce checks and balances in the political system, with measured pluralism permitted by the ruling RPF of Tutsi. About 10,000 Hutu fighters, some of whom took part in the genocide, now hide in eastern Congo; on this pretext in 1994, the Rwandan government invaded that country in pursuit of its rebels. Despite successful elections supervised by the UN in 2006, fighting still goes on, along the northern border with Uganda's Lord Resistance Army, who are given to slaughtering and kidnapping innocent civilians. Within this small country, the Forces for the Liberation of Rwanda are exiles who have yet to negotiate their peaceful return as a political party, while it caused 100,000 people to flee their homes.

- *Uganda* is still recovering from the horrors of the Idi Amin regime that murdered upward of 300,000 people. Because its citizens speak some 50 languages, requiring multiple translations for media and government, innumerable delays are inevitable. Since 1986, Lt. General Yoweri Museveni, who seized power, serves as "president" and pursues social reforms. He has threatened to invade the Congo's Kivi Province, but this time in pursuit of Uganda rebels there. But the good news is that the economy is now growing at 8.9% a year, and the capital of Kampala is booming with construction.

- *Congo* today tries to heal after destructive years of warfare, in which 3.3 million people died since 1998 (see Exhibit 14.4). In the Democratic Republic of the Congo, former soldiers face hearings in the International Criminal Court about their past actions in genocide. Having not had an independent election in over 40 years, 25 million registered voters cast a ballot in a December 2005 referendum; seemingly over 80% of the people voted to accept a draft constitution to set up new institutions that may lead to a functioning government. Remember that Congo is vast, two-thirds the size of Europe, and a former colony of Belgium.

*Pygmies*, referred to above, have lived for thousands of years in tropical rain forests about 4° above or below the Equator.[c] Their jungle habitat

---

[c]Paul Raffaele, "The Pygmies Plight," *Smithsonian*, December 2008, pp. 70-77 (www.Smithsonian.com/pygmies).

## EXHIBIT 14.4
### CONGO: AFRICA'S WORST WAR

Consider African challenges in terms of one country. As a result of invasions and warfare, the Congo lost more than 9% of its population since the start of the twenty-first century. Yet the Democratic Republic of the Congo has abundant resources coveted by the rich nations of the world. But this sad story goes back to 1993, when genocide began on its northeast border in small, neighboring Rwanda. There, the Hutu-dominated government tried to exterminate the Tutsis, a prosperous minority. The slaughter ended when exiled Tutsis, refugees in Uganda, returned in force to drive the killers into the DRC, while gaining control in Rwanda. Soon, six neighboring countries were involved in the cross-border fighting. The senseless game went back and forth, on and on, as marauders from neighboring states and tribes preyed on the poor, especially in the Congo. The latter's economy was disrupted and its infrastructure crumbled. The violence was partially fueled by its greedy neighbors and their warlords seeking the Congo's diamonds, gold, germanium, and other resources.

The United Nations and the European Union decried the situation, especially human rights abuses. The UN's Security Council voted in 2003 to send 17,000 French, Belgium, and Canadian peacekeeping troops into the Congo's Ituri's northeastern province—over the previous 4 years, 60,000 locals in Bunia, its capital, had been murdered, mutilated, or maimed. The African UN secretary general, Kofi Annan, issued a report calling events there a catastrophe for the 4.6 million Ituri inhabitants in the area—600,000 persons had been displaced internally, and half of the health care centers had closed. When neighboring nations withdrew their troops from the Congo, the World Bank and the European Union sent in $2 billion for reconstruction assistance. Projects are under way to renovate the railway from the mineral-rich Katanga to the Benguela port in Angola, which will enable the Congolese to harness their huge, hydroelectric potential. All things are possible if peace can be maintained and the needs of average people met.

In 2006, the Congo is trying to hold its first multiparty election in 40 years. The problem is that 8650 candidates signed up in the capital of Kinshasa to run for the presidency, out of a population of 60 million! And the world's largest UN peacekeeping force is still employed there, attempting to ensure a fair election. Finally, the Mbuti Pygmies in the Congo's Ituri forest have managed to survive the civil war and its chaos, but can they cope in a time of peace with a land rush that might overwhelm them?

*Source*: Case partially adapted from "A Report from the Congo" and "Congo's Wars—Peace They Say, But the Killings Go On," *The Economist*, July 6, 2002, pp. 43-45; March 20, 2003, pp. 41-42. "Congo—A Tantalizing Wait for Vote," *The Economist*, April 15, 2006, p. 48.

stretches from the Cameroon's Atlantic Coastline eastward toward Lake Victoria in Uganda. About 250,000 of these dwarf hunter-gatherers are under threat from their taller Bantu neighbors who have undermined their Bayaka culture by deforestation that destroys the Pygmy clans' source of food and livelihood, while forcing their relocation to villages near logging operations. Their Bantu competitors treat them like underclass serfs, so many of these little people have quit hunting and grow marijuana for income, or, worse still, fall into alcoholism. Their spirit is sustained by dance and music, a unique five-part harmony of song. The Centre for Environment and Development in the Cameroon capital of Yaounde helps them to cope with their changed circumstances. Note that the earliest written reference to the Pygmy is 2276 B.C. when an Egyptian pharaoh led an expedition up the Nile and sent letters home about his encounter with their tribes. Today, geneticists research why these people have evolved to be diminutive, while health care specialists seek to counter their many new ailments resulting from malnutrition and infections. Sadly, nearby gorillas also face extinction, hastened by deforestation and warfare in their once-isolated areas of Africa.

At present, sub-Saharan Africa also suffers from devastating droughts, plus the largest number of people afflicted with AIDS in lands devoid of adequate medical assistance. One country, Kenya, has been chosen for additional cultural analysis. Yet, many of these nations, like the ones described above, are rich in natural resources which foreigners often develop for them.

## Kenya

The Republic of Kenya, as a result of years of British colonial influence, has East Africa's most modern infrastructure, as well as a large expatriate community. It is also a popular tourist destination for its national game reserve, safaris, and golf. The coastal beaches, wildlife, and unique scenery are the main attractions, along with access to the magnificent Rift Valley, a site of early human archeological research. In the global marketplace, Kenya maintains good business and political relations. Representatives from many North American and European countries operate here, using it as a base to access larger markets in both East and Central Africa. The nation's main growth sectors are in agriculture, manufacturing, tourism, and power generation.

Nairobi is not only Kenya's capital, but a huge modern city with a population of some 2,818,000. Its largest slum is Kiberia, inhabited by 800,000 poor but talented citizens who can "fix anything." This is a primary example of Africa's impoverished rural folk flocking to urban centers to seek a better life. The city may have upwards of 25,000 street children, many of whom lost parents to AIDS. Only 80 miles from the equator and at an elevation of 5500 ft, this site began as a Maasai watering hole, then as a camp of workers in 1899 who were building the Mombasa-Uganda Railroad. Nairobi is also where a new generation of young professionals and businesspeople hope to create the "New Africa." In this boisterous metropolis, both the middle class is expanding and educated women are rushing ahead. Nairobi is also home to the first African woman to win the Nobel Peace Prize, Wangari Maathai, ecologist and activist. Unfortunately, modernized Nairobi is surrounded by vast slums of angry, Kalenjin-speaking Muslims. Kenyans are disunited by tribalism and ethnic and political conflict, and the country is in danger of national disintegration! China, which has a large economic stake in the country ($706 million in trade for 2006), has failed to provide diplomacy and help in negotiations among warring parties because of their policy of noninterference. But the Chinese have invested in railroad building, mining, offshore oil exploration, and big infrastructure projects (Exhibits 14.5 and 14.6).

## EXHIBIT 14.5

## AFRICAN WOMEN LEADERSHIP

Hardworking, long-suffering African women may lead the resurgences of this continent in the twenty-first century. Already, a woman has been elected head of state for Liberia, so ravaged by civil war and male power-seekers. In 2004, the Nobel Peace Prize was bestowed on a Kenyan woman for untiring humanitarian efforts on behalf of environmental protection, as well as the prevention of disease, violence, and war. When Wangari Maathal, 64, founder of the Green Belt Movement, received the $1.5 million prize, along with a gold medal and diploma, she responded: *Today, we are faced with a challenge which calls for a shift in our thinking, so that humanity stops threatening its life support system! We are called to assist the Earth to heal her wounds, and in the process to heal our own, indeed to embrace the whole of creation in all its diversity, beauty, and wonder. This will happen if we see the need to revive our sense of belonging to a larger family of life, which we have shared our evolution!*

Hopefully, in Africa, it will be its dynamic women who provide the vision, energy, and leadership to translate such ideals into positive actions!

*Source*: Adapted from "African Environmentalist Accepts Peace Prize," by Doug Mellgran, Associated Press release in *The San Diego Union*, December 11, 2004.

### Business Tips in Kenya

Kenyan firms are developing expertise in international business, and their buyers expect quality and service. Customary business courtesies are appreciated, including prompt replies for price quotations, orders,

## EXHIBIT 14.6

## IMPROVING AFRICAN GOVERNANCE

Although Africa is growing an average of 5% per year, and is receiving increased investments from abroad, positive economic progress requires good governance. Only then will the 300 million who live on this continent in poverty be able to gain access to the most basic resources for survival. Effective administration of the state's resources requires governance that respects the rule of law, creates a functioning private sector, and develops a strong civil society. But we lack a widely held, detailed definition of what constitutes good governance. The public sector needs objective criteria of satisfactory performance. With the support of the Kennedy School of Government and an advisory council of eminent African academics, the Mo Ibrahim Foundation has devised an index of governance which assesses all sub-Saharan countries against 58 objectives measures that together define good governance.

By using the Ibrahim Index of African Governance, it is evident that overall progress is being made in the period between 2000 and 2005. Not all countries in the region improved, and the Index revealed that governance deteriorated in under a quarter of the countries. By yearly updating the Index, a scorecard of national progress has been set forth which engages leaders in how well citizens are governed. This initiative is about Africans taking ownership, developing their own forms of accountability, and delivering change. It is about Africans setting benchmarks that the world can emulate. Improved governance is fundamental to realizing Africa's potential. If we can leapfrog ahead in technology, as demonstrated by the mobile phone industry with its 200 million customers, then we can do the same relative to governance.

The Mo Ibrahim Foundation now gives a major financial award annually to heads of state who demonstrate improved governance. The first Prize for Achievement in African Leadership was bestowed in 2007 upon Joaquim Chissano for his performance as President of Mozambique from 1986 to 2005 (the prize is $5 million over 10 years, and $200,000 a year for life thereafter).

*Source*: Adapted from Mo Ibrahim's "Criteria for a Continent," *The World in 2008, The Economist*, p. 72 (www.economist.com). Refer also to "Kenya—Caught in the Act," *The Economist*, January 28, 2006, pp. 45-46. See also E. S. Wibbeke's *Global Business Leadership*, Burlington, MA: Elsevier, 2008 (www.globalbusinessleadership. com).

and deliveries. Because their markets are price sensitive, ensure that delivery dates are maintained, or that buyers are quickly informed of any delays. Also, be prepared to sell here in smaller lots than is customary in the global market.

Their business executives and managers are relatively informal and open, and they do not mind the use of first names. Friendship and trust are highly valued in a productive business relationship. Maintain a close liaison with local customers, distributors, and representatives.

Basic security precautions are advised, as there is a high crime rate in Nairobi, Mombasa, and Kismu, as well as at coastal beach resorts and in some game parks. The border with Somalia has experienced violent criminal activity, including kidnappings. Recall the terrorist bombing in 1998 of the American embassy in Nairobi, killing 213 persons, and subsequently causing the embassy to relocate. Also, the Kenyan mail system can be unreliable, and monetary instruments are frequently stolen. If driving, autos travel on the left side of the road; generally, road conditions are poor, especially in the rainy season. Realize that local driving habits are unpredictable, and vehicle maintenance is likely to be inadequate. The use of sealed bottled water is recommended.

There are prophets of doom predicting that African population growth and climate change condemn its cities and dry countrysides to continuing crises and collapse. But there are optimists, like Michael Joseph, CEO of Safaricom, a Kenyan mobile phone service owned by the U.K.'s Vodaphone. In 8 years, he has taken this market from 20,000 customers to 400,000 subscribers, and created the most profitable company ($223.7 million) in East and Central Africa. Despite Kenya's political crisis and a 25% government stake, retail investors lined up in 2008 to purchase shares in a 25% public offering of the firm. Joseph's strategy is "pay-as-you-go customers" who pay in advance for mobile airtime, then billing privileges, a strong brand which establishes an emotional connection with its loyal Kenyan clients. By fostering national pride in Safaricom, this Hungarian has proven that outsiders can succeed in African business. Before he retires to a home in Northern Kenya, this executive wants to establish M-PESA services for the transfer of funds, such as to pay for mortgages, and to buy the latest generation of mobile technology. Joseph has demonstrated that Africans are resilient inhabitants of a rich continent, and that good business can advance their economies.

Perhaps this explains somewhat why China has become Kenya's ally with a large and growing economic investment in the country. China's trade with this nation is up 36% to over $706 million. Now, if it could only bring peace to Kenya's warring political parties, and demonstrate to politicians the value of cooperation.

## Humanitarian Role in Africa[7]

According to the latest estimates, there are some 2.3 million refugees spread across Africa, along with 12.7 million internally displaced persons who did not flee across borders. Those figures alone justify that humanity elsewhere seeks to help such unfortunate people whose lives have been disrupted by wars and ethnic cleansing. All of Africa benefits from the exceptional service of international humanitarian organizations, some of which are UN/UNESCO or government-sponsored, while others are under private auspices, foundations, or nongovernmental organizations (NGOs). Exhibit 14.7 provides some insights into the dedication of such volunteers. The first item concerns the tiny country of Benin, the most underdeveloped nation in the world. In West Africa, it is situated between Togo and Nigeria. Although French is the official medium of communication, there are 54 local languages used by the average person, who is largely uneducated. Radio is the means for creating public awareness in this new capitalistic society, especially concerning issues such as malnutrition, health care, and education.

---

## EXHIBIT 14.7

### AFRICAN HUMANITARIAN SERVICES

Not all foreigners in Africa are there to despoil her—for centuries, outsiders have also come to help its people and solve their problems, as the next four examples will confirm:

The Peace Corps has a 45-year legacy of American service to those in need at home and abroad. One such idealistic representative was Benedict Moran[g] of Scottsdale, Arizona. Each day, 7000 PC volunteers like him work in the developing world to fight hunger and disease, to further basic education, and promote economic security. Motivated by a strong work ethic, these unpaid, optimistic Corps members have a commitment to human service, as well as a pragmatic approach in problem solving. After graduation from college, Ben had joined up and was assigned to a very undeveloped Benin in West Africa. There he worked with local community leaders to bring the benefits of information technology to some 6.6 million people who earn on average less than $2 a day. To assist its largely impoverished and uneducated population, his project in the Peace Corps Partnership program was improving and upgrading *Radio Rural Locale de Quake*, founded in 1996. That media broadcasting in the French and major local languages has a significant impact toward improving health care, in girl school enrollment, and in use of sustainable agro-forestry techniques. In his time there, Ben's project replaced deteriorating technical equipment in the Quake station, especially computers, music library, information database, and

*continued*

---

[g]After his Peace Corps service, Ben Moran, son of our senior author, volunteered with a French humanitarian organization for two more years of working in Darfur, Sudan. He recently completed dual degree graduate studies in the Schools of International Public Affairs and Journalism.

EXHIBIT 14.7

AFRICAN HUMANITARIAN SERVICES (CONTINUED)

sound quality. By using the Internet, they were able to reach a larger number of citizens to cover a wide range of subjects for community development purposes. Through computer workshops for employees, the Beninese learned new skills, which further empowered them in their business careers. Moran and other volunteers worked closely with the natives to raise funds, obtain and install new equipment, manage and evaluate this innovative project for maximum benefit of the people, so as to enrich their lives and self-worth.

—Paul D. Civerdell, Peace Corps Headquarters,
1111 20th St. NW, Washington, DC 20526, USA
(www.peacecorps.gov/project#680-120).

In 1999, Medecins Sans Frontiers, or Doctors Without Borders, was awarded the Nobel Peace Prize for their exceptional, global humanitarian service! Within 72 hours, their health care teams responded to 2005 disasters in Southeast Asia. MSF provided two hundred international volunteers and two hundred metric tons of aid supplies to assist people in five countries who were suffering from tsunami damage. Another of their campaigns is *Access to Essential Medicines,* which offers generic drugs to assist 25,000 patients in twenty-seven countries who are coping with the HIV/AIDS—many of these recipients are in Africa.

Among its many projects on that continent is one to support the health care system of Uganda, where conflict has raged for eighteen years. For example, in the Lira District, MSF runs a 350-bed therapeutic feeding center and program, as well as four clinics and two mobile clinics. In the Gulu District, this non-profit organization administers a night shelter for 4,000 children in need of a safe place to sleep on the grounds of Lacor Hospital. The work of these dedicated and selfless medics deserves our readers' support! From their experience, DWB identified ten top humanitarian stories that were most unreported by the global media. Six trouble spots were in Africa—displaced inhabitants of Somalia due to violence; health care crisis in Zimbabwe due to political and economic turmoil; need for effective drugs to combat tuberculosis, as in Kenya and Uganda; combating malnutrition with nutrient-dense ready-to-use foods; worsening conditions in Eastern Democratic Republic of Congo requiring expanded medical services; civilians caught between government troops and rebel groups in Northern Central African Republic are being displaced from their homes. Doctors without Borders are addressing these multiple human needs of Africans.

—Doctors Without Borders, 333 Seventh Ave.,
2nd Fl., New York, N.Y. 1001, USA
(www.doctorswithoutborders.org).

EXHIBIT 14.7

AFRICAN HUMANITARIAN SERVICES (CONTINUED)

New York's Fordham University established an Institute of International Humanitarian Affairs in 2001. Its founding director is an alumnus, Kevin M. Cahill, M.D., who has undertaken medical humanitarian missions for more than forty-five years in sixty countries as a member of the above MSF. Recently, this "visionary grounded in human realities" wrote a book, *To Bear Witness: A Journey of Healing and Solidarity* (Fordham University Press, 2005). Among Cahill's many true stories, it describes how this physician of Irish heritage treated John Paul II after the 1981 assassination attempt on the Pope's life. Dr. Cahill also pays tribute to his late wife, Kathryn, who often worked with him on his Doctors Without Borders undertakings, saying: *Ours was a marriage made in heaven, and honed to perfection in some of the hell holes on Earth!* Such humanitarian efforts took him to many African countries, such as drought-plagued Somalia, and more recently to serve victims in need after the devastation of U.S. Gulf Coast hurricanes; the earthquake in Kashmir, Pakistan, and India, as well from the Iraq war. Here is an excerpt from his new volume: *Those of us privileged to participate in great humanitarian dramas have the opportunity that adversity offers to build a new framework—using and sometimes rediscovering the best of old structures, but realizing that a new spirit and innovative methods are necessary for international discourse in a new millennium.*

—"Nota Bene," *Fordham Alumni Magazine,*
Fall/Winter 2005/6, Vol. 39:1.
*(www.fordhamedu/instituteofinternationalhumanitarianaffairs).*

The Heifer Foundation operates worldwide from its international headquarters in Little Rock, Arkansas. This non-profit humanitarian entity works with communities who seek to end hunger and poverty, while caring for the Earth and its environment. Since 1944, it has helped 9.2 million families move toward greater self-reliance through the gift of livestock, plus training in environmentally sound agriculture. The impact of each original gift is multiplied by recipients who agree to "pass on the gift" by giving one or more of their animals, or the equivalent, to a neighbor in need. For example, an eleven-year civil war in Sierra Leone fought over rich natural resources plunged this West African country into destitution. Many people lost their livestock in the conflict. So, in 2008, Heifer International opened an office in Freetown where they are working with poor Sierra Leoneans to establish programs that develop animal and agricultural projects so as to help the locals to rebuild self-sustaining communities.

—George Bugbee and Sherri Nelson's "Sierra Leone on the Mend,"
*WorldArk,* November/December 2008, pp. 21-26
(www.heiferinternational.org/worldark).

On the Atlantic side of the African continent, the Gulf of Guinea defines the region. Its coastline has a series of exotic names that reveal something of its history—Grain Coast, Ivory Coast, Gold Coast, and Slave Coast. This is an equatorial area of high precipitation (20-40 inches of rain), and high temperatures (75-80 °F). It is a land mass primarily of forest, woodlands, and grasslands, plus mixed use, crop-land, and wetland. It is an expanse filled with wildlife and fauna—the major crops being bananas, cassava, cattle, citrus fruit, cocoa, coffee, corn, fish, forest products, millet, oil palm fruit, pineapple, rice, rubber, sesame seed, sheep, sorghum, sugarcane, swine, tea, and tobacco. The area is also rich in industry and mining—aluminum, gold, manganese, titanium, diamonds, manufacturing, petroleum, and processing. West Africa is in the midst of an oil boom today, but, unfortunately, too many corrupt elite benefit, instead of improving the masses. These natural resources are why so many non-Africans have come here, and why it is a target of foreign investment.

Centuries ago, this region experienced the rise and fall of great African empires, like the Mali from the thirteenth century and the Songhay from the fifteenth. Great rivers, such as the Gambia and Niger, flow from the mountains to the shores through forests, savannahs, and arid plains to an often swampy coastline.

The region is home to some 14 nation-states, all of which describe themselves as republics. However, their rulers range from democratically elected presidents to dictators and military coup masters. The locale extends from Guinea-Bissau in the northwest corner, south of Senegal, to another Congo in the southwest that abuts the Democratic Republic of the Congo. Alphabetically, these countries are called: Benin, Burkina Faso, Cameroon, Congo, Cote d'Ivoire, Equatorial Guinea, Gabon, Ghana, Guinea, Guinea-Bissau, Liberia, Nigeria, Sierra Leone, and Togo. The biggest urban center is Lagos, Nigeria, with a population of approximately 5 million. One country in the region, Nigeria, has been chosen for a cultural analysis. Unfortunately, West Africa is a region of political instability and even civil war, often originating from rebel groups in neighboring countries. Examples are given below:

- *Congo*—In its eastern region, civilians suffer from fighting by Congo troops and rebels. In 2008, 250,000 people had been displaced, while massacres, rapes, cholera, and hunger multiply, despite the presence of 20,000 UN peacekeepers in the area.
- *Cote d'Ivoire*—The central government recently fought northern rebels, resulting in a violent and wasteful civil war until peace was restored.
- *Liberia*—Warlord President Charles Taylor came to power through a coup and killings, but was finally forced into exile with the help

of French and American troops; he now faces prosecution in the International Criminal Court. The days of "big man" may be over now that he is the first African head of state to be indicted for *crimes against humanity*. He has been replaced by Africa's first woman elected President, who has launched a recovery program.

■ *Sierra Leone*—Struggling with postwar reconstruction and trying to contain the smuggling of their famous *blood diamonds* out of the country. As so many widows resulted from the conflict, a positive sign was the formation of the Women's Empowerment Self-Development Association. WESDA is a cooperative at Crossing Village, which helps them farm together so as to raise food for their families, as well as some income.

■ *Togo*—President General Gnassingbe Eyadema, having shot his way to power, is Africa's longest-standing leader, as well as one of its most brutal and corrupt leaders; though his term of office is constitutionally over, his son will succeed this usurper of democratic elections.

The United Nations spends over $50 million in the region annually, running camps for refugees and fugitives, numbering more than 200,000. On the positive side, constitutional and multiparty Ghana, Mali, and Senegal stand out as beacons of stability in the area. Discovery of offshore oil may also improve living conditions in Ghana.

## Nigeria

Nigeria's land mass is approximately 356,669 square miles—about twice the size of the state of California. Despite some border disputes with its neighbors over Lake Chad, this West African nation is bounded by Benin, Niger, Chad, and Cameroon, as well as the Atlantic Ocean on its southern edge.

### Historical Perspective[8]

The cultural history of this country and its peoples dates back to the seventh century B.C. More advanced cultures have resided in Nigeria since the twelfth century A.D. In 1861, the British seized the principal city of Lagos, supposedly to end the slave trade then flourishing there. The English social, financial, and political cultural impacts have been considerable ever since. Even though the locals gained their political independence in 1960, they are still members of the British Commonwealth of Nations, often traveling to the United Kingdom for business, pleasure, or resettlement. English is often the language for business and national affairs, in addition to six local languages.

Its rapidly growing population of over 130 million is composed of 250 tribal groups, of which 65% are the Hausa-Fulani, Ibo, and Yoruba—these also represent three major language groups (Hausa, Zulu, and Swahili). There are five main religious influences present: Muslim (45%);

Protestant (25%); Roman Catholic (12%); African Christian (11%); and traditional African or indigenous beliefs (6%)—all percentages of the population are approximate. As with many African countries, foreign missionaries accompanied European colonists in previous centuries. Today, Christian churches, schools, hospitals, and social institutions have significant influence on the culture, especially in the south, as do comparable Koranic schooling and enterprises in the north. A quota system guarantees students from the latter a share of university places—an undue share, contend the southerners who view their school system as superior.

## Cultural Guidelines for Doing Business in Nigeria

Nigeria's human resources have great potential, and oil is its main income producer today. The literacy rate has risen to 57% as a result of 6 years of compulsory education. Over 14 million students are enrolled in elementary (34,240) and secondary (5970) schools and 48 colleges/ universities. The Nigerian educational system is largely based on the British system. What was generally described at the opening of this chapter about African culture comes into sharper focus in the context of Nigeria, once considered Africa's most advanced nation.

## Social Structure

In Nigeria, the family dominates the social structure. Nigerian tradition places emphasis on one's lineage through the male head of the household. In non-Muslim sections, these familial connections form vast networks that serve as a foundation for one's social identity. Marriage is seen as a way of producing more children to contribute to this lineage or network. Sterility is a ground for divorce. Three forms of marriage exist in Nigeria. Among some Christians and non-Muslims, unlimited polygamy is customary. Wives are acquired through the payment of a "bride price" to the bride's parents. Muslim custom differs in that the number of wives is usually limited to four. The Western Christian marriage is relatively uncommon in rural areas, although increasing in the cities.

The stratification of Nigerian society varies with region. In northern Nigeria, rank is more important than it is in the south. In the east, some egalitarian tradition exists, whereas in the west there is a distinct aristocracy.

## Groups and Relationships

Among the many tribes, the principal ones are the following: (1) Hausa, very religious Muslims; (2) Yoruba, an outgoing, festive people, not secretive about their business activities; (3) Ibo, excellent merchants, extremely resourceful, hardworking, and conscientious, who understand the value of money. These important attitudes exist in Nigeria, affecting business relationships.

*Old family business tradition.* One does not share information, because everyone else is a competitor. (This traditional attitude has often been reinforced by subsequent European influences, as opposed to new American management training which encourages a free flow of information, including the sharing of trade knowledge and more open communications. Many young Nigerian businesspeople are U.S. trained.)

*Muslim attitudes.* Predestination rather than free will; reliance on tradition and precedent; mistrust of innovation; unwillingness to take risks; learning by rote rather than by experiments or problem solving. Some of Nigeria's serious internal strife is not just tribal, but also religious—with Muslims attacking Christians.

## Communications

There are certain words that should not be used by a Westerner in Nigeria, such as *native*, *hut*, *jungle*, *witchcraft*, and *costume*. The connotation behind these expressions tends to be that Africa is still a dark continent. Nigeria, as is true with many other parts of Africa, has made great strides in development and is proud of its advancement. Therefore, it is best to remember that a hut is a home and a costume is really clothing. Nigerians want to be friends with foreign visitors, and they are proud to have them in their homes. They will go to great lengths to be a friend, but they do not want to be patronized.

*Greetings.* Upon meeting a Nigerian business associate, the greeting is Westernized but formal. A simple, "Good morning, Mister Opala, how are you?" is accepted as proper. Asking personal questions about one's family is a common practice. Once you have established some degree of familiarity, you can use a first name if the Nigerian initiates it. Always shake hands when greeting someone. It is extremely rude not to acknowledge a person when entering a room or to shake his or her hand.

*Forms of address.* Nigerians distinguish the levels of familiarity between one another by their forms of address. Friends will call one another by their first names. Older brothers and sisters are very rarely addressed by their first names. An older brother is addressed as N'da__, and an older sister as N'se__, which means "my senior [brother or sister's name]." This is simply a sign of respect toward seniority and age. The expressions *sir* and *ma'am* are always used when speaking to a businessperson, government official, someone older, or someone in a position of authority.

## Social Customs

Nigerians are a proud and self-confident people. Much of this confidence comes from a knowledge that their country is a leader in

Africa in many ways. They are extroverted, friendly, and talkative. Nigerians are known also for their hospitality. Strangers are taken in, fed, and lodged for as long as the guest desires. Consequently, it is possible to make many more long-lasting relationships that are less superficial than in some other cultures.

When a friend, acquaintance, or relative becomes ill, it is customary for that person to receive many, many visitors. Anyone who even remotely knows the sick person will come to visit. It is the Nigerian way of saying, "I want to know for myself how you're feeling."

*Gender.* As in all of Africa, the role of women in Nigeria is changing with modernization, especially in urban centers. Traditionally, women have always performed the major laboring tasks, from farming to road building. Now, with increased education and opportunity, they are moving up in commerce and industry, as well as in government and the professions. Perhaps the Nigerian women achieving positions of leadership and influence in the political and economic arena will also set the example for the liberation of women elsewhere on the continent.

Women play a vigorous role in this society, although domestic authority always rests seemingly with the husband. There is a network of marketing and trading in commodities that occurs throughout the country. This is the exclusive province of women, who run their own businesses the way they see fit.

*Marriage.* When two people are considering marriage, a proper procedure must be followed. The first step is for the prospective groom to send an intermediary to the woman's home to present the idea of marriage to her parents. Gifts are sent to the woman, and then the man himself comes to the woman's parents to discuss the marriage. So far, nothing has been said to the woman about the pending marriage. If everything is in order with the prospective bride's family, the woman then goes to live with the man's family to make sure this is where she wants to live. If so, the marriage can occur. The dowry involved in the marriage is not a fixed amount. It is an insurance against maltreatment for the woman. It is not until the wife dies and is buried in her natal land that the dowry is paid to her husband, if she has been treated well. Christian and Muslim marriage practices and ceremonies may differ from this tribal tradition.

Currently, intermarriage between tribes is rare in Nigeria. It is more common for a Nigerian to marry a foreigner than a member of another tribe. There is still a great deal of rivalry between the tribes, and the intent seems to be to try and keep them pure. However, if such an intertribal marriage should occur, oddly enough, the stranger will be treated almost royally by the members of the other tribe. The reason for this is that the nontribe member is viewed as having made a supreme sacrifice by giving up his or her tribe and their traditions and adopting those of the spouse, as they almost always do in such situations.

Most Nigerian cultures are patriarchal. In some areas, particularly the rural ones, polygamy is still prevalent. However, in urban areas, it is much more common to find one-man, one-woman marriages. Marital age is becoming more of an economic decision. Couples wait until they have an education and can afford a marriage.

## Traditions

Nigeria is growing quickly and becoming more modernized and urbanized, but traditions are still very important to the people. Local customs still play a significant role in Nigerian life. One such ritual, though quickly disappearing, is found strictly in the western portion of the country and has to do with tribal marks. When a child reaches the age of 2 or 3 years, he or she has the appropriate tribal marks burned into his or her face, very similar to the branding process. These marks reflect tribes or family. When one sees the marks, it is not necessary to ask what the person's last name is or from what tribe he or she comes. It is said that if the child cannot withstand the pain during the ceremony, as there is no anesthesia, he or she is not worthy of that family or tribe. The whole process is very unhygienic and dangerous, and seems to be gradually dying out.

Nigeria is a "right-handed" society. As in many cultures, the left hand is considered unclean, as it is the "toilet hand." It is extremely impolite to extend the left hand to others or to eat with it, even if the person is left-handed.

It is important to reemphasize the matter of age in Nigeria. There is a profound respect for one's elders. Older people are not placed in nursing homes when they become ill. They are taken in by their families, looked after, and revered. The importance of the elderly seems to lie in their capability to pass on family history and tradition.

The custom of eating with one's hands is practiced in Nigeria. If there is a big festival, or even in a private home, where there are foreign visitors not used to this custom, allowances are made and silverware is often provided to them. However, an honest effort will be greatly appreciated. A communal bucket is passed around in which they wash their hands prior to the beginning of the meal. Once again, it is important to use only the right hand.

## Governmental and Economic Challenges

Despite the long tribal history within this region, the Federal Republic of Nigeria was not established until 1963. The boundaries provided by the British brought together four peoples who have had a continuous rivalry going on since then. In 1967, the eastern region seceded to found the Republic of Biafra; the subsequent civil war lasted 3 years and caused over a million deaths, mainly from starvation. Since its formation, Nigeria has experienced struggles about whether the government should be ruled by civilians or by the military. In 1985, Maj. Gen. Ibrahim Babangida seized power, and in 1992 when Moshood Abiola, a Yoruba, was elected president, in an election organized by the military, the northern generals annulled the results. Instead, the president was put on trial for treason, and one of the military cabal, Gen. Sani Abacha, became the self-appointed ruler. With his death from a heart attack in 1998, General Abdulsalam Abuubakar was sworn in as Nigeria's 10th head of state, appointed by a provisional Ruling Council of military men.

There is growing consensus that military rule by soldiers who get rich has had its day—28 years out of the nation's 38 years of independence. Politics has been reduced to matters of stealing, or *chopping*, as it is called here. The reality is that multiparty politics, a product of industrialized societies and often based on social class, has yet to succeed here or in the rest of Africa, where loyalties are tribal. Each new general who comes to national power makes noble promises: to break up state monopolies in several industries, to partially privatize big corporations, to introduce competition, and to end the country's crippling domestic fuel shortage. By 2000, a retired general, Olusegun Obasanjo, served as president and tried to cope with eight northern states who declared the adoption of *Shariah*, the Islamic legal code. Like elsewhere on this continent, there is little trust in their unscrupulous "leaders," whose misrule stirs up ethnic chauvinism, undermining national integration. For example, in June 2003, elections were held against a backdrop of a failing economy and religious strife.

As Africa's most populous country, Nigeria represents an enormous market for goods and services. Over a hundred companies are doing business there, with an investment of some $2 billion, two-thirds of which is in the petroleum industry. Its most important international trading partner is the United States, which imports 58% of its oil production. Expatriates from many countries abounded when Nigeria was awash with oil money, especially in the capital of Lagos. Today, though fewer in number, expatriates remaining are businesspersons, construction engineers, agricultural experts, educators, and technocrats.

Besides petroleum, Nigeria's natural resources are tin, columbite, iron ore, coal, limestone, lead, zinc, natural gas, marble, and fish. Agriculture and foodstuffs are big business, along with major industries in beverages, tobacco, vehicles, chemicals, pharmaceuticals, iron/steel, rubber, printing, building materials, lumber, and footwear. Nigeria, like others of the world's hungriest and most populous markets, has needs, tastes, and requirements that will transform the global economy, including how we work and live.

As a young, struggling democracy, Nigeria's greatest challenge is utilizing the country's enormous resources and potential for the benefit of all its inhabitants. If more of the annual national income of almost $10 billion could be diverted into the development of infrastructure, education, and health services, then the new millennium holds promise for this largest, nation in Africa, with one of its lowest standards of living. For progress, these are a few national problems to be addressed:

- *Reversing the culture of corruption* so deeply engrained in this society, as the Economic and Financial Crimes Commission has lost its bite. This pervasiveness ranges from stealing and bribes to scams and swindles, where credit card numbers are subject to theft and fraud. The country is also known for its internal scam artists who often use the Internet to bilk foreigners. Restoring the nation's financial reputation and retrieving its misdirected income are first steps toward regaining the confidence of international investors who now avoid the country. Tales of massive frauds, drug smuggling, money laundering, and embezzlement make it difficult for Nigerians to obtain visas worldwide. Such reforms must begin at the top levels of government.
- *Distributing national income* more equitably, so that the fantastically wealthy elite, many of whom stole shamelessly and without punishment from the public treasury, develop some social responsibility toward the poor in their society.
- *Reforming the public sector*, starting with the electoral, and extending to the criminal justice, law enforcement, and military systems in Africa's biggest and most boisterous nation.
- *Countering criminal behavior and terrorism.* Because local regions do not share equitably in oil profits, there has been much unrest and violence in the Delta region, including kidnapping and ransoming of foreign oil management and technicians. Militants have attacked oil installations, reducing oil output. As a result, nationwide electricity cuts have increased, and infrastructure remains feeble.

## Business Tips in Nigeria

*Meetings.* It will almost always be necessary to deal, in some capacity, with Nigerian government officials. When a meeting is granted, whether with the desired official or someone else, there are important practices to be aware of. First, any significant business transaction is always conducted in person. Any attempt to conduct business either over the telephone or by mail is seen as considering the matter trivial and unimportant. When visiting a colleague's office, tea, coffee, or other refreshments are always available and offered. These refreshments should not be refused, as this may be taken as an offense. Also, refreshments must always be available when the colleague comes to visit the foreign businessperson's office. When commercial visitors are invited to a local colleague's home for dining, if at all possible, the invitation should not be refused.

At state and federal meetings, protocol must be observed. Extreme politeness, respect for authority, and a slower pace are normal. If an authority does not answer your question, it may mean they do not know the answer and do not want to be embarrassed. It is helpful if a foreign businessperson establishes a Nigerian counterpart. One needs expertise in dealing with the Nigerian business community. References should be carefully checked, and choosing someone with influential contacts is important. This local resource will prove invaluable in translating later what was said during a meeting. Even though the official language is English, the Nigerian accent can be difficult to understand. A Nigerian may be insulted when an individual does not comprehend his or her local version of English, often British in origin. It takes a long time to become established in the Nigerian business community, and it is who one knows that will make a difference. Connections are important and should be cultivated. When investing in Nigeria, start at the state government level instead of the federal. Each state operates differently, but all want and need business, and, consequently, are very receptive and can greatly facilitate business formalities.

*Negotiations.* When conducting negotiations with a Nigerian, the tone of such meetings is generally friendly and respectful. Notice should be taken of titles to be sure the appropriate ones are used correctly. Age is highly respected in Nigeria and often associated with wisdom. Therefore, to maximize chances of success, an older person should be sent to meet with prospective businesspersons. Nigerians assume promises will be kept, so be realistic about delivery dates or price specifications. Furthermore, it is not unusual for a Nigerian worker to try to involve his foreign manager or supervisor in politics. It is much better not to participate in these political discussions, as sides will undoubtedly be taken and one's role may be compromised. Subsequently, an air of hostility and tension will be apparent.

*Decision making.* Decision making is based on a centralized system, and delegation of authority is almost nonexistent. Nigerians cling to authority and are dependent on supervision. A Nigerian manager at a high-level position may feel obligated to find jobs for his or her family, and will not hesitate to "pull strings" to employ them. If the Nigerian is very powerful, there is nothing a foreign businessperson can do to stop this practice. This decision-making process based on family responsibilities can be very frustrating to a North American business representative, conditioned to a work environment with a norm of competency and merit selection in advancement and promotions.

*Concept of time.* In Nigeria, this can be summed up as unlimited. Lagos, the center of business, is congested, and traffic jams can hold one up for several hours. Consequently, late appointments are common and usually anticipated, and telephone service is poor and unreliable. Time, therefore, is not of the utmost importance to most Nigerians. As such, punctuality is not prevalent. Although work is important to the Nigerians, so is their leisure. Sports are a favorite way to spend time, including the most popular activities of football, boxing, and horse racing. Hockey, tennis, cricket, polo, golf, rugby, table tennis, and softball are also played.

The southern tip of the African continent encompasses some 11 nations. On the West Coast facing the Atlantic Ocean are Angola, Namibia, and South Africa. The latter is the most modern state bordering on the Indian Ocean, and will be the target for our analysis which follows. Within that country are the small kingdoms of Lesotho and Swaziland. In the region's interior are Zambia, Malawi, Zimbabwe, and Botswana. On the East Coast facing the Indian Ocean are Mozambique, plus the channel island of Madagascar. In this southern area, the largest population centers are along the northwest and southwest coastlines, as well as in the north.

The area's peace and prosperity has been severely constricted by a 30-year civil war in Angola; a lengthy, costly, but successful struggle to overturn the all-white, Afrikaner apartheid government; and the ongoing civil unrest, killings, land grabs, and economic disasters of President Robert Mugabe's administration in Zimbabwe. An exception to this pattern is Botswana, a small peaceful country of only 1.8 million people, just north of South Africa. It has used its vast diamond wealth wisely to foster education, one of the best on the continent, as well as tourism and friendly business environment. This country is known to be the least corrupt state, but its sparking image is marred by a high rate of AIDS, and its mistreatment of a most vulnerable ethnic group, the Bushmen, or San, a hunter-gatherer tribal people.

Off the coast of Mozambique is the island of Madagascar, also a part of Southern Africa. Further east in the Indian Ocean are three small other islands. The second is called Mauritius, an independent republic of some 1.3 million inhabitants (Exhibit 14.8).

## EXHIBIT 14.8

### MAURITIUS: MULTIDIVERSITY PROGRESS

This isolated island state of only 1100 square miles gained its independence from Britain in 1968. Then, it was a sugar-based economy with a GDP of $200 per person. But with freedom, the country's GDP has jumped to $7000 per person and ranks first for good governance on the above Ibrahim index! The World Bank has also given the republic a high ranking as the best African country for ease of doing business. With over a hundred hotels, it is now a peaceful and popular place with tourists who crave sun, palms, and good service. Its capital of Port Louis is an attractive place for offshore banking, hosting nineteen global banks. Furthermore, Mauritius is a low-tax gateway for investment into Asia, especially

*continued*

EXHIBIT 14.8

MAURITIUS: MULTIDIVERSITY PROGRESS (CONTINUED)

India. The economy also includes food processing, sugar milling, chemical and textile manufacturing, fishing, as well as cattle raising plus the exporting of cut flowers and molasses.

With an economic mindset that welcomes competition, its government has slashed commercial red tape and cut taxes, while reforming labor legislation and promoting itself as a desirable business destination. As a result, unemployment and budget deficits are down, and foreign investments are up. Unfortunately, the republic has to import most of its food and energy, while too much of the economy is concentrated in the hands of a few local conglomerates. These factors are being diminished by a new competition commission and development of new industries. With an independent judiciary and democratic elections, three political parties agree on broad policy directions.

A pluralistic population mix of Africans, Chinese, Europeans, and Indians has religious and cultural differences, but has avoided communal divisions. They speak some seven languages, ranging from English, Creole, and French to Hindi, Urdu, Hakka, and Bojoori. Further, adherents of Christianity, Hinduism, and Muslim religions have learned to tolerate one another's beliefs. Surely, a demonstration model for other African nations to emulate!

*Source*: Adapted from "Beyond Beaches and Palm Trees," *The Economist*, October 18, 2008, p. 58.

## South Africa[10]

There are multiple visions of what South Africa has been and should be. One vision is that it is a land of promise—the most advanced economy on the continent, a country with enormous natural beauty and resources. In the twenty-first century, the African continent needs a strong and prosperous South Africa.

South African society is in the midst of a transformation that could lead to prosperity, if both the white citizen minority who had been in control and the oppressed black majority now ruling truly share their nation's sociopolitical institutions and power. By their practice of cultural synergy, both may create a multicultural society of equal opportunity.[11] One small indicator of progress is the "Buppies," the growing, upwardly mobile, black professionals. In this multiracial democracy, they can even be found at gatherings of "high society," such as the J&B Met Horse Race, an annual sports and fashion extravaganza, formerly the exclusive domain of middle-aged white suburbia!

# Historical Perspective

South Africa has a heritage of pioneering, colonization, wars, and building a modern infrastructure. Thankfully, now, *apartheid* is gone—a failed policy of separation of white and blacks that was internationally condemned and finally abandoned in the 1990s. Three centuries ago, this land became home to Bushmen and Hottentots, Bantu-speaking black tribes. In the mid-seventeenth century, the European whites arrived. First were the Dutch, who built a trading settlement at the Cape of Good Hope. They were joined by Germans and French Huguenot refugees in 1688. Together, these colonists would become known as Boers (farmers). The British invaded and captured the Cape in 1806, gaining formal possession of the colony in 1814 as the result of the Napoleonic wars. To avoid English rule, the Boers migrated to the undeveloped interior of the country from 1835 to 1848, defeating the indigenous Zulu and other black tribes in the process. With the discovery of gold and diamonds in that territory, Britain annexed parts of that area that led to the Boer War, which they won in 1902. The British then combined their colonies of Cape and Natal with the Boer Republics of Orange Free State and Transvaal, creating in 1910 the Union of South Africa, today called the Republic of South Africa (RSA).

Thus, this is a nation of four cultural influences or ethnic groups: the native African majority, the minority populations consisting of the Dutch who were to become known as Boers and *Afrikaners*, along with the British and Asian immigrants, the latter mostly from India and designated later as the *Coloureds*. As British power waned, the Afrikaners increasingly took control of the government after the election of their National Party in 1948. During the 1960s, Afrikaners introduced the oppressive apartheid system separating blacks from whites, creating two unequal communities. Another flawed policy was launched that forced settlement for the majority black African population in separate and supposedly independent homelands (e.g., Lesotho and Swaziland). Since the 1960s, domestic turmoil and violence caused by these inhumane political actions brought international protests and boycotts, including trade sanctions by the United States and condemnation by the United Nations.

To fight for black human rights, the African National Congress (ANC) was formed in 1955 and eventually coalesced with other black groups' campaigns against the white power government. Finally, the economic and social impact of multinational sanctions led to the resignation in 1989 of the president of the RSA, P. W. Botha. His replacement, F. W. de Klerk, implemented a series of democratic reforms, beginning with the freeing of political prisoners, the desegregating of institutions, and the legal recognition of the ANC as a political party. The outcome was the signing of a peace agreement between the latter and the ruling elite providing for power sharing, the dismantling of apartheid, and the holding of open elections. In the 1994 election, all RSA citizens voted for the first time, electing ANC leader and former political prisoner, Nelson Mandela, and de Klerk as vice president of a multiethnic government. For their peacekeeping success, both men were awarded the Nobel Peace Prize.

Since then, a political evolution, not revolution, has been under way. The RSA is a laboratory of social experimentation that has implications for the whole continent. With the ascendancy of the ANC leadership to the national government in 1994, and a new approach to white/black power sharing, the inequitable, segregated, apartheid political and social system is very slowly being transformed into a more democratic, multiparty one. Despite an odious and corrosive historical legacy, here the change process and progress are under way. Suffrage policy was at first limited to whites only, and then extended to the *Coloureds*, and now finally includes the blacks, formerly restricted to voting in local "homeland" or township elections. The shift in political parties and power has been from the National Party and Conservative Party to the ANC, the Inkatha Freedom Party (Zulu), and the Democratic Party. Overall, the current government is striving to meet educational and training needs for a global economy and a knowledge society.

Postapartheid presidents have all been from the ANC, and struggle with human resource and economic improvements for all. They have been slow to counter the AIDS epidemic in the country, and to provide human rights leadership relative to nasty regimes elsewhere. With refugees flocking in from nearby Zimbabwe, they have been reluctant to confront its failed president, Robert Mugabe, or to endorse the International Criminal Courts prosecution of Omar al-Bashir, Sudan's president accused of genocide. They have not implemented the vision of the revered Nelson Mandela when he was elected president: *Human rights will be the light that guides our foreign affairs.* Africa's richest nation has yet to become a "beacon of hope" to the world's oppressed. However, the government has been a leading peacemaker in the New Partnership for Africa's Development, which promotes continental democracy and effective governance through a peer-review system. South Africa has sent troops to mediate conflicts in Darfur, Burundi, the Central African Republic, and Congo. At home, it has adopted a progressive constitution, prohibiting discrimination, and promoting civil liberties. Its officials have sought to provide more adequate housing and reproductive health care for citizens. But South Africa must do more to exercise moral leadership in Africa, while contributing to a more equitable world order. As their Nobel prize winner, Archbishop Desmond Tutu observed that turning a blind eye to oppression outside South Africa is *a betrayal of our noble past.... If others had used the arguments we are using today when we asked them for support against apartheid, we might have still have been unfree.*[d]

---

[d]"South Africa and the World: The See-No-Evil Foreign Policy," *The Economist*, November 15, 2008, pp. 55-56.

# Cultural Guidelines for Business in South Africa

Today, there are some 47 million South Africans, equally divided between men and women, who have a life expectancy of only 48 years. This is a relatively young population, about 70% or more are under 50 years of age, with 26% under the age of 10. Approximately 37 million are black Africans (79.3%); 4.4 million are white (9.3%); 1.2 million are Asian (2.5%); and 4.1 million are colored (8.8%). The Black Africans consist of nine tribal groups—Zulu (the largest), Xhosas, North and South Sothos, Tswanas, Shangaan-Tsongas, Swazis, South Ndebeles, and Vendas. Each has its own special cultural heritage, language, and sense of identity. During the apartheid period, tribal groups had been assigned by the racist government to 10 ethnic "homelands" that were supposed to have self-rule, but actually were dependent on the white statecraft—these are being dismantled under the new regime. Although English and Afrikaans (a Dutch derivation) are the official languages, the blacks among the four major tribes speak varying forms of Bantu. The whites have zero population growth, but were reserved 85% of the land under the old system. The whites are divided into two groups— the English-speaking descendants of English, Scottish, and Irish settlers, and the Afrikaan-speaking offspring of the Dutch, German, and French colonials; there are also the English-speaking *Coloureds* descendants of early white setters, native Hottentots, imported Dutch East Indian slaves, and indentured laborers from India (Hindi speakers).

*Religion.* In terms of religious affiliations, most South Africans are Christians, divided among the Dutch Reformed Church of the Afrikaners, and other denominations, such as Anglican, Methodist, Presbyterian, Roman Catholic, as well as African Charismatic, a combination of Christian and traditional African rituals. The Indian community consists of both Hindus and Muslims. There are also a small number of Jews.

*Literacy/Education.* Compared to most other African nations, the overall literacy rate is high but deceptive. The overall literacy rate is 84.6%, which is among the highest in Africa, but 99% of whites as compared to 50% of blacks are literate. (The other two highest African literacy rates are also in the south—Lesotho, 82%, and Zimbabwe, 85%; all three countries are former British colonies in which English is widely spoken.)

Among the black population, 22.3% have no schooling; 25.4% have some or completed primary school; 30.4% have some secondary schooling; while only 16.8% have completed their "metrics"; 5.2% has had higher education. Generally, the Indians (41%), the whites (36%), and the coloreds (7%) benefit by passing metric exams, and moving on to university or college. Formerly all-white institutions, such as Witwatersrand and Cape Town universities, are still excellent. Historically, black universities have been described as atrocious with serious security problems, so reforms are under way among them. Until recently, when Africans replaced Afrikaners in the education ministry, only 3.8% of the GDP was devoted to education and 85% of that went to whites; now, 20% of the national budget is spent on education regardless of color. Today, nearly all children attend primary school—over 8 million students enrolled in elementary schools, 1 million plus in secondary, and 282,000 or so in third or higher levels of education. But the quality of that education is questionable—the new education minister claims 30% of the schools are not fit for use, and there is an acute shortage of qualified teachers. The school system is an adaptation of the British educational model, but is in transition to integrate more black Africans at all levels. Fifty-eight percent of students matriculating in secondary school do graduate. The apartheid legacy lingers among a lost generation who thought education was right, but did not require personal effort and attendance. The situation improves in independent schools, the majority of which charge fees—2000 of them enroll 4% of the student population. The proportion of blacks in them has risen to 60%, and this system is the best racially integrated. Furthermore, parents are becoming educational entrepreneurs, creating their own avenues of learning opportunities for economic and social mobility. Private business is involved in funding initiatives to improve all types of schooling. Overall, South Africa has one educational advantage—its school systems are flexible and opening to customizing programs to meet national and student needs.

## Social Conditions

Consider these cultural insights about contemporary South Africa, especially among the black African majority:

- *Family structure* in the black community has been destabilized by past apartheid policies and its constraints; dislocation caused by job searches contributes to 7 million people living in poverty. In the black extended family, there is normally great respect manifested toward the elderly and obedience to parents. In contrast, the white community's family is nuclear, close-knit, and privileged, though declining in affluence and influence. The Truth and Reconciliation Commission enabled families from both sides to testify or confess about the brutality of 40 years of apartheid regime, and to try and move on with reconstruction.
- *Emerging middle class* is slowly happening among the black community—up to 40% of the total population. Africans have taken over downtown urban centers, formerly only open to them by day. Affirmative action and black empowerment programs have opened up the job market and management positions, but only one black-owned company is a real success—Johnnic Holds, an entertainment, media, and telecommunications group. Today, some 70% of the workforce is black Africans, of which 45% are women and

5% disabled. The black share of personal income has climbed and is rising, whereas that of the whites is declining, falling from 71% (1970) to 50% (2000). With all of the country's problems, including a 36% unemployment rate, the trends point toward greater prosperity for black Africans, even with a 2% annual growth rate in population.

■ *Lifestyle* is better for many black Africans than in the past decade—their society is humming with activity and opportunity amidst poverty. Among the blacks, one can find more vibrancy, naturalness, and brotherhood, but it is sometimes marred by intertribal conflict and power struggles. The government is spending 21% of the national budget on education now, which is 5.7% of the GDP. But the rates of crime, violence, and alcohol abuse are up, again partially because of past Afrikaner practices of uprooting people (e.g., putting migrant laborers into hostels, and paying too many wages in *papsak*, or wine). The dying white-dominated culture kept Africans subordinate, called men *boys*, and undermined their role as protectors, often dumping their wives and children in so-called "homelands." Realistically, postapartgeid South Africa is experiencing serious threats to family life, which is increasingly breaking down with male violence.

Sports are a positive influence among the masses. While a prisoner, Nelson Mandela taught himself about rugby because his Afrikaner jailors were so mad about it.[e] When he was released from jail, Mandela inspired black Africans in many ways, including sports; he coaxed all his countrymen towards more civilized government and behavior. Having studied the culture of his opponents, he promoted rugby as a bridge across the racial chasm. Thus, he overcame some of the tensions between the two racial groups that ultimately resulted in the destruction of apartheid. Now, in 2010, South Africa is hosting the World Cup soccer match!

■ *Work environment* is gradually improving for all employees. However, in government, the ANC, a former revolutionary party, is still authoritarian and prizes political loyalty over competence. Its officials have not mastered the art of administration and science of management, while being deployed from one job position to another. Their public servants are not open to new ideas outside their own bureaucracy. Their current policies discourage blacks from becoming entrepreneurs, so small and medium enterprises languish. Also, there is a severe shortage of native skilled workers, and protectionism in place to prevent the import of technicians from abroad. This shortage of qualified personnel has led to thousands of job vacancies,

---

[e]Note in chapter reference #10, John Carlin's book, *Playing the Enemy: Nelson Mandela and the Game That Made the Nation*, Penguin Books, 2008. Also see "Briefing South Africa—The Long Journey of a Young Democracy," *The Economist*, March 3, 2007, pp. 32-34.

especially in the financial and banking sectors, as well as in delivering services. Presently a plan is under way—Joint Initiative for Priority Skills Acquisition—to develop the needed skill base by recruiting and training more engineers, technicians, and other skilled professionals.

■ *Health care and social services* are beginning to deteriorate, though the country has the most organized and functioning health care system in Africa. The quality of life for average citizens is being severely undermined by the spread of diseases, especially AIDS. The UNAIDS estimates that nearly 4.7 million people here are HIV-positive, yet government "leaders" often live in denial. The administration of President Mbeki was absurdly slow in responding to the epidemic of 5.2 million HIV-infected citizens. With 40% so infected, forecasts are that the AIDS deaths will be up to 635,000 by 2010, bringing a vast increase in orphaned children and dysfunctional families. As a result, by the end of this decade, the public health costs are likely to approach 38 billion rand. The health care and social services systems, until recently, had no effective plan in place to cope with growing numbers of patients and dying people, no less their youthful offspring, who may end up truants, street gang members, and eventually criminals. Within that context, the UN expects South Africa's GDP in 10 years to be lowered by 17%. Except in the gold fields, the nation's workforce is likely to be decimated by this and related diseases, so undermining productivity. With about 1000 dying daily from this illness, the government is finally waking up to the scourge of AIDS and its implications—a comprehensive regime is under way to combat the pandemic with antiretroviral drugs. But the whole health care system is inadequate for coping with this plague, which now infects 5.5 million people.

■ *Criminal justice* is weak in South Africa—the system suffers from too many unemployed criminals who either do not get caught, or when they are arrested, are not likely to be convicted. Although the government is spending more on law enforcement, the crime shows the country to be among the most violent in the world with 50 people killed every day. With a loss of cases by prosecutors of 500 out of 1800 prosecuted, half of the 2.2 million crimes reported go unsolved. However, private investment and research into the processing of accused criminals has produced reforms in the justice system and higher conviction rates. The old hatred of police lingers, along with a legacy of firearms. Poorly paid police ranks are riddled by corruption, inadequate equipment, insufficient training, and ineptness (about a quarter are functionally illiterate, and large numbers do not even have a driver's license to drive themselves to crime scenes). The cost of crime to business is up approximately to 12 billion rand, while the national police budget is about 16 billion rand. Reforms under way include the appointment of a new national prosecutor, establishment of a new elite investigation force, legislation to mandate minimum sentences, and bail. Poverty and the shantytowns it produced, such as Soweto outside of Cape Town and Forman Road in Durban, are home to thousands of struggling black Africans and their uneducated and unemployed youth, many of whom turn to criminal activities to survive. In the 1990s, there was a crime wave, and Johannesburg became known as the "crime capital of the world." But there has been a remarkable turnaround in that municipality with the formation of Business Against Crime (BAC)—it has reduced street crime by 80% after installing 200 surveillance cameras in that city's central business district. Other cities, like Cape Town, have also had success in curbing crime with closed-circuit television monitoring. With a mixture of both private and public sector funding in crime prevention, young professionals have begun to move back into the inner cities, contributing to their renewal. Private security firms have increased and employ some 250,000 people, twice as many as in the regular police force. There are other positive signs, such as an efficient constitutional court and vocal think-tanks. The nation has become a leader in conflict resolution within Africa and the founding of the African Union.

## Economic and Social Challenges

*Economic Development.* South Africa still has the strongest and most diversified economy on the African continent. Although it has only 6% of the sub-Saharan people, it accounts for one-third of its GDP. With a diversified economy and first-world financial services, the economy has structurally changed and is more internationally competitive. It is strong not only in minerals and raw materials, but increasingly in high technologies. A strong central bank and legal system, as well as a fair road and transport infrastructure, all contribute to development. Although foreign investments did not grow as anticipated with the lifting of global economic sanctions and diminishing civil protests, the global companies that have come are pleased overall with their experience and are expanding.

The government has succeeded in reducing the national budget, debt, and inflation, through disciplined, responsible fiscal and monetary policies. It aims to promote growth, employment, and redistribution. The challenge is whether the high standard of living enjoyed by the whites can be shared somewhat by the masses of black citizens, developing in the process a broader middle class. The gross domestic product average is obviously much higher for whites than for blacks, but the GDP is growing too slowly overall. With an employment rate between 25% and 35%, 3 million inhabitants are looking for work. Reducing unemployment and job creation are critical, along with new enterprises, for growth within a new multiracial society. In the past, the economy was largely based on varied agriculture, as well as the mining of diamonds and gold, until the manufacturing industries took hold. South Africa has vast natural resources, including chromite, coal, uranium, platinum, natural gas, and fish. Today, this mixed economy has a large industrial base—from metal products, chemicals, and foodstuffs, to machinery, vehicles, and textiles—all part of a strong exporting program. With a good infrastructure in transportation and communication already in place, as well as an educated population, this nation has great potential for development.

The economic situation is well summarized in the township of Soweto, Johannesburg. In what was once a byword for violence and black deprivation, shiny new cars are parked in front of elegant houses protected by security systems. Shopping malls, banks, and tourists are now visible. Black economic empowerment is evident throughout the country. The GDP is growing by 5% annually. Many companies have become multinational corporations. Although it creates a half-million jobs every year, unemployment ranges from 25% to 40%, and half the total population is classified as poor, with a quarter of them on government handouts. Yes, South Africa is still a young, vulnerable economy.

*Twenty-First Century Needs.* This country produced two of the greatest modern African leaders; namely, Nelson Mandela and Desmond Tutu, both Nobel Peace Prize winners. Mandela, as the first African president, and Archbishop Tutu personified the vision of creating a country with a nonracial future. Together, they established a Truth and Reconciliation Commission, engaging enlightened leadership like theirs, in both the public and private sector. Leadership is South Africa's primary need; leadership that is concerned for the whole citizenry, not just for his or her racial community. That type of leadership would address challenges, such as promoting the following:

■ *Pluralism and inclusiveness*, which allows for reasonable dissent, compromise, give and take, and protection of human rights.
■ *Educational and training improvements* at all levels for the development of a more knowledgeable and competent workforce.
■ *Rebuilding strong family life and child care*, especially in those African homes and villages devastated by past apartheid policies and currently by AIDS.
■ *Economic development* without graft and corruption that improves the whole society, especially the black African and colored poor.
■ *Political diversity and inclusiveness* so that all citizens participate in voting, and other parties than the ANC are given the opportunity for more leadership participation in a government that is less centralized (e.g., Democratic Alliance). As former President Thabo Mbeki stated in 2007, the country needs to pursue a *commonly defined national agenda*, something he was unable to accomplish during his

administration. If such a new mission statement for South Africa is ever written, it should emphasize "bridge building" among the many elements in a still divided society (Exhibit 14.9).

---

### EXHIBIT 14.9
### THE NEW SOUTH AFRICA

---

In the 12 years since the African National Congress triumphantly took power in South Africa's first multiracial democratic elections, the country has plotted its course to relative stability, democracy, and prosperity. It is even beginning to lead the continent in an entirely new way, urging other nations there to emulate its example. Under Nelson Mandela's leadership, the ANC government campaigned to alleviate poverty and degradation of apartheid victims, without resorting to counterproductive populism. While there have been some improvements, there is growing impatience over the pace of change in South Africa. Mandela's vision of a "rainbow nation" has slowed to a crawl.

Yet, from education to foreign policy to crime-fighting, the inhabitants have found creative solutions to their problems. The government has presided over 87 months of economic growth (currently 5% a year), low budget deficits, and low inflation, while trying to encourage free enterprise. Buoyant domestic demand has been accompanied by the sort of foreign investment that some thought would never come. But despite a 5% GDP growth, the unemployment rate has risen and has affected 27% of the population. Governance policy has provided more money for social programs grants, mainly for child support and pensions to some 10 million people, as well as for public works, mainly to stimulate job creation, consumer demand, and tourism.

Furthermore, there are hopeful experiments to benefit children from squatters' camps, such as an extraordinary school called *Sekolo Sa Bonrokgo* in the northern suburbs of Johannesburg. There, 25 dedicated teachers inspire black learners to achieve remarkable academic progress. As the lack of quality education is the single most important factor holding back the country's development, such innovations need to be multiplied.

The continent needs a strong South Africa, one prepared to go beyond traditional agendas, and to make a commitment to good governance, humans' rights, and democracy as enshrined in the goals of the African Union.

*Source*: Excerpted and adapted from Richard Crokett's "Chasing the Rainbow—A Survey of South Africa," *The Economist*, April 8, 2006, 12-page insert (www.economist.com/surveys).

Those observations written 4 years ago are still valid for the most part. Today, there are too much division, factionalism, stagnation, and patronage.[f] The country's potential is being undermined by a high crime rate, food and petrol prices, power cuts, strikes, economic downturn. |The deteriorating situation is fueling a white diaspora among the English-speaking and Afrikaan-speaking population who make up only 9% of the richest and best-educated people. How long these talented émigrés, including mixed race and black inhabitants, will stay abroad depend on how much improvement occurs in the land of their birth. Some professionals are attracted by higher salaries paid in foreign places. But people of all races are put off by myopic regimes which promote greed, corruption, nepotism, and incompetence. The new South African leadership needs to "nurture" Mandela's rainbow vision to build a vibrant, pluralistic society that cares for all its citizens and their progress. The continent possesses the assets to realize this vision—an energetic people who live in a beautiful far country; a model constitution which protects individual rights; a free press and judiciary; a democratic Parliament and separation of powers; and a good infrastructure and banking system.

## Business Tips in South Africa

With a continent as vast and diverse as this, it is impossible to generalize on the preferred business and trade practices. South African business customs, for example, require some flexibility, depending on which ethnic group you are dealing with. The white business protocols are comparable to those of Europe and North America, whereas those of Indian heritage may seem more like the commercial environment found in India. However, in what is typically referred to as *Black Africa*, whether in the west, east, or south, the following observations may prove useful. These observations supplement those made earlier in this chapter on "Cultural Characteristics of Africa."

*Meetings.* Business is normally discussed in an office, bar, or restaurant, but always outside the home. What happens in the home is considered private. When invited to someone's residence for a meal, do not discuss business. When an African is the host of such meetings, he or she will pay for everyone. If a foreigner is the host, he or she should pay. If a foreigner receives an invitation to a *braaivlets,* or barbecue, it is an important part of getting to know better business associates without discussing business per se. It is customary for outsiders to bring a token gift, such as beverage or candy.

*Communications.* Most businesspeople have business cards which are exchanged readily. After some small talk on encountering a foreigner, white South Africans tend to get down to the purpose or agenda for meeting, whereas those of other races may make long inquiries about your health and family before getting down to business.

---

[f]"South Africa—A Future of Division, Factionalism, Stagnation, and Patronage," *The Economist*, August 9, 2008, pp. 43-44. "White Flight from South Africa—Between Staying and Going," *The Economist*, September 27, 2008, pp. 35-36.

*Attitudes*. South Africans generally are more low key in their business discussion, searching for "win-win" opportunities for both parties. They are wary of foreigners who try to take advantage of them, so resist high-pressure and cut-throat types, and emotional appeals. Ordinarily, in the world of commerce and government, people do not like to be rushed into decisions about some deal. The local merchants of Indian or Chinese heritage are experienced and shrewd traders, and may be more aggressive in their negotiations.

*Seniority*. As indicated previously, traditionally, age commands respect. Age and wisdom are seen as identical, and the norms of the elders must be followed to ensure smooth business dealings. Some of this tribal heritage is retained in some business environments.

*Gender*. As women become better educated and involved in business life, the traditional precedent of man before woman is giving way to a more equalitarian approach. This is confirmed by national policy of affirmative action to ensure equal opportunity.

## PROSPECTS FOR PAN AFRICAN SYNERGY[11]

In general, Africans are in transition from their traditional cultures based on a rural, agricultural, and tribal way of life. Rapidly, they are moving toward an urban lifestyle that is based on industrial and technological development. For the past 60 years, international business, professionals, and humanitarian workers have done much to promote greater African prosperity, whether through the United Nation's agencies, their own governments, multinational corporations, foundations, or other financial investment. Some foreigners and their governments have long contributed to the exploitation of Africa's enormous resources for their own greedy purposes, and now there are new players seeking to benefit from the continent's rich resources (Exhibit 14.10).

### EXHIBIT 14.10

### CHINA IN AFRICA

During the Cold War, China entered Africa to encourage solidarity with socialistic states there by aiding with infrastructure projects, as well as supporting liberation movements. Now, China rapidly buys up African oil, metals, and farm products to fuel its own economic growth. Chinese officials, businessmen, and laborers are flocking into this continent in ever-increasing numbers. For example, in 1991 only 300 Chinese foreigners lived in Zambia; in 2008, the number has jumped to 3000. Similar trends can be seen in other African states, such as Algeria, Angola, Congo, Kenya, Morocco, Nigeria,

continued

EXHIBIT 14.10

CHINA IN AFRICA (CONTINUED)

and even South Africa. In 2008, the PRC President, Hu Jintao, not only visited some of these countries, but invited 30 African leaders to a Sino-African summit in Beijing!

With China's economy growing on average 9% annually, and its foreign trade increasing five-fold, it needs African natural resources, more than just ideology and influence. Thus, its trade and investment in Africa is $50 billion or more. China looks for copper and cobalt to the DRC and Zambia; for iron ore and platinum in South Africa; for timber in Cameroon, Congo-Brazzaville, and Gabon; for oil primarily in Nigeria, as well as Congo, Equatorial Guinea, Gabon. Thus, Chinese trade with African sources continually expands (about 10% of all African trade). By 2010, estimates are that these numbers will double. China also contributes aid and investment into this continent (over $10 million yearly), as well as cancelling African debt, thus assisting there the development of infrastructure and housing. Further, China aid is straightforward without the bureaucratic demands of the IMF and World Bank. China builds strategic relationships and agreement with African states. Its assistance includes investments, professional training, and providing Chinese doctors, technicians, and workers to Africa. In sharing its technology, many African states benefit, such as building and launching a satellite for Nigeria. Also, China is becoming a processor of commodities, cheaper goods services, and military hardware to the continent. By buying African, the PRC reduces its own trade deficits, and offers competition to Westerners there. Yet, there are concerns for human and economic rights in China's projects—for example, alleged mistreatment of workers in a Chinese-owned mine in Zambia; technical assistance, which necessitates the Chinese remain to maintain railways and pipelines built mainly with Chinese laborers; support for the Sudan government when it commits genocide against its own people in Darfur; resisting democratic reforms in countries ruled by the "strong man"; and blocking UN reforms and sanctions against failed administrations, such as Robert Mugabe in Zimbabwe. It would appear that this new interloper is no more altruistic than its colonial predecessors on this great continent. In the long term, the ultimate question is: will China contribute to lifting Africa from the third to the first world civilization? There can be synergy between China and its African partners that is "win-win" for both partners.

*Source*: Adapted from "China in Africa—Never Too Late to Scramble," *The Economist*, October 28, 2006, pp. 53-56. Parag Khanna, "China Moves In," *The Second World*, New York: Random House, 2008, pp. 188-190.

For this new millennium, there is much discussion of an *African Renaissance* and rediscovery of its creative past, led by South Africa. If non-Africans wish to participate in that renewal, consider the following arenas to promote:

■ *Effective Leadership*—Replacement with twenty-first century leaders who are better educated and more competent and honest, as well as more socially responsible and foresighted, aware of international interdependence. Such new leadership in governance and public service will promote democratic government, and respect of human and environmental rights. This will require massive cultural changes so that Africans become more goal-oriented and less fatalistic. It means the heads of the 53 states must learn to work together synergistically through the African Union.

■ *Environmental Protection/Rural Development*—Preserving the natural beauty and resources, while stopping further degradation of land and forests. The goal is to manage natural resources for sustainable development and more equitable sharing by the whole population. Less emphasis on urban development and more efforts directed to creating rural opportunity and agricultural production, including providing basic infrastructure for smaller towns and villages (e.g., clean water, electricity, transportation, jobs, education, and health services).

■ *Population Control*—Traditional large families that enlarge tribal power bases have to be regulated, while social security provisions are made for the aged and orphan children. Only then can tough problems related to infant mortality, child abuse, illiteracy, nutrition, and health care be solved in Africa. The internal refugee crisis needs continental solutions.

■ *Continental Health Crusade*—An African Union initiative to control and conquer, with the help of global organizations, the scourges of HIV/AIDS and malaria, to improve water systems and medical treatment, and to provide cheaper drugs. Within Africa, multinational synergistic efforts to defeat the HIV/AIDS epidemic that is devastating Southern Africa, the epicenter of this Pan African tragedy.

■ *Education and Training*—Promote education and skill development throughout the continent suitable for a technological work environment and the knowledge culture. Such human resource development should include environmental education, civic responsibilities and competencies, intertribal and interracial tolerance, as well as management and administrative skills. The aim would be empowerment of the people, particularly of women and minorities.

If synergy is to occur between the more modern, developed world and Africa, there are lessons to be learned from the observations in Exhibit 14.11.

## Exhibit 14.11
## Africa's Poverty

Humanitarian assistance should not be confused with economic development assistance. A rampaging disease that respects no international border threatens the survival of Africa. About 70% of AIDS sufferers worldwide are African, and fighting the disease has overwhelmed African budgets. At a United Nations Conference on AIDS last June, UN Secretary General, Kofi Annan, called for a global war chest of $7-$10 billion to battle AIDS.

The state of postcolonial leadership in Africa is not pretty—a hideous assortment of "Swiss bank account" socialists, military vagabonds, quack revolutionaries, and briefcase bandits. Their overriding preoccupation is not to develop their economies, but to perpetuate themselves in office, loot the treasury, and brutally suppress all dissent and opposition.

Africa is not poor for lack of resources. Its mineral wealth is immense: hydroelectric power potential; the bulk of the world's diamonds and chromium; substantial deposits of uranium; and gold, cobalt, phosphates, platinum, manganese, copper, and vast bauxite deposits, plus nickel and lead resources. There is also vast oil and natural gas. Yet paradoxically, a continent with such abundance and potential is mired in squalor, misery, deprivation, and chaos.

*Africa is not poor for lack of resources. African leaders prefer to blame the West for Africa's poverty. But, in fact, it has little to do with colonial legacies, the slave trade, imperialism, or other external factors. At the 2000 Summit of the Organization of African Unity in Rome, Tongo, Kofi Annan told African leaders they are to blame for most of the continent's problems: "Instead of being exploited for the benefit of the people, Africa's mineral resources have been so mismanaged and plundered that they are now a source of our misery."*

The way out of Africa's economic miasma is through investment. Aid to rogue regimes helps nobody. And to trade, a country must first produce the goods required for international commerce. In 1990, only 4 out of 44 African countries were democratic; this number has now grown to 15. Target aid only to those countries that are democratic. To establish a democratic order, these are most critical: an independent central bank; an independent judiciary; an independent free press and media; an independent electoral commission; a neutral and professional armed or security force; and an efficient civil service.

*Source*: Ayittey, B. N: "Africa's Poverty," *San Diego Union-Tribune*, INSIGHT, June 16, 2002, pp. G1, G6.

Africa covers 20% of the world's landmass and has 10% of its people. Yes, it has problems, but nothing that a north-south dialogue and collaboration cannot resolve, for Africa is a rich continent with great resources. That may explain why the People's Republic of China has stepped up its involvement there. Remember that six centuries ago, Ming Dynasty seafarers reached African shores for trade purposes, and today, Chinese vessels ply those same sea lanes to bring back oil, iron ore, and other commodities to satisfy the voracious needs of its huge, expanding economy. Meanwhile, the West makes insufficient investments in African human and natural resources, while wondering if the Chinese presence will undermine their own efforts there on behalf of human rights, democracy, peacekeeping, health care, and anticorruption. But Africa should be of global concern for humanity, not just of eastern and western nations.

The continent's emerging middle class is taking advantage of technology to improve communications among diverse African people, especially through satellite television and mobile phones. Hopefully, this century will find Africa moving beyond its colonial past and contemporary problems toward self-sufficiency in a more peaceful environment that protects and develops its vast natural and human resources. Recall that it took centuries for another continent to move from feudalism to an effective European Union—here, a comparable African Union may be created in decades!

## CONCLUSIONS

Africa is the cradle of our civilizations, home to every person in the human family, whether they come to this continent as tourists, professionals, humanitarians, or businesspersons. Accept the diversity among Africans, while seeking to understand its inhabitants in an atmosphere of nonjudgmental acceptance.

In this chapter, we examined the immense continent of Africa in terms of its four geographic regions and the multitude of states within it. Profiles of selected countries with the larger populations in each area were presented, along with four in-depth regional case studies. Overall, we also provided general insights into Africa, its current problems and promise, as well as characteristics of its diverse peoples. As a result, global leaders may appreciate the possibilities in Africa. Then, with respect and sensitivity to its inhabitants, synergistic partnerships, such as joint ventures and humanitarian projects, can do much toward contributing to the proper development of the area and its resources.

When comparing cultures, such as the American and African, and how they affect the business environment or humanitarian service, it is necessary to understand that the United States is a low-context culture. It is technologically and futuristically oriented with an emphasis on individual achievement rather than on group participation. In the communication process, a low-context culture places meaning in the exact verbal description of an event. Individuals in such a culture rely on the spoken word. In contrast, Africa's culture is high context. In the communication process, much of the meaning comes not from the words, but is internalized in the person. Meaning comes from the environment and is sought in the relationships between the ideas expressed in the communication process. High-context cultures, more so than low-context cultures, tend to be more human-oriented and to value the extended family.

Perhaps this closing quotation may stimulate readers' thinking about Africa: "No other continent has endured such an unspeakably bizarre combination of foreign thievery and foreign goodwill" (B. Kingsolver, *The Poisonwood Bible*, New York: HarperCollins, 1998). The outside world needs to appreciate and give back to Africa for its enormous contributions to humanity and multiple nations, as confirmed by the election of Barak Obama, the first American president of African heritage!

## MIND STRETCHING

1. Why is it important for all members of the human family, now consisting of 6.5 billion people, to appreciate Africa's past, present, and future potential?
2. How has past European colonialism impacted today's Africans, in contrast to present Asian influence on them?
3. What and where is sub-Sahara Africa, and how do its 48 states differ from the rest of the continent?
4. What is the implication of the fact that in Africa, 900 million inhabitants live in the countryside, while rapid urbanization is under way?
5. How can those who live outside of Africa contribute to development of its human and natural resources, to combating poverty and disease on this continent, and to promoting peace and better governance?
6. What is the connection, if any, between a third of Africa's countries with soaring oil revenues, and cycles of unrest, violence, and civil wars on the continent?

## REFERENCES

1. *Family Reference Guide to the Future Book of the Peoples of the World—A Guide to Cultures.* Washington, D.C.: National Geographic, 2002, 2008.
2. Dowden, R. *Africa: Altered States, Ordinary Miracles.* London, UK: Portobello Books, 2008; Meredith, M. *The Future of Africa: A History of Fifty Years of Independence.* New York, NY: Perseus Books/Public Affairs,

2006; Iliffe, J. *Africans: The History of a Continent*. Cambridge, UK: Cambridge University Press, 2007; Pitcher, G. *Lonely Planet's Africa (A Travel Guide)*. New York, NY: Lonely Planet Publisher, 2007; "Africa—Whatever You Thought, Think Again," *National Geographic Magazine*, Special Issue, September 2005. Guest, R. "How to Make Africa Smile—A Survey of Sub-Saharan Africa," *The Economist*, January 17, 2004, p. 16, www.economist.com/surveys; Oldfield, S. (ed.). *The Trade in Wildlife: Regulation for Conservation*. New York: Earthscan, 2003; Peterson, D. *Eating Apes*. Berkeley, CA: University of California Press, 2003.

3. Salgado, S. *Africa*. New York, NY: Tachen, 2007, www.amazon.com/books; Obradovic, N. (ed.). *The Anchor Book of Modern African Stories*, Second edition. New York: Anchor, 2003; Richmond, Y. and Gestrin, P. *Into Africa—Intercultural Insights*. Boston, MA: Nicholas Brealey/Intercultural Press, 1998; Wiredu, K. *Cultural Universals and Particulars: An African Perspective*. Bloomington, IN: Indiana University Press, 1997; Arnold, M. J., Geary, G. M., and Hardin, K. L. (eds.). *African Material Culture*. Bloomington, IN: Indiana University Press, 1996; Ojisku, U. J. *Surviving the Iron Curtain: A Microscopic View of What It Was Like in a War-Torn Region*. Baltimore, MD: PublishAmerica, 2007, www.publioshamerica.com; Lovejoy, P. E. *Transitions in Slavery: A History of Slavery in Africa*. Cambridge, UK: Cambridge University Press, 2000.

4. Painter, N. I. *Creating Black America: African-American History and Its Meaning*. Oxford, UK: Oxford University Press, 2006; Hill, K. H. *Religious Education in the African-American Tradition*. Danvers, MA: Chalice Press, 2007, www.chalicepress.com.

5. Diagram Group, *North Africa: Islam, and the Mediterranean World*. New York, NY: Frank Cass Publications, 2005; Davis, D. *Resurrecting the Granary of Rome: Environmental History and French Colonial Expansion in North Africa*. Athens, OH: Ohio New University Press, 2007.

6. Diagram Group. *History of East Africa*. New York, NY: Frank Cass Publications, 2003; Fitzpatrick, M. and Parkinson, T. *Lonely Planet's East Africa*. New York, NY: Lonely Planet, 2009; Davitt, N. *Kenya: A Country in the Making*. New York, NY: W. G. Norton, 2008; Marcus, H. G. *History of Ethiopia*. Berkeley, CA: University of California Press, 2008; Johnson, D. H. *The Root Causes of Sudan's Civil Wars*. Bloomington, IN: University of Indiana Press, 2002; Flint, J. and deWaal, A. *Darfur: A New History of a Long War*. New York, NY: Zed Books, 2008; Barz, G. *Music in East Africa: Experience Music, Expressing Culture*. Oxford, UK: Oxford University Press, 2004.

7. Bass, G. J. *Freedom's Battle: The Origins of Humanitarian Intervention*. New York, NY: Knopf, 2008; Obrinski, J. *An Imperfect Offering: Humanitarian Actions for the Twenty-First Century*. London, UK: Walker and Company, 2008; Bolton, G. *Africa Doesn't Matter: How the West Failed the Poorest Continent and What We Can Do About It*. New York, NY: Arcade, 2008; Ginn, J. K. *Circle of Giving*. Little Rock, AR: Heifer International, www.heiferfoundation.org.

8. Ham, A. *West Africa (Multi Country Guide)*. New York, NY: Lonely Planet, 2006; Vansina, J. *How Societies Are Born: Governance in West Central Africa before 1600*. Charlottesville, VA: University of Virginia Press, 2005; Falola, T. and Heston, M. *A History of Nigeria*. Cambridge, UK: Cambridge University Press, 2008.

9. Meredith, M. *Diamonds, Gold, and War: The British, the Boers, and the Making of South Africa.* New York, NY: Public Affairs/Perseus Group, 2008; Murphy, A., Armstrong, K., Firestone, M., and Fitzpatrick, M. *Southern Africa (Multi Country Guide).* New York, NY: Lonely Planet, 2007; Ehret, C. *An African Classical Age: Eastern and Central Africa in World History, 1000 B.C. to A.D. 400.* Charlottesville, VA: University of Virginia Press, 2001.

10. Cockett, R. "Chasing the Rainbow—A Survey of South Africa," *The Economist,* April 8, 2006, p. 12; Grimond, J. "A Survey of South Africa—Africa's Great Black Hope," *The Economist,* February 24, 2001, p. 16; Sadiman, J. *South Africa's "Black" Market—How to Do Business with Africans.* Boston, MA: Nicholas Brealey/Intercultural Press, 2000; The authors acknowledge that the insights for this profile were partially obtained from a "Culturegram for the Republic of South Africa," *Culturegrams,* David, M. Kennedy Center for International Studies, Brigham Young University, 280 HRCB, Provo, Utah 84602, USA (Tel: 801/378–6528); Carlin, J. *Playing the Enemy: Nelson Mandela and the Game That Made a Nation.* New York, NY: Penguin Books, 2008; For further information about this nation and its culture, contact the Embassy of South Africa (3051 Massachusetts Ave., NW, Washington, D.C. 20008, USA) and the South African Tourism Board (747 Third Ave., 20th Floor, New York, NY 10017 or 9841 Airport Blvd., Ste. 1524, Los Angeles, CA 90045, USA).

11. Lewis, R. D. *The Cultural Imperative—Global Trends in the 21st Century.* Boston, MA: Nicholas Brealey/Intercultural Press, 2003; Khanna, P. *The Second World: Empires and Influence in the New Global Order.* New York, NY: Random House, 2008, Chapter 21.

African Resources: Beside a Google search on the Internet for Africa or any country therein, consult www.africaguide.com; , www.joeant.com/DIR/info/get/7375/18588; , and www.sul.stanford.edu/depts/ssrg/africa/guide.html; . A very useful learning system is Africa, produced by Palm World Voices (www.palmworldvoimces.com; ). This compact packet focuses on African peoples and their business. Each package contains a National Geographic map of African peoples and their music; a booklet with pictures entitled Africa the Musical Continent; a visual DVD; and an audio CD on the music of Africa. Inquire about other productions, such as BabbaMaal: Senegal. Specific country reports are available from Reprints Department, The Economist Newspaper Group, Inc., 111 W. 57th St., 10019. New York, NY 10019, USA (www.economist.com/surveys).

Details on every country in the world, including those in Africa, are available in the CIS Fact Book (www.cia.gov/cia/publications/factbook/geos/ct.html; ). The National Geographic Society periodically publishes updated maps on Africa (www.nationalgeographic/africa; ). For example, the map supplement to their magazine in September 2001 was entitled Africa Today, and in September 2005, Africa the Human Footprint. National Trade Data Bank, International Trade Administration, U.S. Department of Commerce, Washington, DC 20230 (Tel: 1/800-USA TRADE #4/5; www.export.gov; —click on "market research" and then "country commercial guide" choosing a particular African state.) For hard copy or diskette of any African country guide, call National Technical Information Service (1-800/553-

NTIS). There is a country code for information on all nations of Unit 2 and this chapter on Africa (telephone hotline, 1-202/482-1064 or 1860). Major U.S. cities also have local offices of USDC with commercial advisors to provide counseling and resources to businesspersons seeking data or connections abroad in a specific country or area within that target culture. Also consult the local telephone directory under "Government Pages" for the nearest listing of the United States Government Offices and the Federal Commerce Department.

# 15

# DOING BUSINESS WITH NORTH AMERICANS

## The United States and Canada

## LEARNING OBJECTIVES

The purpose of this chapter is to provide a historical overview of Canada (to be included on the Managing Cultural Differences Web site) and the United States, as well as some important cultural similarities and differences.

The North American continent has a very diverse human population. Geographically, Mexico is part of this region, but we prefer to cover that country in Chapter 11 on Latin America. These three nations have formed a partnership called NAFTA—the North American Free Trade Agreement.[1]

## Geological Perspectives[2]

Geographically, North America is incredibly old—some 200 million years ago, it separated from Africa when the former supercontinent of Pangaea broke apart. For a time, it was attached to Europe and then broke off into its present landmass. There are stones here that can be dated as 4 billion years old, forming today part of Canada's frozen tundra. In the East, an ancient mountain system, known today as the Appalachians, runs south from Canada into the United States. The region contains what are the world's largest island (Greenland), greatest concentration of water (Great Lakes), spectacular geographical features (e.g., Grand Canyon and Niagara Falls), largest and tallest trees (California redwoods), plus big animals (grizzly bears, moose, and bison). Even before the present dramatic climate changes, this area was known for climate extremes (from sauna-like heat in Death Valley to brutal cold on Greenland's windswept ice cap). After Asia and Africa, North America is the third largest landmass (9.45 million square miles), extending from Kap Morris Jesup (Greenland) south to Peninsula de Azuero (Panama). Both on its eastern and western ends, it also has the longest coastline compared to other continents. The land is surrounded by water (Atlantic Ocean in the east, Pacific Ocean in the west, Arctic Ocean in the north, the Gulf of Mexico and Caribbean Sea in the south). With vast inlets and bays, coastal waters pour into mighty rivers (e.g., St Lawrence, Rio Grande, Yukon, Columbia, Mississippi). Other dominant geographical features are the Canadian (Laurentin) Shield; Western Cordillera that includes the Rocky Mountains, Sierra Nevada, and Sierra Madre; and colossal flatland embracing the Great Plains, Mississippi-Missouri River Basin and Great Lakes region. Its highest peaks range from Mount McKinley in Alaska (30,230 ft) and drops to 282 ft below sea level in California's Death Valley. In addition, the continent has a diverse biological heritage of endless tundra and coniferous forests in the north, to vast deserts and rain forests in the south. However, the continent's huge numbers of wildlife have declined with the increase of human population.

Although North America geographically includes three major nations—Canada, the United States, and Mexico[3]—the continent technically extends from the frigid Arctic Ice Cap in the north to include the tropics of Central America and the Caribbean islands. Chapter 15 covers only the two countries north of the Rio Grande River. As Mexico is culturally and linguistically aligned with Latin America (Central/South America), that nation has been covered in Chapter 12. Recognize that the term "American" can be used by all the inhabitants of that area, but, colloquially, American is more often used to refer to those living in the United States.

## Historical Perspectives[3]

The first North American inhabitants of this continent may have migrated 12,000-30,000 years ago, possibly from southern Asia or even northern Europe. Smithsonian Institution researchers studying other New World human skulls found potential resemblance to archaic Norse populations, as well as the mysterious Ainu aborigine from the Japanese islands. Perhaps these early people originated from multiple migrations. By 12,000 B.C., the Olmec of Mexico were developing what is thought to be "the first civilization in the Western Hemisphere." It was a highly sophisticated culture with a calendar, writing system, and stonework architecture. Similarly, the Clovis people operated in Chile 12,500 years ago. In the southwest of present-day United States, the Ancient Pueblo, or Anasazi, people lived for 2000 years along the Colorado Plateau before climate change in the twelfth and thirteenth centuries forced abandonment of their settlements.

The Eskimos or Inuit ancestors already crossed the Bering Sea and settled in North America long before the Phoenicians, Viking warriors, Irish monks, Polynesians, and Chinese seafarers supposedly reached this hemisphere. Their explorations were centuries before an Italian navigator named Christopher Columbus in 1492 got the credit for finding what he thought was India, but actually a "new world" to Europeans, a continent later to be called America. His landing that year in the Bahamas ushered in an era of European exploration and colonization. For historical perspective, note that archaeologists from the College of William and Mary uncovered an 11,000-year-old spearhead on Jamestown Island, Virginia. The primitive tool was used by Ice Age inhabitants to hunt mastodon and elk. The English only landed in Jamestown in 1607 A.D.

Apparently, the descendants of Asiatic nomads who came to what is known today as Alaska spread throughout Pan America, evolving into distinct tribes and lifestyles as Native Americans who speak some 550 different languages. But it was the European discoveries that changed the cultural landscape of North America during the past 500 years and created a modern civilization. With the coming of the Europeans, followed later by Asians and Africans, permanent settlements evolved, along with written languages, weapons, and metal tools. On the basis of "Old World" models, towns and villages emerged as world-class cities, such as New York, Chicago, Los Angeles, Toronto, Montreal, Vancouver, and Mexico City. The Amerindian tongues gave way to Spanish, English, French, and many other foreign languages spoken today by some 500 million people in North America. Animist beliefs with their emphasis on nature gave way to Christianity in many forms, as well as introduction of Islam, Judaism, and other religions. The newcomers brought fresh ideas and concepts, like individual freedom, democracy, and capitalism, shaping the people with new approaches to intellectual, political, and economic life. Culture was transformed from hunter-gatherers, to farmers and factory workers, to the present-day knowledge culture dominated by communication technologies, as well as by research and development. North Americans gained leadership in the human family by rapid advances in education, business, and industry. Many of their social and technical innovations revolutionized modern life worldwide, and even off-world. In the twenty-first century, North Americans have energized globalization, media, and space exploration. Their exploitation of natural resources has also contributed to serious crises in the environment and climate. Although the continent has approximately only 8% of the planet's inhabitants, their per capita consumption of energy is almost six times as great as the average for all other continents. Their appetite for other natural resources, like timer, metals, and water, is just as voracious. Finally, their emphasis on material prosperity and greed has disenfranchised masses within their own society and that of nearby neighbors, adding to the global recession under way at this writing.

This land body that extends almost from the Arctic to Cape Horn was named "America" after sixteenth century Italian explorer and merchant, Amerigo Vespucci. Trade was a dominant force in the discovery and development of these unknown territories between the Atlantic and Pacific Oceans. Pan America—North, Central, and South—has a diversity of cultural heritages requiring a synergy of sorts. It is like a huge laboratory of human relations in which a mixture of cultures are merging. One tends to think of North America as largely "Anglo-Saxons" who speak primarily English. However, Canada is bilingual with French as its second language, while the United States is moving in that direction with Spanish. The area south of the Rio Grande River is considered Latin America, because the languages there are mainly of Latin origin. Apart from numerous Indian languages, Spanish is dominant in Mexico, Central and South America, while Portuguese is the primary language of Brazil (with some Italian and Japanese being spoken). For our purpose, Pan America will designate that landmass of some 15 million square miles from the Arctic Ocean south to the convergence of the Atlantic and Pacific Oceans at Drakes Passage. The Americas comprise approximately 30 national cultures, plus Eskimo and Native American cultures.

To appreciate the cultural diversity in just North America, consider the matter of language. In Canada and the United States, English is supposedly the official language (along with French in Canada). But the *Atlas of North American English* contends that regional dialects are becoming more pronounced, especially with reference to how accented vowels are pronounced. Social forces among family and friends cause local dialects to develop as a means of expressing identity. So, there are distinct differences in the pronunciation of English in Canada in contrast to the USA, where there are many dialects and accents on the basis of location within that vast country. Linguists claim that people adapt their spoken English to sound more like their family and colleagues, especially in the work environment.[4] Thus, the Amish of Pennsylvania use a distinct dialect and vocabulary of the English language. For global leaders seeking to function effectively in the Pan-American market, it is important to understand the geoeconomic and cultural characteristics that will facilitate business and acculturation.  To better comprehend the Pan-American market, consider the following realities.

## *Economic Development*

International agencies and banks generally consider the North American countries to be rich in terms of annual gross domestic product per capita, whereas most of Latin America, from Mexico southward, is thought to comprise developing economies. Despite economic progress in Latin America, a significant percentage of their population is still classified as poor. This helps to explain the economic dependence of the South on the North in the Americas, as well as the flow of legal and illegal immigrants northward in the search of work. It also points up the problems of these nations with the International Monetary Fund and the World Bank related to difficulties with repayment of loans, rising inflation, and other economic problems. The most significant economic development in the Americas has been the signing of the North American Free Trade Agreement (NAFTA) in 1992, signed by Canada, the United States, and Mexico, to expand trade and financial growth in the three countries. In 2008, the global recession and failures of fiscal institutions have challenged the whole of Pan America.

## Human Resources

Canada and the United States have a combined population of approximately 341 million persons, with a natural population increase of less than 1%. Latin America has more than 560 million inhabitants, and an increase rate of 1–3%; the most populous countries, at 3% or more, are Mexico, Venezuela, Guatemala, Peru, and Paraguay. Obviously, unless expanding population is brought under control in the South, not only will economic growth there be affected adversely, but continuing social unrest, as well as political and military turmoil can be expected. Yet, there are huge human assets in Latin America waiting to be capitalized through education and training.

In this hemisphere, the interface between its northern and southern inhabitants is a contrast in opportunities and problems. The opportunities for mutual enrichment will be achieved through cultural exchanges, scientific collaboration, educational and economic assistance, and efforts promoting peace between the hemispheres. For example, the U.S. State Department sponsors the Fulbright Program and grants to promote the exchange of scholars through the Institute of International Education (www.iie.com).

However, the problems proliferate because social and economic issues cry out for creative solutions from Pan Americans. There need to be more North/South dialogue and synergistic endeavors that benefit the peoples of both continents, such as projects to renew the infrastructures of societies in need, or to provide adequate food and shelter for the poor, or to enact environmental policies that protect natural resources and counter severe climate change.

Instability in countries within Pan America results from archaic political, legal, justice, and economic systems. Insecurity is caused by growing deviant behavior, such as antisocial actions like terrorism and drug trafficking, or the expanding struggle between democratic ideals and totalitarian realities. Inability to establish a meaningful North–South communication and collaborative exchange in the Americas undermines societies, furthering exploitation and dependence in the Southern hemisphere. Yet, for the most part, Pan America is a free-enterprise system and a market of vast potential. It borders the Pacific Rim on the west, and can benefit from the trade shift from the Atlantic to the Pacific.

# NORTHERN AMERICA'S INDIGENOUS PEOPLES

Long before Europeans discovered the Western Hemisphere in the fifteenth century, there were millions of humans already living there, from the Arctic Circle to the tip of Tierra del Forego. These indigenous peoples of varying cultures, languages, and ethnicity are now known as Native Americans. They called themselves *The People*, or by the name of their tribal groupings. They acculturated in unique ways to their environment, depending on such factors as climate, topography, and natural resources. They have been described by outsiders as nature lovers, enchanting, and even mysterious. All of them were and are bound together by a sense of the sacred, or the connection between humans and the animate. They value life as expressed through creative spirits, animals, persons, plants, and places. They have ancient belief systems reflected in diverse cultures manifested in their stories and rules of behavior, songs and dances, rituals and ceremonies, and customs and practices. For thousands of generations, the young listened and learned from respected tribal elders. Organized into some 1000 indigenous tribes, they had about 300 original languages, of which 175 living languages survive. Since 1491, they have experienced their worlds tuned upside down—spiritually, physically, socially—by migrants, primarily from Europe, Asia, and Africa. Among them, whole communities were and are wiped out by the diseases, weapons, and policies brought by newcomers.

Many of these peoples also flourished and became leaders in modern civilization. For example, in 2002, the first Native American to fly in outer space was John Herrington, a Chickasaw astronaut. This Navy commander, pilot, and NASA flight engineer flew on the space Shuttle Endeavor 5.67 million miles off-world at speeds up to 17,085 miles per hour. Circling around earth at 250 miles above, he remembered ancient traditions, so he carried a Hopi pot with a design of corn and eagle feathers, a symbol of prayer to native peoples. Witnessing the cosmos aloft gave him a "spiritual sense of the grand scheme of Mother Earth." Upon his return from orbit, this Amerindian wrote a letter, "To my many friends in Indian country: We have looked over the horizon together, and what lies before us is a universe of possibilities."

## Eskimos (Inuits) and the Arctic Circle[5]

The Arctic Circle lies 66°30 latitude and includes one-third of Alaska. Together with the Canadian Arctic Archipelago, there is a group of

50 large islands in the Nunavut and the Northwest Territories. This is a mountainous region characterized by tundra and ice. The landforms include the Brooks Range across the northern range, giving way to the North Slope to Beaufort Sea and Arctic Ocean. To the west are the De Long and Baird Mountains, which are part of the Noatak National Preserve; to the east, the Endicott Mountains lead into the Arctic National Park and Preserve. The only major road is the Dalton Highway through the American Arctic, running north to Prudoe Bay on the Beaufort Seas. With the current global warming thawing ice in the region, vast resources are becoming more accessible to five countries with territories bordering this polar region at the top of the world. From their shorelines, Canada, Denmark, Norway, Russia, and the United States can claim ownership up to 360 nautical miles under the continental shelf. From the North Pole outward as the ice recedes, these five countries are likely to seek new Arctic sea routes, valuable oil, mineral resources, and much more. Fortunately, they have agreed to allow the United Nations to rule on competing claims to the seabed (www. economist.com/videographics/Arctic). Anticipate extensive litigation from environmental organizations seeking to protect fragile ecosystems, and possibly the native peoples nearby. A harbinger of this is the Natural Resource Defense Council (NRDC), which has been successful in their lawsuits against the Bush Administration and Shell Oil in blocking the drilling of oil in the Beaufort Seas, just off the coast of the Arctic National Wildlife Refuse (www.nrdc.org/naturesvoice). NRDC did this with another NGO, Earth Justice, and a coalition of Alaska Native Organizations in 2008. The suit against the U.S. Department of the Interior resulted in a court order requiring the government to study and disclose "significant harm" that the oil drilling may cause to the sensitive environment, including wildlife, polar bears, bowhead whales, and the Inupiat subsistence way of life.

In these most northern parts of that Americas, there are two indigenous peoples caught in a culture gap—the Eskimos (Inuits), and the Native Americans. Both have been harmed and helped by the rapid advancement of "white civilization" into their lives. With the introduction of United States and Canadian government health and education programs, their life expectancy and educational levels have risen. But so have their frustration, despair, and social deterioration. Many have succumbed to alcoholism and drug addiction, and the rate of suicide is exceedingly high. Their problems and potentials are similar on or off reservations, whether in the U.S. state of Alaska or the Canadian Northwest Territories, or above or below the U.S.-Canadian border.

Of all the Eskimo populations, the Alaskans (54,000) are most numerous and diverse, living from the Arctic tundra to the North Slope to forested seacoasts in the south. Thousands of these hunter-gathers split into two groups—the northern Inupiat and the southern Yupiati, who have a flexible social organization based on the nuclear family, focused on sea mammal or inland hunting and fishing. Extreme weather hardships fostered valuing the elderly for their experience; infanticide or abandoning of newborns, especially female ones; voluntary suicide by the very old; and cherishing of children and their adoption without stigma. Other groups include the Aleut (17,000), a seafaring people who originated in the Aleutian archipelago in the Northern Pacific. Today, they are declining in numbers, and many have been relocated by the American government into scattered villages, sometimes far from their native Aleutians. The Inuit (80,000) have settled now in northern Canada within semipermanent coastal villages. What is common to Eskimo peoples is a similar language; knowledge of human and animal anatomy; exceptional skill in hunting and utilization of animal parts; weaving and basketry; animistic religious practices that include respect for the "soul" in human, animal, and inanimate, along with "taboos" about subsistence. In the Arctic Circle, the Eskimos have demonstrated human ability to survive harsh, atypical conditions (e.g., 20 °F temperatures). For millennia, these intrepid peoples have shown both biological adaptation and environmental innovation in their struggles against Mother Nature and government bureaucrats. For their frigid climate, they have evolved a body frame that is shorter, stockier, and remarkably adaptable.

In 1971, the USA passed the Native Claims and Settlement Act, which granted Alaskan Eskimos 44 million acres and a payment of $962 million. In April 1999, in another attempt to right past wrongs, Canada divided their Northwest Territory in two and established Nunavut, meaning "our land," giving the Inuit title to 135,000 square miles of their traditional territory, plus a $1.1 billion payment. The Nunavut Legislative Assembly was formed for governance of this vast land holding. For Inuits in Greenland, a measure of home rule has been gained from Denmark, but the Danes still control key government positions.

As a result, village and regional corporations were formed by the local natives, and this has encouraged economic growth. With the creation of Nunavut, the Inuit have won some degree of self-determination. What is remarkable is that by conventional measures of political influence, like voting in elections, they control or have access to funds which have enabled the Eskimos to have more power over their own life space. However, using traditional Inuit attributes of patience and compromise, they accomplish their goals without long, drawn-out court battles or violence.

Weatherford discusses how the misnamed "Indians" of the Americas transformed the world, stating that the contributions of the Native Americans to our economy and culture have been consistently underrated, if not ignored. His conclusion is even more telling—the richness of the Amerindian cultures may be lost without learning what they have to teach us. Museums, such as the National Museum of the American Indian in Washington, D.C. or the Anthropological Museum in Mexico City, help to understand the lessons from their cultures. For example, the Inuits have given us the snowshoe, toboggan, and kayak, among other things, while Native Americans introduced maize, potatoes, sweet potatoes, and manioc into our diets. These crops constitute a large portion of today's staple foods. Cotton was also introduced by Native Americans.[6] The Inuit and Native American have much to teach us about the mind, spirit, and body, and about our relationship to the natural world. The Native American philosophy of respect and reverence and cooperation with the earth are finally gaining acceptance in the mainstream.

Tribal or aboriginal peoples everywhere face the same dilemma brought on by accelerating social and technological change. Whether an Inuit in Hudson Bay or a Navajo in northern Arizona, the confrontation with too-rapid cultural change leaves the natives bewildered, confused, and almost overwhelmed. The rate of innovation in traditional societies is slow, while it rises astronomically in modern societies in the midst of transition. The traditional culture is past-oriented, while modern society is future-oriented, interpreting history as progressive movement. Unfortunately, Western ethnocentrism, even among anthropologists, has labeled some of these tribal people as primitive. In fact, these groups are quite developed within their own context, and are more in harmony with nature than many people today. They seem to possess a better sense of ecology, energy conservation, food distribution, and overall happiness than many of their so-called civilized counterparts. In the process of trying to enhance the indigenous peoples of the Americas, one must first appreciate the values and assets in such cultures. One is then in a position to create synergy with them relative to their contributions, and both cultures can work together to meet their needs.

The Eskimos (Inuits) and Native North Americans have paid a high price for acculturation. Many of their people suffer mental and physical as well as economic handicaps. Climate change is causing vast amounts of ice to melt, and threatens both them and their food supply, such as seals and polar bears, but with cooperation and collaboration by their fellow citizens, these proud and resourceful people can create a new place for themselves in a knowledge society.

## Native Americans[7]

Who is the Native American? Misnamed "Indians" by Christopher Columbus, Native Americans are the indigenous people who were the local inhabitants of the Americas when the Europeans arrived. Ancestors of these Native Americans migrated here from Asia, and possibly Egypt and the Viking homelands. There are obvious cultural differences between the descendants of these aboriginal peoples and modern citizens of North, Central, and South America.

In Canada, the Kwakiutl have 30 tribes of some 5000 members who live on the Northwest Coast around the Queen Charlotte Strait in British Columbia. The average annual income is below poverty level, and their unemployment rate is the highest in the country.

When the "New World" was discovered by Europeans in 1492, the Amerindians living in what is now the United States were scattered, and their tribal organizations were largely unrelated. Many early colonists married Native Americans, motivated largely by social and cultural factors. For example, a native wife was an asset to a fur trader in teaching him the language and customs of the tribe from which he bought furs. Before contact with Europeans, Amerindians cultures thrived, such as in Werowocomoco, whose Chief commanded the allegiance of some 14,000 natives. The Powhattans had a prosperous 45-acre village when the English arrived there to build Jamestown. Some tribes moved from place to place, while others lived in fortified towns and built ceremonial centers. They shaped their environment to sustain themselves, so preservation of plants and animals were vital. Up until 1800, their population was estimated a million in eastern North America; from then on, they declined to approximately 178,000, until today, when the total population of Amerindians rebounded to 2.5 million.

The U.S. government, which came into existence with the adoption of the Constitution in 1787, began its imperialistic relationship by considering the various tribes as national entities and negotiating with them for land. For the past few centuries, relations between Americans and the aboriginals have been both cordial and hostile. Many injustices were put upon the Native Americans by wrong or questionable government policies, such as relocation and establishment of the reservation system.

There are many fundamental differences between a tribal culture and the dominant U.S. culture. The following contrasts three of these differences between the mainstream culture and that of Native Americans:

- Time is to be used, saved, and spent. People are paid for their time and generally view time as a continuum. For Amerindians, time is relative traditionally to the rising and setting of the sun, and to the changes in the seasons.
- Decision making is based on authority; some have authority to make decisions and others do not. Authority in Native American cultures is more horizontal than vertical because of the necessity of reaching group unanimity on a decision before any action will be taken.
- Most Americans live oriented to the future. We ask our children what they want to be when they grow up. Native American children are not asked the same question, because they already "are"—they are children and they do not have to wait "to be." Aboriginals are more oriented to the here and now, as well as past heritage.

Understanding the Native American way of life provides outsiders with a challenge and an opportunity. For thousands of years, their children listen and learn from tribal elders who pass down tradition, wisdom, and experience. The connection between the sacred and the real world is important to them. They believe that creative forces formed the universe, and humans are only a small part of that creation. The spirits and power are to be found in nature. Amerindians can learn to develop new skills, but need modern work and practices that do not destroy their dignity, so can change at their own pace. An understanding of Native American history, values, and cultural differences facilitates communication and business with these remarkable First People.

Within the continental United States, many Native Americans have passed into the mainstream culture. Those still living on reservations are extracting oil and other minerals, and starting entrepreneurial businesses. Today, in many states, gaming and casino operations are managed and owned by Native Americans. Some, like the Sycuans in San Diego County, have also built hotels and shopping centers. They not only offer education, jobs, and training to their own, but make significant financial contributions and investments in their neighboring communities. For those who still live on government reservations, painful progress is being made to gain greater control and administration of their own affairs, whether this be in schools and services or within the Federal Bureau of Indian Affairs. With recent financial settlements through the courts over abrogated treaty rights and lost lands, some tribes have established modern corporations to manage their natural resources and to enter into joint ventures with major companies for economic development purposes, even in the field of high technology on the reservations. Native North Americans never had the "white man's" sense of private property. Tribal culture thinks in terms of collective, and assumes responsibility for the preservation of the land and nature's gifts. Today, ecology and environmental movements are catching up to the aboriginal concern for nature.

## Government Reparations

More than a half million Canadians are classified as having native ancestry, and three quarters of these people live on reservations. These are grouped by their government in four categories—status (registered formally under the Indian Act); nonstatus Indians who have not registered with the government; Metis (descendants of mixed aborigine and European ancestry); and Inuits, a distinct cultural group, described above, who generally live north of the tree line and speak primarily their own language (Inuktitut). A 1985 change in Canadian law has caused a dramatic rise in Indian population figures, which includes Indian women who marry Canadians of non-Indian ancestry. Exhibit 15.1 details this historic development.

As described previously and in the above exhibits, North American governments, both in Canada and the USA, have tried to rectify past mistakes made against the aboriginal peoples. But it is the younger generation of Native Americans that is leading tribal peoples into the twenty-first century, as the statement below confirms:

We shall learn all the devices the white man has.
We shall handle his tools for ourselves.
We shall master his machinery and his inventions,
his skills, his medicines, his planning;
But we'll retain our beauty and still be Indian.
                    —*By a young Indian college student, 2000.*


## Private Enterprise and Native Americans

Energy companies, searching for commercial quantities of oil, coal, uranium, and other natural resources, are present on Native American lands. One example of apparent differences has been revealed in the Northern Cheyenne and the outside oil people who work with them.

However, if both groups are respectful and knowledgeable of each other's business motivations, value systems, and other aspects of their cultures, the possibility of working together for mutual advantage is significantly enhanced, as we read in Exhibit 15.1. Some energy companies provide education and cross-cultural training for the geologists and other externals who work closely with Native American people. These educational seminars involve presentations by Amerindian leaders, self-assessment exercises, collaborations, team-building exercises, and the distribution of articles and books on the various tribes.

It is impossible to provide information on all the Native American nations. Next, we have profiled one North American tribe to illustrate the rich background and unique aspects to be considered when contemplating investing in tribal resources, forming joint ventures, or partnerships with Native American tribes. Exhibit 15.2 is a summarized profile on the Northern Cheyenne prepared by R. T. Moran and S. Casey.

In the twenty-first century, the North American Indians are experiencing a cultural renaissance. They are overcoming stereotypes and bigotry; recovering historical land rights; telling their stories in literature and

---

### EXHIBIT 15.2

### HISTORY OF THE NORTHERN CHEYENNE

The name Cheyenne comes from the Sioux word sahiyela or sahyiyena and means "alien speaker." In their own Cheyenne language, however, the name is Tsitsistas.

Originally, the Northern and Southern Cheyenne lived together as one tribe. They were first seen by white men in Minnesota in approximately 1640. In the latter part of the seventeenth century, the Cheyenne began migrating to the Western Plains, where they obtained horses and led basically a nomadic life.

The Cheyenne coalesced into two groups; the Northern Cheyenne who lived in Big Horn and Rosebud Counties in Montana, and the Southern Cheyenne who lived in the Southern Arpaho in Oklahoma. In the mid-1800s, after several bloody battles with the U.S. Cavalry, the U.S. government ordered the Northern Cheyenne to the reservation of the Southern Cheyenne in Oklahoma. The Northern Cheyenne, longing for their homeland in Montana, left Oklahoma. Eventually, U.S. troops captured the returning Cheyenne and moved them to army barracks at Fort Robinson, while the army petitioned Washington concerning their fate. When Washington decided that the Northern Cheyenne should be returned to Oklahoma, about 150 Cheyenne attempted escape and were shot. The remaining Cheyenne were taken to the Tongue River Reservation in Montana that was established for the Northern Cheyenne.

---

EXHIBIT 15.2

HISTORY OF THE NORTHERN CHEYENNE (CONTINUED)

U.S. Congress passed a law permitting all Native American Indian tribes to divide their land among tribal members. Each member would receive approximately 160 acres. After holding the land for 25 years, the individual could sell the land. Land that was not allocated was owned by the tribe.

The Northern Cheyenne believed that the land that their ancestors had fought and died for should not be divided. Land is mother and is holy. The Indian Bureau informed the Cheyenne that if they divided the land, the individuals who owned the land could receive government loans to improve the property. The Cheyenne resisted dividing their land, but in 1926 the tribe gave 1457 members a tract of 160 acres each. The remaining acreage (a little less than half of the reservation) was owned by the tribe. All mineral rights on the land belonged to the tribe. After the 25 years passed, there was great pressure on individual Cheyenne to sell their property. Today, less than 2% of the reservation is owned by nontribal individuals, and 70% is owned by the tribe.

**Governance and Authority**

The Northern Cheyenne are governed by a tribal council that is headed by a president and elected by the tribal members. There are Amerindian courts, Indian judges, and police force. In 1933, the Indian Department became the Bureau of Indian Affairs (BIA). The BIA is the trustee of reservation lands and assets. Native American land is entrusted to the BIA, which is to ensure that the land is used for the best interest of the Native Americans. Historically, the BIA has not always understood Native Americans or acted wisely on their behalf, so today more Amerindians work within this Bureau, many in decision-making capacities.

However, the traditional Northern Cheyenne's view of authority and power was that it was a condition that flowed naturally from one's moral excellence and virtue. Historically, a chief was selected because of his wisdom and honorable actions, and he in turn received the loyalty, respect, and obedience of the tribe.

**The People**

Today, the Cheyenne's world is a mixture of the American world and the European world. Almost everyone speaks English, although many still converse in the Cheyenne language, and in some schools the Cheyenne language is taught.

The Northern Cheyenne and the Plains tribes are fun loving and enjoy good companionship. They love feasts, happy talk, and

continued

EXHIBIT 15.2

HISTORY OF THE NORTHERN CHEYENNE (CONTINUED)

storytelling. The efforts of the Northern Cheyenne to preserve their culture are at their height today. Through education, both in the classroom and through the traditions of the tribe, the Cheyenne are attempting to teach and pass on the Cheyenne ways to their children.

Many nontribal organizations—for example, VISTA Volunteers— have offered programs and assistance to the tribe. Many religious organizations have also provided aid to natives on reservations. But many in the tribe, including parents, are concerned that the exposure to nontribal values from outsiders may create problems or send mixed messages to the young.

**The Culture**

Historically, the Northern Cheyenne men were hunters who provided for their families and tribe. Today, that is a financial impossibility for most, and men and women work on or off the reservation in offices and factories. But such jobs are often hard to obtain. The Northern Cheyenne, and many other tribes as well, perceive their work in combination with their Native American traditions. Work is to be done so that a harmony exists between one's work and the land, nature, and one's family; a balance. Tardiness on the job is often a problem because of the different perception of time for the Cheyenne. Non-native Americans view time as a straight line with a past, present, and future, a fast-moving river. Native Americans view time with recurring phases, with one season flowing into the next and one's life leading into another.

In the Native American system, families are extended to include grandparents, aunts, uncles, and cousins, as well as relatives by marriage. In the Northern Cheyenne tribe, the word for mother is the same word for aunt, and these aunt-mothers are integral to the child's upbringing.

Traditionally, the naming of a child was an important occasion. The first name giving took place shortly after birth. If it was a male child, it was named by the father's family, and a female child was named by the mother's. As a child grew older, a new name would be given, sometimes describing a brave or important event in his or her life. These new names might be given when the young man or woman entered puberty.

Powwows, a social custom of the past, still are held several times a year. During the summer, a powwow can bring together many different tribes or unite the Southern and Northern Cheyenne and the Sioux. Historically, a powwow was a sacred event, a prayer for

EXHIBIT 15.2

HISTORY OF THE NORTHERN CHEYENNE (CONTINUED)

protection to the Great Spirit. Also, traditionally, the powwow was a "giveaway," when horses and goods were shared with others in the tribe. Today, the powwows are for feasting and meeting with old friends and for sustaining old traditions.

Another enjoyable old festivity of the Northern Cheyenne was Distribution Day. In the beginning of government annuities, provisions of beef were distributed on the hoof at distribution centers. A bull was released from a chute and the head of each Native American household chased the animal and killed it with a bow and arrow or rifle. As this was reminiscent of the old buffalo hunting days, the Native Americans enjoyed it immensely. The women would follow and butcher the animal and pack the meat for traveling back to the reservation. At these gatherings, there would be singing and dancing and exchange of gossip and news. Each Native American culture brings a richness and diversity to the world. An understanding and respect for the differences and similarities can only bring mutual benefit.

multimedia; and reasserting their rights to governance and the practice of ancestral traditions. They have their own museum in the Capitol, and pantheons on the National Mall.

## UNITED STATES OF AMERICA

America is great, not because it is perfect, but because it can always be made better—and that unfinished work of perfecting our nation falls to each of us. It's a charge we pass on to our children, coming closer with each new generation to do what we know America should be.
Barack Obama, 44th President of the United States of America.[8]

## The Government

The United States of America is a constitutional republic, a federation of 50 states and other territories. It is a representative democracy in which the rule of the majority is tempered by laws which protect minority rights. The U.S. Constitution is both the supreme legal dictate and a social contract with the American people. This document regulates a governance system of checks and balances centered on the nationally elected President ("White House" Administration); the elected Congress (Legislature) consisting of the Senate (100 members, or two per state) and House of Representatives (435 apportioned by population); and the Supreme Court (judiciary of nine), whose judges are appointed by the President with approval of the Senate. They rule on the constitutionality of laws, which are passed both nationally and by states. The President can initiate or veto legislation by the Congress, and is the Commander-in-Chief of the military forces. This federalist system is the model for government activities at the regional, state, and local levels; the latter powers may be split between county and municipal administrations. State governors and other officials are elected by popular vote. The USA follows the rule of laws which are subject to review and may be declared unconstitutional. The Constitution, amended 27 times, has articles structuring the role and responsibilities of the Federal government in relation to the state governments. It also protects citizen rights, such as in the Bill of Rights and the writ of "habeas corpus." The two major political parties are the Democrats and Republicans, although citizens may vote as Independents or form other political parties.

## Geographical and Historical Perspectives[9]

The mainland of the United States is situated in the central part of North America, south of Canada, and north of Mexico, Cuba, and the Bahamas. It is bound on its west coast by the Pacific Ocean, and on its east coast by the Atlantic Ocean. Its northernmost state is Alaska, which lies above the Arctic Circle and above Canada. Hawaii is the furthest away state, west of the mainland in the Pacific Ocean.

The largest nation in the Western Hemisphere on the North American continent, the USA consists of 50 states—48 contiguous ones are on the mainland, plus the state of Alaska in the northwestern tip of the hemisphere, and the state of Hawaii located west of California in the Pacific Ocean. Washington, D.C. (District of Columbia) is the federal capital the United States. Puerto Rico is a self-governing commonwealth, plus the U.S. Virgin Islands, which is a territory. Since the end of World War II, the United States has administered 11 trust territories in the South Pacific, gradually relinquishing control. Between 1975 and 1980, accords were negotiated with the native islanders to establish the commonwealths of the northern Marianas, the Marshall Islands, the Federated States of Micronesia, and the Republic of Palau. The federal government supervises the national highway and transportation systems, national park and forest systems, national wildlife refuges and grasslands, national marine sanctuaries, national energy and environmental systems, as well as reservations for Amerindians and the military.

The topography of this huge country is varied. On the Atlantic seaboard are coastal plains, forests, and rolling hills of Piedmont. In the East, the Appalachian Mountains divide the eastern seaboard from the Great Lakes and grasslands of the Midwest to the north. The Mississippi-Missouri River system runs mainly north-south; the Great Plains of fertile, flat prairie stretches west, interrupted only by a highland region in the southeast. At the western edge of the Great Plains, the Rocky Mountains extend north-south dividing the country and reaching 14,000 ft in Colorado. Moving westward, there are the rocky Great Basin and deserts of the Mojave. Close to the Pacific coastline are the Sierra Nevada and Cascade Mountain ranges. The offshore states of Alaska and Hawaii are noted for their mountains, volcanoes, and natural beauty. The climate in the whole nation, like its people and ecology, is very diverse—on the main continent, one can experience humidity and cold weather in the north, while in the south it is more humid subtropical. Seasonal tornadoes and hurricanes occur in the Midwest Tornado Alley bordering on the Gulf of Mexico and extending as far south as Florida. Most of Alaska is subarctic or polar, while Hawaii has more temperate weather. Today, the U.S. Fish and Wildlife Service seeks to protect threatened and endangered species and their habitats under the Endangered Species Act of 1973. The Federal government regulates some 28% of the country's land area, while its various agencies manage parks, forests, and wilderness area, including 58 National Parks.

Historically, starting in the sixteenth century, three major European nationalities originally imposed their distinct culture upon the Native American cultures in what is now the continental United States. The Spanish seemingly came first in "La Florida," when Juan Ponce de Leon landed; their culture was to dominate that area and later the whole southwest. French fur traders followed with their New France outposts around the Great Lakes, later extending their claims south through Louisiana and the Gulf of Mexico. The English established their first successful settlement in 1607 at Jamestown, Virginia. At that time, they brought the first African slaves into what was to become their Thirteen British Colonies. Migrations from England were fostered by Pilgrims Plymouth Colony, the Massachusetts Colony, Puritans, and other religious groups, as well as by large trading companies. The English king gave land grants to favored ones, sometimes for religious reasons, resulting in the formation of new government entities (e.g., Delaware and Maryland). In 1614, the Dutch laid claim to New Amsterdam on Manhattan Island along the lower Hudson River. In 1674, they ceded to England that territory of New Netherlands (now known as New York City and environs). Waves of settlers, indentured servants, and African slaves pushed expansion of the original colonies. By 1729, the Carolinas were divided into two entities, and in 1732, Georgia was colonized. In the westward expansion of this nation, territories were transformed into new states, and some divided into two: Virginia and West Virginia, North and South Dakota. In them were ensconced cultural values like free elections for free men, religious liberty, self-government, bonded labor and slavery, especially in the south (one in five Americans at this time was a black slave). Although treaties and agreements were worked out with the Amerindians, for the most part they were excluded from mainstream U.S. life.

Then began a series of wars that would transform these eastern colonies. The American Revolutionary War was fought by the colonists against the British from 1775 through 1781. In June 1775, the "Americans" convened a Continental Congress in Philadelphia, established a Continental Army under General George Washington, and adopted a Declaration of Independence on July 4, 1776. That document, drafted by Thomas Jefferson, proclaimed the new nation's ideals and values, such as "all men are created equal," and are endowed "with certain unalienable Rights." In 1777, the Congress passed an Articles of Confederation with provisions for a weak federal government. When the British were defeated, and Great Britain formally recognized the independence and sovereignty of the United States as far west as the Mississippi River, a U.S. Constitution was ratified in 1788 with provision for a Senate, House of Representatives, and President. The next year, George Washington took office as the first President, and in 1791, the Bill of Rights was adopted forbidding federal restrictions on personal freedoms and guaranteeing various legal protections for American citizens. The Northern States abolished slavery during 1780-1804, leaving only the southern states with that unjust and peculiar institution.

The new country's expansion westward was accomplished through Amerindian wars and resettlement to reservations. In 1803, President Jefferson arranged to purchase from France its Louisiana territorial claims, doubling the nation's size. In 1812, a second war against the British strengthened U.S. nationalism and identity, and corrected certain grievances against the "Mother Country." In 1819, after U.S. military excursions into Florida, the Spanish ceded its claims to other Gulf Coast lands. In 1845, the United States annexed the Republic of Texas, and was militarily successful over Mexico under its new policy of "Manifest Destiny." In 1846, the Oregon Treaty with Britain led to American control of the Northwest and establishment of boundaries with Canada. In 1848, the Americans were again victorious over Mexico in a war that gave California and much of the southwest to the USA. The California Gold Rush of 1858-59, building of transcontinental railways, and Federal land grants spurred westward migration and settlement. Thus, the original Thirteen British Colonies emerged into what are today the 50 states of the United States of America.

By 1860, tensions over slavery between northern and southern states led to violent internal conflicts, the secession of seven slave states, and a Civil War by Union forces against the Confederate States of America, now a rebel government of some 11 southern states. President Abraham Lincoln's Emancipation Proclamation committed the Union to abolish slavery. In 1845, the Union prevailed over the Confederacy, and the Congress passed three amendments to the Constitution ensuring freedom for 4 million African-Americans who had been slaves, and gave them citizenship and voting rights. This all resulted in increased Federal power and a Reconstruction Period that ended with "Jim Crow" laws in the south, which disenfranchised African-Americans until they were reversed by the Civil Rights Act in 1964.

The nineteenth century then experienced further American development through the following:

- urbanization and industrialization;
- waves of immigrants from Southern and Eastern Europe;
- high tariff protection, expansion of national infrastructure, and new banking regulations;
- purchase of Alaska from Russia in 1865;
- annexation of Hawaii in 1898, and then victory that year in the Spanish-American War leading to further annexations of Puerto Rico, Guam, and the Philippines (the only territory to gain its independence from the United States a half century later).

The twentieth century witnessed America becoming a world power, able to assist Europe in winning both World Wars I and II. That last century saw the United States swing from isolationism and nonratification of the League of Nations to internationalism and formation of the United Nations with its headquarters in New York City. During this time, citizen movements ensured (a) the guarantee of women's suffrage by a constitutional amendment granting women the right to vote; (b) the end of prohibition laws against alcohol consumption; and (c) the protection of African-American citizens in the Civil Rights Act of 1964 and the Voting Rights Act of 1965. The attack by Japan on Pearl Harbor in Hawaii on December 7, 1941, mobilized the American people and government to enter World War II. During WWII, the United States and its democratic allies overcame Nazi, Fascist, and Japanese power, ending the war in the Pacific by developing and using a nuclear or atomic bomb (1945). The nation then led in establishing international structures and economic policies, such as the International Monetary Fund, the World Bank, and NATO. During the postwar period, the United States initiated the Marshall plan to help Europe recover; undertook through NASA an Apollo space program that placed satellites in orbit and 12 American astronauts on the moon; and engaged in a geopolitical Cold War with the U.S.S.R. that resulted in the demise of that Communist government in 1991. Unfortunately, the United States, during that period, like Russia, supported dictatorships and proxy government in unwise attempts to defeat each other. The United States was also involved in a series of disastrous regional wars in Korea (1950-1953); Vietnam (1961-1973); Iraq (1991; 2003-); and Afghanistan (2001-). In America, these major military conflicts not only weakened the nation's economy, but resulted in significant countercultural movements and public protests, contributing to altering American behavior, attitudes, and foreign policy.

In the twenty-first century, the attack of Middle Eastern terrorists on September 11, 2001, against New York City's Trade Center and

Washington, D.C.'s Pentagon building became a significant force, changing the nation and its citizens. Most Americans believe that the events of 9/11 were the most serious terrorist acts that violated their sovereignty, prompting a transformational moment in their history. That event led to a declaration of war on terrorism worldwide, and against the al-Qaeda global network of radical Islamic anarchists, in particular. It contributed to the nation's concern about improving security for its citizens, limitations on immigration and human rights, as well as neglect of domestic concerns (e.g., natural disasters). Another consequence was the United States invasion of Afghanistan and again Iraq. These bloody conflicts diminished both the national treasury and the image of the world's only superpower, which was no longer held in high esteem by many foreigners.[10] As a result of these failed policies and a severe economic recession, a new President was elected in 2008. The first African-American in that powerful office is Barack Obama, who has pledged to renew this "land of the free and home of the brave," while restoring fundamental United States values expressed in the Constitution and Bill of Rights.[a] The relatively short history of this nation has both inspired and disillusioned people at home and abroad. Today, the United States has seemingly entered a period of reconciliation and renewal, both domestically and overseas.

*Not exactly; Bush's term was up anyway.*

*Not quite; it's gone the other way*

## *American Cultural Insights*[11]

The citizens of the United States of America refer to themselves as "Americans," although that term may also be claimed by other inhabitants of North, South, and Central America. The fourth largest nation in the world, the United States has been referred to as a "melting pot" culture, where people come from many places and meld into the mainstream European cultures of the United States. The "salad bowl" metaphor is perhaps more appropriate and accurate, for it recognizes the contributions of the Native American, African, Asian, and Latin cultures, with each culture maintaining its unique cultural markers, while striving to work and live in harmony. It is true that it is a land of immigrants—from the time of colonists (British/French/Spanish), plus the African slaves and nineteenth and twentieth century European influx, especially from Austria-Hungry, Ireland, Italy, Poland, and Russia. More recent waves of refugees are from Indochina, China, Cuba, Haiti, Latin America, and the Philippines. Germany alone accounts for 43 million emigres in the last census here. And so, too, did the Scots-Irish proliferate in America. The last census confirmed that nearly 40 million people now in the USA are foreign born. Many of these cultural immigrants try to preserve their beliefs and traditions. Apart from the Native Americans, this is true of groups such as descendents of the Amish from Switzerland, Hutterites from Moravia, Old Believers from Russia, Cajuns from

---

[a]"Renewing America—The 44th President," *The Economist* (www.economist.com), January 17, 2009, pp. 11, 31-33.

Arcadia, Polynesians from the Pacific Basin, Gullahs or Sea Islanders from West Africa, and Vietnamese from Indochina. Growing minorities of Hispanics, Blacks, and Asians, as well as the Native Americans, are rapidly changing the configuration of the population.

By 2050, U.S. census forecasts that minorities in this country will become the majority. By then, the American population is expected to number 438 million, including some 40 million of Asian heritage and 16 million of African roots. It is estimated that by mid-century, whites or Caucasians will make up only 46% of the U.S. population, while one in three Americans will be Hispanic or Latino! This discussion will continue in the section on subcultures. Like the rest of the world, there are more aging Americans as a result of fewer childbirths and longer life spans. Recent surveys reveal that among 450,000 centenarians worldwide, 50,000 now live to be 100 years or more in the United States. Such demographic changes have a significant impact on American culture and society. The composition of Americans has greatly diversified since Kennewick man, a Caucasian, lived some 9300 years ago in what is now Washington State!

Obviously, then, the United States is a multicultural society with many microcultures. In addition to the American form of English, Spanish is emerging as a second language, especially in the Southwest, California, Florida, and Puerto Rico. American speech is as varied as the country's geography. Yet, French is still spoken by many in the state of Louisiana and parts of New England.

## American Cultural Profile

There are some general cultural characteristics associated with Americans. The overview of the dominant mainstream culture reveals that citizens of the United States tend to be as follows:

- *Goal and Achievement-Oriented*—Americans are optimistic, and think they can accomplish just about anything, given enough time, money, and technology.
- *Highly Organized and Institutionalistic*—Americans prefer a society that is strong institutionally, well-organized, and secure.
- *Freedom-Loving and Self-Reliant*—Americans fought a revolution and subsequent wars to preserve their concept of democracy, so they resent too much control or interference, especially by government or external forces. They believe in the ideal that all persons are created equal, though they sometimes fail to live that ideal fully. They strive through law to promote equal opportunity and to confront their own racism or prejudice. Americans also idealize the self-made person who rises from poverty and adversity. Control of one's destiny is popularly expressed as "doing your own thing." Americans think, for the most part, that with determination and initiative, one can achieve whatever he or she sets out to do, and can thus fulfill individual human potential.

- *Work-Oriented and Efficient*—Americans possess a strong work ethic, though they are learning in the present generation to enjoy leisure time constructively. They are very time-conscious and efficient in doing things. They tinker with gadgets and technological systems, always searching for easier, better, more efficient ways of accomplishment.
- *Friendly and Informal*—Americans reject the traditional privileges of royalty and class, but do defer to those with affluence and power. Some Americans are impressed by celebrities created by American mass media. Although informal in greeting and dress, they are a noncontact culture (e.g., they usually avoid embracing in public).
- *Competitive and Assertive*—Americans in play or business generally are so oriented because of their drives to achieve and succeed. This is partially traced to their heritage, having overcome wilderness and hostile elements in their environment. The syndrome is that people are free to achieve any dream in America, and can go "from rags to riches."
- *Values in Transition*—America is a dynamic and open society. Traditional American values of family loyalty, respect and care of the aged, marriage and the nuclear family, patriotism, material acquisition, forthrightness, and the like are undergoing profound reevaluation.
- *Generous and Altruistic*—Although Americans seemingly emphasize material values, they are a sharing people, as has been demonstrated in the Marshall Fund, foreign aid programs, refugee assistance, and their willingness at home and abroad to espouse a good cause and to help neighbors in need. They tend to be altruistic and, some would say, naive as a people. Volunteerism is alive and well in the United States.

## American Social Institutions

In terms of U.S. social institutions, three are worth noting here. Education is viewed as a means of self-development, so participation in the process and within the classroom is encouraged. Education is mandatory until age16, and 97% finish at least elementary school, so the literacy rate is high. There is a public system (largely free of cost) with charter schools that focus on innovation and specialization; and a private school system which is independent, and in some cases sponsored by a religious institution. These schools extend from the elementary and secondary levels through college and university level. Two-year community or junior colleges are popular for the learning of technical and professional skills, as well as for transitioning into 4-year college degree studies.

*Family*—The average family has been nuclear, consisting of only parents and children; however, the number of single-parent and extended families is increasing. Growing pluralism has also led to rising numbers of interracial marriages. There is a strong movement toward same-sex marriages or legal partnerships with or without children. Fifty percent or more of all marriages in this country end in divorce. More than half of American women work outside the home, and women have considerable and improving opportunities for personal and professional growth, guaranteed by law. The society is youth-oriented, and usually cares for the elderly outside the home, in institutions. It is experimenting with new family arrangements, from unmarried couples living together or even in group communes.

*Politically*—The government operates on the Constitution of 1787, which provides a three-branch approach of checks and balances, and two or more political parties as described above. Currently, there is much disillusionment with political leaders, bureaucracy, corruption in public offices, and a counter push toward decentralization or the confederation of states for regional action (i.e., emphasis on states' rights and less government regulation over individual lives, or regional plans to respond to natural disasters). Increasingly, high-tech communications are altering traditional politics, as seen in the 2008 Obama presidential campaign. The many voters and supporters organized across party lines on issues and concerns were made possible by the Internet and new information-exchanging technologies. The current U.S. administration is keeping this electronic network going after elections to gather public support for the President's plans to fulfill campaign promises and bring about needed reforms or programs, despite Congressional opposition.

## Cultural Challenges and Changes in the United States

The Americans, too, are in the midst of profound social change, and even an identity crisis. The following factors have contributed to this maturation challenge.

*National Image*—Being, at the moment, the world's only super power within a global economy experiencing recession has forced a reassessment of the national self-image. After much success in its wars abroad, military conflicts in Korea, Vietnam, Iraq, and Afghanistan proved to be costly and questionable, with citizens influenced by mass media. Support for such military actions is declining. And the focus is more upon international diplomatic solutions, such as cooperation with the United Nations. The country's social fabric was undermined by the assassinations of the country's leaders in the 1960s; growing violence in the streets and social protests; acts of both domestic and foreign terrorism; absurd racist policies and practices in light of growing pluralism and "latinization" of the country; increase in homelessness and creation of an underclass; and erosion of American values and international perceptions abroad, especially from a failed presidential administration over the 8 years of the twenty-first century. These and many other factors are causing people in the United States to reassess their national image.

Transition into a postindustrial society happened first and faster in the United States than in most other countries because of scientific and technological advances. The values and lifestyles brought on by the industrial stage of development are being reexamined, and new replacements are being sought for more effective coping in a knowledge culture.

The impact of such contemporary trends depends on where you are in America, for there are considerable regional differences and subcultures. There is also a big difference between eastern and western lifestyles and attitudes. The eastern United States is thought to be more established, conservative in thinking, overorganized, and deteriorating; the western part of the nation is seen as more casual, innovative, and flexible.

As a result of the 9/11 attacks, more Americans are becoming isolationist, nationalistic, and provincial in their thinking and actions. In an era of globalization, corporate acquisitions, and property purchases in the United States by Canadians, Japanese, Europeans, Middle Easterners, and South Africans are considerable, causing some fear and backlash. The increased influx of refugees, along with legal and illegal immigrants, has strained existing social systems. But most of the newcomers, like Mexicans, Somalis, and Iraqis, are communities of strivers who want only to advance themselves in their new homeland.

Just before the 2008 elections, *Newsweek Magazine* produced a special issue with results of a national opinion poll of American views, and 44% of the respondents thought immigration was good for the country. Exhibit 15.3 summarizes some of the most significant findings,

---

### EXHIBIT 15.3

### AMERICA'S CHANGING CULTURE

- 5.2 million Americans are estimated to be living overseas.
- 5.7 million unmarried, heterosexual couples live together.
- 65% of population is urban, 33.6% suburban, and remainder other (e.g., rural).
- 27% of the high-income males report a work week up to 50 h.
- 33% of the females are college graduates; 25% of the males in age group 25-29.
- 77% work in the service sector; 20% in industry; 3% in agriculture.
- 46% of the workforce are civilian women.
- 67% of children live with two parents; 28% with one parent; 5% other.
- 31% of college freshmen describe themselves as liberal in their political/social outlook.
- 20% of the population will be age 65 or older in 2050.
- 45% of population by 2050 will be white, 31% Hispanic, 14% black. 10% Asian.
- 80% today accept interracial marriage among Americans, while 45% of voters under 30 accept gay marriage rights.

*Source*: *Newsweek Magazine Special Inaugural Issue,* January 2009 entitled "Obama's America—Where We Are Now," 78 pp. Data based on their own opinion poll, plus information from others, such as Pew Research Center, U.S. Census Bureau, Congressional Research Center, Environmental Systems Research Institute.

along with data from other sources which reveal insights on the changing American culture. The disparity between younger and older voters was the greatest ever recorded. That segment of the population between 18- and 29-year-olds was more diverse, more female, more secular, and less politically/socially conservative—20% of this group are children of immigrants.

Obviously, from the brief summary above, it is evident that America is changing almost beyond recognition, and externals need to revise their image of a "typical" American! Assimilation to the United States is not easy, but the constant inflow of immigrants produces a vibrant society with a fluid culture which breaks down barriers among previously estranged groups. The country, on the whole, is also becoming more tolerant on social issues that previously divided its citizens. The increasing numbers who travel, study, work, or live abroad also foster a population more global and open to different perspectives, and less arrogant. Americans are becoming more "borderless" in their attitudes toward environment, energy, trade, and human rights. They are more resilient in coping with climate and weather changes, economic setbacks, and in creating a work environment in which home and office are more integrated. Today's Americans still have a sense of affinity, but are creating new associations and communities more on the basis of common causes, issues, interests of concern that go beyond the traditional organizations. Knowledge and expertise divide these people more than class or wealth. Rebuilding the ladder of upward mobility and historic optimism in hard economic times is a challenge!

In business agreements or partnerships with Americans, Exhibit 15.4 illustrates how cultural values and assumptions may potentially clash.

## EXHIBIT 15.4
## CULTURE CONTRAST

| Host Country Value | U.S.A. Value |
| --- | --- |
| *Japan*: Group orientation | Individualism |
| *Guatemala*: Flexible time sense | Punctuality |
| *Saudi Arabia*: Relationship focus | Task/goal orientation |
| *Switzerland*: Formality | Informality |
| *India*: Stratified class structure | Egalitarianism |
| *China*: Long-term view | Short-term view |
| *Germany*: Structured orderliness | Flexible pragmatism |
| *France*: Deductive thinking | Inductive thinking |
| *Sweden*: Individual cooperation | Individual competition |
| *Malaysia*: Modesty | Self-promotion |

*Source*: Wederspahn, G. M. *Intercultural Services: A Worldwide Buyer's Guide and Sourcebook*. Burlington, MA: Buteerworth-Heinemann/Gulf, 2000, pp. 41-42.

# Microcultures in the United States[12]

So far in this chapter, the emphasis has been on the USA macroculture. In mainstream American society, for example, most people are concerned with "doing." Americans have a preoccupation with time, organization, and the use of resources. In American social relationships, everyone is assumed equal, thus removing the need for elaborate forms of social address. Social relationships are characterized by informality, and social reciprocities are much less clearly defined. In the majority culture, citizens are motivated by achievements and accomplishments. American personal identity and, to a certain extent, one's self-worth are measured by what the individual achieves. Their world is material rather than spiritual, and Americans also see themselves as individual and unique.

However, American culture is in transition, as was discussed above. Because of wars, economic recession, and social changes, many American families are in crisis, especially in the inner cities and suburbs. Some also fear that the centerpiece of American life, the large middle class, is eroding and under economic threat. Violence is increasing, especially among the young gang members, many of whom lack adequate character education and supervision, as well as job opportunities. Their parents' attention is directed toward work and earning a living, and many times there is only a single parent, usually female. Under these circumstances, an expanding segment of the population is prone to homelessness, child or spousal abuse, substance abuse, paranoia, crime, hatred, and intolerance. This distressed underclass is balanced by a majority of Americans who are relatively affluent and well-educated, in contrast to the rest of the world's population—who are generous in their charity and community service; who are into fitness and wellness regimens; who fight for just causes, such as protecting other species and the environment; and who are optimists and futurists. There is growing concern in the United States about the increase in obesity and greed, about community service and volunteerism, about care of the elderly and homeless, about promoting a pluralism that accepts diversity because of race, religion, ethnicity, or sexual orientation. The emergence of a polyethnic society is most evident in Los Angeles, where a cacophony of 160 languages is spoken today. California is now home to up to 2.4% illegal immigrants. The transformation of minorities into majorities is also taking place in Texas, Arizona, New York, Nevada, New Jersey, and Maryland. By 2050, half of the U.S. population will likely be nonwhite.

The exceptional uniformity that characterized American society in the post-World War II period has been supplanted by extreme diversity. The most integrated national market in the history of the world is splintering into an array of niches. Immigration, legal and illegal, has eroded the homogeneity of the U.S. population while multiplying commonalities and connections between American society and other societies around the world. But there are multiple minorities or subcultures in this large country that have their own unique needs and concerns. In the United States, these microcultures—such as those of African-Americans, Hispanics, Chinese-Americans, Vietnamese-Americans, and Muslim-Americans—are socially, economically, and physically challenged by the mainstream culture. Furthermore, there are subcultures that cross national boundaries, such as youth and senior citizens, athletes and musicians, as well as technological nerds and video game players. Each of these groups has aspects of their lives, priorities, or values that may differ in part from mainstream America. To work effectively together and develop authentic relationships among all Americans, it is helpful to be aware, accept, appreciate, and respect the uniqueness of these various subcultures.

Those who have been in the majority, such as Caucasians, will have to change their sense of identity as they become a minority culture and must share power with all those other "people of color." White citizens are becoming less of a privileged group; as minorities move up in this great society, norms or standards and privileges in the mainstream culture will be altered. As this process expands so will the backlash and hatred increase from those losing their privileged position, as is seen in movements like the Klu Klux Klan, white supremacists, Neo-Nazi, and other such alienated groups.

There are two types of minority groups: those that are distinguished by the physical characteristics—racial groups—and those that are differentiated by distinct language, religious, cultural, or national characteristics. According to Gudykjunst and Kim, there are five characteristics of minority group membership:[12]

1. Members of minority groups are treated differently from members of a majority group by members of the majority group. This inequality usually takes the form of segregation, prejudice, and discrimination.
2. Members of minority groups have either physical or cultural characteristics that make them stand out from the majority group.
3. Because minority groups stand out from the majority, membership in them is not voluntary.
4. Members of a minority group tend to associate with and marry other members of their group.
5. Members of a minority group are aware of their subordinate status, which leads to strong group solidarity and gaining a sense of ethnic identity.

Often, minority groups are not recognized as legitimate and distinct. Instead, they are automatically diminished, being judged by their physical appearance rather than with acknowledgment and appreciation of their different culture, language, and ethnic characteristics. When a mass movement of Irish and Italian peoples to the United States occurred in the nineteenth century, there was much bigotry and prejudice practiced against them by the majority because of their poverty and religious beliefs (Roman Catholic in a country that was then largely Anglo-Saxon, Protestant). Today, smaller numbers of immigrants similarly struggle to assimilate into American culture, so as to be accepted by the majority, such as Ethiopians, Sudanese, Laotians, Hmongs, and many other new minorities from abroad.

The major minorities are easily identified by their larger numbers within the United States. At the opening of this chapter, we discussed the microcultures of the Eskimos (Inuits) and Native Americans (Amerindians). Now we will examine two other principal ethnic and racial groupings.

## African-Americans

Since colonial times in America, people from Africa were here as either slaves or freemen, and many of them served gallantly in the Revolutionary War. They became the backbone of the Southern plantation economy; in return for this subservient status, their human rights were denied and their families broken apart. The Civil War was fought to give blacks full citizenship. Although African-Americans today still struggle to maintain their full civil rights and equal opportunity under the law, their economic and social position has advanced. Yet racism against them has become more subtle within institutions, housing, or educational opportunities. Despite their accomplishments and the growth of the black middle and upper classes, unemployment among black teens and deaths from violence within black communities have also risen. There is much to be done together if all African-American citizens are to share in the American dream. Power is not equally shared, and economic access is limited, not equal. Yet, the election of the first African-American president in 2008 has brought new hope to this oppressed community.

Racism entered global consciousness in WWII with the Holocaust and the racist philosophy of Nazi Germany that resulted in the imprisonment and death of millions of Jews. Today, world events have convinced most that racism is a significant problem in all countries, as the ethnic cleansing in former Yugoslavia and genocide in Rwanda exemplify. Law enforcement has also utilized questionable "racial profiling" in world security systems. Whether one focuses on individual, institutional, cultural, or symbolic racism, it is a phenomenon that is deeply ingrained throughout many cultures. Racism is an explosive issue in American life today. To begin a serious dialogue regarding race, one must establish the terms for racial issues. As long as African-Americans are viewed as "them," the burden falls on blacks to do all the "cultural" and "moral" compromising, so healthy race relations are hampered. It is not acceptable under the U.S. Bill of Rights that only certain Americans can define what it means to be American—and the rest must simply "fit in."

Obviously, African-Americans are distinctive by their skin color, but that is simply an example of human adaptability to environmental circumstances. They have made unusual contributions to American military and economic history, as African studies in U.S. colleges and universities underscore. They have enriched American culture in music, dance, art, education, entertainment, and sports. Other Americans need to share their unique qualities for joy and survival, and be transformed by experiencing them as friends, neighbors, and coworkers. Consider these indicators of progress in the African-American community:

■ Since 1970, the proportion of African-American households living in poverty has shrunk from 70% to 46%, while the black middle class has grown from 27% to 37%.
■ The percentage of those who are considered prosperous—earning more than $107,000 a year in 2007—rose from 3% to 17%.
■ The racial wage gap between blacks and whites is diminishing because of increasing deregulation and competition in financial institutions.
■ The number of blacks elected or appointed to office at all levels of government has increased dramatically, including to the U.S. Supreme Court and Attorney General, as well as the presidency itself.
■ The number of blacks completing secondary school, college, and postgraduate studies is rising steadily.
■ African-Americans can be found everywhere in the USA, but their population concentration by states is centered in six southern states—Mississippi, Louisiana, South Carolina, Georgia, Maryland, and Alabama.
■ The African refugees from Somalia, Sudan, and Ethiopia are spreading from urban areas to smaller towns, such as Lewiston, Maine, and prospering while infusing more diversity into these communities.

With one of their own as the present head of the White House, Civil Rights leaders have to develop new strategies to fit within the President's own priorities for economic upliftment. They need to learn how to take advantage of new administration programs that will address these long-standing, unresolved concerns of the African-American community: (1) unequal schools; (2) segregated housing; (3) lagging economic opportunities; (4) disproportionate number of black men incarcerated in prisons; and (5) too many single-mother families and absent fathers. Yet, a 2008 opinion poll conducted after the Obama election reported that 42% of blacks now believe that American society is fair and decent toward them.

A specific example of this minority advancement is evident in the Knowledge for Power Program, or KIPP charter public school network. There are 36 such schools in 19 states, including Washington, D.C. For some 17,000 students (81% from low-income families, 60% African-American, and 35% Hispanic), a typical school day is 9 h in a

6-day week, plus summer study. Of 688 graduates of 8th grade, 576 so far have gone on to college, an 84% matriculation rate. Sending your kids to college is part of the American dream, and programs like this are reversing trends, and galvanizing minority youth to aspire to further education. Good teaching and mentoring, as well as discipline and support services, make it possible!

## Hispanic Americans

Hispanics are moving up in every American business area. Their cultural passion and adaptability with emphasis on family is ideally suited to both the American and global business scene.[b]

Recall the insights on Latin American culture provided in Chapter 12 before this examination of an emerging majority. Broadly defined, a Latino or Hispanic is an immigrant to the United States, or one whose ancestors came from Spain or Latin America. Most still speak Spanish and reflect the cultural images of both Spain and the indigenous peoples of Mexico, Central, and South America. This cultural influence is most evident in California, Florida, Nevada, Arizona, Texas, Puerto Rico, and Guam. However, Hispanics have also been migrating to the Midwest and Northeastern states. From the viewpoint of creating synergy from cultural differences, the Latino expansion and integration into U.S. culture is also in major urban centers such as Denver, Chicago, and New York, as well as in Miami, Los Angeles, and San Diego (all three cities founded over 250 years ago by Spanish colonists). Many Latinos, whose communities here go back to the sixteenth century, consider themselves "native" Americans. Less than 200 years have passed since the United States annexed the southwest after the Mexican-American War, and only a century since it occupied Puerto Rico.

Today, Latinos represent 11% of the U.S. population, having increased by60%, and the percentage is projected to further expand by 75% in 2015. Census forecasters expect a Hispanic population here of 96 million by 2050. Spanish-speaking Americans are heterogeneous in terms of skin color and in terms of origin: approximately 65% are from Mexico; 12% Puerto Ricans; 12% Central Americans and other Latin countries; 8% Cubans; and 5% Dominicans. Hispanics are most diverse in terms of histories, loyalties, and class. Some come from elite and wealthy backgrounds or ancestors in Mexico, Latin America, or Spain, while many others have come as migrant workers, legally or illegally, willing to work hard and long, yet many can find only low-paying and low-status jobs. Once established, they take advantage of American public education and the ability to move ahead economically and socially.

---

[b]Failde, A. and Doyle, W. *Latino Success: Insights from 100 of America's Most Powerful Business Professionals*. New York: Simon and Shuster, 1996.

It is difficult to generalize about Latino-Americans, but they are gaining political power and representation as greater numbers of them vote. Although many are bilingual, they gain a certain cohesiveness through the Spanish language, Roman Catholicism, and family values. They are moving rapidly into middle-class status and home ownership. In most states, the number of Hispanic-owned businesses has doubled, and their purchasing power is likely to triple by the end of this decade. The Hispanic buying power in the United States is estimated to reach $1 trillion by 2010. This has resulted from a rise in the average Hispanic household income from $14,712 in 1980 to $29,500 in 1996 to over $40,000 in 2003. The Latino consumer market—large and growing—has a reputation for brand loyalty, particularly when shopping for food and clothing. Consider that by the year 2000, there were 6.9 million Latino schoolchildren, and most of their parents wanted them to be taught in English. Spanish-speaking America is the world's fifth-largest Hispanic nation. Yet, the dialect of choice for millions of young Latinos is Spanish, for they can switch with ease between Spanish and English.

Presently, Latinos lack strong leaders, especially in the political and financial arenas. Though well involved in baseball, they are not well represented in mainstream American sports, preferring soccer. As they become more assimilated, Latinos are slowly entering the mainstream of cultural and performing arts, the professions, and law enforcement. People of Hispanic background bring a distinct, joyous flavor to the American mainstream, especially in terms of food and music. They comprise a varied tapestry reflecting Spanish, Indian, African-American, and mulatto heritages. In the future, Hispanics will account for the bulk of American population growth—by 2007, Latinos were already 45.5 million in the United States, and their main country of origin was Mexico! By 2050, experts estimate that they may represent 29% of the population.

## Words Matter with North American Minorities

From a majority perspective in any society (i.e., as a white, Anglo-Saxon in Canada or the United States), it is difficult to write about "we the people" in North America, for the population make-up is rapidly changing. Indigenous people need to be addressed first with respect and in a positive manner, and then with openness to the ways we can learn from their cultures and histories. All ethnic groups expect the same treatment in the United States.

Members of the majority and others need to be aware of culturally biased words. *The Color of Words: An Encyclopedic Dictionary of Ethnic Bias in the United States* explains words and expressions used in the United States today that carry ethnic bias.[13] The words listed illustrate the labeling and classifying of people; these classifications are often for "reasons of manipulation or mischief." There are over 1000 words or phrases listed, and the following are some culturally biased examples:

- *Coolie, cooly.* An unskilled Asian laborer or porter. Dating from the mid-seventeenth century, the term was applied by Europeans in India and China to a native laborer hired at subsistence wages. In California, since the 1860s, Chinese immigrants or sojourners were viewed as a "race of coolies" who threatened white Californian labor.
- *Coon.* A shortened form of raccoon. In American English, coon is usually dated to1742. Coon has been used derogatorily to refer to a black person, especially a man since the mid-nineteenth century. Nigger for Negro is another offensive term for African-Americans.
- *Dink.* Derogatory nickname for an Asian or person of Asian descent, but today usually with reference to a Vietnamese. Used by American and Australian soldiers during the Vietnam War. (Note: "DINK" also describes a social/economic group that has "Dual Income, No Kids.")

Thus, to promote intercultural harmony among Americans, speakers have to be careful in their cross-cultural communications. As Donald L. Conover, honored by the U.N. for his world entrepreneurship, has observed in broadcasts and books, words do matter, especially when they reflect ignorance, stereotyping, media bias, and inflammatory language (www.wordsmatterradio.net or .tv). Hate and fear mongering can lead to horrors ranging from community conflict to genocide (www.tsunamiofblood.com). In the past, prejudice, bias, and bigotry have led to urban riots, sometimes blamed on the police. Learning from such negative experiences, the United States has led in the training of its police to be more culturally sensitive to minorities. For example, in the widely used book, *Multicultural Law Enforcement—Strategies for Peacekeeping in a Diverse Society*, police are provided with information and insights about these American minorities: Asian/Pacific, Africans, Latino/Hispanic, Arabs/Muslims, Amerindians.[14]

In their fluid culture, most Americans, especially in educational systems, do endeavor to promote racial harmony. The Southern Poverty Law Center promotes a tolerance program for schools, as well as monitors hate groups and extremist activities in the USA. Often, this results in successful class action lawsuits against such un-American, illegal behavior (www.splcenter.org, or www.tolerance.org, or en.wikipedia.org./wiki/Southern_Poverty_Law_Center).

Some groups acculturate better or faster to American society. American Muslims, for instance, are better integrated and successful. The U.S. constitutional right of freedom of religion enables them to build mosques. In Detroit, Michigan, they are a formidable force in public affairs. Southeast Michigan has the country's largest concentration of Arab-Americans. But this Muslim community represents not only those of Arab descent, but African-Americans and Bosnian-Americans. Their social solidarity has been facilitated by the Arab Community Centre for Economic and Social Service, as well as by the Dearborn Islamic Centre and seven charter schools, like the Bridge Academy. Despite their gains, peaceful Muslims face growing prejudice caused by public fears of Islamic extremists and terrorists worldwide who are a small minority of the global Muslim peoples, as pointed out in Chapter 11 on the Middle East.

The experience of the most racially mixed society in the world, the United States, is that when national, regional, and local policies encourage cultural integration and assimilation, ethnic distinctions gradually vanish. Each generation develops its own American identity from the widest available materials and subcultures. As evolved creatures, human beings are basically one family, which our common DNA confirms! Race has no wider ramifications than intelligence—it simply characterizes the tendency of people living in different parts of the world to have diverse skin and color, as well as physiognomy.

Although mainstream American culture espouses a classless society, the reality is that significant differences do exist between social classes that affect socialization, language, and values.

## Tips for Doing Business and Negotiating with Americans

The following is a profile of an American negotiator, reflecting some of the variables that can occur in business and negotiations:

- *Basic Concept of Negotiation*: American negotiators view conflict and confrontation as an opportunity to exchange viewpoints and as part of the process in resolution, negotiation, and agreement. Americans prefer outlining the issues or problems and a direct approach to determining possible solutions. They are motivated to further the interests of their corporation or government, and have a highly competitive nature regarding the outcome or settlement.
- *Selection of Negotiators*: American negotiators are usually chosen for a negotiating team on the basis of their record of success in past negotiations and their knowledge and expertise in the area to be negotiated. Negotiations that are technical in nature require Americans with very specific knowledge and the ability to communicate their expertise. Individual differences, gender, age, and social class are not generally criteria for selection, but individual differences in character (cooperative, authoritarian, trustworthy) can determine whether one is chosen for an American negotiating team.
- *Role of Individual Aspirations*: As a rule, Americans encourage individual aspirations and individual achievements. When representing

their corporation or country, Americans temper their individualism and seek to accomplish and/or represent the positions of their company or country.

■ *Concern with Protocol*: Generally, Americans are friendly and open. Their etiquette is largely informal, and so is their basic concern for protocol. They are relaxed in their business conduct, and do not often adhere to strict or explicit codes of behavior and ceremony.

■ *Significance of Type of Issue*: The popular American expression "getting the job done" reflects their desire to assess the situation and get results quickly. In negotiations, Americans may focus on the tangible aspects of the negotiation without spending too much time on the more intangible aspects, such as building relationships during the process.

■ *Complexity of Language*: Americans are low-context communicators. The message is primarily in the words spoken, and is not overridden by nonverbal communication—the cues of gesture, eye contact, and silence.

■ *Nature of Persuasive Argument*: Americans usually attempt a rational presentation with detailed facts and figures accompanied by logical and analytical arguments when persuading their counterparts.

■ *Value of Time*: Every culture has different ways of organizing time and using it. Some cultures are rigidly bound by their schedules and deadlines, while other cultures have a relaxed attitude about detailed plans and schedules. Monochronic time emphasizes schedules, segmentation, and promptness. Polychronic time stresses involvement with people and completion of transactions rather than an adherence to a preset schedule. Americans generally have a monochronic time orientation, and for most Americans "time is money." In negotiations, Americans set schedules and appointments and tend to prioritize events and move through the process "controlling" the time allotted them.

■ *Bases of Trust*: In negotiations, Americans generally trust the accuracy of the information being communicated and negotiated, and they assume that the negotiations will have a desirable outcome. If, however, Americans have had a past experience with a counterpart who has not been trustworthy, they will withhold the trust.

■ *Risk-Taking Propensity*: Americans are risk-takers. In light of their history, their perception of themselves as rugged individualists, and the rewards of capitalism, Americans have embraced risk and are not risk averse.

■ *Internal Decision-Making Systems*: Decision-making is becoming more and more decentralized with authority, within predetermined limits, being given to those with negotiating experience. Most of the final decisions must be cleared with senior executives in the organization.

■ *Form of Satisfactory Agreement*: Because the American culture is legalistic, Americans prefer and expect detailed contractual agreements to formalize negotiations. A handshake may conclude negotiations, but the attorneys are always involved.

# CONCLUSIONS

In 1831, a Frenchman, Alexis de Tocqueville, wrote *Democracy in America.* He discovered what he called *habits of the heart,* which form the American character and sustain free institutions—family life, religious convictions, and participation in local politics. Bellah and others then examined individualism and commitment in American life.[15] These authors concluded that rampant individualism within American culture may threaten freedom itself, especially when individual achievement is attained at the expense of the community that provides support, reinforcement, and moral meaning for the individual. The latter proved true in 2008 when Wall Street financiers and corporate CEOs pursued greed over honesty and the common good, triggering an economic recession globally. Furthermore, within North American society, competition is almost a cultural imperative, but Bellah argues that pure selfishness does not contribute to the good of all. Yet, he sees new community forces at work within America, such as leading corporations becoming more personal and participatory, more socially responsible, and so contributing to the renewal of this society and the creation of a new work culture.

In the opening decade of this twenty-first century, many worldwide and in the United States have become disillusioned with American global policies and actions, predicting a waning superpower would be superseded by other nations. Khanna concluded that much of America's global esteem and self-promotion has been on based on its status as the military defender of freedom, the wealthiest society, and the most vibrant democracy.[16] The real lesson of Hobbes and Darwin is that no single power will dominate others; rather, the most adaptive system will prevail. In their 2008 national election, Americans overwhelmingly rejected the previous George W. Bush's administration's arrogant, unilateral policies and actions that so undermined U.S. image and values. As their country's influence diminishes and is buffeted by climate change and hard economic times, they chose to elect Barak Obama, a leader who is pragmatic, multicultural, and a global visionary. The 44th President has set himself the goal of renewing the United States, and once again making it a land of opportunity and hope. It remains for the American people to answer his call for a collaborative spirit that includes more volunteerism and selfless leadership.[17]

We have reviewed in this chapter the diverse cultures of North America—Native Americans, Canadians, and the peoples of the United States. These are complex, cosmopolitan, and changing populations worthy of careful study by foreign businesspeople, visitors, and students who want to understand all that can be properly called "Americans." This concludes our unit on cultural specifics.

## MIND STRETCHING

1. Many Americans seem to be anxious about how the world perceives them, and are disturbed by what seems to be its declining image and position in many countries. Some wonder if the end is near for U.S. dominance or influence. The following are some quotations from recently published materials that are worth considering:

   ■ "In Muslim and developing countries, the image of America is skewed by north/south, east/west economic inequality; by long-standing, direct grievances over foreign policy...."

   ■ "On the surface, President Bush's week-long swing through northeast Asia has been a strong contrast with his recent storming (and, some say, stumbling) excursion with Latin America. While no foreign leader will openly oppose American leadership...beneath the polite appearance, however, there is no less a challenge to American leadership in Asia...."

   ■ "In developing countries...there is much greater awareness now than there used to be of the nature and pervasiveness of imperialism. As a result, in some countries there is mounting reluctance to conform to ideals 'born in the USA'...."

   ■ "One of the trickiest files for the prime minister (of Canada) will be relations with the United States. The two countries are drifting apart."

2. Consider the significance of the 2008 national elections in the USA, and its implications for important changes within this nation. What kind of inspiring leadership is anticipated from the first African-American president, Barak Obama?

## REFERENCES

1. Abbot, J. D. and Moran, R. T. *Uniting North American Business*. Burlington, MA: Elsevier/Butterworth/Heinemann, 2002.
2. National Geographic, *Family Reference Atlas of the World*. Washington, DC: National Geographic, 2002, Chapter on North America, pp. 70–113.
3. Gore, R. "The Most Ancient Americans," *National Geographic*, October 1997, pp. 93–97; Murphy, K. "Skeleton Embodies Debate on Americas First People," *Los Angeles Times*, August 13 1997, pp. 1/3.
4. Hitchings, H. *The Secret Life of Words: How English Became English*. New York, NY: Farrar, Strauss and Giroux, 2008; "North American Dialects," *National Geographic*, December 2005.
5. "A New Deal for One First Nation," *The Economist*, August 8, 1998, p. 34; See also National Geographic Maps: "North American Indian Culture," 2004; and "A World Transformed," 2007, 1–800/962–1643 or www.nationalgeographic.com/magazine0409. For further information on

Eskimos: Huntington, S. *Shadow on the Koyukuk—An Alaskan Native Life Along the River*. Seattle, WA: Graphics Arts Center Publishing Co., 1993; Marshall, R. *Arctic Village*. Juneau, AL: University of Alaska Press, 1991; Lynge, F. *Arctic Wars: Alaskan Rights, Endangered Peoples*. Hanover, NH: University Press of New England, 1992.

6. Davis, W. and Harrison, K. D. (eds.). *Book of Peoples—A Guide to Cultures*. Washington, D.C.: National Geographic, 2008, pp. 256–303.

7. McMaster, G. and Trafzer, C. E. (eds.). *Native Universe—Voices of the Indian America*. Washington, DC: Smithsonian National Museum of the American Indian and National Geographic, 2004; Tedlock, D. and Tedlock, B. (eds.). *Teachings from the American Earth: Indian Religion and Philosophy*. New York: Liveright, 1975; Chihuly, D. *Chihuly's Pendletons and Their Influence on His Work*. Seattle, WA: Portland Press, 2000.

8. Obama, B. "What I Want for You and Every Child in America—A Letter to My Daughters," *Parade—The San Diego Union Tribune*, January 18, 2009, pp. 4–5.

9. Remini, R. *A Short History of the United States*. New York, NY: Harper-Collins, 2008; "United States," Wikipedia Encyclopedia, 2009, 36 pp., http://en.wikipedia.org/wiki/United_States. Thomas, E. "Al Qaeda in America, The Enemy Within," *Newsweek*, June 23 2003; Schama, S. *The American Future: A History*. New York, NY: Ecco, 2009; Brands, H. W. *Traitor to His Class: The Privilege Life and Presidency of Franklin Delano Roosevelt*. New York, NY: Doubleday, 2008; Lewis, A. *Freedom for the Thought That We Hate: A Biography of the First Amendment*. New York, NY: Basic Books, 2008; Fukuyama, F. *America at the Crossroads: Democracy, Power, and the Neoconservative Legacy*, New Haven, CT: Yale University Press, 2006; Lieven, A. *America Right or Wrong: An Anatomy of American Nationalism*. New York, NY: Oxford University Press, 2004; Lieven, A. and Hulsman, J. *Ethical Realism: A Vision of America's Role in the World*. New York, NY: Pantheon, 2006.

10. Maddox, B. *In defence of America*. New York, NY: Little Brown, 2008; Mayer, J. *The Dark Side: How the War on Terror Turned into a War on American Ideals*. New York, NY: Doubleday, 2009; Tyler, P. *A World of Trouble: The White House and the Middle East—From Cold War to the War on Terror*. New York, NY: Farrar, Strauss and Giroux, 2009.

11. Campell, J. *U.S.A. (Country Guide)*. New York, NY: Lonely Planet, 2009. For U.S. Census Information, visithttp://www.census.gov/main.Sayre, A. P. *Welcome to North America*. Brookfield, CT: Millbrook Press, www.millbrook.com, 2003.

12. Gudykunst, W. B., and Kim, K. Y. *Communicating with Strangers: An Approach to Intercultural Communications*, Third edition. New York, NY: McGraw-Hill, 1994.

13. Maharidge, D. *The Coming of the White Minority: California's Eruption and the Nation's Future*. New York: Time Books, 1997; Hine, D.C., Harold, S., and Hine, W.C. *African-Americans: A Concise History*, Third edition. New York, NY: Amazon.com, 2008, with CD-ROM; Giola, T. *Delta Blues: The Life and Times of the Mississippi Masters Who Revolutionized American Music*. New York, NY: Norton, 2008; Rivera, G. *HisPanic: Why Americans Fear Hispanics in the U.S.* New York, NY: Celebra/Penguin Group, 2008; Chan, S. *The Vietnamese—America's 1.5 Generation*.

Philadelphia, PA: Temple University Press, 2006; Kim, I.J. *Korean-Americans: Past, Present, Future*. Elizabeth, NJ: Hollym International Corporation, www.hollym.com, 2004; Herbst, P.H. *The Color of Words: An Encyclopedic Dictionary of Ethnic Bias in the United Sates*. Boston, MA: Nicholas Brealy/Intercultural Press, 1997.

14. Shusta, R. M., Levine, D. R., Wong, H. Z., Olson, A. T., and Harris, P. R. *Multicultural Law Enforcement: Strategies for Peacekeeping in a Diverse Society*, Fourth edition. Upper Saddle River, NJ: Pearson/Prentice-Hall, 2008. McNamara, R. and Burns, R. *Multiculturalism in the Criminal Justice System*. New York, NY: McGraw-Hill, 2009; Toth, R.C., Crews, G.A., and Burton, C.E. (eds.). *Special Populations and American Justice*. Upper Saddle River, NJ: Pearson/Prentice Hall, 2008.

15. Bellah, R. et al. *Habits of the Heart—Individualism and Commitment in American Life*. Berkeley, CA: University of California Press, 1985.

16. Khana, P. *The Second World: Empires and Influence in the New World Order*. New York, NY: Random House, 2008, "Conclusion: The Search for Equilibrium in a Non-American World," pp. 321–342; Gruber, R. "What Europeans Really Think of America," *The New Leader*, August 2002; Sneider, D. "Asia Polite Reception to Bush Marks Declining U.S. Influence," *Yale Global*, November 2005. Kohut, A., and Stokes, B. *America Against the World—How We are Different and Why Are We Disliked*. New York, NY: Times Books, 2006.

17. Obama, B. *The Audacity of Hope—Thoughts on Reclaiming the American Dream*. New York, NY: Three Rivers Press/Random House, 2006; Thomas, E. *A Long Time Coming—The Inspiring, Combative 2008 Campaign and the Historic Election of Barak Obama*. New York, NY: Public Affairs Books, 2009, www.publicaffairsbooks.com or www.obama.newsweek.com.

# INDEX

Note: Page Numbers followed by '*b*' indicates boxes '*f*' indicate figures and '*t*' indicate tables.

preassignment strategies, 145–146
predeparture assessment for relocation, 220
preliminary stage of culture shock, 213
present orientation, 20
Pritchett , P., 123
Pritchett & Associates, 123
privacy
  in China, 337
  in France, 413, 417*b*
  in Germany, 420–421
  in Latin America, 316
  in Middle East, 260, 282*b*
  in South Korea, 378
proactive environmental forces, 116
process model of conflict, 85, 85*f*
process models of communication, 46
profession of faith (*Shahadah*), 255*b*
professional service organizations, 29–30
profile, cultural, 19, 20
projecting self into communication, 44, 45–46
projective cognitive similarity, 76–77
promoters, 196*b*
Protestantism
  in Europe, 393
  in Latin America, 298–299
  in Philippines, 370
  in South Korea, 376
protocol
  defined, 226
  in negotiation
    in Brazil, 82
    in China, 81
    in Germany, 83
    in India, 80
    overview, 78
    in Russia, 84
    in South Korea, 82
psychological contracts, 226–227
psychological environment, 45
PTSD (Post Traumatic Stress Disorder), 93*b*
punctuality, 77
punctuation, English, 62
Putin, Vladimir, 438–439
Pygmies, 471, 472*b*

## Q

Quach Hai Luong, 4
quality initiatives, 105
questioning
  in Argentina, 314
  in China, 336
  in France, 413
  in Latin America, 316
  in Middle East, 282*b*
*Qur'an* (Koran), 254–256

## R

Rabin, Yitzhak, 265
Rachman, Gideon, 396
Rajya Sabha, 342–343
*Random House Dictionary, The*, 27–28
rapport, creating, 54
Rast, D. S., 30
rational behavior, 18
rationale change model, 120
Raynet, 167
reacculturation, 225–226
reactive environmental forces, 117
reasoning, 42
recreational systems, 16
redundancy, avoiding, 62
reeducative change model, 120
reengineering, 121
reentry programs, 225–226
reentry shock, 213, 216, 225–226
referent power, 27
refugees, defined, 158
Reich, Robert, 191
relating to people, as global skill, 195
relationships
  *See also* family
  culture and, 12–13
  global transformations, 30
  in negotiation, 78, 90
relativist approach to diversity and ethics, 161, 166
religion, 13, 15, 110
  in Africa, 466–467
  in Argentina, 313–314
  in Asia, 325
  in Brazil, 303–305
  change in twenty-first century, 112*b*
  cultural patterns, 25
  in Europe, 393
  in France, 411
  India, 345
  in India, 342, 345–346, 348, 349
  in Iran, 275*b*
  in Italy, 428, 433
  in Japan, 352, 357–358
  in Latin America, 298–299, 304–305, 318
  in Mauritius, 489*b*
  in Middle East, 254–255
  in Morocco, 467
  in North America, 512
  overview, 13
  in Pakistan, 363
  in Philippines, 365, 370
  in South Africa, 493
  in South Korea, 375–376, 377
  in United States, 542–543
relocation, 205–231, 212–216
  assessment instruments, 227–228
  in Brazil, 205–208
  business etiquette and protocol, 226–227
  coping with, 209–211